It doesn't matter where you live, or if it's an older house or one that was recently built. Once you've spent some time in your home, you'll probably come up with ideas for ways to improve it. It could be anything, from simple repairs, to redoing a room, building a deck, or even putting an addition on the house. Even with a good idea, many people still hesitate to get started on a project due to a lack of knowledge and experience, while others who jump right in may find that they're in over their heads. That's the reason for this book. Here I'll share what I've learned over the years to help you complete your project with professional results.

I've been working on homes for over thirty years now, and looking back, I'd guess it all started one summer that I worked on the family cabin. Originally, our cabin had been a streetcar in St. Paul, Minnesota. Then after being retired, it was hauled eighty miles and set up next to a lake in western Wisconsin. Over the years a porch was added, and little by little, some of the windows were covered over. One problem with the cabin was that the original walls of the streetcar were in bad shape, so on this project we worked our way around the perimeter, tearing out the old walls and replacing them with new ones framed up with 2x4s. After that was finished, I started helping my brothers and sisters on their houses. Then I started working for friends, and then friends of friends, until it became a regular job. Even today, on most of my jobs I still work alongside the homeowner. This gives me a different perspective than others in my field. It also means that most of the time I have to figure out a way to do a job by myself or with the help of one other person, pretty much the same as most homeowners.

I learned as I went along, so I made a lot of mistakes before I figured out how to do certain jobs. This has always bothered me, and a few years ago I began to consider how much it would have helped if I'd known some of these things back when I first started, so I decided to write this book. There was never a master plan on what was going to be included in it, since that would partly be determined by the different jobs that came up at the time. The main idea was just to put in anything that I thought would be of benefit to someone -- basically to write the book that I wish I'd read years ago.

These days, there's information available on how to do almost anything. If you want to build a wall, plumb a sink, trim a door, etc., it's either in a book or you can find it on the internet. While this will give you the basic idea, it won't teach you the things that are learned from actually doing it. That's where this book is a little different. Instead of quickly going over something, I'm going to concentrate more on how to do a job step by step, and as you do it, what you're looking for, and how to deal with some of the common problems that you'll run into. Since I'm trying to pack a lot of information into the book, I'll try to keep it short and to the point, and to explain it in a manner that's easy to understand.

Neil Tschida

# CONTENTS

BUILDING TIPS FOR THE HOMEOWNER

Copyright 2020 by Neil Tschida

# FRAMING

For many home projects, the first step will be the framing, so that's where we'll begin. I realize that a lot of what's in this section, or others for that matter, may be common knowledge to some of you, but to others it's all new. Different methods may also be used when doing the many jobs that are covered in this book. On the subject of framing, there have been some good books written -- in my opinion, the best being some of the older ones that were published before the use of trusses became so common.

## FRAMING THE WALLS

We'll start with how to lay out and frame up a wall. Anyone can nail a wall together, but the rest of the project will go easier if it's done the right way. Almost everything that follows will be affected in some way by the quality of the framing. That's one thing I quickly learned when I first started working on houses. Everything is connected. If you get a little sloppy, or do something wrong, you'll pay for it later on.

When framing the walls, always consider what's the best way to position the studs. It's generally best to have the studs directly under the rafters, trusses, or floor joists whenever possible. This isn't required with a doubled up top plate, but it's stronger and helps with the rest of the layout. It also lines up the cavities for running the heat ducts and the plumbing. You should also always consider how the layout will affect the installation of the sheathing and/or the sheetrock.

On bathrooms, there's a lot to think about. You have to be able to run the plumbing, which will be determined by the position of the tub or the shower, the sink, and the toilet. You also have to make sure that the studs or framing are positioned correctly for installing any enclosures, the tub or the shower faucet, the shower light, and the exhaust fan. Other things to think about are mirrors, wall lamps, medicine cabinet, etc.

When building a house, or an addition on one, always consider how the window openings on one floor level relate to others that are above it or below it. I've made this particular mistake only once. You learn pretty quick once you've had to reposition the windows after a wall has already gone up.

To show how this is done, we'll frame up a typical wall. For an 8 foot wall, precut studs are generally used, which are 92 5/8 inches long. After adding 4 1/2 inches for the thickness of the bottom plate and a double plate on the top, the wall will actually be 97 1/8 inches tall. This height allows for the sheetrock that's going on the ceiling, and will leave a gap at the floor. There's also precut studs available for 9 foot and 10 foot ceilings

Start by measuring how long the wall has to be, and then cut the top and the bottom plate to that length. Try to use straight boards for this. If the wall is long enough that the plates have to be made up from more than one board, they're generally butted together at the center of a stud. You can also end the bottom plates in door openings, since they'll be cut out in those locations anyhow.

Once the plates are cut, they're laid on the floor, side by side. The bottom plate should lay right side up, and the top plate should be flipped over so the top side is down. How they face can matter if one of the boards has a bad edge.

Now you have to mark the positions of the studs. Let's say that this is going to be an exterior load-bearing wall that starts at the corner of the house. This wall will support the floor or the roof that's above it, so I'd lay it out with the studs centered every 16 inches, starting from the corner end of the plate. This way, the studs will be directly under the joists or the rafters if they're framed on 16 inch centers, and under every other one if they're framed on 24 inch centers. The sheathing will also be centered on a stud if it starts at the end of the wall. Most measuring tapes are highlighted at these 16 inch increments.

To do this, hook the measuring tape on the end of one of the plates, and then make a mark 3/4 of an inch under or over the center of each stud. I always mark 3/4 inch under. That means I make the marks at 15 1/4, 31 1/4, 47 1/4, 63 1/4, 79 1/4, 95 1/4, etc. Now make sure that the ends are lined up on the plates, and use a square to draw a line across both plates, at each mark. Then make an X on the side of the line where you want the studs to go. This way, you position a stud by holding it against the line as the X is covered. If you marked the center of a stud, you wouldn't be able to see the line.

The next thing is to mark the position of any windows or doors on that wall. The studs will be doubled up on the outside edge of these openings if a single jack stud is required. Draw a line marking both sides of the doubled studs, and then put an XX between the lines.

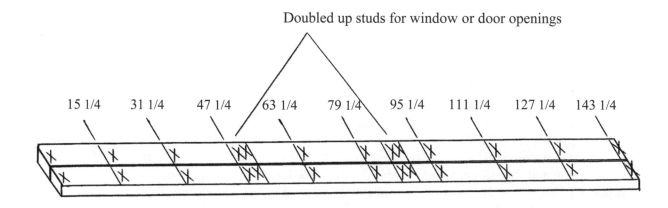

Doubled up studs for window or door openings

| 15 1/4 | 31 1/4 | 47 1/4 | 63 1/4 | 79 1/4 | 95 1/4 | 111 1/4 | 127 1/4 | 143 1/4 |

When laying out the walls, mark the position of every stud, even those that are inside of any window or door openings. This is done for positioning the cripple studs that go above or below these openings. In this drawing, the stud on the right end will overhang the plates by 3/4 of an inch, so the next section will overlap it. The top plate on that section will also be nailed to this stud to lock the two together. On the lower end, I generally toenail the bottom plates together.

4

Any additional sections that are needed to complete this wall will be laid out to maintain the 16 inch centers. The wall that was just done had marks at 15 1/4, 31 1/4, 47 1/4, 63 1/4, etc., and the plates were cut so they ended at the center of a stud. When doing this, the next section will be laid out to the same measurements, again starting at 15 1/4 inches. It won't always be this way. Walls are built on a case-by-case basis, and they're laid out to fit whatever is needed at the time.

## WINDOW AND DOOR OPENINGS

Make sure you have the correct size for the rough openings of any windows or doors. Years ago, I helped one of my brothers put an addition on his house, and the store gave us the wrong measurements for the windows. Because of that, we ended up having to redo every one of the openings. Since then, I always try to have the windows on hand before I build the walls, or at least know that I can trust the measurements I've been given.

When framing for a window, I generally add an extra inch to the width of the opening to give 1/2 inch of clearance on both sides of it. I also add another 1/2 inch to the height, for over the window. Some manufacturers will tell you to only add an extra 1/2 inch to the width, but that may not leave enough room for insulating around the window.

On interior doors, the rough opening will generally be 2 inches wider than the door itself. That means a 32 inch door will need a 34 inch rough opening. Exterior doors may need a little more. For a standard interior door, I generally make the rough opening 82 1/2 inches high, though the height may be changed if hardwood floors or tile is being added.

Door openings on an interior non-load bearing wall only need a single board over the top of the opening, but they should be doubled up for French or pocket doors for more rigidity. Window and door openings in load bearing walls require headers. These days, where I live, exterior walls are framed with 2x6s. For most headers, I'll use doubled up 2x wood. If there's room for it, I'll also put a 2x6 under it for attaching the sheetrock and the trim, which will leave a 2 1/2 inch pocket for insulating the header. When framing a large window opening, you may have to leave out the 2x6 so you can use a bigger header. When doing this, a board will have to be attached to the lower edge of the header for installing the sheetrock and trim. Another option is to build the header using tripled 2x wood. In some areas, boxed headers are required. One way to make them for 2x6 walls is by nailing a 2x3 between the header boards along the upper and the lower edge.

In most rooms, the door's positioned in one of the corners, and swings open against the other wall, so it's out of the way. When doing this, the door opening is typically framed with the two outside studs nailed directly against the corner. With 2 1/4 inch trim, the trim boards will generally end up about an inch off the other wall.

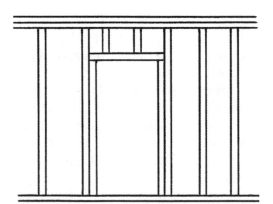
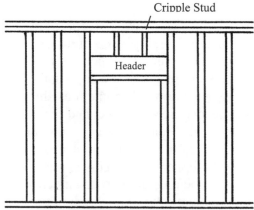

These drawings show how door openings are framed. The one on the left is for a non-load bearing wall, while the one on the right, which has a header, is for a load bearing wall. Except for that, they're framed in the same manner.

For an 82 1/2 inch high rough opening, the inside studs are cut at 81 inches. Then, once they're nailed on, a 2x4 goes over the top of the opening if it's a non-load bearing interior wall. For a load bearing wall, the header would go on at this time. Then any cripple studs that are needed would be installed above the door. The bottom plate is generally cut out on a door opening once the wall has been nailed into place.

When framing a door opening on a taller non-load bearing wall, say 9-10 feet, sometimes I'll use full length studs on both sides of the door for more rigidity. When doing this, the inside studs are nailed first. Then the board is installed over the top of the opening before the outside studs are nailed on. If both studs were installed first, the board across the top would have to be toenailed.

Each stud gets nailed to the plate(s). Then the boards are nailed together on both sides of the opening. When using 2x4s, I'll put a single nail about every 16 inches. On 2x6 walls, I either shrink the distance and stagger the nails, or increase it to around 2 feet and pair them up.

Before framing an exterior door opening, I like to measure the jamb on the door that's being installed. I'll also determine the thickness of anything that will be added to the floor, so I know exactly how high I want the door and/or the threshold to be, which will determine the size of the opening.

Once the inside studs are nailed on, I generally cap off the opening with a 2x6 that's laid flat. Then over that, I'll put the header, which sits flush to the outside edge of the wall. Both the header and the 2x6 are cut 3 inches longer than the width of the rough opening, unless you need two supporting boards on each side. In that case, they'd be cut 6 inches longer. The header is nailed to the outside studs with a double row of nails at each end. The 2x6 is nailed to the outside studs, and also to the header. Then cripple studs are toenailed to the top of the header to maintain the 16 inch centers. When using a header, the studs that support it are called trimmers or jack studs. The outside studs are called king studs.

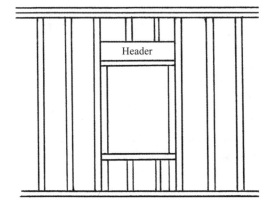
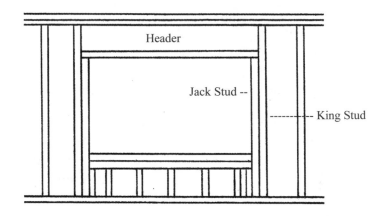

These drawings show two ways to frame window openings. For a small window, sometimes I'll frame it as shown on the left. Here the supporting studs go on in two pieces, with the sill board between them. When framing this way, once I've determined the height for the window, I start at the bottom and work my way up. The header and any cripple studs are done in the same manner as on a door.

For a larger window, I'll frame it as shown on the right for more strength and rigidity. Here the boards that support the header are one piece, and the sill might be doubled up on a wide opening. When framing this way, you can install the boards one at a time, or you can nail the inside members together and then slip them into place as one unit. With a doubled up sill, nail on the lower board first, and do any studs that are beneath it before installing the upper board. This saves you from having to do any toenailing. Then install the 2x6 and the header over the opening, along with any cripple studs if they're needed.

In the drawing on the right, you'll notice that there aren't any cripple studs above the window opening. Commonly, windows are framed with the headers tight against the upper plate. Here there's also only one jack stud on each side to support the header. When framing a large opening, sometimes two, or even three, are needed instead. Tables showing the requirements for headers and jack studs are near the end of this book.

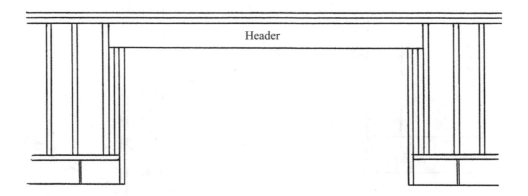

Header

This drawing shows the framing for a double garage door. On a door this wide (16 feet), two studs are required at each end to support the header. Here there are actually four studs at each end of the header, with three of them beneath it. In this case, only the two that rest on top of the sill plate count as supports. The one that runs down on the inside of the block doesn't.

An opening of this size requires a pretty big header. If the door opening is on the gable end (peaked end) of a garage, a pair of 2x12s are needed. On the side that supports the roof, you'll need more strength yet, requiring the use of two 1 3/4 x 14 inch LVLs (micro-lams) on a 24 foot garage with a gable roof. With a hip roof, two 1 3/4 x 12 inch LVLs are required on a 24 foot garage. On larger garages, or ones that have living space above them or a heavy snow load, the header size would have to be calculated.

## CORNERS

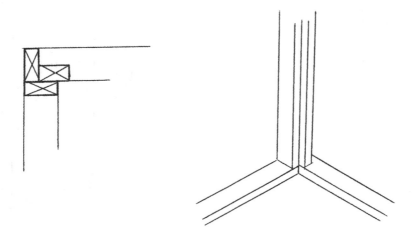

As you frame up the walls, you'll have to consider how the corners are going to be done. This is the way that I prefer to do it. Here the two wall sections are nailed together where they meet at the corner. Then a third stud is added to provide a nailer for the sheetrock. It doesn't matter if this is done when walls are put up, or at a later date, but it's best to install it before you start on the wiring. One advantage of doing a corner this way is that it's insulated from the inside. It's also easier to run the wires when the electrical work is done.

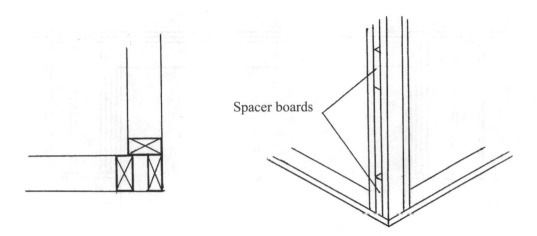

Spacer boards

This is another method that can be used when framing the corners on a 2x4 wall. Here, one side of the corner has a second stud added to the end of the wall, which is spaced out from the first stud using short pieces of blocking. This will give you a 1 inch nailing surface on the inside for attaching the sheetrock. When framing a 2x6 wall, the inside board would have to be 2 inches farther from the corner, so spacer boards generally wouldn't be used.

There are some disadvantages to this method. The corner has to be insulated from the outside, before the sheathing goes on. Also, when wiring, a hole has to be drilled from each side, and then the wire fished through. These corners seem colder to me in the winter. Besides not being able to insulate them later, in case you forget, the insulation can also settle and clump if it gets wet before the roof is on.

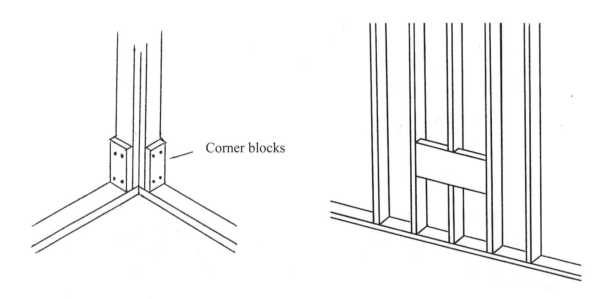

Corner blocks

Sometimes, short boards have to be added to a corner to provide a nailing surface for the baseboard. Blocking may also be needed to provide a backer (brace) for drapes, toilet paper dispenser, wall mounted sink, etc. For a small backer, a board is generally nailed between the studs. For a wall mounted sink, a larger board is needed that may span more than one stud cavity. When installing it, a separate board can be used for each opening, or the center stud, or studs, can be notched so the backer board is installed in one piece.

## NAILING THE WALLS TOGETHER

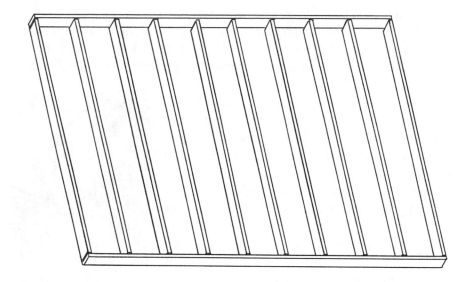

After the lines have been drawn out on the plates, everything is laid out on a flat section of floor. Spread the plates apart with the lines facing each other, and make sure the X's are on the same side of the line. Then slip a stud into place wherever a full length one is needed. This includes the outside studs for any window or door openings. For a flatter wall, crowned studs should all be facing in the same direction. This is assuming that the studs are being covered with a material that isn't strong enough to pull opposing crowns into line, such as sheetrock. Crowns that face in both directions can leave you with a wavy wall, which could be a problem if a countertop is going against it.

Doubled up studs are laid out so that any warps or crowns will oppose each other, which will help to straighten them as they're nailed together.

Before you start nailing a wall together, look it over to see if there's anything that you can do to make the job go easier. Sometimes a stud ends up so close to a window or a door opening that it would be difficult to nail on the header. In that case, I'd leave the stud out to give me room to swing a hammer. Then, once the opening is finished, I'll put in the missing stud.

When framing walls, you'll commonly end up with studs that are close to each other. Most of the time it's caused by window or door openings, though it could also be at the end of a wall. Depending on how close the studs are, and their location, sometimes they can be left out. This is decided on a case by case basis, but this is how I generally do it. Let's say the stud is 5 or 6 inches from the one that's next to it. Here we're talking center to center, not the actual distance between them. When it's that far away, I'd probably put the stud in, since it would be 21 or 22 inches between them if it wasn't installed. Now if it was only 2 inches over so it centered at 18 inches, I'd leave it out, unless the sheathing was going to meet up on that stud. Between those measurements is a gray area, and I'd have to think about it at the time. Things to consider would be the seams in the sheathing, whether or not the stud was actually supporting anything, and what kind of sheathing and/or sheetrock was going over it. Most of the time, the sheathing and the sheetrock can handle a little extra span.

Once the studs have been laid out, you can nail the wall together. When doing this, I start at one end, and hold each stud against the line. Then I make sure the stud is over the X, and nail it with two 16D sinkers. If the studs aren't the same width as the plate, you'll either have to hold them flush to the top of the plate, flush to the bottom of the plate, or centered on it as you nail them into place. It generally doesn't matter which way, as long as they're all done in the same manner. This will give you a flatter wall.

After you've finished that end, switch sides and start nailing the other end of the studs. When doing this end, you may find that some of the studs are twisted. To straighten them, either hold the top or the bottom edge of the stud in place, and drive a nail in to hold that side in position. Then rotate the stud so it's against the line, and put the second nail in.

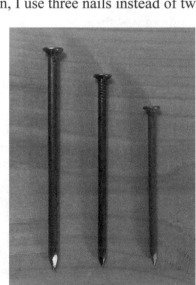

If a stud has a bad twist, attaching a clamp to it will give you more leverage for straightening it. On studs that are twisted, you may also want to add an extra nail, though most of the time you can't totally straighten a stud with a hard twist, since it will still move, even though the ends are securely nailed.

This photo shows a wood clamp being used to hold two studs together when nailing them, which helps when either one or both of them are warped or crowned. It can also be used to help straighten twists, though a bar clamp will give you more leverage.

If you have help, work as a team when framing the walls with a nail gun. Have the most agile person position the studs, while the other shoots the nails. I always want to be the one that holds the studs, so I can't complain if they're positioned wrong. When framing as a team, you have to work out a system so the nailing goes fast, and so no one gets hurt.

I start on one end of the plate, and say the word "good" when a stud is positioned correctly and ready to be nailed. Then I move over to the next stud, and say "good" when that one is in the correct position. If a stud is twisted, I'll either hold the top or the bottom edge in place, and say "good on top" or "good on the bottom," so just that side is nailed. Then I'll rotate the stud into position and signal to nail the other side. Gun nails have a thinner shank than ones you drive in by hand, so when using a gun, I use three nails instead of two on 2x6 studs.

It's important that the person who's positioning the studs keeps their hands away from the end of the boards. Every now and then, a nail may either miss the stud or deflect and come out where you least expect it. Keeping your hands at least a few inches from the plate should keep them safe.

Once the studs are nailed, stand back and look the wall over to make sure that every stud is in the right position. Remember that the X's should be covered. It easier to fix any mistakes now before you go any farther. Then finish the wall by framing any window or door openings.

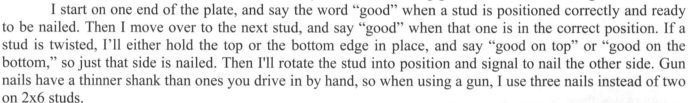

In this photo are the nails that are generally used for framing when hand nailing. On the left is a 16D sinker, which is around 3 1/4 inches long, while on the right is an 8D sinker that's around 2 1/2 inches. The nail in the center is a 3 inch 10D. This size isn't used as often. It's a little longer than an 8D, so it's good when you need a little extra reach, but it has a thin shank, so it bends easier. Sinkers are cement-coated to hold better. The D that follows the size stands for penny, so a 16D nail is actually called a 16 penny.

# TIPPING UP THE WALL SECTIONS

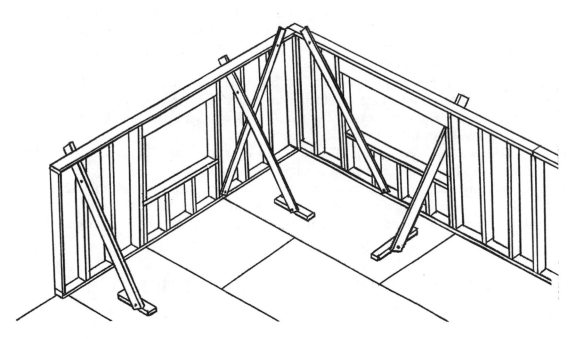

As you nail the wall sections together, they're tipped up into place and secured to make room for the next one being made. Since I normally do this with one other guy, or two if I'm lucky, I've always done it before the sheathing is on. 2x6 framing can be pretty heavy. If I'm alone, or there's only one guy helping, I generally just nail on the outside studs for any window or door openings, and then install the inside studs, headers, sills, and cripple studs, after the walls are in place.

Once a wall section is finished, everyone involved will help to tip it up and slide it into position. Then the wall is nailed to the floor and braced. Use 16D sinkers, and put a nail every sixteen inches. I also put two at the edge of any door openings. If the floor has a straight edge, just line up the wall flush to the edge, and then nail it. If the floor isn't straight, you can either snap a chalk line in advance, for the wall to follow, or check the wall with a string line as you put in the nails. When the wall is heavy, or you don't have enough help, the best thing to do is to lightly nail it to the floor and quickly attach the diagonal braces. Then you can think about straightening the wall once it's safely held up in place.

Most walls will get at least two braces, but the number will vary depending on its length. It's best to use braces that are longer than the length of the studs. To install a brace, hold it at an angle, high up on a stud, and then nail it to the stud with a 16D sinker. Then, while holding the wall plumb, nail a piece of 2x material to the floor, next to the brace, and nail the brace to that board. Screws can also be used instead of nails. When there are just two of you framing the walls, one person will hold up the wall as the other installs the braces. The person holding the wall will also have to check it for plumb as the lower end of each brace is being nailed. Any other braces are put on in the same manner.

When framing exterior walls that rest on concrete, the bottom plates will generally be pressure treated wood, which are slipped over anchor bolts and then held in place with nuts and washers. The holes for the anchor bolts should be drilled and checked before the wall is assembled. On concrete, you won't be able to nail into the floor to install the braces. One option here is to pound stakes into the ground, and then attach the braces to them.

Now that the wall is standing on its own, it's also plumbed in the other direction by pushing on the end of the wall. Then it's held in that position by nailing a 2x4 diagonally across the studs. Again, a longer board works better for doing this.

With everyone working together, this job should go pretty fast. Use at least a 4 foot level for plumbing the walls. A 6 foot is better. A laser level can also be used on taller walls, and is more accurate as long as it's been properly adjusted.

I like to start the walls at a corner, and install the load bearing wall first. This one will generally have the studs positioned on 16 inch centers, starting at the corner, so they're directly under the floor joists or the rafters. The floor joists and the rafters will commonly go across the entire house maintaining the same centers, so the walls should be done in the same manner. This can get a little confusing as you go around corners. If there's ever any doubt, go back and measure from the starting point when doing the layout. You can also use the seams in the floor sheathing as a reference.

Once the first section is braced into position, I'll build the other section that ends at this corner, and then nail the two sections where they come together with 16D sinkers spaced about every 16 inches. This section is braced the same way as the first one. After that, I work off this corner as I build the rest of the wall sections, and tip them up and brace them into position one at a time.

To finish off the walls, a second top plate is added over the first. These boards should be free of crowns, but warps are OK. Install the boards so the joints are overlapped at each corner to lock the walls together. I try to overlap any seams that are in the lower top plate by at least 4 feet. I think 2 feet is the actual requirement. On 2x4s, nail the boards every 16 inches, and put two nails at the ends. With 2x6s, either stagger the nails and shrink the spacing to around 12 inches, or double them up and space them around 2 feet apart.

# BUILDING WALLS IN AN EXISTING STRUCTURE

There are two ways to build walls when working on a house. One is to build the sections on the floor, and then tip them up like we just went over. The other is to build them in place. Generally, the only time that walls have to be built in place is when you're adding them to an existing structure. To do this, I start by laying out the bottom plates, which are positioned by measuring off the existing walls. Then after attaching them to the floor, the lines are drawn to mark the position of the studs. On wood floors, again I'll put a nail every 16 inches, and two on each side of a door opening.

Once the bottom plates are installed, I mark the position of the upper plates on the ceiling or the framing that's above, and then either nail or screw them into place. To find the position of the upper plates, I've used levels, plumb bobs, and a laser level. When using a plumb bob, I hold the string at the top, and then move it around until the plumb bob comes to rest above the edge of the bottom plate. Then I mark that spot. When doing this, it's faster and more accurate if you lay a short piece of 2x4 next to the plate, and then line up the plumb bob on the seam between the two boards.

When using a laser level that projects vertically, I'll position the level so the lower beam just touches the edge of the bottom plate, and then mark the spot where the upper beam hits the ceiling. To check the laser level for accuracy, turn it in the opposite direction. Then aim it at the same point on the bottom plate, and see where it hits the ceiling. Many times you'll find that it hits at a slightly different spot, which means the level is off. This can be corrected by adjusting the level, though you could also just mark halfway between the two points, as this is where the mark should actually be.

These marks can also be made by using a level and a long board. To do this, find a straight board that's just long enough to reach the ceiling, and then attach a 4 foot level to the side of it. You could also just hold the level against it, but taping it on will free up your hands. To make the marks, all you have to do is to hold the board against the edge of the bottom plate, and then mark the ceiling once the bubble is centered.

12

You'll generally need at least two marks for each upper plate. You can check the accuracy of the level the same as you'd do with a laser level, by simply rotating the board 180 degrees. In this case, if the mark doesn't end up at the same point, it could be for a couple of reasons. The level could be off, or the maybe the board isn't actually straight. If it's the level, again the correct point can be found by marking the ceiling with the level turned in both directions, and then splitting the difference between the two marks.

When you start on the upper plates, you might run into a problem. Any plates that run perpendicular to the framing can be attached to the trusses, rafters, or the floor joists, but there won't be anything above the ones that run parallel to it, unless you're lucky and the plate just happens to end up where there's a board. Above the walls where there isn't anything to attach to, you'll have to install blocking between the framing. Besides providing a place for the walls to be attached, they're also used for screwing on the sheetrock.

The blocks are cut from left over ends of 2x4s or 2x6s, or from boards that aren't good for anything else. I generally install them on 16 inch centers, with the boards laid flat, and hold them flush to the lower edge of the joists or rafters. The boards are cut to fit tight and then nailed into place. When hand nailing, sometimes it's easier to use a bar clamp to hold each one in place as it's being attached. Not all clamps will work for this, as some tend to fall off as you're pounding in the nails.

When installing the blocks, their location is determined by the sheetrock. Many times I've had to reposition some of the blocks, or add more, because I forgot to consider this. The correct way to position the blocks is so they're centered where the rows of sheetrock come together. This way, both sheets will be attached to the same board.

Once the upper plates are in place, the lines can be drawn to mark the positions of the studs. I generally check the position of the first stud on each wall with a level, and then find the location of the others by measuring off that one.

After that's done, the studs are cut and toenailed into place, one at a time. This takes accurate measuring and cutting. It's easier to do this with a miter saw, since on many of them you'll have to take a little more off to get the right length. The studs should be just long enough so you have to lightly pound them into place. If they're too loose, they'll be hard to nail. When toenailing, use 8D sinkers, and install four nails on each end (two from each side) if you're using 2x4s. It's easier to get a nail started if you begin by holding it more perpendicular to the stud. Then once it's started, you can give it more angle. This drawing shows how the nails should ideally be positioned. It doesn't have to be nearly that exact, but most people don't put enough angle on the nails, so they don't go far enough into

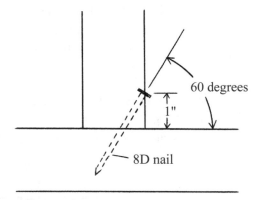

the plate. Toenailing with a hammer takes an accurate swing. To finish off pounding in the nails, I recommend using a large nail set. This will keep you from beating up the wood as you're trying to drive them the rest of the way in. When doing this, hit the nail set hard enough so each nail is driven in with one or two swings, so you're not wasting a lot of time. I still use a nail set most of the time, since I don't toenail that often.

The other problem with toenailing is trying to keep the studs in place as you're pounding the nails in. For this, you have a few choices. Most of the time, I hold each stud so its just off the line -- the idea being that it will move over the correct amount as the first nail is driven in. If it shifts over too far, the next nail will be driven in from the other side to move the stud back to the line. I generally have each stud where I want it by about the third nail. When doing this, on some of the studs you'll have to give them a whack with the hammer to move them over. But ideally, this is done before all the nails are in.

Another way, when toenailing the bottom plate, is to plant your foot on the back side of the board to keep it from moving. On the upper plate, sometimes I'll clamp a board behind the stud for the same purpose. Yet another method is to use a spacer board that goes between the studs as you're nailing. The spacer board will prevent the stud from being driven back, since it's resting against a stud that's already been nailed. You could also use a nail gun. Toenailing with a nail gun takes practice, If you haven't done it, I'd recommend that you toenail a few scrap boards, so you know where to aim on a stud. When doing this, use the same nails that are used for the rest of the framing. When remodeling, you can also use deck screws, with 2 or 3 at each end.

Another option is to assemble the walls on the floor, and then tip them up into place, the same as you do on exterior walls. But building them to fit would be asking for trouble. In a basement, the height of a wall keeps changing and commonly gets smaller when going from one end to the other. Even upstairs, the ceiling height will change once the wood has dried and the house has settled. Another problem is that a wall is actually a little taller when it's slightly tipped to one side. This is because of its width, so even though a wall is the correct height, it may not be possible to tip it up.

The way around this problem is to build the wall short, and then shim it into place. To do this, first you have to measure the height of the opening at several points along its length. Then build the wall a little under the shortest height that you measured. If the measurements were pretty much equal, I'd build the wall about 1/4 inch short, but if the height varied or shrunk down a bit when going from one end to the other, I'd make it about an 1/8 inch under the shortest height to keep the gap that I have to shim from getting too big. You could also lay the plates on top of each other, and measure the height at every stud position. Then cut each stud 1/4 inch short. There's no set rule when doing this. You have to take each wall on a case by case basis.

After the wall is nailed together and tipped up, which commonly involves a little persuasion with a hammer, shims are inserted at a couple of points above the wall to keep it from moving. Then the bottom plate is tapped into position and attached to the floor. An exception to this is where the bottom plate is being glued to the floor. In that case, first I'd make sure that the wall fit. Then I'd take it down, apply construction adhesive, and tip it back up. Once the lower end of the wall is in position, the upper end can be plumbed and shimmed into place. I put shims at each end of the wall, and then every 24 - 32 inches in between, depending on the framing above it. The shims are driven in until they're snug, and are paired up by coming from opposite directions if the gap is large enough. Then the wall is locked into place by driving a 16D nail or 3 - 3 1/2 inch screw through the top plate wherever there's a shim. I prefer to use deck screws or zinc plated construction screws when doing this, as they seem to drive in easier. They're also quieter. Black construction screws tend to make an awful squeal as they're driven in.

When building a wall, sometimes an extra plate is added to one end of it. This could be done for several reasons. Maybe it's just easier to have the plates already in place when the sections of walls are installed, or maybe the studs are a little short, and this will increase the height of the wall. Recently I had to add a second bottom plate to a wall to provide a nailing surface for a shower base. One advantage of having the extra plate at the floor is that it gives you the option of either installing the shims at the ceiling, or between the two lower plates.

Gable ends are commonly framed after the rafters have been installed. Here the studs could go all the way to the floor, or just rest on a lower wall. Either way, the studs are generally notched to fit against the end rafter. When doing this, it isn't necessary for them to go all the way to the top of the rafter.

# INTERSECTIONS OF WALLS

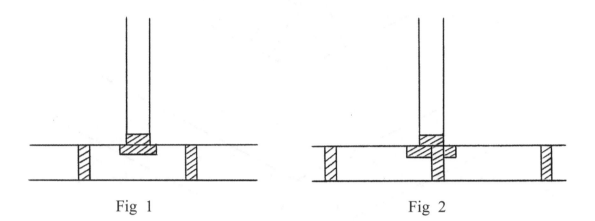

Fig 1                    Fig 2

As you're building the walls, you have to consider how they're going to be connected to each other, and also how the sheetrock is going to be attached at the corners. Shown here are a few examples where an interior partition wall is connected to the middle of another wall. There are several ways that this can be done, depending on whether there's a stud at that position, or if the wall is insulated. In these drawings, the partition wall is framed with 2x4s, and the wall that it's attached to is framed with 2x6s.

Figure 1 shows a partition wall that's centered between the studs. In this case, a 2x6 was installed to provide a nailing surface for the sheetrock.

Figure 2 shows a partition wall that's attached where there's a stud. Here a 2x4 was used on one side to provide the nailing surface, while on the other, only a 2x2 was needed.

Figure 3 shows a side view where a 2x4 block has been installed in the center, flush to face of the studs. I do this to hold the end stud in place, so it's positioned correctly, and/or to straighten it if it's warped or crowned. Then the backer board is installed in two pieces. If there's no insulation, I'll use a 2x6 for this. If there is, I'll either use a 1x6 or plywood, preferably at least 5/8 inch thick, so the sheet rock screws won't strip out. The reason for the thinner board is because it's easier to slip it into place when there's insulation behind it. It also won't compress the insulation as much.

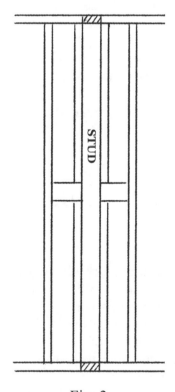

Fig 3

## 45 DEGREE CORNERS

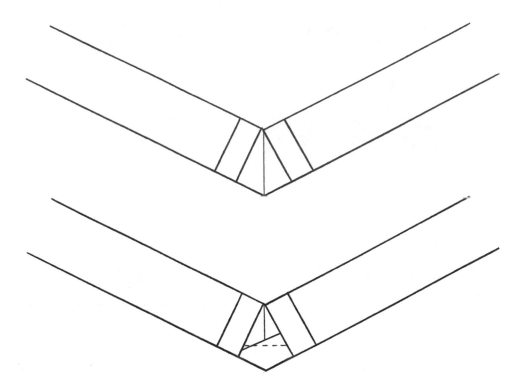

The upper drawing shows a typical 45 degree corner. When framing it, the two studs are nailed together, and then the corner is sheetrocked as is. I never cared for this method, since there isn't anything behind the corner itself on one side of the wall. The nails also have to be held back when installing the baseboard.

The lower drawing shows the way that I prefer to do it. A table saw is used to cut the corner board, and the solid line represents the way that I normally cut it. When doing this, the blade is set at 45 degrees, and it only takes two cuts to make the board. The dotted line shows another way that the board can be cut. This one is a little tougher since the saw blade has to be set at 45 degrees, and also at 22 1/2 degrees. Four cuts are also needed instead of two.

## ATTACHING INTERIOR WALLS TO A CONCRETE FLOOR

When building above grade, the walls are generally just nailed to the floor. That's still an option on concrete if you have a nail gun that's made for this purpose, but there are other ways to do it. Years ago, I used to attach the walls with either a 25 caliber RamSet, or a 22 caliber Remington gun. Sometimes the nails would go in straight, and sometimes the nails would turn when they hit a rock, so there wasn't any holding power. Once in a while, the nails would even turn so much that they'd lift the board off the floor. Because of that, now I use different methods, such as Tapcons, expansion bolts, construction adhesive, and a nail with a wire.

Tapcons ( 1 ) are hardened screws that are specifically designed for going into concrete. When using them to attach the walls, you have to pre-drill the holes, going through the plate and into the floor with the correct size masonry drill bit. A 5/32 inch bit is used for 3/16 inch Tapcons, and a 3/16 inch bit is used for ones that are 1/4 inch in diameter. Use a hammer drill for drilling the holes. The holes must be drilled deeper than the actual distance the Tapcons are going in. The directions say you need an extra 1/4 inch, but in my experience it takes more than that. It also helps to clean each hole with a Shop-Vac to remove the dust to make sure the screw goes all the way in. The best way to install Tapcons is with a cordless impact driver. The photo shows a Tapcon with a Philips head. For this, you should use one with a hex head instead. I just didn't have one with me when the photo was taken.

Expansion bolts ( 2 ) can also be used for attaching the plates. When using them, the drill bit should match the diameter of the bolt. Once the hole is drilled, the bolt is driven into place with a hammer. Then the nut is tightened. This will pull up on the bolt, which will cause the sleeve to expand against the concrete. Again, the hole should be drilled deeper than the length of the bolt, and it helps to vacuum out the hole.

Using a nail with a wire ( 3 ) is another way to attach the plates to concrete. I learned this years ago from a friend who was a building inspector. The idea here is to drill a hole the same as you would for installing a Tapcon, but instead, you slip a piece of wire into the hole and then pound a nail in right next to it. When doing this, I generally use a 16D sinker, and drill the hole with a 5/32 inch drill bit. Once the hole is drilled, I remove the dust and then insert the wire with the upper end folded over, so the lower end sits about a quarter of an inch from the bottom of the hole.

The trick to this method is to use the right diameter wire. If the wire is too thick, the nail will be hard to drive in, and it will probably bend. If the wire is too thin, the nail will go in easy, but it won't have any holding power. One good thing about this method is that the nail can be removed if needed, and it will only leave a small hole, though you may need a crowbar for pulling it. If you plan on removing them, use duplex nails, which will leave you with the second head sticking out. These nails may be thicker, so you might have to use a 3/16 inch drill bit.

These days, it's pretty common for basements to have in-floor heat. This creates a problem for attaching the walls. Since you don't want to risk puncturing one of the loops of tubing by nailing into the floor, the plates will have to be glued on with construction adhesive. When doing this, I'll lay out the plates beforehand, and either draw or snap a line to mark their location.

If the walls are being built in sections, once they're finished I'll apply construction adhesive to either the bottom plate or the floor. Then I'll tip each wall up into place against the line, and nail or screw it to the ceiling. On walls that are being built in place, I do it a little different. Since I don't want the plates to be sliding around and making a mess, I'll glue them to the floor, and then hold them in place until the adhesive sets up. This can be done in a couple of ways. One is to simply stack something heavy on top of the plates. Another method is to cut some of the studs and then temporarily position them along the boards. This will keep pressure on the plates until the adhesive sets up.

## BASEMENT WALLS

When finishing off a basement, there are several ways to do the exterior walls. Newer houses generally have 2x4s that go around the perimeter, which are either nailed to the floor, or glued where in-floor heat has been installed. Framed walls are also needed where plumbing will be installed on the exterior walls.

Years ago, furring strips were attached to the concrete blocks on 16 or 24 inch centers with nails, Tapcons, or construction adhesive. Then foam panels were installed between the furring strips. A more recent method is to use 1 1/2 or 2 inch thick foam that has a notch cut on each edge, with the panels butted up against each other. Then either 2x2s, 2x4s, or strips of 3/4 inch plywood slip into the notches, and get attached to the walls with Tapcons to hold the foam in place. To install the wiring, the foam will have to be cut out for the wires and the boxes using a pull saw and a razor knife, or hot knife. The boxes get attached to either the wall or one of the strips, and the wires are pushed tight against the concrete, so they're out of the way.

# SHEATHING THE WALLS

Once the exterior walls are in place, they can be sheathed. These days, OSB is generally used for this. OSB is short for oriented strand board. I normally use 1/2 inch on the walls, though 7/16 is also available. Years ago, I used 1/2 inch plywood, preferably good quality 4-ply. I used it on the roof too, though 5/8 is better on 24 inch centers. Even though I use OSB, I've never liked it. I just don't like the idea of using a bunch of wood chips that have been glued together. Plywood consists of thin layers of wood, and will stay strong as long as the glue holds up. At this time, decent plywood costs almost twice as much, so that's why I use OSB.

From what I've read, OSB has greater shear strength than plywood. It's not as good though if it's going to get wet, since it tends to swell up. Leave a piece on the ground over the winter, and you'll have a hard time trying to decide how thick it was to begin with. One advantage of using OSB on a roof is that it's flatter, so it's easier to slip into H-clips.

When sheathing the walls, the sheets are generally installed vertically. This way, the sheet will overlap both the top and the bottom plate. If you run it horizontally, like you do with sheetrock, blocking should be installed where the rows come together. Generally, 1x4s or 1x6s are used for this, and they're nailed so they lay flat against the sheathing. If you're using a nail gun, just cut the boards to length so they fit between the studs. Then have one person hold them while someone else nails them from the outside. When doing this, hold the boards in place with a hammer or a piece of wood, so you don't get a nail shot through your hand.

On a two-story house, you'll generally have to install horizontal strips of sheathing to cover the floor joists. When doing this, try to position the sheathing so the horizontal strips and the full size sheets come together on the same board.

If the walls were framed properly, the sheathing on the load bearing walls should center on the studs if the first sheet is matched up at the corner. Any time it doesn't, you'll have to cut off part of a sheet to shift the sheathing over.

# SHIFTING THE FRAMING OVER

On the wall that was framed earlier, the studs were positioned so the first one was centered at 16 inches from the end of the wall. When framing a building, sometimes you'll want to shift everything over. For instance, if the non-load bearing wall that meets up at the first corner was framed in the same manner, the sheathing wouldn't overlap at the corner. Since I prefer to overlap the corners, sometimes I'll shift the studs 1/2 inch over on the non-load bearing walls if it doesn't screw up the other end. So, instead of marking the plates at 15 1/4, 31 1/4, 47 1/4, 63 1/4, etc., I'll mark them at 14 3/4, 30 3/4, 46 3/4, 62 3/4, etc.

Buildings are generally framed on 2 foot increments, such as 40, 54 or 64 feet. This way, the trusses will be spaced out evenly. Sometimes that won't be the case, and then you'll have to decide if it's better to shift the framing over. Let's say you're building a garage that's 27 feet long. If there's only going to be a short overhang on the roof, it doesn't really matter how you frame it, since you'll need the same number of trusses. If the first inside truss is 2 feet from one end, then the last inside truss will be 1 foot from the other end.

If the overhang on the ends was longer, it would be different. In that case, you'd want to shift the trusses over, so they're 18 inches from each end. This would be better for framing the lookout rafters. When doing this, I'd also shift the studs over so the first one was centered at 18 inches. The gap between the first two studs will still only be 1 1/4 inches farther apart than the others.

# CORROSION

Since 2004, treated wood has changed, and they say it's now more corrosive on metal. This requires the use of hot-dip galvanized or stainless steel fasteners. So far, I haven't seen it for myself, so I don't know how much worse it is. I've pulled cement coated nails that have been in the new treated wood for months, and they showed no sign of corrosion. I've also seen plenty of so-called premium deck screws that were partially gone in just a few years, and this was with the previous type of treated wood, which was supposed to be less corrosive. Whichever the case, it always seems that moisture is the problem when I come across nails or screws that are corroded.

The reason for bringing this up is, when is it OK to use standard nails or screws, and when do you have to use ones that are galvanized, stainless steel, or have some other type of corrosion protection? I don't really know the answer to this, but feel that you have to consider it anytime you're building, and then use common sense to decide. Right or wrong, this is what I normally do. Anytime I'm nailing into wood that's going to remain dry, I don't worry about it and use standard nails. This includes treated sill plates. I'll also use regular nails on a basement floor if it's in a heated area and if it's properly drained, -- basically if I think it will remain dry. On the other hand, concrete slabs in unheated garages, and those in cold and clammy basements, will probably sweat. Here I'd only use nails or screws that could also be used on a deck. Basement walls are another spot where there can be a problem. I've removed plenty of furring strips from basement walls that weren't attached anymore, once they got close to the floor. Because of this, I'd rather err on the side of caution and use fasteners that have corrosion protection, at least on the lower part of the wall.

I've read that cedar will react with galvanized nails, so it's better to use stainless steel instead. Based on what I've seen, I'd have to agree with it. On a cabin that I've worked on the last couple of years, galvanized nails were used to install the cedar siding, and there are stain marks around most of the nails on the exterior. Another option here is to use ring-shanked nails that are both galvanized and painted.

# SILL PLATES

When framing over a basement or a crawl space, the first job is generally to build the floor. If you're going over concrete, the floor joists will rest on a sill plate, which consists of pressure treated 2x6s that are attached to the foundation wall with anchor bolts that were left hanging out from the top of it. The sill plate doesn't necessarily follow the edge of the wall. Here it's more important that the boards are installed in a straight line, and have square corners, as they will determine the shape of the building that rests on top of them. When installing the sill, I'd rather have a board overhang the foundation wall, instead of sitting in so far that it interferes with the overhang of the siding. Sills are laid out along a chalk line that's snapped to mark their inside edge. Corners are checked for square by measuring diagonally, or by using the 3-4-5 method.

To drill the holes for the anchor bolts, lay the sill plates into position so they're right next to the bolts. Then use a speed square to mark the outside edge for both sides of each anchor bolt, on the sill plate. Now draw a line across the sill plate that's centered between those marks. To find the distance that each bolt will sit in from the edge of the board, either measure from the center of the bolt to the edge of the wall, or to the chalk line, whichever works the best. Then when drilling the holes, use larger bit. I use a 5/8 inch drill bit for 1/2 inch anchor bolts.

Before the boards are installed, a foam strip is laid around the perimeter to help seal against air leaks between the sill plate and the foundation. Years ago, I just applied a single strip, but every now and then I'd still find spots where you could feel the air getting through. To avoid this problem, check for low spots with a straight edge, and then double up the foam, over even triple it, to make sure it's thick enough in those locations.

# CHECKING FOR SQUARE

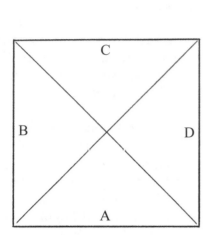
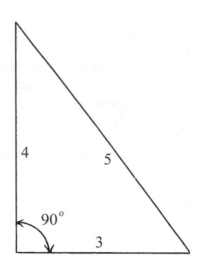
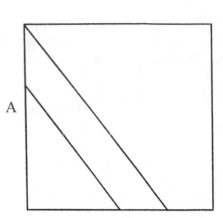

These drawings show two ways to see if the corners are square. This is something that you have to know, since you'll be using it on many of your home projects. On the left is the diagonal method. For this to work, the opposite sides have to be the same length. In this case, A and C have to be the same length, and B and D have to be the same length. Then to check for square, you simply measure from opposite corners to see if the measurements are the same.

The drawing in the middle shows the 3-4-5 method, which can be used almost anywhere. To do this, you measure out an increment of 3 going one way, and then 4 going perpendicular to it. If the corner is square, the diagonal measurement will be 5. Almost always, these measurements will be in feet. If you're checking something smaller, you can just use a square. You don't necessarily have to use 3-4-5 for the measurements; you just have to maintain the same ratio. You can double the measurements and use 6-8-10, or you could multiply by one and a half and use 4 1/2 - 6 - 7 1/2, etc. Use whatever works the best.

Generally, you'll get a more accurate reading if you measure out closer to the far edge, as this will eliminate a bad measurement that's caused by a warped board. You can see this in the drawing on the right. If side A wasn't straight, and you only measured part way out, the diagonal measurement would be off when trying to determine if the corner was square. By measuring out to the corner, the problem would be eliminated.

# FLOOR JOISTS

I remember an article that I once read in "Fine Homebuilding" where a carpenter described how he installed the floor joists. The method he used was to begin by laying out the joists along the top of the wall. Then after cutting them to length, he worked his way across by rolling the joists up into position and toenailing them to the sill plate. Then he installed the rim joists. I do it a little different. I lay out the boards and nail them together first, the same as if I were building a wall. Then I slide the sections into place and nail them to the sill plate.

When doing this, I start by cutting the joists to length, and mark any that are crowned by drawing an X on the crowned side. Then they're laid out along the top of the wall. After that's done, I mark the layout on the boards (rim joists) that I've picked for going around the perimeter. This is done in the same manner as when building a wall, by drawing a line and then putting an X on the side where the joist will go.

Ideally, the boards are straight, but if they're not, I'd choose one with a warp over one that was crowned. Serious crowns should be avoided if possible because the boards can be hard to pull down into place. If more than one rim joist is needed to complete a side, the boards will butt together at the center of a joist.

Once everything is laid out, I get up on the wall and start nailing the frame together. I roll the joists up into place, with the crowns up, and position them against the lines on the rim joist. Then I nail the boards together by putting several 16D sinkers into the end of each joist. Joists that sit noticeably low are lifted up flush to the upper edge of the rim joist before they're nailed on. Any gaps that are beneath these joists can be shimmed later.

After everything is nailed together, each section is slid into position along the edge of the sill plate. These sections are easier to move than you'd think, considering how much they weigh. Most of the time, all you have to do is to pull on each one at several points. For small adjustments, I tap on the edge with a sledge hammer. Then, once the rim joists are in the correct position, I kneel on the floor joists as I work my way around the perimeter, toenailing both the rim joists and the floor joists to the sill plate. For this I use 16D nails, and put two at the end of each joist, and then one every 16 inches around the outside of the perimeter. One advantage to this method is that the boards don't move around as much as when you're toenailing a single board, since they're already nailed together, and also because you're on top of them.

Once the outside walls are finished, I move on to the center wall if the joists are overlapped, and toenail the joists to the top plate. Then I nail the joists together where they overlap, again using 16D sinkers. I've found that it helps to pull any twisted joists into position, so they're square to the center wall, before the two boards are nailed together. I do this by attaching a pipe clamp or a bar clamp to give me more leverage.

After everything is nailed, I go over the framing one last time, looking for any high spots that have to be planed down. This would include boards that sit way above the rim joist, badly crowned floor joists, and high spots where they overlap.

If you're only framing across one room, the joists can probably span the entire opening, going from one wall to the other. In that case, the floor joists will generally be laid out in the same manner as the walls, on 16 inch centers, with the first one being centered at 16 inches from the end. Doing this will put the floor joists directly in line with the studs. It will also position a joist at the 8 foot mark, so every other row of floor sheathing can start with a full sheet.

When framing a house with standard floor joists, they generally come from opposite sides and overlap over a load bearing wall. When doing this, the position of the joists will have to be changed to compensate for the overlap. Otherwise the boards would sit at an angle, making it difficult to install the plywood and the sheetrock. What I do in this case is to draw the lines right at the 16 inch marks on the tape measure. Then to keep the floor joists parallel to the perimeter, the joists on one side of the house are installed on one side of the line, and the joists on the other side of the house are installed on the other side of the line. This will position the floor joists so they offset the studs by 3/4 of an inch, on both sides of the house.

I-joists and floor trusses can be used to span larger openings. Floor trusses are commonly centered every 24 inches, though they could also be centered at a little over 19 inches, which would give you one extra support for every 8 feet. One advantage of using I-joists is that they're more consistent in size, so you won't have the problems that you can have with standard joists, where some of the boards are wider than others. Floor trusses can be made to go across much larger openings. The farther they span, the taller they have to be. Even though floor trusses commonly go across the entire width of a house, there's generally a load bearing wall in the middle. The farthest that I've actually spanned was only around 22 feet. If I remember correctly, those trusses were 18 inches high.

One problem I have with floor trusses is that some of the floors are too bouncy for my taste. You can feel it every time someone walks across the room. To keep this from happening, I'd make sure the trusses were a little over-built. You should do the same when using standard floor joists. You don't want to use joists that are only rated for a span of 14 feet, if that's the distance you're spanning. Even though it meets the code, it would be better to use joists that can span a couple extra feet, so you end up with a more solid floor. When using standard floor joists, they're commonly doubled up under bathtubs to support the extra weight. You should also consider this when stone countertops are being installed, since they can weigh hundreds of pounds.

# SISTERING FLOOR JOISTS

When working on older homes, sometimes you'll find floors that need to be repaired and/or strengthened. Here, some of the floor joists could be rotted, and many times they're also too small by today's standards. You'll commonly run into this problem when converting an attic into a living space, since the joists may not have been sized to be used as a floor. Since replacing undersized boards with larger ones isn't always an option, this leaves you with sistering, which is doubling up the joists that are already in place.

The idea of this is pretty simple; it's just a matter of nailing another board to the side of each joist. In practice, it's not always that easy. The joists may have to be notched, and sometimes the end and/or the upper edge will have to be tapered for them to slip into place. Then, once they're in position, they're nailed to the existing board with at least two nails every 16 inches.

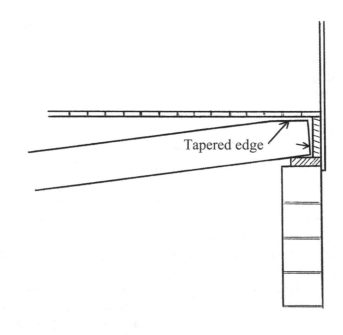

Tapered edge

Before you do this, you'll have to determine if sistering the joists will give you the necessary strength and stiffness. The problem is that very little information is available on this subject, and so far I haven't been able to find anything that shows the maximum span for doubled up floor joists. Because of that, I decided to come up with my own table, which is shown below. I have no training as an engineer, so I used equations that I found on the internet. To test them, I tried the equations on single joists to make sure that the numbers I came up with would closely match what's in existing tables. When doing this, two calculations are needed to determine the maximum span. One is based on deflection, and the other is based on load. After doing both calculations, the number that's used is the smaller of the two results.

On smaller joists that are spaced closer together, they're generally limited by deflection, but as the joists get larger and/or farther apart, load can be the limiting factor. In this table, you can see that the number for a sistered joist at 24 inches is the same as a single one at 12 inches, the exception to this being Southern Pine. Strength-wise, it doesn't matter if the extra joists are nailed to the existing ones, or centered between them. The numbers for single joist Southern Pine are the same as what's found in most tables. When calculating the span for doubled up Southern Pine, I used the same deflection rating, but newer numbers for the load, which are lower. Some of the numbers for the other types of single joists are smaller than those found in most tables, particularly for Spruce-Pine-Fir, the reason being that lumber from the U. S. and from Canada has been combined and given one rating.

So far, I've only worked on two projects where we sistered most of the floor joists. On the cabin that's shown on the last page, we used doubled-up Hem-Fir 2x8s on 19.2 inch centers to span 12 feet. On another project, where we added an upstairs, all there was for floor joists were 2x6s on 16 inch centers, spanning around 11 1/2 feet. The building inspector said we'd be OK if we doubled them up. Both floors feel fine.

| Maximum Span For Doubled-Up No. 2 Floor Joists       40# LL plus 10# DL   L/360 | | | | | | | | | |
|---|---|---|---|---|---|---|---|---|---|
| Joist Size | Joist Spacing | Hem-Fir | | Southern Pine | | Spruce-Pine-Fir | | Douglas Fir-Larch | |
| | | Single Joist | Doubled Joist | Single Joist | Doubled Joist | Single Joist | Doubled Joist | Single Joist | Doubled Joist |
| 2x6 | 12 | 10-0 | 12-7 | 10-9 | 13-6 | 9-5 | 11-11 | 10-9 | 13-6 |
| | 16 | 9-1 | 11-5 | 9-9 | 12-3 | 8-7 | 10-9 | 9-9 | 12-3 |
| | 19.2 | 8-7 | 10-9 | 9-2 | 11-6 | 8-1 | 10-2 | 9-1 | 11-6 |
| | 24 | 7-11 | 10-0 | 8-6 | 10-9 | 7-6 | 9-5 | 8-1 | 10-9 |
| 2x8 | 12 | 13-2 | 16-7 | 14-2 | 17-9 | 12-6 | 15-8 | 14-2 | 17-9 |
| | 16 | 12-0 | 15-1 | 12-10 | 16-2 | 11-4 | 14-3 | 12-5 | 16-2 |
| | 19.2 | 11-3 | 14-2 | 12-1 | 15-2 | 10-8 | 13-5 | 11-4 | 15-2 |
| | 24 | 10-2 | 13-2 | 11-0 | 14-0 | 9-8 | 12-6 | 10-2 | 14-2 |
| 2x10 | 12 | 16-10 | 21-2 | 18-0 | 22-8 | 15-11 | 20-0 | 17-6 | 22-8 |
| | 16 | 15-2 | 19-3 | 16-1 | 20-7 | 14-6 | 18-2 | 15-2 | 20-7 |
| | 19.2 | 13-10 | 18-1 | 14-8 | 18-10 | 13-3 | 17-1 | 13-10 | 19-5 |
| | 24 | 12-5 | 16-10 | 13-5 | 16-10 | 11-10 | 15-11 | 12-5 | 17-6 |
| 2x12 | 12 | 20-4 | 25-9 | 21-9 | 27-7 | 19-4 | 24-4 | 20-4 | 27-7 |
| | 16 | 17-7 | 23-5 | 19-0 | 24-1 | 16-10 | 22-1 | 17-7 | 24-10 |
| | 19.2 | 16-1 | 22-0 | 17-2 | 22-0 | 15-4 | 20-10 | 16-1 | 22-8 |
| | 24 | 14-4 | 20-4 | 15-4 | 19-8 | 13-9 | 19-4 | 14-4 | 20-4 |

Here are the equations I used, so you can calculate what's needed at different spans, at different deflection ratings, or when using boards that aren't a standard size. When doing this, remember that these are maximum spans. It's better to overbuild for a stronger and more rigid floor. If I have a choice, I always try to use joists that have a rated span of a couple extra feet, and I'd want a lot more when spanning a long distance.

L/360   is what's required for floor joists in a home, though L/480 could be used instead to give you a stiffer floor. L/360 is the span in inches, divided by the deflection rating (360). For example, with a span of 12 feet (144"), the maximum deflection that's allowed would be .40 of an inch.  144 divided by 360 = .40  Any floor joists that are used at this length must have a deflection rating that is equal to or smaller than this number.

## TERMS USED

L  -  Length of span in inches            b  -  Width of joist
E  -  Modulus of elasticity               d  -  Depth of joist
I  -  Moment of inertia                    s  -  Spacing of floor joists, in inches.
W  -  Weight supported by the joist

Modulus of elasticity is a rating that each type of wood is given that determines how far it can span. This number will vary, depending on the species and how the board has been graded. For instance, No. 2 Hem-Fir is rated at 1.3 million, while No. 2 Douglas Fir and Southern Pine are generally given a rating of 1.6 million. The modulus of elasticity for No. 2 Spruce-Pine-Fir has recently been lowered to 1.1 million.

The Moment of Inertia of a board is determined by its width and depth. The calculation for this is $b \times d^3/12$   For a 2x8, the calculation would be $1.5 \times 7.25^3$ divided by 12 = 47.6  Numbers for other sizes are:  2x6 = 20.8   2x10 = 98.9   2x12 = 178.

The weight supported by a floor joist is determined by the length of the span, the spacing of the joists, and the load. Most tables are based on 40 pounds per square foot live load, plus 10 pounds dead load. A 30 pound live load is allowed for sleeping areas. Dead load is the weight of the floor itself, while live load is what goes on top of it. Only live load is used to determine deflection. To find the answer, you multiply the span, in inches, by the spacing, in inches, and divide by 144. Then the answer is multiplied by the load. For instance, with a 12 foot span at 16 inches on center, and a 40 pound live load, the calculation would be:

144 x 16, divided by 144  =  16      16 x 40 = 640 lbs

The equation for determining the deflection of a floor joist is   $5WL^3/384EI$
For example, a 12' Hem-Fir 2x8 at 16" would be  $5 \times 640 \times 144^3$ divided by 384 x 1,300,000 x 47.6
9555148800 divided by 23761920000  =  .40   This equals the allowable deflection for a 12 foot board at L/360, so this is the maximum length, based on deflection.

To find the maximum span for sistered floor joists, based on deflection, I ran the calculations on Excel, and changed the length until the deflection for L/360 and the deflection for the joist itself would match up. I had a friend set it up for me, since I know about as much on a computer as a five-year-old. When doing this, the moment of inertia was doubled, since the joist is twice as wide. If you wanted, you could reduce the spacing instead, for example, from 16 to 8 inches. Either way, you'll get the same answer.

To check for load, the equation is $\sqrt{Sbd^2/9W}$ = the maximum length (in feet). To change the answer to inches, multiply by 12.

For this equation, dead load is included, so W = 50 pounds per square foot multiplied by the spacing (in feet). For example, with a 16 inch spacing, 50 is multiplied by 1.3333, which is rounded off to 66.7  At a 12 inch spacing, W = 50, at 19.2 inches W = 80, and at 24 inches W = 100.

In this equation, $S$ is the load value that's been given for that type of lumber. This number will vary, depending on the species, the width of the board, and if multiple joists are used. The numbers used to come up with the table are listed below.

|      | Hem-Fir | Southern Pine | Spruce-Pine-Fir | Douglas Fir-Larch |
|------|---------|---------------|-----------------|-------------------|
| 2x6  | 1270    | 1207          | 1160            | 1270              |
| 2x8  | 1175    | 1121          | 1070            | 1175              |
| 2x10 | 1075    | 997           | 980             | 1075              |
| 2x12 | 980     | 920           | 890             | 980               |

As an example, the maximum length for a No. 2  2x8 Hem-Fir floor joist, based on load is:

The square root of (1175 x 1.5 x 7.25 x 7.25  divided by  9 x 66.7) = 12.42 ft. x  12 = 149 inches

The maximum length, based on deflection, is 144 inches. Since this is the smaller of the two numbers, that's the one that gets used.

# FLOOR AND ROOF OPENINGS

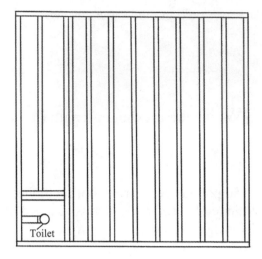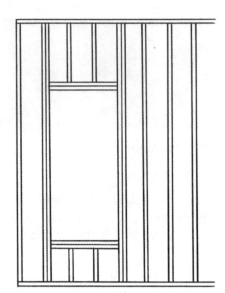

Floors commonly need openings for things such as stairs. On hand framed roofs, they're also needed for dormers and skylights. When framing one of these openings, you have to consider the size of it, and also take into account how many joists or rafters have to be cut, so the floor or the roof will be strong enough once you're finished. Take stairs, for instance. Let's say that two joists have to be cut in order to frame the opening. To get the strength back, you'll have to add two new joists, with one sistered to the last uncut joist on each side. The boards framing the end of the opening will also be doubled up. It's easier to add these boards before you double up the joists, if possible, as this will allow them to be end nailed. If you add them after the joists are doubled up, they'll have to be toenailed. You may also be required to use joist hangers when doing this. Here I prefer to just use nails instead, since it's easier to install the sheetrock without the hangers sticking out. I also hand nail, since the nails are thicker, which gives them greater shear strength.

# FLOOR SHEATHING

Once the framing for the floor is finished, the sheathing can be installed. Before you get started, stretch a string along the outside edge of the end joists to see if they're straight. If they are, you're good to go. If not, the string should be left in place.

When laying the first sheet, I position it right on the corner, and make sure it's even with long edge. Then I'll put the second sheet in place to see how they both look. If the outside edge is even with the last floor joist, or parallel to the string, and the corners of the sheathing are pretty much centered on the other joists, I'll start nailing the floor and then install the rest of the sheets. As I do this, I'll make a mark every 16 inches along the far edge of the sheathing. Then I'll pull the joists into place so they're centered on the mark before I nail the sheathing to that joist. If I'm on a big floor, I'll also snap a chalk line for the first row to follow, to make sure it's straight.

When using tongue and groove plywood, the second row will have to be pounded into place, as will any rows that follow. It helps to stand on the sheet as you're hitting it. Use a sledge hammer when doing this, and lay a 2x4 against the edge to protect it. I prefer to lay the flooring so that I pound on the groove side, as I feel there's less damage this way, rather than beating up the tongue.

Any butt seams should be offset from those of the previous row. I like to offset the seams by at least a couple of joists from one row to the next, but this may not be possible, and you may only be able to offset it by a single joist. Sometimes you can cut off part of one of the sheets to get more offset on that row.

On floors, I prefer to use ring-shanked nails because of their greater holding power. While working on older homes, you see a lot of floors with the nails sticking out. Using ring-shanked nails should keep this from happening. These days, many of the floors that are installed by professionals are also glued. I'm still on the fence concerning this. People will tell you that using glue will eliminate squeaks. I'm sure it helps, but I've still heard plenty of squeaks on floors that were glued. You can't expect glue to cover up sloppy work. My view is that good workmanship is more important for a quiet floor. If the joists are sized correctly, and everything is properly cut and nailed, you shouldn't have a problem. A floor that's glued is probably a little stiffer, but the framing should have been strong enough to begin with.

If you're using construction adhesive, apply it to the joists right before the sheets are laid into place. If the adhesive has time to skin over, it may not bond to the sheathing. Polyurethane construction adhesive costs more than others, such as PL400, but it's stickier and seems to have more working time.

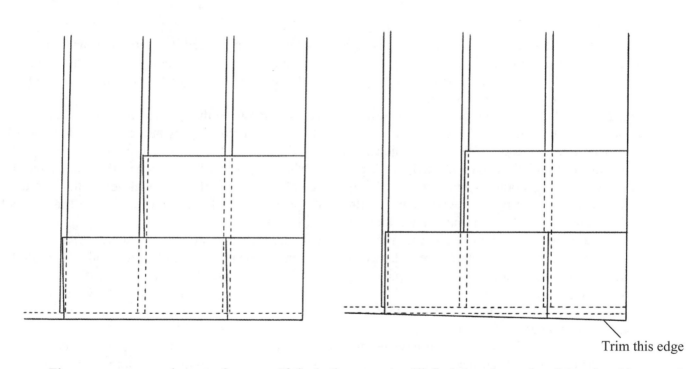

Trim this edge

Floors are commonly out of square. If that's the case, you'll find that the ends of the sheathing won't line up properly on the joists. There are a couple of ways to compensate for this. One is shown in the drawing on the left, where the sheathing is slightly shifted over on a floor that's out of square. When doing this, the seams will angle across the joist. This method will work as long as there's enough nailing surface where the two sheets come together.

The drawing on the right shows another method where the first row is installed at an angle. This will square it up, so the ends of the sheathing will run straight down the joists. When doing this, you'll have to cut off any material that overhangs the side that you start on.

While a floor that's out of square can still be sheathed, if it isn't straightened, you'll have the same problem when sheetrocking the ceiling and sheathing the roof. That's why you'd like everything to be square to begin with.

# ROOF TRUSSES

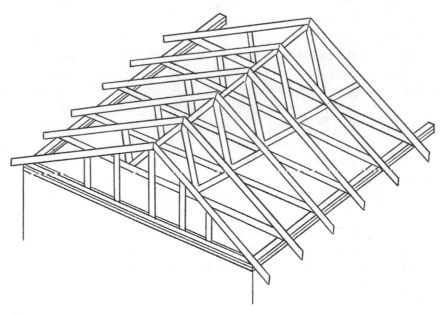

As soon as the walls are up, and they're sheathed and/or securely braced, the top plates are marked to show the position of the trusses. Then the trusses can be installed. If you have enough help, the trusses can be carried into the building and then positioned along the wall. On a gable roof, I just spread them out hanging upside down. This way, they're ready to go.

Then I start by tipping up one of the end trusses, and position it on the edge of the wall. This truss is toenailed so it's flush to the outer edge of the framing, and I generally hold it up by attaching it to long boards that are screwed to the outside of the wall, which extend above it to keep the truss plumb and in line with the wall. If the wall has already been sheathed, small pieces of sheathing should go between the boards and the truss to keep everything straight. On most roofs, I'll put three of them along the end wall before the first truss goes up. To install them, first I screw a long 2x4 flat to the wall, that will reach the top of the truss at that location. Then I'll screw a 2x6 to it, perpendicular to it, to stiffen it up.

You could also brace the truss by using long diagonal boards that are attached to stakes driven into the ground. Yet another option is to start several trusses in, and run diagonal braces to the end wall. Then do the end trusses once the others are braced. Just make sure the first truss is braced securely, since it's going to be the only thing holding everything up for the time being. At this time, the diagonal bracing between the walls and the floor should still be in place. Where this isn't possible, diagonal braces should be installed between the walls at each corner (near the top) to keep them from moving.

Once that's done, the rest of the trusses are tipped up, positioned on their marks, and then toenailed to the walls with 16D sinkers. I put three nails at each end on the inside trusses, with two going in from one side, and one from the other. As they're being installed, someone will have to get up on the trusses to nail a board across the top, called lateral bracing, that holds them up so they're spaced correctly. On a small garage that will be sheathed the same day, sometimes I'll use 1x3s for this, with two 8D sinkers going into each truss, but on a larger roof I'd use 2x4s with 16D sinkers. I generally leave the nail heads sticking out, since the boards will be removed as the sheathing is installed.

When installing the second truss on a 24 inch center, hook the measuring tape on the far side of the end truss, and then nail the brace so the second one is centered on the 24 inch mark. On the trusses that follow, hook the tape on the far side of the last one that was installed, and position the next truss with the near edge on the 24 inch mark. As you go along, every now and then you should reach over as far as you can with the measuring tape to double check the measurements. The end truss on the far end is ideally installed with the distance across the top matching what's on the bottom, but here it's more important that the truss is plumb and in line with the wall.

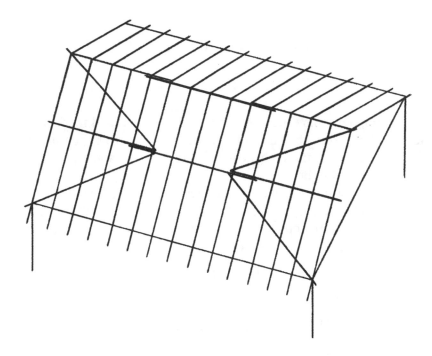

Some guys use 2x4s that are cut at 25 1/2 inches for bracing the inside trusses, and then nail them so each end is flush to the outside edge of a truss. Others put the braces at the top, between the trusses, and cut them at a little under 22 1/2 inches. Either method is fine, as long as the trusses are spaced correctly.

It's important that the trusses are kept in a straight line as they're being installed. If the walls are straight, you can line up the end of the bottom chord with the edge of the top plate, or you could measure to see that each rafter tail overhangs the wall by the same amount. Measure carefully, or you'll end up with a hump on one side of the roof and a dip on the other.

For the best results, whether the walls are straight or not, you can also line up the trusses by using a string line. This is the way that I prefer. I do this by putting up both of the end trusses, and then stretch a string line between them that's just above the peak. Then one by one, the inside trusses are tipped up and centered on the string, and then nailed into place. The first time I helped install trusses, they were positioned by measuring the overhang, and the roof ended up with a hump in it because someone got sloppy. Since then, I like to be the one up on the trusses to see that they're lined up under the string, and also spaced correctly. To check the lower spacing, I only have to look down and see that every other truss is centered over a stud.

Once you have a few of the trusses up, diagonal braces are installed to keep everything from tipping over. How many are needed is determined by the size of the roof, and also by how long it will be before the sheathing goes on. If I was working on a garage, I'd probably only brace one side of the roof, using a long 2x4 on each end that was attached with 16D nails or long deck screws. This will leave the other side ready to be sheathed. Larger roofs will get more braces, and they'll go on both sides. Just make sure that the roof is braced enough so there's no way a hard wind is going to knock it over. The drawing above shows a roof with two rows of staggered lateral braces going across it, along with a pair of diagonal braces on each end. The other side of the roof would get the same, except for the row along the peak.

Normally I'd say that the walls should be braced so they're plumb. One exception to this would be when using scissors trusses. The last time I installed scissors trusses, the trusses were about 40 feet long, not counting the tails. The walls were securely braced, and were plumb before the trusses went up, but after the roof was finished, they were tipped out by almost half an inch in the middle of the wall. The reason this happened was that the trusses sagged a little as more weight went on the roof, which pushed the walls out. When they're 40 feet long, it doesn't take much of a sag to move the wall half an inch. I don't think there's a whole lot that you can do about this, since you don't know how far the wall is going to move. However, the next time I install scissor trusses, I'll set the walls so that they lean in a little, once I'm away from the corners.

## CUTTING THE TAILS

Once the trusses are up, determine the overhang that you want, and mark the cut line on the rafter tail at each corner of the house. Then either snap a chalk line between the marks, or stretch a string between them, and mark the cuts with a pencil. Snapping a chalk line is quicker, but sometimes it won't snap correctly and you'll end up with a line that isn't straight.

After they're marked, you still have to draw the lines for making the cuts. Depending on the angle, this can be done using a speed square, a level, or one of those squares that lets you adjust the angle. These cuts are generally made with a circular saw. If you have a lighter weight saw, this might be a good time to use it. Reaching up and out while hanging on with the other hand gets tiring when you're using an eleven pound saw.

## SHEATHING THE ROOF

At this point, whether or not you can start on the sheathing will depend on the amount of overhang on the gable ends, as this is done in different manners, depending on how far it's going to extend. If you're only going to have around a foot of overhang, you'd start on the sheathing, since no extra framing is needed at this time. Hand framed roofs with rafters are done the same way. When installing the sheathing, it's nailed on with 8D nails or the equivalent in a nail gun, and it should overlap the end trusses far enough to allow for the overhang. Make sure the sheathing is relatively flat where it hangs over the outside edge. A sheet that turns up slightly is OK, but one that has a hard downward curl should be avoided, as this will make it harder to frame the overhang.

The roof sheathing is installed with the butt seams offset from each other, and H-clips are sometimes used between the rows. These clips, which look like an H when viewed from the side, are slipped over the sheathing between each truss. Then the next sheet will slip into the same clips as it's installed. This will lock the rows together, and also leaves a gap that allows the sheets to expand. These clips come in different sizes, but many times they'll still fit too loose on the sheathing. This is easily fixed by pinching down on them.

As the sheathing is installed, the trusses are pulled into place, the same as when working on a floor. Before starting, I always run a string line down each end truss. These will be left in place until the sheathing is finished. This may seem unnecessary, but I've rarely seen an end truss that was actually straight. I also recheck the distance between the end trusses at the peak, and make sure that both of them are plumb and in line with the outer walls.

Many times, roofs are out of square. You could check for this by measuring across the roof diagonally. But, even if it is, there isn't much that you can do about it at this point if the end trusses are in the correct position. Generally a little out of square isn't that big of a deal, since it would be hard to see once the roof is finished.

Years ago, I installed the sheathing a little different than I do now. Back then, I'd put strings on the end trusses, and mark both edges of the sheathing every 24 inches. Then I'd pull the end trusses into place against the string as I went, and center the others on the pencil marks on both the upper and the lower edge of the sheets. On some roofs it worked fine, while on others, everything would be OK until I got close the top. Then I'd hit a point where the trusses wouldn't center on the marks anymore, and anytime this happened, the interior trusses ended up with a bend in them.

It took me a while to figure out what was wrong. It turned out that the roofs were a little out of square, and I was creating the problem by trying to pull the trusses into place. The way to deal with it is to sheathe the roof in the same manner as a floor that's out of square. Either run the sheathing parallel to the lower edge of the roof, and have the butt seams meet at an angle on the trusses, or start the first row of sheathing with it running at an angle to the lower edge, which will square it up to the trusses. Both methods were shown a few pages back.

These days, I rarely check to see if a roof is square, and I've only made a couple of changes that prevents the problem from happening. What I do now is to start by looking for an inside truss that's straight. Then once I've found one, I base that side of the roof off the one truss.

On most roofs, the first row is laid out along a chalk line, and the sheathing will overhang the lower edge to overlap the fascia. I mark the sheets for the first row every 24 inches, on both the upper and the lower edge, and then position the first sheet so either one end of it or one of the upper marks is centered on the truss that's straight. Then it's lightly nailed into place as it's held against the chalk line. Now I can see if the roof is reasonably square. If both ends of the sheet are parallel to the trusses, and the marks seem to line up with the other trusses, on both edges, I'd leave the sheet where it is and then install the one that's next to it, and also lightly nail it into place. While looking them over, I always check the tails to see if they're warped, since that would make a roof that's square appear to be off, and vice versa. If everything looked OK, I'd install the rest of the sheets on the first row, and then nail them off. While doing this, I'd center the trusses on the upper marks, pull the end trusses into place along the string, and center the tails on the lower marks.

Now with the first row is in place, H-clips, if used, go between each truss. Then the second row is installed with the butt seams offset from the previous row, and again, the first sheet is positioned off the straight truss. On this row, and others that follow, just the upper edge of the sheets are marked for positioning the inside trusses. The strings continue to be used at the end of each row to make sure the end trusses are straight. Once you get to the top, the last row is cut to fit. If a ridge vent is being installed, a 1 inch gap is left at the top, on each side.

If the roof appeared to be out of square once the first two sheets were in place, I'd have to make a decision. If it wasn't that bad, I would probably just shift the sheets to one side to compromise on how they overlapped the trusses. Then I'd hold the measuring tape against the truss that was straight as I marked the sheathing for positioning the other trusses. On the lower edge of the first row, I'd straighten the tails by just looking up the edge of them.

Now if the roof was way out of square, which you sometimes get with an older building, I would have dropped one of the ends on the first row, and re-snapped the chalk line so the sheathing was squared up to the trusses. Then I'd cut the lower edge. Sometimes you don't realize how bad a roof is until you get to the second row. That's why it's best to lightly nail the sheets until you're sure that everything is OK.

# FRAMING THE GABLE ENDS

After the sheathing is installed, both sides are marked at the top and the bottom for cutting the overhang. Then a chalk line is snapped between the marks, and the sheathing is cut off at the line with a circular saw. Now the fascia or sub-fascia, depending on whether the boards are getting covered, can be installed. On most houses, these boards are generally 2x6s. It generally doesn't matter if the gable ends or the lower edge is done first, but here we'll start on the gables. These boards can be a little warped, but you have to watch out for crowns. A board with a slight crown facing up should be OK, but I'd avoid anything else. Begin by cutting the ends where they'll meet at the top. Either a speed square or a framing square can be used for drawing the angle of the cuts. You could also hold the boards in place, and then draw the lines using a level.

Once the upper ends are cut, the fascia boards are clamped into place, flush to the outer edge of the sheathing. Then the angle of the cuts is checked, and the boards are either slid up or down until they meet up at the peak. While doing this, you should also lay a straightedge across the sheathing, near the peak. What you're looking for is whether or not the overhang is in line with the rest of the roof. If you find that it either rises up or sags down, it can be adjusted by moving the fascia boards. If the upper end is sagging, tap both boards upward. This should raise the height. When doing this, you may have to pull up on the sheathing at the peak. To lower the overhang, slide the fascia boards down slightly. Once it looks right, mark the position of both fascia boards on the sheathing.

Now the lower cuts have to be marked. If the fascia has already been installed along the lower edge, you only have to mark where the boards come together, and then remove the boards and cut them off at that point, while matching the angle. If the lower fascia boards haven't been installed yet, they should be cut to line up with the end of the trusses. After that's finished, the boards are put back into place and positioned on the marks that were drawn. Then the sheathing is nailed to the boards. At the peak, I also like to install a long deck screw that goes through the sheathing and into both boards to lock everything together. If you only use nails, the seam tends to open up. As you drive the screw in, put your weight on the peak to keep the boards together.

When installing the fascia boards that run along the lower edge, they should be cut so they're flush to the outer edge of the sheathing. Wherever possible, the ends of the trusses should be pulled into position on this board as they're being nailed. This should help to keep the lower edge of the roof straight. Since this board will also support the lower end of the gable fascia, you have to watch out for any crowns on the end of it.

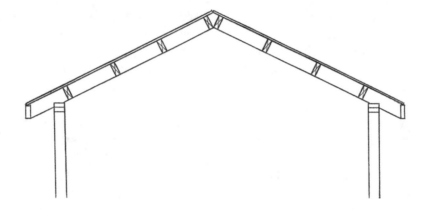

To finish off the peaks, blocks are installed between the fascia board and either the sheathing, the end truss, or the rafter to support the overhang. If possible, the blocks should be the same width as the fascia boards. I generally install the blocks about three feet apart, and cut them to fit tight. Then they're nailed into place by going through the fascia board, and also by toenailing them to the wall. When using this method, install the sheathing so the end of each row is nailed to at least two trusses or rafters.

## LARGE OVERHANGS

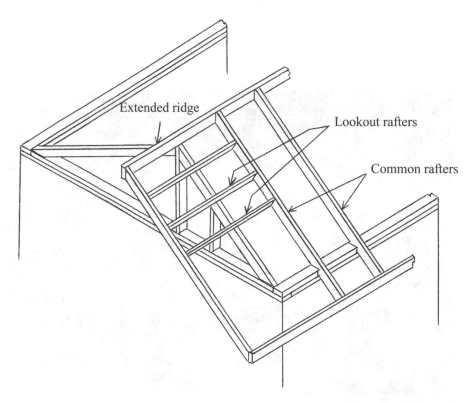

Using blocks to support the edge works fine on a short overhang, but once you get much over a foot, the overhang should be framed before the sheathing goes on. One method is shown in the drawing above. Here the end rafter sits lower than the others, and lookout rafters are nailed to the first common rafter so they cantilever over the end rafter, which gives you a strong overhang. Trusses are done in the same manner, with the end trusses being 3 1/2 inches shorter than the others. When doing this, I frame the overhang with 2x4s on either 16 or 24 inch centers, depending on the thickness of the sheathing, and position the boards so they're centered on the seams between the rows.

When building my brother's cabin, full size rafters were used on the ends, so we cut 3 inch wide by 5 1/2 inch deep notches for the lookout rafters. Then we used doubled up 2x6s and spaced them about every 5 feet. The overhang on the cabin is around 30 inches wide. In this photo you can see the doubled up 2x6s.

On a friend's house in Arizona, the framers used this method for a 1 foot overhang. In this case, notches were cut into the end trusses, which had a 2x6 for the upper chord, and 2x4s

were laid flat on 4 foot centers to support the overhang. Then the sheathing was installed so it ended at the center of each end truss. After that, the 2x4s were cut to length, the fascia boards were nailed on, and sheathing was installed along the edge in narrow strips.

As you frame the overhang, use a straightedge to make sure it's in line with the roof. To adjust it, the lookout rafters can be shimmed up at the end wall, or they could either be raised or lowered on the common rafter.

# HAND FRAMING THE ROOF

I seldom see a roof being framed by hand anymore, which is too bad. While they're more difficult to build, the ceilings on the upper floor of a house that has dormers and a roof with a steep pitch can be truly beautiful, with all the angles that come together.

Roofs framed in this manner generally have collar ties attached to the rafters, though they're not necessary when using a properly sized ridge beam. This supports the extra weight and allows the ceiling to be wide open. Even where the ceilings are going to be flat, a ridge board will still be used, though its main purpose here is to provide a nailing surface for installing the rafters.

Collar ties (collar beams) and ceiling joists are used to triangulate the framing to prevent the roof from sagging down, which would push the walls out. These boards have to be securely nailed to the rafters with several 16D nails (4 - 6) used at each end when framing the roof on a house.

When the ceilings are at wall height, you may want to install the ceiling joists first. This will lock the walls together, and give you something to stand on while working on the roof. These boards are sized according to the load they have to support. With an unused attic above, the only load will be the weight of the sheetrock and the insulation. But where the joists will also be used to support a floor, they'll have to be sized for that purpose. The same holds true for collar ties. The main difference between the two is where the boards are attached. When the ceiling is at wall height, the joists rest on the upper plate and they're nailed to both the upper plate and to the rafters, whereas collar ties sit above the wall, so they're only attached to the rafters.

On my brother's cabin (shown in this photo), we used a combination of these methods when framing the roof. In the middle section, vaulted ceilings go all the way up to the peak, except in the center where there are collar ties on the main roof, 15 feet above the floor. The two ends have flat ceilings. On one end, 2x6 collar ties were installed 10 feet off the floor, with the area above them not being used. On the other end, the collar ties were installed a foot lower, at 9 feet. Here, 2x8s were used, so the area above them can be used as a loft.

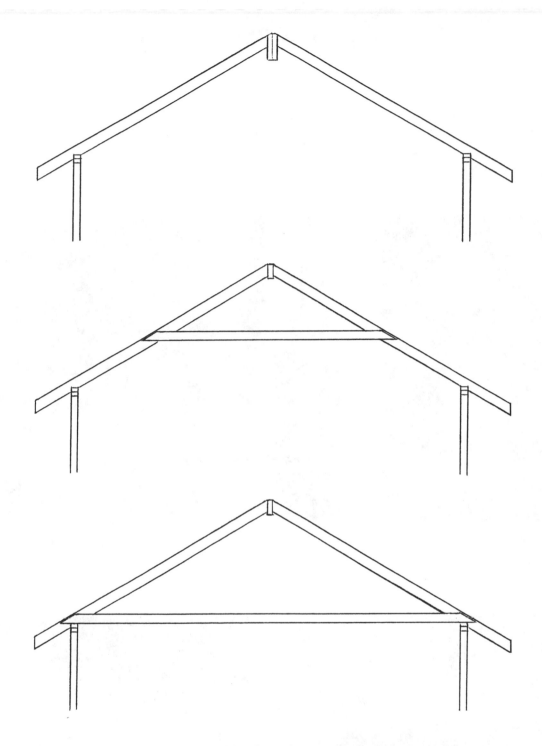

These drawings show some of the combinations that are used when hand framing a roof. In the upper drawing, a ridge beam is used to support the load, so the ceiling area can be wide open. In the second drawing, a ridge board and collar ties are used, but they're high up so you still have a tall ceiling. In the lower drawing, the ceiling joists sit right on top of the walls, so the ceiling is completely flat. When framing a sloped ceiling, you'll need a tall step ladder.

I generally start by calculating the height for the ridge board (beam), since it will determine the pitch of the roof. If I'm having a problem coming up with this height, or determining how long a rafter has to be, sometimes I'll do the layout on the floor. I do this by snapping chalk lines and/or laying boards across the floor. On a house, the ridge board is commonly installed in sections. When using a ridge beam, it has to span the length of the opening, with each end supported by a wall or a post.

# FRAMING A SMALL ROOF

This series of photos shows how the roof was framed on a small shed. Though the size of everything is much smaller than that on a house, the same process is used. This should give you a better idea of what I'm describing on the following pages.

The ridge board supports were installed first.

Once the supports were in position, the ridge board was slipped into place and attached.

The rafter positions were drawn on the ridge board before it was installed.

When installing the opposing rafter, the nails were driven in at an angle through the ridge board.

The upper cut on the rafters

The lower notch (bird's beak)

The rafters, after they were installed

String lines were used to install the collar ties in a straight line, since the ceiling will be attached to them.

A string line was also used to mark the end cuts.

The lower edge, after it was cut

Once the rafter tails were cut, the
roof was ready to be sheathed.

Since I was working alone, blocks were
attached to the end of the rafters to hold
the sheathing in place as it was nailed.

Here the sheathing has been
cut for the overhang.

The lower fascia board was lined up
with the end of the sheathing.

The lower end of the gable fascia

The upper ends were matched up at the peak.

The almost finished roof

## RIDGE BOARD

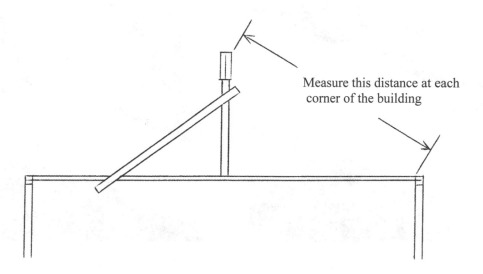

Measure this distance at each
corner of the building

To start on the roof, the first job will be to install the ridge board or the ridge beam, so you'll begin by putting up the studs or the posts that will support it. When doing this, I want a notch for the beam to slip into, at least until the rafters are in place. The notch will serve two purposes: to keep the ridge beam plumb, and to provide a place for it to be attached. If I'm using studs for the support, I'll double them up and cut one stud to go under the board, and a longer one to go along the side of it. For the time being, these supports will be held in position with diagonal braces. Use a level to check for plumb, so the beam is centered. If the beam is higher up, a laser level is generally faster and more accurate.

Once the supports are in position, the beam is lifted up into place and attached to the supports. But before you do this, you may want to mark the positions of the rafters on it. Then after it's up, use the level to make sure it's positioned correctly, and also measure from the beam down to both walls to make sure it's centered between them.

## CUTTING THE RAFTERS

To start on the rafters, first I measure the distance from the upper edge of the beam to the point on the outside wall where the rafter will first come into contact with it (as shown in the last drawing). Measure this distance on both sides of the beam, and at both ends of it. The measurements should be approximately the same. If they're a little off, just split the difference between them. To get the most support, you'd measure to the inside edge of the walls, so each rafter would lie across the full width of the upper plate. You'll notice that this wasn't done in the previous photos. On that roof, the rafters were 2x4s, so there wasn't enough wood to allow it. When cutting the bird's beak, also called bird's mouth, you should leave enough wood so the rafter tails are strong enough.

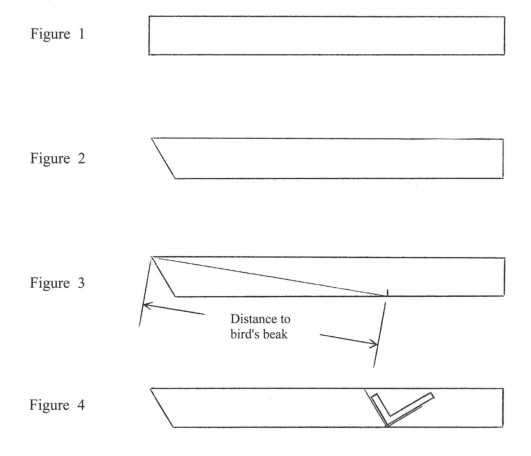

Figure 1

Figure 2

Figure 3

Distance to bird's beak

Figure 4

Figure 5

Figure 6

Figure 7

Figure 8

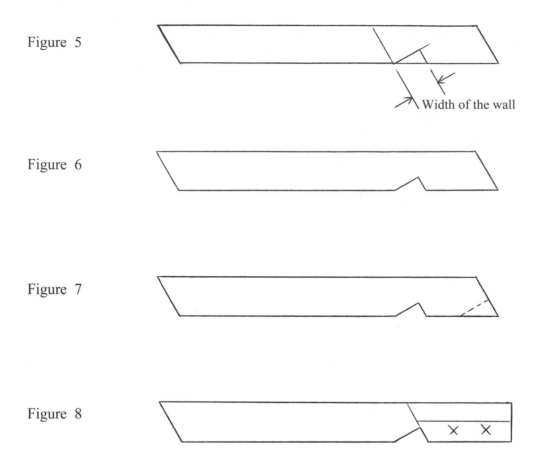

Width of the wall

Looking at the drawings, Figure 1 shows the board that will be used for the rafter. In Figure 2, the upper end has been cut to fit against the ridge board. To draw the line for the cut, either use a speed square or a framing square. You could also hold the board against the end of the peak, and then trace it, or draw a vertical line with a level. In Figure 3, the mark has been made for the start of the bird's beak. This measurement is the one that's shown in the drawing two pages back. Figure 4, after drawing a line at the mark that matched the angle on the upper end of the board, a framing square was used to draw the horizontal line. In Figure 5, the vertical line was drawn for the bird's beak by measuring over the width of the wall. In Figure 6, you can see that the bird's beak has been cut. When doing this, I make the cuts with a circular saw, and then finish them up with a jig saw. Figures 7 and 8 show two ways to cut the rafter tails. In Figure 7, a line has been drawn for the horizontal cut for the soffit, where the fascia board will be smaller than the rafter. Most houses have 6 inch fascia. In Figure 8, the X's mark where the board will be cut. Here the fascia will be smaller yet, and the soffit will run parallel to the roof.

Another method that can be used for drawing the bird's beak is to cut the angle on the upper end of the rafter, and then to simply hold the board in place as you draw the lines by running a pencil along the edge of the upper plate. This only works when you have help or when framing a small roof.

Once the rafter is cut, it's put into place at each corner to check the fit. Then any changes that are needed will have to be made. Since this rafter will be used as a template for cutting the others, it has to fit correctly, and the cuts should be straight. After it's finished, lay it on top of the other rafter boards, with any crowns facing up. Then trace the upper cut and the bird's beak onto each board, and make the cuts. At this time, I don't cut the rafters to length.

The rafters are installed by starting on one end, and are nailed into place with 16D sinkers. On the first rafter, I hold the upper edge flush to the top of the beam, and then nail into the end of it by going straight through the ridge board. On the other side this won't be possible, so I drive the nails through the board at an angle. Another option is to slightly offset the rafters, so the nails can go in straight.

The size of the rafters determines how many nails are needed. On a 2x4 I'd use two, while a 2x12 would get four, or maybe five if it had a steep pitch. I also put three toenails at the bottom, two from one side and one from the other.

Before the rafters go up, make sure the walls are straight and securely braced. When framing a vaulted ceiling, the rafters tend to push the walls out at the top, which will knock them out of plumb. I don't know if you can totally prevent this from happening, but it would help to install collar ties before any more weight is put on the roof, or it has time to settle. Another option would be to nail on a temporary collar tie every few rafters as they're being installed. These boards could be removed later, one at a time, and then replaced by the permanent collar ties. This should have been done on the roof that's shown on the cover of this book. By the time we installed the collar ties, the short wall on the right side of the photo had been pushed out about 1/2 inch, even though the ridge board was well supported from underneath.

As you install the rafters, make sure that each bird's beak ends at the same point on the top plate. This will help to keep the rafters in line, and the ridge beam straight. Then, once the rafters are all up, the lower ends are cut off the same as when installing trusses.

Commonly, the end walls aren't built until the rafters are in place. The advantage to this is that the studs can be run full length, assuring you of a flat wall, where a stacked wall could move where the two sections come together. When doing this, I make the support for the ridge board using studs, so they become part of the finished wall. You'll need longer studs when doing this. On my brother's cabin, studs around 20 feet long were needed at the peaks, and also for the diagonal braces that held up the beams.

On larger roofs, the beam may have to go up in sections, with a support installed under every joint. These supports may or may not be temporary, and are put up and braced in the same manner as those on the ends. Joints that are over walls can be supported by boards that rest directly on top of those walls. Temporary posts that aren't directly over a floor joist should rest on boards that are long enough to bridge between the joists, to prevent the floor sheathing from sagging under the weight of the roof. Permanent posts that are load-bearing should rest on framing that carries down from that point, all the way to the footings in the basement floor.

## ROOF DESIGN

The roofs that we've gone over so far have been gable roofs that have a single peak that goes from one end of the building to the other. Another version of a gable roof that you commonly see on houses is shown in this drawing. Here you have ridges running perpendicular to each other, with a peak on three sides of the house. While this may seem too complicated and beyond your skills, building this type of roof is just a matter of using common sense, and then building it in the right order.

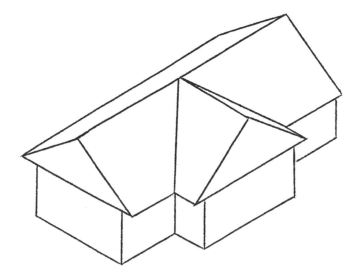

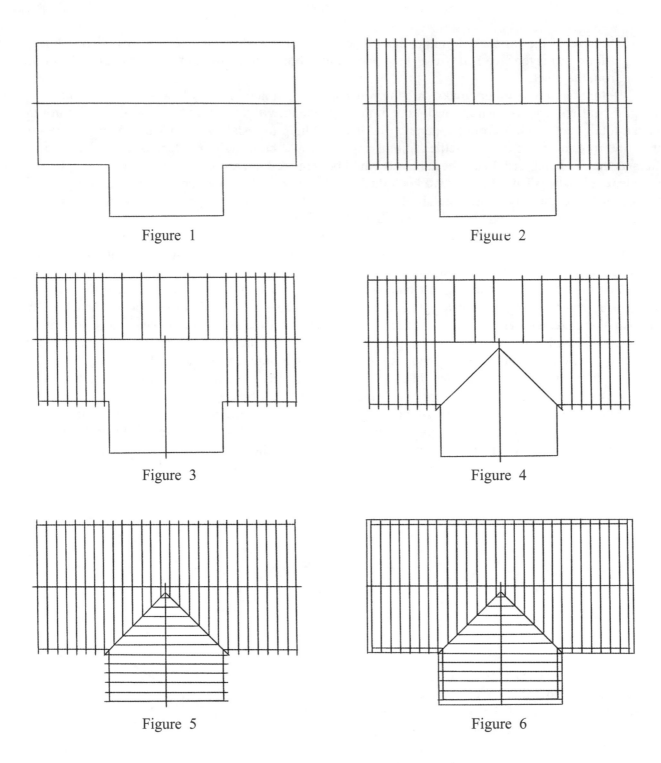

Figure 1

Figure 2

Figure 3

Figure 4

Figure 5

Figure 6

These drawings show the order that the roof would be built. Starting with Figure 1, the main ridge board has been installed. You can see that it extends past the end of the house to help support the overhang. In Figure 2, the common rafters have been put up on both ends, and there's also a few in the middle of the house. This will keep the ridge board straight as long as it's well supported from underneath. In Figure 3, the second ridge board has been installed. In the drawings, this peak is a little lower than the main roof, and the ridge board was extended slightly past the other one. In Figure 4, the valley rafters are in place. In Figure 5, the rest of the rafters have been put up, and in Figure 6, the fascia boards have been installed.

# HIP ROOFS

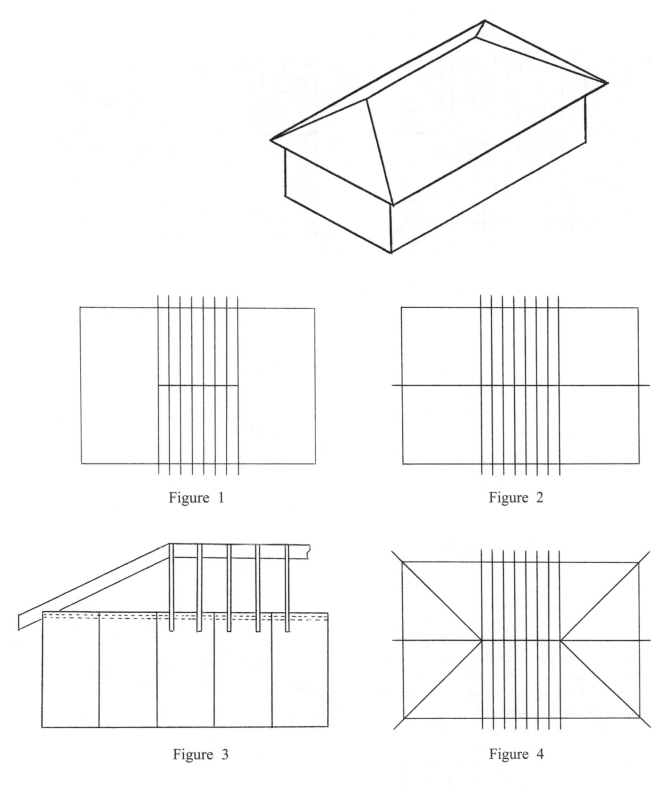

Figure 1

Figure 2

Figure 3

Figure 4

Hip roofs are another common style of roof. To build this one, you start by installing the ridge board on the part that has the standard peak. The common rafters that meet at this board could also be put up at this time as long as the supports are securely held with diagonal bracing. This is shown in Figure 1. In Figures 2 and 3, the center rafters on the end walls are in place. These butt up against the ridge board. In Figure 4, the hip rafters are installed at each corner.  In Figure 5, the rest of the rafters have been put up, and in Figure 6, the fascia boards have been installed.

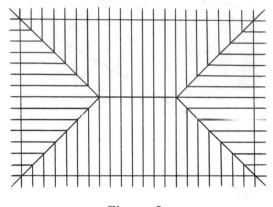

Figure 5

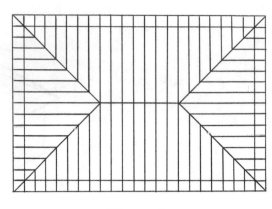

Figure 6

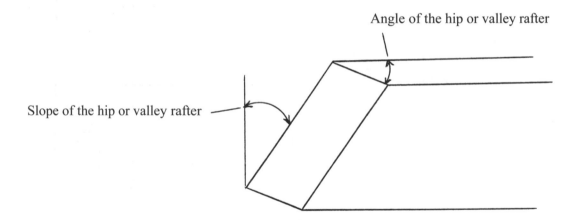

Angle of the hip or valley rafter

Slope of the hip or valley rafter —

The only thing that's different when framing this roof and the one before it are the rafters that run at an angle to the common rafters, called hip rafters and valley rafters. Attached to them are the jack rafters. Hip jack rafters rest on the wall and are nailed to a hip rafter, while valley jack rafters go between the ridge board and a valley rafter. Cripple jack rafters are between a hip rafter and a valley rafter. I had to look this up since I've never been too concerned about knowing the proper terms.

To make these rafters, one end will need a compound miter cut. This is shown in the center drawing. This cut can be made using either a circular saw or a sliding miter saw. With either saw, the blade is tilted to match the angle of the hip or the valley rafter. The hip rafters in Figure 4 on the last page sit at 45 degrees to the outside walls, so the blade would be set at 45 degrees for every cut.

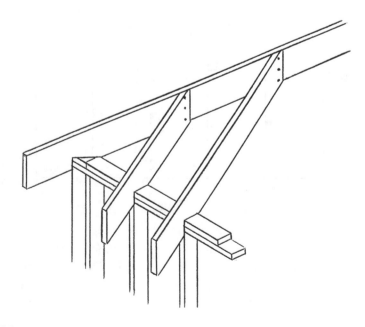

If the angle was different than 45 degrees, let's say 40 degrees on one side of the corner and 50 degrees on the other, then the tilt of the blade would be set at either 40 or 50 degrees, depending on what side you're on. There's a good chance that your saw can't even be set to 50 degrees. In that case, you'd have to finish the cuts with a plane, preferably with an electric planer. This is a good reason to design the roof so the rafters are at 45 degrees.

The other angle you need is for the pitch (slope) of the board that the rafter is being attached to. This is not the same as the slope of the roof, the reason being that the hip and valley rafters sit at an angle, so they're longer and come down at a more gradual pitch. Once you think you have the right angle, it's drawn on the board for the saw to follow. You might have to adjust it a couple of times until you get it right, but once you've found the correct angle, the rafter will sit up straight after it's been nailed into place.

I use a level to find the pitch by holding it horizontal with the upper end resting on whatever I'm checking. Then I measure straight down while making sure the measuring tape is square to the level. Let's say that I measured down at the 2 foot mark and got a measurement of 10 inches. At 1 foot, it would be 5 inches, so the pitch is 5-12.

The bird's beak on hip and valley rafters is longer because it's coming across the wall at angle. The angle for the cuts is also different, since the rafter has a lower pitch.

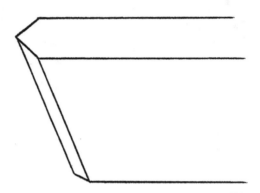

When the upper end of the hip or the valley rafter has to slip into a corner, it's best to cut from both sides, so the point is centered on the board. To make this cut, the line for the pitch has to be drawn on both sides. The problem is, when you make the first cut, you'll cut off the line on the other side of the board. One way around this, when using a circular saw, is to draw a second line farther back on the board. Then make the cut by following that line with the other side of the base of the saw.

It can be difficult trying to follow the line when making compound miter cuts with a circular saw. Here it helps to clamp a board to the line for the saw to follow, or to use an adjustable square. If there are a lot of cuts to make at the same angle, you could also make a pair of cutting jigs for installing the rafters on both sides of the hip or valley rafters (page 398).

If the hip or valley rafters aren't at 45 degrees, sometimes I'll skip the second cut and just line up the upper end the best that I can. On larger roofs, these rafters may also be doubled up, so each rafter would only be cut from one side.

When installing jack rafters, mark their position by measuring off the other rafters. Then draw a line at that point, using a level. To find the length of a hip jack rafter, measure from the line on the hip rafter to the near side of the upper plate. I generally cut the upper end of the rafter first, and then cut the bird's beak. On a valley jack rafter, the length is found by measuring between the line on the ridge board and the line on the valley rafter.

Every rafter should be at the same height where it passes over the outer edge of the wall. This height was set once you put up the first rafters. After that, the depth of the cut for the bird's beak has to be adjusted to maintain that height on every rafter that follows. This is necessary to keep everything in line.

# DORMERS

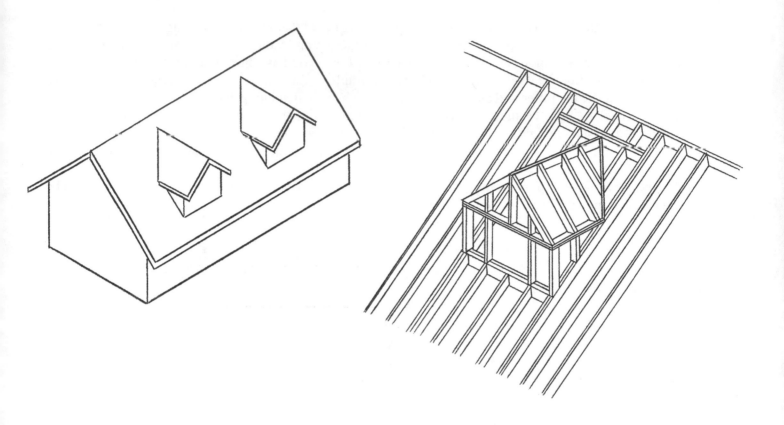

Dormers bring light into the house and also increase the space. You can see in the drawing that they're framed in the same manner as a small building. To build a dormer, the first thing you have to do is to frame the opening. Generally, the rafters have to be doubled up on each side, as will the other boards that form the opening. After that, the order that things are done will depend on the size of the dormer and where it's located. On some dormers, the easiest way is to put up the ridge board first, and then build the dormer around it. If I was building the one that's shown in the drawings, I'd probably frame the lower walls first, and then put up the ridge board and the common rafters. Then I'd install the valley rafters, add the other rafters that were still needed, and finish the peak on the front wall.

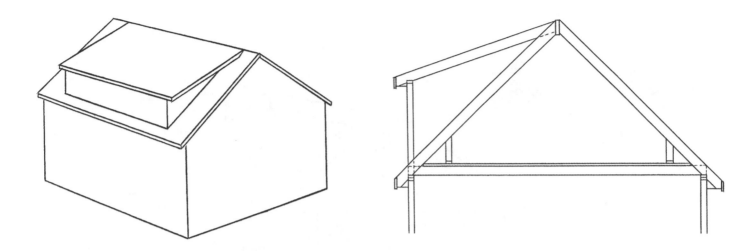

The dormers on the last page are gable dormers. The one that's shown here is a shed dormer. As you can see, the framing is pretty simple since the rafters are supported by the end wall. Without collar ties, there's more load on the ridge board where the dormer is. Because of that, a ridge beam may be needed to help support the roof in this area.

## ENTRYS

Here's the front entry on a house. About the only difference between this and a dormer is that it extends out to provide protection from the weather.

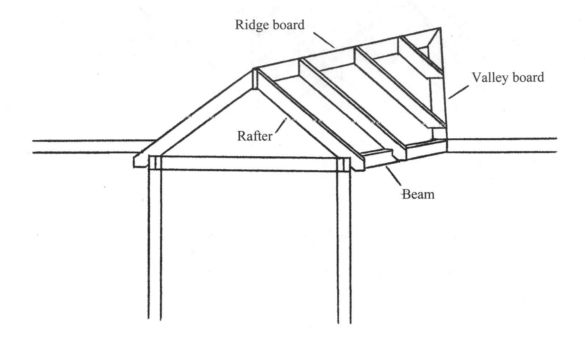

This drawing shows the basic framing for the front entry that was shown on the last page. To build it, the first boards that were installed were the beams coming out from the house, along with the board that goes across the front to hold them together. 2x4s were used to hold everything up temporarily. After that, the ridge board was cut to match the angle of the roof, and then it was installed by supporting it off the front board.

With the ridge board in place, the common rafters were put up, and their tails were cut to line up with the fascia on the house. Then the valley boards were nailed to the roof. When doing this, the upper end was lined up with the ridge board, and the lower end was positioned by laying a straightedge across the rafters that were already in place. I generally use 1 1/2 inch thick boards for the valleys, though 3/4 inch can also be used. These boards should be wide enough to properly support the rafters, and to provide a good nailing surface.

Once that was done, the other rafters could be installed. These were cut to length so the lower end was flush to the outer edge of the valley board. When cutting the lower end, the blade on the circular saw was set to match the slope of the main roof, and the angle of the line that was drawn was determined by the pitch of the entry roof. Once the rafters were installed, the temporary supports were replaced with treated 4x4s. The plan is for them to be covered in the future. When framing the roof that's shown on pages 390-393, it was done in the same manner.

# USING A LEVEL

The level is one of the most important tools that you can own. Unfortunately, most people don't use it often enough. Here I'm also talking about professionals. I'm surprised at how many times I've seen framing that was done by pros that was completely out of level or wasn't plumb.

When framing, most people know that the floors should be level (horizontal) and the walls should be plumb (vertical), but there are other locations that should always be checked with the a level as you're building. Two obvious ones are window and door openings. Another is closet openings.

Walls are generally framed strictly by measurement. The studs, plates, and any other boards that are used for window or door openings are cut to a set measurement. Then the wall is nailed together, and it's tipped up into place and plumbed. The problem here is that you're assuming the floor is level, when many times it isn't, even in new homes.

When framing a window opening, the most important thing is that it's the correct size and to have a level sill, so the window can simply be centered between the sides and then nailed into place. Here all you have to do is to check the floor to see if it's level at that location. If one side is higher, and the supporting studs are being done in two pieces with the sill between them, just cut the lower board on that side shorter to make the sill level. Then cut the other boards the same length as usual. If the supporting studs are done in one piece, cut one side shorter so the header is level. Then measure down from the header and mark the length of the rough opening on both sides, and cut the other boards so the sill is at the same height as the marks.

On a closet opening where you're installing a double bi-fold door, the top of the opening has to be level in order for the doors to hang plumb, at the same height, and with an even gap across the top. If the floor isn't level at the closet opening, just add the board that goes across the top after the studs are already in place. If the board is being doubled up, you could also build the wall by only installing the upper board. Then add the lower one once the wall is up, and shim it as necessary.

Door openings should be reasonably plumb, but here it's even more important that the wall on both sides of the door line up with each other. Otherwise, the jambs might have to be twisted in opposite directions to compensate, which makes trimming the door more difficult.

I recently installed a door where the framing had been done by a so-called professional. This was a closet door in the basement, at the base of the stairs. Before installing a door, I always measure the opening and check it for plumb to see what's needed. What I saw on this one was that the surface of the wall on one side of the door was tipped one way, while on the other side of the door, it was tipped the other way. This is a bad combination, but it got worse as the door itself also had a twist in it, going the wrong way. Wide trim was also going to be installed, which isn't very forgiving.

I tried to hang the door with the jambs twisted in the opening as far as they could go, but it wasn't nearly enough. It turned out that I had to build out the lower part of the wall a full inch on the left side of the door to get it to line up with the jamb. Since the left side was at a corner, that meant I also had to redo the corner bead. This was the worst door opening that I've had to deal with so far. But if the carpenter had only used his level, there never would have been a problem to begin with. There are many other places where it's equally important to use a level. Just keep one handy, as it will save you a lot of time and grief later on.

To get the most out of a level, you have to really pay attention to where the bubble is actually sitting. Though at first glance the bubble may appear to be centered, if you take a closer look, you may find that it's slightly off to one side. That little difference can add up to quite a bit on a long board. There's also a good chance that the board you're checking could either be crowned or have a warp in it. Because of that, you should check it at different heights, and on both sides. Your level could also be out of adjustment. If it is, when something is actually level or plumb, the bubble will be to the left when the level is held one way, and to the right when the level is turned over or reversed. This doesn't mean that you have to throw it away if it can't be adjusted. Quite a few of the levels that I've used had a bubble that was slightly off. You just have to know when they are, and to compensate for it by checking with the level held both ways.

51

In practice, this is all much easier than it sounds. Whenever you're checking for level on a short board, check one way, then turn the level over or reverse it, and check it again, just to make sure. On long surfaces, check it at different points and on both sides, if possible. You'll also get a more accurate reading if you have good light and are directly behind the level. The bubble may appear to be different if you or the light is off to one side.

Levels come in many sizes. Common lengths are 2, 3, 4, and 6 feet. On the short end, you also have the torpedo level, which is around 9 inches long. Also included here would be laser levels. I'm sure that some people have levels in all the different lengths, but most of the time you can get by with only a couple of them. Myself, I do most of my work with a 4-foot and a torpedo level, though I also use a 6-foot and a laser level on occasion. I generally use the torpedo level to check the slope when working on plumbing, since it easily fits into my pouch or a back pocket.

A 6 foot level is a better choice for framing walls and hanging doors, but many of them are heavy and too expensive, considering that you don't need one that often. Years ago, when I needed more length, I taped my 4 foot level to a straight board that was kept just for that purpose. One thing I like about 4 foot levels is that they're lightweight and inexpensive. I bought mine years ago for about 8 dollars. This level has been dropped countless times, sometimes from one floor to the next, and it's never been knocked out of adjustment. While I like quality tools, I'd hate to see an expensive level take that kind of abuse. Besides, I don't think a hundred dollar level could do any more.

Laser levels come in many styles. Some project a spot, while others project a line. Which is better would depend on what you need it for. The one I own isn't that expensive, costing around one hundred dollars. This model projects a spot, both vertically and horizontally.

## STRING LINES

This is another thing that people don't use enough when building. While chalk lines are used to lay out walls and sheathing, and to mark for cuts, string lines are used to project lines and to see if something is straight. For the work I do, I probably use a string line twice as often as a chalk line. You should have one ready to go any time you're framing. After using it, just wrap it around a scrap piece of wood.

## BUYING WOOD

Over the years, I've spent way too much time buying wood. It's a hassle, but you should really take the time to get the straightest wood that you can find. It will make the framing go easier, and there will be less work when you're flattening out the walls later on. The problem is that you never know what you're going to find on any given day. Sometimes you'll find a stack of wood where almost every board is straight. You give the boards a quick check, load them up and go home. Other times it's the exact opposite, with every board having the same warp or crown in it, and you'll go through the whole pile just trying to find a few boards that are reasonably straight. When that happens, if you're looking for 92 5/8 inch studs, check out the 8 footers and see if they're any better. It doesn't take that long to cut them to length. If the 8 foot studs also look bad, you may want to try another store, or come back another day. Some guys will tell you that whenever the wood is questionable, you should frame the walls as soon as possible before the wood has time to warp or twist any farther. There's some truth to that. Once a wall is framed, the boards can't move as much. But in my experience, no matter how well the ends are nailed, a bad stud is still going to move.

# CHECKING THE WOOD

For those of you that are new to this, you check a board by looking down the edge of it, trying to see if it's straight or if it has a curve to it. Look down one edge, then rotate the board 90 degrees and look down that edge also. Bad warps or crowns are easy to see. Mild ones can be a lot harder. You may have to rotate the board several times before you even notice them. As you do this, you also check for any twist. Some people will use other terms such as "crook", and "bow," but I only use four to keep it simple: warped, crowned, twisted, and cupped.

This may take a while to get the hang of it. At first, you might have a hard time trying to spot anything but the most obvious bends and twists, but stick with it as it will get easier as you go. After a while it should only take a few seconds to check each board. Also, look down the side of the board that feels the most comfortable to you. My right eye is the dominant one, and I look down the left edge of a board, checking for curves that go sideways. A friend of mine says he checks the wood by looking for bends that go up and down. Do whatever works best for you. Once you actually know how to do this, I doubt that you'll buy wood again without checking it out first.

Besides checking for straightness, at the same time you should also look for splits, large knots, and other flaws that could be a problem. Don't get so caught up looking for one problem that you miss others that are obvious.

One other thing, -- when you're finished going through the wood, stack it neatly back together. The store shouldn't have to straighten up your mess after you leave. Besides, you should consider other people who will be looking through the same stack, which could be you.

You could also go to a real lumberyard if you don't want the hassle of sorting through the wood. It will cost more, but generally the wood is a little better. Tell the yardman if it's important that you have straight boards for the job you're working on. Hopefully, then he'll give them a quick check, instead of just grabbing whatever's on the top of the pile.

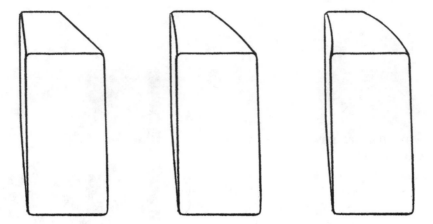

Here are three boards that are being checked to see if they have a warp. The one on the left appears to be straight, while the one on the right has an obvious warp. The one in the middle is just slightly warped, although it's not as easy to see.

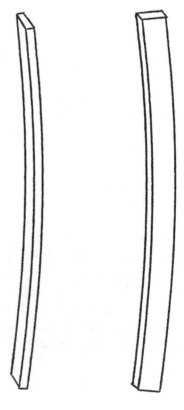

In these drawings, the board on the left is warped. Some people would say it has a bow. The one on the right is crowned. Others might call it a crook, if it was a stud. I call it crowned, no matter what it's used for, to keep it simple.

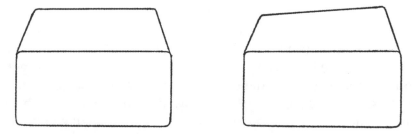

This is how you check a board to see if it's twisted, though in real life you'd hold the near end higher, so you see less of the upper surface. What you're looking for is whether or not the upper edge on the far end of the board is parallel to the one on the near side. Here the board on the left is straight, and both edges are parallel to each other. The one on the right has a twist, which you can see by one side sticking up higher than the other. It's harder to see a twist when the board is also warped, and sometimes you'll have both problems.

When framing with wider boards, you also check to see if they're cupped, like the one in this drawing. It's best to use boards that aren't cupped for ledger boards and beams that consist of more than one board, so you get a tight fit.

END VIEW

## FRAMING WITH WARPED WOOD

On most building projects, you'll have to deal with boards that are warped, crowned, and twisted. You can minimize this problem by buying boards that are straight, and then keep them stacked together until they're used, but there's no way to ensure that the wood is going to stay straight. Here I'll go over the best way to use the flawed wood. By sorting through the boards and then using them in a way that will help to straighten them, or at least minimize their flaws, you'll end up with better framing.

We'll start with the floor joists. The first thing I do before installing them is to quickly go over the pile of wood to see what I have to work with. I'm looking for warps, crowns, bad twists, and also checking the width of the boards. Let's assume that most of the wood looks reasonable. If so, I'd pick out some of the straighter boards that are around the same width, to be used around the perimeter of the floor. If I'm framing a deck, I want the straightest wood for the beams, the ledger board, and the outer members. Any boards that will be used for beams should be around the same width. Try to find boards that aren't cupped for the ledger board, the beams, and also for going around the perimeter.

Once the boards have been picked out, I'll go over the rest of the wood and check it for crowns. Any board that's crowned is marked with an X on the crowned side. This side generally goes up, since you don't want a dip in the floor. There's a rule of thumb that says you should reverse the crowns when the joists are cantilevered, but I still put the crowns up as long as it's a short overhang. I wouldn't use a floor joist with anything more than a mild crown on a long cantilever. The overhanging end on a badly crowned joist would be too far out of line when installing the board that caps the floor joists.

When installing the inside joists, I'm not too concerned about mild warps and twists, since the boards can be pulled straight as they're nailed into place, and the sheathing or decking is installed. Other than crowns, the main problem is with boards that vary in width. This is especially true when using treated wood. A standard 2x10 should measure somewhere around 9 1/4 inches. Treated wood is generally a little wider, and I've built decks where the 2x10s measured anywhere from 9 to 9 5/8 inches. This makes it tough when trying to get everything to line up at the same height.

When building walls, again I'll check the wood first, to see what I have to work with. If most of the boards seem to be pretty good, I'll start laying out the walls after giving each stud a quick check to see if it's straight. Any boards that aren't straight enough for studs are set aside to be cut up for window framing, door tops, cripple studs, and blocking.

If enough of the boards are bad, I'll be forced to use some of them full length. If so, I'll go through the pile of wood and sort them out into groups: straight, crowned, warped, and twisted. Then I'll use them as follows:

Straight boards are for studs and top plates.

Crowned boards are marked with an X on the crowned side. Boards with mild crowns can be used for bottom plates, since they'll be pulled straight as they're nailed into place. They can also be used for door openings and larger windows if they're nailed together with the crowns opposing each other, which will help to straighten them. When necessary, boards with mild crowns can also be used as studs, provided that the crowns are all facing the same direction. This will give you a wall that has a slight curve to it, but in my opinion, that's preferable over one that has dips and humps in it. An exception to this is where something is getting nailed to the wall that's strong enough to pull the boards into line, if the crowns are facing in different directions.

Warped boards can also be nailed together, with the warps opposing each other, and used for window and door openings. Warped boards are also used for plates, since they'll be straightened as the wall is nailed together. When using them for studs, they should be pulled into position when the sheetrock or the sheathing is installed.

Boards with mild twists can be used for plates. They can also be used for studs if they're pulled into position as they're being nailed, but they may overcome the nails and twist again.

Any wood that's left over is cut up for window framing, door tops, cripple studs, and blocking. The worse the board is, the shorter it has to be cut.

# FIRE BLOCKING

When framing, fire blocking may be required, which is used to prevent a fire from spreading from one area of the house to another. This is just a matter of installing boards that are cut to fit between the studs, so the cavities are blocked once the studs have been covered with sheetrock,. One place where it's needed is when building a wall using full length studs, and the stud cavities on one floor level extend into the one that's above it. Here, once a fire got into walls, it could easily move from one level to the next. Another potential spot would be where a wall extends past a soffit. If this provided a way for a fire to quickly spread to another area, then it should also be fire blocked.

Besides blocking the stud cavities, holes should also be plugged if they go from one floor level up to the next. This includes holes that are drilled for the wiring and the plumbing. The holes are filled once the plumbing and the electrical work is finished, and you're ready to cover the walls. These holes can be packed tight with fiberglass, caulked, or filled with foam. Foam may be required if the hole goes through framing that has a vapor barrier.

# FELT PAPER AND TYVEK

Years ago, felt paper was installed over the sheathing before the siding went on. Here it served a couple of functions. It helped against air infiltration, and provided protection from any water that got past the siding. It would also breathe to help get rid of any moisture in the walls. Now, Tyvek is used for this purpose, along with other brands that I don't know the name of. While these materials may appear to be the same, often they're not. Tyvek is made in a way that it has tiny holes across the entire surface. These holes are large enough for vapor to pass through, yet small enough to keep water out. Some of the brands appear to be woven or have small holes punched through the surface for this purpose. For using under stucco, there's a different kind of Tyvek that has a grooved surface for water drainage. There are also other types that are made for roofs, but be aware that some of them don't breathe, in case it matters.

Felt paper is generally used on roofs, but it has it's own problems. Once it's stapled on, it's best to install the shingles as soon as possible. After a couple of days in the hot sun, the material changes. It dries out, changing from black to dark gray, and tends to shrink and pull away from the staples, which means you'll have to restaple it to keep the wind from blowing it off. Other, more expensive forms of felt paper are available. They're designed to eliminate the problems that you have when using standard felt paper. They're advertised as being wrinkle-free, and also allow more time before the shingles have to be installed.

Being wrinkle-free is a big advantage. The best time to install standard felt paper is in the warm sun (not hot) so it lays flat. The problem is that it doesn't stay that way. Every time the felt paper gets damp, which could be from rain, dew in the morning, or even as it cools down in the evening, it will have wrinkles all over the surface. These will fade away as the roof dries out. Shingles can still be installed when it's wrinkled, but it's easier when it's laying flat, especially when you have to snap chalk lines.

# INSTALLING SIDING ON THE PEAKS

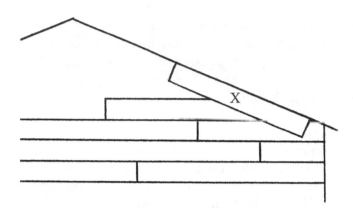

When siding the peaks, you'll have to determine the angle for cutting the ends. There are several ways to do this. One that's shown above is to lay a piece of siding on the top row. Then a second board (X) is held against the peak, and a line is drawn across the first board by following the edge of the second one.

Another method is shown in the drawing below. Here you hold a piece of siding in place with one end tight against the soffit. Then you measure the distance (X) between the end of the piece that you're holding, and where the row beneath it makes contact with the soffit. Yet another way is to hold two pieces in place, with the shorter one on top, and both of them tight against the soffit. Now you just have to measure the distance that they overlap each other. To draw the angle, mark this length on the upper edge of the siding. Then draw a line between that point and the lower corner, as shown in the center drawing.

If the row that you're on is at the start of the peak, the angled cut may only go part way down the board. You can see this on boards 1 and 2 in the lower drawing. In that case, I'd mark the end of the board at the correct height, and then use the method shown in the first drawing.

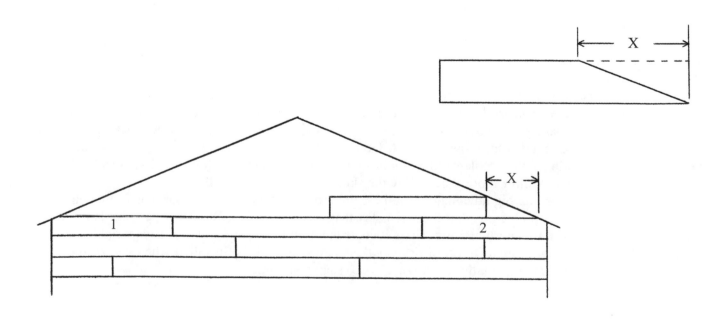

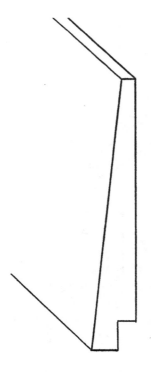

When installing lap siding that's notched on the back, it's done a little different. I had to do this just yesterday while siding a cabin that has a low-pitched roof. On the peaks, it was 35 inches to the start of the taper when checked with the notch in place on the row below it, and 38 1/2 inches when the board was held with the back side out. I used a circular saw, and cut from the back so I wouldn't leave marks on the front surface of the cedar boards To do this, I measured in 38 1/2 inches at the top, and 3 1/2 inches at the notch, and drew a line between the marks. Then I made the cuts by following the line until the notch, and just tried to stay straight so I'd come out right at the corner. When siding the peaks, sometimes it's best to cut each piece a little long to begin with. This will let you make any necessary adjustments to get a good fit on the angled cut. Once that's done, the siding is cut to the correct length.

## DETERMINING THE SQUARE AREA

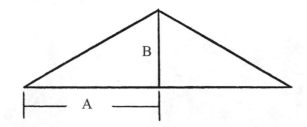
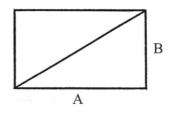

To determine the square footage of a peak, multiply the height by half the width (A x B). You can see in the second drawing that you'd get a rectangle if you stacked the two sides together. To find the area of a single triangle, multiply the width by the height, and then divide by two.

59

# PULLING NAILS

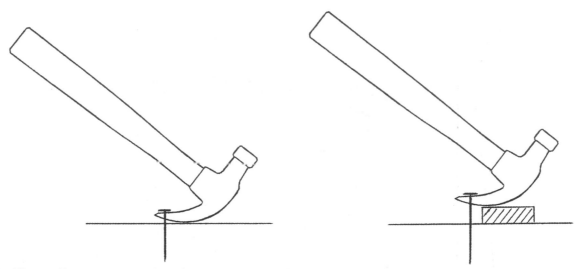

Pulling nails seems easy, but there are some things to know that will help. The trick to doing this is to use leverage, as shown above. In the drawing on the left, the nail head is just above the surface, and the claw of the hammer makes contact with the board close to the nail, which gives it good leverage. In the other drawing, the nail is sticking out farther. If you tried to pull the nail, the hammer wouldn't make contact with the board until it was close to the head. This gives it less leverage, which puts more strain on the hammer. On a small nail, or one that's easy to pull, it wouldn't matter. But, if it's hard to remove, you could crack the handle. Here it's better to put something like a block of wood, or anything that won't be crushed, under the hammer to increase the leverage. It will also help to protect the surface that's beneath it.

On older homes, larger nails were used for the framing, which could put too much strain on a hammer. In that case, it's better to use a crowbar ( 1 ) for pulling the nails. A cat's paw ( 2 ) is needed when the nail is in too far to grab. Use a hammer to drive the cat's paw under the nail head. A Wonder Bar ( 3 ) can also be used for pulling nails, though they generally don't work as well for this, in my opinion.

If you just want to break a nail off, the best way is to grab it as close as you can to the board with a Vise-Grip pliers. Then bend the nail back and forth until it breaks.

When remodeling, commonly you have to remove trim that will be put it back on later. If the nails are right at the surface, you may be able to drive them back out. But, if they're in too deep, the best way to remove them without damaging the board is by pulling them through, from the back. You do this by grabbing them with a Vice-Grip pliers, and then pry them out using the curved side of the pliers.

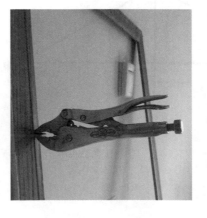
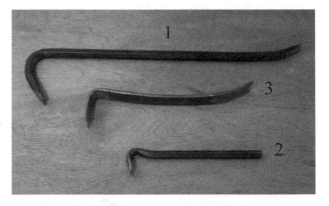

Even though it seems totally wrong, sometimes it's easier to remove cement-coated nails if you drive them deeper first. Doing this will break the bond between the cement and the wood.

# BUILDING STAIRS

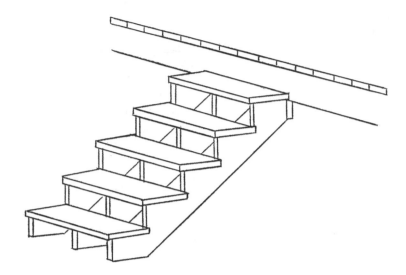

Building stairs is one of those jobs that many people are afraid of. Maybe they're intimidated by the diagonal line of the stairs, or just wouldn't know where to start, but the truth is that it's much easier than you'd think. You just have to be careful when measuring, doing the layout, and the cutting. While doing this, you don't even think about the diagonal line. Your main concern is finding the correct height and width for each step, so they're all the same size. In this section, I'll try to simplify the process by showing in a step-by-step manner, how to measure, do the lay out, and then build the stairs. We'll start with a straight set of stairs for a deck, to show the basics, and then move on to U-shaped stairs for inside the house.

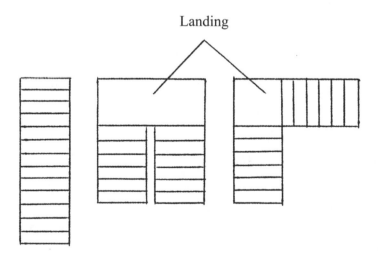

Landing

When you get right down to it, there are two types of stairs that are used in most homes, those with a landing, and those without. Straight stairs are just that, a straight run from the top to the bottom. Stairs that have a landing break the stairs into different sections. One section may turn 90 degrees as it does on L-shaped stairs, or turn 180 degrees on U-shaped stairs. They could also continue on in the same direction, or there could even be a second landing, followed by more stairs. What kind you build is more a matter of what best fits the opening, and the layout of the house. We're not going to concern ourselves with winding stairs at this time.

61

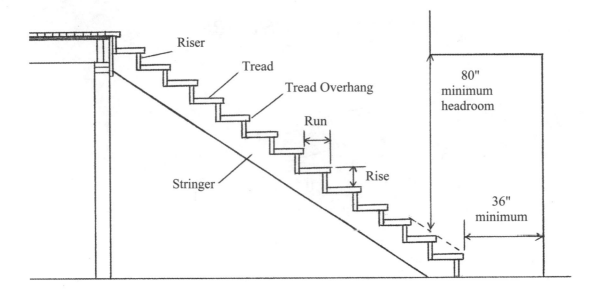

Below is a list of rules to follow when building stairs.

* Maximum riser height is 7 3/4 - 8 1/4 inches, depending on where you live.

* Minimum riser height is 4 inches.

* Minimum stair run is 9-10 inches, depending on where you live.

* Headroom minimum is 80 inches above the nose of the tread.

* Minimum finished width of stairwell is 36 inches between the walls.

* Largest tread width or riser height shall not exceed the smallest by more than 3/8 of an inch.

* Tread overhang is 3/4 - 1 1/4 inch.

* Landing is 36 inches minimum.

* Landing must be as wide as the stairs.

* Balcony handrail minimum height is 36 inches.

* Spacing between the balusters is less than 4 inches.

* Guardrails required on all decks or stairs more than 30 inches above grade or another deck.

* 6-inch sphere can't pass between stairs and the lower lower rail.

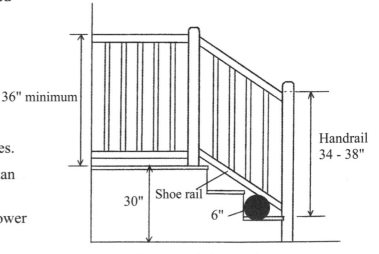

* Stair handrail height is 34-38 inches, when measured vertically above the nose of the tread.

* Stairways having 4 or more risers shall have at least one handrail with its ends terminated or returned in posts or the wall.

Some of these rules may not be required where you live. For instance, the balusters may not have to be so close. Also, the rules concerning the size and shape of handrails could differ, and risers may or may not be required on the stairs.

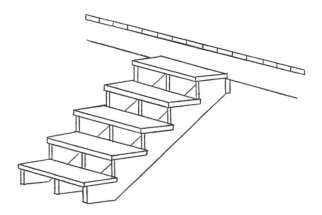

We'll start off by building a straight set of stairs for a deck. These stairs will have three stringers, the outer ones being 42 inches apart when measured to the outside edge, and the treads will consist of doubled up 2x6s. The treads will overhang the stringers by 1 inch on each side, giving them a total width of 44 inches. Risers won't be installed on these stairs, though they may be required where you live. The stairs will land on a cement pad that will be mounted flush to the ground. There isn't anything in front of the stairs that's close enough to limit the width of the treads, but we'll keep it simple here and make the run of each step 10 inches. By using doubled up 2x6s for the treads, with just a small gap between them, it will give us around 11 inches, with a 1 inch overhang in the front.

The stairs described here are not the same as those shown in the accompanying photos. Eleven inch treads are pretty common, and what I'd consider a bare minimum for stairs on a deck. Spacing the 2x6s would increase the width of each tread and make the stairs a little more comfortable, but that would also increase the amount of overhang, so at some point the run would have to be increased. The steps shown on page 370 are 19 inches wide and are very comfortable, both for walking or as a place to sit. On that deck, the wide treads are nice, but if any more were needed, they would take up a lot of room. A pair of 2x8s would also be good for wider steps on a deck, and could be cut down in width if necessary.

There's a rule of thumb that says the riser height and the run of a step should be between 17 and 18 inches when added together. This rule is fine for interior stairs, but on a deck you have more leeway and can install wider treads or go with a shorter riser, if that's what you want. Just remember, when doing this, the stairs will take up more space.

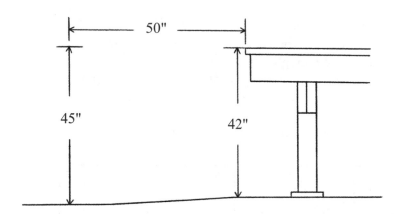

To determine the rise for each step, first you measure the distance from the top of the deck to the ground. In this case, it measures out at 42 inches. Now if each step had a rise of 7 inches, you would step down 6 times, since 6 x 7 = 42. These stairs will be mounted one step down from the surface of the deck, so the stringers will only need five steps.

You still need the height at the spot where the stairs will actually land. Five steps, with a run of 10 inches for each one, means you'll have to measure the height 50 inches out from the edge of the deck. One way to do this is to lay a straight board across the deck, with one end hanging over the edge. Make sure it's level, and then measure down at the 50 inch mark. Another way if you're alone, and especially when you're dealing with a longer set of stairs, is to measure straight down to the ground, and then measure the height difference between the two points. As it turns out, the ground is sloped in front of the deck, and the height at this point is 45 inches. 45 divided by 6 equals 7 1/2. That's still a comfortable riser height, so that's what we'll use. If the ground had too much slope, and the riser height became too high, another step would have to be added, and then you'd have to measure out another 10 inches. When building stairs for a deck, you also have the option of building up the ground to whatever height is needed.

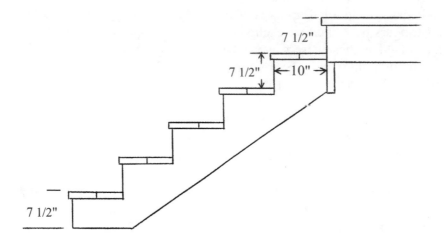

At this point, I always draw out what I'm trying to make. Nothing fancy; scribbling is just fine. I just want to make sure that I'm not making any mistakes.

Now you'll have to determine how you plan to attach the stairs to the deck. The drawing below shows one way to do it, where the stringers are connected to another board, called a hanger board, that's hung from the platform. On decks, you could also attach the stringers to the outer joist, so the stairs are flush to the surface of the deck, which would eliminate the hanger board, though you'd need another step when doing this. This generally isn't done inside the house, since the stairs would be longer. There it's better to use the extra 10 inches for wider treads and/or a bigger landing.

On these stairs, the hanger board is a 2 x 6 that's 42 inches long, which is the outside width of the stringers, and will be installed using short boards that are attached with either lag screws or bolts. The length of the hanger board might be different if there were posts or some other framing that it could also be connected to. The hanger board should be wide enough to reach the lower edge of the stringers.

Once the board is in place, mark the height for each stringer, which in this case is 9 inches below the upper surface of the deck, and center the middle stringer on the board. The riser height will end up at 7 1/2 inches after the treads are installed. If the deck isn't level, mark the center stringer so it's positioned 9 inches from the top, and then level the other two off that mark.

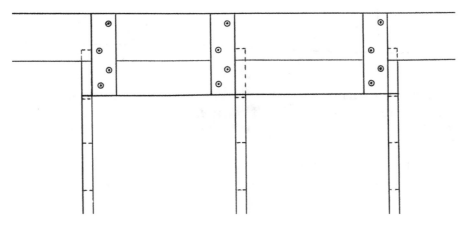

Rear view of the hanger board

This step was hung from the porch floor using short boards that were screwed to the framing. On stairs with more steps, where the load is greater, lag screws or bolts would be used instead of screws.

To build these stairs, you'll need three 6-foot 2x12s for the stringers, either cedar or treated wood. The boards should be straight, and reasonably dry if possible. They should also be approximately the same width, and without any major flaws. Here the lower half of the board is the most important, since that's where the stringers get their strength. 2x10s are used sometimes for short stringers, but I've never done this since I want the stairs to feel rock solid. With 2x10s, you'll have 2 inches less wood where you actually need it.

You're also going to need a pair of sawhorses and a framing square. Two framing squares would be better yet. The inexpensive ones are just fine. You'll also need a pair of stair gauges, or a short straight board with two C-clamps. A calculator helps for figuring out the measurements.

To start, look over the 2x12s and determine which edge is going to face up on each board, and then mark it as such. If a board is crowned, the crowned edge should go up. Then stack the 2x12s on top of the saw horses and line up their top edges. If one of the boards is way off because of excessive crowning, it would be good to plane it down to match the others. With longer stringers, a crown in the center stringer will probably be pulled out as the stairs are assembled.

Now leave one of the 2x12s on the sawhorses, and set the other two aside. Then either clamp a short board or attach stair gauges to the framing square. On the short side of the square, leave 7 1/2 inches exposed. On the long side, leave 10 inches exposed. The framing square should be turned so the shorter side (riser) faces the upper end of the stringer as the steps are being drawn.

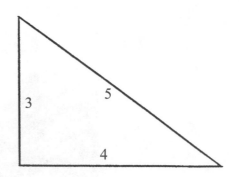

There's still one measurement that's needed, which is for the marks that show the distance from the point of one step to the point of the next. If you laid out the stairs without using these marks, and were a little bit off on each step, by the time you were done you could be way off. That may not be a problem on most decks, but it wouldn't work when building more complicated stairs inside the house.

To find this distance, you use the geometric rule, A squared plus B squared equals C squared. To give you an example, I'll use it on a 3-4-5 triangle. Here, 3 squared equals 9, and 4 squared equals 16. 9 plus 16 equals 25, and the square root of 25 equals 5. For stairs, A and B are the riser height and the run of each step.

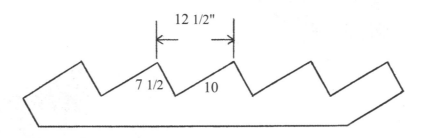

7.5 x 7.5 = 56.25
10 x 10 = <u>100</u>
     156.25    The square root of 156.25 equals 12.5 inches. That should be the distance between the point of each step.

Start each stringer by marking these points along the upper edge of the board. On the first one, I measure from the upper end, and use the best board. Generally the boards will be long enough so the points can be shifted towards one end or the other. Once the first stringer is finished, it can be laid across the other boards to find the best position for marking the points. This will allow you to stay away from any splits, and to work around other flaws in the wood when drawing out the stringers.

Once the marks are drawn, lay the framing square on the board. When it's centered between the marks, the square should run off the edge of the board, right at each mark. If it doesn't, then recheck your measurements. If it looks good, center the square between the marks, and trace a line around it. Repeat this between all the marks. Use a sharp writing pencil when doing this. Sometimes, once you've already started, you'll see that the layout should be shifted over. If you're going to do it, do it now before you go any farther. That's why you should always have a big eraser in your pouch.

Once the initial lines have been drawn, you still have to draw out the top and the bottom steps. This is where most of the mistakes are made when making stringers. On the upper step, the length of the horizontal run is determined by whether or not the stairs are getting risers, and if they are, will one be installed over the upper step. When drawing the bottom step, any adjustment will be to the riser height, this being determined by the thickness of the stair tread. This is where the drawing helps to see how the stringer should be cut.

At this point, it would help to have a second framing square. Then, depending on which line has to be drawn, you can use the square that's still set up, or the other one. To do the top step, center the framing square between the first mark and the upper end of the board, and trace a line around it, if it hasn't already been done. Here, since there aren't any risers to take into account, you just measure out 10 inches and square off the stringer at that point. If 3/4 inch thick risers were being installed above every step, except the upper one, you'd shorten the run to 9 1/4 inches to compensate for it.

To do the bottom step, begin by drawing the line for the riser. You'll need to shorten the height of this step by the thickness of the treads, which in this case is 1 1/2 inches. Mark the riser height at 6 inches, and then square it off at that point. If you forget to do this, the lower step would end up being 9 inches tall. I remember making this mistake on my first set of stairs.

When building stairs for a deck, there's one more thing that I do sometimes. Normally the stringers would be resting on a cement pad, and the bottom edge will often be wet from soaking up moisture from any rain or snow, which could lead to rot. To help prevent this, sometimes I'll take an extra 1/4 inch off the bottom step. Then I'll cut a notch that's 1 1/4 inches deep for a treated 2x6 that will rest on the cement. This will keep the lower edge of the stairs 1/4 inch off the ground. It will also help to straighten the stringers, and will stiffen up the lower posts.

Once everything is drawn out, use a circular saw to cut out the stringer. When doing this, try to split the pencil line, and be careful not to cut past the intersecting lines on the inside corners where the tread and riser come together, as that would weaken the stringer. After you've made all the cuts with the circular saw, finish them up with a jig saw to remove the triangles of wood that were left. Then use the jig saw to clean up any corners that need it.

Now put the stringer into position against the hanger board, and put a piece of 2x material under the notch at the bottom, if one was cut, to see if the stringer looks right. Then check the cuts for the treads with a level. You can expect that some of them will be a little bit off. But if there's anything major, you'll have to find the reason for the problem before continuing. If the stringer looks right, move on and make the other two.

Draw out and cut the other stringers the same way as the first one. Commonly the first stringer is used as a template for the others. It's tempting to do this, but I don't recommend it. Nobody cuts perfect, and you'll just be repeating your mistakes. I've done it both ways and get better results when I draw each stringer separately. Before drawing the other stringers, lay the one that's finished on top of each board to see how it will end up. You may want to shift the stair points one way or the other to eliminate splits or knots.

The stringers are stacked on top of each other to make sure that all the cuts line up.

When the stringers are finished, set them in place, square to the deck, to determine the position of the cement pad. I generally use patio blocks for this. With the stringers in position, I mark the outline where I want them to go. Then I dig out the ground inside the outline, going a little deeper than the thickness of the patio blocks. Sand is added, which is then tamped and leveled with a short 2x4 to form a base for installing them. Make sure the patio blocks are set at the correct height. Sometimes it's easier to do this by pounding in a stake or laying something on the ground that's at the right height, and then adjusting the blocks so they're level with it.

Once the pad is in place, put the stringers back into position, and slip a 42 inch piece of treated 2x6 under the notch that was cut on the bottom of the stringers. Then recheck the tread cuts with a level to see if they still look OK. If they look right, you can attach one of the outer stringers to the deck. Make sure it's at the correct height, plumb (vertical), and square to the deck. Then drive several long screws through the hanger board and into the back of the stringer. For this I use 3 1/2 - 4 inch long deck screws. You could also use stair hangers instead. Now do the other outside stringer, after making sure that it's plumb, square to the deck, and level with the first stringer. When doing the middle stringer, center it between the other two, and check the height by laying a 4 foot level (straightedge) across the top step. To attach the treated 2x6 that's beneath the stringers, 3 inch screws are driven at an angle through the stringers and into the board below. Make sure the middle stringer is centered on the board.

You're going to need ten 44-inch long 2x6s for the stair treads. You'll start by installing the treads at the bottom, and then work your way up, pulling the stringers into place as you go. It's important to get the first step right. If the stringers are twisted, you may need help to pull them into position.

To begin, lay a pair of stair treads across the bottom step. Match up the ends, and gap the boards if you want. Position them so the rear tread overhangs one of the outer stringers by 1 inch, at the back corner. Then hold a level against the side of this stringer, just behind that corner, and check for plumb. Now measure how much the tread overhangs the side of the stringer, near the front of the step. If the stringer is plumb, and the overhang is 1 inch, front and rear, you can screw the treads to this stringer. When doing this, I'll put two 2 1/2 - 3 inch screws through each tread.

If the stringer isn't plumb because it's twisted, the overhang measurements won't be the same. In that case, twist the stringer, and while holding it plumb, recheck the measurements. If the overhang is still off, the stringers may not be square to the deck. Check for square, and slide the stringers across the pad if they're off. Then position the stringer as best you can, and attach the treads to it.

Now move over to the other side, and pull the outer stringer into position so you also have a 1 inch overhang on that side, front and rear, and attach the treads.

Next, mark the center on the back edge of the rear tread. Then hold the middle stringer so it's plumb and centered on the mark, and pin it with the back screw. Before you put in the other screws, measure to see if the stringer is also centered on the front edge. If it's not, pull it into place and then install the other screws.

Work your way up the stairs in this manner, pulling the stringers into position and screwing on the treads. Before installing the treads on the top step, reinforce the stringer attachment to the deck. One way is to use corner brackets that are attached with screws. You could also use joist hangers that are cut in half.

Sometimes you'll have to settle for an overhang that's a little bit off. Even though the stringers are square to the deck, the measurements could still be different if the ends are warped or twisted, the boards are cupped, etc. In this case, the most important thing is that the stairs feel solid and are strong enough.

These stairs are similar to the ones that were described, except that here, risers were installed, and there are also four stringers. The reason that the upper tread is spaced away from the deck is to allow for a trim board that will be installed around the perimeter. For the same reason, the treads and the risers were cut to fit flush against the stringers. Later on, a trim board will be added to both sides to cap them off. The lower photos give you a closer look at how certain areas were done.

69

# U - SHAPED STAIRS

Now that we've gone over the basics, we'll move on to the interior stairs. When we start this project, all there is to begin with is a hole in the floor, and the job will be to build a set of U-shaped stairs to fit the opening. For the time being, the treads will be standard 2x12s, and the risers 1x8s. Once the house is nearing completion, the stairs will be capped with hardwood (finished treads and risers), and the posts and handrails will be installed.

Though similar, the stairs in the photos are slightly different than what will be described. For instance, on those stairs the ceilings were taller, so more steps were needed.

You'll begin by measuring the opening. Double-check each measurement, and write everything down. It's important to get this right, since every measurement has to be accounted for. Once the measurements are taken and the stairs are drawn out, you should be able to add up the measurements for each step, the stair treads, the risers, the landing, and the different thicknesses of flooring, and come up with the same measurements that you get here.

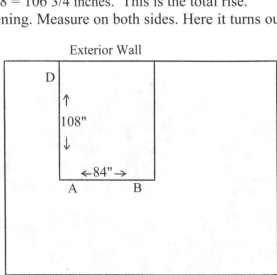

First you need the height of the opening. With U-shaped stairs, the stairs will start at point A on the upper level, and end up at point B at the bottom. You can measure this two ways. You can either go straight down from point A, and then see if the lower floor is level between the two points, or you can measure straight down from point B, and see if the upper floor is level. Any difference in height is either added or subtracted from the original measurement. In this case, the measurement is 107 1/8 inches, and it turns out that both floors are level.

Now consider what's going on both floors. Here the upper level will get 3/4 inch thick tongue and groove flooring, while the lower level will be tiled. After adding up the different layers for the tiled floor, our best guess is that it will be 1 1/8 inch thick. 1 1/8 – 3/4 = 3/8. Since the lower floor will be thicker than the upper one, that means that the total rise will be less. 107 1/8 – 3/8 = 106 3/4 inches. This is the total rise.

You also need the horizontal length (total run) of the opening. Measure on both sides. Here it turns out to be 108 inches on both sides. Then measure the width of the opening. Here it measures out at 84 inches.

Then check the opening to see if it's square. You can do this by using the 3-4-5 method. In this case, the opening turns out to be square. If it wasn't, depending on which side is off, you might have to adjust the length of the upper stringers, or cut the finished stair treads at an angle.

Another thing to check, is to stand on the lower floor, and then use a level to see if the upper half of the back wall is plumb (vertical). Since the opening was measured along the upper floor, but the stairs end at the landing, which will be halfway down the wall, you have to know if the wall is off, since that would change the length of the horizontal measurement. Here the wall is plumb, so the total run will stay at 108 inches.

The stairs will be built from these measurements. Now you have to determine how many steps are needed. To do this, divide 106 3/4 by different numbers to see what the options are.

106 3/4 divided by 13 = 8.21 inches

106 3/4 divided by 14 = 7.625 inches

106 3/4 divided by 15 = 7.11 inches

The answers are the riser heights. For instance, when you divide by 13, that means to go from the lower floor up to the next level, you would step up 13 times, rising 8.21 inches with each step. Dividing by either 14 or 15 will give you acceptable riser heights. By going with 14, you'll have more room for wider stair treads and/or a bigger landing. There will also be an equal number of steps on each set of stringers. 7.625 = 7 5/8 inches. This will be the riser height for making the stringers. Since both the landing and one of the floors count as steps, only six steps will be needed on each stringer.

In this case, the riser height just happened to come out exactly at 7 5/8 inches, but many times you'll have to go with the closest 1/16 of an inch. I don't use any formula for changing decimals to a fraction. I just break the decimal down, and add up the different increments until I get as close as I can to the right number. 7.625 was easy. I just subtracted 7 1/2 (7.5) from 7.625 leaving me with .125, which is 1/8 of an inch. One half, which is 4/8, plus an 1/8 equals 5/8.

If we went with one more step, the riser height would have been 7.11 inches. This is just under 7 1/8 inches. Subtracting 7.11 from 7.125 equals .014, which is a little over one hundredth of an inch, so here you'd go with the 7 1/8 inches. For those not familiar with this, the numbers you'd use are as follows:  1/2 = .5  1/4 = .250  1/8 = .125  1/16 = .0625

Now you have to come up with the run of each step, and the size of the landing.  The minimum run for steps where I live is 10 inches. These stairs will initially be built using 2x12s for the stair treads. 2x12s measure out at around 11 1/4 inches wide. If left full width, that will give you a tread overhang of 1 1/4 inches when going with a 10 inch run.

On these stairs, risers will be installed on every step, except above the upper one on each set of stringers. You'll compensate for this by shortening the run on the top steps by 3/4 of an inch. Since 3/4 inch plywood will be used to hang the upper end of the stringers, this will offset the 3/4 inch that was deducted, so the net result is that the stringers will have a total run of 60 inches. 6 steps x 10 inches for each individual run.

The length of the opening is 108 inches. Subtracting 60 inches from that will leave 48 inches for the landing. From the 48 inches, you have to subtract the thickness of the two layers that are going over the lower riser, a one inch overhang on the finished stair tread, and the sheetrock on the wall. Now you're down to 45 inches. There will also be a newel post installed at the landing for the upper set of stairs, which will take up even more space. To keep moving along, we'll go with these measurements. Here there's room to increase the run of the stairs, but that would also shrink the landing. Try to find the right balance. If I was working with these measurements on a real set of stairs, I'd consider increasing the run to 10 1/2 inches, assuming the finished stair treads were 11 1/2 inches wide. This would shrink the landing by another 3 inches.

|  | | |
|---|---|---|
| 108" | 3/4"  riser | 48" |
| - 60" | 3/4"  finished riser | - 3" |
| 48 inches | 1"  tread overhang | 45 inches |
|  | + 1/2"  sheetrock | |
|  | 3 inches | |

71

The landing will be 48 x 87 1/2 inches, which is 3 1/2 inches longer than the width of the opening. The extra length is needed for a 2x4 wall that will go under one end of it. The hanger board for the lower set of stairs will be overlapped by the 3/4 inch plywood sheathing that's used on the landing. If you use a full sheet of plywood, you'll end up 3/4 of an inch short at the back wall, but the gap will be partially filled by the sheetrock, and then covered up later by the flooring and the baseboard. Tongue and groove floor sheathing is smaller yet. In that case, a thin strip of plywood may have to be added to the back edge.

Before you go any further, draw out the plan to make sure everything looks right, and that nothing's been forgotten. Then add up all the measurements to see if the totals are correct. This is important, as it's easy to get confused when you're working with all of these numbers.

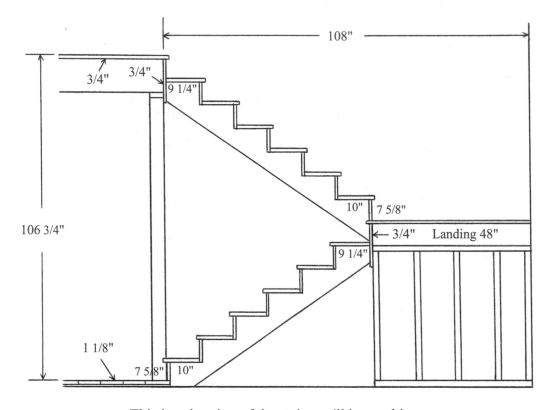

This is a drawing of the stairs we'll be working on.

On these stairs, before you can start on the landing, a wall has to be framed up under one side of the opening. This one will be 108 inches long and end at the edge of the opening. The studs will be spaced on 16 inch centers. Try to start the layout from the end that will put the studs in the best position to help support the landing. In this case, by starting the layout away from the back wall, a stud will be positioned a few inches in from the front edge of the landing.

Now the landing can be built. Since it will have posts mounted to it, you should try to build it in a way that won't interfere with their installation. The most solid way to install the posts is to cut holes through the top of the landing, and then attach them to the framing below. If the boards were doubled up on the front edge, the posts would either have to be moved farther back or they'd have to be notched deeper, which would weaken them. On the landing that's shown in the photos, it was framed using a single 2x8 around the perimeter, with 2x6s used for the interior members. Three 16D nails were used at each stud.

Make sure you don't end up with one of the interior framing members blocking the newel post for the upper stairs. Here, by equally spacing the boards on 17 3/16 inch centers, including the ends, the area where the post will go should be clear.

The landing height will be at the halfway point between the two floors. 106 3/4 divided by 2 equals 53 3/8. But before the height is marked, you should check the upper floor to see if it's level between point A and point D. In this case, point D is 1/4 inch lower. Since the upper floor is already 1/4 inch low, you only have to measure down 53 1/8 inches. When doing this, use a 3/4 inch board to represent the finished floor. Then measure from the top of it, and make a mark on one of the studs. This will be the height of the finished landing. Now make another mark 3/4 of an inch lower. This will be the height of the 3/4 inch plywood. Then make another mark 3/4 of an inch under that. This will be the height of the upper edge of the framing for the landing. Use a level to draw a line at that height around the perimeter where the landing is going.

To help install the landing, supporting blocks can be attached to the studs. This will allow you to build the frame, and then just set it on top of them. To do this, measure the width of the boards that will be used for the perimeter of the landing, which in this case is 7 1/4 inches. Then attach the blocks to several of the studs, 7 1/4 inches under the line that marks the upper edge of the framing. Pick two studs on opposite ends of the back wall, and one near the front edge of the side wall. Use short lengths of 2x4s for the supports. Mount them vertically, and attach them using two or three 3-inch deck screws for each support.

After the frame has been nailed together and laid into place, it will still need a support on the front edge, opposite the wall that was just built. This can be done by clamping on a 2x4 that extends from the floor to the landing. Make sure the frame is on the line, and level in both directions. Then use a couple of deck screws to attach the 2x4, and remove the clamp.

Now cut the 3/4 inch plywood for the top of the landing and set it in place. Overlap the front edge by 3/4 of an inch to go over the hanger board. If everything looks OK, attach the landing to the back wall with one 16D nail per stud, but don't drive the nails all the way in. Then nail the plywood to the framing. I commonly use 8D ring-shanked nails from a nail gun for doing this, even when hand nailing. For now, the 2x4 supports will be left in place. We're going to play it safe, in case something's wrong and the landing has to be moved. Once you see that the upper stringers fit correctly, you can finish nailing the landing.

At this point, it's time to cut the stringers. For these stairs, you can either use six 8-foot or three 14-foot 2x12s. The wood should be straight, dry, and without any big knots, especially on the lower edge. Mark the upper edge on each board, and have any crowns facing up. Then stack the boards on top of each other, and make sure that they all line up reasonably well.

Either stair gauges or a board that's held with clamps will be attached to the framing square, with the riser height set at 7 5/8 inches, and the run at 10 inches. Now you need the distance between the points.

$$7.625 \times 7.625 = 58.14$$
$$10 \times 10 = +\underline{100}$$
$$158.14 \quad \text{The square root of } 158.14 = 12.575, \text{ which is a trace over } 12\ 9/16.$$

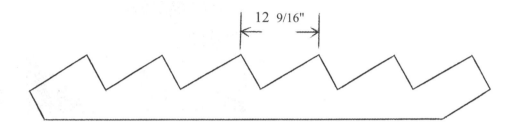

Since the measurement is a little over 12 9/16 inches, I'd multiply 12.575 by six to get the distance between all the points. 12.575 x 6 = 75.45, which is around 75 7/16 inches. Then I'd start the first stringer by making a mark 75 7/16 inches from the upper end of the board, and then make a mark every 12 9/16 inches in between. This is a smart thing to do, anytime you're drawing out stringers. It keeps you from making mistakes, so the stringers end up the correct length. Again, once the first stringer is finished, it can be laid across the other boards to see if the points should be shifted one way or the other to eliminate any splits or bad knots.

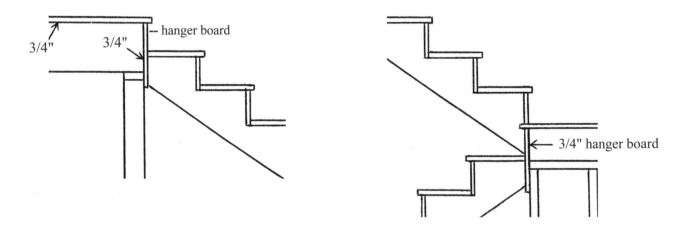

The stringers will be drawn out in the same manner as before, by centering the framing square between the marks. These stairs are getting risers that are 3/4 inch thick, but a riser isn't going above the top step on either section of stairs, so you'll shorten the run by 3/4 of an inch. Mark the run on the top step at 9 1/4 inches, and then square off the stringer at that point. This first stringer is going to be one of the upper ones. So, on the bottom step, mark the run at 10 inches, and then square it off and draw the riser line so it extends all the way to the lower edge of the 2x12. These drawings give you a better look at how everything comes together at both ends of the stringer. Here, the bottom riser on the upper set of stairs has been drawn so it's directly over the hanger board. On the stairs that we're building, it will actually be 3/4 of an inch farther onto the landing.

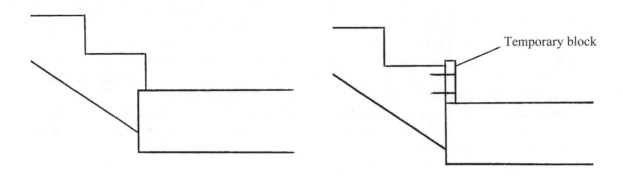

As you're building the stairs, you have to consider how the upper stringers will end at the landing. If the landing is wide enough, the stringers can be notched so they overlap the landing, as shown in the drawing on the left. Doing this will make it easier to position the stringers. Then they're attached by nailing into the ends of them.

If the stringers aren't long enough to do this, temporary blocks can be attached to the lower end. Now they can be laid into place, the same as if they had a notch. This is shown in the drawing on the right.

Yet another option is to have a hanger board on both ends of the stringers. This way, you can nail everything together, and then slip the whole assembly into place at one time. That's how it was done on the stairs that are shown in the photos. Those stairs go from the basement, all the way up to the second floor, so all there was to stand on were a couple of boards that were laid across the opening for the basement stairs. When I built them, I was working alone, so I nailed the hanger boards to the stringers and then lifted everything up into position. Then I made sure that both hanger boards were tight against the floor sheathing, and nailed them into place.

On these stairs, the stringers just make it to the landing frame, but the sheathing extends 3/4 inch past the front edge to overlap the hanger board. This will allow you to cut a 3/4 inch notch for installing the stringers. Since it's easier to install the stringers by cutting a notch at the bottom step, it would seem to be good idea to always make the landing a little bigger to allow it. The only problem is, by doing that, the lower set of stairs will stick out farther. So you have to consider that as well.

Whether you cut notches or use temporary blocks, the stringers have to be at the correct height. You also have to know the measurement for the upper end of the stairs. This is done by drawing it out. I start at the finished height and then work backwards, adding and subtracting the different layers until I end up with the distance needed between the top step and the upper floor, and the bottom step and the landing.

|  |  |  |  |
|---|---|---|---|
| 7 5/8 |  | 7 5/8 |  |
| - 3/4 | T&G flooring | - 2 5/8 | treads (1 1/2 + 1 1/8) |
| 6 7/8 |  | 5 |  |
| + 2 5/8 | treads (1 1/2 + 1 1/8) | + 3/4 | T&G flooring |
| 9 1/2" | stringer height below floor | 5 3/4" | stringer height above landing |

Once you know the numbers, you can draw the notch and cut out the first stringer. Again, cut accurately, and don't cut past the lines on the inside corners.

At this point, the upper hanger board has to be installed. Here the board will be 3/4 inch plywood that's been cut to 40 1/4 inches long to fit between the edge of the opening and the center wall. The hanger board should also be wide enough so it extends to the lower edge of the stringers. After it's cut, lightly nail it into place, leaving the nail heads up. Then measure down 9 1/2 inches from the upper floor, and mark the positions for the stringers. If the floor isn't level at the top of the stairs, measure down to get the height of the center stringer, and then mark the positions of the outer stringers, level to the center one.

After that's finished, the stringer can be lifted into place to check the fit. With a little luck, the top of the stringer will be at the 9 1/2 inch mark, and the tread cuts will be level. If it fits correctly, slide it across to the other end of the hanger board, and check the fit at that position.

If it looks good in both positions, push the stringer tight against the wall and draw a line across the studs, following the lower edge of the stringer. Then take the stringer down and securely nail the hanger board. Also finish nailing the landing by driving two or three 16D nails into each stud around the perimeter. Then cut the other two stringers the same size.

But what if the stringer doesn't fit? First, see if the stringer is at the correct height on both ends. Then make sure that the top stair run is the right length. Also recheck the height of the landing. Laying a level across the cuts for the stair treads will give you a better idea of what to look for. If you don't see the cause of the problem, go back over all of the measurements.

When building stairs, the riser height is the most important thing to get right. If it's wrong, there's no way to make it up, short of changing the height of one of the floors. Remember the rule that says "the largest tread width or riser height shall not exceed the smallest by more than 3/8 inch." You've only made one stringer at this point. If the first one isn't correct, you can always make a new one.

If the stringer length is off horizontally, or if the opening isn't square, there are adjustments that you can make. I have listed a few ways that come to mind.

* If the stringer is long, you can mount the hanger board so it's flush to the framing by notching the studs at the top of the stairs, as was done in this photo. This will give you another 3/4 of an inch. You could also notch the stringers, or go deeper if they're already cut to hang over the landing.

* If the stringer is short, you can build out the landing and/or the hanger board.

* If the end of the stair opening is out of square, the result being that the stringer fits on one side but not the other, you can adjust the length of the top stair run to fit. Then, when the stairs are capped, the top riser can be shimmed out on one side, which will bring it back to square.

* If the landing isn't square to the opening, you can shim out one side to even it up, and if necessary, also notch the stringers.

Any of these fixes will be hidden after the stairs are finished. Once the first stringer fits, cut the other two, while making any adjustments that are necessary. Then finish nailing the hanger board and the landing.

The next thing to do is to build the short wall that goes under the landing. This could have been done sooner, but it might have been off if the landing had to move. Make sure it's plumb and fits flush on the front and the outside edge.

Before the upper stringers can be installed, the center wall also has to be built. This can be done in several ways. One option is to run the wall all the way up to the ceiling. Another is to end it just above the stringers, and then install balusters and a handrail over the top of it. You could also combine the two methods by running the wall full length partway down the stairs, and then install a handrail and balusters from there. On these stairs we'll be using the second method. On the stairs that are shown in the photos, the stairs go from the second floor to the basement, so the center wall goes down to the basement floor.

Here, the height of the wall will be determined by the height of the skirtboard, which is the trim board that runs along both sides of the stairs. The skirtboard will fit tight against the trim board that caps the center wall. The shoerail, balusters, and the handrail will go directly over the trim board. This means the wall should be framed to the same height as the upper edge of the skirtboard. The problem is, on these stairs we don't know what that height is at this time. Skirtboards also look best if they match up with the baseboard whenever possible. At this time, we also don't know the height of the baseboard, or even what kind it's going to be. For now, we'll build the wall so it's 1 1/2 inches above the finished stairs. The height can be changed later, if necessary.

To determine the height of the center wall, put one of the stringers into place against the first wall. Then cut blocks of wood for the top and the bottom steps that show the position of where the finish stair treads will end up, and tack them into place. Remember to account for the risers.

Now lay a straight 2x4 flat across the blocks, and draw a line across the studs, following the upper edge of the 2x4. Then remove the stringer and put the 2x4 back into place against the line, and draw another line across the studs, following the lower edge of the 2x4. Assuming the floor is reasonably level, the upper line represents the height of the center wall, and the lower line shows the length of the studs that are needed.

To build the wall, cut the bottom plate at 60 inches to fit between the stair opening and the landing. Then line it up against the first wall and mark the positions of the studs, matching those on that wall. Now the length of the studs can easily be found by just measuring from the bottom plate to the lower line. The line can also be used to find the angle of

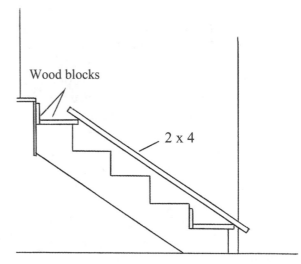

Wood blocks

2 x 4

the cuts with a speed square. You'll still have to determine the length of the studs on both ends, and also the boards for the upper plate. Once the other studs are cut, you can lay the wall out on the floor, square it up, and then project the lines to come up with the correct length for the those boards.

After the wall has been assembled, it's spaced out from the first wall 40 1/4 inches, to center it in the opening, and then it's nailed into place. Since the sheathing overlaps the landing, it will have to be notched for the wall. Then one of the stringers is lifted into position, and a line is drawn across the studs on the center wall following the lower edge of the stringer, to match the line that was already drawn on the other wall.

2x4s will be nailed to both walls, with their lower edge positioned on these lines. The purpose is to create a gap between the wall and the stringer for installing the sheetrock and the skirtboard. Use the stringers as templates to mark the end cuts on the 2x4s. Then install them by putting two 16D nails into each stud.

Now it's time to install the stringers. Do the outer ones first. Lift them up into position against the 2x4s that were just nailed on. Make sure the ends are at the correct height, and then drive three or four 16D nails into both ends of each stringer, where possible. If you're working alone, it may help to clamp the outside stringers to the 2x4s, and then tap them into the correct position.

Also nail the lower edge of the stringers to the 2x4s. I generally put a 16D nail near each end, and then one every foot in between. When doing the middle stringer, make sure it's centered, and that the ends are plumb. Then check the height by laying a level across the treads, and nail the ends in the same manner. If the landing is too thick to nail through, the stringers can be toenailed and/or attached to boards that are cut to fit tight between the stringers. You could also use metal hangers or corner brackets.

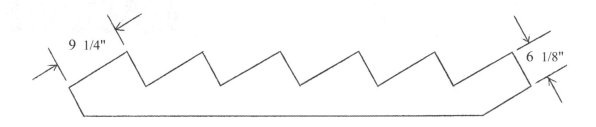

9 1/4"        6 1/8"

Now we'll move on to the lower set of stringers. These are laid out and cut the same way as the upper ones, with one exception. Since the stringers will rest on the lower floor, the bottom risers have to be cut to the correct height. To the right is the calculation that was used to find the riser height.

Before you mark the riser heights, check the floor for level at the base of the stairs, perpendicular to the stringers. If it's off, you'll have to adjust for it. In that case, the bottom riser on the center stringer will be cut at 6 1/8 inches. Then the riser height on the outer stringers will be adjusted so they're level with it.

The lower set of stringers will be attached to a hanger board in the same manner as the upper set. Again, cut the hanger board at 40 1/4 inches, and wide enough to reach the lower edge of the stringers. Then nail the hanger board to the landing, and mark the positions for the stringers 9 1/2 inches from the top.

| | |
|---|---|
| 7 5/8 | finished height |
| -2 5/8 | treads |
| 5 | |
| +1 1/8 | tile |
| 6 1/8 | riser height above floor |

At this point, the stringers could be installed, but it might be easier to build the end wall first. To do this, you have to go through the same process that was used to build the center wall, which is as follows: Put one of the stringers into place against the center wall, and tack on the same blocks that were used to mark the position of the finished stair treads. Then lay a straight 2x4 over the blocks, with it laid flat, and draw a line across the studs following the upper edge of the 2x4. Now remove the stringer, put the 2x4 back against the line, and draw another line following the lower edge of the 2x4.

Instead of the wall being 60 inches long to match the center wall, you could also cut the bottom plate at 60 3/4 inches so the stairs will line up with the end wall once the risers are on, which may help when they're finished off and the newel post is installed. Match the position of the studs in the center wall, and find their length in the same manner, by measuring to the line that was drawn across the studs. After cutting the studs to length, lay everything out. Then square up the wall, and use a square and a straightedge to find the point where the upper plate levels out at the height of the landing. Miter cut the ends where the two boards meet. Then nail the wall together. I use screws to attach the plates to each other if there isn't a stud at that point.

Once the wall is finished, nail it in place 40 1/4 inches from the center wall. It should line up with the edge of the landing. Again, the sheathing will have to be notched for the wall. Now position a stringer against both walls, and draw a line across the studs following the lower edge of the stringer. Then cut the 2x4s that go behind the stringers, and nail them into place.

The stringers can be installed now. Again, do the outer ones first. These are held at the 9 1/2 inch mark on the hanger, and are attached with several 16D nails going into the end of each stringer. Then the stringers are nailed to the bottom plates, and also to the 2x4s that run along the lower edge. Check the height of the center stringer by laying a level across the upper treads, and then nail it into place. This stringer can be toenailed to the floor, or secured between 2x4 or 2x6 blocks that are cut to fit tight between the stringers. After attaching the blocks to the floor, the stringer is either nailed or screwed to the blocks.

On the stairs in the photos, the end wall was built after the stairs were already installed. To build the wall, I attached boards to the steps to show where the finished stair treads would end up. Then the studs were cut to line up with a 1 inch board that was laid across the top, to match the height of the center wall. Here I should have cut the studs to line up with the lower edge of the board instead. At this height, once the stairs are finished off, the walls will be around 3 1/4 inches above the stair treads. To me, this seems a little high, so I might cut both walls lower. To do this, I'd lay a board that was the correct thickness across the original treads. Then I'd hold a pull saw tight against the board as I cut the studs shorter.

On this wall, the studs were turned so they're flat to the wall. This was done to make it as thin as possible to keep it farther away from the door that's next to it. In the photo on the left, you can also see the 2x4 that runs along the lower edge of the stringer. When the opening was cut for the stairs that go down to the basement, the right side was shorter so the lower stringers on the upper set of stairs would have something to rest on.

To finish the stairs, the treads and risers are installed. Here 1x8s will be used for the risers, and 2x12s for the treads. They'll be cut to 37 1/4 inches long. The finished stair treads won't be installed until the house is almost done, so the 2x12s will be left full width, which will give you a 1 1/4 inch overhang.

The risers go on first. Start at the bottom step, and work your way up. The first riser will have to be ripped to fit, since it's shorter than the others. To install it, apply a bead (line) of construction adhesive to the end of each stringer, and nail the riser to one of the outer stringers while holding it flush to the top, and also to the outside edge of the stringer. Then attach the riser to the opposite stringer, again while holding it flush to the top and to the outside edge, if possible. To do the middle stringer, mark the center of the riser. Then pull the stringer into position and nail the riser to it. Do the others in the same manner.

Since the outer stringers are nailed at each end, and also to the 2x4s, they're pretty much locked into place. Even pulling the middle stringer into position can be difficult if it's warped or twisted. By attaching a pipe clamp or a bar clamp to them, it will give you more leverage. Then as long as the stringers aren't cupped too badly, you should be able to get them to line up reasonably well with the risers. Just do what you can, and realize that it will all be covered up later.

Once you've done the first two risers, the bottom tread can be installed. Apply a bead of construction adhesive to the stringers, and also along the upper edge of the riser. Keep the adhesive toward the back edge of the riser, so there will be less chance of it squeezing out the front. Then lay the tread in place, and nail it to the stringers.

Screws could also be used instead of nails, but on interior stairs I generally use nails and adhesive. At this time, I use polyurethane construction adhesive, which is supposed to be stronger. For the risers, I use three 8D ring-shank nails per stringer. On the treads I use three or four 16D nails at each stringer. Here I like to use nails with a thinner shank to help eliminate splitting. Sometimes I'll use nails from a framing gun for the treads and risers, and then hand nail them. I also angle the nails a bit for more holding power. The nail heads should be driven under the surface of the wood, since they tend to come up later as the wood shrinks.

As you work your way up the stairs, it makes no difference whether you install all of the risers and then do the treads, or do one and then the other, as long as the riser goes on first. Once you reach the top of the stairs, you're finished for the time being, unless you plan on installing a temporary handrail. The lower right photo shows a temporary handrail that I built using boards that were just laying around.

# STAIRS IN OLDER HOMES

When I work on older homes, sometimes I'm asked to look at stairs that are too steep and/or have treads that are too narrow, to see if there's something that can be done about it. Almost always, the answer is "No," without it being turned into a major job. The reason has always been the same. There just wasn't enough room for it.

If the stairs are too steep, either the risers are too high or the run of each step is too short, which is the reason for the narrow treads. By shrinking the riser height, you'll need another step. Now the opening for the stairs will have to be longer, the same as what you'd need if the treads were any wider. Since the stairs were made to fit the opening, there generally isn't a simple way to get the extra length that's needed. In older homes, the landing at the bottom of the stairs is generally bare minimum to begin with, so the stairs will have to start farther back. If you're lucky, there will be enough room to do this. But most of the time it's not that easy.

Another thing to consider is the amount of headroom. By having wider treads and/or the extra step, the headroom will be one step lower. Eighty inches is required above the nose of the stair tread, and many times it's under that to begin with. If it's too low, you'll have to increase the size of the opening to get the extra height that's needed. This could be a lot of work if it means cutting into another room that's already finished.

Riser heights have changed over the years. Sometimes there isn't room to install a new set of stairs if you follow the rules that exist today, but there would be if you went by the previous rule. Where I live, the maximum riser height for stairs was 8 inches for many years, until recently. Now it's 7 3/4 inches. That extra 1/4 inch can be the difference of having one less step that could be used for wider treads or a bigger landing. On an older house, the building inspector will probably allow you to build the stairs at the previous height if it's the most practical choice.

When determining the best location for the stairs, you'll need an opening around 6 1/2 feet wide by a little over 8 feet long, at a minimum, for U-shaped stairs with 8 foot ceilings and standard floor joists. On straight stairs, you'll need at least 3 feet for the width, enough length for the stairs themselves, and also a minimum of 3 feet of open space at each end. Sometimes the best choice will be L-shaped stairs, where you go straight and then turn to one side. Whichever one you choose, make sure there's enough headroom where the stairs pass under the upper floor. In some houses, the location and the shape of the stairs is obvious. In others, you'll spend a lot of time trying to come up with a solution that works.

If the stairs are next to an exterior door, make sure they're far enough apart. Over the years, I've helped on several houses where a friend or a family member built a house from the ground up, from blueprints. On two of them, the stairs ended up closer than they should have been to an exterior door. In the lower right photo on the last page, you can see the door that's right next to the stairs. Originally, the stairs would have been several inches closer, but I notched the studs on the center wall, as shown in this photo, so they're only two inches wide on the upper end. I also thinned down the end wall. This wouldn't have been necessary if I'd noticed the problem and either moved the door or the stair opening over a bit.

If you're thinking about capping the stairs with new treads, the first thing you have to do is to measure the riser height on both the top and the bottom steps, to see if it's even possible. Here you're concerned about the rule for the maximum riser height, and also the one that says only 3/8 inch height difference is allowed. If it's reasonably close to that, I wouldn't be the too concerned if the stairs aren't being inspected, since the riser height changes anytime something is added to the floor.

A couple of years ago, one of my sisters wanted to cap the basement stairs in her house. To keep the riser height within reason, she bought stair treads that are only half an inch thick, with a decorative board on one edge. This board wraps around the outer corner to form the overhang, and also hides the other stair tread. Those stairs are shown in the jig section, in the upper photo on page 400.

81

# WIRING

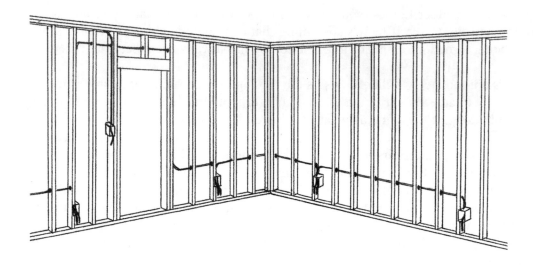

Once the framing is finished and the house is weather tight, you can start on the wiring. I consider this to be one of the easier jobs. To begin, the first thing to do is to plan the layout. On jobs where the homeowners want to help, I always start by telling them the basic rules that must be followed, and then have them staple a bright colored Post-it note every place that they either want an outlet (receptacle) or a wall switch, while still meeting the requirements. When necessary, the Post-its are labeled to show what's needed at that point. When marking the position of switch boxes, indicate the size of the box that will be needed, such as single, double, triple, etc.

While doing this, you have to visualize the house in a finished state. Since you're going to be the one that lives there, set it up the way that you like. On certain walls, or even floors, you may want to add receptacles that are installed specifically for televisions, work areas, etc. Also install any boxes that will be needed for communication lines to the phone, TV, computer, etc. If you're redoing the kitchen, the receptacle for the microwave is generally installed in the cabinet that's above it when the microwave is mounted above the countertop. An outlet is also needed for the refrigerator, that goes directly behind it.

You also have to decide how you want to light the rooms, with ceiling lights or floor lamps? With floor lamps, you may want to have them plugged into switched outlets. Then consider which light switches should be 3-ways, so they can be turned on and off from different locations. Also consider where you need reinforced ceiling boxes for any fans that might be installed. Where are the smoke detectors going, and what about recessed lights or sconces?

In the bathroom, where do you want the exhaust fan, and how about lights over the sink or vanity? Then you have to consider where you want the switches to go that control the ceiling light, the exhaust fan, the vanity lights, and the light over the shower, in case one's going to be installed. These can all go into one box next to the door, or maybe you want them broken up, with the switches for the ceiling light and the fan by the door, and the switch for the vanity lights next to the GFCI receptacle above the vanity. On larger vanities, it might be best to have more than one receptacle box.

On the next couple of pages are some of the basic rules for doing electrical work. Most of them will apply in all areas, but there are exceptions, so you should also check the current rules for your specific area. When remodeling, anytime you open up a wall or a ceiling, you may be required to bring the wiring in that area up to code.

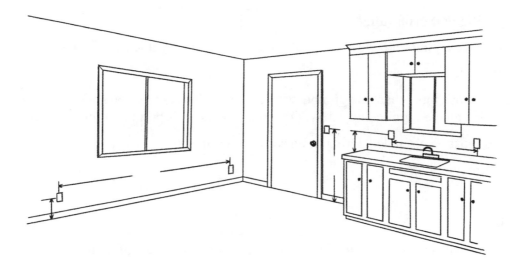

## Required circuits

* Bathroom receptacles: one separate 20 amp circuit

* Kitchen receptacles: two separate 20 amp circuits.

* Laundry receptacle: one separate 20 amp circuit.

* General lighting: one 15 amp circuit for every 600 square feet.

   Most appliances, such as furnace, air conditioner, electric water heater, electric dryer, electric range, dishwasher, disposal, and microwave, require separate circuits.

## Switch controlled lighting

* Most areas, including halls, need switch controlled lighting. Switched or half-switched receptacles are allowed.

* Switch required at top and bottom of stairs.

## Receptacle outlet spacing (maximum distance)

* Kitchen: 24 inches from the beginning of a counter space and then every 48 inches. A receptacle is required for each counter space 12 inches or wider, and at each island counter or peninsula larger than 12 x 24 inches. Counter spaces separated by range tops, sinks or refrigerators are separate spaces.

* Habitable Rooms: 6 feet from the beginning of a wall space and then every 12 feet. Doors are considered wall space. Receptacle is required for each wall space 2 feet or more in width.

* Hallways 10 feet or more in length shall have at least one receptacle outlet.

* All receptacles must be tamper resistant (TR). When outdoors, must be Weather Resistant (WR).

## Size of wire required

* 15 amp: 14 gauge        * 40 amp: 8 gauge

* 20 amp: 12 gauge        * 50 amp: 6 gauge (depends on wire)

* 30 amp: 10 gauge        * 60 amp: 6 gauge

## Wire length, splicing and grounding

* All boxes must have a minimum wire length of 6 inches, and extend at least 3 inches outside box.

* The outer cable jacket must extend at least 1/4 inch into the box.

* If a receptacle box has more than one ground wire, the ground wires must be spliced with a "wire tail" attached to the receptacle's grounding screw. Only one conductor is permitted under a terminal screw.

* All metal boxes must be grounded. Use ground screw or ground clip.

* All splices require wire nuts.

## Strapping cables

* Plastic cables must be strapped within 8 inches of boxes, and at intervals of no more than 4 1/2 feet.

* Plastic cables must be installed no closer than 1 1/4 inches from the face of studs and joists.

* Cables closer than 1 1/4 inches must be protected with metal plates.

* Up to 3 cables may be stacked under a single staple. Over three cables requires a stack staple.

## Under ground wiring

* Direct burial cables (Underground Feeder/type UF) must be in a trench at least 24 inches deep.

* Electrical PVC conduit must be in a trench at least 18 inches deep.

## Junction boxes

* Do not conceal junction boxes. Junction boxes are required to be accessible.

* Make sure box is correctly sized for the device used. (i.e. ground fault receptacles, dimmers, etc.)

## Box volume

| | Box volume In cubic inches | |
|---|---|---|
| | #14 Wire | #12 Wire |
| Each conductor | 2 | 2-1/4 |
| Ground wires in box | 2 | 2-1/4 |
| Each switch in box* | 4 | 4-1/2 |
| Internal cable clamps in box | 2 | 2-1/4 |

*Receptacles have the same rating as a switch.

For example, a 2-gang switchbox with four "14-2 with ground" cable in the box requires:

| | |
|---|---|
| Eight conductors | 16 cu. in. |
| Ground wires | 2 cu. in. |
| Two switches | 8 cu. in. |
| Internal cable clamps | 2 cu. in. |
| Minimum box size | 28 cu. in. |

### Ground Fault Circuit Interrupters (GFCIs) and Arc-Fault protection

* At this time (2016), the current NEC (National Electric Code) rules require GFCI protection for 15 and 20 amp receptacles in the kitchen (that serve the countertop surface and also the dishwasher), bathroom, laundry area, unfinished basements, garage, outdoors, and crawl spaces. Arc-Fault protection is required for 15 and 20 amp circuits in kitchens, family rooms, dining rooms, parlors, libraries, dens, bedrooms, closets, hallways, laundry areas, or similar rooms.

These are the basic tools that are used for wiring, which includes: a hammer, measuring tape, utility knife, needle-nose pliers, wire stripper, electrical tester, wire cutter, and a screwdriver.

After everything is laid out, you can start installing the boxes. There is no NEC (National Electrical Code) rule concerning the height of switch and outlet boxes in the home, with the exception that receptacles can't be more than 20 inches above a countertop. When remodeling, I try to match the height that's used in the rest of the house. On new construction, I generally install the switch boxes so the upper edge will be 48 inches above the finished floor, and outlet boxes around 14 inches to the top.

To satisfy the accessibility requirement of the Fair Housing Act, outlets and switches should be 15 inches minimum to 48 inches maximum from the floor to be accessible from a wheelchair. In the garage or a workshop, you may want to install switches a little higher, so sheetrock or plywood can be stacked against the wall without blocking them.

On switch or outlet boxes, I use a pencil to mark the position for the top of each box. With round boxes, I mark the center. The boxes should be installed so they extend out past the studs the thickness of the sheetrock, and farther yet if anything else is going to be added over the top, though on many boxes you're limited to about 3/4 of an inch. To do this, I use a small piece of sheetrock or plywood that matches the thickness of what's going on the wall. Then I hold it against the face of the stud as the box is lined up with it, and the nails are driven in. It's the best way I've found to make sure they're extended correctly. There are also lines on plastic boxes for doing this, but most of the time they're in the wrong place. It's not a problem if a box sits a little back from the surface of the sheetrock, but make sure that it doesn't stick out too far, or the cover plate won't lay flat against the wall.

Single boxes come in different sizes. When using a plastic box, 18 cubic inches is fine for a switch or a standard outlet with only one or two 14-2 wires in the box, but GFCI outlets are bigger, so a larger box would help. On outlets where three 12-2 wires are in a single box to split the power in different directions, you'll need the deepest box that's available.

Once the switch and the outlet boxes are in place, I start installing the boxes for the lights, fans, and smoke detectors. At this time, I'll also install the recessed lights, bathroom fan(s), and anything else that's needed. This is how I generally do it, but it makes no difference in what order everything is installed.

After that's finished, I map it all out. It doesn't have to be anything fancy. I just want to determine what outlets or lights are going on what circuits, and also whether the circuits will be 15 or 20 amps. This may depend on how many spaces are left in the breaker panel. When determining the circuits, you want to take into consideration how much power you'll actually be using. Generally the circuits will be split up, with the lights on one circuit and the outlets on another, though there isn't any rule that says you have to do it that way. Light circuits in homes are generally 15 amps. 20 amps is more common for the outlets.

One way to determine the number of outlets (receptacles) that go on a circuit is to count each one as 1 1/2 amps, and then only use 80 percent of the available amps. This would let you put eight outlets on a 15 amp circuit, and 10 on a 20 amp. From what I've read, there isn't a NEC rule concerning the number of outlets on a circuit, but there's probably a local requirement.

When you think about it, you don't actually use much power in a typical living room, and even less in a bedroom. Generally you might have a couple of lamps, a television, a computer, and maybe a sound system. For areas like this, I'm willing to put in the maximum amount of outlets that are allowed on a circuit. Now if you're wiring a home workshop, it's a different story. Here you need enough power to run an assortment of different tools, some of which will use up most, if not all of a circuit, all by themselves. Many times there may also be more than one tool running at the same time. For a room such as this, you'll want at least two 20-amp circuits, just for the outlets. I'd also use heavy duty receptacles that have a 20 amp rating.

On 20 amp circuits with only one outlet, a 20 amp outlet is required. If there's more than one outlet on the circuit, then 15 amp outlets are allowed.

As you map out the circuits, remember the 80 percent rule. Even though a circuit breaker may be called a 15 amp, it's actually only designed to handle a steady load of 80 percent of that, which is 12 amps. A 20 amp circuit breaker is only rated for a steady draw of 16. Using a tool or an appliance that draws more amps than that will eventually trip the circuit breaker.

There are also special requirements for the receptacles in certain areas of the house. For instance, you need at least one 20-amp circuit for the bathroom receptacles. If the lights or the exhaust fan are on the same circuit, you'll need a separate 20 amp circuit for each bathroom. This would be a smart thing to do anyhow, since a blow dryer can use up most of the circuit by itself. You're also required to have two 20-amp circuits for the receptacles in the kitchen, and a separate 20 amp circuit for the laundry area. Other appliances, such as the furnace, air conditioner, electric water heater, electric stove, electric clothes dryer, dishwasher, garbage disposal, Jacuzzi, and wall mounted microwave, will require their own circuit.

When mapping out the light circuits, I generally count each recessed light or each light box where a single light bulb will be installed as one amp, even though the actual draw will almost always be less. When dealing with lights that have multiple light bulbs, such as a chandelier or the vanity light in a bathroom, I consider the power draw as if it had the brightest bulbs that were allowed in that particular light. Doing this gives me some leeway in case something has been forgotten, or has to be added to the circuit at a later date. Try to put enough lights on each circuit without overloading it, and then lay it out so it makes sense.

Maybe it'd be best for the lights in the kitchen and the dining area to be on one circuit, the living room and the entry on a different circuit, and the bedrooms on another one. Every house is different. Just try to group them into their individual areas.

Bathrooms lights are not required to be GFCI protected, so they can be on the same circuit as the lights in an adjoining room.

Once the boxes are installed and everything has been mapped out, it's time to start running the wires. Years ago, interior wires were generally white. Now they're color-coded according to size. Most of the time you'll be working with ones that are either yellow or white. White is 14 gauge, which is used for 15 amp circuits, and yellow is 12 gauge, for 20 amp circuits There's also orange, which is 10 gauge and used for 30 amp circuits. The lower the number, the thicker the wire is.

One thing to always remember is that you can't put an undersized wire on a circuit. If you're wiring a 20 amp circuit, every wire on that circuit must be at least 12 gauge. Anything smaller could be a fire hazard, since the wire could be overloaded without tripping the circuit breaker.

NM (nonmetallic sheathed) wire is used for most interior wiring. This wire is also commonly called Romex. For most wiring, you'll be using either 14-2 with ground or 12-2 with ground. This means that there are two insulated wires inside the sheathing (a black and a white), and also a ground wire. Any wire with a three at the end, for instance14-3, also includes a red wire that's used for switched outlets, 3-way switches, smoke detectors, 240 volt circuits, etc. In home wiring, the black and the red wires are the "hot" wires that supply the power, and the white wire is generally the neutral wire that's used to complete the circuit. The green or the bare copper wire is used as a ground for safety. It provides a path for the electricity to run in case of a short circuit. On many of the newer power tools there isn't a third prong on the end of the cord for the ground wire. That's because they have a plastic case that acts as an insulator to prevent you from getting a shock.

For no particular reason, I generally begin by running the wires for the outlets. These are pretty straightforward. To get started, you'll have to drill the holes. Figure out the path that each wire is going to take, and then drill a 3/4 – 1 inch hole through the studs, joists, or the plates where needed. When going between the boxes, drill the holes around 2 feet off the floor, and center the holes in the studs. I usually drill them at about 20 inches. Spade bits work fine for this. Besides the standard length, there's also a shorter version. You may need both sizes, and also a snap on extender to drill the holes. You could also use an auger bit, which is what an electrician generally uses. For this type of bit, you'll need a drill with more torque.

Each circuit starts with a wire that runs from the breaker panel to the first outlet box on the circuit. This wire, called the home run, is brought up to the panel but isn't connected at this time. Just let the wire hang. Be sure to cut it long enough so there's plenty to work with. I usually cut the wire so that it extends to just beneath the panel, if it's coming from above. Use a Sharpie to write on the outer sheathing of the wire, identifying which circuit it goes to.

Then do the rest of the wires on that circuit, with each wire running from one box to the next until the circuit is completed. Sometimes it's easier to run a circuit by bringing the wire into a box and then splitting it off in two directions.

Wire staples (generally 1/2 inch) are used to hold the wires in place, anywhere they run along a joist or down a stud. The wires also have to be stapled within 8 inches of a box. With metal boxes that clamp the wire, the distance is extended to 12 inches. I generally cut the wires so that 6 - 8 inches is left extending from each box.

It's easier to run the wire through the holes if it isn't twisted. To keep from twisting the wire, it should be rolled off the coil. If I don't have a wire dispenser with me, I generally just hold the coil in my hands and unroll it as I back up. On most outlets there's no need to identify the wires, since they'll all be connected together anyhow: black to black, white to white, and ground to ground. One exception to this is a box that's getting a GFCI outlet. This is an abbreviation for ground fault circuit interrupter. In this case, if there's more than one wire in the box, you have to know which one is bringing the power in. I'll write "Power In" on that wire. Myself, I generally bring the power into a box through the hole that's closest to the stud. This way, I know which wire is the hot one, even when they're not labeled. It may not matter on most outlets, but it helps on a switch box that has several wires in it.

Now let's move on to the light circuits. When installing a light circuit, the power is commonly split off in different directions. You also have the option of running the power to the lights first, and from there going to each switch, or to run the power to the switch(s) first, and from there to the lights. I always run the power to the switch first if it's controlling multiple lights.. In boxes with multiple switches, it's common for each switch to be fed by a single hot wire.

When running the light circuits, label all the wires in the switch boxes, so you know which wire brings the power in, and which wire goes to each light. In most cases, 3-way switches on a 15 amp circuit will need a 14-3 wire for going between the switches. In some instances, you'll need two 14-2s instead. The wire that brings the power in only has to be a single 14-2.

In this photo, you can see that all of the wires are coming into the box through a single hole. This was done because paneling will be installed at a later date, and by doing it this way, it should be easier to remove and then reposition the box.

When drilling holes for the wiring, make sure they're big enough for the wires to easily pass through. Also, when drilling through the joists or the rafters, make sure the holes are at least two inches from the edge of the boards.

Smoke detectors that are hard-wired have to be connected together. On a 15 amp circuit, the wire supplying the power to the first smoke detector will be a 14-2. Any wires that go between the smoke detectors will be a 14-3. By having the extra wire, if one smoke detector goes off, they all do.

On 240 volt circuits, you may or may not need a neutral wire. For instance, on a typical 30 amp electric water heater, you'll need a 10 - 2 with ground. In this case, there's no place to attach a neutral wire, so the black and the white wires are both used to supply the power. On newer kitchen stoves and electric clothes dryers, a neutral wire is needed, so the red and the black wires supply the power.

When multiple wires are in close contact with each other for more than 24 inches, it's called "bundling." This is a potential problem because any heat from the wires could be trapped, and if the wires get hot, it lowers their amp capacity. For this reason, there might be a rule in your area on how many romex wires can pass through a hole, regardless of its size. Some electricians say three wires is the most that you can do. In Arizona, a new rule limits it to two wires per hole. I can do pretty much what I want, where I live.

In many cases, this rule seems contradictory to me. For one, I don't remember ever noticing a romex wire that felt warm to the touch. On the other hand, quite often I find extension cords or plug ends that are too hot, which are UL approved Also, if heat is the problem, why is spray-foam insulation allowed on houses, since it would trap any heat that was given off by the wires -- and why are breaker panels installed on the exterior in Arizona, one the hottest places in the country.

In the photo on the right, there's a 5-gang switch box on one side of the wall, and a 3-gang box just below it that faces in the opposite direction. There are also wires running through the wall to a light that's  above the boxes. When you have this many wires, you have to keep things neat and make sure the wires are kept away from the edge of the studs, so there's no danger of hitting them with a sheetrock screw. In order to do this, the wires have to be stacked on top of each other. Wire staples can be used for up to two or three wires. If any of the holes are less than 1 1/4 inches from the edge, a metal plate is needed to protect the wire. Here the switch box has been covered with plastic because the wall is going to be sprayed with foam insulation.

In some houses, Romex wire going to the furnace, electric water heater, etc. is connected to a disconnect box that's mounted near it. From there, metal conduit is used to bring the wire to the appliance. In other homes, the metal conduit ends at the ceiling, and the Romex wire just passes through it. To protect the outer sheathing on the Romex, a plastic sleeve or a metal connector with a plastic nut should be attached to the end of the conduit.

From what I've read, this is one rule that nobody agrees on. Some say that Romex can pass through conduit up to 6 feet in length, and that's it. For anything longer, you'll have to run separate wires through the conduit. Others say that you can do whatever you want, since there isn't a NEC rule prohibiting it. You would think that stripping off the outer sheathing on Romex would solve the problem, but it isn't allowed because the individual wires inside aren't labeled. If there's any doubt, ask the electrical inspector what the rules are for your area.

After the wires have been run, look everything over to see if anything has been missed. Make sure that every outlet box has a wire bringing the power in, and that you've run all the necessary wires to the different switch boxes, and also between the lights. It won't take long to do this, and it will save you the headache of something not working after the sheetrock is already in place. A missing wire isn't that obvious on a box with multiple wires going into it.

I generally install the circuit breakers after all the wires have all been run. This will give me a better idea on which side of the breaker panel to run the wire for each circuit, and where I want certain breakers to be located in the panel. If the wiring is being inspected, you'll probably need Arc-Fault circuit breakers and/or GFCI protection for many of the circuits. A Ground Fault Circuit Interrupter (GFCI) is used to prevent you from getting a shock. An Ark-Fault circuit breaker is used to prevent fires. Combination GFCI - Arc-Fault circuit breakers are available. Where you need both GFCI and Arc-Fault protection, an Arc-Fault circuit breaker can also be used with a GFCI outlet. Many people think Ark-Fault circuit breakers are too sensitive and also not necessary, and just use standard circuit breakers with GFCI outlets in the kitchen, bathroom, etc.

If a permit has been pulled for doing the electrical work, the wiring will have to be inspected at this time. On most houses I just tuck the wires inside each box. Some inspectors want the wires to be stripped and also have the grounds pigtailed together.

Once you've passed the inspection, you can do the insulation and the sheetrock. Then the outlets are installed, along with the switches and the lights. Even though it's easier to hang the sheetrock with the wires tucked inside the boxes, you may want to install some of the outlets and/or lights first, so you can see what you're doing and not have extension cords laying all over the floor. I always test recessed lights to make sure they're working properly before the ceilings are done.

# ELECTRICAL BOXES

These are just a few of the electrical boxes that are available. On upper left is a single and a 2-gang plastic box. To the right of that, you can see the difference between an 18 and a 22 cubic inch single box. The extra depth is needed when several wires are in the box, and helps when installing a GFCI receptacle. Plastic boxes up to 4-gang are available from most stores. 5-gang boxes can be special ordered from Home Depot. You could also gang five metal boxes together.

On the lower left is a box that's used when remodeling. This one is for switches or outlets, but a round version is also available for installing lights. Once a hole is cut through the wall, the box is slid into place. Then the screws are tightened, which rotates the tabs, so they catch on the back side of the sheetrock or the plaster. To the right is a single and a 2-gang metal box. Against the wall are a couple of covers for the larger box. On the right is a blank cover for when it's strictly being used as a junction box. The other cover is used to install a switch or an outlet. Also shown are a couple of Romex connectors for attaching the wires to a metal box.

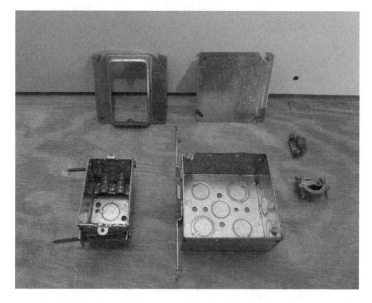

This is a heavy duty box for installing a fan, when you're going between the floor joists or rafters.

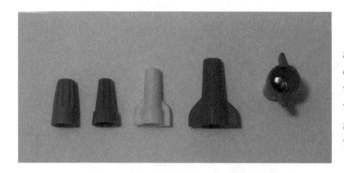

Here are several wire nuts, which are sized according to color. Red and yellow are used most often when wiring switch and outlet boxes. The two on the left are smaller, and they're used for attaching things such as light fixtures. The wings on the yellow and the red wire nuts give you more leverage for turning them.

On the top is a spade bit for drilling holes through the studs and the joists, and attached to it is a snap-on extender to increase the reach. Below that is an auger style self-feed bit. Try not to hit any nails or screws when drilling the holes, or you'll need a new bit. Nail-cutting drill bits are also available in both auger style and spade bits.

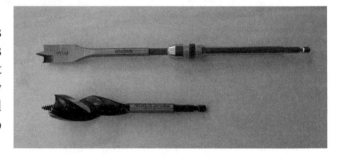

## WATTS = VOLTS x AMPS

The equation above, known as Watt's Law, is one of the basic rules of electricity. But to understand it, first you have to know the definitions of the factors that are used. **Watts** is the amount of energy that's used per second by a light bulb or an appliance. **Volts** is the amount of pressure on the electricity, and it's commonly described like water in a hose. If the pressure is greater, more water will pass through the hose. **Amps** is the amount of current that flows past a given point in one second. As long as the voltage remains the same, the only way to increase the amp capacity is to increase the size of the wire, such as 14 gauge wire being rated for 15 amps, and 12 gauge being rated for 20 amps.

By using Watts Law, you can determine any one of the factors as long as you know what the other two are. For example, a fluorescent light bulb that's rated at 12 watts only uses 1/10 of an amp (12 divided by 120 (volts) equals one tenth). You'll also find that a 120-volt 1500-watt heater uses 12.5 amps (1500 divided by 120 equals 12.5).

The following pages show different ways to wire the lights and outlets in a home. Many of the combinations that are commonly used are shown. Once you have a basic understanding of how this is done, you should be able to figure out other combinations if you just use a little common sense.

# OUTLETS

Here are two ways to attach an outlet. On the left is the preferred method, where the wires are secured by screws. The black wire (hot) is attached to the brass screw, the white wire (neutral) to the silver screw, and the ground goes to the green screw. To the right is an outlet where the wires were attached by just pushing them into the holes in the back. This is easier to do, but the connection isn't as solid. There are also other versions where the wires are held by the screws, but instead of wrapping around them, the wires slip into a hole or a slot that's next to each screw. These are also good.

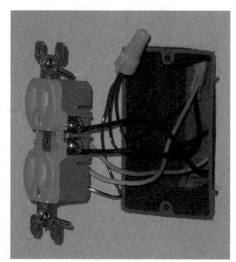

The photo on the left shows an outlet at the end of a circuit, and to the right of it are two views of an outlet with two wires in the box, where one wire brings the power in, and the other goes on to the next outlet. When there's more than one wire going into a box, a piece of ground wire that's about six inches long is attached to the ground screw, and then all of the grounds are twisted together and connected with a wire nut. This is called a pigtail, or wire tail splice.

On this GFCI outlet, the wires were slipped into the holes in the back, and then held by tightening the screws. Always connect the wire that brings the power in to the "LINE" side on a GFCI outlet. To provide GFCI protection to other outlets on the same circuit, attach the wire that goes to those outlets to the "LOAD" side.

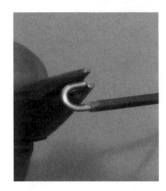

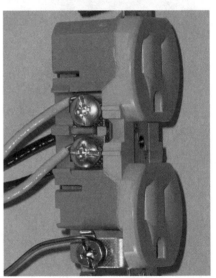

The photo on the left shows a needle-nose pliers being used to form a loop on the end of the wire. Then the loop slips under the screw head and wraps around it in a clockwise direction, This way, the loop will tend to close as the screw is tightened.

In most electrical books, you'll see a drawing or a photo of the wires being twisted together with a pliers before the wire nut is installed. This is seldom necessary. You'll get the same results by just turning the wire nut. When using a pliers, strip the sheathing farther back. Then trim the end once the wires are twisted, and put the wire nut on. When connecting different size wires, the smaller wire won't always twist correctly. This commonly happens when installing lights. Check for this by pulling on the small wire after the wire nut has been tightened. Sometimes it will come right out. When installing recessed lights, you don't want to find out that you have this problem after the sheetrock has already gone up.

When installing a switch or an outlet, the wires connected to it are generally bent so they fold vertically (like an accordion) as it's pushed into place and then screwed to the box. Where several wires are attached together with a wire nut, it's generally best to run them in a circle. When doing this, I split the wires up into groups before they're connected. Then I generally do the ground wires first, and push them to the back of the box. This will keep them away from any screws that could short it out. Then I'll do the neutral and the hot wires, and push them as far back as necessary. Where you need all the room you can get, cut the sheathing farther back so there's no more than an inch inside the box. Then cut the wires so they don't extend out more than 6 inches. When stripping the individual wires, don't go any farther back than necessary.

I use a utility knife to split and remove the sheathing, and keep the blade centered on 10-2, 12-2, and 14-2 Romex. Some people think this method is dangerous, and will tell you how they sliced open their hand while doing it, but so far, I haven't cut myself. I quit using a cable ripper years ago because sometimes it would cut through the sheathing on one of the wires if the Romex was twisted.

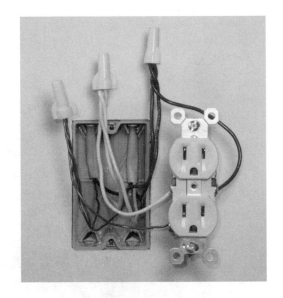

Another way to install an outlet is by attaching short lengths of wire to each screw, and then pigtailing everything together.

This outlet box has three wires coming into it. One brings the power in, and the other two are used to split it off in different directions. When doing this with 12-2 wire, you have to use the deepest box that's available to meet the size requirements.

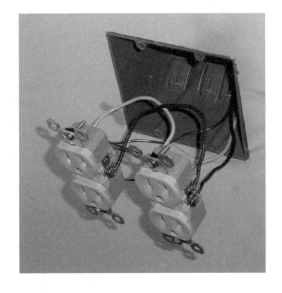

Here are two outlets wired together. The wire that brings the power in is connected to one of the outlets, which is then attached to the other with wires that go between the two. Both outlets have short wires attached to the ground screws that are pigtailed to the ground wire coming into the box.

# SWITCHED OUTLET

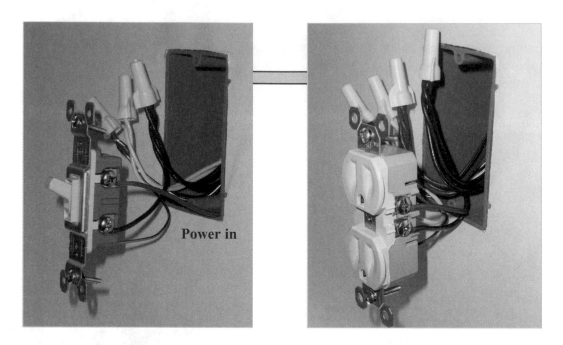

Power in

These photos show a switch being used to control the upper receptacle on an outlet. On a 20 amp circuit, a 12-2 wire brings the power to the switch first. Then a 12-3 wire goes from the switch to the first outlet, and another 12-3 wire goes from that outlet to the next, etc. Starting in the switch box, the hot wire is connected to the black wire that goes to the outlet, and also to a short wire that's attached to the switch. Then the red wire is attached to the other screw on the switch. To finish, a short wire goes to the ground screw, and then the neutrals and the grounds are connected together.

In the other box, short wires are attached to the outlet. Here, the black wire goes to the lower screw, so the lower receptacle will always be hot, while the red wire is connected to the upper receptacle, so it can be turned on and off. Only one wire is needed for the neutral screws. Then the wires are pigtailed together according to color.

You don't have to control every outlet with the switch. By having the extra wire, it gives you the option of doing it wherever you want. To control both receptacles, only attach the red wire. For both to always be hot, just attach the black wire. On outlets where you only want to control one of the receptacles, break off the tab on the hot side, so the receptacles aren't connected. If you aren't using one of the wires, put a wire nut on the end of it.

# METAL BOXES

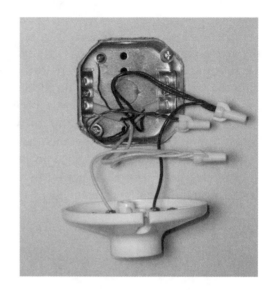

Metal boxes should always be grounded. To ground the box on the left, the ground wire was cut extra long so it could also wrap around the ground screw. The box on the right was grounded with a separate wire that was pigtailed to the other grounds. Metal boxes generally have a threaded hole in the back for the ground screw.

# SINGLE POLE SWITCH

Power in

A single pole switch is used where you want one switch to control the light(s). To install it, the hot wire goes to one screw, and the black wire that goes to the light is attached to the other. I always connect the hot wire to the lower screw, although it doesn't really matter.

More lights can easily be added by running another wire to the light box. Multiple lights can be run in a series, or by splitting the wires off in different directions, if that's an easier way to do it. In any light box with more than one wire going into it, just attach short lengths of wire to the light, and then pigtail everything together according to color. On some lights there isn't a place to connect the ground wire. In that case, just push it up out of the way, so it's there for the next light that gets installed.

# MULTIPLE SWITCHES

Even a small house will generally have several boxes that contain more than one switch. The easiest way to wire them is by running the power to the switch box first, with one wire supplying the power to every switch. In the 2-gang box that's shown here, the hot wire is pigtailed to the black wires that go to the lower screw on both switches. Connected to the upper screws are the black wires that go to each light. A ground wire was also attached to each switch, and then the neutrals and the grounds were pigtailed together. The same method can be used, no matter how many switches are in the box. The only limiting factor is how much power you're drawing, and the number of wires that can be attached together. If there are too many wires to fit under a wire nut, or they're too far apart, you can split the wire off in different directions. By breaking it up into two groups, you shouldn't have any problem wiring a 5-gang switch box. When there's more than one circuit in the box, the neutral and the hot wires from each circuit have to be grouped separately.

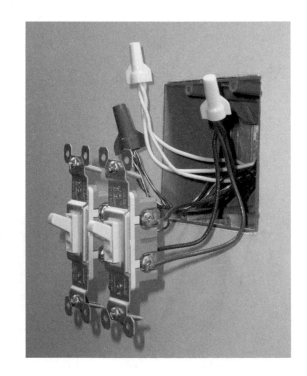

On multiple-gang boxes, make sure the box is level across either the upper or the lower edge. Otherwise, the cover plate will sit at an angle.

# SWITCH LOOP

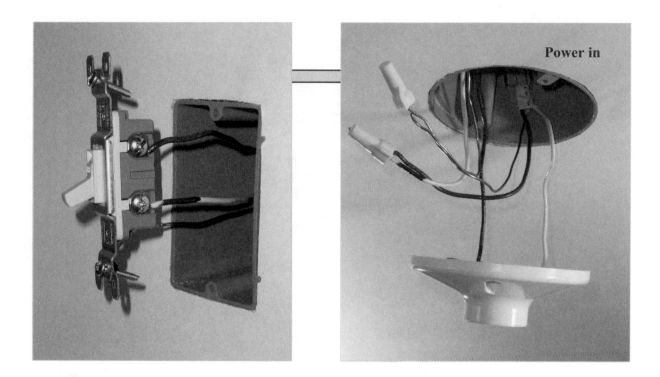

Power in

When wiring the lights, the power is commonly run to the light(s) first, and from there down to the switch. This is called a switch loop. To do it this way, the hot wire coming into the light box is attached to the white wire that goes to one of the screws on the switch. Both ends of this wire are colored black with a Sharpie to show that it's being used as a hot wire. Then the black wire in the switch box is connected to the other screw on the switch, and at the other end it's attached to the light. The neutral wire in the light box goes directly to the light.

A switch loop can also be used when wiring the outlets. To do this, just run a wire from the outlet that you want to control to a switch. Then instead of attaching the hot wire to the outlet, connect it to the white wire that goes to the switch. The black wire coming back from the switch gets attached to the outlet.

There are only two wires going into the light box that's shown above: the one that supplies the power, and the one that goes to the switch. Commonly there will be one or two more that go to other lights. Then, depending on whether you want the other wire(s) to be hot all the time, or on the same switch, the black wire is either attached to the hot wire coming into the box, or to the wire coming back from the switch. In either case, the neutral and the ground wires are all connected together.

Switch loops are generally wired with the power going from one light to the next across the ceiling of one room, or even several rooms. The lights can be run in a single series with the switch connected to the first light box, or they could be broken up into different series, with each one having its own switch.

Examples of a single series would be the basement lights controlled by one switch, or a dozen recessed lights spread across the living room ceiling that are also controlled by a single switch. If you wanted to add more lights to the ceiling that were controlled by a different switch, just run a run a wire to the first light box in the series, and attach the black wire to the wire that's always hot.

If the switch can't be connected to the first light in the series, then a 14-3 wire (15 amp circuit) will be needed to go between the lights until you get to the box that the switch is connected to. Here the extra wire is necessary because one wire will be used to bring the power to the light box that the switch is connected to, and the other will be used to go back and power the other lights.

97

# SWITCH LOOP WITH MULTIPLE LIGHTS

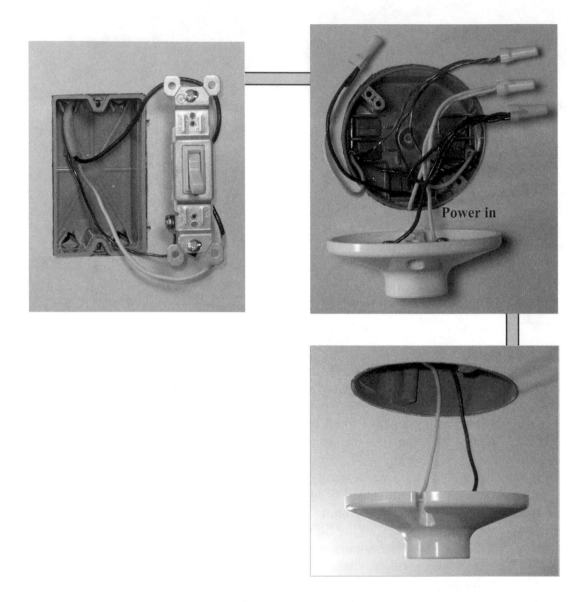

Power in

Here are two lights that are wired with a switch loop, where the power comes into the upper light box. Again, the hot wire is connected to the white wire that goes to the lower screw on the switch. But, in this case, the black wire that goes back to the light is also attached to the black wire that goes on to the next light. The neutral wire in the upper light box is connected to the neutral wires that go to both lights. More lights could also be added by running a wire to either light. When doing this, just pigtail everything together according to color.

When wiring these lights, the power could also have come in through the lower light, but there's a problem with that. When doing it this way, an extra wire would be needed for going between the lights, since you need a wire to get the power to the switch, another wire to bring the power back, and a neutral wire for the second light. When done in this manner, the wire between the lights would have to be a 14-3. You'll run into the same problem with 3-way switches if you do it in the wrong order; though, in that case, you'd need two 14-2 wires instead of a 14-3.

# 3-WAY SWITCHES

3-way switches are used to control a light from two locations. These switches have three screws for attaching the wires, not counting the ground screw, which means a 14-3 wire will be needed for going between the switches on a 15 amp circuit. Only a 14-2 is needed to supply the power to the switches. The black or copper colored screw is the common terminal. In these photos, and the ones that follow, the common terminal will be on the upper right corner of the switch. Depending on the switch, this terminal may not always be in the same place.

In every combination, the hot wire that brings the power in is attached to one of the common terminals, while the neutral wire goes to the light. The black wire connected to the other common terminal also goes to the light. Sometimes this can be difficult to keep track of if the wires change color as they go from one box to the next.

A 3-way switch is different than others, in that it doesn't actually turn on and off. Instead, it switches the power from one side to the other.

The wires attached to the other screws are called travelers. Generally the travelers will be connected to the same corner on both switches. If the red wire is on the lower right corner of one switch, it will also be on the lower right corner of the other. Although it's typically shown this way, it isn't actually necessary.

It turns out that the position of the travelers determines the position of the switches. If they're wired the same way, the light will be off if both switches are either up or down. If one switch is up, and the other down, then the light will be on. If the wires are reversed, it will be the opposite.

14-2

Power in

Common

Common

14-3

3-way switch, with power going through both switches first, and controlling one light.
Multiple lights are easily added with this layout by running the other lights off this one.

99

3-Way Switch, power coming in through the light

Power in

14-2

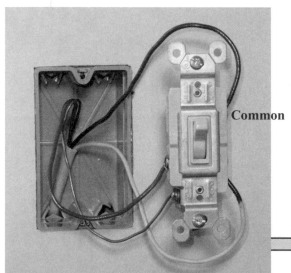

Common

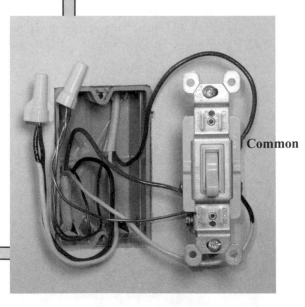

Common

14-3

With this combination, the hot wire is attached to the black wire that goes to the common terminal on the nearest switch, and the neutral wire is connected to the light. The black wire attached to the other common terminal is connected to the white wire that goes back to power the light. The ends of this wire are blackened, as are the ones on the white wire (traveler) that's connected to the lower right corner on both switches. The red wire (traveler) is attached to the lower left corner on each switch.

3-Way Switch, power coming in through the light, with switches on both sides

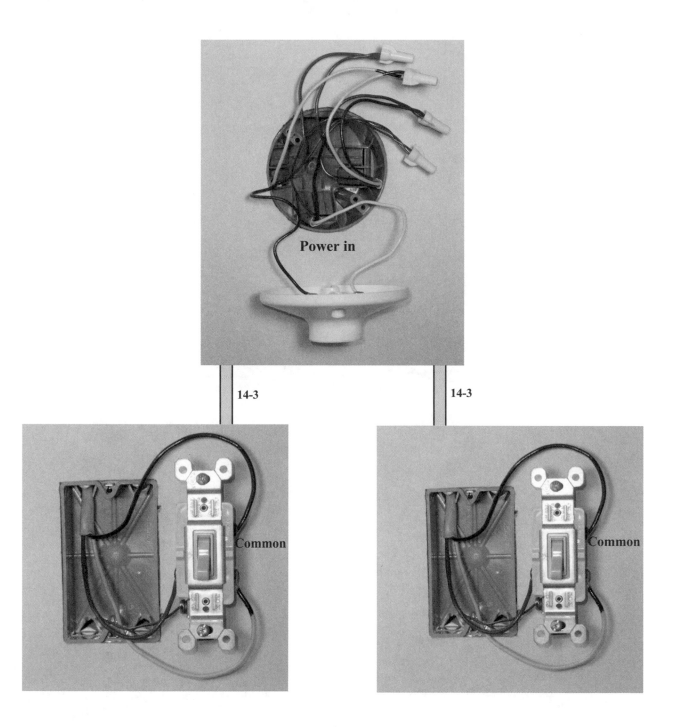

This one is pretty simple. Here the hot wire is connected to the black wire that goes to the common terminal of the switch on the right, and the neutral is attached to the light. The black wire attached to the common terminal on the other switch also goes to the light. The rest of the wires in the light box are matched up according to color and connected together.

3-Way Switch, power coming in through the switch, with the light between the switches

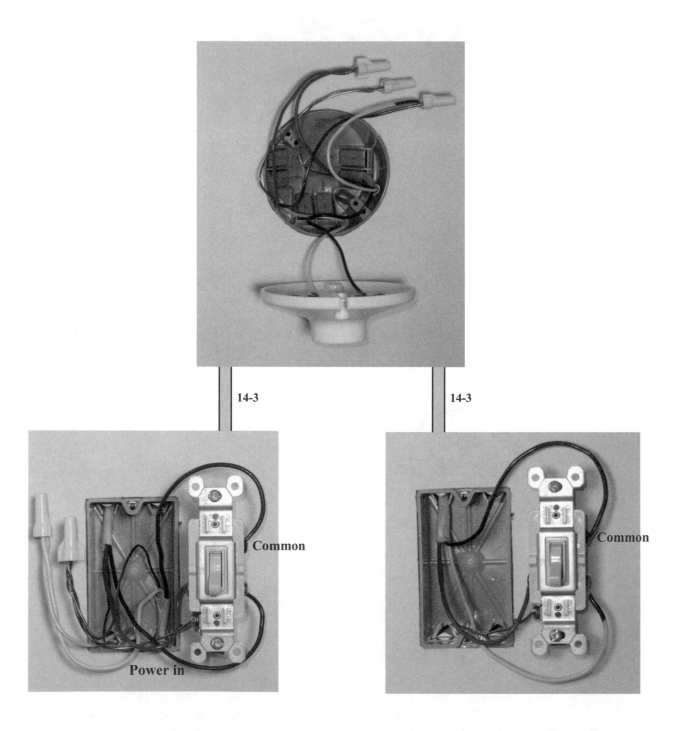

With this layout, the hot wire is connected to the common terminal on the first switch, and the neutral is attached to the white wire that goes to the light. The red wires connect to the lower left corner on each switch, while the black wire that's attached to the lower right corner of the switch on the left is connected to the white wire that's attached to the same corner of the switch on the right. This wire has its ends blackened. The black wire connected to the common terminal of the switch on the right goes directly to the light.

In every combination that's been shown, a 14-3 wire is used to go between the switches. But, if you look at an electrical book, you'll see that two 14-2 wires are needed instead to go between the lights when there are multiple lights between the switches. An easier way to add lights without having to do this is to install the 3-way switches with a single light, and then run the wire for the new light(s) by pig-tailing it to the wires that go to the other light.

No matter how you do it, -- when installing 3-way switches, just follow the same rules. The hot wire connects to the common terminal on one of the switches, and the neutral goes to the light. The wire attached to the common terminal on the other switch also goes to the light. The other wires (travelers) generally match up on the same corner of each switch. When using a neutral as a hot wire, you should blacken the ends with a Sharpie to mark it as such.

## 4-WAY SWITCHES

4-way switches are used when you want to control a light from three locations. For example, I installed one at a friend's house for a ceiling light that's located on the second floor, above the stairs. These stairs are at the end of a hall that goes to several bedrooms. By having three switches, the light can be controlled at either end of the stairs, and also at the far end of the hall.

About the only difference between this and a 3-way switch is how the travelers are run. Instead of attaching them to the other 3-way switch, the travelers are connected to opposite ends of a 4-way switch.

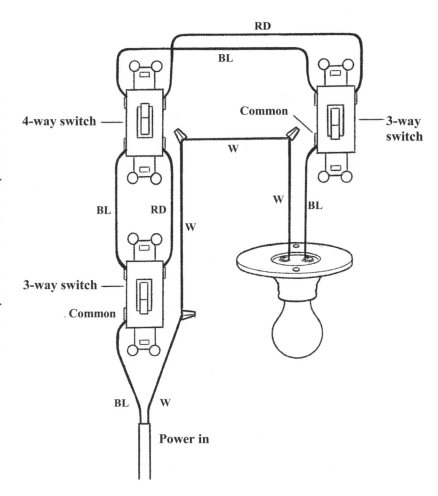

103

# BREAKER PANEL

To finish roughing in the wiring, you have to install the circuit breakers. You can see that this breaker panel has been filled up, which happens pretty often when remodeling. On this particular job, Arc-Fault circuit breakers were required for any new areas that didn't have GFCI protection. The new breakers are at the lower end of the box. The wires were also labeled using short pieces of the plastic sheathing to match the original work.

The safest way to install the circuit breakers is by shutting off the main breaker in the panel, which will kill the electricity to the whole house. Before you do this, turn off any computers or electric appliances that might be affected by it. With the main breaker off, you may need a headlamp or someone holding a flashlight to do the work. Myself, if I'm only adding a few circuits, and the panel isn't too cluttered, I generally leave the main breaker on. This isn't something that I can recommend, but my feeling is that unless the power is shut off outside the house, there's always the possibility of getting a shock when you're working inside the breaker panel. You just have to be aware of what's hot, and to keep your hands away from it.

When I'm running new wires in the panel, I try to keep things neat and generally follow the same pattern that was used by the electrician who installed it. Once the sheathing is stripped, I attach the neutral and the ground wires first. While doing this, I bend the other wires out of the way to give me room to work. Notice how the wires run down the outside of the box, and then turn ninety degrees right before they attach to the circuit breaker or the ground/neutral bar. When done in this manner, it's easy to fold the wires out so you can get behind them.

On the main breaker panel, the ground and the neutral bars should be connected (bonded), so you should be able to attach the neutral and the ground wires to either bar. On a sub panel, they have to be kept separate. Only one neutral wire is permitted under a screw. Depending on the breaker panel, you can generally put two or three ground wires under the same screw, as long as the wires are the same size. If you run out of terminals to attach the wires, you could also add another ground bar. This is easy to do. Just drill a couple of holes, and then screw one into place. This bar is only for the ground wires, not the neutrals.

To attach the hot wire, you can either connect the wire to the circuit breaker and then snap the breaker into place, or install the circuit breaker first and then attach the wire, while first making sure that it's in the "off" position. If the main breaker has been turned off, none of this matters, since the only place there's current is where the main wires are attached.

If you've pulled a permit for doing the electrical work, you'll probably have to install Arc-Fault circuit breakers. When remodeling an older house, that can be a problem. Besides the cost, this type of circuit breaker is a lot bigger. With standard circuit breakers, if there aren't any open spaces left, sometimes you can replace some of the breakers with the skinny ones that are only half as thick. With Arc-Fault circuit breakers that isn't an option, which means you may have to install a sub panel or replace the breaker panel.

This breaker panel is in a house that I've worked on in Wisconsin. Notice how the wires enter the box through large conduit, instead of small holes. In some areas, this would be considered bundling and wouldn't be allowed.

Since there are some open spaces left in the panel, it gives you a good look at the points where you could get a shock. There are several spots that you have to avoid. The photo above shows the large wires that supply the power. There are three of them, two hot wires and a neutral that's on the right side. The position of these wires isn't always the same. Just remember that the hot wires feed the breakers, and the neutral wire goes to the neutral bar. The one place that you can get a shock, whenever there's power to the house, is where the hot wires connect to the main breaker (1).

The other three spots are only hot if the main breaker is in the "ON" position. In the lower left photo, you can see the bars that the breakers attach to (2). They supply the power to the breakers, so stay away from them. The bars are attached to the bottom of the main breaker (3), so stay away from there too. The lower right photo shows the breakers themselves. The screws where the wires attach (4) are hot whenever the breakers are in the "ON" position. By knowing these points, it's safe to work inside the breaker panel, as long as you pay attention to what you're doing.

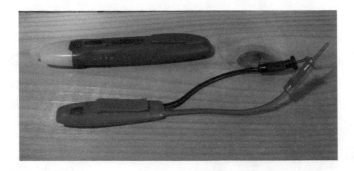

Anytime you're working around electricity, you have to know what to look out for to keep from getting a shock. It's easy to say to always turn the power off, but many times that isn't practical. On the last page I went over the breaker panel, but it's unlikely that you'll ever get a shock while working on one. Most of the time, you'll get a shock when you least expect it.

If you're hanging the sheetrock or paneling the walls, sometimes the outlets have to be pulled away from the wall and then reset once you're done in that area. If the power is still on, the side where you could get a shock is on the right, when the ground is facing down on the receptacle, since that's the side the hot wires are connected to.

When wiring the outlets or the lights, the circuit breaker is generally off, so you're safe. But watch out for junction boxes, and switch boxes that have multiple switches, because the wires may be on more than one circuit. I seldom get a shock, but I've made this mistake a couple of times. On both occasions I turned the breaker off, and then got zapped when I started working on the wiring.

After the circuit breaker is turned off, use a voltage tester like the upper one in the photo to make sure the power is actually off. They cost less than ten dollars and are simple to use. Just hold it next to the wire, outlet, switch, etc. and push the button. If there's any current, it will start beeping. This type of voltage tester is very sensitive. If you're testing a wire that's in close contact with a wire that's still hot, it may still go off. The other voltage tester that's shown, lights up. To use it, touch one of the contacts to whatever you're testing, and the other contact to a ground. If there's current, the bulb will light up.

## OLDER HOMES

According to the rules, anytime a wall or a ceiling is opened up, and you make changes to the wiring, it may have to be brought up to code. Years ago, the wires were run by suspending them from porcelain insulators. If you find this type of wiring, called knob-and-tube, it should automatically be torn out and replaced.

In homes that were built a little more recently, metal boxes are used in conjunction with flexible metal conduit (Greenfield). Inside this conduit, separate wires are run to the different outlets, switches, and lights. Because they're run separately, some of the wires may pass through a box, and not end at every one the way they do now when using Romex. When wired in this manner, the boxes are grounded as long as the conduit runs in an uninterrupted path all the way back to the fuse box or breaker panel. Sometimes there will also be a thin wire inside the conduit that acts as a ground.

When I work on an older house, I prefer to remove all of the old wiring. This may not always be practical, in which case I'll have to tie into it and bring it up to code at the same time. How I'd go about this would depend on the condition of the wiring itself.

Sometimes the wires inside the conduit are sheathed with plastic, pretty much the same as what's used today. But there are also older ones where the wires are covered with some sort of a fabric material. This material can get brittle, sometimes so much that it's hard to even work with it, without the insulation falling off. Where possible, I'd strip out and replace any wires that are covered with this material.

Any of the old wiring that remains in areas that have been opened up will have to be properly grounded to bring it up to code. Where the conduit is missing a ground wire, a new one can be run to each box, going all the way back to the breaker panel. You may need a fish tape for doing this.

If that isn't possible, a box can also be grounded by running a wire to a metal water pipe. This pipe must be metal all the way back to where it enters the house in order for it to act as a ground.

A ground wire should be connected to every metal box. This wasn't done in the past. Back then, the boxes were grounded by the conduit, and the switches and the outlets were grounded by attaching them to the box.

# WORKING ON EXISTING WIRING

Before you can add on to the existing wiring, or make any changes, first you have to determine how it was run. Once you have a basic understanding of how to wire a house, you should be able to pull the cover on almost any switch or outlet box and determine what's what by just using a little common sense. If you're having a problem, use a voltage tester to determine which wires are hot. Then by flipping the switches as you test for power, you can also determine which wires are switched, and what they're used for.

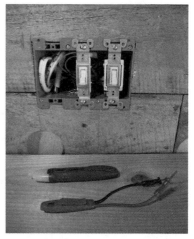

Starting with the outlets, two wires in the box generally means you're in the middle of a circuit, with one wire bringing the power in and the other going on to the next outlet, though it could also be going to a light. One wire generally means you're at the end of a circuit. Switched outlets have an extra wire, so you have the option of whether you want it to be switched, or not. I use the word "generally" because there are always exceptions when wiring.

Switch boxes can be a little harder, but you should still be able to figure them out. If you find a wire that's pigtailed to multiple wires, which are connected to the different switches, you know that's the hot wire bringing the power in, no matter what color the wires are. The other wires that are connected to each switch will be going to the different lights. When a white wire is attached to a switch, or there's only one wire in the box, it's either a 3-way, or a switch loop where the power goes to the light first. Any other white wires are neutral wires, and they all get attached together if they're on the same circuit. If there's more than one circuit in the box, then the neutral wires for each circuit should be grouped separately. This is especially important with Arc-Fault circuit breakers, as it will trip the breaker if they're connected.

When you're dealing with 3-way switches, remember that a 14-2 wire, on a 15 amp circuit, is used to bring the power in, and the hot wire gets attached to the common terminal on one of the switches. The wire attached to the common terminal on the other switch goes to the light A 14-3 wire is used to connect the 3-way switches together. Any white wire that's connected to a 3-way switch is probably being used as a traveler.

On the switch box that's shown in the photo, the wires had been roughed in the previous year, so I had to go through the same process to install the 3-way switch that's on the right side. Here I had to look over the wires in this box, and also in the box where the other 3-way switch was going, to remember how it was supposed to be installed. In this case, all I had to do was to find the wire that went to the light, which meant the hot wire would get connected to the switch in the other box.

In older homes, sometimes the wires look pretty much the same, so you don't know which one is hot and which one is the neutral, without testing them. There may also be different colored wires inside the conduit, such as blue, brown, yellow, orange, etc. In either case, you'll have to determine what each wire is being used for before you can make any changes.

# PLUMBING

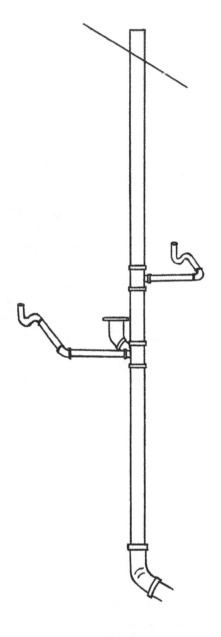

Out of all the jobs that have to be done on a house, the plumbing is one of the harder ones to get right. By that, I don't mean installing it so it's good enough to work, -- but by also doing it in a way that meets the requirements for your area. For years, whenever I worked on a bathroom, I'd have someone else do the plumbing, until I finally bought a book to learn the basics. My first attempt worked fine, but I made a couple of mistakes that would have kept it from passing a plumbing inspection.

The problem was the book I'd purchased. It was an older one that showed the plumbing as it would have been laid out in an older house. Here the tee fittings were drawn without having any slope to them, so I had to guess how everything should go, and ended up facing some of the sanitary tees for the vents backwards. I continued doing it the same way for quite a while, without anyone correcting me, including a couple of building inspectors, though I do remember seeing a strange look on the face of one of them as he looked at the vents. He probably thought he was doing me a favor by not mentioning the mistake, but it would have been better if he'd told me the correct way to do it.

Years ago, the plumbing in a typical house was much simpler than it is today, with many homes only having a single bathroom. That's how it was where I grew up. We lived in a three-story house with eight kids and only one bathroom. These days, a house that size would probably have at least three or four bathrooms.

In those older homes, a large cast iron pipe would come up from the basement with the drains for the bathroom fixtures clustered around it as it went up to the roof, similar to that in the drawing. When done in this manner, called stack venting, extra venting isn't needed for the fixtures. Commonly there would also be a smaller stack for other fixtures, such as the kitchen sink. That pipe would cross under the basement floor and connect to the main drain pipe.

In newer homes, the plumbing tends to be a lot more spread out. Because of that, it gets a little more complicated, and there are more rules that you have to follow. I think it's easier to get a better understanding of this when you can see how it's laid out in an actual room, so I've shown the layout of several bathrooms, and also included anything else that I can think of that will help.

# BUILDING A NEW BATHROOM

When deciding on the location for a new bathroom, one of the first things you have to consider is the layout of the plumbing. To start off, there are a couple of things that you have to look for. The first is, how are the drain pipes going to be run, and is there a drain pipe in the vicinity that you can connect to, or do you see a way to run a new one? For a toilet, you'll need a 3 inch pipe. The second question is, how is the plumbing going to be vented? Where I live, that means either locating a 2 inch (minimum) vent pipe to connect to, or finding a way to run a new one up to the roof. Once you've figured this out, you can start working on your plan for the bathroom.

As you determine the layout for the bathroom fixtures, you have to visualize how each one will be both drained and vented. A plumber once told me that running the drain pipes was easy; it was the vents that were the problem. Sometimes, even though you can run the drain pipes, it isn't possible to put a fixture in a certain spot because there's no practical way to vent it at that location. In many houses, the drain pipe for the toilet has to run parallel to the floor joists, or straight down, because the joists aren't big enough for drilling the large holes that are needed for the 3 inch pipe to pass through them, though you shouldn't have this problem with I-joists or floor trusses. On drain pipes that run parallel to the floor joists, because of the slope, you're still limited by the size of the joists. Anytime the location of a fixture is questionable, you should check it out with a tape measure and a level to make sure there's room for the necessary fittings and for the drainpipes to be sloped properly. When drilling through the floor joists, the holes have to stay at least 2 inches away from both the upper and the lower edge. In the last section of this book are the rules concerning the maximum size of notches and holes for going through the studs and the floor joists.

While designing the bathroom, you have to consider how everything is going to come together. Besides the position of the bathroom fixtures, and how the drain and the vent pipes will be run, you must also consider the supply lines for both the hot and the cold water. Then you have to think about the exhaust fan and how it will be vented, the medicine cabinet if there is one, and also the wiring, lights, switches, and outlets.

Depending on the circumstances, you can install the drain pipes and the supply lines by starting where they connect to, and then work your way out to the fixtures, or you could start at the fixtures and then work your way back. When using the second method, you have to start at the correct height, so the drain pipes will have the proper slope. This is easy to calculate. If you want 1/4 inch per foot slope, and the length of the drain pipes, including elbows, is 20 feet, you'll need a 5 inch height difference from one end to the other. The size of the drain pipes may also change, so take that into consideration. You can't always set the height by measuring off the framing. On one job, I drilled holes through the new I-joists for a drain pipe, and adjusted the height of each hole by measuring off the bottom of the joist, so I'd have 1/4 inch per foot slope. Then once I slipped the pipe into place, I found that it was level, which meant the new floor was way off. So don't assume anything, and check the floor joists with a level before you mark the positions of the holes.

One of the problems with plumbing is that the rules are different from one state to the next, or sometimes even between adjoining cities. One reason for this is because there's more than one plumbing code. The two that are followed are the International Residential Code (IRC) and the Uniform Plumbing Code (UPC). Another reason is that the plumbing code is updated every few years, and the rules can change.

Generally, the rules concerning the drain pipes are pretty much the same, the main difference being how many fixture units are allowed for the different size pipes. Vents are where they really differ. The reason for having vents is to help prevent the water from being siphoned out of the traps. The water in the traps prevents sewer gas from getting into the house. Where I live, common vents are only allowed in a few instances. In other areas, common vents are used more often. The distance allowed between the vent and the trap for the fixture may also be greater. A common vent is one that vents more than one fixture. A wet vent is a pipe that's used both as a drain and as a vent. Where common vents aren't allowed, each fixture must be vented before the drain pipes are connected together. Where horizontal vents aren't allowed, vents have to stay within 45 degrees of vertical until they're at least 6 inches above the flood rim of the fixture they're venting. You'll see this in most of the photos, as these are the rules that I generally have to go by.

109

# COMMON WAYS TO PLUMB BATHROOM FIXTURES

## TOILETS

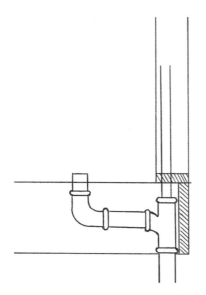
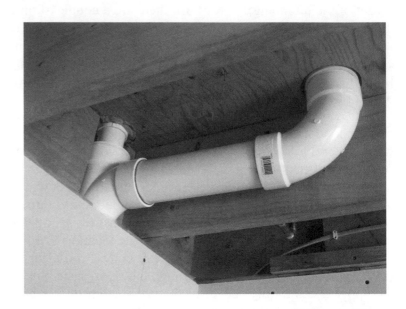

One way to plumb a toilet is to run the drain pipe down the nearest wall. In this case, it's an exterior wall, but here the walls were framed with 2x6s, so there was still room for insulation behind the pipes. As you can see, a 3 inch elbow and a short length of pipe are connected to a sanitary tee. From there, the 3 inch drain pipe goes down to the basement. To vent the toilet, a reducer bushing was glued into the sanitary tee for a 2 inch pipe that goes up to the roof. For the time being, a short pipe will extend above the floor and be capped off. When the floor is finished, the pipe will be cut off flush to the floor, and the toilet flange will be installed. In the photo, the toilet flange is just temporarily laying in place, since the floor still has to be tiled.

Commonly a floor joist will be positioned right next to where you want to install the elbow for the toilet. So in order to make this work, you'll have to keep everything as close as possible to the joist. That's why a 3 inch elbow was used here. A 4x3 closet elbow would have put the hole a little farther out. When the floor joist is directly in the way, you'll either have to box off the floor joist, or shift the toilet over. By moving it, it might be too far from the wall, but one option then is to build out the wall in that area.

Here's a toilet drain that's running parallel to the floor joists. When doing this, it's generally vented up the first wall that it passes by, which in this case is the shower wall. Where I live, a toilet has to be vented within 4 feet (now 6 feet), so that's a limiting factor on where they can be located. Here, the sanitary tee for the vent pipe is turned so it's sloped towards the sewer. When there's no place to run the vent, a short partition wall can be built to enclose the area around the toilet. This will provide a place for the pipe to come up, and from there it can run up the wall behind the toilet.

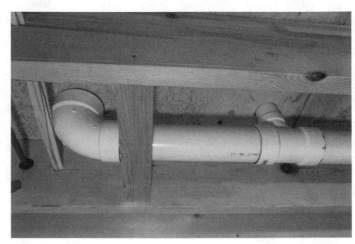

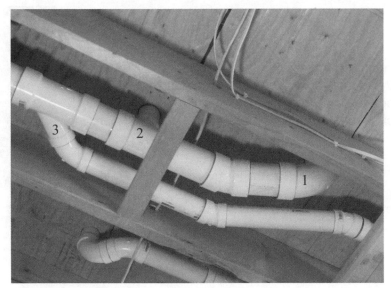

This is another drain pipe for a toilet that's going between the floor joists. Once the toilet (1) had been vented (2), the drain from the shower (3) was connected to the pipe.

## SINKS

The easiest way to run the plumbing for a sink is to have the drain pipe come up from the floor, and then use a sanitary tee. From there, the vent goes straight up. The supply lines typically sit to both sides and just above the drain, though they could also stay out of the wall and come up through the floor. This is better if the sink is on an exterior wall in a cold climate, so the pipes are less likely to freeze. In the lower photo, you can see how the pipes were installed beneath the floor.

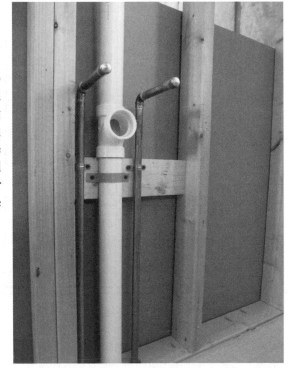

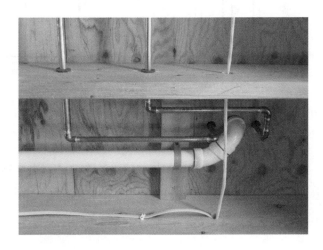

111

This photo shows the drain pipes for two sinks that are connected to a cross tee. In this case, a 2 inch cross tee was used to match the pipe that's coming up from the floor, along with a 2 inch cleanout. The individual drains are 1 1/2 inch, the same as the vent pipe.

The supply lines are PEX tubing that's attached to 90 degree stub outs. These were held in place by screwing them to blocking that was nailed between the studs. Commonly one of the supply lines will have to be shifted over to clear a stud.

# REVENTING

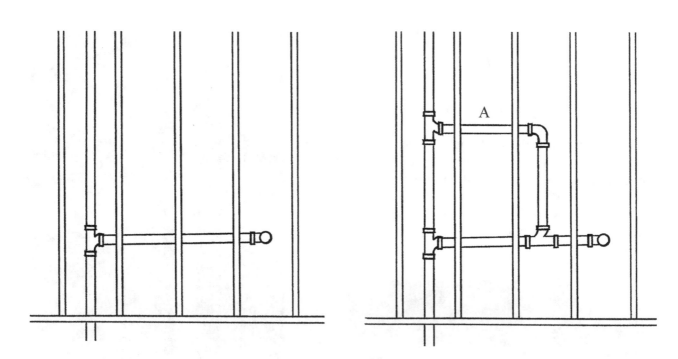

Sometimes the drain pipe for a sink, laundry tub, etc. has to be run horizontally. When doing this, the distance from the trap to the vent can't be over the amount that's allowed for that size pipe, or another vent has to be run. This is called reventing. In these drawings, the vent pipe is three studs over from the elbow for the sink, or around 48 inches. With 1 1/2 inch pipe, the farthest it can be from the trap to the vent is 42 inches (UPC), so the pipe would have to be revented.

Vents can't run horizontally (A) until they're at least 6 inches above the flood rim of the fixture they're venting. If this vent pipe was connected to the vent pipe for a different fixture, it would have to be attached at least 6 inches above the flood rim of the other fixture also.

# ISLAND SINK VENT

IRC  Island Sink Vent

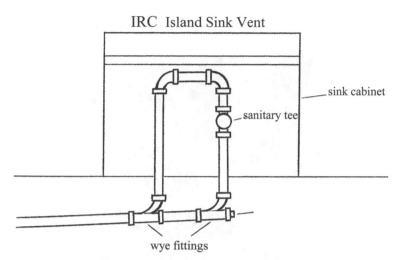

sink cabinet

sanitary tee

wye fittings

When I ran the drain pipe for the sink that's shown above, I originally planned on using an island vent, since that's how it was done in the first place. But once I looked it over, I realized that because of the way the other pipes were run, there wasn't any way to do it that would meet the requirements for that area. Once I started thinking about an alternative method, I measured the distance to the outside wall and found that it was only 5 feet away. By increasing the size of the pipe from 1 1/2 to 2 inches, it allowed me to run a horizontal drain, and then vent it up the wall.

The vent shown in this drawing may also require another cleanout. UPC island vents are done in a different manner and have to be connected to a regular vent. That was my problem, since the nearest vent was too far away.

# AAV VALVES

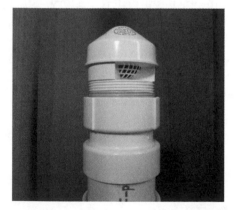

An AAV valve, properly called an air admittance valve, can be used where it's either not possible or practical to vent a fixture in a conventional manner. These are also called cheater vents. At this time, they aren't legal in all states, though the number of states where they can be used is increasing. An inspector could also allow one if there isn't any other way to vent a fixture. The AAV valve that's shown here costs around 20 dollars. Less expensive ones are also available. In the photo on the right, an AAV valve is being used to vent an island sink.

## ESCUTCHEONS

Escutcheons are used to cover the gap where the drain for a sink or a bathtub either enters the wall or goes through the floor. These days, they don't seem to be used as often, since the drain is often hidden by the vanity or a kitchen cabinet. In these locations, no one is going to notice how the plumbing looks, so generally a hole is cut through the wall and/or the back of the cabinet, and the drain pipe is run through as is. This might also be a good time to use flexible supply lines and plastic traps for the same reason.

When installing a wall-mounted or pedestal sink, or a clawfoot bathtub, it's a different story. Since everything is going to show, an escutcheon is used to give the plumbing a more finished look. For the escutcheon to fit, the trap adapter has to be the correct distance out from the wall or the floor. There are two types of trap adapters, as shown below. One gets directly glued into a fitting, such as an elbow or a sanitary tee, while the other generally goes over a short section of pipe. The purpose of the trap adapter is to provide a watertight connection for the trap or the drain assembly that allows it to be removed and/or adjusted.

## TRAP ADAPTERS

 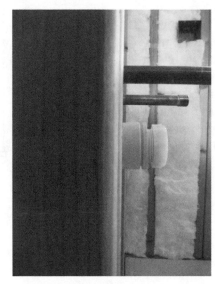 

In these photos, you can see that using a trap adapter that slips into the sanitary tee will keep you closer to the wall. This is generally the one that I use when installing an escutcheon. But every job is different, so I'll buy both types to see which one works the best. You don't have much leeway here. The nut has to be far enough out from the finished wall, so it can be tightened, but still be close enough to clear the escutcheon. When installing the drain pipes for a sink, laundry tub, bathtub, etc., I generally dry-fit everything to see how it's going to work. Sometimes I'll find that it's necessary to shift the pipe farther back in the wall. The trap adapter on the right slips over a section of pipe that's glued into the sanitary tee, so it can stick out as far as you want. I generally use it on vanities where a hole has been drilled through the back.

## TUBS AND SHOWERS

Here's a shower drain. It would be nice to have everything out in the open, but commonly the plumbing has to be run in tight locations. On this shower, the drain pipe had to rise up between the vent and the trap, for the trap to clear the wall beneath it.

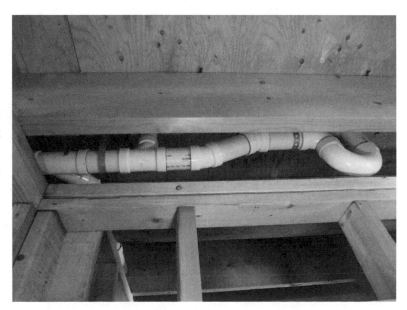

115

This drawing shows how a shower is plumbed. Two inch pipe is used, and a trap is needed, which is centered on the drain. With a factory base, you'll also need a hole around 5 inches in diameter through the floor or the concrete slab, so the drain can fit. If the shower is being handbuilt, the drain should be at the correct height for making the base. In this drawing, the shower is vented up the first wall that it passes by.

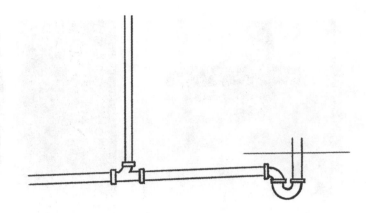

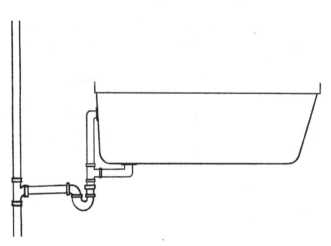

Here's the plumbing for a bathtub. The main difference between this and a shower is that the trap is at the end of the tub. The hole through the floor also has to be a lot bigger if it isn't a clawfoot bathtub. On a bathtub, the drain assembly gets attached to the drain, and also to the overflow. This assembly slips into a trap adapter that's been glued to the end of the trap. Since part of the drain assembly is beneath the tub, the hole in the floor has to be large enough for it to slip through. The hole also has to be big enough so you can work on the drain in the future if it's necessary.

When installing a bathtub on an upper floor, I generally use 1 1/2 inch pipe to match the size of the drain assembly. If the tub is in the basement, or the plumbing code requires it, I'll use 2 inch. Two inch pipe is needed beneath a concrete slab.

In this drawing, the bathtub is vented through the drain for the bathroom sink, which is now being used as a wet vent. It could also be vented through the drain for the kitchen sink or a laundry tub. When doing this where horizontal venting isn't allowed, the wye (pronounced as Y) must be tipped up at least 45 degrees. Two inch pipe is needed for the section that's being used as a wet vent, along with a 2 inch wye and sanitary tee. The vent pipe above the sanitary tee can still be 1 1/2 inch.

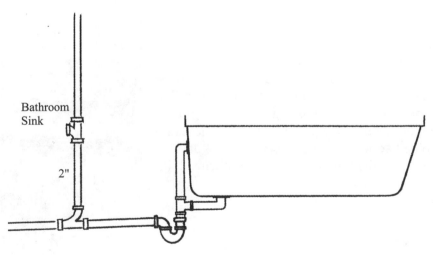

Bathroom Sink

2"

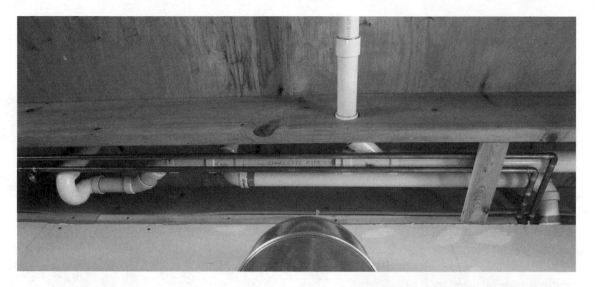

I spent all day running these drain pipes for the bathtub that's shown on page 124 because they're right over a stove with a large vent hood. It's hard to see, but again the tub was vented up the nearest wall before the drain from sink was connected to the pipe. Here the other pipe is a vent for the washing machine.

On the left is a standpipe for the washing machine, with a washer box on top of it. To the right of it is a horizontal drain for a sink. On both, the vent pipe was run up above the ceiling and then connected to the other vents.

# TRAPS

Traps for tubs and showers are different than those used for a sink because they're glued into place. When using this type, there are two styles. Both consist of two pieces, but on one, the parts are glued together, while the other has a threaded connection. This allows you to pivot the trap, so it lines up better. On a shower, I generally use the style that's glued together, and just make sure it's turned in the right direction. When I'm plumbing a bathtub, I want the other kind, and glue a trap adapter to it. This way, I can remove it if I have to work on the drain assembly.

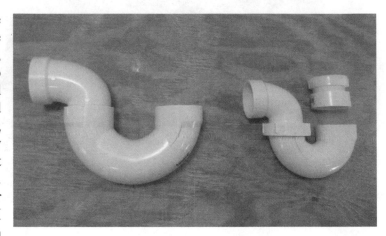

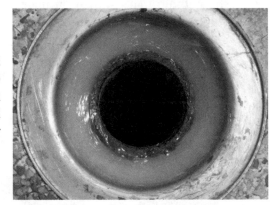

A rubber boot is commonly used to go between the drain pipe and the base of the shower, on a factory-made base, to create a seal. This photo shows an old shower where the drain pipe is held in place with silicone caulk. A plumber once told me that he preferred to use silicone caulk, instead of a rubber boot, because it's easier to remove if there's ever a problem.

When installing the drain for a hand-built shower, you generally want to mount it as low as possible, since the higher it is, the thicker the base has to be. Here, a 4 1/2 inch hole was drilled, so the drain would lay tight against the floor.

# PROPER USE OF FITTINGS

One of most common mistakes that people make when installing their own plumbing is using the wrong fitting. Here are some of the more common fittings, and how they're used.

**Sanitary Tee**: This fitting is used on most jobs. It's used to connect a sink, toilet, etc. to a vertical drain pipe, and it's also used where a vent is attached to a horizontal drain. Sometimes people use it incorrectly to connect a drain pipe to a horizontal drain. A wye is needed for this.

**90 Degree Elbow**: You have a few choices here. There are vent elbows, short sweep elbows, and long sweep elbows. Vent elbows are as short as you can get, and they're strictly used for vent pipes. Standard elbows (short sweep) are the least expensive, so they're used whenever possible. On 3 or 4 inch drain pipes, long sweep 90s or 45 degree elbows should be used to make the turns. Even on the smaller sizes, a building inspector will want you to use long sweep elbows on the drain pipes wherever you can.

**45 Degree Elbow**: Also called an 1/8 bend. These are used whenever a pipe has to be turned 45 degrees, or in pairs to make a 90 degree turn. Street 45s are commonly used with a wye to turn it either parallel or perpendicular to the pipe that it's connected to.

**Street Elbow**: Street elbows slip inside of other fittings, which allows you to make a tighter bend. It also eliminates the short length of pipe that's normally needed to connect the fittings.

**Wye**: Wyes are used where a drain pipe is connected to a horizontal drain. They're also used where you want a horizontal drain pipe to gradually flow into one that's vertical.

**Traps**: P-traps are used for sinks. They're connected using slip joints, so they're adjustable and can easily be removed. 1 1/4 inch traps are generally used on bathroom sinks, while kitchen sinks and laundry tubs need a 1 1/2 inch trap. Traps for showers and bathtubs are glued into place.

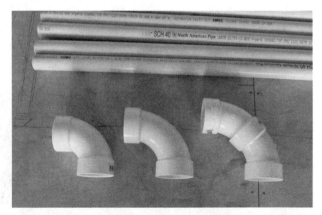

In this photo, you can see the difference between a standard 90 degree elbow, compared to a long sweep elbow, or a street 45 that's connected to a standard 45 degree fitting. Standard 90 degree elbows are allowed for drain pipes up to 2 inches to go through the framing. Once you're larger than that, 45 degree elbows or long sweep 90s are required when making a turn on a horizontal drain pipe, or where a vertical pipe turns horizontal.

A 4x3 closet elbow can be used instead of a 3 inch for installing a toilet. When doing this, 4 inch pipe will be glued into the fitting. Then the toilet flange will slip into the pipe. This makes it easier to glue the toilet flange. On 3 inch pipe, the toilet flange generally goes over the pipe. Because of that, the hole in the floor has to be large enough to apply the glue, since the pipe will be cut off flush to the floor. Toilet flanges that fit inside of 3 inch pipe are also available, though on some of them you won't be able to use a standard wax ring, because the hole is too small for the plastic flange on the wax ring.

# S-TRAPS AND IMPROPER USE OF A WYE

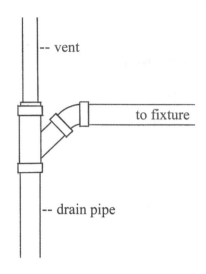

-- vent

to fixture

-- drain pipe

S-traps should not be used on sinks because water could be siphoned from the trap, which would let sewer gas into the house. The reason is because they lack a horizontal arm. Traps should be at least two pipe diameters away from the vent. A vertical-leg fixture drain is allowed because it has a horizontal arm, and an increased size in the vertical drain.

This drawing shows a wye being used, instead of a sanitary tee, to connect the pipe that goes to a fixture. This is incorrect because the fixture won't vent properly, as there isn't a straight path for the air to pass. When a wye is used in this manner, the fixture(s) has to be vented before it's connected to the other drain pipe.

Here, a wye was used where the 3 inch drain pipes from two bathrooms come together.

When installing the plumbing, sometimes one of the holes will have to be shifted over, or even redrilled, so it's larger. This is hard to do, because once a hole has been cut, there isn't anything to keep the hole saw in place as you drill. That's what the pilot bit is used for.

This photo shows one way to deal with the problem. By drilling the correct-sized hole through a scrap board, the board will keep the hole saw contained as the hole is redrilled. When doing this, position the board over the existing hole, and then hold it in place with nails, screws, clamps, or by just kneeling on it.

## VENTS

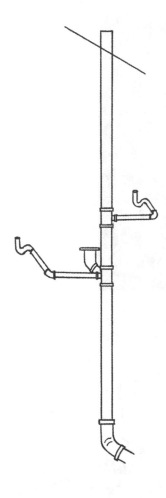

In older homes, the bathroom fixtures are commonly clustered around the main vent pipe. When installed in this manner, they're stack-vented, and here's the rule for it.

### STACK VENTING

A group of fixtures consisting of one bathroom group and a kitchen sink or combination fixture may be installed without individual fixture vents at the uppermost branch interval of a stack, if each fixture drain connects independently to a stack at least three inches in diameter extended full size through the roof, and bathtub or shower stall drain enters the stack at or above the same level as the water closet drain, and in accordance with requirements in part 4715.2620, subpart 4. Where the trap arm distances are exceeded, the fixtures must be revented. When a water closet discharges to a sanitary tee in the vertical position, and a bathtub or shower on the same floor level also discharges to the sanitary tee through a side inlet, the water closet vent must be at least three inches in size unless the bathtub or shower is revented.

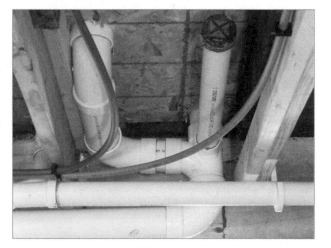

Though it looks a little different, this photo shows the drain pipes for a toilet and a future bathtub that are stack-vented. In this case, the plumber used a 3 inch sanitary tee that has a 2 inch side inlet. Above this fitting, the 3 inch pipe goes straight up and connects to the original cast iron stack.

When going through holes that were drilled in the studs or the floor joists, the pipes generally have to be installed in short sections, with a coupler between each one, unless there's a way to slip the pipe in from one side.

In both of these photos, two vent pipes were connected by using a sanitary tee, so only a single pipe went up to the next level. In the photo on the right, one of the pipes had to be shifted over in order to make the connection.

Here the vent pipes for a bathroom were connected together before they went up to the roof. Number 1 is a 2 inch vent for the toilet that I ran up the shower wall and then over the top of it. Attached to it is a 1 1/2 inch vent for the shower (2) that comes up the outside wall of the bathroom. The 1 1/2 x 2 inch sanitary tee that's used to connect them is turned so it slopes towards the roof, as is the next 1 1/2 x 2 inch sanitary tee that's used to attach the vent for the sink (3). When using vent tees, it doesn't matter which way they face, since they aren't sloped.

Sometimes vent pipes have to be run in a different manner. Pipe number 1 appears to be a drain pipe, but it's actually the vent for a kitchen sink where the plumber ran it across the ceiling and then connected it to another vent pipe, from above. This generally isn't done if there's another option, since sewer gas could get trapped in the pipe.

# ROUGH-IN DIMENTIONS

**Toilet** - Center of drain is typically 12 inches out from the finished wall. You should also have at least 15 inches of clearance on both sides, from the center. If the toilet will primarily be used by children, 12 and under, then 12 inches on each side, but not more than 18, is acceptable. The supply line is generally around 6 inches to the left of center and 6 inches above the floor, if it's coming out the wall. This height should be changed if the pipe is too close to the edge of the baseboard. Toilets are also made for different rough-in dimensions, with 10 inches being pretty common. This may help when a floor joist is in the way.

**Bathroom sink** - In the book that I bought years ago, the rough-in height for the drain on a bathroom sink was 19 inches on center above the floor, and the supply lines were at 22 inches, on 8 inch centers. These days, if you go by those measurements, most of the time you'll have to add a tailpiece extender when installing the trap. The reason for this is that sinks are generally taller now.

When I'm installing the drain pipe for a vanity sink, I generally raise the height of everything by a couple of inches on a 34 inch tall countertop, since I'm normally about 2 inches low on a 19 inch rough-in. But here you also have to consider whether it's an undermount sink, and if the vanity will go over the tile, or the tile will go around it. If there's any doubt, I'll keep the drain at 19 inches to be safe. When installing a pedestal sink, I always look up the factory recommendations for the rough-in, since everything is going to show.

**Shower and Bathtub** - For either one, I look up the factory specifications for the particular model that's being installed. The drain is hidden on bathtubs that are mounted against the wall, but a large hole still has to be cut for the drain assembly, since the tub will rest directly on the floor. In order to do this, the bathtub has to run parallel to the floor joists. If it doesn't, it will have to raised up on a platform, unless the floor joists can be notched deep enough.

I don't remember the size of the holes that I've cut for drain assemblies, but from what I've read, 8 or 9 inches wide by 12 inches long is needed. There should also be an access panel that's at least 12 x 12 inches to work on the drain. When there's no place for an access panel, there has to be another way to get to the drain assembly, such as cutting a hole through the ceiling.

Clawfoot bathtubs are another alternative, since the drain assembly is above the floor. Here, everything is going to show, so I'd also want the factory specifications for the rough-in. The drain connection on a clawfoot tub is hid by an escutcheon, so the trap adapter should be just above the finished floor level.

When a shower is being handbuilt, it's best to go over it with the guy that will be doing the work. Here you need to know where the drain should be centered, and how high the drain assembly should be above the floor, since the height of the drain determines how thick the base is.

**Kitchen sink** - I had to look this one up, since I seldom do the rough-in on kitchen sinks. On the last one that I worked on, the drain had to stay under 17 inches (center height). There are a few things that will determine the height needed: the height of the sink cabinet, how thick the countertop is and whether the sink is mounted above it or below it, whether it's a standard depth bowl or extra deep, and if there's a garbage disposal and/or a dishwasher.

According to what I've read, 18 inches above the floor is the standard height for installing the drain on a sink without a garbage disposal. With a garbage disposal, on a sink that's mounted beneath the countertop, 16 inches is needed. If the sink has an extra deep bowl, 14 or 15 inches is better. I recently worked on a sink that didn't have a garbage disposal, but needed a place for the dishwasher to be attached. On that one, I reset the sanitary tee so it was centered at around 15 inches to allow for a sink with a deeper bowl in the future.

The supply lines are typically 21 inches high, on 8 inch centers. One plumber made a good point by saying it's better to spread the supply lines way out, or to put them off to one side, in order to clear the hose for the spray nozzle. I've worked on a few sinks where the hose always catches on the shutoffs.

**Washer box** - This is a plastic box that's attached to the drain pipe (standpipe) for the washing machine, where the supply hoses also get connected. The height of this isn't critical, and plumbers seem to vary between 36 to 42 inches to the bottom of the box.

**Laundry tub** - The numbers that I've seen are 12 inches above the floor for the drain. The supply lines should be at 14 inches, on 6 or 8 inch centers.

The photo on the left shows the rough-in for the clawfoot bathtub that's shown to the right of it. Once the floor had been tiled, the trap adapter was installed. In this case, the drain pipe had to be cut 1/2 inch below the surface of the floor, so the trap adapter would be just above floor level to fit under the escutcheon. The supply lines also have escutcheons, so the copper pipes were cut off flush to the floor for attaching 1/2 inch female adapters. To raise the pipes up for cutting, gluing, and soldering, I cut a hole through the ceiling under the tub.

Another example is shown in the lower photo, where the escutcheon has been raised up to show the trap adapter. On this tub, the shutoffs are right next to the floor, so the supply lines were cut a little over an inch above the tile.

# RULES FOR VENTS AND DRAINS

## FIXTURE UNITS

Every plumbing fixture in your house ( sink, toilet, shower, etc.) is given a rating that determines the size of the pipe needed for the drain. Because of that, anytime you're installing the drain pipes, you have to consider the total number of fixture units that will go through each pipe to make sure the pipes will be large enough. For instance, let's say you're running a 2 inch horizontal branch drain pipe for the fixtures in a bathroom and an adjoining laundry area. This will not include the toilet, since a toilet needs a 3 inch pipe. Where I live, until recently, a 2 inch horizontal drain pipe would handle 6 fixture units. That means I could drain the bathroom sink (1), shower (2), and clothes washer (2) with a single 2 inch pipe, since they add up to 5 fixture units. Once the number got over six, I would need another drain pipe or have to increase the size to 3 inch.

## FIXTURE UNITS AND MINIMUM TRAP SIZE

| Fixture | Fixture units | Minimum trap size |
|---|---|---|
| Toilet > 1.6 gal flush | 4* | |
| Toilet < 1.6 gal flush | 3* | |
| Bathroom Sink | 1 | 1 1/4" |
| Shower | 2 | 2" |
| Bathtub / Shower | 2 | 1 1/2" |
| Dishwasher | 2 | 1 1/2" |
| Kitchen Sink | 2 | 1 1/2" |
| Clothes Washer Standpipe | 2  (3 UPC) | 2" |
| Laundry Tub | 2 | 1 1/2" |
| Floor Drain | 0 | 2" |

*A recent change gives toilets a rating of 6 fixture units.

| Vent Pipe Sizes, Critical Distances | | | |
|---|---|---|---|
| Size of Fixture Drain | Minimum Vent Pipe Size | Maximum Trap To Vent Distance | |
| | | UPC | IRC |
| 1 1/2" | 1 1/4" | 3 1/2' | 6' |
| 2" | 1 1/2" | 5' | 8' |
| 3" | 2" | 6' | 12' |
| 4" | 3" | 10' | 16' |

## BUILDING DRAIN AND SEWER SIZING

| Maximum Fixture Units | | | | | | |
|---|---|---|---|---|---|---|
| Pipe Diameter | Slope per ft. | | | | | |
| | 1/8" | | 1/4" | | 1/2" | |
| | IRC | UPC | IRC | UPC | IRC | UPC |
| 2" | | | 21 | 8 | 27 | 8 |
| 3" | 36 | 0 | 42 | 35 | 50 | 35 |
| 4" | 180 | 172 | 216 | 216 | 250 | 216 |

## SIZES FOR HORIZONTAL BRANCHES AND STACKS

| Maximum Fixture Units | | | | |
|---|---|---|---|---|
| Pipe Size | IRC | | UPC | |
| | Horizontal | Vertical | Horizontal | Vertical |
| 1 1/2" | 3 | 4 | 1 | 2* |
| 2" | 6 | 10 | 8 | 16 |
| 3" | 20 | 48 | 35 | 48 |
| 4" | 160 | 240 | 216 | 256 |

* No kitchen sinks or dishwashers.

These numbers were taken from "Code Check Plumbing." The first table on this page is for sizing the building drain and sewer pipes, which are the lowest pipes in the system. Building drains are generally under the basement floor, while sewer pipes are outside the building. As you can see, the numbers will vary depending on which code you're going by, and the amount of slope. Four inch pipe is generally used for the main building drain. Any drain pipes that are under the basement floor should be at least 2 inch.

The second table is for horizontal branches and stacks. Toilets require at least a 3 inch drain pipe. Where I live, 3 inch pipe used to be rated for only two toilets. Now it's three. Anything over that requires 4 inch pipe. Two inch pipe is required for kitchen sinks and/or bathtubs in some areas. There are different opinions on this. Some people think the larger pipe is better, while others say the faster flow in a 1 1/2 inch pipe will give you better scouring action.

1 1/2 and 2 inch drain pipes are typically sloped at 1/4 inch per foot. 1/4 inch per foot is the minimum. It can be steeper than that if you want. 3 and 4 inch drain pipes are generally sloped at 1/8 to 1/4 inch per foot. On these larger pipes, the amount of slope is more critical to prevent solid waste from being left behind in the pipe. I've been told that 1/4 inch per foot is preferred over 1/8 inch for today's low-flush toilets. Where you need 3 or 4 inch pipe to drop quicker than the slopes listed, it should be at an angle of at least 45 degrees.

To keep things simple in the Plumbing section, any pipe that's used as a drain will be called a drain pipe, regardless of its location and whether it's actually a building drain, horizontal branch, or stack.

There is no specific slope requirement for vents. They only have to be sloped enough so that water will run out towards the sewer. I generally slope horizontal vent pipes at about 1/8 inch per foot. An exception to this are PVC vents on furnaces. They should be sloped at 1/4 inch per foot.

## PIPE  SUPPORT  INTERVALS  (maximum distance)

|  | Vertical Support Interval | Horizontal Support Interval |
|---|---|---|
| Copper | At every story | 6 foot intervals |
| PVC | At every story, if enclosed | 32 inches - 4 foot |

Metal straps shouldn't come into direct contact with PVC or ABS plastic pipes, as it may cut into the pipe. Hangers should resist upward thrust.

## PROTECTING THE  PIPES

All plastic or copper pipe that's within 1 1/4 inches of the edge of a stud should be protected with a metal plate.

The maximum fixture units for vent pipes wasn't shown, since it's unlikely that you'll exceed it. For 1 1/2 inch pipe, the maximum is 8 fixture units, For 2 inch pipe it's 24, and for 3 inch it's 84.

Some fixtures have different rules. For instance, where I live, toilets have to be vented within 6 feet. It used to be 4 feet. When going by IRC rules, the length for the toilet vent is unlimited. Where horizontal vents aren't allowed, vents have to stay within 45 degrees of vertical until they're at least 6 inches above the flood rim of the fixture they're venting.

Because of these differences, it's best to know what the rules are for your area. Many times you can find this on the internet. If you look up the plumbing code for your state, you'll probably find that it's around 200 pages long. Most of the pages won't concern you, since the code is also for commercial businesses. I quickly scroll through until I get to the ones that show the requirements for sizing pipes, which fittings are allowed, and specific ways that you can vent a system. Once you have a basic understanding of how to install the plumbing, the code isn't as intimidating.

Even though your local code is based on the one for the state, it may not be the same. Some rules may be strictly enforced, while others aren't required. It depends on which rules have been adopted. A building inspector could also OK things that normally wouldn't be allowed.

The rules concerning plumbing can change at any time. The 2015 Minnesota Plumbing Code made quite a few changes that effect homeowners. These are the ones that I know of.  Basement bathrooms can now be vented horizontally. -- Kitchen sinks require a 2 inch drain pipe. -- 8 fixture units are allowed on a 2 inch horizontal branch line. -- Spacing of supports for horizontal PVC pipe has been increased to 4 feet -- Shower waste outlet 2 inch minimum. -- Only 1 fixture unit is allowed on a 1 1/2 inch horizontal branch line. -- Three toilets (water closets) are allowed on a 3 inch horizontal branch line, at a minimum 1/4 inch per foot slope when possible. -- Residential dishwashers must have an air gap fitting above countertop -- Floor drains must be individually vented. Under the old rule, a floor drain didn't require a separate vent if the fixture branch was less than 25 feet in length, and it was connected to a vented main or branch. -- A backflow valve (backflow preventer) is required for a basement bathroom. This is a one-way valve that prevents sewage, from the main line in the street, from backing up into the house. Contractors that I've talked to don't like this rule, since the flapper on the backflow valve tends to get stuck. Homeowners also don't like having an extra hole drilled through their new countertop when installing a dishwasher.

# SUPPORTING THE DRAIN PIPES

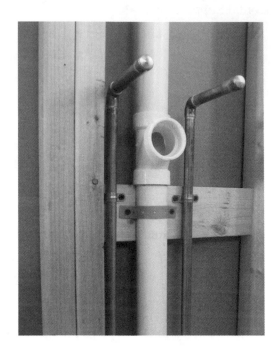

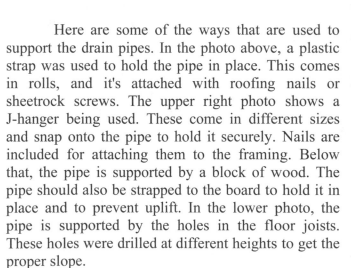

Here are some of the ways that are used to support the drain pipes. In the photo above, a plastic strap was used to hold the pipe in place. This comes in rolls, and it's attached with roofing nails or sheetrock screws. The upper right photo shows a J-hanger being used. These come in different sizes and snap onto the pipe to hold it securely. Nails are included for attaching them to the framing. Below that, the pipe is supported by a block of wood. The pipe should also be strapped to the board to hold it in place and to prevent uplift. In the lower photo, the pipe is supported by the holes in the floor joists. These holes were drilled at different heights to get the proper slope.

# CLEANOUTS

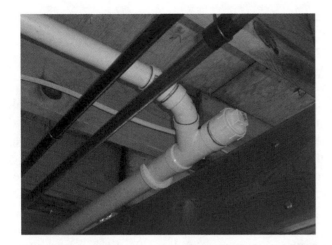
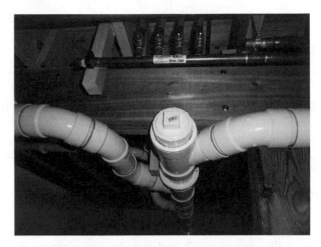

Drain cleanouts are installed at accessible locations for removing obstructions from the pipes. They're generally needed where you have a change of direction, but aren't necessary if you can access the pipe by going through a fixture. This would include: going through the sanitary tee on a sink, the trap on a shower, going through the toilet, etc. Cleanouts should be the same size as the pipe they're attached to, until you're over 4 inches. In the photo on the right, a 3 inch cleanout is at the end of a 4 inch pipe, which looks better, but isn't correct.

When the pipes have to turn at an odd angle, other than 22 1/2, 45, 60, or 90 degrees, it may take more than one elbow to make the turn. In this photo, two 90 degree elbows were used to turn the pipe up a vaulted ceiling. Since this is a vent pipe, short elbows were used. On a drain pipe, long sweep elbows should be used wherever possible.

# CUTTING PVC

PVC pipe can be cut with a handsaw, Sawzall, or a miter saw. I generally use a miter saw for this. If one isn't available, I'll mark the length every couple of inches around the circumference on larger pipe, to keep me square, and then cut it with a pull saw. Plumbers use a Sawzall, but I tend to cut at an angle if I don't have something to follow. When using a miter saw, the inside of the pipe will have to be cleaned out. On 1 1/2 or 2 inch pipe, I just take a deep breath and blow the chips out. On 3 inch, I hold the pipe up at an angle, and then run a scrunched up plastic bag down it by setting a short section of smaller pipe on top of it. I also clean up the end with a 4-in-1 file to remove any burr.

The lower photo shows a cutting box that I recently made for remodeling a bathroom. On this project, a miter saw wasn't available, and I had a lot of cuts to make with a hand saw. Then I remembered the simple, wood boxes that were used years ago to make the miter cuts for trimming windows and doors. So I bought a 6 foot 1x6 and quickly assembled one using two boards on each side, with a small gap between them. This idea worked so well that I might use it in the future, instead of a miter saw.

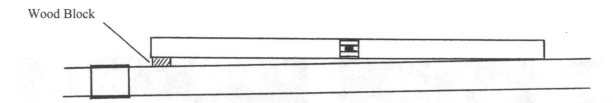

Wood Block

To check the slope on a drain pipe, raise the level up so the bubble is centered, and then measure the gap on the end that's raised. For a 1/4 inch per foot slope, the gap should be 1 inch with a 4 foot level, and 3/16 with a 9 inch torpedo level. To set the slope on a long section of pipe, sometimes it's easier, and more accurate, to put a 1 inch block of wood under one end of a 4 foot level (for a 1/4 inch per foot slope) as shown in the drawing. Then the height of the pipe is adjusted so the bubble is centered on the level.

Once you know where the bubble should sit, you can also check the slope by holding the level against the pipe itself. When doing this, the slope is determined by how far the bubble hangs over the line. This method isn't as accurate, so I just use it on shorter pipes, or to give them a quick check.

When a sanitary tee is used for a sink, it's generally turned so it's square to the wall. When I install the tee, I like to have a 2 to 4 foot level within reach. Once the glue in applied, I put the fitting on and turn it so it looks close to square. Then I quickly grab the level and hold it against the tee, and rotate the tee so the level is parallel to the wall.

# GLUING PVC

When I'm gluing PVC, sometimes I mark the pipes with a pencil to show how far they should go into the fittings. Then I apply the primer so it's just over the line. This way, I can see if a fitting is all the way on by just looking at it. I also know that the pipes will line up with any holes that have been drilled. The cement should be applied while the primer is still wet. Some people like to prime more than one fitting at a time, but the joint isn't as strong if the primer has time to dry, according to one of the manufacturers. Once the glue has been applied, quickly put the fitting on, and then rotate it so it lines up correctly. Then hold it in place for about 20 seconds or until it won't move. On horizontal pipes, I generally wipe the bottom of the joint with a paper towel to remove any excess glue.

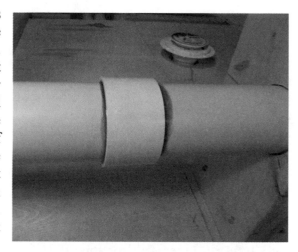

Here, several pieces were glued together before they were installed. When doing this, all you have to do is to line up one of the marks on each fitting, so it's turned in the right direction. When a section of pipe has writing on it, I'll line up the marks with either the upper or the lower edge of it. If there isn't any writing, I'll use a level or the edge of a board to draw a line across the pipe, and then use that for lining up the marks.

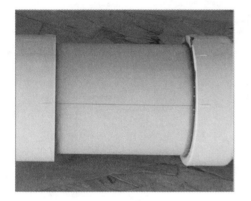

When the fittings are farther apart, or you change direction, they're installed one at a time using a torpedo level. If the fittings are tight, or you're working overhead, you might need both hands just to push them on and to hold them in place The lower photos show one way to deal with it, by taping the torpedo level to the fitting. This way, you can glue the fitting, and then watch the bubble as you rotate it so it's turned in the right direction. The photo on the left shows a level being used to install a sanitary tee for a vent. Commonly the fittings have to be turned so they're slightly tipped up or down for the slope, which was the case for the 45 degree elbow that's shown on the right.

The following pages show how the plumbing was laid out in several bathrooms. Included is a description and photos of the finished rooms.

## BATHROOM 1

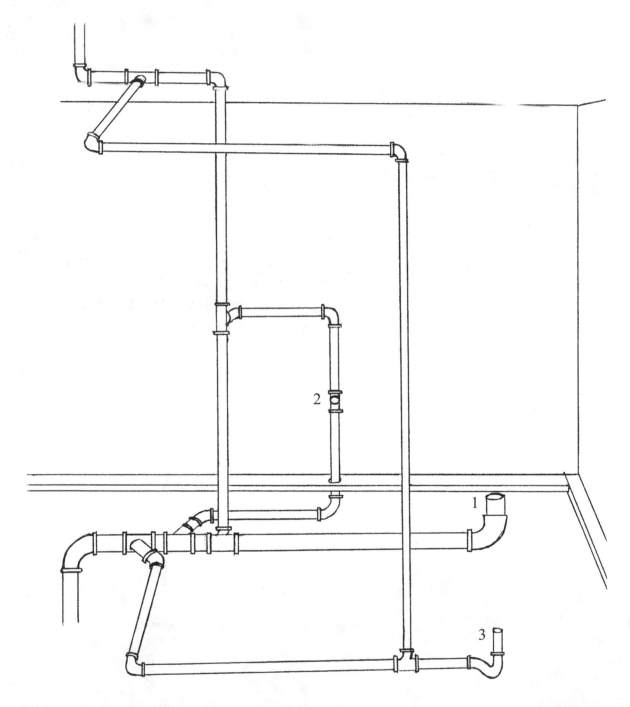

When I installed the plumbing for this bathroom, I considered running the 3 inch drain pipe for the toilet down the nearest wall. But after looking it over, I decided it would be easier to run it between the floor joists and then over to the kitchen wall, and from there down to the basement. As it was, I barely had enough room to get the proper slope and still clear the beam between the kitchen and the dining area.

132

Rather than label all the parts in the drawing, I'll just quickly describe how everything was laid out. On this bathroom, I started at the toilet (**1**). As I said, I barely had enough room to get the proper slope, so I used a 45 degree toilet flange, thinking it was my only choice. Later on, I realized a 4x3 closet elbow would have worked if I'd raised it up into the floor sheathing. The 4x3 elbow is the better choice, so that's what's shown here. From there, the 3 inch pipe goes to a 3 x 2 sanitary tee that was used to vent the toilet up the wall, and from there up to the roof.

Once the toilet was vented, using 2 inch pipe, the other drains could be attached. The next fitting is a 3 x 1 1/2 inch wye for the sink (**2**). From that fitting, 1 1/2 inch pipe goes over and then up to a 1 1/2 inch sanitary tee, using a 45 and a long sweep 90 degree elbow. Above the sanitary tee, the vent pipe goes up and then over and connects to the 2 inch vent pipe with a 2 x 1 1/2 inch sanitary tee. The vent pipe couldn't run horizontally until it was at least 6 inches above the top of the sink bowl.

The next fitting on the 3 inch pipe is a 3 x 2 wye for the shower (**3**) with a 45 degree elbow attached. From there, holes were drilled through the floor joists for the pipe to pass through, and then a long sweep 90 degree elbow was used to turn it parallel to the joists. After that, the 2 inch pipe goes to a 2 x 1 1/2 inch sanitary tee for the vent, and then a 2 inch trap for the shower drain. From the sanitary tee, 1 1/2 inch pipe goes up the wall and then across the ceiling and connects to the other vents with another 2 x 1 1/2 inch sanitary tee.

After the wye fittings, the 3 inch drain pipe goes down to the basement using a series of 90 degree elbows. All 90 degree elbows that were used for the drains were long sweep whenever possible. Standard elbows were used for the vents.

In this photo, you can see the dining area below the bathroom, and the beam that I had to go over. The drain pipe passes through the boxed-in area between the beam and the upper cabinet.

# BATHROOM 2

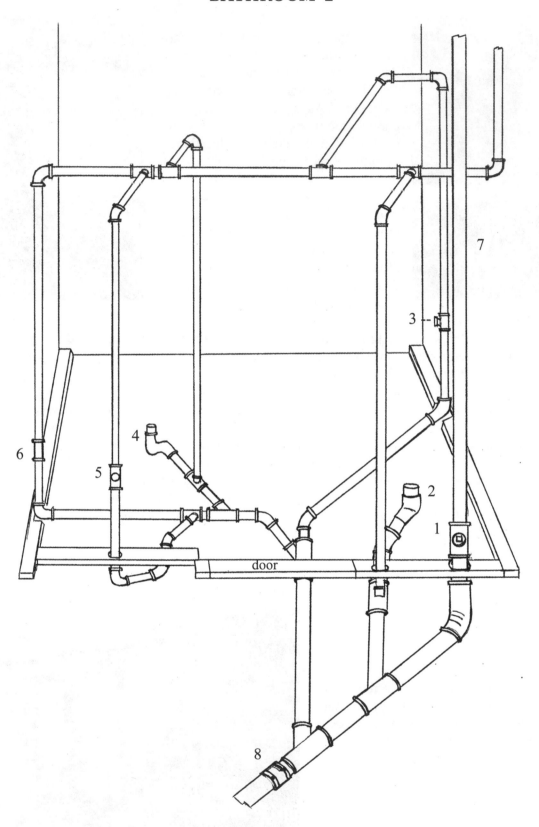

door

This bathroom is in a basement, and also includes an adjacent laundry tub and a standpipe for the washing machine. On this one, the first thing I looked for was a drain pipe to connect to, and then I had to figure out how it could be vented. Luckily, there was both a drain pipe and a vent in the immediate area.

Once I knew where to connect the pipes, it was just a matter of coming up with a workable plan, and laying out some of the fittings to see where everything would go. Then we cut out the floor. I generally cut strips that are about a foot wide to give me enough working room, and make the cuts with a circular saw that has a diamond blade attached. Most of the time, the cuts won't be deep enough to get through the concrete, so it has to be broken up with a sledge hammer. Then the dirt is dug out after the concrete is removed.

Sawing concrete floors creates a tremendous amount of dust, but you can contain most of it by hanging a plastic sheet around the area that you're working on. When making the cuts, you'll need safety glasses, hearing protection, and a good dust mask so you don't breathe it in. Then, as you saw, have someone hold the hose from a Shop-Vac right next to the saw blade to suck up as much of the dust as possible before it has a chance to spread out. While doing this, keep the Shop-Vac itself outside of the plastic, so the exit port doesn't blow it around. This should eliminate a big part of the dust. After finishing the cuts, leave the hose inside the plastic enclosure, and keep the vacuum running until the air is clear. It also helps to put a fan in a basement window, with the fan blowing out.

To cut the old pipes, we rented a chain-breaker and started by removing a three inch cast iron pipe that was in the wall, and then cut out a section of the 4 inch pipe in the floor.

Starting on the PVC, short sections of pipe were glued to the ends of two 4x3 wyes, which were attached to the 4 inch drain pipe with a rubber coupler (8). The wyes were positioned so that one of the 3 inch pipes would go through the door opening, while the other would pass under the wall. Once the wyes were in place, the 4 inch pipe was turned up the wall with a long sweep 90 degree elbow. Above that went a 4 inch test cap (1) to be used as a cleanout. Then a reducer bushing was glued into the top of the test cap, and a 3 inch pipe (7) was run up the wall.

Now starting at the wye for the toilet (2), there's a short length of 3 inch pipe, followed by a 3x2 sanitary tee that was used to run the 2 inch vent pipe up the wall. After that, a 45 degree elbow turned the pipe, and then a 4x3 closet elbow was used for the toilet.

On the other wye, the 3 inch pipe runs into the bathroom and then splits off in different directions using a 3x2 wye. Coming straight out of the wye, a 3-2 reducer bushing was used to shrink the pipe down to 2 inches. Then a 45 degree elbow turned the pipe, and a long sweep 90 degree elbow was used to run it up the wall. Once it was above the floor, the pipe was reduced to 1 1/2 inches, and then goes up to a 1 1/2 inch sanitary tee for the sink (**3**). From there, the vent pipe runs up to the ceiling.

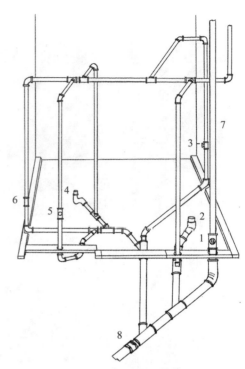

Now coming off the side of the 3x2 wye, the first fitting is a 45 degree elbow that was used to turn the 2 inch pipe parallel to the wall. After that comes a pair of 2 inch wyes, one for the shower (**4**), and the other for the laundry tub (**5**). For the shower, a 2 inch sanitary tee was used to vent the pipe up the wall, and after that is a 2 inch trap. The vent pipe was reduced to 1 1/2 inches once it was above the floor.

For the laundry tub, two 45 degree elbows and a long sweep 90 were used to bring the 2 inch pipe over to the wall, and then up to a 2 x 1 1/2 inch sanitary tee. From there, a reducer bushing was used to run the 1 1/2 inch vent up the wall.

To finish off the drains, the 2 inch pipe continued from the end of the last wye. At the wall, it was turned up with a long sweep 90 degree elbow, and goes to a 2 inch sanitary tee for the washing machine (**6**). In this case, 2 inch pipe was also used to vent the washer.

The vent pipes were turned at the ceiling using standard 90 degree elbows. Then as the 2 inch vent for the washing machine went across the room, sanitary tees were used to connect the vents from the other fixtures. A 2 x 1 1/2 inch sanitary tee was used for the shower, laundry tub, and the sink, while a 2 inch was used for the toilet. Here I could also have used a 1 1/2 inch vent for the washing machine, and then increased the size to 2 inches once I got to the vent for the toilet.

There are a couple of things that aren't shown in the drawing. The reason there's a 3 inch pipe in the wall (**7**) is because it's a drain pipe for the toilet that's in the bathroom directly above this one. The 2 inch vent for this toilet goes up the back of a closet wall, and had to stay tipped up at least 45 degrees until it was a minimum of 6 inches above the toilet bowl. The 2 inch vent that goes across the ceiling also runs up the back of the closet wall, and tees into the other vent a little over 2 feet above the floor. Also not shown in the drawing is the standpipe for the washing machine. The drawing below shows the layout of the room.

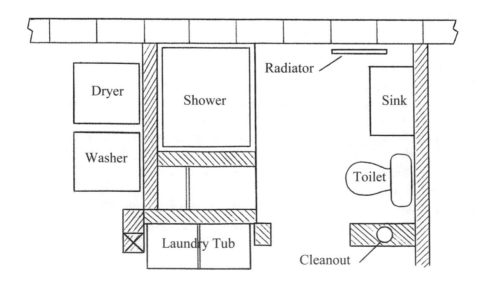

Here's the laundry tub that's next to the bathroom. This one, which hangs from the wall, is very solid and nicer than others I've seen. It's made by Mustee.

In the photo on the left, you can see how the pipes were boxed off at the ceiling. This is pretty common when remodeling. The photo on the right shows the cleanout for the 4 inch drainpipe under the floor. There are also covers available that snap into place, if the cleanout is farther back in the wall.

A washing machine box sits on top of the standpipe.

# BATHROOM 3

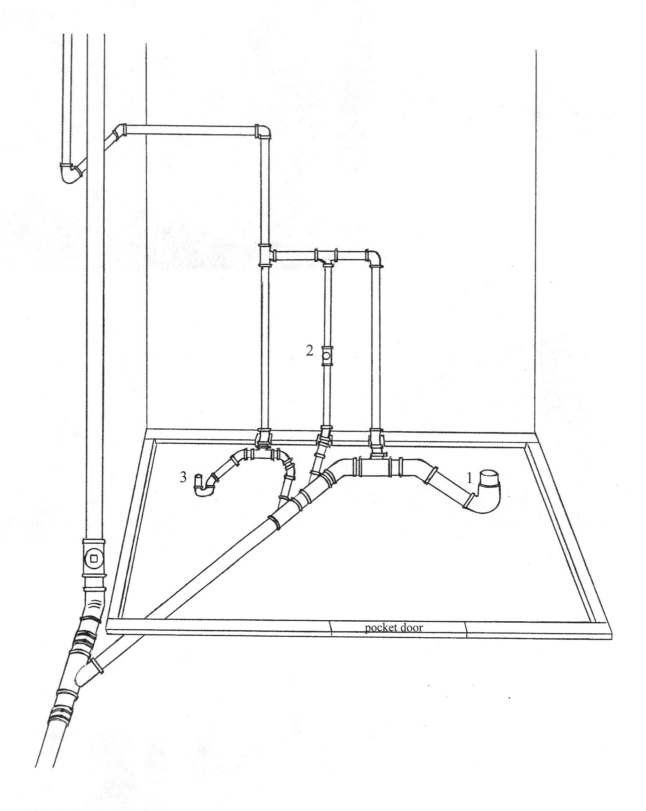

This is another basement bathroom where I helped install the drain pipes. When I first looked it over, the original plan was to run the drain pipes for the toilet and the shower straight across the floor, and then vent them up the wall that has the door. But, with a pocket door, the distance was too far for the toilet vent, so we changed the plan and vented everything up the back wall.

138

Once we determined how to run the pipes, the concrete floor was cut out Then anything that was going under the floor was laid out and dry-fitted before it was glued together. Here a 4x3 closet elbow was also used for the toilet (**1**). Attached to it is a short length of 3 inch pipe, followed by a 45 degree elbow that turned the pipe parallel to the back wall. The next fitting is a 3x2 sanitary tee for the toilet vent. This was tipped up at 45 degrees, and then a 45 degree elbow turned the 2 inch pipe up the wall.

After the toilet vent, a 45 degree elbow was used to turn the 3 inch pipe away from the wall, Then the next fitting is a 3x2 wye. From the wye, a pair of 45 degree elbows turned the 2 inch pipe up the wall. Once it was above the floor, the pipe was reduced to 1 1/2 inches, and goes up to a 1 1/2 inch sanitary tee for the sink (**2**). Then the vent for the sink was connected to the toilet vent with a 2 x 1 1/2 inch sanitary tee.

A 3x2 wye was also used for the shower drain (**3**). From the wye, the 2 inch pipe was turned parallel to the wall using two 45 degree elbows, and then it was vented with a tipped-up sanitary tee, along with a 45 degree elbow. This pipe was also reduced to 1 1/2 inches once it was above the floor, and then it was connected to the other vents with a 2 inch sanitary tee that had a  2 – 1 1/2 inch reducer bushing glued into the bottom of it. From there, the vent goes up and over until it connects to an existing vent. Normally I wouldn't have reduced the size of the shower vent for such a short distance. The reason it was done here was to create more room for the supply lines that go to the sink faucet.

Going back to the floor, once the shower drain was past the vent, a 45 degree elbow was used to turn it away from the wall. Then a 2 inch trap was installed for the shower.

From the wye for the shower drain, the 3 inch pipe goes to an existing 4 inch cast iron pipe. To make the connection, short lengths of 4 inch pipe were glued to both ends of a 4x3 wye. Then the glued-up section was laid into position to determine where the cast iron pipe had to be cut. You want a little slop for the new section to slip into place, something around 1/4 of an inch on each end.

We used a chain-breaker to make the cuts. Snapping a cast iron pipe of this size is a lot easier than sawing it, so it's worth the cost of renting a chain-breaker to do the job. You may be able to rent one for only 4 hours. This tool is simple to use. All you have to do is to wrap the chain around the pipe, and then crank on the ratchet like you're tightening a nut or a bolt. This will tighten the chain until the pipe breaks with a loud pop. There was a problem with the last one I rented. While using it, I cranked so hard that I was afraid the tool was going to break, and the pipe still wouldn't crack. Before I returned the chain breaker, I lubricated the threads with oil and tried again. This time, the pipe broke with hardly any effort.

Once the section of pipe had been removed, we slid a rubber coupler over each end of the wye assembly, and then glued it to the 3 inch pipe. Then the couplers were centered on the joints, and the hose clamps were tightened. Sometimes the  rubber couplers fit tight and don't want to slide on. When that happens, it helps to lubricate them with soapy water.

On the bathroom that was just described, we ran into a problem because it was next to an exterior wall, and the footing was in the way. Since horizontal vents weren't allowed, the vent pipes had to be tipped up at least 45 degrees until they were a minimum of 6 inches above the flood level of the fixtures. In order to do this, we had to run the drain pipes close to the footing, and then angle the vents and the drain for the sink up into the new wall.

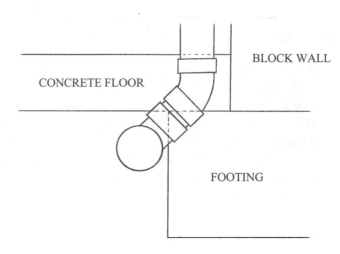

This drawing shows the problem that you might have when installing the plumbing next to a concrete wall or a supporting post. As you can see, the footing is in the way because it sticks out farther. To work around this, you generally have to tip the sanitary tee or the wye so it's at 45 degrees, and then use a 45 degree elbow to turn the pipe up the wall.

No matter how tight you stay to the footing, you may still end up with the pipes hanging out above the floor. In that case, the first thing to do is to use a diamond blade in a circular saw or a grinder, along with a chisel, and notch the upper corner of the footing to put the pipes farther back into the wall, as shown in the drawing. If that doesn't work, you'll have to find a way to hide the pipes. On the last bathroom, every one of the pipes stuck out from the lower edge of the wall. The vent for the toilet and the drain pipe for the sink were hidden by the vanity, which was notched out in the back, and the shower vent ended up being covered when the shower floor was installed.

The photos on the right show how PVC was attached to a cast iron drain pipe for a basement bathroom. In the upper photo, you can see how the pipe looked once we removed the dirt. In the second one, a section has been removed by cutting the pipe in two places with a pipe breaker. The lower photo shows the new drain pipe after it was installed. Here, short sections of pipe were glued to both ends of a wye. Then a street 45 was used to turn the pipe perpendicular to the other one. After the glue had set up, rubber couplers were slipped over each end. Then the whole assembly was slipped into place, with the proper slope, and the clamps were tightened after centering the couplers over the joints.

To remove a section from the lower part of a cast iron stack, the stack has to be supported from above, so it can't drop. In the photo above, you can see how it was done using a steel riser clamp, which grips the pipe by tightening the bolts. Then it's supported by the framing. In this case, threaded rod was used, which was attached to blocking that was securely nailed to the floor joists.

# HORIZONTAL VENTS

In some areas, horizontal vents are allowed for basement bathrooms, and the toilet and the shower and/or bathtub can be vented through the drain for the sink (X) as shown in the upper photo. When doing this, 2 inch pipe should be used for both the drain and the vent on the sink.

The lower photos show the drain pipes for a bathroom in Sioux Falls, South Dakota, where horizontal vents are allowed, as long as the vents are taken off above the center of the drain pipes. In this case, that's how the original plumbing was done. Unfortunately, the plumber didn't allow enough room for the shower, so the homeowner decided to install a tub/shower on the other side of the room. Because of the changes, and how the vent pipes had to go through the framing, we ended up having a separate vent for each fixture. I've read that dry-vents aren't allowed when venting in this manner. Since I didn't know if that was actually the case, we called the building inspector. He said horizontal dry-vents were fine as long as wyes were used instead of sanitary tees. This way, it's less likely for anything to get caught at the edge of a vent opening. In the upper left photo, the toilet flange is just being used to temporarily cap the pipe.

On this basement, I helped a friend install new plumbing for a remodeling project. Once the floor was removed, we took out the cast iron drain pipe and replaced it with PVC. We also moved the laundry tub and the washer and dryer to the other side of the room. In the photo, you can see the drain pipes for the laundry tub and the washing machine, and also for a floor drain. At this time, we also poured a footing for a new post, and reinforced the beam. This is shown on page 394. Then before the new floor went in, my friend leveled out the area and installed 2 inch foam, and ran PEX tubing for in-floor heat.

## BOXING OFF CONCRETE

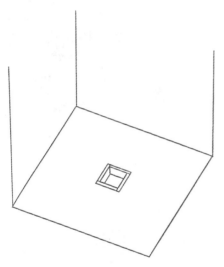

When showers or bathtubs are installed in a basement, the area around the drain pipe is commonly boxed off before you patch or pour the concrete floor. In the photo on the right, a board was used to leave an opening for the drain assembly on a corner tub/shower. For shower bases, you'll need about a 5 inch opening that's centered on the drain, as shown on the left. The boards are removed once the concrete has set up.

## TEMPORARILY INSTALLING A TOILET

On some of the projects that I've worked on, it was months, or even years, from the time a bathroom was started until the walls were finished and the floor was tiled. When that happens, I generally install the toilet temporarily, so it can be used in the meantime. To do this, I glue everything together until I get to the last section of pipe (vertical) that the toilet flange will be attached to. On the last piece, I measure the length needed, and cut it about 1/4 inch short. Then I dry-fit the parts, and attach the toilet flange to the floor with sheetrock screws. Everything should fit tight, so there aren't any leaks. When the time comes to tile the floor, I take everything apart by rocking the pieces back and forth until they come out, and then cap the pipe. After the floor is tiled, a new section of pipe is cut to the correct length, and the toilet flange is installed permanently.

142

# CLEARANCE MINIMUMS FOR BATHROOM FIXTURES

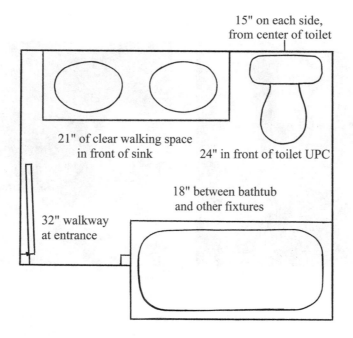

15" on each side,
from center of toilet

21" of clear walking space
in front of sink

24" in front of toilet UPC

18" between bathtub
and other fixtures

32" walkway
at entrance

# STANDPIPE

This drawing shows the standpipe for a washing machine that has a washer box installed above it. Here the supply lines are attached to the top of the box, but they could also be on the bottom instead.

There are a few rules that you have to follow on a standpipe. **A** is the length of the vertical pipe. It has to be 18 - 30 inches long according to the UPC. The IRC allows up to 42 inches. **C** is the height above the floor, which has to be from 6 - 18 inches according to the UPC. **B** is the distance between the trap and the vent. A trap has to be at least two pipe diameters away from the vent for it to work properly. This rule applies to all traps, including those on sinks.

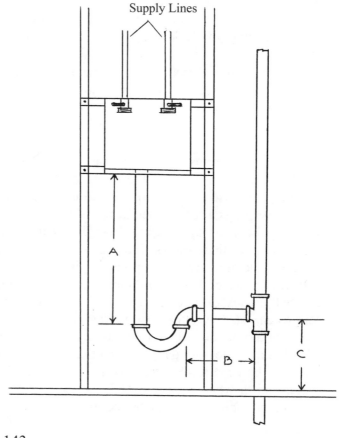

Supply Lines

143

# PRESSURE TESTING THE SYSTEM

Anytime you pull a permit to work on the plumbing, you may be required to pressure test it to check for leaks. Where I live, it's a simple procedure where you cap off the lower end of the drain pipe, the vents, and any place a fixture is going, and then pump air into the system. The standard test is to pump it up to 5 pounds. Then it has to hold steady at that pressure for 15 minutes. In some areas, the plumbing is checked by filling the pipes, and the bathtubs, with water.

In order to do this, the end of the pipe at each fixture should be left in a way that it can be easily capped off. How this is done will depend on what you have to plug the ends. I had a problem the first time I pressure-tested a system. I bought plastic caps, called test caps, and glued them to the open ends of the pipes. The pressure test showed a slow leak, but we couldn't find it, even after applying soap solution to all the joints. We ended up finding the leak(s) by putting a little perfume into the system, and then smelling where it came out. It turned out that half of the test caps leaked, so I never used them again. These days, I buy rubber caps that slip over the end of a pipe, that are tightened with hose clamps. I generally keep a few of them in different sizes. Besides being used for pressure testing, they're also good for capping the pipes to prevent sewer gas from getting into the house. On large jobs you may need quite a few. Sometimes I'll buy what I need and then return them to the store once I'm done, since they're as good as new, along with the other fittings that weren't needed.

Rubber caps are used for plugging open pipes, such as those that extend above the floor for the toilet and the shower, or for capping the vents on the roof. For other locations, such as an open sanitary tee, inflatable plugs are used. These are slipped into the fitting, and then air is pumped into them to lock them in place. Inflatable plugs are also used at the cleanouts where the drain pipes go through the basement floor. The one shown on the next page goes through the cleanout and slips into the pipe itself. There's also another type that's easier to use, that screws into the test cap and then gets inflated. Inflatable plugs don't always seal properly; so, if the pressure is dropping, this is one of the first places I'd look.

When you've added on to the original plumbing system, try to cap the pipes so they're separated from the ones that already existed. This way, you won't have to pressure test the entire system. This is especially important when you're working on an older house that has cast iron pipes, as those joints tend to leak air.

The photo on the left shows an inexpensive pressure tester that was bought at a plumbing supply store. It's basically just a pressure gauge with a Schrader valve attached, the same as what's used on a tire. The same tester can also be used to pressure test the gas lines. All you have to do is to add the necessary fittings, so it can be attached to whatever needs to be tested. When doing this, use Teflon tape on the threads to prevent leaks. For the plumbing, you may be required to use a gauge with one tenth increments.

Several years ago, I had a little incident while working on a friend's house. After the drain and the vent pipes were installed for the plumbing, I pressure-tested the system and found that there was a leak. It was large enough that I could watch the gauge slowly go down, yet small enough that I wasn't able to locate it, since the new pipes were spread out across the basement and two upper levels. I spent hours spraying soap solution on every fitting, without finding the leak. Then I got the bright idea to look for it by filling the system with water. To do this, I removed the cap where a toilet was going on the second floor, and then used a bucket to fill the pipes with water. As I recall, it took thirty or forty gallons by the time I was finished. Then I kept checking the system for a day, but the leak never showed.

After that didn't work, I realized that now I had the problem of how to get rid of all the water, with the drain pipe in the basement being blocked by an inflatable plug in the cleanout. After looking it over, I figured if I was fast enough, I could let some of the air out of the plug, and then quickly pull it out, which would allow the water to run down the pipe. What I never considered, though, was the weight and the force of all of that water. As soon as I released a little air, the plug slid farther down into the fitting and took my hand with it. Then with my hand stuck, and the only place for the water to go directly facing me, I was pounded by it as it gushed out and hit me in the chest. It was like standing in front of a fire hydrant.  Luckily, there happened to be a floor drain nearby, or I could have had a bigger problem. As it turned out, the only thing hurt was my ego, and I thought it was kind of funny after I dried off.

Once the mess was cleaned up, I still had to find the leak. Then I remembered that one day, the homeowner had called me upstairs and showed me where he'd nicked the main four inch vent pipe with a Sawzall. I looked it over and told him it wasn't a problem, as he had barely cut into the pipe. It turned out that I'd been wrong, and after pressurizing the system again, that's where I found the leak. Even though the pipe was only nicked, it had a cellular core, which means it has a hard inner and outer skin, with a different material in between, and somehow air was getting through. Since this was a vertical vent pipe that was close to the roof, my main concern was that it passed the pressure test. To fix it, I attached the hose from a Shop-vac to one of the pipes. Then I kept brushing PVC cement over the cut until enough of it was sucked in to seal the leak. Since then, I always try to use solid pipe, which is heavier and uses the same plastic throughout. It's a little more expensive, but I've been told that it's quieter, though all plastic pipe seems noisy to me.

Since I have a little space to use up, I'll mention another minor screwup on this house. One day, as soon as I walked in, I started getting crap from everybody for causing a water leak. When I left the night before, I had turned off the shutoffs for a second floor bathroom that I was working on, but didn't turn them far enough so they were all the way off. The pipes had been empty, but during the night they slowly filled, and by morning there was a puddle on the floor.

Once everything started to settle down, I went down to the basement and got to work. Then the guys that were installing the sheetrock called me upstairs, saying there was still a leak. I never saw the first leak, but now there was water on the dining room ceiling, and also a puddle on the floor. So now I was going back and forth trying to figure out where it was coming from, since there wasn't any water on the second floor. This went on for probably around twenty minutes. And just about the time that I was thinking I'd have to cut a hole in the ceiling, the sheetrockers started cracking up. It turned out that they thought this would be a good time to spray some water on the ceiling.

# SUPPLY LINES

After the drain and the vent pipes have been installed, it's time to run the supply lines to the different fixtures. I generally use copper or PEX, but if you plan on using CPVC, the idea is basically the same. When doing this, the first thing I do is to look for the nearest hot and cold water pipe that I can tee into, preferably 3/4 inch. If I'm working on a bathroom that's close, with a shower instead of a bathtub, I'll run 1/2 inch lines the whole way. But, if the bathroom is farther out, and has a bathtub or a Jacuzzi, or if I'm going to tee into the lines to supply something else, then I'd use 3/4 inch, if possible, and reduce it to 1/2 inch at the first point it branches off to the individual fixtures.

If you're adding a bathroom to a house that's being lived in, you'll want to plumb it in a way that the water only has to be shut off for a short amount of time. In that case, I'd run the pipes by starting at the fixtures, and work my way back to the lines that I'm connecting to. Then once I've gone as far as I can, I'd drain down the water in the house and tee into those pipes.

Where it's possible, it might be smart to install shutoffs on the pipes that are supplying the bathroom, as shown on the right. This way, you can work on the plumbing without affecting the rest of the house. You can also shut off the water if there's ever a problem.

As the supply lines are being run, the horizontal pipes should be given a slight slope if possible, so the water can run out without being trapped when the system is drained. This is especially important if the building won't be heated in cold weather.

When using copper, street elbows make the job a little easier. Standard elbows go over the pipe on both ends, while street elbows go over the pipe on one end, but are the same size as the pipe on the other, so they'll slip into another fitting. Ninety degree street elbows are commonly used when the pipes have to cross over each other. For instance, when supplying the water to a sink, the pipes are generally run through holes that are centered on the studs. If the pipes are crisscrossed, by using a street elbow along with a standard elbow, one of the pipes can cross over the other one.

The lower right photo shows the valve body for a shower faucet that has PEX for the supply lines. Threaded PEX adapters were used to attach the tubing to the valve body. Then PEX SnapClips were used to hold the tubing in place against the studs. The shower head arm connects to a drop ear elbow. Different styles are available for sweating copper, using PEX, or with a Quick-Connect on one end.

On the right is a shower faucet with copper supply lines. When installing it, I dry-fitted the pipes and used threaded adapters to attach them to the valve body. Then I removed the adapters and the first two sections of pipe on each side when soldering, and installed the whole unit at one time after it was assembled using Teflon tape.

Tub and shower faucets are generally screwed to a board that goes between the studs. When installing a new faucet, the instructions should show the correct distance that it should stick out from the wall. A plaster guard may also be included. This should be close to flush with the finished surface. The plaster guard isn't needed, unless the faucet is

being attached to the shower wall itself. The position and the thickness of the board that the faucet is attached to will vary, depending on the brand of the faucet, and how thick the wall is. Sometimes a 1 1/2 inch board will work the best, and sometimes there's only room for one that's 3/4 inch thick.

Shown above is the valve body for a shower faucet, where copper pipes were soldered to it instead of using screw-on fittings. Nipples have also been attached for connecting PEX tubing. When soldering, the cartridge should be removed from the valve body.

The board was turned around for the photo, so you can see the valve body. It will actually be facing in the opposite direction and line up with the hole in the shower wall.

This photo shows a shutoff with a flexible supply line connected to the toilet. For the shutoff, the rule of thumb is for the pipe to be stubbed out from the wall 6 inches above the finished floor, and 6 inches to the left of center on the toilet. These measurements can't always be followed. If a stud is in the way, you'll have to run the pipe on one side of it or the other. More important is the height. Here, short baseboard was used, so the shutoff is well above it. That won't be the case with wide baseboard. And the last thing you want is for the pipe to be too close to the edge of the board, which would mean cutting off part of the flange. Anytime this is going to be a problem, look it over, and then either move the pipe so it's higher, or go lower and come through the baseboard itself.

When the pipe is coming up through the floor, make sure it's far enough out from the baseboard, and also from the shoe rail if it's being installed.

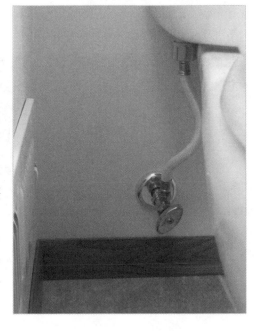

# SOLDERING

When soldering, three things are needed for a good joint that doesn't leak. First, make sure that both the pipe and the fitting have been properly cleaned. This is done with either a wire brush or emery cloth. A 4-in-1 wire brush works good on new copper, but emery cloth is much faster on old pipes. It's also needed when you're redoing a joint and have to remove the old solder. The second thing is to apply flux to both the pipe and the fitting. This is necessary for the solder to be drawn into the joint. The last one is to properly heat the joint. This is done by concentrating the heat on the fitting itself, not the pipe. Once the fitting is hot enough,

the solder will be drawn throughout the joint by capillary action, by just touching the solder to the edge of the fitting. On 1/2 inch and 3/4 inch horizontal pipes, I generally heat the fitting from the bottom, and then apply the solder to the top of it. On fittings that are larger than this, I like to heat from more than one side, so I know it's hot enough all the way around. If you don't do this, the solder may only be pulled partway into the joint. There's a rule of thumb that says a 1/2 inch joint will need 1/2 inch of solder, a 3/4 inch joint will need around 3/4 inch, etc., but this is just a general rule. Once the joint is filled, solder will start coming out at the bottom.

If you plan on doing a lot of soldering, using Mapp gas instead of Propane is a little quicker, since it burns hotter. Push button torches are much nicer to use. Once you've used one, you won't go back to your old torch. Also, anytime you solder, make sure there isn't any water in the line that could run down at the wrong time. If that happens, the joint could leak, and then you'll have to redo it. Make sure that something is left open when you solder the last joint. Air expands as it's heated, and if the line is closed, it could force its way out through the solder before it's hardened, which would also cause it to leak.

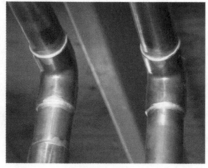

For a better looking joint, use a rag to wipe off any excess solder before it hardens. For this, I generally tear a piece from an old terrycloth dish towel. Courser material works better. If the solder has already hardened, but it's still hot, it should only take a little more heat to resoften it. Both the center photo and the one on the left show how much nicer the joints look if they've been wiped down. After the joint is finished, cool it down with a wet cloth, and then use it to remove any flux residue.

On large ball valves, like those used on boilers, it can be more difficult to heat the ends when soldering. If possible, I'll dry-fit the pipes, and then remove the valves when soldering them to the pipes that they connect to. When doing this, I'll tip the valve up and hold it in place with a wood clamp. Heat tends to rise, so I can quickly heat the end of it, and then apply just enough solder to fill the joint. Here it also helps to have another person with a second torch. Once it's been cooled, I'll turn the valve over and do the other side. Then I'll reassemble everything, and do the other joints.

A few years ago, I was installing shutoffs in a friend's basement when I made the mistake of telling him that I'd never had a leak when soldering. So, of course, when the water was turned back on, both shutoffs leaked, and water literally sprayed out from one of them. Soon after that, I had a leak on another shutoff, so I should have kept my mouth shut. I think the first two were caused by old flux that was contaminated, as it had a funny look to it. The last one was close to a ceiling, and for some reason it didn't leak for two months. After removing the shutoff, I could see that there wasn't any solder at the very top of the fitting, so I must not have got it hot enough at that point.

There are a couple of problems when soldering shutoffs. The first is that you want to quickly heat the ends, so the valve doesn't get too hot. The other concerns the brass itself. It seem to me that the brass on forged shutoffs is a lot harder than on ones with the regular cast body that's thicker. When using a wire brush on a forged shutoff, you can barely scratch the brass. Because of that, now I always use a new piece of emery cloth to prepare the surface for soldering.

## SOLDERING IN TIGHT QUARTERS

When soldering next to studs, or anything that you want to keep from burning, the best way I've found to protect it is by using a piece of sheet-metal flashing. Sometimes the metal will stay in place by just bending it, and sometimes it will have to held with a nail. In stores, you'll also find a woven pad that's made for this purpose, but in my opinion, they don't work. I've burned a lot a wood when using mine, and the first time I used it, the torch burned a hole right through it.

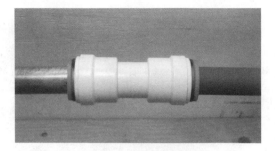 

Quick-Connect couplers, tees, and elbows can also be used to attach copper, CPVC, or PEX tubing. When using them, you just push the pipes into the fitting, and then install a collet clip on each end. With PEX, a tube stiffener (shown in the upper right corner) is needed for internal support. Metal Quick-Connects are also available.

In this photo, a hole saw was used to cut through the floor, and also to notch out the rim joist for the 3 inch sanitary tee. To keep me going straight, vertical lines were drawn on the joist. Normally there would be enough room for the fitting with a 2x6 wall, but in this case, the rim joists were insulated with 2 inch foam around the outside of the perimeter.

 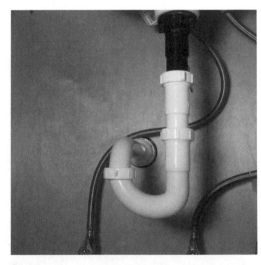

When plumbing a bathroom sink, the drain is generally centered on the sink. That was the original plan on the left, but when the vanity was installed, it was shifted over so the drain ended up being 4 1/2 inches off center. That was a problem, because a P-trap can only reach over about 3 1/2 inches. To make it work, I used a 1 1/2 inch adjustable trap that's normally used for a bathtub. Then I added a 22 1/2 degree elbow to increase the reach, and glued a trap adapter to each end. The trap works fine, but I made one mistake. The trap adapter that's attached to the sink is too low, so it's always under water. I should have added a short section of pipe to raise it up, and then used a trap adapter that went over the pipe.

The photo on the right shows another drain for a bathroom sink that's off center, where a tailpiece extender was needed to make the connection. This is pretty common these days, since many sinks are taller.

# WATER HAMMER

Water hammer is the banging sound you hear sometimes that comes from the supply lines on the plumbing. Many houses don't have this problem, but when they do, it's from the water being shut off quickly to one of the fixtures, which causes a shock wave that makes the sound. In order to fix it, first you have to locate the source of the problem. This is done by paying attention to when you actually hear it. It could be caused by flushing the toilet, using the washing machine, turning off a faucet, etc.

To prevent it, a water hammer arrester is generally installed (using a tee fitting) on either one or both of the supply lines, as close as possible to that fixture. This will act as a shock absorber to keep it from happening. There are several types of water hammer arresters. The simplest one is just a vertical pipe with air trapped in it, which is soldered into place. Another style, like the one in this photo, has a piston to contain the air. Yet another version has an air bladder, the same as a much larger expansion tank.

# DIELECTRIC UNIONS

Dielectric unions are sometimes required when different types of metal are used for the supply lines, -- for instance, in a house where some of the galvanized steel pipes have been replaced with copper. The reason for using dielectric unions is to prevent corrosion. Based on what I've read, this is what causes it.

When different types of metal pipes are used, there can be some level of electrical current flow between the materials, due to their different levels of electrical current potential. All metals, when immersed in an electrolyte, such as water, have a voltage potential. This voltage varies from +3.0 volts to -3.0 volts, depending on the metal. Those with a negative voltage potential corrode the fastest. Iron has a voltage potential of -0.4 volts, while copper has a voltage potential of +0.35. When metal with a negative voltage potential is connected to metal with a more positive voltage potential, the metal with the lower voltage potential will sacrifice itself (corrode) to protect the metal with the more positive voltage potential. In theory, putting a dielectric union between the different metals will keep this from happening, but, as it turns out, the circuit is generally completed through the water.

By using the same material for the pipes, this won't be an issue. As for myself, I've used copper when replacing galvanized steel pipes that were plugged on quite a few houses, and so far I haven't had a problem with corrosion. On one of the houses, I asked the building inspector if dielectric unions were required. He said "No -- dielectric unions have their own problems."

On most water heaters, sacrificial anodes are used to protect it. This is based on the same idea of a metal with a negative voltage potential sacrificing itself to protect one with a more positive voltage potential.

# SUPPORTING THE SUPPLY LINES

On this page are several ways to support the supply lines. On the upper left are hangers that consist of hard wire that get pounded into place. To the right is a more expensive type that holds the pipe securely and gets attached to the framing with either nails or screws. In the center is another style that holds the pipe just off the edge of the board. These can also be used for PEX tubing.

In the lower photos, the pipes are going through holes that were drilled in the framing. In this case, the holes were drilled extra large, so short lengths of foam insulation could be slipped into them to hold the pipes more securely. Depending on the thickness of the foam, a 1 3/8 or 1 1/2 inch spade bit is used for 1/2 inch pipe.

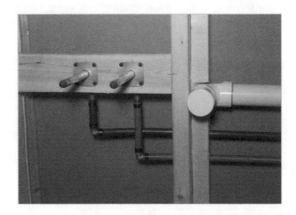

In the photo on the left, the position of the sink was changed, so both stub out elbows were installed on one side. To the right is the supply line for a toilet.

## WATER HEATERS

Here are several ways to connect a water heater. In the lower right photo, dielectric unions were used to attach the supply lines. This makes it's easy to remove the water heater without having to cut the pipes. Above that are fittings specifically made for installing a water heater with PEX tubing. They have a rubber washer on the bottom, so you just have to tighten the nut. On the upper left, copper adapters were used. The one on the left had a slight leak, probably caused by poor threads. You can see that the pipe is a little crooked. To redo the fitting, I'd have to completely drain the lines, cut the pipe, retape the fitting, and then reattach the pipe by soldering on a slip coupler. With dielectric unions, I could drain the lines and replace the washer without having to be concerned about whether a little water remained in the pipes.

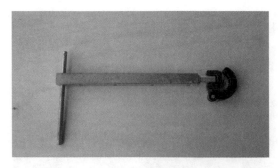

On the left is a tool that's used to tighten the drain on kitchen sinks. To the right is a basin wrench, which is used to reach up behind a sink to work on the supply lines.

## REPAIRING AN OLD STYLE FAUCET

These photos show an outdoor faucet that had been leaking for quite a while. To repair it, first the water was turned off. Then a wrench was used to take the faucet apart. You can see in the lower left photo how the rubber washer is totally shot. Faucet washers can be found at most hardware stores or home building centers. They come in different sizes, and are either beveled or flat, so you have to know which kind you need. The one that's shown here is flat. I generally buy an assortment pack, and pick through it to find a washer that matches. Then I remove the screw, and replace the old washer with the new one. The screws can also come loose. I've used faucets that acted erratically and found that the only problem was a loose screw that let the washer move around. Many of the older style faucets in a home are repaired in the same manner.

On this 4 inch cast iron wye, a rubber coupler was used to connect the PVC cleanout. If the job was being inspected, I would have used a coupler with a stainless steel outer sleeve instead, since it's required when above grade. But I prefer this style.

A rubber boot was used where the 4 inch pipe slips into the lower part of the wye. One is shown in the center of the lower photo. To the left of it is a 4-3 reducer coupler.

Once the new boot was in place, I spent a couple of hours trying to push the pipe into the fitting. In the past, I've been able to do this without a problem when replacing floor drains. But here, even though I lubricated both the pipe and the boot with dish soap, I couldn't get it in much more than about an inch, and I needed at least three. What finally worked

was to taper the end of the pipe with a block plane and a file, as shown on the upper right. Then after lubricating it, I gently tapped it into place with a sledge hammer. I used one hand when doing this, and gripped the handle right next to the head. Once that was done, I cut the pipe to length with a pull saw.

## OLDER HOMES

If you live in an older house, you might have to deal with galvanized steel water pipes. The main problem here is a lack of flow and low water pressure caused by deposits that have built up over time inside the pipes. To find the source of the problem, first you have to isolate it. You do this by turning on the faucets, one at a time, to determine the flow in the individual lines. Sometimes you'll find that the water pressure is bad at every faucet, for both the hot and the cold water. In that case, you'd start near the water meter.

At other times, there will only be a lack of flow at one or two of the faucets. There could be several reasons for this. Let's say there's a problem with both the hot and the cold water on two of the faucets, and they're on the same side of the house. In that case, the first thing I'd do is to remove the screen on each faucet, and then clean them to see if it helped. If there was a lack of flow for just the hot water, or the cold, on both faucets, I'd look is for a single pipe that supplied that water to both faucets. On newer faucets, if there's only one faucet that doesn't have hot water, it's probably a bad cartridge. On sinks, you can check this by disconnecting the flexible supply lines to see what the flow is before the faucet.

It's also possible that either one or both of the shutoffs are plugged. Sometimes small rocks break off the material that's building up on the inside of the pipes, and then lodge at the first point they're restricted. To check this out, you'll have to shut off the water and drain the lines, and then look inside the shutoffs.

This is a common problem in older homes. Anytime you turn the water on at the meter, you run the risk of these deposits breaking free and plugging something up. I have the same problem where I live at this time, as I have two faucets where the water is being restricted because someone turned the water off and then on again.

To help prevent this from happening, when you turn the water back on, just open the valve part way to slowly fill the pipes. Have the faucets turned on when doing this to let the air out, and then turn them off as the pipes fill, starting in the basement and working your way up. Once the pipes are filled, open the valve the rest of the way. Doing this will eliminate the sudden rush of water that can cause the problem.

If the restriction turns out to be inside the pipes, you'll have to go in and take a look. Before you start, make sure the water is turned off and the pipes have been drained. Most of the time, there isn't going to be a union where you want it, so you'll start by sawing through one of the pipes. Either a hacksaw or a Sawzall (reciprocating saw) will work for doing this. Once the first cut is made, the pipes can be removed by using a couple of pipe wrenches, though a Sawzall is generally faster.

Let's assume that the whole house has bad water pressure, and you sawed through one of the pipes just after the water meter. When looking inside this pipe, you'll probably see that it's partially, if not almost completely plugged. With a little luck, you'll only have to replace the first couple of pipes to get the flow back to an acceptable level. Ideally, you'd replace any pipe that was partially plugged, but that isn't practical unless you're remodeling the whole house and plan on opening up the walls.

If there's a problem with the water line before the meter, you could still have bad pressure after replacing some of the pipes. This would mean calling a plumber. You can check the flow at this point by opening up the main valve to see what comes out from one of the first pipes, and use a bucket to catch the water.

To keep going, we're going to assume that you only have to replace the pipes between the meter and the first point the pipe splits off in different directions. The new pipes will connect to the old ones at a threaded fitting, so you'll have to remove the last section on each end with pipe wrenches.

The old galvanized steel pipes are generally replaced with copper, PEX, or CPVC. If the new pipes are copper, you may be required to use dielectric unions where the different materials come together.

When using copper, solder any threaded adapters that are needed to attach them to the original plumbing before applying pipe thread compound or wrapping the threads with Teflon tape. The end sections are installed first, and then the rest of the pipes are laid out and soldered into place.

On the supply line that's shown in this photo, the copper pipe was originally connected to a galvanized steel pipe that went up to a second floor bathroom. This pipe supplied the hot water, and was plugged so bad that the water only dripped out. To repair it, we cut the copper and soldered on a PEX adapter. Then we cut a hole in the wall upstairs to remove the steel pipe, and screwed a threaded PEX adapter into the fitting. After the PEX tubing was installed, the hot water had a little over half the flow of the cold water, which is as good as it was when the homeowners bought the house. To get at the other pipes, the bathroom would have to be redone.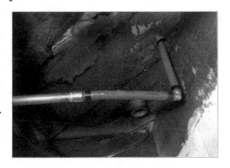

# DRAINING THE WATER PIPES

Anytime you're working on the supply lines, that part of the system will have to be drained down. If you're working in the basement, you might have to drain the entire house. This is especially important when soldering, since you don't want any water coming down at the wrong time.

To do this, turn the water off at either the meter or one of the shutoffs, and then open up all the faucets. Every faucet should be on. Those with a single handle should be centered, so both the hot and the cold side are opened up. The reason that the faucets have to be on is to let air into the pipe. This is the same idea as how you can hold water in a straw by plugging the upper end with your finger. As long as you keep your finger on the straw, the water will stay put, but as soon as you remove it, the water runs out.

When draining down a house, I'll also turn off the shutoff at the water heater. Year ago, sometimes it took way to long for the water to run out. After a while, I realized that water was being pulled (siphoned) from the water heater.

When draining the pipes, I generally leave the water in the toilets. This should give them enough for one flush. If the water is going to be off for awhile, I'll fill a couple of buckets with water to be used for refilling the tanks, if needed.

After the pipes have been drained, it's common for a little water to remain in the horizontal lines. If I need to remove it, so I can solder, I'll use a torch to get it out. When doing this, the first thing I do is to heat the end of the pipe to see if there's any water present. If water starts to boil out, and continues for some time, I'll pull down on the end of the pipe to see if that helps. Then I'll move the torch over and work my way back to the open end. This helps to push the water along the inside of the pipe. As you do this, water and/or steam should be coming out. It could take several passes with the torch before it's all out. You can tell if there's still water in the pipe by just looking at it. If there's any water, the color of the pipe will stay about the same as you heat it. But, if it's dry in that spot, the color of the copper will change within a few seconds if the torch is held close to the pipe. Once you make a pass without anything coming out from the end of the pipe, it should be ready to clean and solder after it cools down.

Sometimes, no matter what you do, you won't be able to get all of the water out. Every time you think the pipe is dry, more water comes running down. When that happens, you'll have to stuff bread into the pipe to hold the water back while you solder the fitting. White bread seems to work the best for this, without the crust. It doesn't take much to dam up the water. I'd guess that, most of the time, I use maybe half a slice or a little more. I use a pencil to shove the bread up the pipe. The bread will get flushed out once the water is turned back on. One place where I won't use bread is on a pipe that supplies cold water to the water heater. When using bread, it's a good idea to remove the screens from the faucets before you turn the water back on, or you might have to remove some of them to clean out the bread residue.

# BAD FITTINGS

In the last few years, there seems to be more problems with threaded pipe fittings that leak. Here are two examples. A couple of years ago, I helped my brother-in-law install a water heater in a cabin that he and my sister had just bought. After installing it, one of the copper fittings at the water heater had a steady drip once we turned the water back on. So I drained the system and redid the fitting, again using pipe thread compound. Then I went to bed, after making sure that there weren't any leaks. In the morning, now there was water around both fittings, so I threw them away, and we drove 20 miles to the store and bought new ones. This time, I used Teflon tape when redoing the fittings, and that stopped the leaks.

Another case happened to a friend a couple of months ago when he installed a new shallow well pump. While telling me about it a couple of days later, he was still mad. After installing the pump, when he turned the water back on, the fittings leaked. So he retaped the fittings and tightened them a little more. They still leaked. This went on for several times. Finally, he went out and bought the thickest Teflon tape that he could find. Now everything held, but with all the installations, the pump had a hairline crack where the pipe attaches to it.

So what's causing this? My guess is that the problem is strictly poor quality threads, and that several wraps of heavy Teflon tape is just thick enough to compensate for it. I don't think pipe thread compound is the problem, since it's been around a long time, and also because the new stuff is probably better than it was in the past. When using Teflon tape, I generally go around the pipe four times. On plastic threads, sometimes I've had to use as many as six wraps to keep a fitting from leaking. At this time, steel pipes and fittings that are made in America have better threads. At Home Depot, Menards, etc, they're generally manufactured in China. Check local hardware stores for American made galvanized and black steel pipes and fittings.

# PLUMBING LEAKS

If you work on your own house, you're going to have to deal with plumbing leaks from time to time. Generally they'll be found at the faucets, the shutoffs, the drains, and the traps. We'll start with the shutoffs. Shutoffs commonly leak in two places. Shutoffs with compression fittings are attached by tightening a nut that compresses a ring (sleeve) around the pipe. With this type, sometimes you'll have a leak that comes out right behind the shutoff. Normally this is stopped by tightening the nut a little more, which squeezes the ring tighter around the pipe. But once in a while this doesn't work, even if you tighten the nut another time or two. The way to fix it then is to turn off the water, and remove the shutoff by loosening the nut. This will leave the nut and the ring still attached to the pipe. Now apply a little pipe joint compound to the edge of the ring where it gets squeezed against the shutoff. Then put the shutoff back on and retighten it. I've seen instructions where they recommend using pipe joint compound when you first put the shutoff on, but I've only used it to stop leaks when tightening the nut didn't help.

Another place where shutoffs can leak is around the stem (round shaft), just behind the handle. This is also a common problem on some of the older style faucets that don't have a cartridge. To prevent leaks, some of them have a thick string or cord that's wrapped around the shaft, called packing. Then a nut goes over the packing, which compresses it around the shaft to keep the water from leaking out. If it does leak, generally the packing just needs to be compressed a little more. To do this, tighten the nut by turning it in a clockwise direction. You shouldn't have to turn it very far to stop the leak. If that doesn't help, the packing may have to be replaced. You can find it at the store, in the same area where the faucet washers are. Then to replace it, or add more, turn the water off and remove the nut, wrap a short length of the new packing material around the shaft, and replace the nut. Newer style shutoffs are made a little different. On some of them, if there's a leak, you tighten the same nut that you'd remove to take the shutoff apart. On others, there isn't anything that you can tighten. Ball valves can also leak around the shaft. To get to the nut, first you have to take off the handle.

Drains are another place where leaks can occur. Kitchen sinks commonly have stainless steel drains that may or may not be connected to a garbage disposal. Plumbers putty is generally used to install the drains. To do this, roll the putty between your hands until you have a piece that's long enough. Then the putty is either wrapped around the perimeter of the hole, or under the lip of the drain, which ever works the best. After that, the drain is slipped into place, and then you push down on it. If you used enough putty, there should be excess that gets squeezed out all around the hole. Now slip on the rubber gasket, followed by the washer and the nut, and then tighten it. The excess putty will easily come off and can be reused. Plumbers putty doesn't have to dry, so the sink can be used right away.

When installing the drain on a bathroom sink, the instructions that come with the sink will commonly tell you to use caulk instead of plumbers putty, because plumbers putty could damage the material. In that case, I always use silicone caulk. When using caulk, be sure to use enough so that it gets squeezed out all around the hole. Then wipe off the excess with a paper towel, and clean up the residue with paint thinner. Then give it a day to dry.

Bathroom sinks can also leak at the bottom. The drain has to be sealed at both ends because there's an overflow hole on most bathroom sinks. The lower part of the drain is sealed by a thick rubber washer. Here, most of the time, you just have to tighten the nut until the rubber is tightly compressed against the sink. I've installed a couple of sinks where the hole wasn't round, and also had to use caulk or plumbers putty to get the leak to stop. If the water is coming out at the threads, loosen the nut and apply Teflon tape. Then retighten the nut.

Bathtub and shower drains vary, so you should always read the instructions from the manufacturer of the tub or the shower, and also for the drains. But even after following the instructions, some of them can still leak. Often the problem is caused by the hole itself being poorly made. Either the area under the hole is too rough, or the hole is the wrong shape, so the drain doesn't fit right. This is also a common problem on some bathroom sinks. Here, the only answer is to stop the leak with either caulk or plumbers putty, depending on the material.

Traps will commonly leak, even when using new parts. When that happens, the first thing to do is to make sure the nuts are tight enough. Something may also be crooked and/or out of position, so the parts are meeting at an angle to each other. Another common reason is caused by the pipe itself. Look at the tail piece that comes with a new faucet, and you'll find that it's smooth on the outside. Now compare that to the typical plastic trap that you find at a local building center. The trap will most likely have a small ridge on both sides of each piece, that I assume is caused by how it's made. The problem here is that a compression washer may not get a good seal against the ridge, which could cause the joint to leak. To stop the leak, I generally wrap the washer with Teflon tape, by going around the pipe, and then put the nut back on. The Teflon tape is soft enough to fill the small gap at the edge of the ridge.

The photo on the left shows a faucet that has a separate packing nut (1), which is tightened if water leaks around the shaft. Number 2 is the nut for taking the faucet apart. On the right is a shutoff with one nut (3) serving both functions.

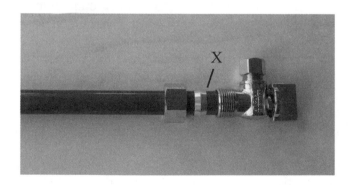

Shown above is a 90 degree quarter-turn compression shutoff that's used for sinks and toilets. A compression fitting is attached by tightening the nut, which compresses the brass ring against the pipe. If the shutoff leaks, even after tightening it farther, put a thin layer of pipe thread compound around the edge of the ring (X) where it meets the shutoff, and then retighten the nut.

Small leaks may also stop on their own. Sometimes I'll have a shutoff, or one of the fittings on a water heater, etc. where a drop of water slowly keeps appearing after I've retightened it. Then after letting it sit overnight, the leak is gone. I wish I could say I planned it that way, but the truth is that I was just tired of working on it.

# HEATING

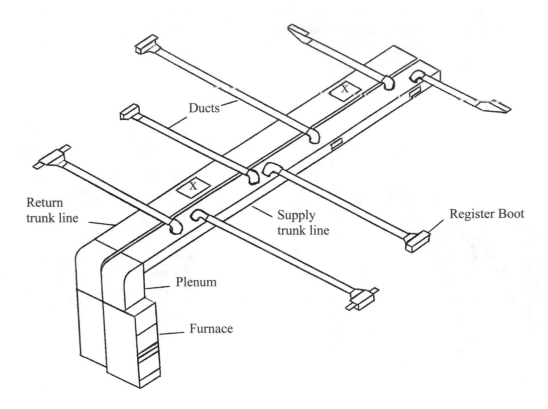

Ducts

Return
trunk line

Supply
trunk line

Register Boot

Plenum

Furnace

On projects where you're creating new rooms, such as when finishing off a basement, you'll have to consider how the areas are going to be heated and/or cooled. We'll start with forced air heat. Adding on to one of these systems is a pretty straightforward job that most anyone can do, and doesn't require a lot of knowledge or expensive tools.

The drawing above shows a typical forced air heating system. Here, warm air from the furnace goes through the plenum and then across the horizontal trunk line. From there, it passes through the different ducts and comes out the heat registers. At the same time, air is pulled in through the cold air return registers and either goes through ducts, or stud or joist cavities that are connected to holes cut into the return trunk line (x), as it returns to the furnace to complete the loop. If the forced air system includes an air conditioner, the rooms would be cooled in the same manner.

In unfinished basements, commonly the only heat is from a couple of grills that are mounted over holes that were cut into the bottom of a trunk line. Most of the time this isn't enough, and once the walls are framed, you'll have to come up with a plan for the heating system. When the furnace was installed, it should have been sized to allow for heating the basement, so you should be able to add new ducts to the existing trunk line. Heat registers that are already installed can still be used, or they can be removed, and the holes covered with sheet metal.

Upstairs, heat registers are generally at floor level, but that doesn't work in a basement. I've been in houses where the heat ducts for the basement have gone across the ceiling and then down an outside wall, but, from what I've seen, this doesn't work as hardly any air came out. For the best air flow, ducts should take the shortest route possible, and elbows should be kept to a minimum.

In smaller rooms where the trunk line has been framed off with 2x2s and covered with sheetrock, I like to heat the area by installing registers on the side of the trunk line, as shown in these photos. I generally prefer the side, rather than on the bottom, as I feel it does a better job of distributing the warm air across the room.

To do this, I draw the outline of the hole on the trunk line, and then measure in how much is needed for folding the metal out. This distance is partly determined by how tight the framing is to the trunk line. Then I drill a hole to get started, and cut out the center of the hole (x) following the inside lines. After that, I cut diagonal lines that end at each corner. This is shown in the drawing on the left.

Once the cuts have been made, I clamp a board along each line and then bend the metal out ninety degrees. If you don't get a tight bend, make sure the board is securely clamped, and then work your way along the edge, lightly hitting it with a hammer. That should tighten it up. Once the edges have been folded out, it's just a matter of framing around the hole, nailing the folded edge to the framing, and installing the sheetrock. In the drawing on the right, you can see the boards that were added.

The same tool that's used for bending the ends on a trunk line can also be used here. It's designed for a 1 inch bend, so the center should be cut out so it's 2 inches smaller than the finished hole.

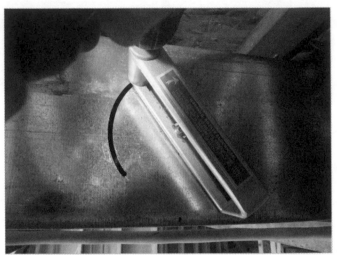

To heat a larger area, holes are cut into the trunk line (generally 6 inch). Then ducts are attached to bring the heat across the room, where it comes out through register boots that are either attached to the ceiling, or to holes that have been cut in the floor if you're heating the level above.

Years ago, I used to cut the holes in the trunk line with a tin snips. These photos show how it's done using a cordless drill with a hole cutter. This one costs a little over thirty dollars. After marking the center of the hole, the cutter bit is used to drill a hole at that spot. Then the center pivot slips into this hole, and another one is drilled along the outer edge of the six inch hole. Now the drill is kept running as you rotate the hole cutter so it goes around the perimeter of the hole. After that's done, the starting collar is slipped into place, and it's held by bending the tabs over. The starting collar shown here is extra long and has holes for installing a damper.

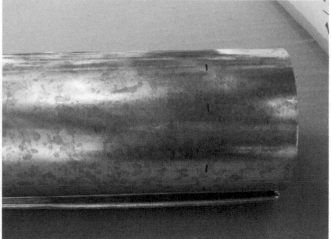

Once the starting collar is in place, the duct can be installed. Here, two sections of pipe were needed for it, a 5 foot length and also a short piece. The 5 foot section was slipped over the starting collar, and then attached with three self-piercing sheet metal screws. These screws are spaced out around the perimeter, and go through the overlapping layers to hold the parts together. After that, the length was measured for the next piece, which was marked with a Sharpie and then cut with a tin snips. Then the pipe was snapped together, and it was slipped into place and also held with three screws. In tight spots, sometimes there's only enough room for a couple of screws.

The ducts are cut to length by cutting off the smooth end, and they're installed with the tapered end facing away from the trunk line, so the air will flow smoothly over the joint. The lower photos show the completed duct. The register boot that was used here is designed for ceilings and has adjustable hangers that attach to the framing. The duct is also supported by an expandable brace that's attached to the framing.

Here are some of the parts you'll need for installing the ducts. Notice that one of the register boots runs perpendicular to the duct, while the other is parallel to it.

The last two pages show a duct that's mounted to the side of the trunk line, but more often, the hole will be on the top and an elbow will go on after the starting collar. There are also elbows that directly attach to the trunk line.

Elbows are used whenever the pipe has to change direction, and can be adjusted to any angle between 0 and 90 degrees. Sometimes it takes two elbows that are connected together to make a turn.

Insulated flexible ducts can be used to go across areas that aren't heated, such as attics or crawl spaces. Flexible ducts are also used in places where it would be difficult to run a standard duct. When using them, they should be extended all the way out for the best air flow.

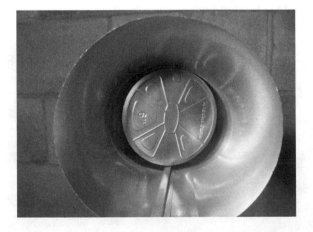

Dampers are used to balance the system. Though many systems don't have any dampers, they're required in some areas. To install one, first you drill a hole in the duct. Then the damper is slipped into the hole, and a wing nut is used to hold it in place. If you want to restrict the air flow in that duct, the damper is turned to partially block the hole.

This photo shows an elbow that's directly attached to the trunk line, with another elbow connected to it. The joints have been sealed with foil tape to prevent air leaks.

Oval pipes can be used to fit into smaller cavities. Six inch oval pipe is about 3 1/4 inches thick, so it will fit between the sheetrock with 2x4 framing. Next to the oval pipe is a register boot that's used when the heat is coming out at the floor. Here you can also see where oval pipe was used for the heat register in the wall. The CFM flow rating for oval pipe is around 20 percent less than for round pipe of equal size.

The tool on the right is a crimper. It's used to taper the end of a pipe, so it can slip into another one. Having this tool allows you to use the pieces that are cut off from other pipes. On the left is a bender. It's used to fold the ends over on a trunk line, or anywhere else that you want to make a sharp bend.

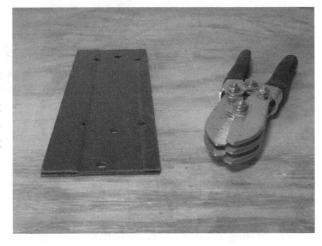

Shown here is a magnetic nut driver that's used to hold the screws for attaching the pipes. When doing this, I prefer to use self-piercing screws over self-drilling because I think they strip out less. When using a cordless drill, set the torque setting low. On this drill, number 4 is about right.

165

# RUNNING HEAT TO AN UPPER LEVEL

 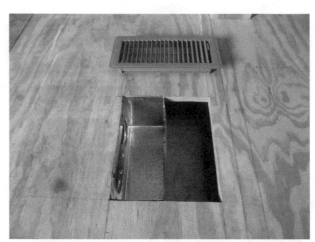

These photos show how the ducts were run to bring heat to a second floor addition. On the lower right, two 6 inch ducts (round) were attached to the trunk line. Then round-to-oval elbows were used to go up the wall. To the left, you see the oval pipes going up the stud cavities, and above that, how elbows were used to bring them across the ceiling in opposite directions. In the upper right photo, the holes for the 4x10 register boots were cut extra large. Here it was necessary in order to slip them on and to attach them to the ducts. The floor will be patched in later. In this case, the top of the boots also had to be cut shorter so they were flush to the floor. Once they were attached to the duct, the boots were nailed to the floor sheathing to hold them in place.

On this addition, because of the layout, we were only able to run two heat ducts up to the second floor, with a cold air return at the top of the stairs. Normally I'd go by the rule of thumb that says you need one 6 inch heat duct for every 100-125 square feet of floor area. In this case, the area isn't that large, and heat will also be coming up the stairs

When heating a basement, I generally tend to wing it, and try to install about the same amount of heat registers as an equal area upstairs. If I had to choose, I'd rather put in too many, than too few, since the registers are adjustable for air flow and can always be turned down if necessary. Of course, this could all be calculated, but I've watched professionals, and they do it about the same way, as in let's put a couple of heat registers on the long wall, one over here, and then another in the bathroom, etc. A flow chart for the different size ducts and trunk lines is used when you need to be more exact.

# COLD AIR RETURNS

Cold air returns are used to bring the air back to the furnace to complete the loop. Ideally, the supply and the return air registers are installed so that warm air will enter a room and then flow across it before it goes out through a return. The preferred location for the heat registers is near the windows on an outside wall, where the heat loss is the greatest. The best place for the returns is at the interior walls on the other side of the room. Kitchens and bathrooms generally don't get cold air returns, to keep from pulling in smoke or unpleasant odors. Instead, these areas should have an exhaust fan.

For the heating system to be balanced, the size of the returns (total area) should be equal to one-third larger than the supply ducts. I've worked in basements where there weren't enough cold air returns, and everything still worked fine, but I've also been in others where the ducts put out very little heat. When areas don't have a cold air return, you have to compensate for it somewhere in the system.

Cold air returns are different, in that metal ducts aren't always necessary. To bring the air across a basement ceiling, sheet metal or foil-faced cardboard can either be nailed or stapled to the floor joists to create a path for the air to travel. On a wall, a sheetrocked stud cavity could also be used as a return. When doing this, the top and/or the bottom plate has to be cut out so the air can pass through. Then a wall register can be installed at that location by simply cutting a hole through the sheetrock.

In some areas, this method isn't allowed anymore, and ducts are needed for both the supply and the return lines. The reason that's given is to have more control of the air flow, to keep the air cleaner, and to keep from pulling in outside air.

When the framing is used for a cold air return, wires can go across the cavity, but can't be stapled along the length of it. There's a rule that says wiring can't pass through a cold air return, but in this case, they're actually talking about drilling a hole through a metal duct and then running the wires through it. There's an exception to this rule that allows for the wiring to pass through when the framing is being used for the return.

Cold air registers in the basement should be down by the floor. To do this, you'd typically use a stud cavity on an interior wall. In basements where this isn't practical, another option is to install the cold air register right at the furnace, attached to either the plenum or a trunk line. If the furnace is in a utility room, another register will have to be added to an outer wall on that room, so the air can get through.

When the furnace has been installed in a closet or small utility room, sometimes holes have to be cut in the wall to provide air for combustion. When doing this, two registers are needed, with one high up on the wall, that's within a foot of the ceiling, and another one that's down low, within a foot of the floor.

The upper photo shows a stud cavity being used for a cold air return, where the work was done by professionals. Here a floor joist was in the way, so the hole had to extend a little bit into the room, instead of staying inside the framing as it normally would have been done. As you can see, the stud cavity has been sealed off using foil-faced cardboard and some kind of metal channel, but it would have been better if they just put a board between the studs.

The lower photo shows a central cold air return where the return trunk line comes up through the floor, and has one opening near the floor, and another one next to the ceiling. From what I've read, in most houses, the height of the cold air returns on the upper floors (levels) doesn't matter. In the basement, or a cold climate, low returns pull in cold air that's near the floor. Where warm air is trapped against tall or vaulted ceilings, high cold air returns would help to remove it. With high cold air returns you don't have to be concerned about putting furniture in front of them.

Ideally, most rooms will have heat registers and also cold air returns, but that's not always possible if the framing runs in the wrong direction, or obstacles such as stairs are in the way. When installing individual returns isn't an option, you'll have to run heat ducts to the different areas, and then have a central cold air return that's sized accordingly. In the photos above, the one on the left shows a central cold air return that's in a basement where the framing wouldn't allow individual returns. In rooms without a cold air return, make sure there's a large enough gap under the door for air flow. In the other photo, an 8 inch flexible duct was used for the cold air return. This one is in the utility room, and pulls air from the main area of the basement. Flexible ducts may not be allowed when going from one floor level to another.

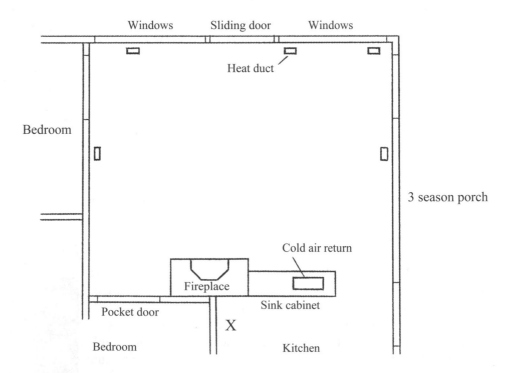

This drawing shows the position of the heat registers for the living room/dining area of a cabin that I've been working on. As you can see, there are five heat ducts, but only one cold air return. This room sits over an enclosed crawl space, and the X shows the location of the furnace that's in the basement. Because of the way the cabin is laid out, it wasn't possible to have individual returns in this area, so we decided to put a central cold air return under the sink cabinet. Since new cabinets were being made, we had this one modified so air could pass through a large register on the back side.

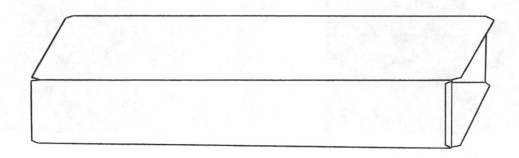

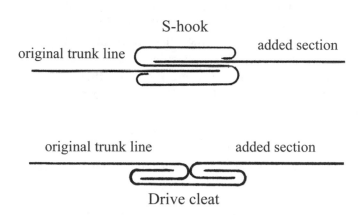

original trunk line

S-hook

added section

original trunk line

added section

Drive cleat

S-hooks

Drive Cleats

Trunk lines are the rectangular ducts that are connected to the plenum on the furnace. On most remodeling projects, you'll be able to attach any new ducts that are needed to the existing trunk lines, but once in a while the trunk lines will have to be lengthened or modified in some way. Normally this is pretty easy to do. It's just a matter of taking off the end cap, or a section that has to be removed, and then adding the new parts.

Each section of a trunk line consists of two identical L-shaped pieces that snap together. Once they're connected, 1 inch cuts are made at each corner, and then the side edges are folded over using the bender that's made for this purpose.

The sections are attached to each other using S-hooks and drive cleats. To do this, S-hooks are slipped over both the upper and the lower edge on one of the sections. Then the next section will slide into the opposite side of each S-hook as the two are pushed together. To lock it in place, drive cleats are driven over the edges that were folded over, and then bent over at the corners. When a trunk line has to be cut to fit, allow for the overlap on the end.

In the upper drawing, you can see how the two sections of trunk line slip into the S-hook from opposite directions. The lower drawing shows how the drive cleats lock them together.

The trunk lines are attached to the floor joists using metal brackets. The
photo on the right shows how the drive cleats are folded over at the corner

There's a rule that says heat ducts shouldn't be attached to the end of a trunk line. The reason for this is that most of the air could come out the end duct, since that's the easiest place for it to go. In some cases, doing this can actually reverse the air flow in the other ducts on the same trunk line. Instead of the air coming out, it could be sucked in, with everything going out the duct on the end. While this rule sounds good, sometimes it has to be broken. If you need another heat duct, and this is the only place where it can go, then you don't have much choice in the matter. When I've done it, everything has still worked fine. If there was a problem, I would think that you could fix it by restricting the air flow in the duct on the end.

Anytime you work on a heating system, make sure that it works properly before anything gets covered up with sheetrock. Every system is different. In some homes you'll have good flow from the basement ducts, so it's easy to heat the area, while in others the flow will be too weak. This could be caused by a lack of cold air returns, though that's not always the answer.

One problem with forced air heat is that it's harder to control. When heating with radiators or in-floor heat, you commonly have multiple zones, so the different areas are heated as needed. With a forced air furnace, generally every room gets heat at the same time, so the system has to be balanced. But this can be difficult to achieve. On a cold night, every room will need heat, but during the day it's a different story. Let's say it's a sunny day during the winter. While the rooms on the south side of the house may not need any heat, or could even be too warm, those on the north side might be cold. With one thermostat, it's difficult to maintain an even temperature.

While sitting here, I can think of quite a few houses with forced air heat that have certain rooms or areas that tend to be too cold. There isn't just one solution when you have this problem. If a room is too cold because of leaky windows or a lack of insulation, you can bring in more heat, but the area will quickly cool down once the heat is off, so here you'd be better off taking care of the problem first. Running a new heat duct to that room might be an option, but it's only practical if there's a way to do it without tearing up the walls and/or the ceiling. It may also be possible to turn up the fan on the furnace, or to install a separate fan that fits inside of the duct for that area to increase the air flow.

Another way is to rebalance the system. By restricting the air flow to the areas that are the warmest, more heat will go to the ones that are colder. With a little luck, rooms that were comfortable to begin with should stay that way, and areas that were cold should be noticeably warmer. This is done by partially shutting the heat registers, or adjusting the dampers if they've been installed and you still have access to them. The handle on the damper is parallel to it, so the damper is wide open if the handle is parallel to the furnace duct.

In the homes that I've been in, the ones that have the biggest problem with this have been split-levels. Here you have an exterior door at a landing, and stairs that go to both the upper and the lower levels. There's also a walkout with a patio door. In the winter, many of these basements tend to be cold. Cold air from the entry door goes down the stairs, and any heat that comes out the ducts seems to leave and go upstairs. It's also cold around the patio door.

Since I don't have much experience at balancing the system in one of these homes, these are just my thoughts on the subject, and bear in mind that I live in Minnesota. To begin, I used to think that the problem was the door between the two levels, and the easy path for the heat to rise upstairs. But now I'm not so sure. As I've worked on more heating systems, I've noticed in homes that are heated with radiators or in-floor heat, heat on one level tends to stay where it is. With that in mind, this is where I'd start.

One thing in common in the houses where I've seen this problem is that none of them had insulation under the concrete. Floors that aren't insulated are going to suck the heat right out of the house during the winter. Concrete floors are also colder, the closer they are to ground level. Since they can't be insulated after the fact, the best that you can do is to use carpeting with a thick pad. But even though the floor might feel OK, it will never be as good as having two inches of foam under the slab. Any windows or patio doors that have air leaks should also be repaired. Here I'm assuming that the walls are insulated properly. If they're not, you can't expect the basement to stay warm, since too much of the heat will be lost.

Once that was done, I'd make sure that plenty of heat was going to the lower level. To do this, I'd add more ducts if it was necessary, and make sure they had good air flow. I'd also have enough cold air returns on the lower level. In homes where most of the cold air returns are upstairs, I wonder if you're actually pulling the heat out of the basement.

## FLOW RATINGS FOR DUCTS

| Dimensions, Round Pipe | Approximate CFM | Square Inch |
|---|---|---|
| 4" | 30 | 12.57 |
| 5" | 60 | 19.64 |
| 6" | 100 | 28.27 |
| 7" | 150 | 38.48 |
| 8" | 200 | 50.27 |
| Square or Rectangular | | |
| 3 1/4" x 10" | 100 | 32.50 |
| 8" x 8" | 300 | 64.00 |
| 8" x 10" | 400 | 80.00 |
| 8" x 12" | 500 | 96.00 |
| 8 x 14" | 600 | 112.00 |
| 8 x 16" | 700 | 128.00 |

Rule of thumb: In general, one CFM (cubic feet per minute) is required to heat or cool 1 - 1 1/4 square feet of floor area.

Rule of thumb for sizing trunk lines, also called an extended plenum: A simple formula is used to determine the width needed for an 8 inch trunk line. When using 6 inch round pipe for the ducts, add up the number of ducts, multiply that by 2, and then add 2 more. For example, if there were five 6-inch ducts, you'd multiply 5 by 2, and then add 2 more, so you'd need a 12 inch wide trunk line. When using 8 inch ducts, you multiply the number of ducts by 3, and then add 2 more.

Forced air heat seems to be out of style at this time, but there's a lot to be said for it. For one, it's easily installed, and there isn't the possibility of a pipe breaking and causing major water damage. Another reason, if you plan on having central air, it uses the same ducts that are installed for the heat. One house that I've worked on has two separate heating systems. The first floor is heated with a boiler, which was originally used for radiators, but has since been converted to in-floor heat. The second floor is heated with forced air and has central air conditioning. That system also has registers installed on the ceiling of the first floor. They're closed during the heating season, but are open in the summer to help cool the rest of the house.

Forced air systems can also be zoned the same as when using a boiler. This is more expensive, and from what I've read, it's less efficient if the system isn't designed properly. If you're interested in this, I'd make sure the installer had a lot of experience with this type of system.

# SIZING THE SYSTEM

When installing a forced air heating system, both the furnace and the ducts should be sized by using calculations. While that may be the case, this isn't necessarily how it's done. When an experienced furnace guy walks into your house, I would bet that most of the time he already knows what size furnace he's going to install within a couple of minutes, regardless of what the heat calculation form says. The form will give you a specific number for the size of the furnace that's needed, but furnaces only come in a few sizes. You also have some leeway on this. When I filled out a heat calculation form for one of my brothers, the furnace installer didn't even look at it. He said it didn't matter, and that he only had to come within 50 percent of the number. Better furnaces will also have a two-stage burner, so the size isn't as important.

Several years ago, I was finishing off the basement in a recently built house, and had planned on running the new heat ducts until I realized the trunk line was too small for the six ducts that had to be added. So the homeowner called the guys that did the original work. When they showed up, they started installing the new ducts without even considering how many were already on the trunk line. When I mentioned that I'd thought the trunk line was too small, they said it didn't matter because the fan would automatically speed up to compensate for it. So much for flow charts.

Recently, three contractors stopped by at a cabin that's owned by the same guy to give bids for installing a forced air heating system. The interesting thing about this was that they had different ideas on how to size the trunk lines. While two of them pretty much followed the rule of thumb, the first guy said he based the size on static pressure. The difference was quite a bit. The last two would use a 14-16 inch trunk line, while the other would use one around 10 inches.

The guy that ended up installing the system was the one that based the size on static pressure. When I first saw the furnace after it was installed, I was surprised at how small one of the trunk lines looked. Here he used a 10 inch for the supply line and a 14 inch for the return line. It doesn't seem right that a 10 inch trunk line can supply enough air for six or seven ducts, but the system works fine, so I guess he knows what he's doing.

One thing the contractors mentioned was that the thermostat on a high-efficiency, forced air furnace shouldn't be set lower than 60 degrees. Below that temperature, the returning air could condense and quickly wreck the furnace. I'd never heard this before. Based on that, you can't have a high-efficiency, forced air furnace at a cabin where the thermostat will be set at a low temperature when you're not there. I looked this up for myself to see if it was true, and it was. According to one of the manufacturers, the temperature could be turned down intermittently, such as during the night, but continuously running it below 60 degrees would void the warranty.

# HEATING WITH WATER

While doing my job, I see different types of heating systems. In most of the older homes where I work, radiators are used, while the newer houses generally have forced air heat. These days, in-floor heat is being installed in many new homes, and others are being converted to include it as part of the heating system. This is always an option once there's a boiler in place to heat the water. The water used for heating the floors is normally at a lower temperature than what's used for radiators, but that can be adjusted with the use of a mixing valve. While in-floor heat has its good points, and many people love it, it may not be quite as terrific as some would want you to believe. Its main selling point is that the heat is even, and having warm floors makes a home feel more comfortable. It's also quieter than forced air heat.

There's also some misconception concerning in-floor heat. I've read and heard that this form of heat is a lot cheaper because, by having warm floors, the thermostat can be set to a lower temperature. While this may be the case, it can't be set that much lower. If anything, I'd say you could set the thermostat a few degrees cooler at the most, and that's when the heat is on. One thing to remember is that with most heating systems, the heat is not constant. It's turning on and off as needed, so the floors aren't always going to be warm. As the floors cool down, you aren't going to have that warmth at your feet, so 70 degrees from one system is going to feel pretty much like 70 degrees from another.

Another problem with in-floor heat is the installation. It's not quite as simple as you might think. While installing the tubing can be relatively easy, many people don't realize how much is needed, and when it's stapled under the floor, insulation has to be installed under the tubing in order for it to work properly. So you're also looking at the time and the money for doing that.

The best place for in-floor heat is either a concrete floor, that has insulation beneath it, or under tile. The main problem occurs when the tubing is installed under wood or carpeted floors. Here there might not be enough heat on a cold winter day, since these materials act as an insulator. Adding rugs over the hardwood floors would normally make it more comfortable, but in this case will only add to the problem, since that's another layer for the heat to go through. The first system that I helped install was under a wood floor. That one could only keep up down to a little below zero. To be fair, that house has 2x4 walls on the exterior, but we also added extra aluminum plates to pull more heat from the tubing.

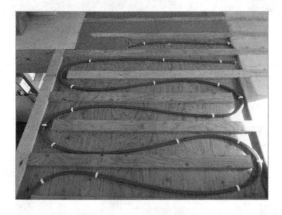 

When you're heating an upper floor, you'll have to decide whether the tubing is going under or over the floor sheathing. When it's stapled to the bottom of it, shorter nails have to be used if you're installing hardwood floors, so you don't hit the tubing. Systems are also available for installing the tubing above the sheathing. The ones that I've seen advertised also use aluminum for spreading out the heat. On the floor that's shown in these photos, we stapled PEX tubing between plywood strips that were glued and nailed into place. Then mortar was installed between the strips to help draw out and distribute the heat. When in-floor heat is installed in a building where the heat isn't always on, or where it could go out without anyone knowing, such as at a cabin, antifreeze is added to provide freeze protection.

# ADDING RADIATORS

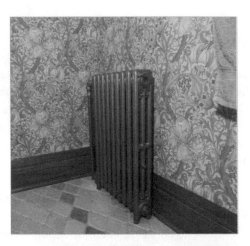

Whether you're remodeling or there's an area that's just too cold, some rooms could use extra heat. Different types of radiators can be used for this. The upper photo shows a small old-fashioned radiator that was installed in a bathroom. The others are more modern looking and also much lighter. The one on the left is next to a rear entry door that's at the top of the basement stairs. The center photo shows a heated towel rack that's also used to heat the room. To the right of it is a radiator that's used to heat the area next to an exterior French door.

When we worked on the lower heating system on page 188, we also installed several used radiators in the basement. On the first two, we used standard fittings for attaching the radiators that included a union, and a boiler valve so the system could be drained. One is shown below, in the photo on the right. On the last radiator they didn't fit, so we went to a plumbing store and bought parts that were actually made for it. In the other photos, you can see how much nicer it looks. The cost wasn't that bad, either.

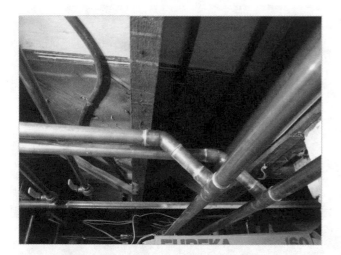 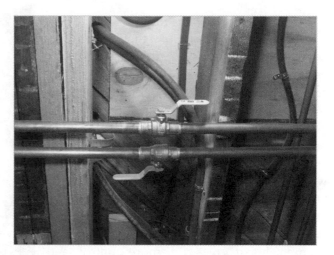

These photos show how the pipes were installed for a new radiator. Here it was just a matter of teeing into the supply and the return line, and then adding shutoffs before the radiator. When doing this, one of the main concerns is the size of the pipes. Water is always going to take the easiest way possible, so you may have to restrict one of the lines, or add an extra pump to get the flow where you need it. In this case, the pipes are the same size, so it wasn't a problem.

Here, a 1 inch line that supplies three radiators is attached to the original 2 inch pipe. In this case, very little water was going through the three radiators, so a small auxiliary pump was added to the new line. Auxiliary pumps should be connected (wired) to the main pump for that zone, so they'll turn on and off as needed.

This radiator is thermostatically controlled. To do this, the manual valve that controls the flow was removed, and then replaced with one that's connected to a thermostatic control on the wall. The line between the valve and the control appears to be a wire, but it's actually a tube filled with fluid. As the temperature changes, the fluid will expand and contract, which will open and close the valve. This isn't the same as having the radiator on a separate zone, since it will only get heat when the pump is running, but it gives you more control, and can prevent the area from getting too warm.

On the left, you can see the original heating pipes that were hanging below a basement ceiling. To make it less of an eyesore, we sawed off the pipes close to the wall, and then ran new copper lines between the floor joists. When making the cuts, we marked the length by wrapping masking tape around each pipe, and cut along the edge of the tape with a Sawzall. Then we rented a pipe threader to cut new threads on the ends. Reducers were used to connect the 3/4 inch copper to the 2 inch pipe.

# INSTALLING IN-FLOOR HEAT

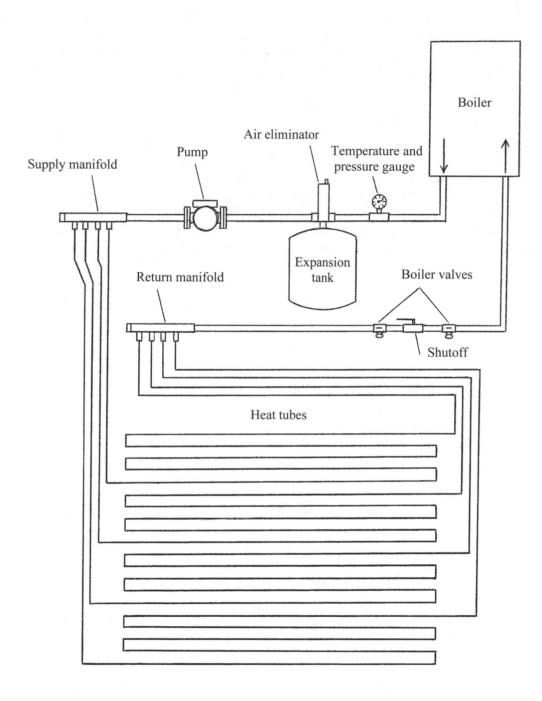

For a couple of reasons, this section wasn't originally going to be in the book. The first is that I didn't consider myself qualified, and the second is that I considered it beyond the capabilities of most homeowners. Since then, I've learned more from working on other systems. I've also found that homeowners are taking on the job of installing in-floor heat, regardless of whether or not they know what they're doing.

To begin, the first thing that needs to be done is to design the system. It starts with what you'll be using to heat the water. Options would include: a gas boiler, electric boiler, a standard water heater, or a water heater that's specifically designed for this purpose, with a separate loop for the heating system.

There are two types of gas boilers, condensing and non-condensing. Non-condensing boilers have been around for a long time. They're designed to heat the water to a high temperature, and are vented up the chimney. For that reason, they aren't as efficient, since the exhaust has to remain at a high enough temperature to prevent it from condensing. If the exhaust cools down enough for that to happen, acids will form, which will quickly corrode the boiler. Since this type of boiler is designed to heat the water to a high enough temperature for radiators, the water will generally have to be cooled down when used for in-floor heat. This is done by using a mixing valve.

Condensing boilers are more expensive, and they're designed to run at a higher efficiency by using more of the heat that otherwise would have gone up the chimney. With this style, the exhaust goes out the wall through a PVC pipe. Condensing boilers can also be adjusted to heat the water to a certain temperature, so a mixing valve may not be needed to cool the water to a lower temperature. There are also condensing boilers that serve two functions, for heating the building, and also to provide hot water for the house.

The drawing on the last page shows the basic layout of an in-floor heating system. Starting at the boiler, the water passes by the air eliminator and the expansion tank. From there, it goes to the pump that's used to circulate the water. After that, it splits up at the manifold, and then runs through the different loops of tubing, where it gives off its heat to warm the house. Then it comes back to the boiler to complete the circuit.

Depending on the system, there may also be unions, shutoffs, relief valves, check valves, faucets, temperature gauges, pressure gauges, mixing valves, and zone valves. As you can see, there's a lot of potential parts. It's important to get everything laid out right, so the system works properly. I'll go over the parts, one at a time, to give you a better idea as to their use.

Expansion tank - On newer systems, there's a small expansion tank with a rubber bladder inside that's under pressure. Older tanks were a lot bigger and had no bladder. Regardless of which one you have, the idea is the same, which is to maintain a pocket of air. Water expands as it's heated. Without an expansion tank, the pressure would increase as the temperature goes up. By having a cushion of air to push against, the pressure will remain relatively the same. Expansion tanks with a bladder should be precharged to the same pressure that you plan on running the system at. For heating systems, they generally come from the factory precharged to 12 pounds.

Air eliminator - An air eliminator is used to remove air from the system, and generally sits directly above the expansion tank. This is simply a brass valve that's designed to expel any air that passes by. Air is what causes the noise in a heating system, and can also prevent the heat from coming out. When using radiators, any air in the system will become trapped in them, so they have to be bled every now and then. With in-floor heat, there's no way to get rid of the air, so that's why the air eliminator is needed.

Pump - A pump is used to circulate the water through the system. These are designed to quietly run year after year with a low power draw. Ideally, a pump will have shutoffs on both ends, so it's easy to replace without draining the system.

Relief valve - Water heaters have a relief valve that will open if the pressure gets too high. A boiler also needs a relief valve, though it's set to open at a lower pressure of around 30 pounds.

Unions - Unions are installed so that you can get into the system to work on it, or to replace something without having to cut the pipes.

Check valve - A check valve is a one-way valve that's used so the water can only flow in one direction. When needed, sometimes they can be included with one of the shutoffs at the end of a pump.

Pressure and temperature gauge - Every system should have a combination pressure and temperature gauge. You may also want another gauge to show the temperature of the water on the return line.

Shutoffs - Full-Port ball valves are used to manually shut off the water. Your system could have only one, or well over a dozen, depending on its design. They're used so you can shut off part of the system to make repairs, and for filling it. They can also be used to balance the system by partially shutting the valve, or as a mixing valve by installing it between the supply and the return line.

Faucets - Faucets are used for both filling and draining the system. Boiler drains could also used for this, which are faucets with a quarter turn on/off.

Zone valves - These are solenoid shutoff valves that open and close as the thermostats call for heat. This will allow you to supply the heat where it's needed.

Mixing valve - This is commonly used when you want to lower the temperature of the water, or need the water at two different temperatures. One example would be where hot water was needed for the radiators, and also water that's a little cooler for in-floor heat. The mixing valve allows the water from one pipe to flow into another, to lower the temperature to what's needed. On a boiler, the return water is mixed with water coming directly from the boiler. On systems where the water has to be cooled for household use, cold water is mixed with the hot.

Manifolds - Manifolds are used on each zone to connect the different loops of tubing to the supply and the return line.

Once you have the basic understanding of what's needed, you can keep the design simple, or make it as complicated as you want. This will also depend on the number of zones. Either way, every system will start with the boiler. Attached to it will be a relief valve, for safety, and close by, on the supply side, will be a combination pressure and temperature gauge. Whether or not there are unions and shutoffs at the boiler is up to you, and may depend on which type of pipe you're using.

From there, you'll have an air eliminator, which has a fitting for attaching a bladder style expansion tank beneath it, and **after** that goes the pump. Systems can vary quite a bit, and the number of pumps that are used is again up to you. There arc several ways to do this. You can have a single pump for the whole system, or one for every zone. There could also be primary and secondary loops, where the boiler has its own pump. Two of the systems shown on the following pages have a single zone and one pump. Another has one pump for five zones on the main system, and another pump for the auxiliary boiler. The last system has two pumps, with one for each zone, so there would still be some heat if one of the pumps break down,.

A mixing valve, if one is needed, is installed before the pump. This way, the returning water will be pulled in to lower the temperature.

Zone valves (solenoid shutoffs) are necessary when one pump is used for multiple zones. When doing this, each zone will have it's own thermostat and a solenoid shutoff. Anytime heat is called for, the pump will turn on, and the valve for that zone will open.

Check valves are sometimes needed in multiple zone systems. One, for instance, is the two-pump system shown on page 188. On that system, if only one of the pumps was running, besides pulling water from the boiler, it would also be trying to pull the water backwards through the other pump. By having a check valve at each pump, it prevents this from happening.

You're also going to need faucets or boiler drains (actually called a boiler drain valve) and a shutoff for draining and filling the system. In a multiple zone system, there should also be a shutoff on both the supply and the return side of each zone. This way, you can shut a zone down if there's a problem and allow the rest of the system to keep running.

A shutoff and a check valve are needed when the heating system is being connected to the main water supply, for filling it. In this case, the check valve prevents the water from going the wrong way, so the heating system can't contaminate the water for the house. On systems that are filled with antifreeze, I don't take any chances, and just have a faucet in the area so I can connect a hose to fill it.

Manifolds are used to connect the tubes for each zone. Each zone needs two manifolds. Commonly, one will have shutoffs, while the other doesn't, and they're available in different sizes, depending on how many loops of tubing each zone has. There are a couple of options here when using PEX tubing, as there are manifolds where the tubes are attached with crimp fittings, and others that have compression fittings.

A relay is used to turn the pump on when the thermostat calls for heat. On a one-zone system, sometimes all you have to do is to attach the wires from the thermostat, and then run the wire to the pump. Multiple zone systems will require a different setup, and may have more than one relay. I know very little about this, and have only followed other peoples instructions when working on the relays, so I can't help you on this one.

There are a couple of choices for the tubing used to heat floors. The most common is PEX, which is cross-linked polyethylene with an oxygen barrier. Another one that you don't see very often is Onix, which is sold by Watts. Onix looks like rubber fuel hose and has several advantages over PEX. One is that it's easier to work with, since it doesn't have memory like PEX, so you're not constantly dealing with tubing that's still curved from being rolled up. Another is that it's easy to attach, using either spring-loaded or screw clamps, and it's not affected by the sun. PEX isn't supposed to be exposed to direct sunlight for more than a few weeks. In my opinion, PEX can also be noisy. When I stay at my brother's cabin, I always notice when the heat first comes on, because I hear the tubes as they're expanding. The noise is coming from where the tubing runs through holes in the floor joists, not the floor itself. Other people don't seem to notice, so I'm probably just sensitive to it. One disadvantage of Onix is that it's quite expensive. It's also a little thicker for its size.

Depending on the floor, the tubing may be installed under the sheathing, or above it between wood strips. There are advantages and disadvantages to both methods. When used under tile, you also have the option of stapling the tubing to the upper surface of the sheathing, and then covering it with self-leveling mortar.

A pneumatic stapler is commonly used to staple the tubing to the sheathing. When going between the floor joists, the tubes will generally run down one side of a cavity, then turn around and come back on the other side. A series of holes will have to be drilled to get the tubing to the different floor cavities. Here you have to follow the rules concerning the size and location of the holes (page 446). Keep large holes away from the edge of the wall, even with standard floor joists. There's a lot of weight on the end of the joists, and holes would weaken them. Once the tubing is installed, you'll also have to insulate between the joists. Four inches of fiberglass insulation is recommended, with a gap between the tubing and the insulation. Friends of mine have also used foil-covered bubble wrap, instead of fiberglass.

On my brother's cabin, we attached 3/4 inch thick plywood strips to the floor and installed the tubing between them. Then we filled the area between the strips with mortar. This took a lot of time, but enough heat comes through to keep the cabin warm when it's way below zero, even though insulation wasn't installed between the floor joists. This also gave him the option of installing either hardwood floors or tile. Tongue and groove flooring was nailed directly to the plywood strips. Where tile was used, Durock was installed with screws and thinset before the tile went on.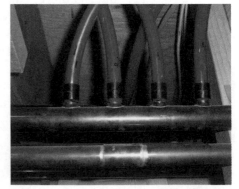

One mistake we made was to secure the tubing using plastic wire staples, since I'd read that they worked fine. On sections where the mortar wasn't installed yet, the staples broke within a couple of months, even when the heat wasn't on. So use the correct staples. On this job, we also had a problem with leaks where the tubing connects to the manifolds. A friend, who's in the business, recommended that we double up the crimp rings, and that stopped the problem.

Before you install the tubing, the length of each run (loop) should be predetermined. This is necessary because, in order for the water to flow equally between the different loops, the length of each one should be within 10 percent of the others on the same zone. When installing the tubing between the floor joists or plywood strips, determine what's needed to go across the room and then come back. Then multiply this by the number of cavities that you can do, while also taking into consideration the distance from the manifold to the starting point, and also to where you'll end up. When going between plywood strips, across and back is considered one cavity. This is where we screwed up on one of the loops at my brother's cabin. Because we didn't allow enough to get back to the return manifold, only part of one of the bathrooms has tubing in it.

A roll of 1/2 inch PEX is generally 250 - 300 feet long, which is about as far as you want to go on each run. When determining the length of each run, when going between the floor joists, you will seldom use the entire length of a roll. PEX can be spliced together, but I'd rather throw a little away than have a splice that I couldn't get to without destroying the floor, in case it leaked.

If one of the loops ends up shorter for some reason, partially turning off a shutoff could compensate for the difference in length.

# FILLING THE SYSTEM

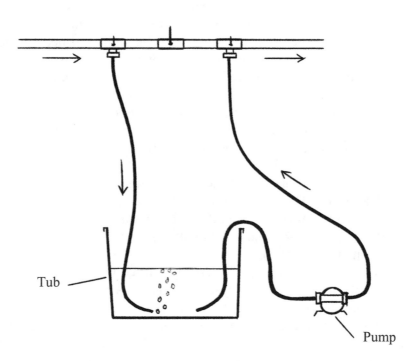

When designing an in-floor heating system, you'll need a way to fill it, and also a way to get the air out. This takes two faucets or boiler drains, and a shutoff that's between them. These faucets don't necessarily have to be close to each other. Sometimes they're installed just for this purpose, though many times you can use a shutoff or a faucet that's already there. Since every system is different, you'll have to find a spot where you can pump the water in, and then have it come out at the another point after it goes through the entire system. The reason for the shutoff is so the water can only go one way when it's in the "off "position.

The drawing above shows a simple way to fill the system, and for getting the air out. In order to do this, you'll need something to hold the water or antifreeze mix, three washing machine hoses, and a small utility pump. Depending on the size of the system, and whether or not antifreeze was being added, I've used anything from a joint compound bucket to a plastic 30-gallon trash can for the container (tub). As you can see, the hoses are connected to the faucets or the boiler valves on one end, while the other end is under water. Here, two hoses are used on the supply side, with the pump sitting between them. If you use a pump that sits in the water, you'll only need one hose for that side.

181

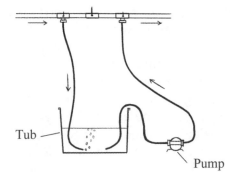

Once the hoses are attached and the container has water in it, turn the pump on so it starts filling the system. On most systems, if every zone was left wide open, some of the tubing wouldn't get filled, so it's best to do them one at a time. This is done by turning off the shutoffs on the other zones, or by just opening the solenoid shutoff on the zone that you want to fill. Solenoid shutoffs have a lever on one end, so they can be locked in the open position. Now that only one zone is open, the different loops of tubing are opened and closed one at a time by turning the shutoffs on the manifold.

As the water is being pumped in through each loop, the air will be forced out. You'll see this as bubbles coming up through the water in the container. Once the tube is filled, it will taper down to only a few bubbles every now and then as the rest of the air works its way out, until they finally stop. At that point, the loop is closed, and the next one is opened. After every loop has been filled, that zone is shut off and the next one is opened, and the process is repeated. Once I've gone through the entire system, I generally go through it one more time to see if I can get a little more air out. You'll never get all of it by doing this. That's one reason for installing the air eliminator.

Now that most of the air is out, the faucet on the return side is shut off so the pump can build up pressure in the system. Then the other faucet is closed, and the pump is turned off and the hoses are removed. The pumps I've used have maxed out at around ten pounds. The job is finished by adding water to the system until you've reached the correct pressure. The recommended pressure for most homes is 12 -15 pounds.

In-floor heating systems can also be filled by just using a faucet from the main water supply, as long as there's another hose that goes to the floor drain or a laundry tub. We used this method on the first system that I helped install, and ended up with a lot of air remaining in the tubes, so I can't recommend it. Here it would help to put the end of the hose in a bucket, so you can see the bubbles. The main water supply runs at a much higher pressure than the heating system, so turn the faucet only part way on, and keep your eye on the pressure gauge.

If the heating system was just installed, sometimes the first thing I do is to attach a hose to it, and then run water through it to clean it out. The water coming out could again go down a floor drain, laundry tub, or anywhere else that's handy. While doing this, the different zones are opened and closed to keep the water at a higher velocity. Then on systems that are being filled with a mixture of antifreeze, an air hose is used to blow out most of the water that remains in the lines.

When using antifreeze, the heating system has to be filled with a pump. In order to do this, first you have to calculate the amount of water that the system holds. This is done by determining the length of the tubing, the length of the pipes, and what it takes to fill the boiler itself. Tables on the internet will show how much each foot of the different size pipes and tubing will hold. Once you know how many gallons it takes, you just have to determine the correct ratio for the antifreeze, and then calculate the amount needed. Antifreeze used for in-floor heat is different than what's used in cars, and the same ratio doesn't offer the same freeze protection.

Now put that amount of antifreeze into the container, but only part of the water if the system was flushed out, in case there's still some water remaining in the lines. You want to make sure that all of the antifreeze gets pumped in. Then turn the pump on so it starts to fill the system. On a large system, antifreeze, and then water, will have to be added to the container when it gets low. Again, the loops are opened one at a time before moving on to the next zone, so you know each one is full. Then finish by adding water to the system until you have the correct pressure. Sometimes you won't be able to accurately calculate the amount of water that a system holds. In that case, you'll have to add the water and antifreeze in increments. For instance, for a 50/50 mix, add one gallon of antifreeze for every gallon of water.

When using a pump, some of the water and/or antifreeze will be left sitting in the container, since the hoses have to stay under the surface, so they don't pick up air. Because of this, the mixture could be different than you originally planned. If you use a small container, or tip a larger one to its side, the amount that's left in it shouldn't be much of a concern. If it is, then the ratio should be changed to compensate for it.

# FILLING A HEATING SYSTEM WITH RADIATORS

Heating systems with radiators are generally filled by opening the faucet that's connected to the main water supply. This will push the air into the radiators, where it can be let out by opening the bleeder valve on each radiator (using a radiator key). Then as each radiator is filled, the remaining air will be forced out until it's full, at which point you'll get a stream of water. Use a rag or a towel to catch any water that comes out, and then close the bleeder valve and move on to the next radiator. Older style radiators hold a lot of water, so this may take awhile. Start at the lowest radiator and work your way up. Here it helps to have a second person, with one manning the faucet and checking the pressure, and the other going from one radiator to the next. If there's more than one floor level, it's easier to keep in touch by phone, rather than yelling. If you're alone, bring the water up to the correct pressure or a little higher, then bleed, and repeat this if you run out of pressure. Once the radiators are filled, add water to the system until you've reached the correct pressure. Then turn the heating system on and open each bleeder valve one more time to see if there's any more air, and recheck the pressure.

## THE RIGHT WATER

It's important that the water used in a heating system has the proper pH to prevent corrosion or scaling. pH stands for potential Hydrogen, which is a measure of how acidic or alkaline the water is. A pH of 7 is considered neutral. When the number is lower than that, the water is acidic, and above that it's alkaline (basic). For a heating system to have a long life, the water should be alkaline to prevent corrosion, but not so much that foaming occurs or deposits build up inside the system, which could restrict the flow and also cut down on the amount of heat that is transferred. A common recommendation is for the water to have a pH of 8.5, though manufacturers of heating systems may vary on what they prefer. The materials used for installing the system could also determine what the proper pH is.

Natural, unpolluted rain or snow is slightly acidic and has a pH between 5 and 6. Pollution in the atmosphere (sulphur dioxide and nitrogen oxides) from coal burning and automobile engines makes it more acidic. So does decomposing leaves and pine needles. As the water passes over and through limestone and dolomite, minerals are dissolved in it, and the pH goes up. Hard water has a high mineral content. Soft water is the opposite.

City water (not softened) is often the best choice for a heating system. Where I live, in the Twin Cities in Minnesota, the water is considered good, right out of the tap. To make sure the correct water is used, it should be tested, or you could ask the building inspector or a furnace guy what's used in your area. When I worked on the heating system that's shown on the next page, containers of water were brought from home. Then I used a 12-volt battery powered pump to fill the system, which also built the pressure up to 10 pounds, and well water from a faucet was used to pump it up the rest of the way.

Just recently, I read that fresh water, which typically has a pH between 6.0 and 8.5, tends to stabilize to about an 8 pH in a pressurized, closed heating system, independent of beginning pH. This level is acceptable for all common system metals.

## GALVANIZED METAL

When using steel pipes to install a heating system, black pipe is generally used. Since it's a closed system, corrosion on the inside of the pipes shouldn't be a problem. When using antifreeze, make sure galvanized steel isn't included in the system. The zinc coating can react with the glycol in the antifreeze to form sludge. I've worked on systems that have a piece or two of galvanized pipe, and years later everything still seems fine, so I don't know what the tolerance on this is.

# INSTALLING THE HEATING SYSTEM

Once you get started on installing the heating system, you'll find that you can't always lay everything out as you planned because of size and space restrictions, so sometimes you'll have to make it up as you go. Just make sure that everything is in the proper order. On the systems that I've helped install, the pipes attached to the boiler were anywhere from 3/4 to 1 1/4 inch in size. The pipes supplying the individual zones were 3/4 inch. On the next few pages are several systems that have been installed to give you the basic idea.

This is the heating system for my brother's cabin. I'll describe it by starting at the boiler, which in this case is electric, and runs on off-peak hours. The boiler puts out just under 100,000 BTUs, and it needs three 60-amp 240-volt breakers to run it. On the supply side, there's a shutoff, followed by the expansion tank and air eliminator, and then the pump. There's also a temperature gauge that's visible through a hole on the side of the boiler. After the pump, the pipe splits off in different directions for five zones. Each zone has it's own solenoid shutoff and a boiler valve, followed by a shutoff. From there, the pipes go to the different manifolds that are connected to the loops of tubing that go throughout the building.

At the other end of the tubing are the return manifolds. On this system, the supply manifolds have shutoffs, while the return manifolds don't. From there, each zone has another shutoff, and then the pipes are connected together. After that, there are two faucets with a shutoff between them, a combination temperature and pressure gauge, and then another shutoff next to the boiler.

This is how it looks from the other side. Now you can see how each zone has it's own solenoid shutoff and a boiler valve. Connected to the solenoids are the wires from the relays. There's a lot going on in this area. Besides the heating system, there's also a 3 inch drain pipe, two supply lines for the water, and a gas pipe, so I tried to keep it all organized.

As with any other job, there are some things that I wish were done a little different. When I first started on this, the boiler and the pump were already in place, and manifolds were connected to the tubing in the basement floor. Pipes were also stubbed off for three other zones. That was a problem, since four zones were being added, so I had to solder another tee to the supply line, and then try to run the pipes in a manner that didn't look too out of place.

The main problem, though, is that the supply line next to the boiler is too short. When the auxiliary boiler was added, there was barely enough room for it. My brother would also like to change the pump, so there's a shutoff on each end, but I can't do it without moving some of the other pipes.

The lower photo shows the auxiliary boiler. This model runs on propane and gets vented out the wall. Since the other boiler is on off-peak hours, this one will start up whenever it's needed.

In the drawing on the next page, you can see how the auxiliary boiler is connected to the heating system. For this to work, the auxiliary boiler needs its own pump. In this case, there's already one inside of it. The pipes also have to be right next to each other (within 4 pipe diameters). When installing them, the inlet pipe has to be on the correct side, so the returning water will be pulled into the auxiliary boiler. If you did it the other way, the water that was just heated would be pulled back in and heated again. When the auxiliary boiler is on, both pumps have to be running at the same time. The main pump keeps the water flowing throughout the building, while the smaller pump is just used to supply the hot water from the auxiliary boiler.

On systems where the main boiler has its own pump, it would be installed in the same manner, with one pump used to supply the heat from the boiler on one loop, and the other pump(s) used to circulate the water through the loops of tubing and/or radiators on a different loop(s). I've read that condensing boilers are more efficient with primary and secondary loops.

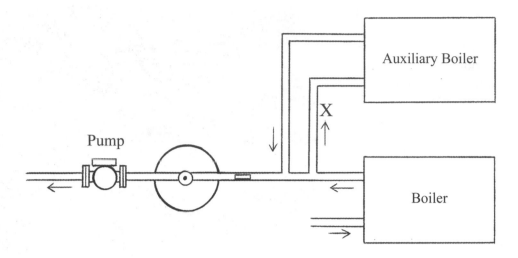

The X shows where the pump would go for the auxiliary boiler, if one was needed.

The next system has a dual-purpose water heater with a separate coil for heating the building. The foam-covered pipes are for the heating system, while the others are for the water supply. PEX tubing will be attached to the manifolds for the different fixtures, such as the shower, sink, etc.

On this setup, a high-velocity forced air heating system is in the attic, and hot water from the coil is pumped up to it, where it runs through a heat exchanger to heat the air. From there, the warm air passes through insulated, flexible ducts and comes out through registers at the ceiling.

Antifreeze was used in the first three systems that are shown here. With antifreeze, you'll have more problems with fittings that leak. When using it, I prefer to have soldered joints wherever possible, and use teflon tape instead of pipe thread compound, since antifreeze tends to sneak past the pipe thread compound over time.

186

This gives you a better look at how the system was installed. Starting at the upper hole on the side of the water heater, there's a union and a shutoff, followed by the air eliminator and the pressure tank. After that is the pump. This one has a shutoff on each end, so it can easily be replaced without draining the system. A combination pressure and temperature gauge is next, and to the right of it is a relief valve that has a pipe attached to it that ends near the floor, in case it goes off. Then the pipe goes up to the attic.

Here, everything is supported by brackets that were screwed to the wall. The return line isn't shown very well in either photo as it goes back to the water heater. In the previous one, you can see the temperature gauge where the pipe turns horizontal. There's also a union and a shutoff at the water heater.

A mixing valve was attached to the water heater because the temperature needed for the heating system is too hot for household use. In this case, it cools it down by mixing cold water with the hot.

Here's another system that uses a water heater for the boiler. On this one, it's a standard water heater that's being used to heat the floor in a pole barn. This system only has one zone, and it's about as simple as you can get.

Starting on the supply side is the pressure tank and the air eliminator, followed by the pump. After that are the manifolds and the tubing. In this case, there are eight loops, and a combination temperature and pressure gauge is installed between the manifolds. On the return side are the manifolds, followed by two boiler valves that have a shutoff between them. Then the pipe goes back to the water heater.

The only problem with this system is the amount of antifreeze that it required. Since the water heater doesn't have a separate coil, antifreeze had to be used to fill the entire water heater, plus the tubing in the floor.

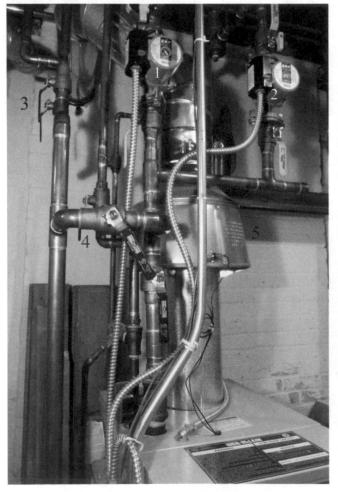

On the left is a standard non-condensing boiler. The original system had one zone. Now it has two zones, with a separate pump for each one. Both pumps (1 and 2) have a shutoff on each end, and they're teed into the supply line. There's also a check valve on each zone to prevent the water from flowing backwards through a pump. We also left room for another zone, in case one is needed in the future.

Radiators are used to heat the house, so there isn't an air eliminator or a separate water temperature gauge, and the expansion tank is next to the ceiling.

From the pumps, copper pipes go to the radiators, which are teed into the supply and the return lines, so each one can be adjusted as needed. On the return lines, shutoffs (3) were installed near the boiler.

Number 4 is a bypass valve that goes between the supply and the return line. This is pretty much the same as a mixing valve, and it's required on high volume systems, such as radiators.

Number 5 is a power damper that's used to prevent heat from going up the chimney when the boiler isn't on. Once the thermostat calls for heat, the damper will open. If it doesn't, the boiler won't come on.

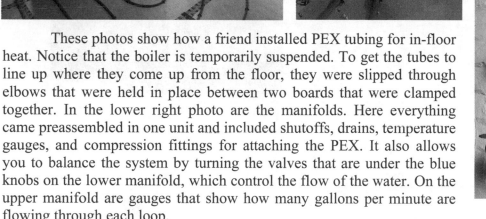

These photos show how a friend installed PEX tubing for in-floor heat. Notice that the boiler is temporarily suspended. To get the tubes to line up where they come up from the floor, they were slipped through elbows that were held in place between two boards that were clamped together. In the lower right photo are the manifolds. Here everything came preassembled in one unit and included shutoffs, drains, temperature gauges, and compression fittings for attaching the PEX. It also allows you to balance the system by turning the valves that are under the blue knobs on the lower manifold, which control the flow of the water. On the upper manifold are gauges that show how many gallons per minute are flowing through each loop.

## INSULATING THE BASEMENT FLOOR

No matter which type of heating system you have, you'll get better results if the house is properly insulated and any air leaks have been taken care of. This is just common sense, as less heat will be needed, and you won't have as many problems with areas that are colder. Where I live, basement floors generally aren't insulated unless they're getting in-floor heat, in which case, foam insulation will be installed beneath the concrete. From what I've seen, by insulating the floor, little heat is necessary. In some cases, I'm not sure if it's even worth the time and the money for installing the tubing for in-floor heat. When saying this, I'm talking about buildings that have more than one story and are heated all winter.

To back this up, I'll use two of my brother's places as examples. One was in Duluth, Minnesota. On this house, an addition was put on, and the basement floor was insulated with 2 inches of foam. The original plan for the basement was to use baseboard heat, so pipes had been installed and stubbed off for that purpose. In the end, the baseboards were never installed. The heat coming from the boiler, the water heater, and an enclosed hot tub that had a thin cover kept the temperature at a comfortable level without any extra heat. If you took away the hot tub, a small radiator or a couple of short baseboards would have been all that it needed. The other place is his cabin, which is also in northern Minnesota. Here the basement floor is insulated with 2 inches of foam, and in-floor heat was installed. The interesting thing about this one is that heat is seldom needed for the concrete floor. Enough heat radiates down from the level above to keep the basement comfortable. In both of these places, the walls are well insulated.

A friend of mine built a house around eight years ago. This is a pretty nice house, costing more than seven hundred thousand dollars to build. One problem with it is that the basement is too cold in the winter. More than half of it is above ground, yet insulation wasn't installed under the slab because he has forced air heat. I talked to the building inspector about this, and also the contractor who built the house, and neither one thought it was necessary. As far as I'm concerned, they're both wrong.

189

A drip tee is needed where the gas line attaches to the boiler, furnace, or a water heater. It's purpose is to catch any particles that could plug an orifice.

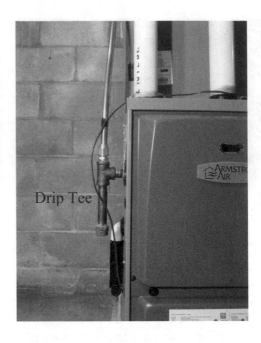

Drip Tee

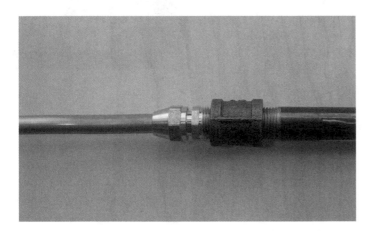

When flexible copper tubing is used for gas, it's connected with a flare fitting, as shown in these photos. A flaring tool is used to shape the end of the pipe to match the fitting. The lower left photo shows how it goes together. Sometimes a flare fitting will leak, no matter how tight it is. It's generally caused by a scratch on the fitting, or the flare itself. This is easy to fix. Just apply a thin layer of pipe thread compound to the fitting where the flared end will make contact (X).

X

This photo shows the manifolds on a system where Onix tubing was used. Here everything was mounted to the wall and then hidden behind doors.

Foil tape should be used when sealing the joints on furnace ducts. You would think that standard duct tape would be the best choice for this, since that's what it's called, but that's not the case. Standard duct tape works on almost everything, except furnace ducts, because it tends to come off after a while.

Here are three types of tip snips that are used for cutting sheet metal. Starting on the left is a left-cut offset aviation snip (red), followed by a straight-cut aviation snip, and a right-cut offset aviation snip (green). I cut right-handed, and use a left-cut offset snip for most jobs. It's good for going in a straight line, and is also used when you're cutting a hole in something, going counter clockwise The right-cut version (green) is used for going in a clockwise direction.

Shown here are frost-free vents, which are used to cover the vent pipes that go through the roof. The vents comes in standard and steep-pitch, and consist of two parts that includes a base and a cap that goes over the pipe. When installing them, the base should be adjusted so the vent is plumb. On the left is the steep-pitch version, and it's adjusted about as far as it can go on a roof with a 14-12 pitch. On the right is the standard version. This one was adjusted so it's about as flat as it can go on a roof with a 3-12 pitch.

# PILOT LIGHTS

Every gas appliance in your home either has a pilot light or uses electronic ignition to light the burner(s). Those with electronic ignition put out a series of sparks until the flame is lit. That's what the clicking noise is when you light the burner on a modern kitchen stove. Other appliances that have them are gas driers and newer furnaces. A manual form of electronic ignition is the push-button igniter on a gas grill.

Any gas appliance that doesn't have electronic ignition has to have some type of pilot light. Older kitchen stoves either have a pilot light in the center, or one near each burner. There may also be another one for the oven. Sometimes the pilot light will get blown out. There isn't any real danger if this happens. You'll smell gas, but the gas isn't going to hurt you, and there isn't enough here to blow up. The reason that gas smells the way it does is because mercaptan was added to it by the gas company. Natural gas itself, or propane, has no odor.

This type of pilot light is fine for appliances that you turn on manually, but doesn't work where the flame has to turn on and off by itself. That's where the gas valve comes in. Appliances that have them, such as water heaters and furnaces, are thermostatically controlled, so the burner only comes on when needed.

As a safety mechanism, gas valves are designed to shut off the gas if the pilot light goes out. This is done by using a thermocouple that's right next to the pilot light. One is shown in the upper photo (just above the flame) and also in the photo on the left. The heat from the flame (pilot light) causes the thermocouple to generate a small amount of electricity. The electricity goes to a coil that holds the gas valve open. If the pilot light goes out, the gas shuts off within seconds.

Furnaces, and also some gas fireplaces, have remote thermostats. This requires more electricity. Furnaces have a transformer that provides electricity for the thermostat, but gas fireplaces use a thermopile. A thermopile is made by stacking thermocouples together, so more electricity is produced. The photo on the right shows the pilot light for a gas fireplace. Here number 1 is the thermocouple, number 2 is a thermopile, and number 3 is the igniter.

To light this type of pilot light, you start by turning the knob so it's pointed towards PILOT. In this position, you should be able to press it down. If so, press the knob down, and then hold it there as you light the flame with either a match or a lighter. Some appliances may also have a separate button that you push down. Gas valves may also have a push-button igniter. If yours does, then push the button every few seconds until the flame is lit. If the appliance has been off for a long time, it may take a while (several matches) for it to light.

On water heaters or furnaces, the pilot light could be way back. If so, you might have to use one of those lighters that are made for lighting a grill, or you may have to attach the match to a wire to reach back far enough.

Once the flame is lit, you'll have to hold the knob down until the thermocouple warms up, which is generally around half a minute. Then let it back up. If the flame goes out, push the knob down again, and relight the pilot. On some appliances it has to be held down much longer than on others. Once the flame stays lit, turn the knob to the ON position. The burner should come on at this time, provided the thermostat is calling for heat.

Let's say that you've just replaced the gas line for an appliance, and now, even though you held the button down for some time, the pilot still won't light. This is probably caused by the gas line being full of air. There are a couple of ways to deal with this. One is to keep holding the button down, and then try to light the flame every so many seconds. This will eventually work, but it might take awhile if the line is very long. You could also loosen the cap on the end of the gas line, or loosen the nut on a flared fitting, next to the appliance, until you start to smell gas. Then retighten it, and try to light the pilot again.

If you can get the pilot to light, but it keeps going out when you let up on the button, you may have a bad thermocouple. You should be able to find one at the hardware store or local building center. Where I used to live, sometimes I'd have to hold the button down for several minutes when lighting the pilot on the furnace. But once it was lit, it stayed on all winter.

For those of you that are interested in doing their own work, the output on a thermocouple should be 25 - 30 millivolts. On a thermopile, it should be 400 - 450 millivolts at the thermopile terminals with the thermostat off, and 150 - 250 millivolts with the thermostat on. 500 millivolts is 1/2 of a volt.

In order for a thermocouple or a thermopile to work correctly, the pilot light has to put out enough heat. If the flame is too small or the wrong color, the orifice could be partially plugged with rust, dirt, spider webs, etc.

The following pages go over how to do a heat loss calculation for installing a furnace. Though you may be tempted to skip over this section, by going through it, you might learn something that will help when remodeling or working on the house. For instance, when a concrete slab is near ground level in a cold climate, the best place to insulate it is along the outer edge. Another interesting thing is that the net insulation value of a framed wall or ceiling is less than the rated value of the insulation itself when insulating between the studs, joists, or the rafters.

# HEAT LOSS CALCULATION

When a permit is required for installing a new furnace, a heat loss calculation may have to be done. This will help determine the correct size furnace by calculating the heat loss for every exterior surface on the building. This includes the walls, ceilings, floor, and any windows or doors. Then the heat that will be lost through air infiltration is added to the other numbers to come up with the amount of BTUs (British thermal units) per hour that will be needed to heat the house on a cold winter night.

How complicated this is can vary quite a bit. Sometimes there will be a simple form where all you have to do is to fill in the square footage for everything. The U values are already provided, so you just have to pick the one that best applies. In other areas, although I'd don't think they'd admit it, they try to make it more difficult for you to do it on your own. That's how it is where I live. I also know from personal experience that homeowners are sometimes held to a higher standard than if the furnace was being installed by a professional.

If you're installing your own furnace, there are several options for doing the heat loss calculation. You could pay someone to do it. You can pay for the use of a one-time calculation on the internet, or you could just do it yourself. Paying someone else will probably cost at least several hundred dollars. And if you do the calculation on the internet, you'll still have do all the measuring. Since I wanted to learn how to do this, I bought a copy of Manual J Residential Load Calculation, and also spent some time on the internet trying to figure it out. At this point, I'd say that I know just enough on the subject to describe the basics of how it's done, so I'll do the heat loss calculation on a small building to go over the process.

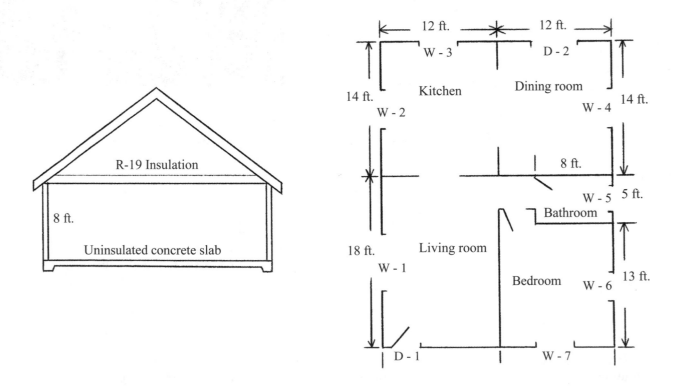

The house shown above only has five rooms. The floor is a concrete slab that's on grade, and the ceilings are flat, with the insulation laid out across the attic floor. To do the calculation, I'll determine the heat loss for each individual room. Then I'll calculate the heat loss from air infiltration, and add everything together to get the total. The reason I'm doing each room separately is because that's how the form is that they give you to fill out in St. Paul, Minnesota. I've seen other forms where the house is just broken up into the different levels.

194

To begin, first you have to know the outdoor design temperature for your area. This temperature is what's considered a cold winter night where you live. You can look this up, or ask the building inspector. Temperatures are listed for every area of the country. Where I live, the number is 15 degrees below zero. The numbers shown by furnace companies may be slightly different from that of your local government. Once you have the number for your area, subtract it from 70 degrees, which is the indoor design temperature. This gives you the heat temperature difference for your area. Mine is 85 degrees.

|  |  |
|---|---|
| 70 degrees | Indoor Design Temperature |
| - 15 below zero | St. Paul, MN. Outdoor Design Temperature |
| = 85 degrees | Heat Temperature Difference |

Now you need the U values for everything. I've read that U factor is actually the correct term, but it's called U value more often than not, so that's what I'll use. The U value is the inverse of the R value. For instance, if the R value of a door is 5, then the U value is .20. And if the R value of a wall is 10, then the U value is .10. To find the U value, divide 1 by the R value. To find the R value, divide 1 by the U value. Windows are already ready rated in U values. A window that has a U value of .30 has an R value of 3.33. Once you start looking up R values and U values, you'll find that the numbers from one source may be different from that of another.

Following are some basic U values from the Manual J Residential Load Calculation. These are default values. Where possible, you'd be more exact. For instance, new windows have labels showing their U value, so you'd use that number instead of what's listed below. The U values are for the whole window unit, not just the glass. The U values for walls or vaulted ceilings take into account the studs or rafters, insulation, sheetrock, sheathing, and the siding or shingles. When looking up R values and U values, windows are listed under Fenestration, and doors and walls are listed under Opaque Panels.

## R VALUES PER INCH FOR INSULATION

Cellulose  R = 3.40

Loose Fiberglass  3.00

Fiberglass Blanket  3.14

Mineral Wool  2.60

Loose Vermiculite  2.13

## CEILINGS BELOW ROOF JOISTS

(vaulted ceilings)

Foam board insulation    R-10 U = 0.076

Blanket or loose fill insulation

| R-11 | 0.084 | R-21 | 0.047 |
|---|---|---|---|
| R-13 | 0.076 | R-30 | 0.034 |
| R-15 | 0.069 | R-38 | 0.029 |
| R-19 | 0.051 | | |

## WALLS

2x4 studs on 16 inch centers

R-11 insulation   U = 0.097

R-13   0.091

R-15   0.086

2x6 studs  R-19   0.068

R-21   0.065

## CEILINGS UNDER ATTIC

Insulation

| None U = 0.408 | R-19 | 0.049 | R-30 | 0.032 |
|---|---|---|---|---|
| R-11   0.081 | R-21 | 0.044 | R-38 | 0.026 |
| R-13   0.070 | R-25 | 0.038 | R-44 | 0.022 |
| R-15   0.061 | R-28 | 0.034 | R-56 | 0.018 |

195

## CLEAR GLASS WINDOWS

(wood, wood with vinyl, or metal cladding)

Single pane, fixed sash    $U = 0.90$

Single pane, operable    0.98

Single pane window with storm    0.57

Double pane operable window
or sliding glass door    0.57

Double pane, fixed sash    0.56

* French doors    0.60

* the window category is used when the
glass area is greater than 50%

## CONCRETE FLOOR

Insulation under floor
2 feet or more below grade,  R-3 or higher

width of shortest side of slab   20 ft.  $U = 0.019$

24 ft.    0.017

28 ft.    0.015

## DOORS

Solid core wood    $U = 0.39$

Solid core wood with metal storm door    0.28

Wood panel door    0.54

Wood panel door with metal storm    0.36

Metal door with polyurethane core    0.29

Metal door with polyurethane core    0.17
and metal storm door

## CONCRETE FLOOR

2 feet or more below grade
No insulation

width of shortest side of slab   20 ft.   $U = 0.027$

24ft.    0.025

28 ft.    0.022

## CONCRETE FLOOR

(**F values** are given for concrete slabs on grade)

Slab on grade, no insulation

heavy moist soil   $F = 1.358$

heavy dry or light wet soil    1.180

light dry soil    0.989

## CONCRETE FLOOR

Slab on grade, insulation covers outside
edge and extends down 3 feet          R-5  heavy moist soil   $F = 0.589$

heavy dry or light wet soil    0.449

light dry soil    0.289

R-10  heavy moist soil    0.481

heavy dry or light wet soil    0.355

light dry soil    0.21

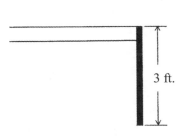

3 ft.

## CONCRETE FLOOR

Slab on grade, insulation
extends 4 feet under slab

R-5  heavy moist soil   F = 1.266

heavy dry or light wet soil   1.135

light dry soil   0.980

R-10  heavy moist soil   1.221

heavy dry or light wet soil   1.108

light dry soil   0.937

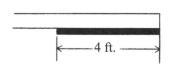

## CONCRETE FLOOR

Slab on grade, insulation covers edge
and extends 4 feet under slab,

R-5  heavy moist soil   F = 0.574

heavy dry or light wet soil   0.442

light dry soil   0.287

R-10  heavy moist soil   0.456

heavy dry or light wet soil   0.343

light dry soil   0.208

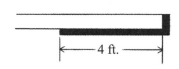

When determining the heat loss for basement walls that are below grade, the walls are broken down into sections, and for each section you'll use a different U value as the wall gets farther below grade. In the Manual J, foundation walls that are less than 2 feet below grade are part of the above-grade wall. Walls that are deeper than two feet are broken down into 2 foot strips. Commonly the ground will be sloped along the edge of a basement wall. In that case, you'd average out the depth on that part of the wall.

The thickness of the basement wall doesn't matter, since the same numbers are used regardless of the size of the blocks that were used. I would assume that you use the filled-core numbers for a poured concrete wall, as I don't see any numbers that are specific for this type of wall.

## BASEMENT WALLS

Block wall, above grade, no interior
or exterior finish

open core   U = 0.584

filled core         0.304

## BASEMENT WALLS

Block wall, above grade, board insulation
plus interior finish, open core

| with stucco or siding | with brick veneer |
|---|---|
| R - 3   U = 0.167 | R - 3   0.174 |
| R - 4   0.143 | R - 4   0.148 |
| R - 5   0.125 | R - 5   0.129 |
| R - 7.5   0.095 | R - 7.5   0.097 |
| R - 10   0.077 | R - 10   0.078 |

## BASEMENT WALLS

Block wall, above grade, board insulation
plus interior finish, filled core

| stucco or siding | with brick veneer |
|---|---|
| R - 3   U = 0.132 | 0.136 |
| R - 4   0.017 | 0.120 |
| R - 5   0.105 | 0.107 |
| R - 7.5   0.083 | 0.084 |
| R - 10   0.069 | 0.070 |

## BASEMENT WALLS

Block wall, above grade plus 2x4 wall
finished interior, no exterior finish

| | open core | filled core |
|---|---|---|
| R - 11 insulation  U = 0.103 | 0.088 | |
| R - 13   0.096 | 0.082 | |

## BASEMENT WALLS

| Block wall, below grade, no interior or exterior finish, | | 2' | 4' | 6' | 8' |
|---|---|---|---|---|---|
| | open core | 0.257 | 0.185 | 0.0148 | 0.125 |
| | filled core | 0.170 | 0.132 | 0.110 | 0.095 |

## BASEMENT WALLS

| Block wall, below grade, no interior or exterior finish, | 2' | 4' | 6' | 8' |
|---|---|---|---|---|
| R - 4 closed cell foam board to floor, open core | 0.114 | 0.094 | 0.081 | 0.072 |
| filled core | 0.094 | 0.079 | 0.069 | 0.062 |
| R - 8 closed cell foam board to floor, open core | 0.074 | 0.064 | 0.057 | 0.052 |
| filled core | 0.065 | 0.057 | 0.052 | 0.047 |

## BASEMENT WALLS

| Block wall, below grade, 2x4 stud wall plus interior finish | 2' | 4' | 6' | 8' |
|---|---|---|---|---|
| R - 11 insulation to floor, open core | 0.074 | 0.064 | 0.057 | 0.052 |
| filled core | 0.065 | 0.057 | 0.052 | 0.047 |
| R - 13 insulation to floor, open core | 0.070 | 0.061 | 0.055 | 0.050 |
| filled core | 0.061 | 0.054 | 0.049 | 0.045 |

## FLOOR OVER CRAWL SPACES

No insulation, tile or wood   U = 0.368

| carpet | 0.295 | R-19 | 0.049 |
|---|---|---|---|
| R-11 | 0.073 | R-21 | 0.045 |
| R-13 | 0.065 | R-30 | 0.034 |
| R-15 | 0.058 | R-38 | 0.029 |

Now that you know some of the basic U values, we'll get started on the heat loss calculation. I'll begin by measuring the exterior walls, and also the length and the width of each room. While doing this, I also measure the windows and doors. In this case, there's only floor level, and each room is 8 feet in height.

The walls are measured on the outside of the building. The length of the walls is measured to the nearest foot. The height is measured to the nearest 1/2 foot. Use the outside dimensions for exposed walls, and the centerline dimensions for interior partitions. I don't know if the framing for the floors, between levels, is considered an interior partition. Either way, it should be included somehow in the measurements, on either one or both floor levels.

Measurements are changed to decimals before multiplying. For instance, 9 feet 6 inches would be 9.5, 3 feet 4 inches would be 3.33, and 4 foot 3 inches would be 4.25. To find the square footage of a triangular area, multiply the length by half the height.

## SPECIFICATIONS FOR THE BUILDING

Outdoor Design Temperature is 20 degrees, so the Heat Temperature Difference is 50 degrees.

Walls are framed with 2x4s on 16 inch centers with R-11 insulation, U value is 0.097

Attic is insulated with 6 inch, R-19 fiberglass insulation, U value is 0.049

Slab is on grade and not insulated, the soil is light and dry, F value is 0.989

Windows are double pane casements, unknown quality, U value 0.57 will be used

Entry door is metal with a polyurethane core, unknown quality, U value 0.29 will be used

Patio door is a double pane sliding glass door, unknown quality, U value 0.57 will be used

|   |   | Exterior Walls | Windows | Doors |
|---|---|---|---|---|
| 1 | Living Room | 12 ft, 18 ft | 6ft W x 4ft H (center fixed) | 3 ft W x 7 ft H |
| 2 | Kitchen | 14 ft, 12 ft | 4 ft W x 4ft H, 4 ft W x 4 ft H | |
| 3 | Dining Room | 12 ft, 14 ft | 4 ft W x 4 ft H | 5 ft W x 7 ft H |
| 4 | Bathroom | 5 ft | 3 ft W x 1 1/2 ft H | |
| 5 | Bedroom | 13 ft, 12 ft | 3 ft W x 4 ft H, 4 ft W x 4 ft | |

Starting with the living room, you can see that it has two walls on the exterior of the building. To begin, I'll calculate the square footage for each exterior wall, and then subtract the area of the rough opening for the window and the door. Then I'll multiply those numbers by the heat temperature difference (50 degrees), and also by the U value (0.097) to come up with the heat loss, in BTUs, for each wall.

**Square Footage  x  Heat Temperature Difference  x  U Value  =  BTUs**

**HEAT LOSS CALCULATION**

The heat loss for the windows and doors is done in the same manner. Default U values will be used, since the manufacturers are unknown.

Here the attic is insulated with 6 inches of R-19 fiberglass, so I'll use the proper U value that's shown in "Ceilings Under Attics".

This house has a concrete slab on grade for the floor. For this, F values are used instead of U values. To determine the heat loss, the F value is multiplied by the heat loss factor, and also the length of the edge of the slab (in feet).

**Edge Of Slab (In Feet) x Heat Temperature Difference x F Value = BTUs**

## LIVING ROOM

|  | BTUs |
|---|---|
| Wall 1   12 x 8 = 96   minus 21 (door) = 75 square ft.    75 x 50 x 0.097 = 363.75 | 364 |
| Wall 2   18 x 8 = 144   minus 24 (window) = 120 square ft.   120 x 50 x 0.097 = 582 | 582 |
| Window   6 x 4 = 24 square ft.    24 x 50 x 0.57 = 684 | 684 |
| Door   3 x 7 = 21 square ft.    21 x 50 x 0.29 = 304.5 | 305 |
| Ceiling   12 x 18 = 216 square ft.    216 x 50 x 0.049 = 529.2 | 529 |
| Floor   12 + 18 = 30 ft.   30 x 50 x 0.989 = 1483.5 | + 1484 |
| Total | **3948** |

## KITCHEN

|  | BTUs |
|---|---|
| Wall 1   14 x 8 = 112 minus 16 = 96 square ft.    96 x 50 x 0.097 = 465.6 | 466 |
| Wall 2   12 x 8 = 96 minus 16 = 80 square ft.    80 x 50 x 0.097 = 388 | 388 |
| Window 1   4 x 4 = 16 square ft.    16 x 50 x 0.57 = 456 | 456 |
| Window 2   4 x 4 = 16 square ft.    16 x 50 x 0.57 = 456 | 456 |
| Ceiling   14 x 12 = 168 square ft.    168 x 50 x 0.049 = 411.6 | 412 |
| Floor   14 + 12 = 26 ft.    26 x 50 x 0.989 = 1285.7 | + 1286 |
| Total | **3464** |

## DINING ROOM

|  | BTUs |
|---|---|
| Wall 1   12 x 8 = 96 minus 35 = 61 square ft.    61 x 50 x 0.097 = 295.85 | 296 |
| Wall 2   14 x 8 = 112 minus 16 = 96 square ft.    96 x 50 x 0.097 = 465.6 | 466 |
| Patio Door   5 x 7 = 35 square ft.    35 x 50 x 0.57 = 997.5 | 998 |
| Window   4 x 4 = 16 square ft.    16 x 50 x 0.57 = 456 | 456 |

Ceiling   12 x 14 = 168 square ft.     168 x 50 x 0.049 = 411.6          412

Floor   12 + 14 = 26 ft.     26 x 50 x 0.989 = 1285.7               + 1286

                                                    Total     **3914**


## BATHROOM

                                                              BTUs

Wall   5.5 x 8 = 44 minus 4.5 = 39.5 square ft.     39.5 x 50 x 0.097 = 191.575          192

Window   3 x 1.5 = 4.5 square ft.     4.5 x 50 x 0.57 = 128.25          128

Ceiling 5.5 x 8 = 44 square ft.     44 x 50 x 0.049 = 107.8          108

Floor   5.5 ft.     5.5 x 50 x 0.989 = 271.975               + 272

                                                    Total     **700**


## BEDROOM

                                                              BTUs

Wall 1   13 x 8 = 104 minus 12 = 92 square ft.     92 x 50 x 0.097 = 446.2          446

Wall 2   12 x 8 = 96 minus 16 = 80 square ft.     80 x 50 x 0.097 = 388          388

Window 1   3 x 4 = 12 square ft.     12 x 50 x 0.57 = 342          342

Window 2   4 x 4 = 16 square ft.     16 x 50 x 0.57 = 456          456

Ceiling   18 x 12 = 216 - 44 (bathroom) = 172 square ft.     172 x 50 x 0.049 = 421.4          421

Floor   13 + 12 = 25 ft.     23 x 50 x 0.989 = 1236.25               + 1236

                                                    Total     **3,289**


                                                              3948
                                                              3464
                                                              3914
                                                              700
                                                            + 3289

                Total BTUs of heat lost through exterior surfaces     **15,315**


   We still have to determine the amount of heat that will be lost through air infiltration. There are several ways to do this. One is to pick the air change per hour value that best represents the quality of construction, and then use this number to calculate the amount of heat that will be lost. Another way is the crack method, where you add up the distance around the windows and doors. Other options are to run a blower door test or to use the component leakage area method.

# AIR CHANGE PER HOUR METHOD

To find the heat loss using the first method, you multiply the square area of the building by the height to get the cubic feet, and then multiply that by the value for the air changes per hour. When doing this, you're only concerned with the living space in the building. For instance, the attic wouldn't be counted if it wasn't being heated.

Below are some default air change values for houses with three or four exposures, and descriptions, also from the Manual J. These may not even be needed if the form that you fill out already has a default number for air infiltration. One form that I downloaded from the internet uses 0.52 for the air change per hour value. Another uses 1.2 for houses built before1980, and .6 for houses build after 1980.

| Air Changes Per Hour  (Heating) | | | | | | | | | |
|---|---|---|---|---|---|---|---|---|---|
| Floor area of heated space (square foot) | Tight | | Semi-Tight | | Average | | Semi-Loose | | Loose | |
| | 1 or 2 - Story Construction | | | | | | | | | |
| | 1 | 2 | 1 | 2 | 1 | 2 | 1 | 2 | 1 | 2 |
| 900 or Less | 0.21 | 0.27 | 0.41 | 0.53 | 0.61 | 0.79 | 0.95 | 1.23 | 1.29 | 1.67 |
| 901 - 1500 | 0.16 | 0.20 | 0.31 | 0.39 | 0.45 | 0.58 | 0.70 | 0.90 | 0.94 | 1.22 |
| 1501 - 2000 | 0.14 | 0.18 | 0.26 | 0.34 | 0.38 | 0.50 | 0.59 | 0.77 | 0.80 | 1.04 |
| 2001 - 3000 | 0.11 | 0.15 | 0.22 | 0.28 | 0.32 | 0.41 | 0.49 | 0.63 | 0.66 | 0.85 |
| 3000 > | 0.10 | 0.13 | 0.19 | 0.25 | .28 | 0.37 | 0.43 | 0.56 | 0.58 | 0.75 |

Description of Tight:  All structural panels, joints, corners, cracks and penetrations are meticulously sealed with air barrier film, tape or caulk. Windows and doors are rated at less than 0.25 CFM (per running foot of crack at 25 mph wind speed). Recessed lights, if any, have a negligible amount of leakage around the fixture. Exhaust fans for bathrooms, and kitchen and dryer vents, have backdraft dampers. All furnaces, water heaters, dryers, etc. have to be direct vent. No range hoods over 150 CFM, unless they have their own source of makeup air. Any fireplaces get combustion air from the outdoors, and have tight glass doors.

Average:  All structural panels, joints, corners, cracks and penetrations are reasonably sealed with air barrier film, tape or caulk. Windows and doors are rated between 0.25 and 0.50 CFM. Recessed lights, if any, have a minor amount of leakage around the fixture. Exhaust fans for bathrooms, and kitchen and dryer vents, have backdraft dampers. No envelope openings are required for combustion air. No range hoods over 150 CFM, unless they have their own source of makeup air. Fireplaces can receive combustion air from the indoors, but have tight glass doors and a chimney damper.

Loose:  Inadequate sealing of corners, cracks, and penetrations, and/or a large amount of leakage around recessed lights. Windows and doors are unrated, or have a rating greater than 0.50 CFM. Some of the exhaust fans or the dryer vent, may not have backdraft dampers. Range hoods over 150 CFM, without their own source of makeup air, still require a way to get it. Fireplaces receive combustion air from indoors and do not have glass doors or a chimney damper.

If your house is somewhere in between, use semi-tight or semi-loose. Based on these descriptions, I've never worked on a house that would be considered tight. Most would probably only rate a little above average to semi-tight for air infiltration. Newer homes tend to have a lot of recessed lights, and many are built with poor workmanship. Since the house that we're doing the heat loss calculation on doesn't actually exist, I'll use 0.52 for the air change per hour value.

**Width x Length x Height x Air Change Value = Infiltration Loss In BTUs**

This is the equation used to come up with the heat loss when using the air exchange method, and the answer that I came up with.

$$24 \times 32 \times 8 \times 0.52 = \mathbf{3194.88} \text{ BTUs}$$

For one fireplace, add 13 cubic feet per minute for Semi-Tight, 20 for Average, 27 for Semi-Loose, and 33 for Loose. For an additional fireplace, add 7 CFM to these numbers. If more than that, add 10 CFM (total) to the first number. To convert this to something that you can use, multiply the number by 60. Then divide that by the cubic feet of the house. The answer is added to the air change value. The calculation for the house that we're on, with one fireplace, would be: 20 x 60 divided by 6144 = 0.19 This would be added to the 0.52, so the value would now be 0.71, assuming the construction of the house is average.

# CRACK METHOD

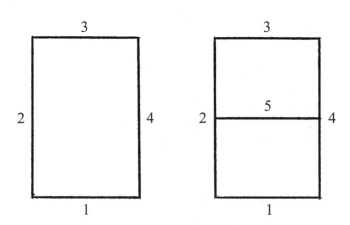

Next is the crack method, which is used for the heat calculation form in St. Paul. To do this, you add up the distance (in feet) around the perimeter of the windows and doors, and then use those numbers in the calculation. On windows, you measure around the outside edge of the sashes. On a double hung window, you also include where the sashes overlap. Patio doors are done the same way.

To keep it simple, I'll do all of them at one time, instead of doing each room separately. I'm also going to use the outside measurements as the perimeter, since there isn't anything to actually measure.

Some of the following numbers are from The Handbook of Air Conditioning, Heating and Ventilation. Here it shows a rating of 39 cubic feet per hour for the average double hung window that isn't weather stripped. Another source gives the same window a rating of 59 cfh. Casement windows are also given the same rating as a double-hung, but casements are generally considered to be tighter. The rating for a double hung window, with a storm, wasn't shown in the book, but concerning exterior doors, it said weather stripping will cut down on air infiltration by about half. Adding a storm will also cut air infiltration by about half, whether it's weather stripped or not.

New windows and doors have much better ratings for air infiltration than the default numbers shown on the next page. They're now required to have a rating of no more than .30 cubic feet per minute, which is 18 cubic feet per hour when you multiply .30 by 60. The last casement window that I installed had a rating of 12 cubic feet per hour. Some are lower than that.

**HEAT LOSS CALCULATION**

Finding the U values and the air infiltration rating for windows and doors can be difficult sometimes. Finding the U value is much easier on windows, and many times it's right on the label. Generally the air infiltration rating isn't shown, and you may not even be able to find it. In that case, I'd use 18 cubic feet per hour (.30 cfm) as the default number on new windows and doors. On older ones, or where the weather stripping isn't as good, I'd use the numbers below.

Double hung window, no weather stripping,   39 cfh  (cubic feet per hour)

with weather stripping,   24 cfh

Casement, no weather stripping   39 cfh

Casement, with weather stripping   24 cfh

Exterior doors, weather stripped, no storm   56 cfh   with storm   28 cfh

French doors   56 cfh

Sliding patio door   56cfh    I couldn't find a default number, so I used the same one as the other doors.

New sliding doors are rated at .30 cubic feet per minute or less. (18 cfh)

**0.018 x Q x Heat Temperature Difference x Crack Length = BTUs**

This is the calculation that's used to come up with the heat loss from air infiltration, using the crack method. The first number is the specific heat of air. Q is the air leakage rating for that particular window, or door, in cubic feet per hour. Below are the actual calculations.

|  |  | BTUs |
|---|---|---|
| Entry door   3 + 7 + 3 + 7 = 20ft.    0.018 x 56 x 50 x 20 = 1008 | | 1008 |
| Window 1   2 + 4 + 2 + 4 + 2 + 4 + 2 + 4 = 24ft.    0.018 x 24 x 50 x 24 = 518.4 | | 518 |
| Window 2   2 + 4 + 2 + 4 + 2 + 4 + 2 + 4 = 24ft.    0.018 x 24 x 50 x 24 = 518.4 | | 518 |
| Window 3   2 + 4 + 2 + 4 + 2 + 4 + 2 + 4 = 24ft.    0.018 x 24 x 50 x 24 = 518.4 | | 518 |
| Patio door   2.5 + 7 + 2.5 + 7 + 2.5 + 7 + 2.5 = 31ft.    0.018 x 56 x 50 x 31 = 1562.4 | | 1562 |
| Window 4   2 + 4 + 2 + 4 + 2 + 4 + 2 + 4 = 24ft.    0.018 x 24 x 50 x 24 = 518.4 | | 518 |
| Window 5   3 + 1.5 + 3 + 1.5 = 9ft.    0.018 x 24 x 50 x 9 = 194.4 | | 194 |
| Window 6   1.5 + 4 + 1.5 + 4 + 1.5 + 4 + 1.5 + 4 = 22ft.    0.018 x 24 x 50 x 22 = 475.2 | | 475 |
| Window 7   2 + 4 + 2 + 4 + 2 + 4 + 2 + 4 = 24ft.    0.018 x 24 x 50 x 24 = 518.4 | | + 518 |
| | Total | **5,829** |

Here's The Total For Everything, Using Both Methods

Air Change Per Hour Method   15,315                    Crack Method   15,315
                             + 3194                                  + 5829
                             **18,509**  Total BTUs                  **21,144**  Total BTUs

# AIR EXCHANGERS

An air exchanger is needed if the house is too tight. They say the point where you need one is once you get down to around 0.35 air changes per hour. By looking at the air changes per hour table, you'll find that a medium sized home that's only average in tightness can hit that number, but here you also have to consider that air is exchanged as people go in and out of the house.

The purpose of the air exchanger is to bring in fresh air from outside, while at the same time, stale indoor air goes out. To eliminate part of the heat that would be lost in cold weather, the air that's coming in is heated by the air that's going out..

The idea here is to start with a tight house, and then use the air exchanger to control the amount of air that's changed -- versus a house that isn't as tight, without an air exchanger, where you have no control at all. The main problem is that you're going to lose a lot of heat if too much air is exchanged.

A friend of mine lives in a very nice house that was built around 2000. It has around 4000 square feet of living space, and since it was recently built, it's well insulated. This house doesn't have an air exchanger, but the one that's next to it does. One day I was talking to the guy that owns it, and asked him how much it cost to heat his house in the winter. I was really surprised when he said $800 a month. His house is larger, but the only way to use that much heat was if the air exchanger was set to run way too often.

One problem that some houses have in the winter is moisture collecting against the windows. Sometimes it can get so bad that the windows start to rot. I'm not sure why this happens in some houses and not in others. It isn't always the number of people that are living there. I know of homes that need an air exchanger with only two adults in the house, and others of similar construction where there are several kids, with no air exchanger, and there aren't any problems with moisture. One of my sisters had to replace some of the windows in her house for this reason. In her case, the moisture collected when the drapes were closed. One advantage of having an air exchanger is that it will quickly dry out the air, though many people would rather keep the moisture, so the air wasn't so dry during the winter, if they're weren't any problems.

# FINISHING OFF THE DORMERS AND VALLEYS

When framing a roof, your main concern is that everything lines up on the exterior of the building, so the roof can be sheathed. Once the house is weathertight and you start working on the interior, you'll find that the framing won't match up on the inside of the dormers and the valleys. Shallow-pitched roofs, framed with smaller sized rafters, may only be off a little bit. But as the pitch gets steeper and/or the boards get wider, the difference will become greater. This roof has a 14-12 pitch, and 2x12s were used for the rafters, so the framing was way off.

To show how this is done, I'll start by shimming out the dormers to prepare them for hanging the sheetrock. The upper photo shows one of the dormers before the work was started.

To begin, a board is installed across the top of the opening to tie everything together. Use a table saw to cut the angle on the board where it's needed. Here the lower edge was cut at the same angle that was used on the upper end of the rafters. Once it's cut to length, the board is lined up as close as possible with the different rafters, and then it's nailed or screwed into place. Now there's something for the boards that follow to match up with.

In the lower photo, you'll notice that the board appears to have been cut short on the right side. It was, but since it was long enough to be attached, and matched up nicely, I left it in place. This was the first dormer that I'd finished off in quite a while, so it was a learning process. I finally had everything figured out by about the third one. While doing this, I used screws for attaching most of the boards, in case something had to be changed.

Once the upper board is in place, strips can be attached to the valley rafters. To do this, first you'll have to find the angle that's needed for the strips to line up with the other rafters. I do this by trial and error. I take a guess at the angle, and cut it on a scrap board. Then I check the fit, and adjust it from there. Because of differences in the framing, what works in one spot may not work at another, so you'll have to come up with the angle that's the best compromise for both sides. If I remember correctly, I cut these boards at around 33 or 34 degrees for the first dormer, and then switched to 35 degrees on the others.

The strips are cut on the table saw, with the blade set at the correct angle so they line up with both sides. Then by running each board through the saw, and then turning it over and running it through again, you'll end up with identical angles that are centered on the boards.

On dormers that have a different pitch than the main roof, each side of the strip may have to be cut at a different angle. In that case, the fence on the saw will also have to be readjusted to center the cuts.

To determine how thick the strips have to be, measure at different points, and then cut a scrap board to see how it fits. Ideally, there's a height that will line up with the rafters on both sides, but most likely that won't be the case, and again you'll have to go with the best compromise. When doing this, remember that it's generally faster and easier to shim a board out than to plane the others down. On these dormers, I ended up cutting all of the strips at two inches, and then adjusted them to fit.

When installing the strips, do whatever it takes so one side of the strip lines up with the main rafters or the board that goes across the top of the opening, and the other side lines up with the dormer rafter(s). You'll commonly have to shim out one end, as shown on the left. In the photo on the right, the strip had to be notched on the lower end to shift it to the right. A shim was also added where the other rafter sat in too far at the corner.

Sometimes, no matter how they're cut, the strips won't line up with both sides. This generally means the valley rafters are out of position. To solve this, the strips are attached off center on the rafters, with one side hanging over the edge. In the photo on the left, the strips only needed a small adjustment to bring everything into line. On the right, it was a different story. Here they needed a major shift, and a short board also had to be added to support one of them. While doing this, I remembered that I'd noticed the problem when sheathing the dormer. When it was framed, I installed the valley rafters on one side of the line, when they should have been centered on it, or vice versa.

Another problem is that sometimes the rafters are lower on one side of the dormer than on the other. To keep both sides at the same height, attach the first strip to the valley rafter on the side that's lower. Then mark where the lower end of the strip makes contact with that side, and use a level to mark the same height on the other side of the dormer, and also on both sides of the exterior wall. This way, you know where to attach the lower end on the other boards.

Once the strips are in place, you can start on the outside wall. Here the first thing I did was to put a stud in the center. Then I did the insulation, and installed the boards that form the peak (1 and 2). Depending on the dormer, either a straightedge or a level is used to determine the height where they connect to the ridge board. On the upper end, they're toenailed or attached by driving screws through the ridge board that go into the end of each board. On the lower end, they're nailed or screwed to the wall, and the marks that were just made are used to set the height. In this case, plywood was used as a backer (3) for installing the sheetrock.

In the photo on the left, you can see where one of the boards ended up being a little short when it had to be repositioned. This isn't a problem as long as the edge of the board still projects out to the mark. On these dormers, the lower corners also had to be built out, as shown on the right.

This is how it looked after the boards were added. The hard part has been done, but a little shimming or planing may still be needed on the rafters. This will be followed by the insulation and the vapor barrier, and then the sheetrock can be installed.

The valleys are finished off in the same manner, though here it's more difficult to match up with the different rafters on both sides. In this case, the strips were also wider and thicker than those on the dormers, because the valley rafters were doubled up. The lower photo shows the height difference where the boards came together.

Ideally, this is done before the insulation is installed, but here it wasn't possible since it was the middle of winter.

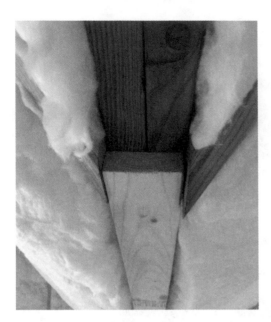
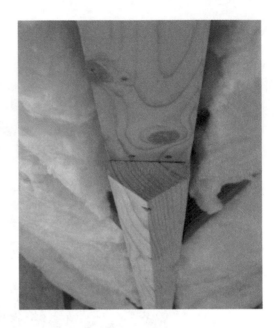

To get started, first you have to determine the angle needed for the strips. Then you try different thicknesses to find out what works the best. On these valleys, I ended up using strips that were 3 inches wide, and 2 1/2 inches thick at the center. To make it easier, I used two boards to make up the strips. For the first one, I ripped 2x4s down to 3 inches wide by 1 inch thick, and then nailed them on with a row of nails going down each edge of the board, and spaced around a foot apart.

The second board was also a 2x4 that was ripped down to 3 inches in width. Then the angles were cut by running each board through the saw, and then flipping it over and running it through again. These boards were attached with screws that were centered on the boards, and were also spaced about a foot apart.

On one of the valleys, the strip was flush to the rafters on one side, while on the other it was about 1/4 inch off. Whenever this happened on the dormers, I could fix it by moving the strip over so it lined up with both sides. That didn't work here, so instead, I cut another 1/4 inch off one of the angled surfaces.

Once the strips were in place, the corner boards were installed around the perimeter of the room. These boards were positioned by laying a straightedge across the rafters. Then after the corners were finished, I laid the straightedge across each side, and either planed down or shimmed the rafters as needed. Here the tolerances didn't have to be quite as tight because of the height, and also because the framing was on 24 inch centers, so any dips or humps were spread out a little farther apart.

One of the problems when framing with wide lumber is how much the width of the boards can vary. While working on this ceiling, I found boards that varied in width from 10 15/16 to 11 3/8 inches. With this much difference between the boards, everything you do is a compromise.

After the wiring, the plumbing, and the heating are roughed in, it's time to go over the framing to see what still needs to be done before you can start on the insulation and/or the sheetrock. While doing this, add any corner boards that are still missing, along with any blocking that's needed as a backer. Some examples of this would be corner blocks for attaching thick baseboard, blocking at the upper corners of windows for hanging drapes, a small backer board for attaching a toilet paper dispenser, or a large backer board for hanging a wall-mounted sink.

For the best results, you should also flatten the walls and the ceilings before they're covered. Start by pounding down any nails that stick out. Then lay a straightedge across the studs or the ceiling joists. I generally use a 4 foot level for doing this. A 6 foot straightedge will give you a better overall look on larger walls or ceilings. Move the straightedge back and forth, and check in the middle, and also high up and down low, while trying to determine what's needed to bring the boards into line. High spots on studs that are crowned should generally be planed down. Any dips that are

over 1/16 of an inch can be filled with either commercial shims or wood strips that are cut on a table saw. Commercial shims are stapled on, while thicker wood ones are glued and nailed.

The lower photo shows a ceiling that was flattened by stapling shims to one of the joists, and then planing off the high spots on the boards that are on each side of it. This type of work is where a planer will quickly pay for itself, since it can be used to remove any high spots, and also to taper wood strips that are used for shimming.

Commercial shims can also be tapered. For instance, on a stud the dips in, a single strip could be used across most of the dip, while in the center, two or even three layers are used. Generally, once it takes more than two strips, I'll use wood that is glued and nailed, unless it's just a short length that has to be tripled up.

Other spots that have to be checked are the corners of any windows or doors. Here, depending on how far the jamb extends past the framing, high spots where the framing sticks out are planed down, or low spots are shimmed. The upper photo shows the planes that are used for flattening walls and ceilings.

I know some guys in this business that wouldn't use a shim unless it was wood that was glued and nailed, but I've never had a problem with commercial shims, which are basically just strips of compressed paper. On the jobs that I've been on where the screws had either popped out or sunk in, it was always caused by the wood shrinking, or where the screws were driven too deep to begin with, so they had no holding power. On ceilings, sometimes there also weren't enough screws.

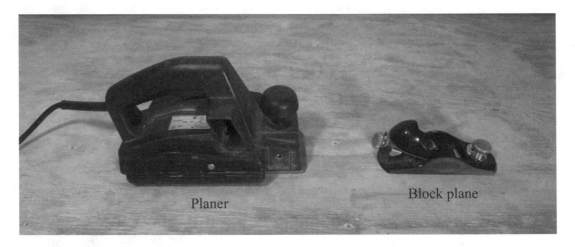

Planer                    Block plane

Studs that are badly crowned should be straightened. There are a couple of ways to do this. One is to cut partway through the stud, near the center of the bend. Then pull it straight, and attach another board to the side of it. Another method is to cut about halfway into the stud, on the side that dips in. Then, while pulling on it, slip a shim into the saw cut to hold the stud in that position. You may have to pound the shim in as you keep pressure on the stud. To finish, drive a nail or a screw down through the cut at an angle, and then cut the shim off flush to the stud. The trick to straightening a stud in this manner is to slightly over-straighten it, since it will tend to bend back when the nail or screw is driven in. This is an old method that's good to know.

Corners over arched windows should be filled in for attaching the sheetrock and the trim.

# INSULATION

It's best to install the insulation after the walls and the ceilings have been flattened. This way, it's easier to check the different surfaces with a straightedge, and to plane off any high spots on the studs or the joists. Even though it's pretty simple, there are still some things to know about installing insulation that will help you do a better job and make it go easier.

Besides the stud cavities, insulation is also needed between the floor joists around the perimeter of the building, and for the headers, if there's room for it. Where I live, a minimum of R-19 insulation is required for wood-framed walls. R-10 is needed between the floor joists On this building, R-19 unfaced fiberglass was used for both. There's also 2 inches of foam on the outside of the rim joists. Foam has to be covered with sheetrock, plywood, etc. since it can burn.

When using fiberglass insulation, the cavities should be completely filled. You might think that stuffing a bigger piece into an opening would be better, but that isn't the case. What you should do instead is to cut each piece of insulation just a little big, so it has to be slightly compressed to fit into the cavity. Anything more can cause it to buckle, and that could leave gaps. Over-compressing the insulation also makes it less effective, since it works by creating dead air space.

For standard walls that are framed on 16 inch centers, the insulation is 15 inches wide. That's 1/2 an inch wider than the width of a stud cavity, which is 14 1/2 inches. This is a good rule to go by. Cut the insulation an extra 1/2 inch wide for a normal stud cavity. For smaller stud spaces, shrink it down proportionally, and for wider spaces, increase it. The insulation doesn't have to be cut to an exact width. Just make sure the cavity is filled, and that it isn't crammed too tight.

215

When cutting it to length, you have to add even more to keep from having a gap on the upper end. For 8 foot walls, I'll generally add an extra 1 1/2 inches when using unfaced insulation. I've also worked with insulation that was so soft that even more was needed for both the length and the width.

Insulation comes in different widths, depending on whether it's going between wood or steel framing. For trusses or rafters on 24 inch centers, the insulation is around 23 inches wide. 24 inch is also available for going over the top of it. When insulating between steel studs on 16 inch centers, use 16 inch instead of 15. When a stud cavity is too wide for the insulation to fit, sometimes it's best to cut the insulation into smaller pieces, and then run it horizontally with the pieces stacked on top of each other.

Before you start on the insulation, open up one the bundles and give it a few minutes to expand. Sometimes that's all it takes for the insulation to expand out to its full thickness. At other times, it needs a little help. Tipping a batt on its edge, and then tapping it against the floor will generally get it to come out. If that doesn't work, hold it on edge and hit it back and forth between your hands.

When installing the insulation, push it into place so it's tight against the wall, and then gently fluff it back out to fill the cavity. With unfaced insulation, by pushing to one side in the middle of a piece, the other side will pull away from the stud, so it can expand out. You can also stick a knife into the insulation at an angle, and then pull on it. This works better than grabbing it with your fingers. With Kraft paper-faced insulation, it's expanded out by pulling the paper tight as it's being stapled.

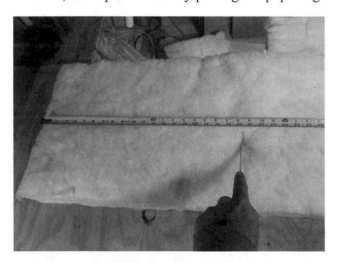 

For cutting the insulation, the best thing to use is either a razor knife with a long blade, or a boning or fillet knife, which also have a thin blade. At this time, I generally use a razor knife with the snap-off blades that can be extended a few inches, and then locked in that position. One is shown on the next page. This is better than using a standard utility knife, since you don't have to compress the insulation with a board to get a clean cut. For years, I used a 5 inch Chicago Cutlery boning knife from my kitchen (shown here). When using a knife, the insulation will quickly dull the blade, so it has to be resharpened when you're finished.

In the upper left photo, I'm using a measuring tape to mark a piece before cutting it. As you can see, 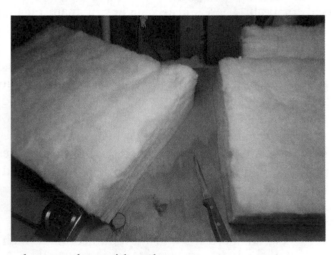 the insulation doesn't have to be compressed very much, and you end up with a clean cut.

When insulating, I do the cutting on top of a scrap piece of plywood. I use a scissors for cutting any Kraft paper facing, and also for things such as electrical boxes. When making long cuts, you may want to use a board as a straight edge. Myself, I generally use a measuring tape and a scissors to make a small cut every couple of feet, and then finish with a knife, using the cuts as a guide.

The insulation can also be cut in place, without measuring. To do this, hold it against the stud cavity, and then cut it to the correct width by running the knife down the stud. To cut it to length, install the insulation by holding it tight against the top of the cavity. Then cut it along the bottom plate, and make sure it's long enough.

In most rooms, there's generally a wire for the outlets that runs around the perimeter about two feet off the floor. There are several ways to insulate this area. You can split the insulation up to the wire, slice through the back half of it at this height, or install the insulation in separate pieces.

Splitting the insulation is my least favorite way. It's fine for a short split, but splitting it two feet back and then dragging it past the wire tends to hack it up. Once that happens, the insulation doesn't want to fluff back out.

Slicing it works fine. You just have to find the correct height to make the cut. Since the insulation is cut a little longer than the height of the opening, the cut for the wire should be higher up than the actual distance from the wire to the bottom plate.

Another method that's used when insulating around this wire, or going around electrical boxes, is to use separate pieces. This way, you can see that the insulation has filled in behind the box and/or the wire. And with a clean cut, you shouldn't have a problem getting the two pieces to fit tight together. Another advantage is that it's easy to run another wire, in case one has been forgotten. Use a scissors or a sharp razor knife to cut out for the box, and make the opening a little small, so there won't be any gaps in the insulation around it. When using this method, I generally add an inch to the length of the lower piece, so it's tight to both the wire and the bottom plate. In this photo, the insulation was cut to end at the top of the box. The next piece will either be sliced or split to go around the wire.

On both of these windows, the header was insulated with 2 inch extruded foam. Since neither one had a 2x6 beneath it, a board was attached to the lower edge of each header to provide a nailing surface for installing the sheetrock and the trim. The easiest way to cut the foam accurately is by using a table saw. Another method is to use a straightedge and a razor knife, like the one shown here.

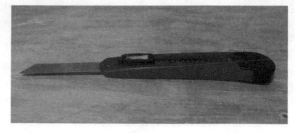

217

# USING A CARVING KNIFE

When insulating the peak on a steep roof, you either have to cut the insulation at an angle, or use small pieces to fill the upper corners. The second method is used most often. When doing this, you have to make sure the cavity is filled, and that the insulation isn't compressed too much. Trying to cut the insulation at an angle is a problem. It's hard to get much of an angle when using a knife, because the insulation has to be compressed to make the cut. Using a scissors will work, but it's a slow process if you're cutting a thick batt.

For a while now, I've had the idea that an electric carving knife might be the answer, since you wouldn't have to push down when making a cut. So, on this job, I finally bought one to try it out. It turns out that it works really well, although it doesn't cut quite as fast as I had hoped it would. Once I used the carving knife, I quickly realized how much of a help it was. Now, instead of forcing a piece of insulation into a tapered opening, I can cut the angle on it and get a much better fit. It's also good for notching pieces. So far, it's the best way I've found for installing thick insulation on a roof with a steep pitch.

# INSULATING AROUND WINDOWS AND DOORS

Years ago, you'd insulate the jambs on windows and doors by stuffing in fiberglass insulation. Now the best way is to use spray foam. The main advantage to this is that it seals off any air leaks. It also locks the jambs into place. The only way that you're going to remove a window or a door where foam has been used is to saw through the foam.

When you buy the foam, make sure it specifies that it's for windows and doors. If you use the wrong kind, it could hump out the jambs. Then while spraying the foam, hold the can upside down, and work your way around the perimeter with the end of the straw near the back of the cavity. Only fill the cavity a quarter to one third full, since the foam will expand around 3 to 4 times in volume. People always use way too much the first time they do it, and overfill the cavities. Once the foam has hardened, cut off any excess that sticks out. When doing this, I use the same razor knife that's used to cut insulation. Make sure the blade is sharp. On larger jobs, as you're going around the windows, use the same straw for each can of foam. Then save the others for using on partially filled cans at a later date.

Spray foam is one of the stickiest materials that you'll ever work with. Don't let it come into contact with anything that can't be cleaned by either scraping or sanding. When it's first applied, you may be able to remove it with acetone or paint thinner, if you're lucky. But once it's hardened, there isn't anything that will dissolve it. If it gets on your skin, it will probably have to wear off.


# INSULATING A CONCRETE FLOOR

I've already gone over this in the Heating section, but I have more to say on the subject. In my opinion, one of the best things that you can do when building a house in a northern climate is to put foam insulation under the basement floor. I'm a little surprised at the number of people who think it isn't necessary, and this includes many people in the building industry. Most homes don't have it, and about the only time it's used is when in-floor heat is being installed.

This is one way to cut the costs, but I think it's a mistake. Once you've lived in a house where the basement floor is insulated, you'll appreciate how much warmer it feels. A thick pad and carpeting certainly helps if it isn't insulated, but there's still a noticeable difference. Putting two inches of high density foam under the concrete will also save on the heating bill. How much you save would depend on where you live, and what type of house you have. If the basement floor is six feet below grade, you won't save that much, at least according to the numbers on a heat calculation form, but the floor will feel a lot better. Those heat calculation numbers may also be misleading, since they're based on the heat loss for a cold winter night in your area. Daytime would be a different story, because then you'd have higher outside temperatures, and also solar gain from the sun, while the heat loss through the basement floor would remain the same. With a forced air furnace, this could be a problem, since the whole house is generally heated at the same time. With the thermostat located on the main floor, where less heat is needed, the furnace wouldn't come on as often, and the basement would get cold. Concrete floors that are on grade, or basements with a walkout and a patio door, have the greatest heat loss, since the ground is colder near the surface. The concrete may also be losing heat directly to the cold foundation. Foam insulation is more cost effective in this case.

You can see the difference that insulation makes in the section on doing a heat loss calculation, at the end of the Heating chapter. There I did the heat loss calculation for a small building that had an unheated slab. On that building, around 25 percent of the heat was lost through the floor alone, and that's including the heat that was lost through air infiltration. If you didn't include that, then it would be one-third of the heat.

# VAPOR BARRIERS

These days, vapor barriers are a controversial subject, and we're having problems with them in some parts of the country. In the winter, warm air from inside the house tries to work its way out. In the summer, the process is reversed, and it tries to come in. That's how it works; heat from a warmer area moves towards one that's cooler, although sometimes you'd think the opposite was true.

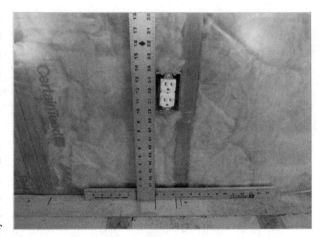

The problem is that air can hold a lot of moisture, in the form of vapor. When the air moves from one place to another, the moisture goes with it. In cold weather, moisture from inside the house can get into the wall cavities through diffusion or from air leakage. Sometimes it will freeze against the sheathing, forming a thick layer of ice. In the summer, it's the opposite. Now it's trying to get into the walls from the other side.

In older homes, this generally wasn't a problem, because any moisture that got into the walls could eventually work its way out. Now that houses are tighter, and we're required to staple plastic on the inside of the framing (up north), the idea being to prevent moisture from getting into the walls, it is a problem because moisture still gets through. With plastic on the inside, and the exterior sheathed with materials such as OSB, this moisture can be trapped in the wall. Because of that, many homes are having problems with mold and rot. This is an expensive problem to fix, sometimes costing hundreds of thousand of dollars.

According to experts, vapor barriers, more correctly called vapor retarders, are rarely needed. From what I've read, they were originally required because of politics and technical errors. It started back in the 1930s, when painters complained that paint was peeling from buildings that had been insulated. While it was true that the exterior siding on insulated houses was wetter, which caused the problem, it wasn't because the insulation caused more moisture to pass through the walls. It turns out the siding absorbed more moisture from the air because it was colder, which would happen no matter what, once the walls were insulated.

I've also read that the main reason moisture gets into the walls is because of air leakage, not diffusion, which is vapor passing through a solid surface. In one test, 1/3 of a quart of water passed through a 4x8 foot sheet of sheetrock, in an entire heating season, while under the same conditions, 30 quarts passed through when there was a 1 inch square hole in the sheet. Here the sheetrock was unfinished. Once it was painted, very little moisture would get through from diffusion.

Going by this, the best thing to do is to skip the vapor barrier, and to make sure that any openings are sealed off. This would include any gaps around boxes for the lights, outlets, and switches. Without a vapor barrier, the walls could dry out quicker.

Unfortunately, even knowing this, you may still be forced to install a vapor barrier. One option is to use a recent product called MemBrain, that's available from Certainteed. It's called a smart vapor barrier. This material is designed to retard the passage of moisture in the winter, while letting it pass through during the summer. The only problem is that it's expensive. When I first used it, I paid six times more for it than for the standard plastic. Since then, the price has come down quite a bit. Although it's expensive, this amount is nothing compared to what it would cost to repair the walls.

Because of the price, I only use MemBrain on walls where the moisture could be trapped. On ceilings with a ridge vent, I use standard 4-mil poly. Here I would think that any moisture would quickly work it's way out.

In newer homes, they're now using air exchangers to bring in air from the outside, the same way it's done on a commercial building. This should cut down on the problem. While this might be a good idea for homes that are being made at this time, that still leaves a lot that have already been built with this potential problem.

# INSTALLING A VAPOR BARRIER

The vapor barrier should be installed so it lays flat, without any major wrinkles. Over the years, I've seen a lot of them that have been put on pretty sloppy. I don't know if the people just didn't know how to do it, or if they didn't care how it looked. In case you've never done it, I'll describe how I install the vapor barrier on a wall. Ceilings are done in a similar manner.

First off, when installing a vapor barrier, the plastic has to be thick enough so it doesn't fall off as it's being stapled. Generally, this means a minimum of about 4-mils thick. Then while installing it, only do one wall at a time. If you try to do more than one wall, sometimes the corners end up with the plastic stretched across them, instead of laying flat.

To begin, I cut a piece of plastic off the roll that's a little longer than the area being covered. The next sheet of plastic will overlap this one, so they should overlap at a corner, or at one of the studs. Try to cut the plastic reasonably square.

I generally start at one of the upper corners, and hold the plastic so it overlaps the other wall by at least a few inches. Then I work my way across the wall, stretching and stapling the plastic along the upper edge.

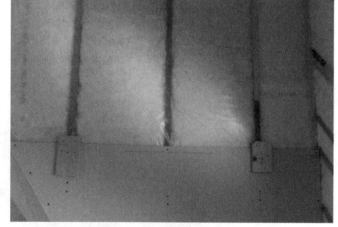

These staples are spaced about a foot apart, and at this time, I only attach the plastic to the one wall. Anything that overlaps the corners will be done later. It's important to get the first side in a straight line. While doing this, it helps to follow the edge of a board.

Now the plastic has to be stretched vertically, without pulling it to one side or the other, so I'll grab the plastic at the bottom edge and pull straight down. I do this near a stud that's close to the center of the wall. Then, while stretching the plastic, I staple it to the stud, starting at the bottom and work my way up.

After that, I move over to the outside edges. Depending on the size of the wall, I either work my way down each side, pulling down and out as I staple the plastic, or I go directly to the lower corners, and give each one a few staples after stretching the plastic down and out. Once the lower corners are finished, I just pull straight out or straight down when attaching the rest of the perimeter. Then I staple the remaining studs, and also around any windows or doors.

Once the wall is finished, I'll do the corners where the plastic overlaps. This is done by pressing the plastic tight into the corner, and then stapling it to the other wall. Now the sheetrock can slip into place without having to stretch the plastic.

After the perimeter is stapled, it's common to have some wrinkles near the top. Generally, these can be removed by pulling the plastic free on a few of the staples, and then restretching it in that area. This doesn't necessarily mean that the edge of the plastic isn't straight. It could also be caused by stretching the plastic, or maybe there's a curve in the plastic itself. The same thing happens when installing felt paper on a roof. There are rolls where one edge keeps wrinkling, even though you can see that it's on in a straight line.

Now that's in place, you still have to cut the plastic around the windows and the outlet boxes. To do the outlets, use a sharp utility knife to cut around the perimeter, along the inside edge of the box. Then stretch the plastic over it. This should give you a nice tight fit. When doing this where the outlets are already installed, either shut off the circuit breaker, or be careful that the utility knife doesn't come into contact with the hot side of the outlet, so you don't get a shock. When doing the windows, just cut the plastic by following the edge of the opening or the outside edge of the jambs.

The vapor barrier is installed in the same manner on the rest of the walls. Depending on where you live, you may be required to tape any overlapping seams, and also around the boxes. There's tape made specifically for this. It's basically colored packaging tape. The brands I've used are either red or pink, the pink being sold by Owens Corning. There's also white tape that's made by Tyvek, but it costs more.

The plastic used for 8 foot walls is actually 8 feet 4 inches wide, so any extra that overlaps the floor will have to be cut off. When doing this, sometimes it helps to lay a straightedge along the edge of the wall.

You may also be required to seal the vapor barrier to the lower edge of the wall. Acoustical sealant is generally recommended for this. Standard caulk won't work because it doesn't stick to plastic once it's hardened. I can't find acoustical sealant at any of the local building centers, so I get it from a drywall distributor. When using it, apply it to the bottom plate by pulling the plastic out of the way, and then push the plastic against it.

If you're finishing off the basement, plastic may also be needed between the studs and the outer wall. Here, the reason for the plastic is to keep the insulation dry, in case the concrete gets wet. To install it, staple the plastic to either the sill plate or the floor joists, and let it hang against the wall.

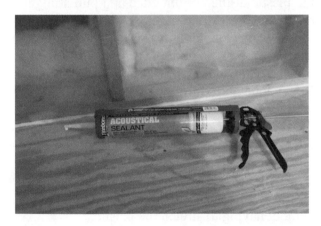

# SCREENS

When installing screens with a staple gun, it's done in the same manner as the vapor barrier. Again, start on one of the long sides, and make sure the screen is attached in a straight line. Then after the first side is finished, grab the opposite edge near the center, and stretch the screen across the opening. Make sure it's square to the opening, and then staple it into place. Now work your way towards the corners, pulling out and towards the corner as each staple is driven in. Once the corners are done, anything that remains is just pulled straight out as it's being attached.

When installing a screen, put a staple every few inches. A scissors works good for cutting the screen to size before it goes on, and a utility knife can be used to cut off the excess after it's been installed.

# SHEETROCK

I always underestimate how long it will take to get to the sheetrock because there are so many things that have to be done first, such as framing, wiring, plumbing, heating, etc. But once you've flattened out the walls and the ceilings, and then insulated, you're ready to get started on it.

Sometimes I think back and remember how it was the first time I installed sheetrock. This was around forty years ago, when we were rebuilding the walls on the family cabin. Back then, I didn't know that you could cut sheetrock with a utility knife. Actually, at that time, I didn't even know what a utility knife was, so I did all of the cutting with a hand saw. Taping the sheetrock was even worse. I remember mixing the joint compound by hand. This was not the quick-setting stuff that you buy today, just standard joint compound. I have no idea where it even came from. I also had an old book that said you were supposed to sand the joints between every coat. Of course, every time I sanded, I'd hit the tape. Needless to say, the job went very slow.

Luckily, today there's a lot of good information available on how this is done. There's nothing complicated about installing sheetrock, but in case you're new to it, there are some things to know that will make the job go easier.

In houses, the sheetrock is generally installed horizontally on the walls. The ceilings are done first, so the outer edge is supported by the walls.

Since I got started on the book, lightweight sheetrock has taken over the market. In the past, 1/2 inch sheetrock was used if the framing was on 16 inch centers, and 5/8 was used if it was on 24 inch centers. Now, 1/2 inch lightweight sheetrock is generally used for both. Besides being stiffer, it's advertised as being thirty percent lighter than standard 1/2 inch sheetrock. I also think it's easier to cut and to shave the edges.

Because it weighs less, I would think that sound would pass through it more easily, but I haven't found any information on this You could also use 5/8 sheetrock instead of 1/2 inch for a better sound barrier, but when used on the walls it would create more work, since standard window and door jambs wouldn't be flush to the surface of the wall. 5/8 sheetrock is required, though, between an attached garage and the house, as a fire barrier.

By using longer sheetrock, you'll have less butt joints to tape. Use 12 foot sheets when you can, though in some basements you'll have a hard time even getting 8 footers down the stairs. Fifty four inch wide sheets are available for doing 9 foot walls.

To cut the sheetrock, cut through the face with a utility knife. Then snap it by pushing from behind, and finish by cutting through the paper on the back. If the sheetrock is standing up, I hit it with my knee to help fold it. You'll get a cleaner edge if you bend the sheet past 90 degrees before you cut through the back.

Always have a Stanley Surform rasp on hand to clean up the cuts. A 4-in-1 file can be used to clean up the holes for round electrical boxes. On holes for small pipes, use a pointed sheetrock saw and a utility knife.

Don't trust the sheetrock square, since they get abused and quickly get knocked out of line. Mark the length of a cut on both the top and the bottom of a sheet. Generally it's easier to measure and cut the sheetrock if the sheets are leaned up against the wall. This also opens up the floor area. Then hold the square in place with one hand, and pin it with both your foot and your knee as you cut with the utility knife.

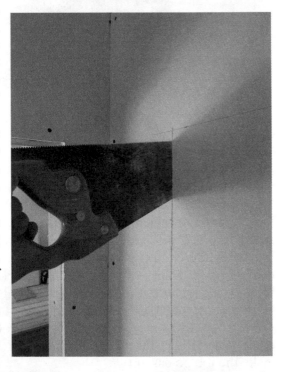

It's good to have help when making long cuts that are parallel to the tapered edge. Once the face has been cut, lay the sheet on the floor, face down, by supporting it as the sheet is being lowered. Then snap it by lifting up on one side, and finish by cutting through the back.

Just recently, I learned a simple way to do this when you're alone. After cutting a 10 foot sheet lengthwise, I was trying to figure out how to lower it to the floor without snapping it, when I noticed two pieces of scrap plywood laying against one of the walls that were around 8 inches wide by 5 feet long. So, for the heck of it, I held them against the sheetrock, with one in each hand and my arms spread out, as I lowered the sheet to the floor without any effort. I just wish that I'd thought of this 30 years ago.

To make an L-shaped cut, one of the sides has to be cut with a hand saw. I use an old crosscut saw for this. Then a utility knife is used to cut and snap the other side. To make a U-shaped cut, two sides have to be cut with a hand saw.

When going around an interior door opening, it's easier to hang the upper sheet so it goes across the opening, and then cut it out. This is assuming that the door hasn't already been installed. To cut the opening, saw both sides by holding the hand saw against the framing. Then cut the top edge from behind with a utility knife, and snap the piece and cut it off. Drywall cut-out tools can also used for going around any openings.

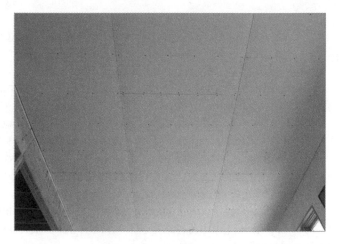

Any butt joints should be staggered between the rows. Don't ever put them at the corners of windows or doors, since they're more likely to crack at those locations. It's OK to have a seam once you're away from the corner, as shown in the center photo, but go easy on the joint compound, because it's hard to get the trim to lay tight against the jamb if the wall sticks out too far.

If possible, have the sheets come together where a board dips in. This way, there won't be a hump in the wall or the ceiling after the sheetrock's been taped. If the board already has a shim stapled to it, just pull it off before you install the sheet.

When hanging the sheetrock on walls with a flat ceiling, do the top row first, and hold it tight against the ceiling. Then either use a pry bar, or a tool that's made specifically for this job, to lift the bottom sheets up so they're tight to the one above them. If I'm doing a wall where the ceiling is sloped, and the upper row will be cut at an angle, I generally do the lower one first, and hold the sheets about a 1/2 inch off the floor by laying them on plywood blocks or small pieces of sheetrock. Then I measure and cut the top row, and use a Stanley rasp to shave it to fit. By holding the sheetrock up off the floor, it will help to prevent it from absorbing moisture, and also provides a space for thin underlayment, linoleum, or carpeting.

Use 6 x 1 1/4 inch coarse thread screws for 1/2 inch sheetrock with wood framing. 1 5/8 inch screws are for 5/8 sheetrock, though some people use 1 1/4 inch for both. Sheetrock screws should be driven in so the heads are just below the surface of the sheetrock. They should be deep enough that you aren't hitting them when you apply the first coat of joint compound. But you also have to be careful that they're not too deep, since they have little holding power if they're in too far.

When installing the sheetrock on walls, I put seven screws at the butt joints, five or six at the corners, and use five on the other studs. Around windows and doors, I generally space them around 10 inches apart. On ceilings that are framed on 16 inch centers, I'll add an extra screw to each joist or rafter in the field (center) for extra holding power. If they're framed on 24 inch centers, I'll pair up the screws instead. When doing this, every screw in the field has a second one added that's 1 1/2 - 2 inches from the first. This used to be standard practice years ago when the sheetrock was nailed on. To me, this still makes good sense. The sheetrock is commonly heavier and/or holding up insulation, and the framing is spaced farther apart. I've seen too many ceilings where the sheetrock wasn't held up tight when attached with single screws.

Try to seam the sheetrock over a single board, even if you have two boards nailed together at that point. The joint is more likely to crack if the sheets are attached to different boards. When I have no choice but to do this, I'll glue the two boards together.

On inside corners where there isn't a wood backer, metal clips can be used to support the sheetrock, instead of floating the corner.

When doing the ceilings, consider using a sheetrock jack,. This way, you can easily make adjustments if a sheet doesn't fit right, and the quality of the job is going to be better. If you don't use a jack, your arms are going to get tired from holding the sheets up over your head, and eventually you're going to say "just screw the damn thing," even when it isn't quite right. Make sure that everything is ready to go before you go out and rent one. Another option is to buy a sheetrock jack, or to go in on it with a friend. The price has really come down, and I've seen some good deals on them in the last couple of years.

Try to install the sheetrock so that the tapered edges are butted up against each other. This isn't critical, but it makes the taping go easier.

On windows and doors, it's generally best if the sheetrock stops at the edge of the framing, and doesn't run tight to the jambs. If the sheetrock is too close, it's hard to get the trim to lay tight against the jamb, in places where it sits back from the surface of the wall. It's also harder to insulate around the jambs.

Holes for outlet and light boxes can be cut out by hand with a sheetrock saw or by using a drywall cut-out tool. When cutting by hand, measure carefully to avoid having to repair holes that are cut in the wrong spot. On round boxes, draw the outline of the cut by either using a compass or a spare box that's used as a template. For a compass, I use the tool that's shown in this photo, though it was actually designed to cut the paper on the sheetrock to knock the circle out.

When using a drywall cut-out tool on a ceiling, the sheetrock should be held up so it's tight against each box as a hole is cut around it. Put in enough screws to hang the sheetrock, but keep them away from any boxes. Go easy on the pressure, especially if the box is nailed directly to the framing, since it won't flex up like recessed lights. Otherwise, the sheetrock will break as you cut the hole. Make sure the wires are pushed up out of the way.

Start the hole by plunging the bit through the sheetrock at a spot that was marked to show the approximate center of the box. Then slide the bit over until it touches the side of the box. Now pull the bit out, and come back in on the outside edge of it. Then while holding the bit against the box, go around it in a counter-clockwise direction until you complete the cut.

When using this tool to cut around the wall outlets, the sheetrock is hung by the upper screws. Then the sheetrock is held against the box as you make the cut.

You have to feel your way around each box. This is a little tougher with the inexpensive ones, since the plastic is thinner, and the bit can go right through them and screw up the cut. I don't use a cut-out tool that often, and there are days when I just don't have the touch. More than once, I've marked the outline of a box to prevent screwups. I'd rather do this than waste time repairing the holes.

You won't be able to use a cut-out tool when the switches or outlets have already been installed. Instead, you'll have to draw and cut out the holes before the sheet is hung. Measure across to find the vertical lines, and draw them using either a straightedge, a level, or the sheetrock square. Then measure off the other sheet or the ceiling, to find the height measurements. One exception to this is on the lower outlets when the bottom sheet is being installed first. In that case, you'd measure off the floor. Make sure you allow for the gap between sheetrock and the floor.

Cut the holes with a pointed sheetrock saw, and then clean them up with a rasp. The switches and outlets can be left where they are if you tip them out so the sheetrock can slip over them, as shown in the last photo.

After the holes are cut, hold the sheetrock against the wall at the correct height to see if the holes are in the right spot. Assuming they are, hang the sheetrock by the upper screws. Then use a utility knife to shave the edges where it's needed, so the sheetrock will slip over each box.

To avoid a potential shock, you can turn the power off when working with tipped-out switches and outlets. You could also use electrical tape to cover the screws. Myself, I generally don't worry about it and leave the power on, and just try to stay away from the screws on the hot side. I can't recommend this, but it's pretty rare that I trip the circuit breaker, and I've never got a shock from it.

 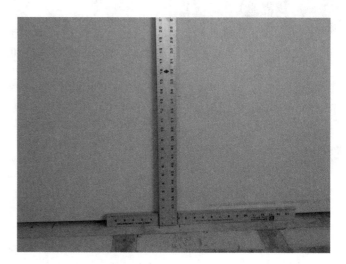

These photos show another way to mark the location of an outlet box, using the sheetrock square. Before you hang the sheetrock, hold the square against both sides of the box, and then mark each position on the floor. At the same time, write down the measurements that show the height of both the upper and the lower edge of the box. When doing this, I use a measuring tape, though you could also use the marks on the sheetrock square. Then hang the sheetrock by the upper screws, and lay the square against it. Draw the vertical lines by using the marks on the floor. Draw the horizontal lines based on the measurements, using a torpedo level. Once the lines are drawn, the lower edge of the sheetrock is pulled out from the wall just far enough to cut the hole.

How you screw the sheetrock along the edge of the floor will determine how well the baseboard lays against the wall. The goal here is to keep the wall as flat as possible. On walls where the bottom plate is either flush to the studs, or sits back from them, put the lower screws into the studs, not the plate. Center the screws on the studs, and put them at a height where they'll be hidden by the baseboard. When doing it this way, the lower screws aren't covered with joint compound, so they'll mark the position of the studs.

If the bottom plate is sitting back from the studs, and you screw into it, the screws would either pull through or the sheetrock would dip in between each stud, depending on where the screws were put. Since the baseboard gets nailed to the studs, there could be gaps between the baseboard and the wall.

On the other hand, if the bottom plate extends out from the studs, you should put the lower screws into the plate, and keep the others high enough so they don't pull through the sheetrock.

227

# WORKING ALONE

If there's no one to help, sometimes you'll have to use a little ingenuity to install the sheetrock. Many times, doing the ceilings can be easier than the walls, if you have a sheetrock jack. When using one, what I actually have the most trouble with is trying to measure the length I need. This is about the only time that I wish I owned one of those extra wide tape measures, so I could reach farther out without the tape collapsing.

Years ago, I'd just pick up a 12 foot sheet and lay it across the sheetrock jack, while trying not to break it. Doing this was a little awkward, and more than once I strained a shoulder or a back muscle. Finally I realized that it's easier to release the pivot on the top section of the jack, and then rotate it so it's vertical. This way, all you have to do is to set the sheetrock on top of the hooks, and then lay it back down so it's horizontal.

In the photo on the left, the sheetrock is being supported by the hooks, while on the right, it's ready to go up. You do this by turning the wheel. There's also a spring-loaded release that keeps it at the same height. You have to hold the release to lower it back down. Sheetrock jacks can be used on ceilings up to 11 feet, and 14 if you use an extension. When using one on vaulted ceilings, the top is left unlocked, so it can pivot against the ceiling. There are also locks at the floor, so the jack won't move.

Just carrying the sheetrock can be a problem when you're alone. Eight foot sheets aren't bad, especially the new lightweight stuff, but 12 footers are a lot harder if you have to carry them from another room. For this, there are a couple of things that can help. One is shown on the left. This simple device, called a panel carrier, makes it a lot easier to carry sheetrock or plywood. You just slip it under the sheet, and then carry it by the handle. The other photo shows an inexpensive dolly that's commonly used for furniture. It also works for moving the sheetrock from one room to another, by holding the sheet upright as it rests on the dolly.

228

 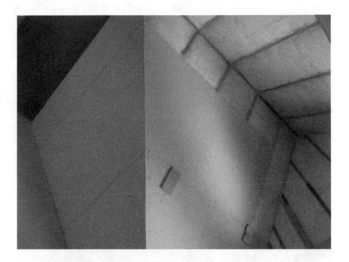

Holding the sheets up by hand while they're being attached is another problem. These photos show how it was done on a vaulted ceiling. Here the first piece was pretty small, so it was easy to hold it in place while I put in a few screws. On the ones that followed, I attached plywood blocks that overlapped the upper edge. Then all I had to do was to slip the next sheet into place, and hold it with one hand until I put a couple of screws at the top. Metal brackets are also available for this purpose.

You'll have the same problem when working alone on the walls. It's hard to hold up a full sheet, without it moving, while you're trying to put the screws in. Since the upper sheets are generally installed first, sometimes I'll screw a 2x4 block to one of the studs at each end, so they're a little over 4 feet from the ceiling. This way, the sheetrock can rest on the blocks. Then each end is raised up so it's tight to the ceiling as a screw is driven in.

I generally lock the sheets into place, and then use a 4 foot level to draw lines that show the center of the studs, trusses, or rafters. The position of each stud is marked on both the floor and the ceiling before the sheets are installed. When doing the ceilings with a sheetrock jack, I generally put a screw into each board around the perimeter. Then I draw any lines where the jack isn't in the way, and put in enough screws so it can be lowered. Then the other screws are done to finish off the sheet.

Sometimes it's easier to draw the lines before the sheets even go up. This way, you can quickly put the screws wherever they're needed, without having to guess where the boards are.

Although you may be tempted to not draw the lines, I don't recommend it. Unless you do this every day, you're going to miss the board every now and then. Then you're going to waste time trying to find out where it is, and also to get the screws out.

When you're working alone, make sure that everything you'll need is within easy reach. The last thing you want is to be holding up a sheet, and then have to take it back down because you forgot something. The screw gun should be right next to you, preferably hanging from your tool belt or a pocket. It could also be left on the ladder, if you'll be standing on it. It's also good to have a screw in the gun, ready to go.

Though I've done it myself many times, my biggest screwup happened one night when I was working alone on a friend's addition. I had just lifted a 12 foot sheet into place on a wall, when I realized that I didn't have the screw gun on me. I tried to grab it while keeping one hand on the sheetrock, but it was just out of reach. Here there was also another problem, since the lower edge of the sheet was almost five feet off the floor, and I couldn't get it off the one that it was resting on to take it back down. As it was, I didn't have any leverage, and had to push pretty hard just to keep it in place. After reaching for the gun, one last time, I was just about ready to call for help, when I realized the sheet was tipping over. Normally it would be easy to push it back against the wall, but here, it was too high up, so all I could do was to get out of the way and let it crash to the floor. It was a little embarrassing when people came out to see what happened, but nothing was hurt except for one end of the sheetrock.

# CUTTING OUT DIFFICULT SHAPES

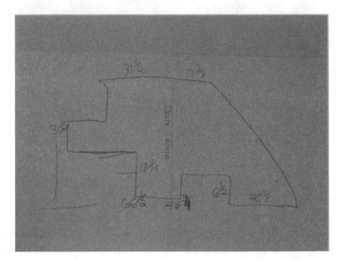

When installing sheetrock, sooner or later you'll have to cut out a difficult shape, like the one that's shown here. The best way to do this is to determine a base line, and then measure everything off of that.

Generally, when I'm cutting a difficult piece, where there isn't anything to measure off, I'll set a square on top of the sheet below it, floor, etc., so it's lined up with something above it (even a pencil mark). Then I'll mark where the square sits, and measure the distance to those points from both sides, and mark it on the sheet that I'm cutting. For the last piece at the top of a triangular-shaped peak that doesn't have a right angle (90 degrees), I'll put the square on top of the sheet below it so it's lined up with the peak, and mark that spot. Then by measuring the length of the lower edge, the distance the mark is from one side or the other, and the vertical distance from the lower edge to the peak, I can determine the shape that's needed.

Here, this wasn't an option because of the window jamb, so I used one of the studs on the left side of the window for the base line instead. Then I drew it out on a scrap piece of sheetrock, and based every measurement off of either that stud or the lower sheet.

# TRUSS UPLIFT

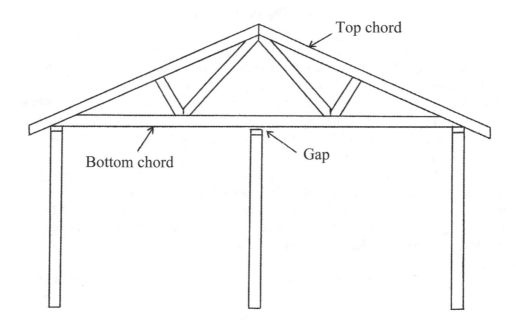

Truss uplift is something that you have to be concerned about when installing the sheetrock on the upper floor of a building that has trusses. It's just what it sounds like, where the trusses actually raise up, which can create a gap where the ceiling and the upper edge of an interior wall come together. This happens in the winter. From what I've read, it's caused by the top chords of the trusses absorbing moisture from the cold air, making them longer, while at the same time, the bottom cords are kept warm and dry, buried in the insulation. With the upper cords growing, and the lower ones possibly even shrinking, the trusses arch up in the middle and lift off the walls.

While there isn't anything that can be done to keep the trusses from lifting, you can do something to prevent the corners from cracking. One way is to use L-shaped truss clips to attach the trusses to the walls. These are nailed to the top of the wall, with the slotted side against the truss. The nail going through the slot is left slightly loose, so the truss can move up and down. On walls that are running parallel to the trusses, but are going between them, the truss clips are attached to boards that are installed between the trusses.

To allow the sheetrock to bend if the trusses lift up, the screws are kept away from the corner. On walls that run perpendicular to the trusses, the sheetrock isn't attached to the trusses until it's about 16 - 18 inches away from the wall. On walls that are parallel to the trusses, the sheetrock is attached to the nearest truss, unless it's too close. In that case, you'd screw it to the next one over.

In either case, boards are nailed to the top of the wall for attaching the outer edge of the sheetrock. Some people use metal clips instead, or don't even attach it, and just rest the ceiling on top of the sheetrock that's screwed to the wall. Another method is to install decorative molding along the upper corner. When doing this, the molding is attached to the ceiling, and not the wall, so the gap will be hidden if the trusses raise up.

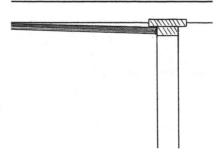

So far, the only house that I've worked on that has a problem with truss uplift is one that I helped a friend build. Since I thought this might be an issue, the walls were attached in a way that the trusses could lift. Unfortunately, my friend couldn't resist, and put the screws too close to the edge. Now every winter, a crack appears at the top of the kitchen wall, and then goes away in the spring.

# TAPING THE SHEETROCK

## CORNER BEAD

Once the sheetrock is in place, corner bead is installed on the exterior (outside) corners to protect them. Here there are several choices. There's metal, plastic, and also paper-faced corner bead that has metal or plastic under it. Paper-faced is attached with joint compound, while adhesive is used for plastic corner bead. I generally install paper-faced corner bead after the tape has been set. Metal corner bead is installed with nails, staples, screws, or it's crimped into place. I think screws are the worst choice, since they have to be sunk pretty deep so they're not in the way.

Crimping is used by many professionals, where the corner bead is held in position and then attached by laying the crimper on top of it and hitting it with a rubber mallet, which drives a piece of the corner bead into the sheetrock on both sides of it. On the last basement I worked on, I helped the homeowner install the sheetrock, but the taping and texturing were done by a crew. They stapled the corner beads on with a narrow crown staple gun. Both of these methods are fast. My only problem with them is that you can't adjust the corner bead once it's in place.

That's why I prefer to use nails. Sometimes, after it's been installed, you'll find that the corner bead isn't straight. Commonly it will dip in at the middle, or at one of the ends where the sheetrock is tapered. It could also hump out, or the corner could be out of square if the end stud is either warped or twisted. Depending on how square the corner is, and how much pressure was used when installing it, the corner bead could stick out farther than you want, or the edge where you nail could actually stick out farther than the corner itself, which is something you don't want. This is checked by sliding a 4 foot level along the corner, on both sides of it, and by laying a short straightedge across it at different points, and checking on both sides.

By using nails, the corner bead can be shifted over. If you want to drive the corner bead tighter against the corner, lay a board over it to protect it, and then hit the board with a hammer. Driving the corner bead out is a little harder. For this, either use the same 6 inch knife that's used for taping, or a pry bar, whichever works the best. Here the tool has to push against the inside edge of the corner bead, in order to drive it back out. Then it's checked as you go along with a straightedge.

According to one of the companies that manufactures the corner bead, nails or crimps should be spaced no farther apart than 9 inches. Crown staples should be spaced 6 - 10 inches apart. I use sheetrock nails for attaching the corner bead, and generally go through the holes that are already there. Depending on how far the holes are spaced out, I may only use every other hole. At the ends, I just put the nails where I think they're needed.

## KNIVES, TROWELS, AND HAWKS

Which tools you use for taping the sheetrock is both a matter of preference and experience. Let's start with what's used to hold the joint compound. Here your choices are either a mud box or a hawk. Myself, I've always preferred a hawk. I've tried using a mud box a few times, but I never felt comfortable with it. I'm sure there are others who feel exactly the opposite. This is strictly preference, as either one will do the job. One advantage of using a mud box is that the joint compound won't dry out as quickly.

Since I've always used a hawk, this is what I'll describe. If you ever watch a professional, you'll notice that they keep things moving. The knife or the trowel is loaded, and then the joint compound is spread out along a joint or a row of screws. Then the excess is wiped off, and the process is repeated, To do this quickly, the blade has to be properly loaded. This takes practice. It's not something that you can learn by just reading about it.

If you're new to this, my advice would be to practice using the hawk. Just put some joint compound on it, and then move the pile around and mix it by coming from underneath and turning it over As you're doing this, keep cleaning the knife by scraping it across the edge. Once you get the feel of it, you're ready to learn how to load a knife or a trowel. This is important, and it's done exactly the opposite as you'd think. Most beginners will scoop up the joint compound by sliding the knife beneath it. The correct way is to come over the top. Grab the amount that you want, and then scrape off any extra on the edge of the hawk. This way, you can control of amount of joint compound, and where it sits on the blade. By loading the right amount, you can apply it in longer strokes, which is how a professional does it. As long as you keep things moving, you shouldn't have much of a problem with the joint compound falling off. That's not to say it won't happen. Sometimes, if you're not paying attention, and especially when using a thin mix, a big gob will fall off the hawk or the blade and land on the floor. If the floor is clean, just pick it up and use it. If it isn't, throw it away. Some people have a hard time learning how to properly load a knife or a trowel, and quickly go back to the way they did it before. But you're only holding yourself back if you don't learn how to do it the right way.

Years ago, before I owned a trowel, I used a 6, an 8, and a 10 inch knife for taping, along with smaller ones for getting into tight spots. These days, besides the smaller sizes, I only use the 6 and the 8 inch, and use trowels for anything larger. About the only time the 8 inch is used is for applying the first coat on the tapered seams when using Durabond. The 6 inch knife is the workhorse. It's used for mixing, setting paper tape, covering the screws, doing inside corners, etc. Mine has a metal cap on the end of the handle, so you can either pound with it, or on it, if needed. Some guys use a 4 inch knife for inside corners, and say it's much faster. Beginners tend to use knives that are too small, which makes it more difficult to get a smooth surface.

Once you get over 10 inches, trowels are generally used. Having a wider blade makes it easier to smooth out the butt joints. Trowels are also stiffer than a knife, so the joints end up being flatter, without dishing in. My first trowel had a curved blade, since I thought it'd be better for doing the butt joints. I never liked it, because the amount that it curved would change from stroke to stroke, depending on the pressure, and also because it wasn't good for anything else. Now I use a 10 and a 12 inch trowel, both with straight edges. Most guys don't have the smaller size, but I find it useful for the fill coat on tapered seams and exterior corners. Any coats that follow will be done with the 12 inch. The 12 inch trowel is almost always used on the butt joints. Some guys will use larger ones yet, such as a 14 inch, but I've never tried one that big.

## FIBERGLASS TAPE

For almost thirty years, I've used fiberglass mesh tape on many of the jobs that I've been on. The reason that I started using it in the first place was because I'd seen too many places where the paper tape had come loose. Sometimes I could grab one end of it and just rip it right off the wall. Now I'm sure that any professional taper will tell you that it won't happen if the tape has been set correctly. That's probably true, but I've seen it too many times, and some of those jobs were done by professionals.

These photos show a ceiling where the paper tape came loose across the whole peak. Since the ceiling has been textured, about the only way to fix it without redoing the entire ceiling is to glue it back down.

This isn't going to happen when using fiberglass tape. The main problem with fiberglass tape is that it's less resistant to cracks, but that's easily solved by using the proper joint compound. I always use setting type joint compound that's made by Sheetrock (USG) -- not the lightweight stuff, but the heavier version of Durabond that comes in the brown bag with the green label. It comes in 20, 45, and 90-minute mixes. There's also 210, which is hard to find. I almost always buy the 90. This will give you, on average, at least one hour of working time before it starts to set up. Using 210 will give you around twice the working time. 20 and 45 set up much faster, so they're good for patching and small jobs.

Watch out for bags that have been sitting around too long, as the mix tends to become inconsistent. Besides having clumps, the working time can vary quite a bit. The first time I used 210-minute mix, I had 2 1/2 hours of working time. The next time I used it, it varied from 2 hours, down to 20 minutes. I'd swear the same bags were sitting on the pallet the second time I bought it, a year later. When the mix sets up too fast, all you can do is to throw it away, wash the bucket and the tools, and then make a new batch.

I'd been using fiberglass tape for only a short time when a friend, who was a professional taper, told me that it didn't matter what kind of joint compound you used with it. He said it wasn't necessary to use setting type. "If a joint is going to crack, it will crack no matter what kind of joint compound you use" is how he worded it. That turned out to be terrible advice. After listening to him, I taped a basement for one of my sisters using mesh tape and Sheetrock Plus 3. Within a week, every inside corner cracked. She repaired the corners by applying a thin bead of caulk to each one, and you'd never know there was a problem. Since then, many times I've seen people use regular joint compound for setting mesh tape. I even saw it being done on "This Old House," years ago. This is a mistake. Read the directions that come with the tape.

Some guys use fiberglass tape on the flat surfaces, and paper tape in the corners, but I use it everywhere. It's slower this way, but I feel that corners done with fiberglass tape and Durabond are actually stronger and less likely to crack than when using paper tape.

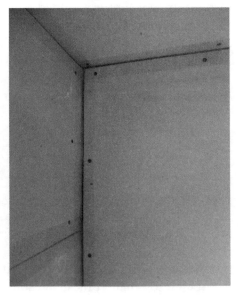

When laying out the tape, I generally do the butt joints first, followed by the tapered seams, and then the corners. To do an inside corner, I lay the tape along one side of it first, and try to hold it so the tape will be centered on the corner, once it's in place. When using standard width tape, you should hold it just under an inch off the corner. I lay the tape in increments. I start by unrolling about a foot of it, then press it to the wall and slide a finger along it to lock it into place. Then I unroll about a foot more and apply it in the same manner, and keep doing this until I get to the end of the corner. Once I get to the end, I cut the tape to length with a scissors. Then I work my way back, pushing the tape into the corner with a 6 inch knife, while at the same time, sliding my hand along the other side, pressing the tape against the wall.

Another way to push the tape into the corner is by sliding the knife along the edge of the wall. This method is faster, but it's easier to cut the fibers if the knife is sharp. You'll know when this happens if you start to hear a popping sound. Another problem with this method is that sometimes the tape isn't as tight in the corners.

One thing about the adhesive on fiberglass tape is that it tends to creep. Try to do the first coat on the corners on the same day the tape was laid. The next day, some of it may not be tight, and it will have to be pressed in again. I always slide the knife along both sides of the corner, after the tape is in place, to make sure it's tight against the wall. While doing this, I stay away from the corner itself. This will hopefully cut down on how much it creeps.

When applying the tape to the flat part of the walls and the ceilings, it's done in the same manner, but in longer increments. Here it's either pressed into place with a knife or the palm of your hand. Cut the tape to length by holding the knife against it, and then give the tape a quick pull. Make sure it's long enough to overlap the other tape.

Bad cuts around outlet and switch boxes are easily repaired with fiberglass tape. Just run the tape along the edge of the box. Then squeeze the joint compound through the mesh when doing the first coat. Small holes are repaired by just putting tape over the hole. On larger ones, sometimes I'll push the tape part way into the hole. Then after the hole is filled, I'll put another layer of tape over the top.

Once the holes are more than a couple of inches, it's best to patch over the opening with sheetrock, and then tape around the perimeter. If there isn't a stud or a joist to screw into on each side of the patch, then plywood blocks or short boards will have to be added in order to attach it. I generally use plywood blocks for this that are around 5 inches wide, and screw them to the back of the sheetrock by going through the face of it. Then the patch is attached by screwing into the blocks. For small patches on walls, another method is to use a Stanley rasp to taper the edge on opposite sides of the hole, so the back of the hole is smaller than the front. Then make a patch with the same taper, so it fits just past flush in the hole. To install the patch, put joint compound on the tapered edges, and push it into place. Then tape around it.

Another place to use fiberglass tape is on metal corner beads. Apply it to each side so it's about 1/4 inch off the actual corner. This helps to prevent cracks from forming along the inside edge.

Once the tape is on, it's time to start mixing the Durabond. With 90-minute mix, you don't want to make any more than you can use up in an hour. Start by mixing small amounts until you get a feel for how much will actually be needed. You'll find that you go through a lot more when filling tapered seams and outside corners. Inside corners don't need very much.

Durabond can either be mixed by hand or by using a mixing blade in a drill. Start by making it thicker than you actually want it to be, and then let it sit for a couple of minutes. Most of the time, it will thin out once you start mixing it again. At this point, add water until it reaches the right consistency.

I generally start on the tapered seams, and then do the upper corners where the walls meet the ceiling. Then I'll let that set up before I continue. I do the tapered seams with an 8 inch knife, and wipe them down with the blade held almost perpendicular to the sheetrock. On this first coat, I'm trying to get it close to flat and not leave any high spots.

It's hard to get a smooth finish with Durabond, especially when doing thick fill coats. Some bags are much worse than others, and have chunks that leave craters and grooves in your work. Don't spend too much time trying to clean it up. Just keep moving along. You can always go over any bad spots after the first coat has hardened.

When using Durabond, it's important that you clean up both sides of the joint, because it sets up like plaster once it hardens. Also, don't go any thicker than you have to, otherwise you'll be left with a hump. This rule should be followed anytime you're taping, but it's especially true when using Durabond, since it's hard to sand. For the same reason, you should scrape off the ridges between coats.

Inside corners are done one side at a time. I use a 6 inch knife for this. If there's a trick to it, it's to lay a smooth coat on the first side, without chatter marks, so there's a smooth surface for the knife to follow on the second side. Make sure the outside edge is feathered out. Where the edge of the sheetrock is tapered at the corner, the joint compound should be applied so it's thick enough to help flatten it out. Otherwise, it should just be thick enough to cover the tape. I tape left-handed, and it's easier for me to do the right side of a vertical corner, so I like to do that side first. On corners that have a gap, the Durabond should be squeezed through the mesh to fill in behind it. I do this by making several passes, and reload the knife before each pass. I'll also do this on any other joints that are gapped. Once the first side has dried, you can do the other side of the corner. While doing this, scrape off any joint compound that gets on the other wall.

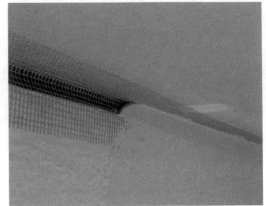

On corners where there's a large gap, it helps to install the fiberglass tape so that it's slightly dished in, and not flat to the surface. This will give you a thicker coat that's less likely to crack, and makes it easier to get a smooth finish.

I always check a butt joint first, to see how flat it is, before applying the Durabond. This will show me the best way to apply the first coat. I generally use a 12 inch trowel for this. I find it's easier to get a flat joint if I start out wide to begin with. If any tape shows through on the first coat, I'll give it another one before I move on to the regular joint compound.

I also use a trowel to do the first coat on the outside corners, though here I generally use the 10 inch.. I find that using a trowel is a little faster. It also doesn't flex as much, so the joint compound will end up a little flatter after the first coat, versus using a knife. When doing this, I apply the Durabond to one side by going perpendicular to the corner, and then change direction as I smooth it down.

When patching or repairing small holes, the Durabond should be applied so it's thin enough that you can still see the tape. This way, there won't be much of a hump once it's finished. Larger holes have to filled in stages, because the Durabond will sag if it gets too thick. To make it easier, you can mix up a small batch that's extra thick, or fill the hole at the end of a mix when it's starting to set up.

After you've done a joint, don't go over it again until it's had time to dry. If the previous mix of Durabond has set up, but isn't dry, it can cause next one to set up prematurely by just coming into contact with it. Sometimes you don't have a choice, and have to go over these spots as the different seams crisscross each other. Just be aware of what can happen, and try not to do it until you're getting close to the end of a mix. For the same reason, you should always thoroughly clean the mixing bucket and any tools that you've used before you mix up a new batch.

Once I'm finished with the Durabond, I switch over to all-purpose joint compound and do the first coat on the screws using a 6 inch knife. While doing this, I also fill any bad spots that I find on the tapered seams. I may also do another coat on the exterior corners, if they're dished in, and widen out the butt joints where it's needed. Then I generally switch over to lightweight or topping compound for the rest of the job.

While doing the first coat on the screws, take care of any problems that you find, so you don't get slowed down by having to do them later. Any screws that you hit with the knife should be tightened, so they're a little deeper. Also put screws where they're missing, and remove any that missed the studs or the rafters. Beginners tend to put little dabs of joint compound over the screws. That's wrong. The idea is to flatten out the surface, so you have to go bigger than that. It's hard to give an actual measurement, but instead of the size of a quarter, it should be more like the size of your fist.

On the finish coats, your only job is to flatten and smooth everything out. Inside corners should get another coat on each side of the corner. I generally do two more on the tapered seams, one with the 10 inch trowel, and the last with the 12 inch. Screws will need two more, the same as when using paper tape, or until the dent is gone. Exterior corners also get one or two more, depending on what's needed. Butt joints get whatever it takes, so they're smooth and there isn't a noticeable hump. They can end up being anywhere from a foot wide if the joint had dipped in, to around three wide if it was already humped out before you started.

When using fiberglass tape, it takes longer on anything but a small job. Inside corners have to be done twice, once with Durabond, and then again with regular joint compound. You're also going to spend a lot of time mixing, and then washing out the bucket and cleaning the tools after every batch. You'll find that it's much easier to clean the bucket if you do it before the mix starts to set up. The mixing blade should be rinsed off as soon as you're done using it. Durabond will even harden under water, so before you wash anything, scrape off any Durabond that you can and throw it in the trash. Then keep the water running long enough to flush everything out to prevent clogging the drain pipes.

## SKIMMING THE WALLS

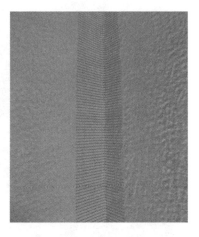

On an older house, the existing walls and ceilings will commonly have to be repaired before they can be painted. How much work this involves depends on the number of cracks, how flat they are, and whether or not the walls and the ceilings have been textured. If you're lucky, there will only be some holes and a few small cracks to deal with. Sometimes that won't be the case, and you'll having to go over everything with several coats of joint compound.

Before starting, check each surface to see if it needs to be cleaned, so the joint compound will stick to it. Flat paint may be OK as it is. Shiny paint will have to be scrubbed with something like TSP, though sometimes I've still had a problem after doing this. On jobs where I think this might be an issue, after washing the surface, I like to go over everything with an orbital or random orbit sander and coarse sandpaper.

These photos show a job that I'm on at this time. Here the walls had been textured, so it took two or three coats of joint compound to flatten them out. There were also a few spots where the joint compound didn't stick, so it had to be redone. Of course, many times this problem won't show up until after the second coat.

Before the walls or the ceilings can be skim-coated, any cracks, holes, or seams have to taken care of first. On this room, mesh tape and Durabond were used to repair the cracks. When applying the tape to the inside corners, make sure it lays as tight as you can get it.

After that's finished, the first skim coat is applied using a trowel and all-purpose joint compound. Which direction you go on the first coat depends on that particular area. You may find that you get a smoother finish by going sideways, rather that vertically, or vice versa. If there isn't any difference, go the direction that's easier for you.

Once the first coat is on, you'll be left with a series of ridges if you're going over texture or a rough surface. To fill between them, do a second coat perpendicular to the first.

After the second coat, it might be flat enough to sand, so you have to be concerned about any air bubbles that are in the finish. These could show up right away, or it may take a bit for them to work their way to the surface. To remove them, after smoothing down a small area, apply joint compound to the area that's next to it. Then go back to the other one and give it a final smooth down. This should get rid of the majority of the bubbles. In spots where they keep coming back, there's a good chance that the surface is dipped in at that point, so it may need another coat at that spot to flatten it out. Depending on how rough the surface was, the walls and/or the ceiling might need a third coat. Then once they've been smoothed down with a trowel, go over the corners with a 6 inch knife to finish them off. After that's done, they're ready to be sanded.

This series of photos shows a textured wall that was smoothed down. The first photo shows the original finish. In the second one, you can see the vertical ridges that were left by applying the joint compound going sideways. Photo three shows an area where the texture was particularly rough. In the next one, the same area doesn't look nearly as bad once the joint compound has dried. In the fifth photo, there isn't much to see. The second coat has been applied, perpendicular to the first, and the area is ready to be sanded. The last photo shows a corner that still needs to be finished off.

Corners that are right next to windows or doors can be difficult. Many times you can't find a putty knife that's the right width, and when you do, it's so stiff that you can't feather out the edge of the joint compound. Here, sometimes it's better to make your own tool by cutting one out from a piece a steel flashing. When doing this, you'll find that it's easier to get a smooth coat, since the sheet metal is more flexible. Flashing can also be cut to fit for doing sharp corners, such as under stairs.

One of the things you have to learn, by just doing it, is the angle that the knife or the trowel is held at when taping. When applying the joint compound, the knife is held at a low angle. Then, to remove the excess as it's being smoothed down, you hold it slightly higher.

On screws, it's held at a steeper angle. Since they'll get three coats, the blade is held high enough so that only a thin layer is left behind on each one. This generally take two passes: One to apply the joint compound, and then another to remove the excess. When you watch someone who's inexperienced, they try to remove the excess joint compound by just pressing harder. This is wrong. You do it by raising the angle of the blade. I generally do each screw separately on the first coat, and take care of any problems I find. Then I'll connect them by using longer strokes when applying the joint compound on the other coats.

## PAPER TAPE

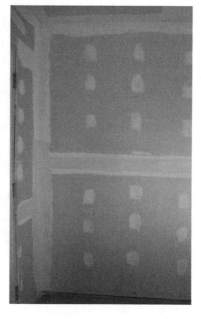

The main difference between using fiberglass mesh or paper tape is how it's attached the wall. Most professionals use paper tape. While setting-type joint compound is needed for the first coat with fiberglass tape, standard all-purpose joint compound is generally used to set paper tape, which is a big plus. It would be hard to argue that paper tape isn't the better choice on larger jobs.

If you ever watch professionals taping sheetrock, you'll be amazed at how fast they can go. They do this for a living, so they use the best tools that are available. For this job, there's a variety of tools that you can buy, for everything from setting the tape to filling the joints. The problem is that you can't justify their cost for a single job, so, as a homeowner, you'll have to get by with simpler tools and go a little slower. This isn't all bad, since you'll save some money, and also have the satisfaction of doing it yourself.

239

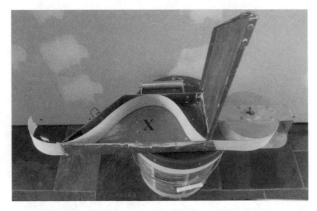

To speed things up, there are a couple of tools that a homeowner can use. One is a banjo, which is used for setting the tape. It's basically just a box that's filled with joint compound, and on one end of it sits a roll of paper tape. When using it, the tape passes through the box, where it's covered with joint compound on one side and then comes out the other end. The X marks where the joint compound goes. The price of a banjo varies. I bought one that's made out of plastic and paid around thirty bucks for it. Metal ones are about eighty to one hundred dollars. If you're doing a lot of taping, it would be smart to buy one.

When taping with a metal banjo, center the tape on one end of a seam, and hold in place. Then pull more tape from the banjo, lightly stretch it, and press it against the sheetrock a couple of feet farther down the seam. This process is repeated, pulling out more tape and pressing it into place, until you reach the end of the seam. At that point, the tape is either cut or torn to length. The plastic banjo that I own has a wheel with teeth on it. When using it, after the tape is started, all you have to do is to roll the banjo along the joint.

Once the tape is in place, slide a knife along the seam to squeeze out the excess joint compound. I generally use a 6 inch blade for this, The tape will try to slide at the start of each joint, so you'll have to hold it in place. On inside corners, use the knife to gently push the tape into the corner, and then do one side at a time. When squeezing out the excess, don't overdo it, so there's still enough to form a good bond. Then scrape off anything that has to be removed.

When setting tape without a banjo, use a knife to lay a bed of joint compound along the seam. Then press the tape into it by sliding the knife along the seam. Make sure there's enough joint compound behind the tape to begin with, so there aren't any dry spots where the tape won't stick. If you find a spot that doesn't look right, pull the tape away from the sheetrock, and use the knife to slip more joint compound beneath it. Do the same when using a banjo, as there could also be dry spots if the banjo is getting low on joint compound.

Something that I haven't tried, but plan on buying, is a roller that's used for applying the joint compound on inside corners, when using paper tape. If you ever tape corners without a banjo, you'll realize how much time it takes, just to apply the joint compound. I watched a video yesterday that shows how fast it is when using a roller. It's not as fast as using a banjo, but on small jobs, it would really speed things up. The rollers are inexpensive. A 3 inch roller for inside corners, from Marshalltown, is around 10 dollars. I would think a roller could also be used for setting the tape on flat seams. When doing inside corners, without a banjo, sometimes it's easier to cut the paper tape to length in advance, so it's ready to go.

Joints that have larger gaps should be filled before the tape goes on. If they're less than 1/4 of an inch, I'll use standard joint compound. On ones that are bigger than that, sometimes I'll use setting type.

Some professionals use a utility knife to cut a V into the butt joints, and then fill them before taping. They say doing this creates less problems. I don't know if that's necessary, but at the very least, you should cut off any paper that's loose or curled over, and make sure that nothing sticks out.

When setting paper tape, I always use regular Sheetrock All Purpose joint compound. For this, the joint compound should be thin enough so the excess can be easily squeezed out. When using a banjo, it has to be thin enough so that's it's easy pull the tape through without tearing it. New buckets of joint compound will have to be thinned out for setting the tape. To do this, add water in small increments as it's being mixed until you reach the desired thickness.

When setting the tape, I generally do the butt joints first, followed by the tapered seams, and then the corners. This way, the ends are tucked under other tape. The tape should be cut long enough so it overlaps where it meets another piece.

Paper tape has a crease in it for doing the inside corners. This should be turned so that it's facing the wall on flat seams. This way the crease will dip in, instead of sticking out, after the joint compound dries.

Once the tape has been set, some people recommend that you go over it with a light coat of joint compound. In general, I consider this to be a waste of time, since the joints don't look much different after the joint compound has dried. When doing it, I've also had more problems with the tape not staying flat.

After the tape has been set, let it dry overnight. Then it's time for the fill coat. Again, I generally do the tapered seams first, and use the 10 inch trowel, since they'll still get another coat with the 12 inch. Then I'll do the upper corner on each wall where it meets the ceiling. Ideally, inside corners will only take one coat, so I'll use a 6 inch knife and make sure the tape is completely covered, and then feather out the outside edge. Any spot that doesn't come out right will have to be touched up later. At this time, I'll also do the first coat on the screws, and any other spots where I won't disturb the joint compound that's still drying.

Then once it's dry, I'll use the 12 inch trowel to do the first coat on the butt joints, and also do any exterior corners with a 10 inch. I'll also do one side of the inside corners on the walls, the second coat on the screws, and touch up any bad spots that dip in too far on the tapered seams.

At that point, the other side of each inside corner still has to be done, and everything else needs at least one more coat. I generally give most of the butt joints two more. Then I'll look it over, and give anything that needs it another coat. I don't have any photos that show the tape, once it's been set. This one shows how it looked after the fill coat with a 10 inch trowel.

After setting the tape and doing the first coat on the screws, and the fill coat on the tapered seams, butt joints, and exterior corners, I generally switch over to lightweight or topping compound for the rest of the job, for easier sanding. The last time I talked to a professional I know, he said he was using Sheetrock All Purpose to set the tape and do the first coat on the screws. Then he'd switch over to Lite Blue.

When patching, or doing small jobs, you don't want to waste a lot of time waiting for the joint compound to dry. This is where 20 and 45-minute setting type mixes really help. When doing this, sometimes I'll use the lightweight version of Durabond, which is smoother and can be sanded if necessary. This type can be used with either paper tape or fiberglass mesh. Don't use a banjo with setting joint compound, or you might have a big problem trying to clean it if the mix starts to set up. Also, I wouldn't use lightweight setting type with fiberglass tape on inside corners, since it's not as strong. If the job is small enough, I'll do each coat as soon as the previous one has set up. Then once it's dry, I'll use standard joint compound for the last coat, so it's easier to sand. I also use a fan when I'm in a hurry, so the joint compound dries quicker.


## SANDING JOINT COMPOUND


The quality of your sanding will determine how well the job turns out. Of course, this also depends on how good the taping is, -- but many times a good sander can make a bad taping job look pretty nice, while a bad sander can easily wreck the best work. In my opinion, if you want to do a good job, you have to highlight the flaws. I do this by holding a light as I sand, and keep it at a low angle to the surface. I generally use a trouble light for this, with a 100-watt equivalent bulb (no LED). If the trouble light is made out of plastic, I'll line the inside with aluminum foil to keep the light out of my eyes.

If the walls and/or the ceiling have been properly taped, the surface is basically flat, so all you're really trying to do is to remove any ridges or lap marks, and to make sure the edge of the joint compound is feathered out where it meets the sheetrock. A bad taping job is much harder. On some of them, you spend most of your time sanding out humps and ridges, and just hope you'll be close to flat before you hit the tape.

On tapered seams, I generally start by going along both edges to make sure they're feathered out. Then I'll quickly go over the whole seam, using light strokes, to remove any ripples or lap marks. When using mesh sandpaper, I sand at an angle. The sander itself is held parallel to the seam, but the strokes are at an angle. This helps to prevent the sandpaper from cutting grooves into the joint compound.

Butt joints are done in the same manner. Then once they're sanded, I'll see if I can feel a hump where the actual seam is. If I can, I'll sand along the seam, going perpendicular to it, and try to flatten it out. But once you start to hit the tape, that's as far as you can go.

When sanding inside corners, I feather out the outside edge, and then lightly go over them while looking for lap marks and dips in the actual corner where there isn't enough joint compound. There may also be a ridge along one side of the corner, opposite the side that was done last. For feathering out the edges and removing lap marks, I generally use a large sanding pad with mesh sandpaper. On the corner itself, I use a sanding sponge, since it's less likely to cut a groove into the joint compound on the other side of the corner. Sometimes it's difficult to do the very corner where the walls meet the ceiling. Here it's generally easier to scrape it out by using a knife.

Sanding the screws should go pretty fast. If there isn't a noticeable hump, just make sure the edges are feathered out, and then lightly go over the center. I don't want to be able to see where the screws are, so I do as little as possible over the screws themselves.

Once I'm finished, I use a towel to knock the dust down. On large areas, I wipe it down by folding the towel over a broom, and tape it to the handle. Then I use the light to quickly go over everything, and look for spots that I've missed or where the joint compound needs to be touched up. Some guys just brush out the corners and then paint, but I think you end up with more mistakes showing when doing this.

## LIGHTWEIGHT JOINT COMPOUND

Years ago, I ran into a problem on one of my jobs that I couldn't figure out. I had just finished the taping, and was starting to paint. After the first coat, everything looked fine. But after the second, there were dimples all across a ceiling where the screws were. I wasn't sure what to do about it, so I put on a third coat of paint, and the problem got even worse. Now I was really confused, since the walls looked fine. The only difference I could think of was that the sheetrock on the ceilings was a different brand than what was used on the walls. In the end, I went over the dimples with more joint compound, and then repainted. The ceiling ended up looking just fine.

A couple of years later, it happened again, this time on a basement ceiling. Here there was also a little dimpling on the walls, but nothing compared to how bad the ceiling looked. Both the sheetrock and the paint were different brands this time, but the joint compound was the same, Sheetrock Plus 3, made by USG.

Right now, some of you may be thinking that it was the quality of my work, or the lack of it, and that the screws were over-sanded, but that wasn't the case. I called USG, the manufacturer of the joint compound, and asked what was going on. They said they'd never heard of such a thing.

After that, instead of starting with primer, I'd put on two coats of good quality paint, with the first coat always being flat. That seemed to take care of the problem. Later on, I talked to a couple of guys who do this for a living. One said he'd never seen it, and the other had, but didn't know the cause. Then one day, while on a job, I met a couple of painters named Bob and Vern. I told them this story, and they said "That's easy, it's the lightweight joint compound. We see it all the time. It shrinks when it gets wet." Then they added, "We never had this problem until that stuff came along."

Since then, I try to stay away from lightweight joint compound, except for the finish coats, and use a good primer. I recently talked to a friend about this, who's been in the business for most of his life, and he said it didn't make any sense because Plus 3 is recommended for going over the screws. In the same conversation, though, he mentioned that joint compound has changed. In the past, buckets of mix would get thicker over time. Now, sometimes it gets thinner. This reminded me -- at the time it happened, I was having a problem with the mix being too dry when some of the buckets of joint compound were first opened. Sometimes it was so bad that I had to add water right from the start. Maybe that was the reason for the shrinkage.

# PAINTING

These days, I seldom do the painting on the jobs I'm on, but over the years I've learned a few things that may help. When remodeling, sometimes you have to work with sheetrock where the surface has been damaged. One example of this would be on a wall where the tile has been removed. This is a problem because, once the surface is damaged, the paper that's left tends to peel off in layers, which may cause it to blister after you skim coat it and then paint the wall. Here the best thing to do is to apply Gardz by Zinsser, which will seal the surface and lock everything together. Do this before you tape or do the skim coat. This product is also good for sealing new drywall in high moisture areas, such as bathrooms, before you paint.

A few years ago, I was repairing a porch, and the homeowner wanted me to use oil-based primer to seal the wood. Since I'd recently been using the latex version from the same company, this gave me an opportunity to compare the two. Based on that job, I'd never use oil-based primer again. Anytime something scraped against the primer, within a few days of when it was applied, the paint would simply peel off and you could see that it hadn't penetrated the wood at all, even though it was labeled as a deep penetrating finish. When I cut into boards where the latex primer was used, it was exactly the opposite. Here the finish went way down into the wood. This primer was the one that was recommended by Bob and Vern, who said they use it all the time. It's call Fresh Start, and it's made by Benjamin Moore. There are several versions for interior and exterior work. It's not cheap, but it's high quality. Don't use your favorite paint brush when priming with it, because it's hard to get it out of the bristles.

A good way to touch up small spots on interior walls is to simply dip the end of a scrunched-up paper towel into the paint, and then dab it on the surface. This should work as good as anything else. If you use a paint brush on a rolled surface, the brush strokes will generally stand out.

One thing that I hate to see on finished walls and ceilings is lap marks, so anytime I paint, I try to avoid leaving them. Lap marks are made in a few ways. One is by using too much paint and/or the wrong roller cover. Another is at the end of a stroke, as you go back and forth with the roller or a paint brush. Yet another is where the paint overlaps an area that's already starting to dry, so it sits on top of it, instead of blending in. To prevent this, you have to keep a wet edge going. This means starting on one end of a wall, and not stopping until the wall is finished. To help avoid lap marks, as I work my way across, I finish up each section with long strokes of the roller that go from the floor to the ceiling wherever possible.

On a wall, this isn't a problem, but for the final coat on a ceiling, it's another matter. When painting a large ceiling, if you started a 2 foot wide strip, and then continued it across the room before starting another one, the paint would have already set up where you first began. To prevent this, if you're alone, you have to work fast and have a few strips going at the same time as you work your way across the ceiling. Here it would be a big help to have a second person.

Since the main reason for lap marks is the amount of time that it takes to paint, the faster you go, the less of a problem it should be. When rolling, a large percentage of the time is spent filling up the roller, so anything that can be done to reduce that time will speed things up. This is where sprayers and power rollers come in. You have a few options here, and it's more a matter of how much you want to spend. Starting on the low end are rollers that store the paint inside a hollow handle. I have one of these myself that I bought for painting the walls in an office building. On mine, you have to pull a lever when you need more paint, and it holds enough to do an average bedroom wall. The only problem was that it started to leak a bit after about 20 gallons, and the part it needed wasn't available at the store. I think I paid a little over twenty dollars for the roller. I see that a battery-powered version is now available.

Another option is a power roller that works by pumping the paint directly from the can. A friend of mine bought one of the less expensive versions for painting the addition on his house. The first one had a problem, but after returning it, the second one worked fine. The more expensive ones are made for spraying, but can also be used for rolling the paint with the proper attachment. If you have help, one person can either spray or roll the paint, to get it on, while the other follows with a roller, using long strokes.

How much time can you save by using one of these rollers? I never kept track, but with mine, I would guess it's about twice as fast, and it'd be faster yet if I didn't have to stop to refill the handle.

Ceiling paint is generally flat, since it's less likely to show flaws, such as lap marks. Flat paint is also used for the primer because paint has a hard time bonding to a shiny finish. If you're going over glossy paint, the surface should be sanded, or at least thoroughly scrubbed. There are products made for scrubbing the walls and ceilings, and also primers that are designed to stick to most surfaces.

Anytime you have new walls or ceilings, you have to expect some screw pops. This is caused by the framing drying and shrinking, which pushes the screws out from the sheetrock. For this reason, it's better to just do the primer until the wood has time to dry. Then any screws that pop out are either turned in farther, or removed and then replaced. After patching the holes with joint compound, the patches are primed, and then the walls and ceilings can be painted.

Years ago, I used to cut-in the corners before I primed the walls and ceilings. Now I roll on the first coat, and then do the corners. I find it to be faster this way, since the first coat soaks right in.

Whenever you paint, another thing to consider is the temperature and the humidity. Paint dries faster when it's hot out, and you're only asking for trouble if you paint a large surface under these conditions. I remember a house that I was hired to paint, years ago. That week, the temperature was at least 90 degrees every day. When I painted the lap siding, I used a large brush and only did two rows at a time, and still got lap marks. If you're painting outdoors on a warm day, stay on the shady side. Sometimes, speed is the only answer. One day I was looking at some interior trim that Vern had painted, and I asked him how he got such a perfect finish, without any visible lap marks. His reply was "paint fast."

Professional painters will often finish the trim in place, since doing it this way looks better. I don't know what word to use to describe it, so I'll just call it "seamless" in how everything comes together. If you're not that good of a painter, you might be better off doing at least the first coat with the boards laid across saw horses, to keep from making a mess of it. Then touch up anything that doesn't look right once they're installed.

When using a clear finish on oak trim, I like to apply it before the trim is installed. This will let me see the boards in their finished state. With oak, you'll get boards that finish up a light tan, some a much darker brown, and others with a distinct red tone. The boards will also have different grain patterns. I think you get better results if you lay out the trim after it's been finished, and then pick matching boards for each window and door.

When finishing wood, the first coat should be lightly sanded to remove any whiskers. 220-grit sandpaper is used for doing this. When using varnish or polyurethane, a tack rag is used to clean the surface before the next coat is applied. These are found in the paint department at most stores.

# INSTALLING DOORS

Installing a door looks easy, since it would seem that all you have to do is to hold it up in the opening, and then nail it into place. Unfortunately, that's not the case, and many homeowners install their own doors without knowing all the things that you have to get right, and end up making mistakes. Because of that, it's best to be taught how to do it before you ever get started. As for myself, I learned as I went along, and installed way too many doors incorrectly until I started to figure out some of the things that you had to watch out for.

Before you begin, the first thing you should do is to take a minute and go over the door opening with a measuring tape and a level. Measure the height on both sides, and also the width, at both the top and the bottom. Then go over the opening with a level to see if the sides are plumb. Check the floor for level, and also at the top. Then lay the level on the wall itself to see if it's plumb, and check on both sides of the opening. Also check both sides to see if the framing is square to the opening. What you're trying to do is to get an overall feel for what you have to work with, so you know the best way to proceed.

Then before you get started, you also have to consider if the jambs should be held up off the floor, how much of a gap is needed under the door itself, and does the height of the upper jamb have to match another door, or a window, so the trim lines up. In case you didn't know, the jamb is the frame that goes around the door that the hinges are attached to. The door stop is the board that's attached to the jamb, near the center of it.

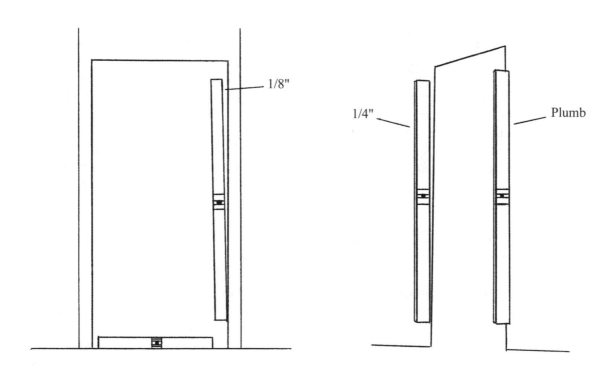

To describe how this is done, I'll go through the process of installing a door. Let's say that this is going to be a 30 inch door at the end of a hallway. The hallway itself is a little over 37 inches wide. The floor is sheathed with 3/4 inch plywood that's pretty close to level, and will be carpeted later. When measured, the door opening was 32 1/4 inches wide, at both the top and the bottom, and it's 1/8 inch off plumb. The height is 82 1/2 inches on both sides. Also, when laying the level across the sheetrock and checking for plumb, the hinge side was dead on, while the other side is about 1/4 inch off. The framing itself is square to the opening on both sides.

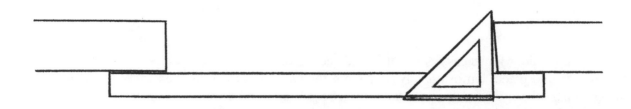

This drawing shows how you check to see if a stud is twisted, by laying a level or a straight board across the opening, and then using a speed square. Here you can see that the right side of the door opening is out of square. In this location, the shims would be positioned to compensate for it, so the jamb is square to the opening and the door isn't hinge-bound.

To get started on the door, first I'll put a 1/2 inch thick plywood block on each side of the door opening to rest the jambs on. This will provide a gap for the carpeting to slip under. Any other doors that are in the hallway will also be raised up to keep everything at the same height.

Typically, a door is placed in the opening, and then shims are inserted around it and adjusted until the gap is even around the perimeter of the door. I generally do it a little different. I install the shims on the hinge side, before the door is put into place. I find this easier to do when I don't have to fight the weight of the door. When doing this, I start by removing an inner screw from each hinge, on the side that's attached to the jamb. This will let me attach the jamb to the door opening by driving long screws through the same holes.

Shims will be going behind each hinge, so I'll measure from the bottom of the jamb to where each screw was removed, and then mark these heights on the side of the door opening. If it's a two-hinge door, I'll also put a shim in the center Remember to allow for the height difference if the jamb sits above the floor.

On the door that's being installed, the jamb is 31 1/2 inches when measured across the top. The opening is 32 1/4, so I have 3/4 of an inch to work with when shimming. Since this door is at the end of a hallway, I want to center it in the opening so the door trim is evenly spaced off both walls.

In this case, I'll do the center shim first, and put it where the mark was just made. This shim should be about 3/8 of an inch thick to center the door in the opening, and I'll tack it into place using a 3D or 4D finish nail. Thinner shims can be stapled on. Once the shim is in place, a level is used to determine the thickness of the others. After they're installed, the shims should be plumb to each other and in a straight line. Here, one of the shims will be a little thinner than the one in the center, while the other will be thicker, to compensate for the opening being out of plumb.

Ideally, a 6 foot level is used for doing this, though it's not a necessity. You can also use a shorter level if you hold it against a board that's straight enough to be used as a straightedge. For years, I installed doors with a 4 foot level that was taped to the side of a board that was kept just for that purpose.

The shims are installed in opposing pairs, unless the stud is twisted at that location. In that case, they'd either be turned the same way, or a shim could be paired up with a parallel board, in order to square up the jamb. When the gap is too small for a standard shim, you can use a thin strip of wood or a drywall shim.

Once the shims have been tacked on, I'll set the door into place on top of the blocks, and hold it there by inserting shims at the upper corners. Then I'll center the jambs on the wall, and see how the door lines up with the door stop. From checking out the door opening beforehand, I already know there's a quarter of an inch difference between the two sides, so I'll twist the jambs in opposite directions until the door makes even contact with the door stop. When doing this, the limiting factor is that you still have to be able to trim the door. By adjusting both jambs, the amount of twist that's needed on each side will be kept to a minimum.

After I've found the best position for the jambs, I'll attach the hinge side. To do this, I open the door and support the end of it with wood blocks, shims, or anything else that's handy. The height of the blocks will adjust the angle of the jamb. Then once it's in the correct position, I'll put a 2 1/2 inch screw through each hinge to pull the jamb up tight to the side of the door opening.

I generally predrill each hole, and go just deep enough to get through the shims to keep them from splitting. Long sheetrock screws should be a close match to the original screws, if they're black. There are also plated versions that will closely match screws that are gold or silver-colored.

At this point, the door is held in place, so I'll close it and check the gap over the top of it (between the door and the jamb). If I find that it's off, I'll adjust the height of the block that's under the other jamb, so the gap is the same on both sides of the door. I'm not concerned about the gap in the center at this time.

Then I'll start on the other jamb by installing the first shim a little ways down from the upper corner. When doing this, I adjust the thickness of the shim to match the gap at the upper corner. Many times, the gap on this side of the door will appear to be the wrong size. If it's too big, the latch won't work properly, and on an exterior door, it won't make good contact with the weather stripping. If it's too small, the door will end up sticking if it ever swells up. When I see this, I check the gap above the upper hinge on the other side of the door, since this is where the problem generally starts. To change the gap, I'll adjust the shims that were used at the upper corners to hold the door in place. By increasing the gap on one side, it will get smaller on the other.

The jamb still needs to be adjusted so the stop lines up with door. Once it looks right, I'll drive a nail through the upper shim. When hand nailing, I use two 8D finish nails or 2 1/2 inch hardened trim nails at the three main shim locations. The lower shim is next. Here the shim is adjusted to match the gap on the upper part of the door. Then I make sure that the door hits the stop evenly, and nail the jamb into place. A shim is still needed just above the door knob. Again, I'll match the gap, and then nail through the shim.

After that's done, I'll remove the shims from the upper corners, and also take out the blocks that are under the jambs. Then I check the gap around the door, see how it hits the doorstop, and open and close it to find out if it's hinge-bound. Then I'll readjust any shims that are wrong, and add new ones where it's necessary, until the gap is even and the door works properly. At this time, I also add a nail to the side of each screw.

While doing this, you'll commonly find that either one or both of the lower corners have to be shimmed. Upper corners that had to be adjusted may also shift over once the shims are removed. To keep this from happening, the shims can be nailed into place, though a better option is to install a shim over the center of the door. This may be needed anyhow if the gap is off. Then once it's been nailed, the shims can be pulled from the corners without anything moving. Just take your time when going over the door, and do it right. At a later date, you can cut off the bottom of the door or shorten the jambs if it's necessary, but it would be tough to change anything else once the trim is nailed on.

Sometimes the center of a jamb will stick out from the wall on one side, and be in on the other, which means that either the jamb or the wall has a curve in it. If it's the jamb, nail or screw both ends first, and then push on the middle of it when you do the center. If the wall is the problem, and it's already sheetrocked, about the only thing that you can do is to slightly shift the jamb to one side to compensate for it.

Although it isn't as solid, installing a door with a trim gun (finish nailer) is much faster. Another advantage is that the gap tends to stay about the same. When hand nailing, sometimes the jambs sink in farther than you want. Since these nails are quite a bit thinner than 8D finish nails, I wouldn't use anything smaller than 2 1/2 inch nails in a 15 gauge gun. When doing this, at the very least, put a long screw through the upper hinge of the door to help prevent it from sagging. Screws can also be used instead of nails on interior doors, if you pull the door stops, and then position the screws so they'll be hidden once the stops are nailed back on.

Years ago, I was installing an oak floor in a new home at the same time that a carpenter was installing the doors. We talked quite a bit as we worked, and he's the one that showed me how to hang a door by driving screws through the hinges. By watching him, I also learned that the jambs could be adjusted a lot farther than I ever thought possible. This is where skill and experience comes in, by knowing how far a jamb can be adjusted, while still being able to trim it. There isn't a set amount that this can be done, and it also depends on the location, and what kind of trim you're using. Narrow trim is more forgiving because it's tapered, so it's harder to see when a board isn't laying flat against the wall. The lower end of a door can generally be adjusted farther in or out than on the upper end, since you don't have a corner to be concerned about, and also because it's less noticeable down by the floor.

Once the door is finished, use a hand saw to cut the shims flush to the wall. Then it's ready to be trimmed.

# HINGE-BOUND

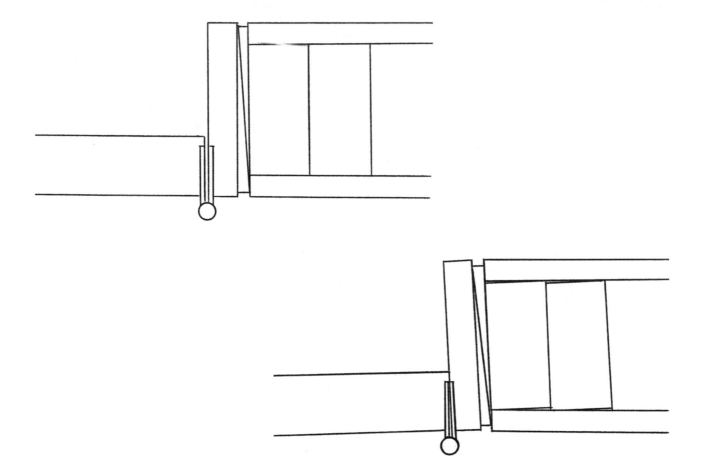

These drawings show the hinge side of a door jamb. In the upper drawing, the studs are square to the opening. The door is closed, yet there's still a gap between the two sides of the hinge. In the lower drawing, you can see that both the studs and the jamb are twisted. Even though the door isn't quite closed, the sides of the hinge are already touching, and the door is tight against the jamb, which means it's hinge-bound. When you close the door, it flexes the jamb and tries to rip out the screws. And anytime the door is shut, it will try to spring open if it doesn't latch.

If a door tends to open when you close it, this doesn't necessarily mean that it's hinge-bound. You'll have the same problem if the door is hitting the jamb or the door stop on one end, a hinge screw is sticking out, or a hinge pocket is cut wrong, so the hinge either sticks out or one side is deeper than the other. It's also possible that the wall isn't plumb, so the door either opens or closes by itself, depending on which way it's leaning.

This photo shows where two bi-folds and a pocket door were installed with the upper trim boards at the same height. The problem here was that the floor wasn't level. In order to do this, the first door was installed where the floor was the lowest. Then a level was used to draw a line around the perimeter at the top of the jambs. When installing the other doors, the jambs were cut to end at the line, and the doors were shortened where it was necessary.

## INSTALLING DOORS OVER WOOD OR TILE FLOORS

When installing a door over an existing wood or tile floor, the jambs will rest on top of it. To do this, you'll have to find out how level the floor is by laying a level across the door opening, and by also checking perpendicular to the wall, on each side of it. If one side of the opening is a quarter of an inch higher than the other, then the jamb on that side will have to be cut a quarter of an inch shorter. You may also have to cut the jambs at an angle if the floor isn't level perpendicular to the opening, or scribe the ends so they fit tight when over tile. The jambs can be cut with the door still on the hinges by tipping up the side that needs to be shortened, and then cutting from the back. Square cuts are easily made with a circular saw and a speed square. Angled cuts should be drawn, and then carefully cut freehand. Use a smooth cutting saw blade to help prevent splinters. The jambs are the correct height when the hinge side is plumb and the gap over the top of the door is even.

## DOORS SETTLING

Once I got started on the book, I began to take a closer look at some of the work I've done in the past, to see how it's held up. One thing that surprised me is how much a few of the doors have settled. I'd expect to see this in an older home, but not on a door that was installed in the last few years.

When this happens, the gap increases over the door, and may also be tighter on the side that has the door knob, near the upper corner. By looking the door over, sometimes the problem is obvious, such as screws that have loosened. Other times, I've found that the door itself has settled. One example of this would be an old-fashioned wood screen door. It's common for these doors to sag, so they generally have a metal rod with a turnbuckle that's tightened to keep this from happening. Panel doors can also sag, though, on a newer door, the amount is probably very small. Sometimes you'll come across a door where you can't find the cause of the problem. The screws are still tight, the door itself hasn't changed, and yet the gap over the door has obviously grown.

If the door itself has sagged, there's isn't much that you can do about it without resetting the jamb. But, if the door sticks or is too tight at the upper corner, it might be caused by the gap increasing at the upper hinge. This is generally an easy fix. Here the first thing to do is to make sure the screws are tight, and that the fit of the hinge pin isn't too sloppy. I'd also remove the long screw from the upper hinge to see if a hole was drilled through the jamb, so the screw can draw it up tight. If there isn't a long screw, I'd install one. Sometimes this is all it takes to fix the door. If that doesn't work, another option is to set the upper hinge a little deeper. To do this, remove the hinge, and use a chisel to cut the hinge pocket. This can be done on just one, or to both sides of the hinge, depending on how much is needed.

Sometimes you'll have the opposite problem where a larger gap is needed on the hinge side. This could be for looks, or to move the door farther out if it's hinge-bound. This one is pretty simple. Just remove the screws from the hinge, and then build it out by putting pieces of felt paper beneath it.

On some doors, there's a good chance that they're going to move, so it might be smart to install them in a manner that deals with the problem before it occurs. One example would be bathroom doors. I would guess, that in the houses I've worked on, at least half of the bathroom doors had to be planed down at one time or another because they were sticking. It's almost always in the same place, on the side that has the door knob, and generally near the upper corner. Even though there was plenty of gap to begin with, the doors expanded that much from the moisture. Heavy doors, in general, tend to sag over time. Even if the door itself hasn't moved, the hinges get sloppy, and sometimes the opening seems to change. By knowing this, on a bathroom door, allow a little extra for the gap on the side of it. When installing a door that's heavy, have the gap a little tighter over the top, on the side that's above the door knob, and a little larger near the top, on the side of it.

# EXTERIOR DOORS

If you install an interior door incorrectly, besides how it looks, the only problem that you might have is that it sticks or it's hinge-bound. With exterior doors, it's important to get it right, since the doors are generally insulated and weather-stripped.

When installing an exterior door, I start by measuring the opening, and then check the floor to see if it's reasonably level, since the threshold is going to rest on it. Assuming that everything is OK, I'll slip the door into place, and while holding it plumb, press it tight against the wall to see if the door is parallel to the other jamb, or if one end of the jamb has to be shimmed out so it lines up. While doing this, I also decide if the door should be centered in the opening, or tight against one side or the other.

If the floor isn't level, I'd also have to determine how much to shim up one side, so there was an even gap over the top of the door. If there's a hump in the floor, both sides may have to be raised up.

After that's done, I'll take the door out. Then I'll run two or three beads of caulk along the length of either the bottom of the threshold or the base of the door opening, and put the door back into place, while trying not to smear the caulk.

Since I already know what to do, the rest of the job should go pretty easy. Once the door is positioned, I'll put shims behind the hinges and replace one of the screws on each hinge, the same as I do on an interior door, though here I'd use a 3 - 3 1/2 inch drywall or construction screw instead. Then I'll shim the rest of the door while maintaining an even gap around it, and nail through the shims with 8D or 10D finish nails.

Some guys install exterior doors by just holding them up in the opening, and then nail them to the wall by going through the brick molding with 10D or 16D galvanized finish nails. Although this works, and I've done it myself on occasion, you're better off shimming and nailing through the jambs. Another option on exterior doors is to push the weather stripping out of the way, and then install screws so they'll be hidden behind it. When using the first method, it's easier to use long trim screws instead of nails for going through the brick molding.

## CHECKING FOR AIR LEAKS

Exterior doors that let air get through can waste of lot of energy. There could be a few reasons for this: torn or missing weather stripping, a striker plate that's either missing or out of position, or a door that's been installed wrong. All of these are easy to check, and will show up as air leaks that can be felt on a windy day, or seen as light around the edge of the door.

If you can see light coming in, the first thing to do is to check the weather stripping. Any that's torn or missing should be replaced. If that isn't the problem, close the door, and then push on it while watching the light around the edge. If the light completely disappears, with only a light push, this could indicate a problem with the striker plate. Whether it's missing, bent, or installed wrong, the result is the same, where the door isn't closing far enough to make good contact with the weather stripping. The striker plate could also be at the wrong height. In order to move it, the screws will have to be reset. Sometimes the best option is to use a file to shave down one side of the opening on the striker plate.

Light that only appears towards one end generally means the jamb is twisted, which means it's either too far in or out on one end. This is checked by seeing how the door lines up against the door stop, or the edge of the jamb, if that's easier. An exception to this is where the light is only coming in close to the bottom. This could be caused by the strip that's sometimes stapled on at that location. If the light is near the center, see if the gap is too big on that part of the door, which would prevent the weather stripping from making contact with it.

To fix either one of these problems, the jamb will have to be adjusted. If the door has already been installed, you'll have to slice through the caulk, and also saw around the jamb if spray foam was used. Then, how you move the jamb, depends on how it was installed and what needs to be done. If the door was installed by nailing through the brick molding, the jamb can be pushed out on one end by simply laying a board against it, and then hitting it with a hammer. On doors that were shimmed and nailed through the jambs, you can adjust the gap by either adding shims to shrink the gap, or by knocking out the ones that exist, and then replacing them with thinner ones to increase it. With any other combination, you'll probably have to saw through the nails in order to move the jamb in the direction that it has to go.

Another place where air can get through is between the bottom of door and the threshold. Depending on the door, the weather strip could be attached to the threshold, or to the door itself. On some doors, the height of the threshold can be adjusted to make better contact.

Exterior doors commonly have flimsy aluminum thresholds that sag when you step on them. If you have one like that, see if you can put something underneath it to support it. Depending on the circumstances, I've done this with shims, boards, mortar, caulk, and have also injected foam.

## FRENCH DOORS

When installing an exterior door, the jambs are held in place by the threshold, so a French door isn't much different than a standard single door. Interior doors are different, since they don't have a threshold attached. With French doors, there's also two doors to deal with, which makes them a little more difficult to install. So that's what I'll be describing here. As with any other door, you should begin by measuring the opening, and then go over everything with a level to see what you have to work with. On these doors, how level the floor is, is one of the most important things to check. Since there are two doors, the difference in height between each side will be twice as much than with a standard door.

When the floor is close to level, the door is installed with the side jambs plumb, and the upper jamb level across the top, the same as you'd do on a standard door. But on floors that are farther out of level, you'll have to make a decision, as there are a couple of ways to deal with it.

The first option is to shorten one of the side jambs, so the doors will be level across the top. There are a couple of problems with this. One is that the gap will be off under the doors, so the lower edge will have to be cut on each one to even it up. Also, as the doors are opened, the gap under one of them will get tighter, while on the other, it will grow larger.

You could also ignore the level, and install the door as is by not having the jambs plumb. This can be tough to do once you're used to doing things the right way, but sometimes this might be the best choice. Now the gap will be even under the doors, and it should stay about the same as they're opened and closed. Again, there are a couple of problems when doing this. One is that the doors may not stay in place. Since they aren't level, one door may open by itself, while the other could close. Another problem is that it might be too noticeable if the door is close to something that is either level or plumb.

On floors that are way off, I generally combine the two methods. I'll shorten one of the jambs, and then install the door with the sides tipped, and the upper jamb out of level as far as it can be, where I'm still comfortable with it. Then I'll cut both doors to even up the gap at the floor.

If the floor isn't level, and you decide on the first method, the first thing to do is to determine the height difference between the two sides of the door opening. Then cut off that amount from the jamb that's on the high side, so the upper jamb will be level.

After the jamb's been cut, the door is placed in the opening, and then held by inserting shims at the upper corners. On doors where the jambs don't have to be cut, you go directly to this point. If carpeting is being installed, the jambs will again rest on 1/2 inch thick plywood blocks.

Now with the door in place, the jambs are positioned so they're flush to the wall, so you can see how the two doors meet up. If neither one has a door stop, just see how they line up with each other. Most likely, the jambs will need a little adjustment. This is done the same as on a standard door. Again, it's better to adjust both sides a little bit, instead of adjusting one by a lot.

One thing that's different about a French door is that the upper jamb is installed first. Begin by shimming and nailing both ends of it. While doing this, if either side has to be adjusted, then the upper jamb may have to be slightly twisted to allow for it. After the ends are nailed, install shims at two points between them, and make sure the jamb is in a straight line.

Once the upper jamb is attached, the sides can be adjusted. Here the shims are installed behind the lower hinges first. Adjust the thickness so the doors are at the same height and the gap is even over the top, and also between them. Then twist the jambs, if needed, so the doors line up with each other, and either nail the jambs, or drive a screw through each lower hinge. After that's done, shims are placed behind the other hinges. Then look the door over, add shims where needed, and make any changes that are necessary.


# POCKET DOORS


Pocket doors are a good choice where there isn't room for a standard door to swing open. They're also good for installing on both sides of an archway, since they'll be hidden from view when they're open. The only requirement is that there's enough room for the frame. For a pocket door, you'll need around 2 inches over twice the width of the door itself.

Frames for pocket doors come in two different styles. On one, the upper and the lower plate are installed first. Then small metal studs, with wood inserts, are attached to both sides of the plates. The other style is the one that I prefer. On this one, the frame is made out of wood and comes preassembled, though you may have to nail the top on. Then all you have to do is to make sure it's plumb, and either nail or screw it into place. Once that's done, brackets are attached to the top of the door, and the door is hung from the rollers.

Years ago, sometimes I'd install a pocket door that ended up being much noisier than I expected. I used to blame it on cheap rollers. Since then, I've found that the weight of the door is what determines how quiet it is. This means no hollow core doors. Stick to heavy solid core, or panel doors.

# STRAIGHTENING A DOOR OPENING

Every now and then, you'll come across a door opening that's off so much that the door can't be installed by simply adjusting the jambs. When this happens, there are several things that you can do. These include: moving the wall, building out the wall, or moving the door stop.

We'll start with moving the wall. I skimmed through a book recently where this was the recommended way to get a door to line up with the door stop. I think that's wrong. I feel this method should only be used in certain conditions, and most of the time I'd consider it a last resort. The best place to do it is where the door opening is away from any corners, and on a wall where the bottom plates don't line up.

The easiest way to move a wall is to lay a block of wood against the base of it, near the edge of the door opening, and then hit the block with a big hammer. By pounding on the side that isn't plumb, you should be able to straighten the wall and plumb it up at the same time. Once it's been moved over, the wall is locked into place with a couple of long screws that angle down through the end of the lower plate and into the floor. Generally, I'd only consider doing this on a wall that was sheetrocked. On a plaster wall, I think there'd be too great a risk of getting cracks. Even with sheetrock, I'd expect to get a few screw pops.

Another option is to pull the door stop, and then reattach it, following the edge of the door. This would seem to be the easiest method, but I only use it when I have to. The problem here is that even though the door lines up with the door stop, the door isn't going to line up with the edge of the jamb, -- though you might not even notice it if the stop didn't have to be moved very far.

You could also build the wall out if the door opening is next to a corner. On an inside corner, it's pretty simple to do. Just install the door, and then build out the corner with joint compound. Doing this on an outside corner is harder. I had to do this to the corner at the bottom of the stairs that are shown in the photo. This wall had to be built out almost an inch at the base to get it close to plumb. It was done by attaching pieces of sheetrock that varied in thickness, and then taping and applying joint compound, until there was straight edge going up to the ceiling. Then I installed a new corner bead, and after all that, I still had to adjust the door stop to get it to line up with the door.

By adding a second corner bead over one that's already been installed, it will build out the wall farther on both sides. This may put a noticeable dip in the wall, unless the joint compound is feathered out extra wide. You could also tear off the original corner bead before the new one is attached, if it's not too much trouble.

The problem with this method is that the wall is thicker where it's been built out, so the jamb won't be flush to the wall on the other side. If you're installing extension jambs, this shouldn't be a problem, since you won't even notice it if one is slightly tapered. Otherwise, you'll have to figure out how you're going to trim the other side of the door.

# TRIM

Most everyone has something that they're more critical of when looking over a house. It could be anything: the furniture, the color of the paint in the different rooms, the layout of the kitchen, etc. Myself, I'm very particular when it comes to the trim, and it's one of the first things I notice. I just hate seeing gapped joints, or corners where the boards were cut at the wrong angle. I figure that since you're going to be seeing it every day, you should take the time to do it right.

It's been said, "The mark of a good carpenter isn't whether or not you make mistakes, but how well you cover them up." When trimming, you're constantly making adjustments to bring the corners together. When I first started trimming, I assumed that all you had to do on mitered corners was to cut the boards to the correct length, with the ends cut at 45 degrees, and then nail them into place. Although occasionally that's true, if that's how you always do it, you'll never be any good at it. Wood isn't an exact material, and the boards that you're working with may vary in width and thickness. The corners could also be at slightly different angles, and the jambs will often stick in or stick out. Because of that, you have take the corners one at a time, and do whatever's necessary to get a tight fit on each one, before you move on to the next corner. Also, no matter how careful you are, sooner or later you're going to cut a board wrong. Nailed on as is, the corner's going to look bad, but with a little work, you won't even notice that there was a problem to begin with. Wood filler is good for filling nail holes, but don't count on it to cover up your mistakes. Even when painted, most of the time you can still see if a corner wasn't tight to begin with.

Some people just aren't cut out to do quality trim work. Even though they have the knowledge, they still do a lousy job. Maybe it's a lack of patience, or not caring. In my opinion, the main requirement is that you have to be picky. Since this isn't a job where strength is an issue, the best trimmer could be anyone, and in some of the homes where I've worked, I think the wife would be a much better trimmer. The only problem is that men are generally more confident using power tools.

This problem is easily cured. You just have to get comfortable using a miter saw. The way to do this is to start with a good quality saw, and then make lots of cuts, without anyone looking over your shoulder. Set the saw to different angles, and practice cutting to the line, to get the feel of it. You may also want to make something to build up your confidence. Besides being used to protect your hearing, wearing ear protection can make a power tool less intimidating, by quieting everything down. My advice would be the same for learning how to use other tools.

# PATIENCE AND LOCATION

Besides knowing "how" to trim, there are two things that will greatly determine the final result. The first one is patience. I'm sure you've heard this before, but it bears repeating. To do quality work, you have to take your time and concentrate on what you're doing, and not be thinking about other problems. Myself, I tend to work faster if I just relax and not watch the clock. If you want good results, your goal should be to get each joint perfect. Although that's not going to happen very often, and sometimes you'll have to settle for a lot less, you have to at least make the effort to get each one as good as you can.

The second thing is probably not what you're expecting. It's the location of the miter saw. For the best results when installing trim, you should have the miter saw close to the work. I prefer to have it in the same room in which I'm working, or in the one next to it, the location being determined by the size of the rooms. If you have to go too far to make a cut, it's more likely that you're going to say a joint is good enough and then nail it, when, with a slight adjustment, the joint could look perfect.

# CUTTING WOOD ACCURATELY

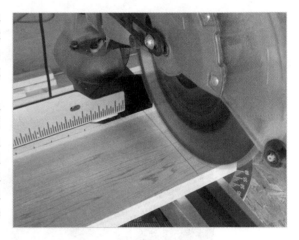

When installing trim, the difference in length between a board that fits correctly, and one that clearly doesn't, is almost immeasurable. Since one of the keys to doing quality work is the ability to cut a board to exactly the right length, anything that you can do to be more accurate will help.

Start by using a sharp writing pencil, so you have a thinner line to begin with. When cutting a board to length, I generally mark it by drawing a line that's around a quarter of an inch long, so it's easy to see. Some guys will use a square, and then draw a line across the entire board, but I consider this a waste of time. In the time it takes to draw the line, you could have already made the cut. An exception to this is when the board is pretty wide, or it's being cut at an odd angle.

From there, you have to fine tune your cutting. After marking a board, decide exactly where you want to make the cut, in relation to the pencil line. Being specific, do you want to miss the line, nick the line, split the line, or remove the line.

My favorite measuring tape is a 25-foot Stanley. One of the reasons that I like it is because the marks are at 1/16-inch increments, all the way to the near end. I feel that measuring tapes with marks at 1/32-inch increments are unnecessary and harder to read.

When measuring, make sure the measuring tape is straight, and that it's being held square to the board or the wall. If the tape is held at an angle, it will throw off the measurement.

When measuring to get the length of a board, most of the time, if you look real close, you'll see that it's is not quite on a 1/16-inch mark on the measuring tape. Let's say that it's slightly over 16 and 9/16 of an inch. I would call this 16 and 9/16 plus. If it was under the mark, I would call it 16 and 9/16 minus. Doing this will get me down to the 1/32 of an inch. If I need to be more exact, I'll break it down even farther by determining whether it's sitting in the middle between two marks, or closer to one mark than the other.

No matter how carefully you measure, you can still be slightly off. If I'm installing trim, and the length of a board has to be exact, I cut it a trace long to begin with. Then I'll check the fit, and cut off a bit more if necessary.

In the last few years, I've been seeing more saws that have a laser attached that projects a line where the blade will cut. So far, I've only used a couple of saws that have this feature, but based on that, I'd have to say I don't like it. On both saws, the projected line made it difficult to see the pencil mark. Maybe I'm wrong, and the laser was simply adjusted incorrectly. But in order to do precise work, you have to clearly see the line, and what the saw blade is doing.

When making a cut, start the saw and then lower it to the board, so the blade has time to get up to speed. Then make sure that the saw blade is lined up correctly by barely touching the board, before you cut it. This way, if you're off a little bit, all you have to do is to slide the board over, and then make the cut. Some guys will set the saw blade against the board to line it up, and then turn the saw on and cut as fast as they can, as if they're trying to impress someone. All this does is cause sloppy work. The position of the saw blade when it's stopped, and where it actually cuts, aren't always the same. I generally start with the blade lined up so it looks like the cut will be a little long. Then I'll start the saw, and many times I'll find that's it's right on the line.

Commonly, you'll make a cut, and then find that you still have to take a little more off. When that happens, I just slide the board over until it touches the blade. Then I turn the saw on and cut it at that position. That should take a bit more off. If I need more than that, I'll press the board against the blade, hard enough to slightly flex it, and then make the cut. It takes a little practice to do this, and every saw is different.

# SCRIBING AN EDGE

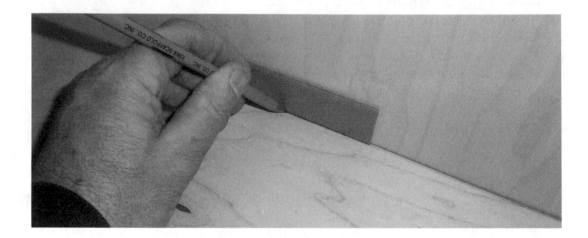

To get a tight fit, sometimes the edge of a board has to be scribed. This is done by drawing a line along the edge of the board that you're cutting, that parallels the surface that it has to match up to. Then you cut to the line. Some places where this is needed would include: fitting a stair tread against the riser, cutting a counter top or a cabinet to fit against a wall, or shaving a board to fit against the back of a built-in book shelf, as shown in these photos.

Depending on the circumstances, you can draw the line by simply dragging a pencil along the edge, by laying a spacer against the surface and then drawing the line along the edge of that, or by using a compass or some other tool that's made for this purpose. In the photo above, the pencil was held against a drywall shim, as the shim was slid along the back edge.

The line can be drawn on the very edge, so it's removed as the board is cut, or it could be in from the edge, so the board is cut parallel to the line.

Generally, a block plane or a belt sander is used for shaving the edge. A jig saw or a planer could also be used when there's more to take off. Check the fit as you go, so you don't remove too much in one spot.

## JAMBS

When trimming windows and doors, you should always go over the jambs in advance to see how they line up with the surface of the wall. These days, most interior doors have jambs that are veneered, which won't allow you to plane down any high spots.

Windows commonly have solid wood jambs, so they can be planed down where they extend out from the wall. When doing this, use a block plane, and keep checking your progress with a straightedge. Try to keep the plane flat to the wall. Then plane in the direction that gives the smoothest finish, and try not to gouge the wood. Be extra careful when doing the corners. When finished, the jambs should be close to flush with the surface of the wall, and be reasonably straight, so there won't be any gaps between the jambs and the trim, once it's in place. This means that sometimes you'll have to leave a bad spot as it is, since planing it down would do more harm than good.

Sometimes a jamb will sit in from the wall, instead. If it's in so far that the trim won't make contact with it, you'll have to soften the edge of the sheetrock. This is just a nice way of saying that you lightly pound on the edge of the sheetrock with a hammer, until the trim will lay flat against the jamb.

In the photos above, the one on the left shows a typical door with a jamb that's veneered. The photo on the right shows an extension jamb that's made out of solid wood, so it can be planed down, the same as most windows. When the jambs are solid wood, I like to go over them with sandpaper, smoothing the wood and lightly rounding off the inside corners, before the trim is installed.

# DOORS

I'll start by describing how to trim a door using standard 2 1/4 inch trim, with mitered corners. Before you begin, go over the trim boards and match them up to determine where they should go. Then decide whether or not the boards should go all the way to the floor. With carpeting, again I'd raise them up about a half inch. On wood or tile floors, I prefer to have the floor finished, and then run the trim tight to the floor. If I'm installing trim over a floor that's going to get wet, I'll seal the lower edge with paint or polyurethane, before it's installed, to help prevent it from absorbing moisture. On floors like this, I generally cut the boards so they're just off the floor, and sometimes I'll fill the gap with caulk to keep water and dirt out.

Before I start, I also check the corners on the jambs to see if they're square. You would think the corners would always be square, so the trim would be cut at exactly 45 degrees. But many times they're not, and the angle of the cuts will have to be adjusted. It's also possible that your miter saw is off. Over the years, I've used quite a few saws in the homes where I've worked, and I can't remember any that were dead on.

To check a miter saw, cut a short length of 1x4 with the saw adjusted to 45 degrees to the left, and another with the saw adjusted at 45 degrees to the right. Then hold the boards together, and check the corner with a square. If the corner is square, and both cuts are the same length, you're good to go. Sometimes you'll have a square corner, but one edge will be longer than the other, which means the base of the saw is on crooked. If this sounds like your saw, read the owner's manual to see if it can be adjusted.

If the base can't be adjusted, and either one or both sides are off, you'll have to determine where 45 degrees actually is. I do this by cutting two boards with the saw adjusted to 45 degrees to one side, and then change the angle until the corner is square when the boards are held together. Then I'll do the same on the other side. Most of the saws I've used have been off by at least half a degree on either one or both sides, and the angle had to be adjusted for every cut. Also check the saw for square cuts.

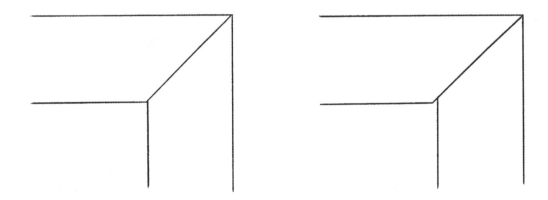

These drawings show the problem you'll have when the boards are cut at the wrong angle. Let's say that the correct angle to trim a corner is 46 degrees. If you've already nailed on the first board with the end cut at 45 degrees, then the other board will have to be cut at 47 degrees. Although the joint would be tight, the boards wouldn't match up on either one or both sides, and you'd have to do a little planing and hand sanding to make the corner look decent. By determining the angles beforehand, you'll get better results and also save time. In the drawing on the left, the correct angle was used and the boards match up, while on the right, the angles are different, so one of the boards overhangs the other. The reason for this is because the edge gets longer as the angle increases.

You'll have the same problem when trimming a square corner if the miter saw is off. If you didn't know it, and cut the first board with the saw set at 45 degrees, then you'd have to change the angle on the second one, and one edge could be longer than the other.

I generally trim a door by installing the side boards first. This way, I can lay the top board in place without having to hang on to it, and it lets me glue both corners at the same time. Others may do it in a different order. I also do the miter cuts first, in case something goes wrong, and then cut the boards to length. If I've determined that the corners are close to square, I'll set the angle at 45 degrees, assuming that the saw is reasonably accurate. If they're not square, I'll change the angle of the cut to best fit each corner.

Many times, the correct angle will either be 44 1/2 or 45 1/2 degrees. This can be a problem if you can't lock the saw at this angle. Miter saws have an indent at 45 degrees. On some of them, if you try to adjust the angle so it's a little off 45 degrees, it will keep falling into the indent. You'll have the same problem if you're trying to set it just off 90 degrees. When that happens, the best way to make the cut is to hold the trim board at an angle to the back of the saw (fence) by placing a shim behind the board, as shown in the photo.

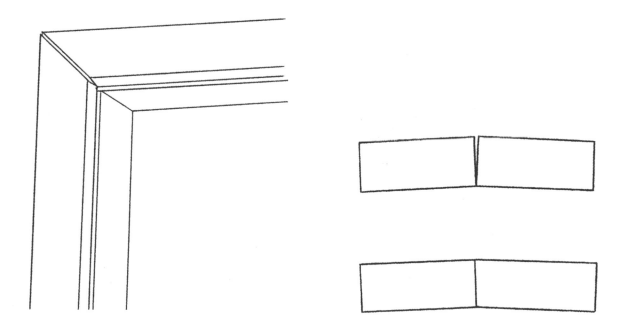

On corners where the wall has a hump in it, or the jamb sticks out from the wall, the trim will have to be back-cut to get a tight fit, which means that wood is removed from the back side of the joint. In the drawing on the left, and also the upper one on the right, you can see the gap that you'll get when the boards aren't laying flat to each other. The ends can be back-cut with either the miter saw or a block plane. In the lower right drawing, the board on the right was back-cut to tighten up the joint. On corners that are way off, it's generally better to back-cut both boards.

259

There are two ways to back-cut the trim with a miter saw. It can be done by adjusting the angle on a compound miter saw, or by shimming up the end of the board as you make the cut, as shown in this photo. By holding the board up, it's cut at an angle. To get more back-cut, use a thicker shim. Positioning the shim farther away from the saw blade will also raise the board so it's higher up.

This photo shows a mitered end that was back-cut with a block plane. In this case, the joint was only a little loose, so it wasn't necessary to go all the way to the front edge. Doing this is quicker if the angle is close, and you know what you're doing with a plane.

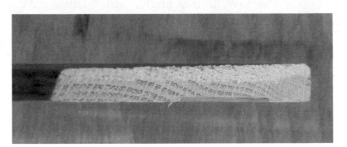

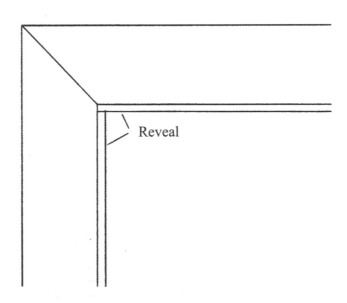

Reveal

After the miter cuts are done, I cut the boards to length so that I have the correct reveal at the top of the door. Reveal is how much the edge of the jamb shows, once the trim is in place. 1/8 - 3/16 inch is generally used for this type of trim. To check the size of the reveal at the upper corner, sometimes I'll hold a scrap board that has a miter cut against the other board to give me a better look. To stay consistent, I'll cut a board (shim) to the same thickness as the reveal, and then use it to check the gap as I go along.

To cut the boards to length, I either measure to the reveal, and then mark the boards on the inside edge, or I make a mark 2 1/4 inches above the reveal, and then measure to that, and mark each board on the outside edge.

When using the first method, you won't be able to hook the measuring tape on the inside edge to mark the length of the boards. Here I generally hold the tape against the side of each board with the 2 inch mark at the start of the miter cut, and add 2 inches to the measurement. This is more accurate than using the end of the tape.

Once the length is correct, the side boards are nailed on with two rows of nails. The inside row attaches the board to the jamb. I generally space these nails about 16 inches apart. The outside row goes into a stud, with the nails spaced about every 24 inches. I also add extra nails wherever it's necessary. Start by positioning each board so the reveal is correct at the upper corner. Then do the inside row first, as you work your way down, maintaining the same reveal.

The trim can either be nailed on by hand, or with a trim nailer. Hardwood trim should always be predrilled when hand nailing. For thinner trim, such as this, I'll use 1 1/4 inch hardened trim nails for the inside row, and 2 inch for the outside row. These nails are the same diameter, so a 5/64 drill bit can be used for both.

If you're using a trim gun, you'll want shorter nails for doing the inside row. Here you also have to watch the angle of the gun, so the nails don't come out on the inside of the jamb. Don't get too close to the mitered end, or you might split the board. When doing this, I like to have two guns set up, a 16 gauge with 1 1/4 - 1 1/2 inch nails for the inside row, and a 15 or 16 gauge with 2 - 2 1/2 inch nails for the outside row.

If the board is warped (crowned), you'll have to start by nailing one end, and then pull the board into place as you go. When hand nailing, I generally leave the nails at the upper corners a little loose for now. If I'm using a trim nailer, sometimes I'll leave them out until I see how the upper board fits. The others are nailed down tight, and finished off with a nail set, when hand nailing.

Now that both sides are on, I can do the top (upper) board. If this board was cut to the right length, using the same angle that was used for the sides, I'd be lucky if it fit correctly. So instead, I cut it about an 1/8 inch extra long to begin with. Then I'll lay it in place with an even reveal going across the jamb, and with the outside corners overlapped by an equal amount. Now I can check each corner to see what changes have to be made to get a tight fit. Maybe one of the ends needs a slightly different angle, or one might have to be back-cut. If so, I'll recut it and check the fit. This is one place where you need to be very picky. Here, taking the extra couple of minutes is the difference between a hack job, and one that you can be proud of. By cutting the upper board a little long to begin with, there should be enough length for a few adjustments.

Adjustments can also be made by planing the mitered ends. This requires some skill and a sharp block plane, so unless you know what you're doing, you're generally better off just using the miter saw.

Once the joints look good on both corners, the board can be cut to the correct length. In this case, just shorten it on the end where the last cut was made, before changing the setting on the miter saw.

Now that it's the right length, there's still one more thing to check. While holding the board in place, press it tight against the wall at each end. When doing this, many times you'll find that one of the boards will sit a little higher than the other. Small height differences are easily corrected by shaving a little wood from the back of the board, or by adding shims that are cut from a piece of felt paper. The shims are stapled on, unless they're going under the side boards, in which case they can just be slipped into place. It doesn't matter if the shim hangs out. After the trim is nailed on, anything that shows will be cut off with a utility knife.

If the top board is being hand nailed, I'll predrill it first. Then I'll apply glue to one side of each corner, and quickly put the board into place. Then the corners are squeezed together as the board is nailed on. At the same time, I also do any nails that were either left out or not driven in all the way on the side boards. Then the excess glue is wiped off, so I can see how the corners look. If anything needs to be changed, it will have to be done quickly, since there isn't much time before the glue sets up.

If one of the boards sticks out where they come together, the first thing to do is to lightly hit it with a hammer to drive it tighter against the wall, and see if that helps. Before doing this, lay a shim or a scrap of wood over the board to keep from denting it.

When that doesn't work, the board that's lower will have to be shimmed out. If there's a gap between the lower board and the wall, I'll drive a wood shim under it, and then hit the face of the board that's higher to get them to line up. When there isn't a gap, I'll pry the board out by using a chisel with a shim under it to protect the wall. Then, as it's being held out, either felt paper or a wood shim is slipped beneath it.

261

Sometimes the boards move as they're being nailed into place, and one of them has to be driven over to get them to line up again. When that happens, lay something against the wall to protect it, such as thin cardboard or a piece that's cut from something like a cereal box. Then slide the hammer along it as you tap on the board that sticks out.

While doing this, try to match up any pattern that's in the trim. If one of the edges is longer, you probably won't be able to match up the corners and the pattern at the same time. In that case, you'll have to make a judgment call as to what looks the best.

If there's a gap in the joint after the corner's been nailed, see if it can be squeezed tight by hand. If so, you should be able to tape it together. Before you do this, see if the joint needs any more glue. If it does, hold the tip of the glue bottle tight against the joint, and try to push a little more in. Then squeeze the joint together, and while holding it, wipe off any excess glue with a damp paper towel, and stretch pieces of masking tape diagonally across it and around the edge of the corner to hold it tight together. Once the glue has dried, the tape is removed.

Sometimes, the only way to tighten a corner is to nail the two boards together. When hand nailing hardwood trim, you'll have to predrill using a drill bit that has a slightly smaller diameter than the nail. Use something to protect the wall when drilling the hole and pounding in the nail.

After the glue dries, if you're still left with a small tip hanging out, just sand it off. While doing this, hold the sandpaper parallel to the shorter board. If it's only a small tip, it shouldn't be too noticeable.

When the tip is larger, you'll also have to sand the outside edge of the board that sticks out, so you won't be able to see where the tip was sanded off. Make sure that you don't just sand the very end of the board. What you're trying to do is to fool the eye by sanding back far enough so the board is tapered, but it doesn't appear that anything was done.

These photos show both sides of the top board, after it was cut long and then laid into place. Here the left side is pretty tight, except right at the inside corner, so I might leave that end as it is. On the right side, the angle is slightly off, as there's a small gap that gets larger at the outside corner. In this case, I'd probably set the miter saw so it had about 1/2 of a degree more angle, and then recut that side and check it again. Then if the fit was good, I'd cut the board to length at the same end.

Commonly, the corners won't be this tight to begin with, and instead of half a degree, they could be off by one or even two degrees if the saw is off. When changing the angle, remove as little as possible. If you're increasing the angle, the cut should end right at the outside corner, and vice versa.

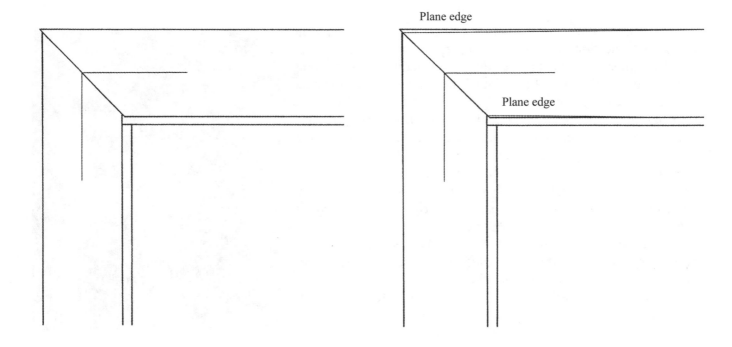

Plane edge

Plane edge

These drawings show a mitered corner where the boards don't match up. This is generally caused by the angle of the cuts being different, though it's also possible that one of the boards is wider. Either way, you'll have the same problem where one of the boards overlaps the other on one, or even both edges. Here the first thing to do is to line up any pattern in the trim, and then make sure the boards are flush to each other along the joint. Shim, if necessary. Now that the boards are in the correct position, you can see what has to be done. When there isn't much of an overlap, you can generally leave the inside corner as it is, and just sand off the tip on the outside corner once the board has been nailed into place. If the overlap is any bigger, you'll have to remove some wood. On the outside corner, I'd plane off as little as possible, and keep it at a gentle taper so it won't be noticeable. I'd do the same on the inside corner, but here you also have to consider the amount of reveal.

## GLUING THE CORNERS

When I first started trimming, I never glued the corners. I assumed that once a joint was tight, it would stay that way. That isn't the case. Houses expand and contract, so a tight joint can still open up over time. By gluing the corners, that generally won't happen.

263

# WINDOWS

Trimming the windows isn't much different than doing the doors. Again, the first thing to do is to prepare the jambs, and then check the corners to see if they're square. I generally start by doing the bottom board first. Once I've found the right angle for the cuts, I cut the board to length so that I have the correct reveal on each side. Sometimes I'll check the size of the reveal by putting a miter cut on both ends of a scrap board, and then hold it against each side. You could also mark the reveal at each corner with a pencil. If the jamb sticks out from the wall at either corner, then that end of the board will have to be back-cut. If it sits in, you'll have to soften the edge of the sheetrock. Once the board looks right, it's nailed on in the same manner as it was on the door trim.

The side boards are next. Cut both ends on one of the boards, using the angles that have already been determined. Again, it should be cut a little long, so there's enough room to make adjustments. Then hold the board in place, parallel to the jamb, to see how it looks. On a jamb that's straight, this is easy. Just make sure that the reveal is the same at both ends. When the jamb is curved, the board may have to be held a little different. Let's say that this is a large window that's already been insulated with spray-foam, and the jamb has a slight curve in it. Since the jamb is locked into place, if the trim board was installed in a straight line, the amount of reveal at the center of the window would be a lot different than it is on the ends. Here it's better if the board follows the jamb, so I'd hold it so there was an even reveal for the first couple of feet when checking the corner. Sometimes the trim board itself will be warped (crowned), in which case, you'll have to compensate for that too.

Now your main concern is how the lower corner matches up. If the angle is a little off, recut it and try it again. If the angle looks right, but you still have a gap, it will have to be back-cut. Also check the thickness by pressing the lower corner tight against the wall to see if the boards match up. Then make any adjustments that are necessary. Once the joint is tight, the board's cut to length so you have the correct reveal on the upper jamb. Again, this can be checked by holding another board against the upper corner.

When hand nailing, I generally predrill the board first. Then I apply glue to one side of the joint, and nail the board into place as I hold the corner tight together. By going in at an angle with the outside nail at each corner, it will help to drive the boards together. On jambs that aren't straight or the trim board is warped, once I've gone a couple of feet, I'll pull the board into place as I go, so it lines up with the jamb.

If there's anything wrong with the joint, once it's been nailed, any changes will have to be made before the glue sets up. Tape the corner if you have any doubts about it staying tight together. Then move on to the other side, and do it the same way.

The upper board is installed in the same manner as it was on the door, by measuring and cutting it long to begin with, and then trimming it to its final length once the correct angle has been found for both ends.

There are a couple of methods used to determine the length of the bottom and the side boards. One way is to do the miter cut on one end, and then hold the board in place with that end positioned correctly as you mark the inside edge on the other end, so it has the correct reveal, and then make the miter cut so it ends at the mark. You could also cut the boards to length strictly by measurement. On windows with 2 1/4 inch trim, measure the distance between the jambs. Then add 4 1/2 inches, plus the reveal on each side, and mark the length on the outside edge of the boards.

When trimming a large window, it's hard to check the corners if you're working alone. You have to match up the corner on one end, and then hold the board in place as you move over to the other side to see how it looks. When doing this, sometimes I'll put one of the nails part way in to keep the board from moving.

# WIDE WINDOW AND DOOR TRIM

I've always liked wide trim, because it gives an old-fashioned quality look to a house. Unfortunately, as money is running low towards the end of a project, narrow trim is often used instead, since this is one way to cut the costs. The upper photo shows windows that have wide trim, which includes a sill (stool), apron, and a back band. A door would be trimmed in the same manner, minus the sill and the apron. I realize that in books, the base of the window is called a stool, but I grew up calling them window sills, so that's what they'll be called here. In the next few pages, I'll describe how to trim a window. Most of the photos that are included aren't from a window, but the idea is exactly the same.

As with the previous trim, you'll start by planing down any jambs that extend out from the wall. But when installing this trim, it's a little different. Since the boards are wider, and you'll be using butt joints, here it's more important that the jambs line up with the wall several inches over, since that's where the outside edge of the trim will actually be.

When installing wide trim, the wood is generally around 3/4 of an inch thick. You won't be able to bend it like you can with narrow trim, so the edge of the jamb should be straight, if possible. This is especially true for the bottom jamb, because the sill will be attached to it. Make sure that the upper corner on this jamb has a nice sharp edge, and that it's square to the wall.

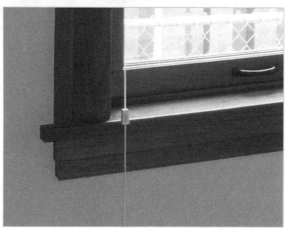

The sill will be installed first. To determine how long it has to be, measure the distance between the inside edge of the jambs. Then add to that: the width of the trim boards, the reveal on both sides of the window, and also the back bands, not counting the part of the back band that overlaps the other board. Then add to that measurement, how much overhang you want on each end of the sill. Generally it's about 1 inch per side. Add this up, and then cut the sill to that length.

Now mark the center on both the sill and the bottom jamb. Then line the marks up, and hold the sill tight against the jamb. While doing this, you may find that the ends have to be notched. Once the sill fits, hold it in place, and then check for any gaps that are caused by high spots on the jamb. Any high spots will have to be planed off.

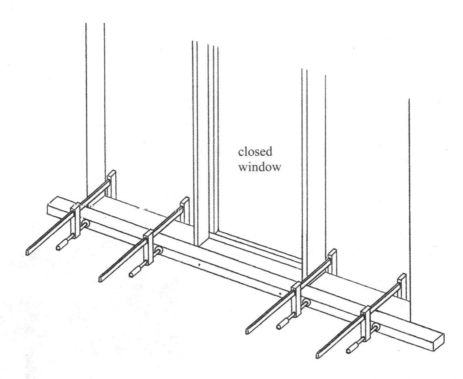

closed
window

The sill is going to be glued, flush to the upper surface of the jamb. I always dry-fit the sill. Then, while holding it in place, predrill it for 8D finish nails where needed. It's easier to do this now, before the glue is applied. I try not to use any more nails than I have to, whether they're for positioning the sill or for driving it tight.

Ideally, the window can be opened. In that case, apply glue to the sill, and then clamp it tight to the jamb while matching up the upper surface. This could take a lot of clamps if you're doing several windows. Borrow what you need from friends. Make sure that the clamps won't harm the window, and pad them if necessary. Clamps for doing this should be some type of a bar clamp that's long enough to pass through the window opening. Pipe clamps may not have enough depth for this job. When part of the window can't be opened, as shown in the drawing, the only way to do that area is to drive the sill tight by nailing it.

When you install a sill in this manner, you want a perfect glue line without any gaps. Nail or clamp any spot that isn't tight. Then use a nail set to sink the nail heads, and let the glue dry. At this time, don't wipe off any of the excess glue that squeezes out the top of the sill. The glue will shrink down as it dries, and removing it now could leave a dip at any spot where there's a gap between the sill and the jamb. Sometimes I'll slice off most of the excess glue, once it's at the point where it's hard and rubbery, to save on the amount of scraping that I'll have to do later.

The clamps can be removed once the glue has set up. Then after letting it dry overnight, use a scraper to remove the excess glue, while being careful not to put any deep scratches into the wood. I use a chisel to clean up the corners, and then scrape them flat using an old blade from a block plane. After that's done, the window sill is sanded, so you end up with a smooth flat surface.

This photo shows a sill that's been glued flush to the jamb. It would have been easier to lower the sill and to have a reveal instead, since it would eliminate any gluing, but I think this looks better. By having the boards at the same height, it also gives you a wider surface to set things on. On this sill, red oak was attached to a pine jamb, which was then stained and varnished.

The side boards are next. To do them, set the miter saw at 90 degrees, and cut one of them to length, again leaving it a little long. Then lay it in place, following the edge of the jamb, to see how it fits against the sill. If the bottom cut is off, redo it so it fits tight. Then check the cut on the upper end by laying a board across the top of it. While doing this, make sure that both boards are being held parallel to the jambs. Once the angle is right, the board can be cut to length so that you have the correct reveal on the upper jamb.

Wide trim generally has around 1/4 inch of reveal, so I mark the jambs with a pencil. Then I use the marks for positioning the boards, and also for cutting them to length. I also cut a piece of wood that's the correct thickness to check the reveal, to stay consistent. If you plan on using varnish or polyurethane, make sure that you erase any pencil marks, since the marks will show through the finish.

After the board has been cut to length, nail it in place, but leave out the top nail on both sides. Then do the other board in the same manner.

When hand nailing hardwood, I predrill, and use either 6D finish nails or 2 inch hardened trim nails on the jamb side, and 8D finish or 2 1/2 inch hardened trim nails for nailing into the studs. When using a trim nailer, I'd use 2 inch nails in a 16-gauge gun on the jamb side, and 2 1/2 inch nails in a 15-gauge gun for going into the studs.

This type of trim may have one side rounded off, while the other edge is square. In that case, the side boards are generally installed with the rounded edge facing in, so it shows. But the upper board should have the square edge down, in order to get a tight joint. Later on, it can be rounded off with sandpaper. Here the trim boards are just maple 1 x 4s, so the edge is square on both sides.

After the side boards are nailed on, the top board is cut to length so it ends at the outside edge of both sides. Then it's laid into place. This cut doesn't have to be exact, since it will be hidden by the back band.

Once the board is in place, there are two things that you have to check. First, see how the boards match up where they come together. If either one sits low, it will have to be shimmed out, so they match up across the entire width of the seam. Use felt paper or wood shims for doing this. Shims that go under the side boards should stay in place by themselves. If any are needed for the top board, they can be stapled on.

The boards also have to be in line with each other. Check this by laying a straightedge across the corner, as shown in the upper photo. If the upper edge of the top board is tipped back, it will have to be shimmed out to bring it into line.

Sometimes you'll have the opposite problem, and the top board will stick "out" on the upper edge. In that case, instead of shimming it out, it will have to be planed or sanded down. If top board is only a little out of line, it might be easier to sand it down after it's been nailed on. If it's off more than that, then the back of the board will have to be planed.

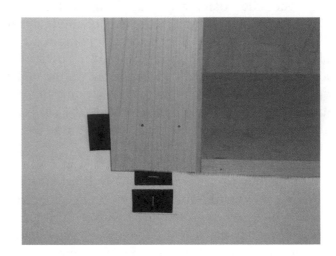

Here, both sides had to be shimmed out, so the lower board would match up.

Once you've finished doing any necessary shimming or planing, apply glue to the top of the side boards, and lay the upper board in place. Then nail it on while pulling the corners tight together. At the same time, also put in any nails that were left out on the side boards. After nailing it, wipe off the excess glue to see how it looks. If any adjustments have to be made, do it now before the glue sets up.

After that's finished, use a random orbit sander to smooth down the seams and to flatten out the corners. I'll start by using 60 - 80-grit sandpaper, if the corner needs a lot of work. Otherwise I'll use 100 - 150-grit. These sanders can quickly get you into trouble. Keep the sander moving, and keep checking your progress with a straightedge, so you don't end up putting a dip in the wood. If one of the boards has to be sanded down, make sure that you go far enough back, so it has a gradual taper that won't be noticed.

Generally, I like to apply the finish first, if I'm trimming with oak that has a clear finish. But since the corners are sanded with this type of trim, it wouldn't be practical here, so you'll just have to match up the wood as best you can.

Now the back band can be installed. I generally do the sides first. To find their length, I lay a section of the back band over the top board, and then measure from the upper edge of it down to the sill. Since the back band is pretty narrow, I cut the upper end at 45 degrees, and make any adjustments to the board that goes over the top. I also cut each one long, so it sits a trace high at the upper corner. If the board is even a little bit short, it would prevent me from getting a tight joint. In that case, the side board would have to be held up off the sill. Having a small gap at the sill is less noticeable than a gap in the mitered joint.

Ideally, the back band will fit tight against the face of the trim boards around the entire perimeter. When it doesn't, it's generally because the top board isn't in line with the sides, or one of the boards has been thinned down. If it's the second reason, the back band will have to be planed down on the back side, so it fits better.

When using a trim nailer, I try to nail the back band to the main trim, from the side, and use a 16 gauge gun with 1 1/2 - 2 inch nails. Then I angle the gun so the nails don't come out the face of the trim. If there isn't room to do this, I'll nail into a stud using a 15 gauge gun with 2 1/2 inch nails. When hand nailing, I'd predrill if it was hardwood, and then nail into the stud using 2 1/2 inch hardened trim nails.

The top board is next. Start by cutting it a little long. Then check the fit, and adjust the angle of the cuts, if necessary, before cutting the board to its final length. Then before it's nailed, push each end tight into place to see if the corners match up on the front edge. If they're off, either shim the boards, take wood off the

back, or do whatever it takes to make the corners come together. If you're hand nailing, and the upper trim board was shimmed out from the wall, you'll probably have to do the same with the back band. Once the fit looks good, glue the corners, and nail the board into place. When necessary, also nail the corners together. Lay something against the wall to protect it anytime you drill or hand nail a corner.

To finish off the window, you still need the apron that goes under the sill. This is cut to the same length as the outside width of the back bands. Then a return is generally glued on each end. Nail the apron to the studs, with two nails going into each one.

# EXTENSION JAMBS

When remodeling, commonly the jambs end up being too narrow on the windows and doors for installing the trim. To solve this, extensions have to be added to the existing jambs. I generally give the extensions a small reveal. I've also glued them flush to the inside edge of the jamb, but found that it wasn't worth the trouble. Several examples are shown here.

Extensions were needed for this window, once the tongue and groove paneling was added. Here the choice was to make the extensions out of pine, to match the jambs, or ash to match the paneling. We decided to go with ash, since it was already on hand, and it had a nice look to it. To install the boards, each jamb was measured on both ends, and also in the middle, to see how far it sat in from the surface of the wall. Then the boards were cut (ripped) to the largest measurement, using a table saw, and planed where needed with a block plane. After that, each one was sanded, and then nailed into place with a trim gun. As you can see, these extension jambs only have a small reveal that's around 1/16 of an inch, while the trim has a reveal of 3/16.

This French door is in the same room as the window that's shown above. On this one, the jamb was too narrow to begin with. Then after sheathing and paneling were added to both sides of the wall, the jamb had to be extended a full 3 1/2 inches. Here I wanted to match what was already in place, so I bought three pieces of veneered jamb and cut them to width. Then I shimmed and nailed the boards into place about every 16 inches while maintaining an even reveal around the existing jamb.

These extensions were needed because the wrong door was installed. This one was made for a 2x4 wall, and the wall was framed with 2x6s. Here, 3/4 inch clear pine was used, and was cut to 2 inches wide. On both the top and the right side of the door, screws were used to attach the extensions. To do this, the holes were predrilled, and then long screws were driven into the original jamb.

On the left side of the door there was a problem, because there wasn't room for the board to slip between the hinges and the side of the opening. To make it fit, the board was thinned down to 1/2 inch thick by ripping it on the table saw. Then it was nailed to the side of the opening, and shimmed out where necessary.

If the door had the correct jamb to begin with, the hinges would extend out from the wall, which is necessary for a door to open all the way. If this was an interior door, I would have installed it so the jamb was flush to the wall on this side, instead, and then attached the extensions to the other side of the jamb. Here there wasn't a choice, because of the threshold. In this case, there's also a short wall next to the door, so it wouldn't have opened all the way anyhow.

These photos show how to put a return on the end of a trim board. It's easier to do this by cutting the return from a different piece of wood, although you can also do it by starting with a board that's extra long.

When using separate boards, start by cutting the trim board to length, and cut the end(s) at 45 degrees where you want a return to go. To make the return, the other board is also cut at 45 degrees, on the end that's opposite the return. For instance, if the return is going on the left side of the trim board, it's cut from the right side of the other board. After cutting the end at 45 degrees, measure in the thickness of the board, and then cut off the end at the mark, with the blade set at 90 degrees, and see how it fits. The trim board, shown here, is just under 3/4 of an inch thick, so that's distance the mark was made from the end of the board.

When cutting the return from the same board, both ends are cut at 45 degrees. Then you cut off one end, and attach it to the other side. If you want a return on both ends of the board, a return has to be cut from each side. In either case, the board isn't cut to its final length until the returns have been cut.

It may take several tries until you get a return that's the right size. Then it's glued on. I prefer to do this before the board is installed. After wiping off the excess glue, sometimes I'll use tape to hold the return in place until the glue sets up. Another option is to install the board first, and then glue on the return(s). Either way works fine.

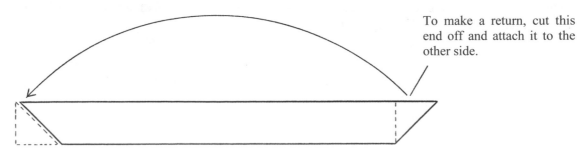

To make a return, cut this end off and attach it to the other side.

When windows are right next to each other, they're generally trimmed as one unit, even though they may not be directly attached. This photo shows two windows that were installed side by side, with a center trim board going between them. When doing this, the center board is generally a little thinner than the board it butts up against. In this case, it's 5/8 inch thick, while the outer trim is 3/4 inch.

This window was made up from four smaller ones that were attached together. Here the outer trim is 3/4 inch thick. The board that runs down the center is 5/8 inch, and the two horizontal boards are 1/2 inch thick.

# EGRESS WINDOWS

When an egress window is being finished off with wood, plywood is generally the best choice. On this window, maple plywood was used to match the rest of the basement. In the past, I've tried using standard wood, but had problems with the boards cupping within a short period of time. Since the openings are seldom square, the boards have to be shimmed into position so there's an even reveal around the window. In the lower photo, the X's show where the shims were positioned on each side to support the plywood.

A table saw, along with a sliding miter saw, works best for cutting the boards. You could also use a circular saw if you're careful not to splinter the ends. Cutting from the back will help in this regard. Applying masking tape where you're making the cut, before the line is drawn, also helps.

I generally install the bottom board first. Since it will be overlapped on both sides, it doesn't have to be the exact length, but cut the board a little wide to begin with. Then once you see how it fits, it can be cut to size so that it lines up with the wall. On this window, maple veneer was attached to the edge of the plywood that faces the room. This was necessary because there will be a reveal along the inside edge of the trim.

The board will have to be shimmed at several points along the edge of the window. Use felt paper, drywall shims, or strips of wood to build it up to the correct height. Then put a nail at each location. In this case, 2 inch finish nails were the longest ones that could be used, to keep from hitting the concrete blocks that surrounded the opening.

The upper board is next. This is done in the same manner as the lower board, with the exception that it's also lightly nailed along the edge of the wall to keep it in place.

The side boards will slip between the ones that were just installed. Cut them to length so they fit tight at the back edge, and make sure the back corners are square. Again, these boards should be cut a little wide to begin with.

In this case, the upper board was a different width than the one on the bottom, so the side boards had to be tapered. A table saw was used to cut the tapers, though it also could have been done with either a circular saw or a plane.

On a table saw, this is pretty easy to do. Let's say that you want the board to taper 1/4 inch, from one end to the other. After drawing a line to mark the cut, staple a parallel strip of wood to the board so it's tight on one end, but gapped 1/4 inch on the other. Make sure it's parallel to the line that was drawn. Ideally, the strip should be at least as long as the board that's being tapered. Staple it from the back side, so the front surface won't be damaged. After that's done, adjust the fence on the table saw so it cuts to the line. Then cut the board by holding the strip tight against the fence.

In the upper photo, you can see that the strip is a little short. To compensate for it, the size of the gap was reduced to end up with the correct taper.

Before they're installed, the side boards have to be shimmed along the edge of the window to maintain the same reveal. Here they were shimmed out at four points, and then nailed at those spots.

Then a framing square was used to square up the boards to the window, on both the upper and lower corners, as shown in the drawing. Shims were used to hold them at that position, and then the corners were nailed. To do the inside shims, a straightedge was held against each side as it was shimmed and nailed, to make sure it was straight.

Once the side boards were in place, shims were used at each corner to push the upper and the lower board tight against the sides. Then a straightedge was used for shimming the middle. After that was done, the edges were nailed, and the shims were cut off flush to the plywood.

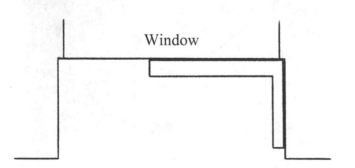

Window

275

When the end of a board is cut at an angle, the length of the edge becomes longer. And the steeper the angle is, the longer the edge becomes. This becomes obvious when looking at the lower left photo. You wouldn't think that the two boards that cap the baseboard are the same width, but they are. Although it isn't nearly as severe, the corner trim on the ceiling in the upper photo has exactly the same problem. Here the trim was laid flat to the wall, so there was a difference in width whenever a horizontal board met up with one that was coming down at an angle. In this case, the difference between the two boards was about 1/8 inch.

To bring the corners together, I planed both edges on the boards that were on the sloped part of the ceiling, and started far enough back so it wouldn't be noticeable. This wasn't possible when doing the corner in the lower photos, so a board was cut to fit.

Out of all the ceilings that I've worked on, this is my favorite, While measuring and snapping the chalk lines to mark the positions of the rafters, I noticed that the wall for the entry door was way out of place. It turned out that there was a 2 1/2 inch difference between the left and the right side, and it had to be made up in the last few feet. What I ended up doing was to use this design to fool the eye. I don't have any good photos that show it, but one side has an extra board. A similar design was also used on the flat area over the piano.

# COVERING A POST

Houses commonly have posts that are used to support an upper level. In basements, they're generally either treated wood or steel, and are spread out along a beam that runs down the center of it. Since leaving the posts as is wouldn't look very nice, the best thing to do is to cover them up. There are a couple of ways to do this. One is to build them into a wall by running the studs in line with them, so they'll be hidden once the sheetrock is in place. Of course, this only works if you want a wall at that location. Another option is to cover the posts with some type of wood. Here are a few examples of how this was done.

The upper photo shows the post that's on the last page. Originally, it was just several 2x6s that were nailed together. The

shape of this one is a little odd, since it's not symetrical, and it has five or six sides to it. Oak boards were used to cover the 2x6s, and the outside corners were just butted together. Here the joints were both glued and screwed, with the screws recessed for plugs. I remember that applying the glue was a problem, because the post is 17 feet tall. Since I wanted the plugs to show, I cut them from hardwood dowels, because the end grain looked darker once the oil finish was applied.

The second photo shows a post that was covered with maple. This one has notched butt joints, but what's different is that it also has an outlet on two sides of it. This

was possible because the original post was an I-beam, so there was room for the wire and the boxes. In this case, it turned out that a second outlet wasn't needed, since the one that you can see is seldom used.

The post in the lower photo was originally one of those round metal ones that are adjustable for height. On this one, I covered it with oak plywood. One advantage of using plywood over solid wood is that the joints will stay tighter over time. This post was covered years ago, and the joints are still as tight as they ever were.

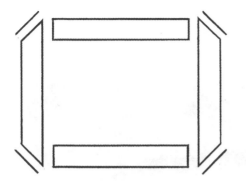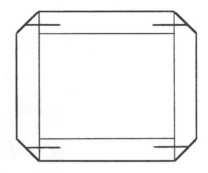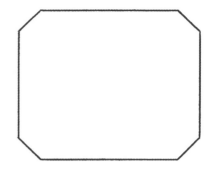

The upper drawings show how the last post was covered. After the different pieces were cut to size on a table saw, I applied glue to one of the boards, and then held the first corner together as small finishing nails were driven through the edge that was cut at 45 degrees. Once that was finished, the second corner was done in the same manner. On the last board, both sides

were glued at the same time, so I had to work fast before the glue set up. Then any glue residue was wiped off, and the post was left to dry overnight.

The next day, I used an iron to attach the veneer to the 45 degree corners. After that, it was just a matter of cutting off the excess veneer with a utility knife, redoing any spots where it wasn't tight, and then sanding the post.

In the lower drawing, two of the boards are notched. One reason for doing this is that it makes the 45 degree edges narrower. It also makes it easier to assemble the post, since the notches will hold everything in place. This photo gives you a closer look at one of the corners.

In the basement that's shown in some of the photos, there was an old wall that was originally an exterior wall, which had been framed out with 2x4s. In this case, there was enough distance between the concrete and the face of the studs that we were able to use the space for shelves. Maple plywood was used for the back and the sides of the openings, and also for the shelves. On the back, we attached the plywood to the concrete with construction adhesive. For the shelves, 3/4 inch plywood was used, with veneer attached to the front edge.

As you can see, two of the openings have doors, while one was left open. To build the doors, the frames were constructed using maple 1x4s that were doweled together, and the panels were cut from thin maple plywood. The center opening also has shelves, but the doors on the right hide the manifolds for the in-floor heating system.

# BASEMENT WINDOWS

When finishing off a basement, you'll commonly have to deal with those small windows that are right next to the ceiling. Depending on if the window was being replaced, how straight the opening was, and whether or not the concrete would stay dry, I've used sheetrock, Durock, and plywood to finish off the openings. Sometimes the material was directly attached to the side of the opening, but more often it was screwed or nailed to furring strips that were attached with Tapcons or construction adhesive. These photos show how it was done in a few houses.

In the upper photo, sheetrock was used, and the opening still needs a little work with joint compound to finish it off.

In the center photo, the window was replaced. Then maple plywood was used to cover the bottom and both sides. The outside edge of the plywood had to be veneered, since there's a 1/4 inch reveal along the edge of the trim.

The bottom window was also replaced. In this case, the opening is slightly lower than the ceiling. Here, both sides and the top were sheet-rocked and covered with wallpaper. Then oak plywood was used on the bottom.

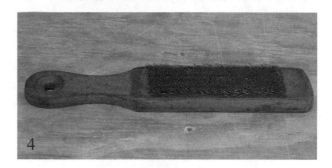

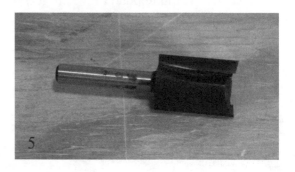

Here are some other tools that may be needed for working on the house. Number 1 is a forstner bit, which drills flat-bottomed holes. This particular one is used for installing European style hinges on cabinet doors. Number 2 is a doweling jig. I don't use one very often, so I haven't got around to buying a biscuit cutter, but a doweling jig still works fine. It's used for building cabinets, making doors, or anywhere you need to glue boards together with a strong connection.

Number 3 is a seam roller for hanging wallpaper. But I use it for applying veneer to the edge of plywood. If I don't have the roller with me, I'll slide a board (with rounded edges) along the veneer as I press down.

Number 4 is a file card (cleaner). When you use a file, the grooves between the ridges get clogged up. The file card removes the material that's causing the problem. Files are designed to cut in one direction, by pushing forward or away from yourself if the handle is towards you. People commonly just go back and forth with a file, but this is wrong. It's the same when using a hand saw. Even though you're going back and forth, you only apply pressure when going in the direction that it cuts.

Number 5 is a router bit that cuts a flat-bottomed slot. This particular one is just under 3/4 of an inch, so the plywood will fit tight if I'm using the bit for installing shelves. This type of bit is also used for installing hinges. When doing this, it's easier to use a jig. One that I can recommend is made by Ryobi.

If I don't have a jig with me, I'll just mark where the hinges go, and then use one of them to draw the outline with a sharp pencil. Then I'll set the depth on the router, and cut the hinge pockets while staying just inside the pencil line. Once that's done, I'll finish up the edges with a sharp chisel.

# INSTALLING BASEBOARD

Baseboard has changed quite a bit over the years. In older homes, it generally consists of two parts, with a wide lower board and an ornamental cap on top. Commonly, there will also be base shoe running along the edge of the floor. In newer construction, baseboard is generally much shorter, with only a single board being used. The two most common styles are ranch and Colonial. No matter which type you have, the best way to install it is by coping the inside corners. Mitering them would seem to be an easier way, but a mitered corner tends to open up as the baseboard is nailed into place. Learning "how" to cope a corner is pretty easy. The hard part for most people is having enough patience to do to a good job. Using this method may be a little difficult at first, but once you get the hang of it, you'll quickly get better and faster. There will also be days where everything seems to go right, and days when even an experienced trimmer has to fight for every joint.

To best describe how to trim in this manner, we'll work our way around a room installing one-piece baseboard. Before starting, you have to know what's going on the floor. With carpeting, the baseboard should be raised up about a half inch off the floor, so the carpeting can slip beneath it. When going over wood or tile, the floor is generally installed first. Then the baseboard will be installed tight to the floor, and base shoe is added if necessary.

Buy the wood ahead of time, as it has to sit in the house to acclimate. If you're trimming an upper level, the wood should be stored on an upper level, and not in the basement. How long it has to be in the house before it's installed would depend on where it comes from, how thick it is, and how dry the climate is. Where I live, I'd like at least a few days for the wood to acclimate, if it came from inside a store. If it had been in the garage or came from an unheated warehouse, I'd want at least a week, and two would be better. Of course, sometimes you can't wait as long you'd like, but it's important to give it enough time, so the wood doesn't shrink after it's been installed. If that happens, you'll end up with gaps in the corners. Without a moisture meter, this is all just a guess, so here it's better to err on the safe side.

These are the tools you'll need for doing the job: hammer, nail set, coping saw, files, drill and drill bits, staple gun, scissors, miter saw, and also a trim gun (finish nailer) and a compressor, if you're using one. A jigsaw can also be used to make the coped cuts, although I've never tried it myself. My favorite files for coping are a 4-in-1 file along with a small rectangular one that has a course edge to cut faster, as shown on the right. Rat tail files (round) are hard to control, and tend to take off too much in one spot, so a file that's flat is better in most cases.

You'll also need 1/2 inch thick plywood blocks, wood shims, fifteen-pound felt paper, and either 2 inch hardened trim nails or 6D finish nails. If you're using a finish nailer, you'll need 2 - 2 1/2 inch nails in a 15 or 16 gauge gun. When installing 3/4 inch thick baseboard, increase the size of the nails to 8D, or use 2 1/2 inch hardened trim nails. With a trim gun, I'd use 2 1/2 inch nails in a 15 gauge gun.

Before you start, you should always go over the boards to see what lengths you have. Also, look for any bad warps or crowns, and check for flaws such as splits and knots. Then determine which piece is going where, and the best way to cut up the boards, while taking into consideration the lengths you have to work with and any flaws in the wood.

Then determine where to begin, and whether to go in a clockwise or a counter-clockwise direction. I saw left-handed with a hand saw, and it's easier for me to cope the left side of a board. So here, we'll be going in a clockwise direction.

At this time, I also cut a board that will be installed later on one of the shorter walls. I cut it a few inches extra long, and make sure it's square on both ends. For the time being, it will used to square up the baseboard. We'll call it the test board.

I've always read that it's best to start in the closets or little used areas, until you get in practice. This sounds like good advice, but I have a problem with it. Even though the boards were checked in advance, sometimes you'll still find flaws in the wood after you've already started. On occasion, you're also going to screw up a cut. I generally start on the longer walls. This way, if I find a bad board or botch a cut, I can just grab another board, and use the bad one on a shorter wall. If you started on the shorter walls, you may not have this option.

I always start a new area by marking the location of the studs, since it's easier to do it now before the baseboard is in place. If you're lucky, the lower sheetrock screws will still be visible, so all you have to do is to mark their positions. If not, you'll have to use a stud finder, or locate the studs by measuring and then pounding small nails through the sheetrock. Some walls will have extra studs for windows, doors, etc. In that case, you only have to mark the studs that are needed for installing the baseboard.

To mark the center of a stud, you have to find the edge of it first. To do this, once you've hit a stud with the nail, keep moving the nail over a little bit at a time, until it either doesn't hit any wood, or you can feel the nail slide off the edge of the board. The center of the stud should be 3/4 of an inch to the side. When checking this way, the holes should be close to the floor, so they'll be covered up by the baseboard. But make sure you're high enough, so you're hitting the stud and not the bottom plate. Then as you locate each stud, mark its position on either the floor or the wall, depending on the circumstances. Just make sure that the marks will be visible once the baseboard is in place. On floors or walls that are already finished, I mark each stud with a piece of masking tape. Otherwise you could just use a pencil.

If the room is getting carpeted, plywood blocks are laid out along the first wall, with a block going at each end, and then one every few feet in between. This is also done for a short ways on both adjacent walls. The blocks will be moved as you work your way around the room.

To begin, the test board is laid against the first wall, and slid tight to both sides. This will let you see if the first piece of baseboard can be cut square, or if either one or both ends have to be cut an angle. The upper corners should fit tight at each end. A gap that's lower down is OK, since it will be hidden by the board that overlaps it.

Once you know this, the first wall is measured, and the baseboard is cut to length so that it just fits into place. If the inside corners of the walls are rounded off, I'll also round off the back edge on both ends of the board. Now with the first board in position, push each end tight against the wall as you slide the test board against it (on the adjacent wall) to see how it fits against the first board.

If sheetrock was used to cover the walls, the baseboard will commonly be slightly dipped in at the bottom. Because of that, if the baseboard was nailed on as is, you'd have to cut the next board at an angle to match up with it.

An easier way is to square up the first board by shimming out the lower corner with felt paper. This only works where the board sits in too far at the bottom, since installing shims higher up would hold the upper edge of the baseboard away from the wall. Here the lower corner had to be shimmed out. In the center photo, you can see that the boards are now square to each other. By having two test boards, every corner could be checked and shimmed in advance.

If you're hand nailing, predrill the baseboard if it's hardwood, and use either 6D finish nails or 2 inch hardened trim nails. Put two nails into each stud. On corners where the lower edge will be held in place by the overlapping board, I generally only put in the upper nail. This will keep the lower corner from dipping in again, as it sometimes does if it's nailed. To help prevent splitting, I'll use a thinner nail at the corners, and either use a 2 inch hardened trim nail or a 4D finish nail. These nails will generally have to be angled towards the corner to hit the framing.

With a finish nailer, I'd use 2 - 2 1/2 inch nails in a 15 or 16 gauge gun. On corners where I'm right next to the edge and/or the nails have to be driven in at a hard angle, I'll still hand nail.

To do the second wall, the left end of the board has to be coped. First, recheck the corner to see if the first board is still square to the floor once it's been nailed on, since the next board will have to match this angle. Assuming it's good, make a square cut on the left end of the next board with the miter saw set at 45 degrees. This will show the profile needed to cut the end at. Make sure the board is long enough for coping the end, and to also allow for any mistakes in case it has to be recut.

When installing Colonial baseboard, the miter saw can also be used to cut the lower part of the board, which means you'll only have to cope the upper corner. Set the miter saw to around five degrees off square to get a slight back-cut. Then turn the board upside down, and cut to the end of the flat section, following the edge of the profile.

A coping saw is used to cut the curved part of the profile. When doing this, stay just off the line, and tilt the saw to give it a back-cut.

To finish the cut, you may also have to saw from the opposite direction. The photo on the right gives you a good look at the cuts that were made with both saws. Here I could have gone a little farther with the miter saw. But, if you go too far, you'll have to recut the end.

When the cut is finished, see how it fits against a scrap piece of the baseboard. Then file off any high spots, and check it again. This is repeated until the joint is tight. One potential problem when doing this is that some of the boards may be slightly different, in which case, the coped edge could fit tight against the scrap board, but still have a sloppy fit once the board was in place against the wall. To keep this from happening, try to use a scrap that's cut from the same board you're trying to match.

Sometimes you'll get a tight joint on the first try, while on others, it seems to take forever. You could also make one of the cuts too deep, which will screw up the profile. If that happens, just recut the end with the miter saw, and try again. When checking the profile, the boards should fit tight together, and also line up at the same height.

This is how the corner looked, before and after the high spots were filed off.

Once it looks right, measure the wall, and cut the board to length after you've checked the next corner with the test board to see if the end can be cut square. At first, I cut the board a little long, so there's room to make adjustments if the coped end doesn't fit right. Then I check the fit on that end by either flexing the board into place or holding it at an angle, depending on the length of the wall.

If the profile is just slightly off, file down any high spots, while being careful not to remove too much wood. In the photos above, you can see how much the fit was improved after doing this. But, if the profile is way off, because the angle is wrong or the scrap board was different than the board you're trying to match, you'll have to decide whether it's easier to do a lot of filing, or to recut it and start over.

Once the joint looks good, the board is cut to its final length. Here you want it to be long enough to put pressure on the coped joint, but not crush the sheetrock. When cutting a long board, it's the correct length when the ends are tight and the middle of the board is slightly curved out from the wall, so it snaps into place.

Before the board can be nailed on, the right side still has to be checked for square, and then shimmed out with felt paper if needed. It isn't necessary for the coped end to be square, but it should be close enough so that it looks good visually. This board is nailed on with two nails going into each stud, and also two on the coped end, but with only a single nail at the upper corner on the right side.

Here the back of the board was rounded off to match the corner.

287

The third wall is done the same as the second. The last wall will be a little more difficult, since both ends will need a coped cut. Coping the right side is more awkward for me because I saw left-handed. When cutting this end, sometimes I'll clamp the board into place to make the job easier.

Some rooms will also have an exterior (outside) corner, in which case, one of the boards could be coped on one end and mitered on the other. When cutting these boards, I generally do the coped side first. After that's done, I'll cut the ends on two scrap pieces of baseboard, with the miter saw set at 45 degrees. Then I'll lay them against the corner to see how they fit. You want the joint to be tight on the outside edge, but have a slight gap at the wall. If it isn't, readjust the angle on the saw, and try again.

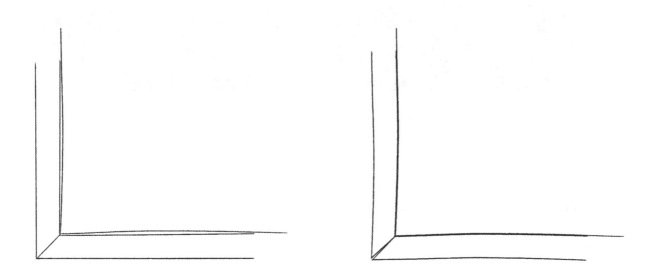

You'd think that the best way would be to cut the exact angle, so the boards would be tight across the whole joint, but that isn't the case. Sometimes the boards will sink in as they're nailed, and your perfect corner will open up and leave you with a gap, as shown in the drawings above. The reason for this is because the wall commonly dips in at an outside corner. This is generally caused by the knife or the trowel flexing as the joint compound is smoothed down, or by not feathering it out wide enough. By starting with a slight gap on the inside of the joint, this is less likely to happen. When the joint is finished, a small gap on the inside is less noticeable than it would be if the gap was on the outside edge of the corner.

You can check for this by using a straightedge before you get started on the corner. When I find corners that dip in too much, if I have the time and the walls are still getting painted, I'll straighten them out with joint compound and a wide trowel.

Once the angle has been determined, hold one of the scrap boards in place against the corner, and use it to measure the length of the other board. When doing this, hold the measuring tape against the flat part of the board. Then cut the board to length at the angle that was determined, and again, cut it a little long to begin with. Then lay the board in place to see how it looks. While holding it tight against the other corner, you want it to be a trace long on the mitered end. Here you're main concern is how it fits on the upper part of the mitered corner. Generally it doesn't matter if the board is long at the bottom, since you won't see it once the corner is finished. It's also better to have a square corner anyhow. Just make sure that the board isn't too short at the bottom.

Recut the mitered end if the board needs to be shortened, or to change the angle Then nail the board into place as you hold it tight against the inside corner. On the mitered end, the nails should go into the last stud. Keep them close to the outside edge, and allow for the sheetrock and corner bead when positioning them.

The other board is also cut so it's a little long. Then it's held in place, tight against the inside corner, as you check the fit on the mitered end. By having a little extra, you should still be able to adjust the angle of the cut if it's necessary. Once the angle looks right, cut the board to its final length. Again, you want the board to be just a trace long, so there's a small gap at the corner of the wall when the boards are matched up. This will allow for a little movement, in case the inside corner sinks in when the board is nailed.

Now apply glue to the mitered end, and nail the board on. Then quickly wipe off the excess glue to see how it looks. If the corner looks good, you're done. But if one side sticks out, lay a small board against that side, and then lightly hit it with a hammer. With the boards cut slightly long, you can generally get them to match up. Once the corner looks right, use a damp paper towel to wipe off any glue residue.

When doing outside corners, there are a couple of problems that you'll have to deal with. The most common is shown on the right, where one of the boards slightly overlaps the other. Here the first thing to do is to sand off the overhanging tip, while holding the sander flat against the board. Then look it over. If you can barely see what's been done, move on. But if it's too noticeable, then the side that was long (x) will also have to be sanded. This is where many people screw up the corner, by rounding it off. What you have to do is to sand farther back on that side, so you end up with a sharp corner, without seeing that the tip was sanded off.

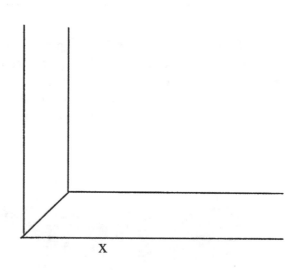

X

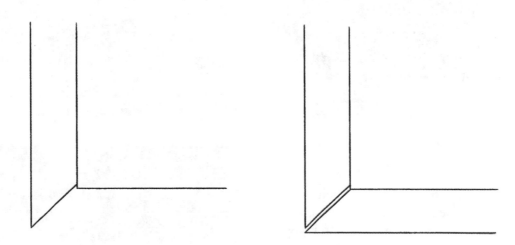

Another problem is shown above. Here you can see that the first board was cut a little short, so the second board can't even meet up with it. If the first board has already been nailed on, you'll have to do whatever it takes to bring the corner together. In this case, I'd start by laying something over the second board to protect it, and then lightly hit it with a hammer a few times to see if that would bring it up tight. If that didn't work, the next thing I'd do would be to scrape off any extra paint or joint compound from the corner.

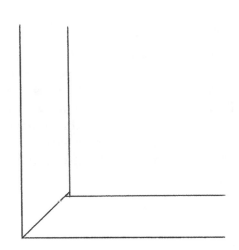

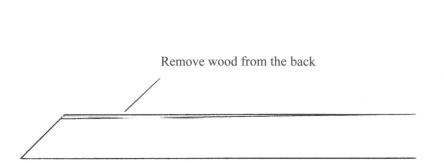

Remove wood from the back

If there's still a gap, then I'd remove a little wood from the back of the second board. Baseboard generally has ridges on the back side, so it's easy to shave it down with a block plane. Remove a little at a time, and keep checking the fit. Plane far enough back so it's at a gradual taper. The drawing on the right shows the finished corner. Here you can see that the second board is a little thinner than the first, and there's also a small hole on the inside of the corner. But the joint itself is tight, and that's what people really notice.

These photos show ranch style baseboard. When installing it, the entire edge has to be coped with a hand saw. But it's pretty easy with this type to get a tight joint.

## WIDE  BASEBOARD

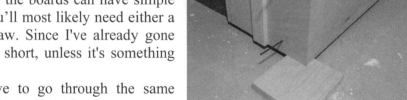

Installing wide baseboard isn't much different than doing the narrow type. It just takes a little longer. When using a separate cap, I generally go around the room and nail the lower boards on first. Then I do the cap. If the lower boards have square corners on the upper edge, or are just lightly rounded off, then coping the joints isn't necessary, and the boards can have simple butt cuts. Because of their width, you'll most likely need either a sliding miter saw or a radial arm saw. Since I've already gone over some of this, I'll try to keep it short, unless it's something new.

Before you start, you'll have to go through the same process of going through the boards to look for flaws and to determine where each one is going. At the same time, you should also mark the location of the studs, determine which direction you're going, and where you'll begin. If the floor is getting carpeted, the boards will again be raised up on 1/2 inch thick plywood blocks. If the baseboard is being installed over a wood or a tile floor, it generally runs tight to it. Here you don't have to be too concerned about any gaps that are beneath it, as long as you plan on installing base shoe.

3/4 inch maple plywood was used for the lower boards that are shown in these photos. This is less expensive than solid maple, but it has several disadvantages. One is that it takes longer, because veneer has to be attached to the lower edge of the notch, so the plywood doesn't show. Another problem is the length, since a splice will be needed on any wall that's over 8 feet wide. Also, when splicing it, the veneer is very thin, so the splice has to be almost perfect to begin with.

I like to start on one of the longer walls that will preferably be done in one piece. On this one, cut the first board so that it just slips into place. Here the main concern is that the upper edge fits tight, since any gaps that are lower down will be hidden by the overlapping board. It also helps to lightly round off the back edge on each end to fit the corners better.

291

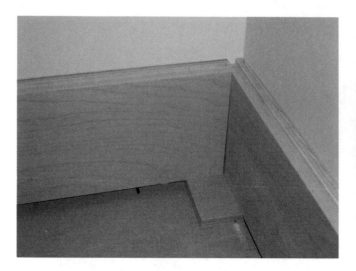 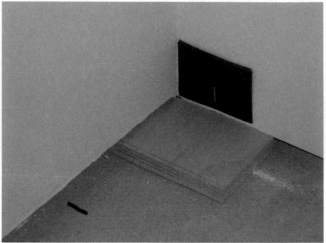

Before the board can be nailed on, you have to see if both ends are square to the floor. This is done by pushing each end tight to the wall as the test board is held against it. This will be done on every corner as you go along. Again, the corners are shimmed out with pieces of felt paper.

Generally, only the lower edge can be shimmed out, since the upper edge should stay tight against the wall. In the photo on the left, you can see a gap between the boards, so shims were needed. I know I'm repeating myself here, but this step is even more important with wide baseboard.

Once it looks right, the board nailed on with two nails going into each stud. For this, I use either 8D finish nails or 2 1/2 inch hardened trim nails when hand nailing, or 2 1/2 inch nails in a 15 gauge gun. On each end, I generally only nail the top of the board, since the lower part will be held in place by the overlapping board. One exception to this is on a corner where the lower edge of the baseboard sticks out. In that case, I'd put both nails in, and also try to drive the lower part of the baseboard tighter to the wall by laying a board against it and then hitting it with a hammer.

Before you start on the second wall, recheck the corner with the test board to see if it's still square. If it's moved, the angle of the cut will have to be adjusted to get a tight fit. Once you know, measure the length of the wall. Then cut the board with a slight back-cut, and again, leave it a little long.

Now hold the board against the next corner, and try to push it into place by sliding it along the baseboard. It should be a little too long to fit at this time, but it will let you see if any adjustments have to be made. See where two boards make contact. If they only touch at the top, then the angle of the cut has to be readjusted so more is taken off the top, and vice versa. This is where it's good to have a sharp, low-angle block plane. Once the angle is right, cut the board to it's final length. It should fit tight, but not so much that it crushes the sheetrock. When doing this, it's generally better to take a little off at a time, rather than risk cutting off too much. The difference between a board that fits correctly, and one that's either too long or too short, is very small. Here, 1/32 of an inch would make a big difference. This is easier than it sounds, and after a while you'll get a feel for how much you have to remove from a board.

When installing the lower boards, it's also important that they meet up at the same height at the corners. If one of the boards is sitting too high, then the lower edge may have to planed before it can be nailed on. Here it might help to scribe the edge by dragging a pencil along the floor to show you where the wood needs to be removed. This generally isn't a problem when the baseboard is sitting on top of blocks, since the height can be adjusted.

Once the board fits, you still have to check to see if it's square to the floor, and shim it out if necessary. Again, this is more important on the new corner. On the other end, where it overlaps the first board, it isn't as important, though with taller baseboard it's more noticeable when the board isn't square.

Nail the board into place, the same as the first one, after making sure that the upper edge matches up at the corner. Then install the rest of the boards in the same manner.

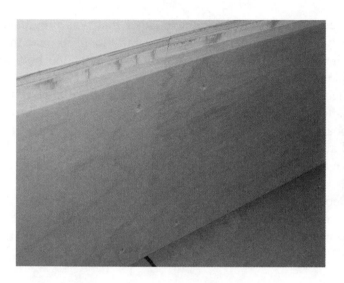 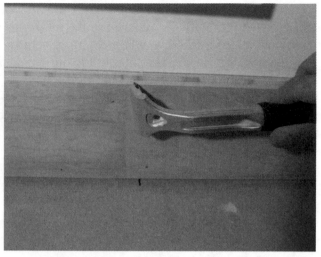

If the wall is too long to use a single board, the baseboard will have to be spliced together. When doing this, I generally cut the spliced ends at 45 degrees, though the angle doesn't really matter as long as the two boards are cut the same way, and the joint is tight.

Cut the first board so it ends about a quarter of an inch before the far end of a stud. The next board will overlap it. Make sure that you don't cut the second board too short, or it will sit in too far after it's been nailed. I generally cut the second board so it's just a bit long to start with. Then I'll glue the joint, and drive the splice together as I nail it. Once I'm finished, I'll wipe off any glue that gets squeezed out. Then after letting it dry, I'll scrape off any high spots and sand the joint.

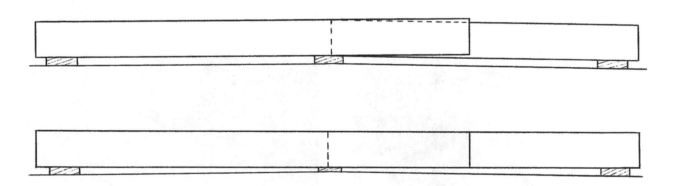

On walls where you're splicing the baseboard, check the floor to see how flat it is. I do this by coming from both sides with a straight board, so they overlap in the middle. Commonly, the boards won't be parallel, and you'll see that the ends are either rising up or falling away from each other, as shown in the upper drawing. When that happens, you either have to adjust the height of the boards to bring them into line, or change the angle of the cuts on the spliced end.

Bringing them into line is easy if the floor is getting carpeted, since the boards will be resting on blocks. Here all you have to do is adjust the height of the center block, as shown in the lower drawing. If the baseboard is tight to the floor, you'll have to plane the lower edge of the boards.

When installing wide baseboard, outside corners are done in the same manner that was previously described. Just remember to determine the angles in advance, and to cut the boards a little long, in case they settle in at the corners. Newer homes are generally sheetrocked, so the walls tend to sink in at the bottom. Again, the best thing to do is to ignore the dip on outside corners, and cut the boards square.

Older homes are different, because many of them still have the original plaster on the walls. Here the lower edge doesn't sink in as often. Sometimes it will stick out instead, which makes it a little harder to install the baseboard. In that case, I'd start by laying a scrap board against the lower edge of the plaster, and then hit it with a hammer. When doing this, I'm not too worried about hurting anything, since it won't be seen once the baseboard is in place. If I'm lucky, the plaster will move and the corner will be square. If not, the end of the baseboard will have to be cut at an angle.

To determine the correct angle on an outside corner, I'll cut the board extra long, and then draw the angle by laying a board against the other side of the corner. On an inside corner, I'll use a different board, if possible. For instance, I might cut the angle on the end of the test board to see if it fits, before I cut the baseboard that will actually be going there.

## INSTALLING THE UPPER CAP

Once the lower boards are in place, the cap is installed. To begin, measure the length of the wall that you're starting on. Then cut the cap so it fits tight between the walls. Again, you only have to be concerned with how it fits at the upper corners, since the rest of it will get covered. You'll also have to notch both ends on the first one to clear the lower board. Round off the back edge, on the ends, to fit the corners better. Then nail the cap on by putting a single nail into each stud. If I'm hand nailing, I'll predrill if it's hardwood, and use either 6D finish nails or 2 inch hardened trim nails. When using a trim nailer, I'd either use 2 inch nails in a 16 gauge gun or 2 1/2 inch nails in a 15 gauge gun, depending on the wall and how thick the cap is.

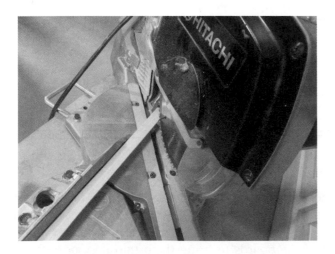 

On the second wall, the cap will have to be coped on one end to fit against the first board. Start by cutting the cap so it's a couple of inches longer than the length of the wall. Then cut one end at 45 degrees to get the profile. Since it's easier for me to cope the left side of a board, I generally install the cap by going in a clockwise direction.

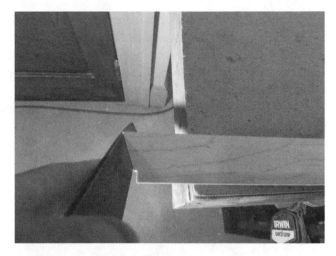

Use a coping saw to cut the profile. Try to stay just off the line, and tip the saw to give it a back-cut. Then use a file to clean up the cut.

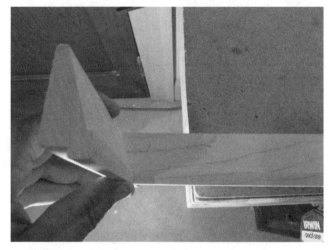

Check the fit, and then make any adjustments that are necessary.

On this corner, the joint is tight, but there's a small hole at the lower end of the tapered section. This happened because the profile was checked with a board that was slightly different than the one I was trying to match.

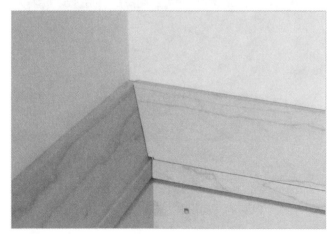

Once the end has been coped, measure the length of the wall. Then cut the board so it's a little long. On this cap, you'll still have to notch the other end to clear the lower board, as shown in the upper left photo. Then slip it into place to check the fit. At this point, the board should be too long to fit, but it should be close enough to allow you to check the shape of the profile. Look the joint over, and make any adjustments that are needed. Then cut the cap to its final length and nail it into place. The others are done in the same manner.

Sometimes one of the boards will end up being a little short after it's been cut to length. Here the most important thing is to have a tight joint. So if it can't be replaced, just push the board over before nailing it. Putting a shim at the other end will help to keep pressure on the joint. If the shim is left in place, cut off anything that hangs out after the board is nailed on.

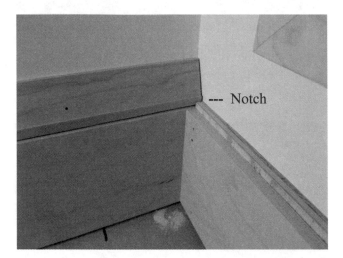 

--- Notch

In these photos, you can see that the end of the cap is quite a bit short, but the joint itself is tight. The gap is only noticeable when looking down on it, and can easily be filled.

When I spliced this cap, it didn't settle in as much as I thought it would. Once the glue dried, the overlap was scraped off and the cap was sanded. You can see in the second photo that the wall was nicked while using the scraper. This is easily repaired with joint compound.

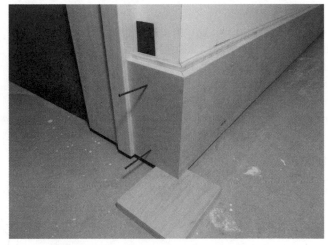

On this corner, when I checked the fit of the lower board that's next to the door, I found that it stuck out farther on the bottom than the top, so the board had to be tapered. This was done by shimming out one end with felt paper as the board was cut on a table saw.

After nailing the board into place, tape was stretched over the corner until the glue set up. Then the cap was installed to complete the corner. Sometimes, even though a mitered corner fits perfect when it's dry-fitted, it may still end up with a small gap once it's been nailed. Many of these joints can be pulled together and held tight by using masking taping. The lower photo shows how tape was also used on the corner over the landing, along with a temporary shim to hold the cap at the correct height.

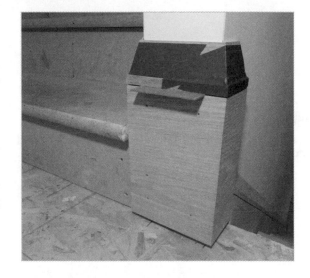

Baseboard that's crowned will either dip down or hump up in the middle. When it's low in the middle, I'll start nailing from one end, and push the other end down to straighten the board as I go. If the board humps up, I'll nail one end, and then push down in the middle to help straighten it. Doing this may take a lot of weight. If I'm alone, I'll lay a stiff board over the baseboard, as shown in the drawing. Then I'll put my knee on it, and push down while nailing the baseboard on both sides of it.

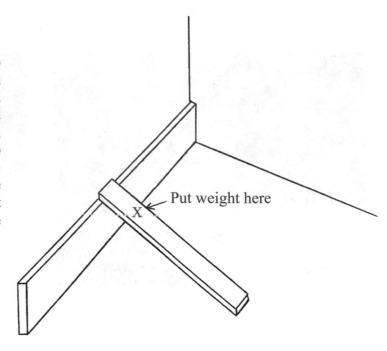

Baseshoe is commonly installed when the baseboard is over wood or tile floors. Baseshoe and quarter round are pretty much the same thing, the difference being that baseshoe is 3/4 inch high by 1/2 inch thick, while quarter round on floors is generally 3/4 by 3/4. Either one can be used, though I prefer the look of baseshoe. When installing it, I just miter the ends and adjust the angle to get a tight fit, as I've found that I'm faster and get better results this way, instead of coping the joints. Then I nail it on with 2 – 2 1/2 inch hardened trim nails if I'm hand nailing, and predrill if it's hardwood. With a trim nailer, I'd use 1 1/2 – 2 inch nails in either a 16 or an 18 gauge gun. Drive the nails so that they angle down into the wall. You want the floor to be able to move, independent of the baseshoe.

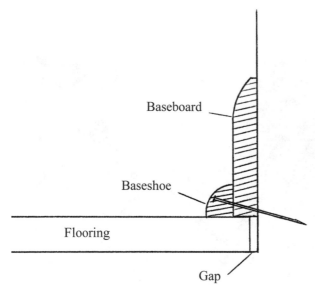

This drawing shows one way to finish off a floor, where it meets up with an exterior door. Here the flooring was cut a little short, so there was room for the spacer board, and still leave a small gap. This way, the trim board can be attached, while still letting the floor expand and contract.

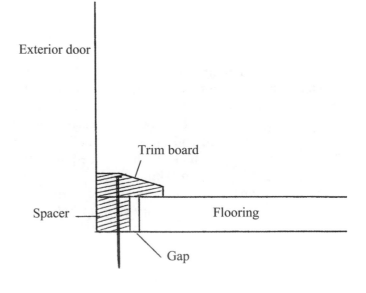

# FINISHING THE STAIRS

When the time comes to finish off the stairs, the posts, handrails, balusters, and the skirtboards will be installed, and also the risers and the stair treads if the stairs are being capped. Here we'll be working on a different set of stairs than the ones that were shown in the section on how to build them. Those stairs won't be finished off for some time, but these are similar. The main difference is that, on these stairs, the center wall runs up to the ceiling, so only the lower half needs posts and balusters. These stairs are also getting carpeted, so treads and risers won't be needed. On this house, the basement and the lower stairs will be finished off using maple, up to the edge of the landing. From that point on, it will switch over to oak to match the trim on the first floor.

To get started, the first thing that has to be done is to determine the height of the skirtboards. If you remember, when building the short wall for the U-shaped stairs, its height was determined by the height of the skirtboard. In turn, sometimes the height of the skirtboard is determined by the height of the baseboard. This house is getting two-piece baseboard. If possible, I'd like the skirtboard to line up with the baseboard at the base of the stairs. Depending on the style and the height of the baseboard, this may not be an option. Either way, at this point, you'll have to decide how the skirtboard is going to meet up with the baseboard.

To find the height, you'll need a short length of the baseboard, and also a piece of plywood or sheathing that's a few feet long and the same width as the skirtboard, which in this case is 9 1/4 inches. Here the baseboard will be raised up 1/2 inch off the floor, since the floor will be carpeted. If the stairs are being capped with new treads and risers, then boards would also have to be laid into place to show the position of the finished stair treads, once they're installed. Now by holding the plywood against the wall, to represent the skirtboard, you can determine which height looks the best, and what's needed for it to line up with the baseboard. Then you compare that to the height of the end wall. This will also be done on the upper section of the stairs.

There's no rule that says the skirtboards have to be the same height on opposite sides, but it's probably best if they're close. On these stairs, the skirtboard on the right side will be capped with the same trim that's used for the baseboard, while the one on the left will butt up against the trim board that goes over the end wall. Here it turned out that the skirtboard had to be 2 1/4 inches above the stair treads in order to line up with the lower part of the baseboard. On the upper section of the stairs, the baseboard was way too short at this measurement, so I decided just to go with the 2 1/4 inches, and then make a short piece of taller baseboard for that location. In this case, the end wall was already at the correct height. If it was too short, a board would have been nailed to the top of it to build it up. Once the height has been determined, either write it down or mark it on the walls, and then move on.

# INSTALLING THE POSTS AND HANDRAILS

Now you can start on the posts and the handrails. When it comes to doing the layout, every set of stairs is different, so you'll have to spend some time trying to figure out the height and position for everything to make it all come together. Some of the things you have to determine are the height and the position of the different posts, the height of the handrail over the stairs, the height of the handrail over the landing, how far the posts extend above the handrails, and how does the height of the handrail that's over the stairs compare to the handrail that's over the landing where they come together at the same post. Also consider that by moving a post either forward or back, you're changing the height where the handrail runs into the post.

To do this, I lay it all out with 2x4s, so I know exactly how it will all match up. The 2x4s are either screwed or clamped to hold them in place. Remember that the height of the handrail over the stairs must be between 34 and 38 inches, when measured vertically above the nose of the stairs, and that the handrail over the landing must be at least 36 inches above the finished floor. When doing this, also take into account that the height of the landing and the position of the stair treads may be changing. Here the stairs and the landing are getting carpeted, so I'll allow about an inch for that. If wood flooring was going over the landing, I'd lay a board in place to represent the finished floor. I duplicate the position of the finish stair treads by putting a 3/4 inch thick board against the riser, and then lay one of the stair treads in place. If a trim board is going over the end of the short wall, a temporary board will also have to be added there when doing the layout. Once you have the positions of the posts and the heights figured out, write the measurements down. Then put the posts into place, and using a sharp pencil, draw the outline for each one to mark its location.

The most solid way to install the posts is to attach them to the framing that's beneath the floor or the landing. Check the framing at these points, before you do the layout, to see if there's enough room for each post. Don't expect the space to be wide open. More often than not, the post will have to be notched. Then it's just a matter of how much it can be notched and still have enough strength. When I'm working with 3 1/2 inch posts, I try to not take off more than 1 1/2 inches.

You may also have the opposite problem, where you're between the framing. In that case, blocking will have to be installed between the floor joists to give you something to attach to.

I generally cut the posts to length on a miter saw. You'll probably have to cut from both sides to get through the post. Then I look each one over, and consider which way I want it to face before I draw out the notch. The end of the notch is either cut on a table saw, or with a speed square and a circular saw. The most accurate way for doing the rip cut is with the table saw, though a circular saw will also do

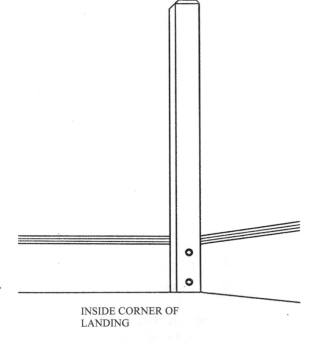

INSIDE CORNER OF
LANDING

a good job if you're careful. While doing this, don't cut past the end of the notch. When using a table saw, it helps to make a mark that shows when you've reached the end of the cut, since you won't be able to see the saw blade. Once that's done, the cut is finished by using a hand saw, and then cleaned up with a sharp chisel and a block plane.

You'll need a clean cut when making the hole for a post to go through a finished floor. Start by drilling a starting hole. Then use a jig saw with a sharp blade in it, and cut to the line. Make sure that you don't cut the hole too large. Then put the post into place to see if it fits, and shave a little more off where it's needed. A sharp chisel and a file can also be used to clean up the edge.

If the floor is getting covered, it's better to cut the hole a little big. This makes it easier to slip the post into place without scraping off the construction adhesive. On a hole that's tight, I'd use a thinner type of glue, such as Gorilla Glue or Elmer's Ultimate. These are polyurethane glues, and expand as they harden, so less is needed. No matter which type is used, I'd tape off the floor if it was finished to make the cleanup easier.

The posts will be attached with lag screws, and should feel rock-solid once they're installed. If they're over the landing, the lag screws go into the framing beneath it. On an upper level, the lower newel post is generally attached to the floor joists or to blocking that's been installed between them. If the post is screwed to a floor joist, blocking may still be needed to reinforce the area. Use screws and construction adhesive to install the boards.

Once the post has been cut, it's slipped into place and held with a clamp. Then after making sure that its plumb, two 1/4 inch holes are drilled through the post and into the framing. These holes are drilled in the direction that gives the most strength, though sometimes you won't have a choice if there isn't much room for the drill. Then the holes through the post are drilled out to 3/8 inch. The safest way to do this is to remove the post. When drilling out a post that's still in place, I wrap masking tape around the drill bit to mark the depth needed, so I don't go past the post.

After the holes have been drilled, the post is attached with 3/8 inch lag screws with flat washers, and then checked with the level. If it's off, the post will have to be shimmed and rechecked. Once it looks right, the post is removed. Then glue or construction adhesive is applied, and it's reattached and checked again with the level. Then it's left alone until the adhesive sets up.

Since the stairs that are shown here are over a concrete floor, the lower newel post had to be attached to the end wall. To stiffen up the wall, a second riser was installed over the first. This board was cut extra long so that it crossed over the end wall to lock it in place. Here, 3/8 inch plywood was used, so it would have less effect on the amount of tread overhang. Then the riser was installed by applying polyurethane construction adhesive to both the existing riser and the end wall before it was nailed on. By overlapping the end wall with the riser, this is a very solid way to mount a post, much better than if the two weren't attached. If the skirtboard wasn't installed yet on the right side, a gap would have been left for it to slip into place. I used the same method to install the lower newel post on the first floor, since an I-joist was directly beneath it. Those stairs are shown in the photo on page 326, and also on page 328.

Before you can do this on stairs that are getting capped, the lower stair tread will have to be cut off flush to the existing riser. Then the skirtboard on the side that's opposite the post will be installed before the finish riser goes on. When cutting the finish riser to length, it should fit tight against the skirtboard and also overlap the end wall. Cut it to width so that the finished stair tread will be level as it rests on top of it. Also make sure that the riser is plumb, so shimming isn't needed when the post is attached. I'll describe how to do the skirtboards later, though, depending on the stairs, it might be better to install them before or after the posts and the handrails. On these stairs, I installed the lower skirtboards first. I started by doing the one on the right, since it determined the height of the others. Then I did the one that's against the end wall because it would sit behind the riser that was added, and also be covered by the trim board that goes over the top.

At this time, the trim boards that cap the end wall have to be installed. Here they consist of maple 1x8s that were cut to width on the table saw, and were done in three pieces. The width of the boards was determined by adding up the thickness of the wall, the skirt board, the trim board that runs along the outer edge, and also the overlap on both sides.

After the boards were ripped to width, they were installed by starting at the bottom. These boards also needed a miter cut where they came together at the corners To do this, the angles were first determined by cutting them on 3/4 inch thick scrap boards.

Since the newel post will be attached to the end wall, the lower board has to be plumb. It should also be glued to make it as solid as possible. Here, after cutting the mitered end, the lower board was cut to length. Then construction adhesive was applied to the end of the wall, and the board was nailed into place with the nails spaced out along both sides of it.

Once that was done, the other boards were cut to fit. Then the corners were glued with regular wood glue, and they were nailed on in the same manner. You can use the same boards that were used to determine the angles to help measure the length of these boards.

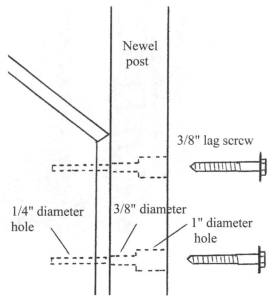

Newel post

3/8" lag screw

1/4" diameter hole

3/8" diameter

1" diameter hole

Now the lower newel post can be installed. This is cut to length, based on the measurements that were taken when everything was laid out. If it's going to rest on top of a finished floor, the lower end should be cut so it fits tight against the floor. Look the wood grain over. Then decide which way you want it to face.

This post will be attached with two lag screws, with one above the other, that go through the post and screw into the end wall. To begin, draw the position of the holes on the post, and then mark them by using a nail set as a center punch. When using 3/8 inch lag screws, 1 inch diameter holes are drilled first to countersink the screw heads. These holes are generally at least 1 inch deep, the actual depth being determined by the length of the lag screws and the size of the post.

Then a long 1/4 inch drill bit is used to go through the rest of the post. Make sure the drill bit is centered on the 1 inch holes.

These holes should be square to the post. Use a drill press if you have one. It also helps to have someone stand to the side, so they can tell you how the angle looks.

Now position the post against the end wall, using a level, and hold it securely as you continue the 1/4 inch holes through the trim board and into the end wall. These holes should be deep enough so the lag screws don't bottom out. After that's done, remove the post, and drill the holes in the post out to 3/8 of an inch. Then put the post back into position, slip flat washers over the lag screws, and tighten the post down with a socket wrench. Check the fit, and use the level to check for plumb, in both directions. If the post is tipped in or out, it can only be shimmed a little bit before the gap would be too noticeable. If it's tipped to the side, just loosen the lag screws. Then push on the post and retighten them. If there isn't enough movement to allow this, the holes in the post will have to be enlarged.

Three-eighth inch flat washers are commonly too big to fit into a 1 inch hole. In that case, try a 5/16 washer. The hole is generally large enough for a 3/8 lag screw.

Once it looks right, the post is installed permanently. Remove it, and apply construction adhesive where it makes contact with the end wall. Then reset the post and tighten it down. Check it for plumb, and adjust it if necessary. Make sure the lag screws are tight, and then don't disturb the post until the next day to let the adhesive set up.

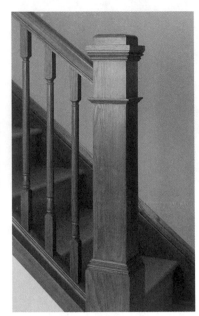

The post that was just installed is solid wood, while others, such as the one on the right, may be hollow. This post was made by gluing boards together to form the perimeter. It also came with an insert that matched the shape of the interior, which was glued into the base before the holes were drilled to install the post.

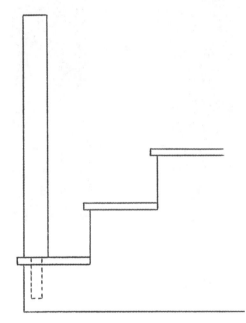

There are a couple of other methods that are also used to install the posts. One is to drill out the end of the post, and then glue in a large dowel that's 1 1/2 - 2 inches in diameter. The dowel is then glued into a matching hole that goes through the stairs. I've never tried this method, so I don't know much about it.

Another method that I "have" tried, consists of a matched pair of metal brackets, with one being attached to the end of the post, while the other is connected to the floor. To install the post, it slips into the bracket that's attached the floor, and then it's tightened by driving the post sideways. There are a couple of problems when doing this. One is that the post can still move if the floor isn't solid enough. In my case, I had to screw a metal plate to the floor to stiffen it up. The post would also loosen up over time, so every now and then I'd had to give it a kick to tighten it.

Sometimes a corner post can be installed by just nailing it to the floor. On this handrail, we couldn't cut into the floor, so we just toenailed the post with 10D finish nails. This was possible because it's held in one direction by the other post, which was bolted and glued into place, and from the other direction, by the wall.

Instead of having a factory-built post on the upper end of the stairs, here one was glued up using maple 1x4s. Only three of the sides were glued together to begin with. This allowed the handrail on each side to be attached from within, using lag screws. The lag screws were set at slightly different heights, so there was room to slip them into place.

The uppers photos show how the post was glued up. After dry-fitting the boards to check the fit, two of the corners were glued, and the post was assembled. There weren't enough clamps available at the time, so strapping tape was used instead to pull everything together. After it was taped, the post was slightly out of square. This was taken care of by applying a clamp to opposite corners on one end of the post, as shown in the photo on the right. Then after letting it sit for a day, the tape was pulled, and the excess glue was scraped off.

This post goes from the end wall up to the ceiling. To install it, a plywood block was attached to the end wall, and another to the ceiling. Then the

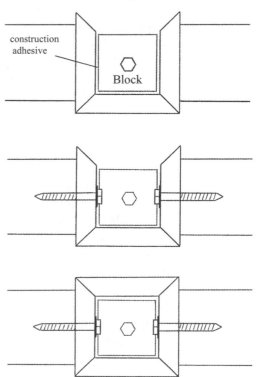

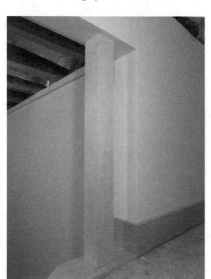

post was slipped into place, over the blocks. After the handrails were cut and dry-fitted, everything was taken down. Then I had to work fast as construction adhesive was applied to the outside edge of the blocks, the post was slipped into position, the handrails were glued and reinstalled, and the last side of the post was glued and clamped into place. After letting it sit overnight, the excess glue was scraped off, and the post was sanded.

To install the handrails, I use a 2x4 to find the correct length and angle of the cuts. Here the first thing to do is to mark the position of the upper edge of the handrail on both posts, and then clamp a 2x4 to the posts so the upper edge is lined up with the marks. Now use a sharp pencil to draw a line along the inside edge of each post, and cut the 2x4 to length with a miter saw, following the lines To check the fit, clamp a board to each post to support the 2x4 at the correct height. Then slip the 2x4 into place.

Once it looks right, the handrail is cut to match the 2x4. Start by cutting one end at the same angle that was used on the 2x4. Then measure the length and cut the other end, and again, match the angle. You may want to play it safe by cutting the handrail a little long to begin with to allow for any minor adjustments.

The length of the handrail can affect how the posts will sit. If it's cut a little long, it will push out on the posts. If it's cut short, it will pull them together. If either one, or both of the posts are a little out of plumb, you may be able to use this to your advantage and bring them closer to where they should be.

Now the handrail is slipped into place, and the boards that support it are adjusted to hold it at the correct height. The handrail will be attached to the posts with lag screws. On the lower post, as shown in the drawing, the lag screw is positioned 1 inch under the upper edge of the handrail. To begin, a 1 inch diameter hole is drilled to countersink the lag screw. The depth of this hole is determined by the size of the post and the length of the lag screw, so it doesn't bottom out. Then a 3/16 inch hole is drilled through the rest of the post, and 1 1/2 inches into the end of the handrail. Once that's finished, the post is drilled out to 3/8 inch.

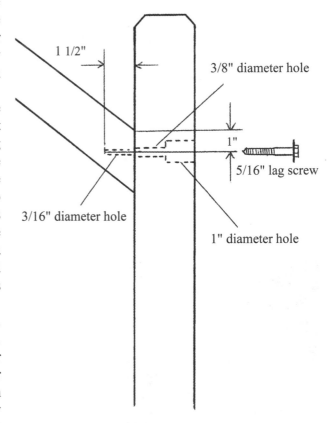

Then the handrail is installed to see how it looks. Assuming that it's OK, it can be mounted permanently. You can generally do one end at a time if you loosen or remove the lag screw, and then either push on the post, or raise or lower the handrail far enough to put glue between the handrail and the post. Then retighten that end. Any glue that squeezes out should be wiped off with a damp paper towel. If any residue is left, it could affect the finish.

When you're installing the handrails, the holes have to be drilled accurately, so it's good to have someone else to help hold them in place, and to also watch from the side, telling you to raise or lower the drill, so it's square to the post. If you're alone, it helps to mark the position on each side of the post, and then drill the smaller hole from both sides. It could also be done on a drill press before the post is permanently installed. When you drill into the handrail, make sure it's centered on the post.

The lower edge of the handrail should be square to the post. This can be checked by holding a square against the post, or by using a torpedo level.

306

This drawing shows how the upper end of the handrail is attached to the post. The holes are drilled in the same manner, with the 1 inch hole drilled first, followed by the one that goes through the post and into the handrail. Notice that in all of these drawings, a 3/8 inch hole is drilled for a 5/16 inch lag screw. Since the holes are generally drilled by hand, some of them might be a little crooked. By having a larger hole, it's easier to pull the handrail up tight.

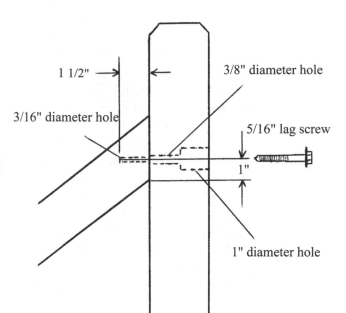

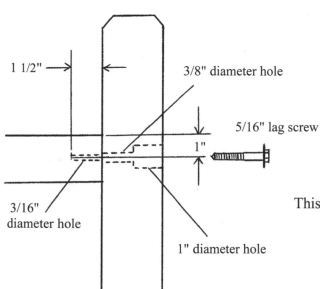

This is one way to attach a handrail that goes over the landing.

These drawings are from instructions that I got over twenty years ago. The measurements are general recommendations, and don't always have to be followed. For instance, the position of the holes can be changed as long as it's strong enough, and you stay away from the edge of the handrail. A 3/4 inch hole could also be drilled instead of a 1 inch if you use a smaller washer. The lag screw could also be changed to a LedgerLok screw or a similar type of hardened fastener. This would also shrink the size of the holes.

To see other styles of posts, handrails, and balusters, and for instructions on how to install them using different methods, information is available from the manufacturers. That's how I learned to install them. That, along with books from the library, and a little common sense.

Sometimes you won't be able to drill through a post to attach the handrail. This generally happens when the post is at the top of the stairs where it meets the landing. Since a handrail will be connected to both sides, the method that's already been described can't be used, unless they're at different heights.

Another way to attach the handrail is shown in these drawings. Although this method can be used almost anywhere, I generally only use it when there's no other choice. To do it this way, a 3/16 inch hole, that runs parallel to the handrail, is drilled 2 inches into the post. Then a 5/16 inch threaded stud is screwed into the hole. It's hard to get the angle right when doing this, so it's better to have someone watching from the side as the hole is drilled. The drill bit will also try to slide across the post when drilling at an angle. In that case, it helps to begin by going in straight. Then, once you're started, tip the drill to the angle that you want.

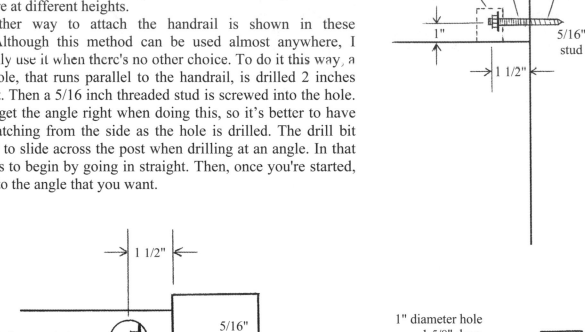

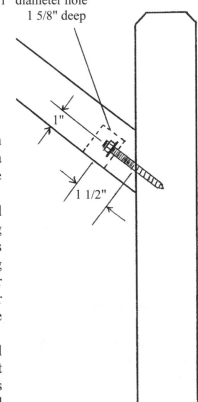

To insert the stud, two nuts are threaded onto the end of it. Then they're tightened together, which locks them into place. Now you can use a wrench to screw the stud into the post. Once it's in place, the nuts are loosened from each other and then removed.

On the handrail, a 3/8 inch hole that lines up with the stud is drilled into the end of it. Then a 1 inch hole is drilled from the bottom, intersecting the first hole. To install the handrail, it's slipped over the stud, and then it's pulled tight with a nut that goes over a washer. The wrench used for doing this is shown on the next page. You should have two of them. The center drawing gives you a better look at how this is done. Notice, in the lower drawing, that the position of the 1 inch hole is a little different when the handrail is over the stairs.

After the holes are drilled, everything is assembled to see how it all fits together. Then, if it's OK, the handrail can be taken down or just loosened far enough so glue can be applied to the end of it. Then it's retightened or reinstalled, and any glue that squeezes out is wiped off, and the handrail is left alone until it dries.

308

Stair wrenches

Threaded stud and a lag screw

When using this method over stairs, the handrail tends to end up a little lower than you want on the lower end of the stairs, and higher on the upper part. Take this into consideration when marking the holes. I haven't shown a drawing of the handrail over the stairs being attached to the upper post, since it's more difficult to do that end. If you have to do it, use the same measurements that are used on the lower end.

Sometimes you'll find that the handrail can't be slipped into position with the stud sticking out. This generally happens when one end is attached to a rosette or a half post. In that case, you'll have to insert the stud after the handrail is already in place. This is easier to do if the stud has been inserted and then removed, so the threads have been cut.

To install the handrail this way, it will have to be supported on one end to free up both hands. This can be done by clamping a board to the post. Then before the handrail goes on, glue the end of it and attach the rosette permanently, and then slip the handrail into position and screw the rosette to the wall.

The 1 inch hole is normally just big enough for the stud to be slipped into place. Once it's through the 3/8 inch hole, the flat washer goes on, and the two nuts are screwed onto the end of it and tightened together, using the stair wrenches. Then the stud is screwed into place, and one of the nuts is removed. Before the handrail is locked into position, the end of it has to be glued. Here I generally just push on the post, and then squeeze some glue into the crack that was created. Then the nut is tightened, and the excess glue is wiped off.

When handrails are being attached to opposite sides of the same post, and they're at the same height, one of the handrails can be attached by drilling through the post if one of the holes is drilled a little higher than normal, and the other is drilled a little lower, so they clear each other. Since the hole for the lag screw has to get covered by the other handrail, use the smallest size drill bit that will work to countersink the head and allow it to be tightened. At the top of the stairs, I prefer to drill through the post when attaching the upper end of the handrail. Then I'll use the other method to attach the handrail over the landing, if necessary.

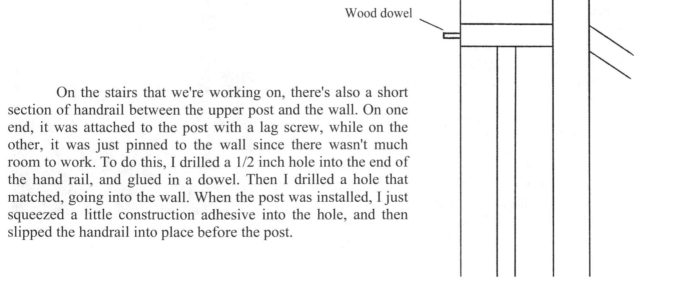

Wood dowel

On the stairs that we're working on, there's also a short section of handrail between the upper post and the wall. On one end, it was attached to the post with a lag screw, while on the other, it was just pinned to the wall since there wasn't much room to work. To do this, I drilled a 1/2 inch hole into the end of the hand rail, and glued in a dowel. Then I drilled a hole that matched, going into the wall. When the post was installed, I just squeezed a little construction adhesive into the hole, and then slipped the handrail into place before the post.

## ROSETTES AND HALF POSTS

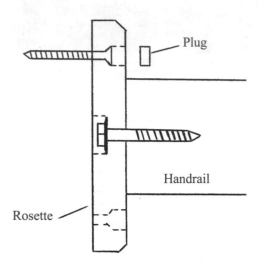

Where the handrail ends at the wall, it's generally attached to a rosette or a half post. A rosette is a small board or decorative piece of wood, while a half post is just what it's called, a board that looks like it was cut off the side of a post. When using either one, you start by temporarily attaching it to the wall. Use screws, and position them so they'll go into the wood framing, but won't interfere with the placement of the handrail. Drill the holes just large enough for the screws to slip through, and countersink them with a 3/8 inch drill bit, so you'll be able to plug the holes at a later time.

To keep it simple, when describing how to install the handrail, I'll only use the word rosette. But its done in the same manner if you're using a half post.

Once the rosette is attached to the wall, a 2x4 is cut to fit between the rosette and the post. Then the handrail is cut to length, using the 2x4 as a template, and it's slipped into place. When doing this, clamp a board to the post to support one end.

Now hold the handrail in the correct position, and draw its outline on the rosette. Then take the handrail down and remove the rosette. The handrail will be attached to the rosette with a 5/16 inch lag screw. Measure off the outline that was just drawn to mark the position of the lag screw. Then drill a small pilot hole through the board at that location. Now coming from the back, drill a 3/4 - 1 inch hole, going just deep enough so the lag screw will be below the surface of the wood. Once that's been done, the pilot hole is drilled out to 3/16 of an inch. Then the rosette is held in position against the handrail, and the 3/16 inch bit is used to drill a hole into the end of the handrail. Make sure the hole is deep enough so the lag screw won't bottom out. After that, a 5/16 inch bit is used to drill out the hole in the rosette. Then the rosette can be installed on the end of the handrail.

310

# SHOE RAIL

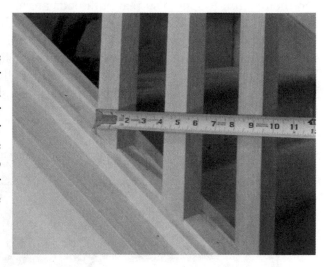

Now we'll move on to the shoe rail and the balusters. The shoe rail is the board that holds the lower end of the balusters in place. Here it was nailed to the end wall and went on in three pieces, with a mitered corner between two of them. When doing this corner, the miter saw was set at the same angle that was used for cutting the trim boards that are beneath it. After the boards were cut to length, they were centered on the posts. Then the corner was glued, and the shoe rail was nailed on with a single row of nails going down the center.

# BALUSTERS

Once the shoe rail is in place, the balusters can be installed. The style that we'll be using here will slip into a groove that's been cut into both the shoe rail and the hand rail. Then going between each baluster will be a strip of wood that's called a fillet (shown in the drawing).

To begin, the first thing to do is to determine the spacing between the balusters. This is done by spreading the balusters out across the floor, and then moving them around until the spacing is found that has the right look, while staying under 4 inches between each one. This pattern is then transferred onto a board, called a pattern board, that's at least 6 inches longer than the horizontal distance of any section you'll be working on. To do this, start at one end of the board, and mark the position of each baluster along the entire length, while making sure that the distance between each one is correct.

Using the pattern board will help in laying out the balusters, whether you're doing one section, or several. For instance, let's say you're working on a section that goes across a landing. You've already determined the spacing between each baluster, but what you don't know is how big the gap is at each end. To figure this out, measure the distance between the two posts, or the post and the wall, whichever one it is. Then lock your measuring tape to this length, and lay it across the pattern board. By moving it back and forth, and using a second tape measure, you can quickly see what the spacing will be on each end. Generally I center the balusters, so both ends are equal, but every section is different. Just make sure that the gap stays under 4 inches. A building inspector won't allow anything over that at any point along the handrails. You can see how this is done on page 376, in the section on building decks.

When installing the balusters over the stairs, measure the horizontal distance between the lower newel post and the one that's above it. On a short section of stairs, you can do this by holding the measuring tape near the top of the lower newel post, and as low as you can go on the post at the edge of the landing. On a longer set of stairs, you'll have to hold a straightedge against the lower post to extend the line. Then lock the tape at this measurement and lay it across the pattern board, the same as you would for a section that's over the landing. The slope of the stairs is not even considered when determining the spacing of the balusters.

Now the first baluster can be cut to length. Here it was measured by holding the tape against the lower newel post. This can be a tough spot to get an accurate measurement. Start by cutting the baluster a little long, and then trim it to length so that both ends are an equal distance from the post, once it's in place. The ends are cut at the same angle that was used on the end of the hand rail.

When installing balusters that have been turned on a lathe, you'll have to decide which way they should go, and how much to cut off on each end, since the pattern is generally closer to one end than the other. By locking the measuring tape to the correct length, and then laying it alongside one of the balusters, it should help to see how they will look. Remember to consider the angle that will be cut on each end, if the balusters are going over stairs.

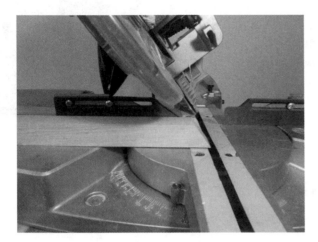 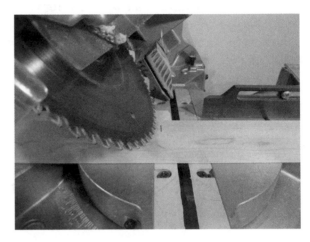

After cutting one end, the baluster was flipped over and then cut to length. On these
stairs, one of the balusters was used as a template for marking the length of the others.

Once the first baluster is cut, it's checked in the middle, and also at the top, to see if the length has to change as you work your way up the stairs. Then the baluster is held in place so that it's spaced the correct distance off the lower newel post, and its position is marked on both ends.

Fillets are cut to end at these marks, using the same angle that was used to cut the baluster. Then the baluster and the fillets are slipped into place to check the spacing, and to see if the baluster sits plumb. The upper fillet may have to be clamped or held in place with masking tape.

If the fillets are the right length, glue and nail them into place. Predrill for hardwood, and use 3D finish nails, or short nails in an 18 gauge gun. Use a single nail for each fillet. On these stairs, I glued and nailed the bottom fillets, but only used glue on the upper ones, since there were enough clamps to hold them in place until the glue set up.

Now, both ends of the baluster are glued, and it's pivoted into place. Then while it's being held in position, the upper corner is predrilled and nailed with a 3D finish nail. I use 1 1/4 inch hardened trim nails for doing this, and also for attaching the fillets. By keeping the nail close to the end of the baluster, it should be hidden by the next fillet. The lower end of the baluster is also nailed, by either going through the inside corner, or coming from the side that works the best. You may need a longer nail for this. Hardened trim nails are the same diameter between 1 1/4 and 2 inches. Use a nail set to sink the nail heads. When predrilling, use a drill bit that's just under the diameter of the nail.

The purpose of the nails is to lock the whole assembly into one unit. If every baluster was cut to the exact length, the glue would hold it all together, and the nails wouldn't be needed. Generally this isn't the case, and some of the balusters will end up being a little shorter than the others. By nailing the ends, it assures you that they'll stay in place, so you can keep moving along.

Before you can install the next baluster, you'll have to determine how long the fillets have to be to get the spacing that you came up with earlier. This length will be used for the rest of the balusters on that section, except at the ends, or where adjustments have to be made.

It's done in the same manner as before. Hold the next baluster in place, so it's spaced out the correct distance. Then mark it's position on both ends, and cut two fillets that end at the marks. Now dry-fit the baluster and the fillets to see if the spacing is correct, and the baluster sits plumb. If everything looks OK, the other fillets are cut to the same length.

Once that's finished, the baluster and the fillets are glued and nailed into place. From there, you'll work your way up the stairs, installing the others. Measure as you go, so the last baluster ends up at the right point. Then cut the last two fillets to fit.

The balusters are cut to fit as you go along. Commonly, one of them will end up being a little short, which shouldn't be a problem, since it will be nailed and held in place by the fillets. Just make sure that none of the balusters are too long. That would push up on the handrail, and you'd end up with a hump in it.

When installing the balusters over a landing, the upper end will have to be cut at a slight angle, so the corner doesn't bind against the handrail as it's tipped into place. If the balusters have been turned on a lathe, or have some other type of pattern, again you'll have to decide how much to cut off on each end, and which end should face up. Check the length that's needed at different points along the handrail.

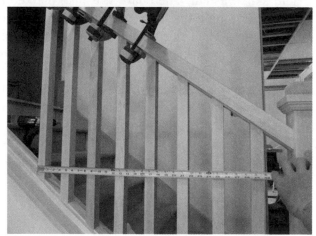

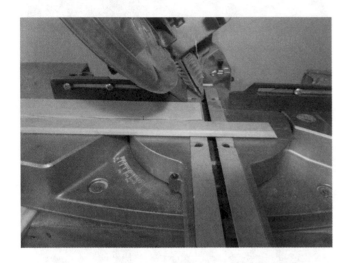

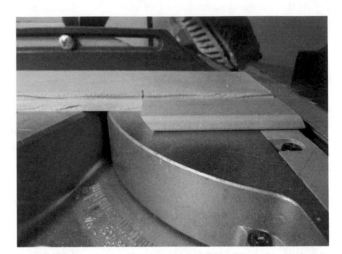

These photos show how the fillets were cut to the same length. To do this, I started by clamping a board to the saw that was tight against the back fence. Then once I found the correct length for the fillets, a piece of blue masking tape was attached to the base of the saw to mark where each fillet had to be held as it was cut. The board was also marked to show where to hold the last piece on each section of fillet material. Then one of the fillets was marked with an X, to be used to check the length of the others.

Once you get started, the fillets are all cut the same length, unless the balusters start to get out of plumb, or if the spacing is off. I check for this by using a level, and measure after every second or third baluster. If something is off, the length of the fillets is adjusted to bring the balusters back into position.

 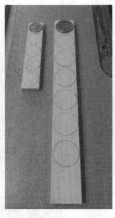 

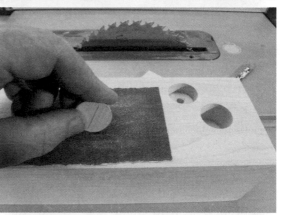

After the handrails have been installed, the holes can be plugged. On these stairs, the newel post needed three plugs. One was 3/4 inch in diameter, and the other two were 1 inch. The plugs should be face-grained and also tapered. Years ago, I used to buy them at the store, but it was hard to find a plug that matched the post when doing it this way. These days, I make my own, and feel that I get much better results this way.

When making your own plugs, try to use wood from the original post. Begin by cutting a 1/4 inch thick piece off the side that best matches where the plug is going. Then draw a series of circles in the sizes that are needed. Here I used coins for drawing the circles.

If the plugs are going to be hand-filed, it would be best to cut them out with a coping saw, and try to stay just outside the line. If you have a sanding wheel, they can be cut square.

When filing, I use the smoother side on a 4-in-1 file, and hold the plug by pinching it between my thumb and my index finger.

On this project, I used a random orbit sander by clamping it to a table. With either method, work your way towards the line, while also putting a slight taper on the plug. Then use coarse sandpaper to make any final adjustments.

Check the fit as you go, and keep removing wood from the high spots until the plug can be inserted a little over half of its thickness into the post.

Once the plug is finished, determine which direction it should face to best line up with the wood grain, and mark it with an arrow. Then apply glue, and tap the plug into place, while making sure that it doesn't go past flush. Wipe off the excess glue, and use a damp paper towel to remove any residue.

After the glue has dried, carefully scrape or plane the plug until it's flush to the surface. Then sand the post. When done properly, with matching wood, the plug should be almost invisible.

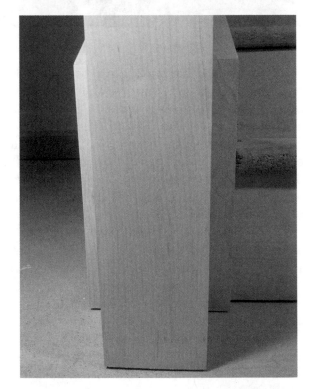

# USING A PLUG CUTTER

A plug cutter is used to make the plugs for rosettes and half posts. Almost any kind of a drill can be used for doing this, though a drill press would be ideal. The plugs should be cut from a board that closely matches the one on which they're being used. Start by drilling a series of holes across the board with the plug cutter, without going all the way through. Then remove the plugs by snapping them off with a screwdriver.

To install a plug, first clean up one end with a chisel. Then apply glue to the side of the plug, and turn it so the grain is lined up before it's tapped into place. Use a damp paper towel to wipe off any glue that runs down the board. After giving it time to dry, cut the plug flat to the surface with a sharp chisel. Don't try to slice it off in one pass, or you might take off too much. Then finish up by sanding the board. In the lower right photo are two types of plug cutters. The upper one is more expensive and cuts tapered plugs.

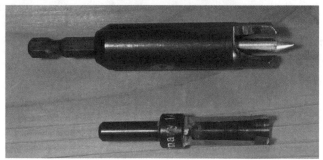

# SKIRTBOARDS

The skirtboards are next. On stairs that are being capped with finished stair treads, the overhang on each tread should be cut off flush to the riser before the skirtboards are installed. When installing the skirtboards, every edge should fit tight, unless it will be covered up later by a riser, stair tread, or carpeting. If you're installing wide baseboard, ideally, the skirtboard and the baseboard will line up with each other. It helps to figure out the cuts by drawing a line across the wall that shows the position of the upper edge of the skirtboard. On a difficult cut, sometimes it's better to cut it out first using a thin piece plywood, and then use that as a template for making the real skirtboard. The template doesn't have to fit perfectly; it just has to be close. You can make any adjustments that are needed when you make the final cuts. For instance, let's say the lower corner on one end of the plywood fits nice and tight, but the upper corner has a gap. Here all you have to do is to mark the spot that's short, and then write on the plywood how much to add at that point when drawing out the skirtboard.

317

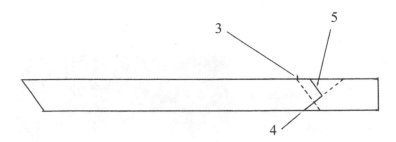

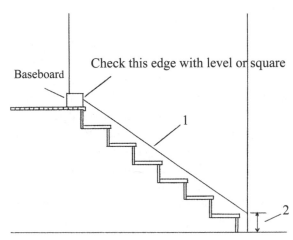

These drawings show the steps used when cutting the skirtboards. Before starting, a line is drawn across the wall that shows where the upper edge of the skirtboard will be. The best time to do this is when you're doing the layout. Once the height of the skirtboard has been determined, draw the line by laying a straight board against the wall, and then run a pencil along the edge of it.

To get started, you'll need two measurements. The first one is the length of the line between the baseboard at the top of the stairs, and the edge of the wall at the bottom. (1) The second is the distance from the line to the floor, when measured along the edge of the wall. (2)

The upper end of the skirtboard is cut first. To do this, start by laying the board across the stair treads. It doesn't matter that it's sitting above the line. It only has to be parallel to it.

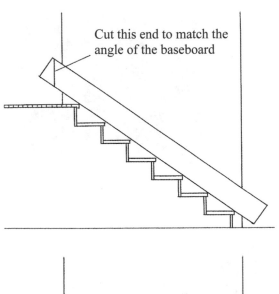

There are a couple of ways to determine the cut on the upper end of the board. If the edge of the baseboard is square to the landing or the upper floor, then a square can be held against the floor as you draw a line across the end of the skirtboard. Another way is to use a level. To do this, hold the level against the surface that the skirtboard is going to butt up against. Then look closely to see exactly where the bubble sits. Now hold the level the same way as you draw the line on the skirtboard. Once the end of the skirtboard has been marked, it's cut off at the line.

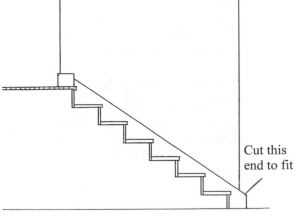

To cut the lower end of the skirtboard, the two measurements are used. (upper drawing) Begin by measuring from the upper corner, and make a mark at the first measurement. Then use a speed square to measure the angle of the cut that was just made on the upper end. Using the same angle, draw a line across the board at the mark. (line 3) Now measure down the line, and make a mark at the second measurement. Then draw a line that's perpendicular to line 3 at this mark. (line 4) These lines represent the end of the wall and the floor.

The cut for the floor has to be made before the skirtboard can be slipped into place. Then, if adjustments are needed on the upper end, it will shift the board towards the landing, which will raise it up off the floor. This isn't a concern if it's going to be carpeted, since the final cut will be a half inch off the floor. When going over wood or tile, you'd start by cutting it a little off the line to allow for any adjustments. At this time, the board will also be cut so that it extends a couple of inches past the end of the wall. (line 5) This will allow for the miter cut where it meets the baseboard

After cutting both ends, the board is laid into place to check the fit. If it's off on the upper end, that cut has to be adjusted first. Then the lower end is marked by drawing a line across it, and the skirtboard is cut to it's final length.

If the skirtboard was ending at the wall, you'd draw the line by following the edge of the wall with a sharp pencil. In this case, the line was drawn by laying a short length of baseboard against the wall, and then following the edge of it with a pencil. Then the line had to be transferred to the other side of the board to make the miter cut. When drawing the line, if the corner had dipped in at the bottom, the upper edge would be marked, and the line would be drawn with a level instead, so the mitered corner would be square to the floor.

On these stairs, I also could have drawn the line by just following the edge of the wall, which would mark the inside edge of the miter cut, but there's a problem with that. If the corner was rounded off, the board could end up being short. By having the baseboard in place, you know exactly where to make the cut. When cutting the board, again it should be a little long to begin with.

In this drawing, the skirtboard needs a second cut on the upper end to fit against a trim board. When doing this, I'd start by making the vertical cut. Then I'd hold a square against the cut, and draw a line at the point where the upper edge was equal to the top measurement. ( 6 ) If the riser and the trim board weren't square to each other, I'd either use a square that was adjustable, or take my best guess, and then adjust the cut if I was off. Either way, the skirtboard would be cut long enough so I could make any adjustments that were needed.

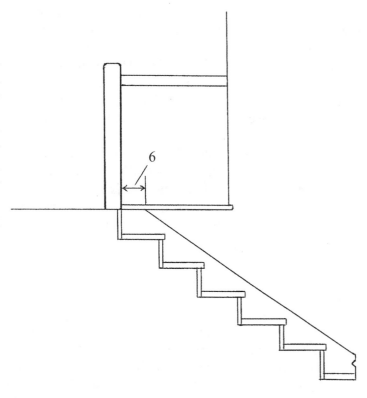

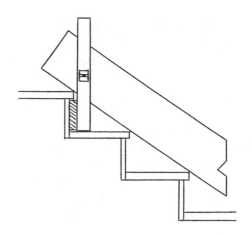

To match the angle of the stair riser if the tread is in the way, lay a block of wood against the riser. Then hold a straightedge against it as you draw the line across the skirtboard.

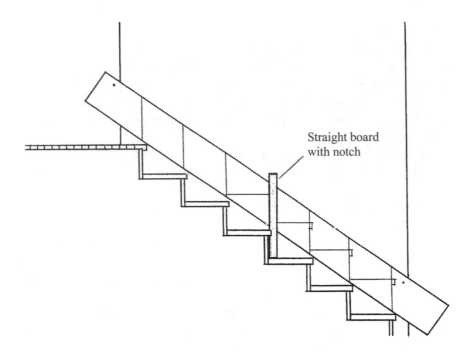

Straight board
with notch

On stairs that are tight against the wall, the skirtboard(s) will have to be cut to fit around the treads and risers. In order to do this, lay the skirtboard across the stair treads and lightly nail it to the wall, as shown in the drawing. Now the stairs can be drawn on the skirtboard by drawing each step so it's directly above the actual stair. The vertical lines for the risers will be drawn first. To begin, you'll need a straight board that's been notched to clear the tread overhang. This board should also be marked on both sides, showing the distance that the skirtboard is above its actual position. For instance, if the skirtboard has to drop 7 3/4 inches to be at the correct height, then the marks would be 7 3/4 inches from the bottom of the board.

If the risers were all plumb, the vertical lines could be drawn by simply following the edge of the notched board with a pencil as it's being held against each riser. Most likely, that won't be the case, and some of the risers will be tipped. Then the notched board would also be tipped, and the lines would be drawn to one side or the other of where they actually should be. To check this, use a level on each step to see if the notched board is plumb. If it's plumb, the line is drawn by following the edge of the board. But, if the riser is tipped, you'll have to compensate for it when drawing the line. To do this, draw a light line as the notched board is held against the riser. Then hold the notched board so it's plumb, and mark the skirtboard where the riser sticks out the farthest. If the lower part of the riser sticks out farther, the mark should be at the same height as the marks on the notched board. But if the upper edge sticks out, the mark should be at the bottom of the next tread, going up. Now draw the line for the riser by starting at the mark, and make it parallel to the light line that was just drawn.

The horizontal lines are drawn by using the marks on the notched board. These are marked as you're drawing the lines for the risers. When doing this, make sure the notched board is being held plumb. Two marks are needed for each step, and also for the floor at each end of the skirtboard. Then use a straightedge to draw the horizontal lines between the marks. Extend the lines far enough to allow for the overhang.

The lines for the overhang on the treads are still needed. To draw the vertical lines, measure the width of each tread by holding the level against it. Then mark the distance, and draw the line on the skirtboard. To check your work, measure between the riser and the end of the tread to make sure you end up at the same point. The lower edge of the overhang is also done by measurement. Measure the thickness of each tread, and then draw it on the skirtboard. If the stairs are being carpeted, the skirtboard could be cut at this time. Otherwise, the shape of the overhang will have to be drawn before it can be cut out. When doing this, I generally look for a coin or a metal washer that has the right amount of curve to it.

You could also skip the last step by cutting off the overhang at the end of each tread, using a hand saw and a chisel, so the skirtboard just fits behind it. Once the skirtboard has been cut out, it's slipped into place, and any adjustments are made, if needed. Then both ends are cut to fit.

Now that we've gone over the basics, I'll describe how the skirtboards were installed on these particular stairs. I'll start at the top, and then quickly go over how everything was cut and laid out to bring it all together.

These photos show the skirtboard coming down from the first floor. As you can see, the board was cut to line up with the baseboard over the landing. To determine where the two would come together, lines were drawn that represented the upper edge of both boards. The skirtboard was cut first, and was temporarily nailed into place. On the upper end, the only place where I had to be concerned about a tight fit was against the door trim, since the stairs were getting carpeted. On the lower end, the skirtboard was cut off square to the floor at the point where the two boards would meet up.

Then the baseboard was cut to length, while making sure that the joint was tight between the two boards. In this case, it turned out that there wasn't a stud at that location, so the boards were glued and doweled together. To do this, after drilling the holes for the dowels, everything was laid out across the stairs. Then the two boards were glued and assembled, and quickly dropped into place. At that point, several nails were put in to hold the boards in position, and a shim was inserted between the end of the baseboard and the wall to keep pressure on the joint. Then the excess glue was wiped off with a damp paper towel.

After letting it sit overnight, the nailing was finished off using two 2 1/2 inch nails per stud, where possible. Then the joint was cleaned up with a scraper and sanded.

On the other side of the stairs, the skirtboard was cut and just tacked into place. Again, at the top it had to fit tight against the door trim, while on the lower end, it was left a little long for the miter cut. Once it was tacked on, a line was drawn across the back of it to mark the outer edge of the next piece. Then the board was taken down, the end was cut, and it was put back up and nailed into place.

This corner is the one where the baseboard was too short, so a piece was made to match the height of the skirtboard. The board that caps the end of the wall needed a miter cut on both sides. The one after that also needed a miter cut on each end, but the cut on the right side was for gluing on a return. Once that was done, the corners were glued, and the boards were nailed into place.

Now we'll move on to the skirtboard that's attached to the end wall on the lower stairs. To make it easier, this board was cut before the riser was added to stiffen up the wall. To cut the upper end, it was laid across the stairs to determine what was needed for it to meet up with the landing. The cut for the floor was done by measurement. After that, the board was tacked into place, and lines were drawn to show where it stuck out from the wall. Then it was taken down and cut off at the lines. Once the riser was installed, the lower corner of the skirtboard was notched to clear the riser. Then it was nailed into place, and the trim boards were installed over the wall.

On the other side of the stairs, the skirtboard only needed a single cut at the top, where it butted up against the baseboard at the edge of the landing. Then the lower end was cut long, so that it overhung the wall, and the board was tacked into place. After marking the length, using a scrap piece of baseboard, it was taken down and the miter cut was made. Then the skirtboard was nailed into place. To finish the corner, a short section of baseboard was cut to go between the skirtboard and the door trim. Then the corner was glued, and the board was nailed on.

Once the skirtboards were in place, the cap was installed. We'll begin where we left off, on the right side of the lower set of stairs. Here the cap was cut to fit tight against the baseboard on the upper end, and then tacked on with the lower end hanging over the wall. After marking where the wall ended, the cap was taken down and cut to length with a mitered cut. Then it was nailed into place.

That left me with a corner that was a problem, as you can see in the upper left photo. At first glance, you'd think that the cap over the stairs is narrower than the one over the baseboard, but it's actually the same size. I ran into the same thing when finishing off the

stairs on the main floor of this house. After going over the options, I ended up cutting a wider cap for that spot. At first, I was concerned that the size of the cap would stand out, but most people don't even notice it unless you point it out to them. I did the same thing here, and it was just a matter of using a table saw to cut a cap that matched up at the corner. If I remember correctly, it took several tries before I ended up with a piece that fit. Then after gluing the corner, the cap was nailed on.

Moving back to the upper set of stairs, we'll start on the left side as you're looking up. Here, the cap that goes over the skirtboard butts up against the one that's over the baseboard on the landing. I determined the angle where the two come together by cutting it on a couple of short pieces of the cap. Then once I had a tight fit, I made a mark at the point where they met up.

The cap over the stairs was installed first. After cutting the upper end to fit against the door trim, the board was cut to length using the angle that was just determined, so it ended at the mark. Once it was nailed into place, the cap over the baseboard was cut to match up at the joint, and then trimmed to fit tight against the wall. Then after gluing the butt joint, the cap was installed, and the excess glue was wiped off. Since there wasn't a stud to nail into behind the joint, construction adhesive was applied to the back of the boards where they came together. When going over the photos, I couldn't find any that were taken of this area when the cap was first installed, so I used one that shows how it looked after it was finished.

Moving over to the other side, these photos show how the cap comes down the stairs, and then wraps around the end of the wall. To begin, the cap over the stairs was cut to fit tight against the door trim on the upper end, and again, it was tacked on with the lower end hanging over the wall. Then after marking where the wall ended, it was taken down and cut to length with a mitered cut, and nailed into place. At this point, a taller cap was needed for going over the end board, and also for the one after that, so the two caps were cut from a board that was the same size as the one used for the lower stairs. To have a more finished look, a return was also put on the cap where it ends above the edge of the landing. Then the corners were glued, and the boards were nailed into place.

# TREADS AND RISERS

Now the finished treads and risers can be installed. This wasn't done on the stairs that we've been working on, since they're getting carpeted, so I'll only be able to describe the process. Generally, the risers go on first, and then the treads are installed with the back edge butted up against the riser. This way, the risers can be raised up, and the gap at the bottom will be hidden by the treads. If you wanted, you could also do it in reverse, and install the risers after the treads, but the disadvantage to this method is that you're covering up part of the stair tread, so there would be less for you to walk on. The risers would also have to be cut to the exact width on each step.

Before you can start, you'll have to cut off the overhang on the existing stair treads, if it hasn't already been done. It's best to do this is before the skirtboards are installed. These cuts are easily made by using a circular saw and/or a quality jig saw with a sharp blade in it. When using a jig saw, the blade should just barely scrape against the riser. If the saw can't make it all the way to the end of the treads, you'll have to finish up the cuts with a handsaw. Then clean them up with a planer, block plane, and/or a chisel.

When building stairs for an average deck, the length of the stair treads and the risers isn't that critical, but on interior stairs with a skirtboard on each side, the cuts have to be exact. The best way to do this is by using a jig that's specifically made for the job. One that's easy to make is shown in the jig and scaffold section towards the back of this book. To use the jig, just lay it in place where the new board is going. Then loosen the wing nuts, extend the ends so they're tight against the skirtboard on both sides, and retighten the wing nuts. Now all you have to do is to lay the jig on the new board, and draw the lines for the end cuts by following the edge of the jig with a sharp pencil. Then cut the board to length, and slip it into place.

Before you install the new risers, check the ones that you're going over with a straightedge and a level to see if they're straight and reasonably plumb. A torpedo level and a straight board work good for doing this. Any dips should be shimmed out with felt paper or wood shims. Humps can be evened up by shimming on both sides of them. The lower edge of the riser is where it's more important for it to be straight, since the finished stair tread will butt up against it at that point. Shims can also be used to tip out the whole riser, if the one that's beneath it is noticeably out of plumb.

If the finished treads and/or risers are going directly over the stringers, the stringers should be shimmed so they're either level or plumb, and in a straight line. When installing the treads, the back edge gets shimmed where it's needed. But, if the front edge is low, it's generally left as it is, since it will be supported by the riser. If the front edge is high, the stringer(s) can be planed down.

When standard lumber is used for the stringers, the stair treads tend to have a downward slope. This is caused by the wood shrinking as it dries. Since the stringer is at it's widest point near the end of each step, that's where the greatest amount of shrinkage will occur, so the treads will commonly be lower at the overhang.

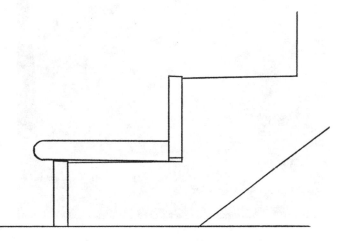

The risers should support the finished stair treads in a level position. Before you install each riser, lay a level across the stringers or the existing stair tread, perpendicular to the riser, to see how it sits. Then, depending on the width of the riser, you'll either have to cut it to the correct width, or raise it up so the new tread will be level as it lays across the top. You can see how this was done in the drawing. This should be checked both ways, parallel and perpendicular to the stringers. If the floor is off, the first riser will need a tapered cut on the lower edge, so the upper edge is level.

Before the risers are installed, sometimes I'll use a table saw to put a slight back-cut on the upper edge. This way, it's easier to get a tight fit against the stair tread, and less adhesive will squeeze out. If bullnose trim has already been installed on either the landing or the upper floor, make sure the riser fits tight against it to help support the overhang.

Install each riser by first applying construction adhesive to the stringers or the board that it's going over. Then predrill if it's hardwood, and nail it on with 6D finish nails. You could also use 2 1/2 inch nails in a 15 gauge trim gun. When hand nailing, I put two nails into each stringer. If possible, I like to keep the bottom nails low enough so they'll be hidden by the stair tread. Once the first riser is on, install the others in the same manner.

If you want, after the first two risers are in place, you can start on the stair treads. These may have to be cut to size to get the correct amount of overhang. When doing this, I rip the treads to width on a table saw, and set the blade just off square to give the back edge a slight back-cut. The stair jig is used to determine the end cuts, the same as it was for the risers.

After cutting a tread or a riser to length, check the fit against both ends, and use a low-angle block plane to remove any high spots. The board should fit tight, but make sure that it's not too long. If that happens, it will push out on the skirtboard, and there will be a gap next to the boards that have already been installed. On a stair tread, you also have to check the fit against the riser. If there are any gaps, the back edge will have to be planed to get a tight fit. Scribing the edge may help when doing this.

To install the treads, apply construction adhesive, and then lay them in place. If I'm going over an existing tread, I put a line of adhesive near the back edge, a thinner line along the upper edge of the riser (towards the back), and then a series of lines going across it. I want the tread to be securely glued, but at the same time, I don't want to see adhesive squeezing out.

Predrill, and nail on the tread using 8D finish nails, when hand nailing. With a trim gun, I'd use 2 1/2 inch nails in a 15 gauge gun. I'd rather not have any nail holes in the center of the step, preferring to let the adhesive do its job, so I'll put two or three nails on each side, but only one in the center if there are three stringers, and try to keep that one towards the back. The rest of the treads are installed in the same manner.

On the stairs that are shown on the previous page, the treads and risers were sanded, and the first coat of finish was applied before they were installed. This made it easier for the painter, and once the adhesive set up, the stairs could be used without worrying about scratches and stains.

Trim detail on the end wall. In the photo on the right, the cap hasn't been installed yet on the short piece of baseboard. The lower photos show the stairs on the main floor.

## OTHER STAIRS

On these stairs, the handrail was installed by someone else. Originally, the treads and risers ran all the way to the wall. To give it a more finished look, I installed a matching skirtboard. I also glued a thin layer of oak plywood over the risers.

While helping a friend install the skirtboards on these stairs, I noticed that the lower end of the wall had way too much movement to it. Here it wasn't possible to stiffen up the wall by running the riser across the front of it, without rebuilding the end of the wall. So what I did, instead, was to cut a notch into the back side of the 2x4 using a hand saw and a chisel. Then I applied polyurethane construction adhesive, and installed an oak riser that overlapped it. I nailed it to the stairs, but used screws to attach the riser to the 2x4. Once the wall is finished off with oak trim, it should be pretty solid.

329

Here the height of the skirtboard was adjusted so the upper end would line up with the baseboard. Since there was no way that the lower end could line up with the baseboard, I cut the skirtboard flush to the wall and glued veneer to the end of it.

You may be required to put returns on the end of the handrail(s). This is easy to do. Cut the returns from the opposite end, and then glue them on.

On these stairs, the carpenter used a piece of corner trim to break up the two sections of skirtboard.

I finished off these stairs about twenty-five years ago. Originally, they were the just simple basement stairs with three stringers, 1 1/2 inch thick pine treads, and open risers. The interesting thing here is that most of the work was done with a circular saw and a low-angle block plane.

On these stairs, I started by removing the old treads, so the riser height would be OK once the new ones were in place. Then I shimmed the riser cuts on the stringers to even them up, and cut a piece of oak plywood to width for the fascia board that caps the outer stringer. After both ends were cut, the board was lightly nailed into place. Then the outline of the stringer was drawn on it.

The lines for the treads were drawn as is, unless the tread wasn't level. If that was the case, I drew the line so it **was** level, and then either planed down or shimmed up the stringer at that spot. For the risers, I held a piece of plywood riser material against the stringers, and then drew a line along the outer edge of it.

Once the lines were drawn, the board was cut to shape. The cuts for the treads was the easy part, since it was just a matter of clamping on a straightedge, and then cutting along the line with the circular saw.

The cuts for the risers were miter cuts. In order to make them, first I had to transfer the lines to the other side of the board. Then after clamping on a straightedge, I had to make each cut by going backwards, since the blade only tips one way. On these cuts, the blade was held just off the line. This way, I'd be sure that the corners would come together.

Once that was done, the cuts were finished up with either a hand saw or a jig saw, and the fascia board was nailed into place. At this time, the skirtboard was also installed on the outer wall.

The risers were next. These were cut to size, and then any necessary adjustments were made by planing the edge. Once they fit, the mitered edge was glued, and the risers were nailed into place.

These treads have returns on them, which gives them a more finished look. After cutting them to size, the back edge was planed to fit tight against the riser. Then the treads were nailed into place. To finish, a decorative edge was installed on both the skirtboard and the fascia board.

331

I recently built this handrail, where I needed to come up with something that was inexpensive, yet also be sturdy and not look too cheap. I think it came out pretty good. Here the total cost was only around twenty dollars. The only thing that I had to buy were the 4x4 posts and a few lag screws. The other boards were all cut out from some old 2x10s that I found in the garage.

The handrails, shoe rails and the fillets were cut first, from the board that had the straightest grain and the fewest knots. After that, the rest of the wood was cut into balusters that were 1 3/8 inch square. Then I picked through the pile to find the ones that looked the best.

In this case, the posts were already rounded off, so they only had to be notched and then cut to length. The hand rails (3 1/4" wide) and the shoe rails (1 1/4" tall) had square edges, so I went over them with a router using a 3/8 inch rounding bit. 1 3/8 inch wide by 1/4 inch deep cuts were made for the balusters and the fillets. I didn't have a dado blade with me, so I made a series of shallow cuts on the table saw, and then used a chisel to remove the strips of wood between the cuts. The balusters were lightly rounded off with a block plane and sanded.

In the second photo, you'll notice that the hand rail is directly attached to the wall. Since the other side of the wall wasn't sheetrocked yet, I drilled through one of the studs with a 3/16 inch bit. Then I held the hand rail in place as I attached it with a hardened lag screw.

The lower left photo shows the corner post with the holes for attaching the handrails. One hole is 1/4 inch above the other, so the lag screws would clear each other. On the lower end, the corner post was toenailed to the floor.

Here I used 5 inch lag screws, 1/4 inch in diameter for attaching the hand rails, and 5/16 inch for mounting the end post. A 3/4 inch spade bit was used for countersinking the heads, and a 5/32 inch drill bit for doing the pilot holes.

# INSTALLING TONGUE AND GROOVE FLOORING

Years ago, I learned how to install wood floors from a book I got at the library. That book, and others I've looked at since then, have always showed that you start on one side of a room, and then work your way across to the other. While this might be the best choice when there's a straight wall to start against, many times that isn't the case.

This drawing shows the outline of the floor that we'll be working on. As you can see, the wall is broken up on the long side, so it'd be difficult to start the floor at different points and have the rows come together exactly right. On the other side, the wall is also broken up, and there's a

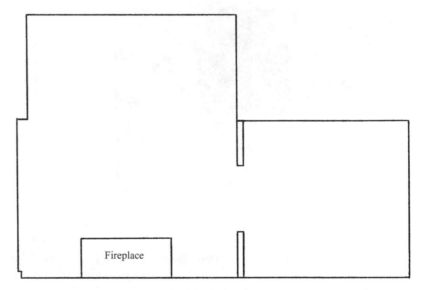

Fireplace

good chance that the edge wouldn't be straight enough by the time you got past the doorway. So, in this case, it's better to start the floor in the middle of the room, and then work back towards the walls.

The installation that follows is a little different than most, because the floor is heated by PEX tubing that's been installed above the floor between plywood strips that were nailed to the floor sheathing. The area between the strips has been filled with mortar to help draw and spread out the heat. Since the flooring will be nailed to the plywood strips, their location has to be drawn out on the rosin paper to keep from hitting the tubes. Rosin paper gives you a smooth surface to work on, and also acts as a dust barrier. Years ago, sometimes I'd use felt paper instead, but felt paper is sticky, so you end up with footprints all over the floor.

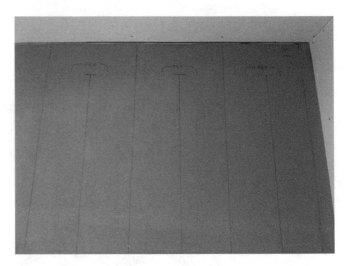

The photo on the left shows the floor before I got started on it. The other photo shows how the location of the plywood strips were drawn out on the rosin paper. Since every other strip was cut short for the loop in the tubing, the ends of those strips also had to be marked. It's important that you lay out the first row of rosin paper where the floor is being started, and then to do the following rows by going in the same direction that you'll be installing the floor. This way, the boards will smoothly slide over the overlapping seams as you pull them into place. I generally overlap each row of rosin paper by a couple of inches. Then I lightly stretch it so it's laying flat, and staple it to the floor.

The TV and the computer modems were left in place, so they could still be used as the floor was being installed. In order to do this, they were mounted on dollies, so I could move them around as needed.

After laying out the rosin paper, a string was stretched across the room between nails to represent the edge of the first row of flooring. Here the first row was started just off the edge of the door opening. Then measurements were taken from the string to the opposite walls in both rooms, to find the line that was as close as I could get to parallel to the different walls. It turned out that I was pretty close on the first try, and the string only needed a small adjustment.

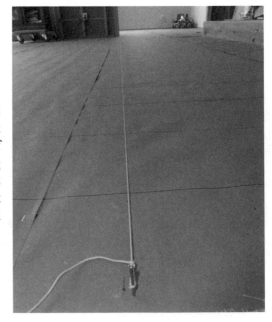

Now with the string was in place, 3/4 inch thick plywood blocks were laid out along the length of it. Since the blocks will be on the groove side of the flooring, they have to be tall enough to make good contact with the wood above the groove. Here I used blocks that were about 5x8 inches, and put one every 16 inches. Then each block was held in place with three screws that were long enough to go into the floor joist beneath it. While installing the blocks, I also made sure that they didn't push against the string, which could move it over and cause the remaining blocks to follow the same mistake, so the line wouldn't be straight

The blocks have to be securely attached to the floor, since the nailer is designed to drive the rows tight together. If they can't be screwed to the floor joists, I generally space them about every 12 inches.. Although I prefer plywood blocks, there's no reason that you couldn't use whatever's available, as long as it's securely attached and installed in a straight line.

Once the blocks were in place, the string was removed. Then a board was installed to cap the end of the floor, to give the edge a more finished look. Here a single 2 1/4 inch board was used, with the tongue cut off and the grooved edge facing towards the blocks. To make sure it was straight, it was nailed along a string line. 8D finish nails were used to attach it, and were spaced about a foot apart. Although I prefer to install the border at this time, sometimes you'll have to do it after the floor is finished. Since this is purely for looks, almost anything can be used for the edge.

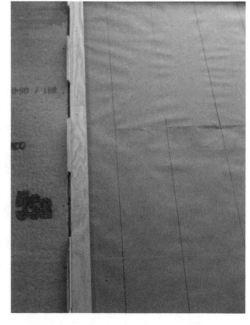

Every row of flooring that's installed along the end board is going to be driven tight against it. With only the nails holding it in place, there's no way that the board will stay in position. Also, every time it's driven back, gaps will appear between the board and any rows of flooring that have already been installed. To keep this from happening, shims were used to support it from behind. Here it was possible because Durock had been installed for the tile floor. Blocks can also be used if there isn't anything to shim against. When neither one is an option, you'll have to be extra careful when starting each row. Any time the board gets pushed back, it will have to be driven back into place with a block of wood and a hammer before the next row is started.

At this point, some of the flooring can be laid out. I generally begin by opening up two or three of the bundles to see what I have to work with. Every bundle is different, and some will have a higher percentage of a certain length. By having more than one bundle open, it's easier to spread them out.

For the first row, I want boards that are straight and reasonably long. In this case, the board that caps the end of the floor will be on the right side to begin with, so the tongue on the first board of each row will slip into it. Then once I've selected the boards for the first row, I'll lay out a whole section of the floor. This is much faster than picking them out one at a time as they're being nailed into place.

While laying out the rows, try to use up the different lengths equally, so you don't end up with a pile of short boards at the end of the project. I once read that you should keep the ends of the boards at least 3 inches apart on adjoining rows. I prefer to keep them at least 6 inches apart, but that depends on the length of the boards that you have to work with. The main thing is to keep the seams random. Spread them out, and try not to get into a pattern. For me, what works the best is to lay the boards out quickly, so there isn't much time to think about it. Then as I'm doing it, I look for areas without any seams, and try to find boards that are the right length to end at those spots.

After an area has been laid out, I'll stand back and look it over. I'm looking for seams that are too close together, or if there's anything else about the pattern that bothers me. You don't want to get too critical here, since the idea is to keep the pattern random. But if something isn't right, this is the best time to change it. Once you start nailing, it's easy to install a board that's obviously wrong, since you'll be paying more attention as to whether each row is tight, rather than watching for any mistakes in the layout.

Here each row was started against the board that caps the end of the floor. A gap should be left between the boards that are being laid out, and the blocks or any rows that have already been installed. This space is needed for the flooring nailer, and to leave room for pulling the boards into place.

When you get to the end of each row, try to find a board that's close to the right length, so there isn't too much waste. Then the last board on each row is overlapped to show where the seam will be.

Two views of the first section

Once the boards have been laid out, it's time to nail them into place. Here the first board was held against the blocks, and slid tight to the cap. Then it was nailed every 8 inches with the flooring nailer to hit the plywood strips. When nailing to the floor itself, the nails are spaced every 10 - 12 inches, except on extra wide boards where the spacing would be closer. By keeping the nails an inch or two from the end of each board, it should help to prevent them from splitting.

After the first board is finished, the second one is slid tight to the end of it, and then nailed. The others are installed in the same manner. Then once I've done a few boards, I generally get the other rows started. It goes faster this way, doing multiple rows at the same time, since you don't have to move around as much. To start the second row, the board is pulled from the layout and slid into position. Then it's driven tight against the first row by hitting it with the rubber end of the hammer. Now the metal end is used to hit the end of the board to slide it against the cap. Then it's nailed into place. For most of the floor, that's how it's done. Pull a board from the layout, and slide it into position. Then hit it with the rubber end of the hammer, so it's tight against the last row, and drive the ends together with the metal end before nailing it into place. Once you get a rhythm going, the boards go on fast.

When driving the ends together, the hammer is slid along the floor to keep from denting the upper corner of the board. While doing this, sometimes the hammer will catch on the rosin paper and tear it. If this happens, just staple the paper back into place. You can cut down on this problem by rounding off any sharp corners and smoothing down the rough spots on the hammer.

Once I got started, I had the first six rows going at the same time. Then as I worked my way across, I hit a point where I couldn't go any farther until I started cutting the boards to length at the far end. On this floor, the plan was to space the flooring 5/16 of an inch off the wall, so I laid a board (spacer board) that was that thickness against the wall, and then measured off of it to get the length of the last board on each row.

Whenever possible, I prefer to install the flooring by starting on the left side of each row. This way, I don't have to measure to find the length of the last board. To determine what's needed, the board is simply turned lengthwise and held against the spacer board. Then it's marked at the point where it meets the board that it's going to butt up against, and cut off at the mark. If you start of the right side, the tongue will be in the way when you turn the board around.

Since the last board is next to the wall, you'll need a pry bar to push it tight against the previous board. The photo on the left shows the board being pried from the top. This works when you're at a stud or there's wood to pry against. Here the spacer board is being used for leverage and to help protect the wall. The photo on the right shows the pry bar coming from the side. This way, it's pushing off the bottom plate. Again, the spacer board is used to protect the wall. Even when the board is being used, the sheetrock can still be dented or broken if you're not careful.

Sometimes the last board will move as it's being nailed into place, and you'll be left with a gap at the other end. By putting scraps of wood under the pry bar, it will keep tension on it when it's nailed.

Once I finished the first six rows, I removed the plywood blocks and started in the other direction. In order to do this, slip tongue was inserted into the groove on the boards that were used for the first row. Then after tapping it into place, the boards were also nailed on this side in the same manner. Sometimes the fit is a little loose, so the slip tongue has to be held in place as its being nailed. You can do this by holding your foot against it, or by using a second hammer, in which case, the nailer will have to be held with your foot. Once it's been nailed, you wouldn't even notice the difference.

Going in this direction, the rows were started on the left side. Since there's a groove on this end of the boards, slip tongue was also needed for the board that caps the end of the floor. In this case, I didn't want to disturb the board by pounding on it, so I glued the slip tongue into place the night before I started in the other direction

Slip tongue is inexpensive and generally comes in sticks that are a few feet long. I buy it at hardwood flooring distributors. When I've asked for it at local building centers, they don't even know what I'm talking about. The last time I bought it, I paid a little over twenty cents a foot for it.

When starting against the wall, the spacer board can also be used to start each row. It doesn't matter if it's laid horizontal or vertical. Just don't let it get stuck between the flooring and the wall.

As the floor is being installed, sometimes the rows will start to curve in at the ends. This is caused by the boards being compressed more in this area. To keep this from happening, I generally put the last nail around three inches from the end of each row, and don't drive it in quite as hard.

Keep laying out more sections as you go along. The floor nailer is used as long as possible, until you get so close to the wall that you can't swing the hammer. My favorite floor nailer is the Porta-Nailer. It has a ratcheting action, so the nails don't have to be driven in with a single swing, which lets me get a little closer to the wall. By the time I'm on the last row that I can do, I'm holding the hammer with both hands and taking three or four short swings to do each nail. When using the Porta-Nailer, I generally take two easy swings, instead of one hard one, even if I'm in the middle of the room. I've found that I get a tighter floor by doing it this way. You can tell when you're driving the boards tight, by the thump in the floor as each nail is put in.

After you've gone as far as you can with the floor nailer, the remaining rows are hand nailed; however, there are a couple of other options. Floor nailers are also available for working next to the wall. They do this by driving the nails straight down into the floor. I used one for half an hour once, and then returned it to the store because there were gaps between the rows. If you want the rows to be tight, they have to be driven together with the nails going in at an angle.

Trim nailers can also be used. I used one on a couple of floors, years ago. For speed, and being easier on the knees, there's no question that the trim nailer is better. But it doesn't drive the boards together, and I don't know how long the floor will hold up since the nails are so thin. When doing this, use a 15 gauge gun with 2 1/2 inch nails. After trying each method, I've found that you end up with a better floor by hand nailing, so that's how I do it.

Generally I can get about a foot from the wall when using the flooring nailer. That leaves me with around six rows left to do if I'm installing 2 1/4 inch flooring. Of those six, I can do four by driving the nails in at an angle, just above the tongue. The last two rows will be face-nailed. For these last rows, make sure the boards are straight. This is hard enough without having to be fighting warps.

When nailing above the tongue, I generally use the nails from the Porta-Nailer. The fastest way to get them is to hold the Porta-Nailer up and keep hitting the rubber end with the hammer, which will give you one nail for every time it's hit. The advantage of using these nails is that you generally don't have to predrill, but it takes a clean swing to drive them in by hand. While doing this, the nails are less likely to bend if you squeeze them between your fingers as you're pounding them in. If they're still bending, you'll have to drill pilot holes through the flooring. When a nail bends, and it's in too far to pull it back out, the best thing to do is to bend it back and forth with a pliers until it breaks off.

As you're pounding the nails in, stop just before you hit the upper corner of the board, as one too many swings will dent the surface. Then finish driving them in with a large nail set, as it's less likely to bend the nail. You'll be right next to the wall, so use the shortest nail set that you can find. If you're drilling pilot holes, keep a vacuum handy for picking up any wood chips that could get caught between the boards.

When doing the last couple of rows, it's easier to do both at the same time. With both rows in place, squeeze them tight, and then hold them in that position with the pry bar and blocks of wood. These boards will be face-nailed with 8D finish nails. With a 3/4 inch plywood subfloor, I'd space the nails about a foot apart, and not worry about the location of the floor joists. If the subfloor was questionable, I'd make sure that I nailed into the joists, wherever possible. On this floor, the nails were spaced every 16 inches on the second row, to hit the plywood strips, and every foot on the last row.

These nails should also be driven in at an angle, if possible. On the second row, keep the nails close to the side with the tongue. The holes should be predrilled by just going through the board. When doing this, I use one of the 8D finish nails, instead of a drill bit, and then change the nail when the point gets dull. When using a drill bit, it should be close to the diameter of the nail. Sink the heads below the surface with a nail set.

When tightening the rows, it's best to pry off each stud. If the gap between the last row and the wall is too big, put a piece of wood behind the pry bar to get better leverage. To pry between the studs, use a board that's long enough to bridge over the stud on each side. The board will also help to prevent damage to the wall.

The last row is generally cut to fit, so there's a 1/4 - 3/8 inch gap between the end of the floor and the wall. Then it's nailed into place. Sometimes the last row will end up a little short, instead, as shown in this photo. Here I shrunk the gap by cutting thin strips that were glued to the last row, so I ended up 5/16 of an inch from the wall.

Short strips can be glued and quickly slid into position. With longer strips, it's easier to loosely set them in place, and then squeeze the glue into the gap between the two boards.

Press the boards together with the pry bar. Then put opposing shims behind the boards to keep pressure on them. To apply more pressure, lay the pry bar or a piece of wood against the end of one of the shims, and then tap it over with a hammer. Remove the shims in the same manner, after the glue has set up.

Once the shims are in place, scrape off the glue that has squeezed out to make sure there aren't any gaps between the boards. Then tighten the shims, or add more, if needed.

This is how you want to end up, with a tight glue line and no gaps.

A couple of photos showing the installed floor

The finished floor

# STARTING AGAINST THE WALL

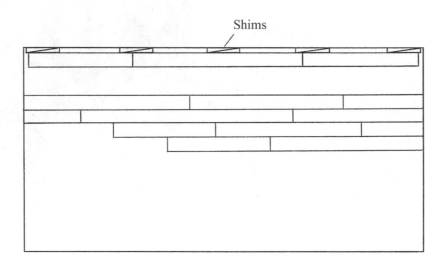

Shims

If there's a straight wall to begin on, the floor is generally started on one side of the room. To do this, begin by measuring the width of the room at both ends, and decide if the flooring should run parallel to the wall, or if one end should be closer than the other. Then find boards that are straight, and lay out the first row using shims to space the boards off the wall at each end, while taking into account the measurements that were just taken. Now put a nail at each end, and stretch a string between the nails to represent the edge of the first row. Then predrill the boards, and nail the first row into place with 8D finish nails, following the string. Once they've been nailed, shims are placed behind the boards to keep them from moving. I generally put shims behind every seam, and a pair every 12 - 16 inches in between.

How the first row gets nailed would depend on the sub floor and the width of the flooring. When using 1 1/2 inch boards, I'd run the nails down the center of the board and space them about a foot apart, if the subfloor was good. If it wasn't, I'd nail into the floor joists, and also put an extra nail between each one if the joists were on 24 inch centers. With 2 1/4 inch boards, I'd do the same, but stagger the nails so they were be closer to both edges. When using 3 inch boards, I'd face-nail along the back edge, and also nail just above the tongue about every 12 inches, once the shims were in place.

The next few rows will have to be hand nailed, just above the tongue, until you're far enough out from the wall to use the floor nailer. By just putting a few nails into it at a time, the spring-loaded slide on the floor nailer will be in as far as possible, so you can get closer to the wall. This could save you from having to hand nail a couple of rows.

When starting against the wall, it's always a little awkward at first. Because of that, I wouldn't lay out a large section of floor until there was plenty of room to work.

The lower drawing shows a floor that's being started on one side, but here there's also an opening in the wall for a closet, pantry, etc. In this case, a combination of the two methods is used. Against the wall, the first row is shimmed and nailed in the same manner, but blocks are attached to the floor to go across the opening. Then slip tongue is used to run the flooring in the opposite direction.

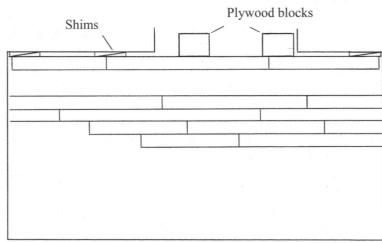

Shims

Plywood blocks

When installing a floor, where the doors are already in place, you have two options. You can go around the jambs, or go under them. To go under them, the jambs, and also the trim if it's been installed, have to be cut off so the floor boards can just slip beneath them. To do this, use a thin-bladed saw, and make the cuts as you hold the saw blade against a board that's the same thickness as the floor being installed. Although a scrap board is shown in the photo, I generally use a couple of the floor boards for doing this.

If you're going around the jambs, the boards have to fit tight against them, so there isn't a gap showing. When doing this, I'd still cut off the trim and the door stops to make it easier. This way, you only have to stay tight to each jamb until you're past the reveal.

Sometimes a floor will change direction as it goes from one room to another. One way to do this is to start one of the areas off plywood blocks or an end cap, the same as it was done at the beginning of this section. Then the floor in the next room is installed perpendicular to the first. When remodeling a home, you may also have to add on to wood floors that are already in place. Depending on the direction they run, this could mean sawing off one end of the floor, and then starting from there. This was done on the floor in the photo, where part of the wall was removed to connect the two rooms.

To make a straight cut, use a cutting jig or run the circular saw along a straight board or a straightedge. Most of the time, you'll still have to finish up the cut at each end. I generally use a pull saw for this by laying a straight board along the line. Then I kneel on the board, and hold the saw blade tight against it as I cut. When doing this, sometimes there's hardly any room to make a stroke, so the baseboard may have to be removed if it hasn't already been done. You could also finish the cut with an oscillating saw or a good jig saw that has a sharp blade in it, if you're real careful. To keep from cutting into the subfloor, the jig saw will have to be raised up by putting a board under it. Then once the cut is finished, clean up the edge with a plane, a sharp chisel and/or a coarse file. After sawing off the end of the floor, it may also have to be renailed. Here the boards could be face-nailed, though another option is to hide the nails by driving them down at an angle through the end of each board.

One thing to mention here is that there's always the possibly of hitting a nail when you saw into a floor, or any board for that matter, when remodeling. Even though I try to be careful, I still end up having to replace the blade on my pull saw every year or so, because of this. Whenever you're using a pull saw or a jig saw, and it feels like you're just starting to hit a nail, stop cutting and take a look. If it is a nail, most of the time you can drive it out of the way by using a nail set.

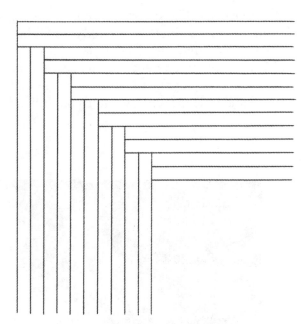

Years ago, I helped install a couple of floors where we changed the direction by using a herringbone pattern. On one of them, we used it where the front entry merged with the hall. This drawing shows the pattern we used, where the boards are doubled up.

## REPAIRING A FLOOR

When remodeling, sometimes you have to patch or repair wood floors. Here the upper drawing shows a floor with an opening that needs to be patched over. You would think that all you have to do is to replace the sheathing, and then cut the boards to fit the opening. But, if you did that, the patch would be too obvious. In this case, the boards that are numbered will either be removed or trimmed to square up the ends to make it blend in.

Boards 1 - 4 are removed. Start by using a circular saw, with the depth set for the blade. The idea here is to cut out the center of the board, so it's easier to take out the rest of it. There isn't a set way to do this. Use a circular saw, jig saw, oscillating saw, hammer, pry bar, chisel, pliers, vise grip, etc. -- whatever it takes to get the job done. Just be careful not to hurt the other boards.

Boards 5 and 6 are too long to be removed, so they'll have to be trimmed if the ends aren't square. Use a circular saw with a speed square, if there's room for it. Otherwise, use a jig saw with a speed square, or an oscillating saw. To make a square cut with an oscillating saw, position a board where you want to cut, and then run the saw blade along the edge of it.

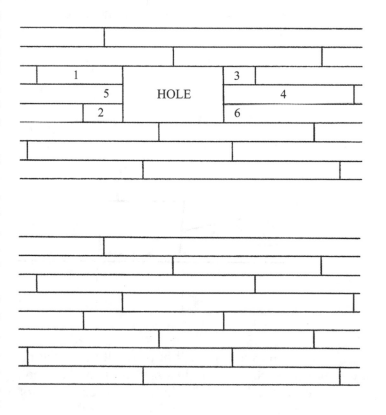

Once the boards have been removed, the new ones can be installed. This isn't as simple as when working on a new floor. Commonly you'll have to remove the lower part of the groove to get a board to slip into place. You may also have to taper it with a block plane. If the board is a trace long, you can generally get it to fit by slipping one end into place, and then pounding on the other end with a hammer. When doing this, lay another board against it to protect the end. Then, when nailing the boards, use the floor nailer wherever you can, and hide the nails when it's possible. Some of the boards will have to be face-nailed.

This floor had to be patched to fill in where a wall had been. While doing this, two boards on each end were also removed to help break up the pattern.

## PLUGS

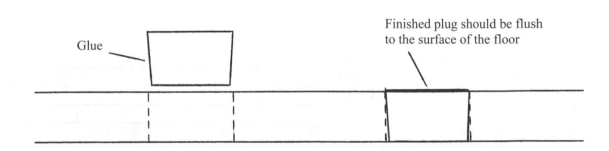

Glue

Finished plug should be flush to the surface of the floor

Sometimes a floor will have small holes that need to be plugged, which generally occurs when pipes are removed, such as for radiators. Normally these holes are small enough that it's not worth the trouble to remove the entire board. The holes could be either round or square, depending on whether the pipes were installed before or after the installation of the floor. Either way, I generally fill the holes using square plugs.

To change a round hole into one that's square, use a sharp chisel or an oscillating saw to cut the sides of it. Then once the hole has been cut to the right shape, make a tapered plug for it by either using a table saw or a compound miter saw. Since the plug is tapered, it doesn't have to be the exact size. It only has to be small enough to get started in the hole, and large enough so it fits tight.

To install the plug, apply glue to each side, and then tap it in with a hammer. Make sure that you don't go too deep. Then wipe off the excess glue, and let it sit for a day.

The plug will generally end up sitting above the surface of the floor. If it's up quite a bit, shave it down with a block plane. When doing this, adjust the plane for a fine cut, and try not to cut into the floor. Then once you're close, use a scraper to clean it up before it's sanded and finished.

## Here Are Some Other Things To Know About Installing A Tongue And Groove Floor.

The subfloor determines the direction that the flooring can run. When it's installed over 3/4 inch tongue and groove plywood, you can run it any direction that you want. If the plywood was any thinner, it would have to run perpendicular to the floor joists. If the subfloor consists of 3/4 inch boards that are laid diagonally, the flooring can be run either parallel or perpendicular to the floor joists. When the 3/4 inch boards are laid perpendicular to the floor joists, you may be forced to run the flooring perpendicular to the 3/4 inch boards. Older homes tend to have big gaps between these boards, and the boards may also vary in thickness. Either one could be problem if you ran the flooring in the same direction as the subfloor.

Before you get started, look over the subfloor, and renail any areas where the nails are missing or the heads are sticking up. Loose nails that are pounded down tend to come back up again. Ring-shanked nails hold the best.

Most warped boards can be used. If you're using a Porta-Nailer, take an easy swing to get the nail started. Then finish with a hard swing, and put your body into it. On bad warps, you'll have to use more nails. Sometimes you'll still be left with a small gap, but that should shrink as you install more rows.

Sometimes a board won't slip into place. First, make sure that there isn't a chip of wood between the two boards, and also check for a tongue or a groove that's either split or crushed, as it could be getting in the way. Then lay a scrap piece of flooring against the board that's tight, to protect it, and hit it hard with a hammer to drive the board into place.

If the left side of a board is bad, cut off that end, and then use the board on the left side of the room. If the right end is bad, it gets used on the right side. If it has a bad spot in the middle, cut out the bad spot, and use the two pieces on both ends of the room.

To remove a floorboard, pry it up gently with the claw of a hammer. Move the hammer from nail to nail and gradually raise the board, so you don't break the tongue.

Though the metal end of the hammer is normally used to drive the boards together lengthwise, the rubber end can also be used by hitting the upper surface at an angle.

If you dent the edge of a board, putting water on it (with a wet cloth or paper towel) will help make it swell back to its original shape. Putting spit on it will also do the job if water isn't available. Do this when it happens. If you plan on coming back to it later, it probably won't get done.

Years ago, I'd run a narrow gap around the perimeter of the floor when thin baseboard was being used, without baseshoe. On one job, as we finished installing a white oak floor, I cut the last row so tight that it had to be pounded into place. Then a problem came up when one of the boards wouldn't slip over the tongue. We also couldn't get it back out, and eventually had to leave it where it was. Since then, I try to leave enough room, and generally cut the boards so that I end up with a 1/4 - 3/8 inch gap, so they can be removed in case something goes wrong. Looking back, I could have removed that board by driving a screw into it and then pulling on the screw with a pry bar.

I've read that you should allow a 1/16 inch gap for every foot of flooring. That sounds good, but if a large floor actually moved that much at the perimeter, the nails would be sheared off. When a floor expands, every seam is compressed. Myself, I've never seen a major change along the outside edge. Sometimes you don't have a choice, and have to install the flooring right next to something. I've also seen a lot of floors that were installed tight against tile without a problem. Wood shrinks and expands all the time. When you install it so it's tight on one side, give it room to move on the other. About the only place where this isn't possible is when you're going around door jambs. Floating floors that snap together are different, since they aren't attached to the floor.

Commonly, the last row will have to be tapered. These cuts can be made with either a circular saw or a jig saw. I'll also freehand them on a table saw if one is available. If it's a mild taper, the boards can be staggered along the edge. For instance, the first board could be cut at 1 3/4 inches, the second at 1 5/8, the third at 1 1/2, etc.

On a box of 2 inch flooring nails, it says that 1000 nails are good for installing about 200 square feet of 2 1/4 inch flooring. In my experience, it's more like 150.

When installing a floor over 3/4 inch sheathing that has tubing stapled beneath it for in-floor heat, you'll have to use shorter nails so you don't go through the sheathing. 1 1/2 inch nails are available for floor nailers, though they may have to be special ordered. When using the shorter nails, I space them a little closer.

Pneumatic nailers can also be used to install flooring. I haven't used one yet, but I've been told that staples hold better that nails.

Without a moisture meter, it's always a guess as to when the flooring can be installed. In the past, when we used to get it from a warehouse that was humidity-controlled, we'd install it after it sat in the house for only a couple of days, and never had a problem, but then Minnesota doesn't have that dry of a climate. Once you get it home, store the flooring in the same area where it will be installed, so it can acclimate. It doesn't have to be in the same room, but storing the wood in the basement, and then installing it upstairs, wouldn't work at all. I like to keep it in the house for at least a week, even when I think it's dry. In a dry climate, it may need a lot more time. The boards will acclimate faster if you open up the bundles and spread them out, but they'll take up a lot of space. Sometimes it seems that the longer the bundles are open, the more you have to deal with warped boards.

When going over a heated floor, you have to be more careful concerning shrinkage. I installed maple on one a couple of years ago, which wasn't recommended, and didn't have a problem with shrinkage after letting the wood sit for three weeks. On the oak floor that was installed in the previous photos, just a few of the boards from one of the 23 bundles showed a little shrinkage. This was after sitting for 13 days.

Even though a floor is tight to begin with, it doesn't mean it will stay that way. For instance, the oak floor that was just mentioned was tight for the first couple of years, but now, there are some small gaps. The floor shown on page 346 is the opposite. That one is still tight, years later. The reason is that the house is air-conditioned, so the humidity level is more consistent. The other floor is at a lake cabin where the windows are open most of the summer, so the wood swells up from moisture in the air, compressing everything together. Then in the winter, the wood shrinks from the lower humidity, and also because of the in-floor heat, which is the reason for the gaps.

Prefinished flooring is being installed in many homes at this time. While it's nice to have the finish already applied, I prefer unfinished flooring. This way, any high spots will be sanded off, and there won't be a small groove around every board that holds dirt.

This landing was done after the floor above it was finished, and all that was left were some short boards. Here I started in the middle and then circled my way around to the outside edge.

## INSIDE BORDERS

These photos were taken by a friend, back in 1992, as I was packing up to leave a job. Here the floor is red oak, and the boards that were used for the inside border are Brazilian cherry. The idea here was to mimic the edge of the corner cabinets that would go in later. Installing an inside border like this can be a lot of work. I spent a week on this floor. I never saw it after this day, so I don't know how it turned out once it was sanded and the finish was applied.

There are a couple of ways to install a floor with an inside border. One is to do the center section first, and then cut it to size. Then the border is installed, followed by the boards that go around the perimeter. Another method is to install the border as you go, and then cut the other boards to fit tight against it. The second method is the one that I used here. This way, I made sure that the rows stayed in line with each other on both sides of the border.

351

# DECKS

Besides finishing off the basement, building a deck is one of the most common projects that a homeowner will take on. There's already a lot of information available on this subject; but, as it turned out, I worked on several decks at the time this book was being written, so I'll go through the process of building one.

## MATERIALS

When designing a deck, one of the many things that you have to consider is what material to use for the upper surface, and also for the framing, the stairs, the balusters, and the handrails. These days, you have many choices. For the upper surface, I've used treated wood, cedar, redwood, tigerwood, and composites. Myself, I prefer to use real wood, cedar probably being my favorite. It has more upkeep, but I like working with it, and to me it just feels better.

Wood is also stronger and stiffer than any composite that I've worked with. Carry a 20 foot composite board on your shoulder, and the ends will just about drag on the ground. When using it, you can't space the joists over 16 inches on center, and you have to make sure they line up, since composite boards aren't stiff enough to pull the joists into place. On the plus side, the material is more consistent, and some of the more expensive brands have a quality look to them. But for about the same money as expensive composite, you could probably use teak or tigerwood.

No matter what's used for the surface of the deck, the framing will be some type of rot-resistant wood. Treated wood is used most often. Cedar and redwood are other choices, though I've only used redwood on one deck for the framing. That was years ago in Rapid City, South Dakota, as it was strongly recommended to me when I was at the lumberyard. I was told that treated wood would warp in the hot, dry climate. There, at that time, it only cost a little more. Where I live, you seldom even see redwood anymore, and cedar is pretty expensive, so I generally only use it where it's going to show. By looking at a framing table, you can see that cedar and redwood aren't as strong as treated wood, which is generally made from southern pine in my area. This has to be taken into consideration when designing the deck.

# THE PLAN

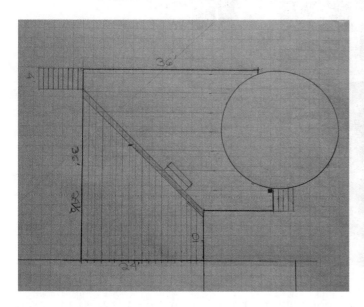 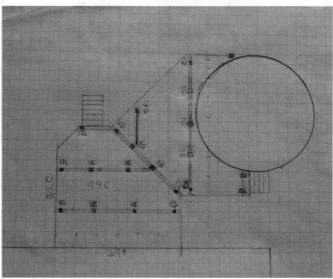

Most decks start with a plan. These are the drawings for the deck that's shown in the photos. The drawing on the left was the original idea. But after realizing how big the deck would actually be, we changed the shape and went with the plan on the right, and then moved the stairs when it was built.

When doing this, draw the deck to scale and/or use graph paper to help determine the length of the boards, and the size of the footings that will be needed. To keep it simple, on this deck we spaced the footings so 2x8s could be used for both the beams and the joists, and so none of the footings would be over 16 inches in diameter. On the corners, we still used 12 inch form tubes for the concrete, even when they could have been smaller, since we were using 6 inch posts.

If the footings will be installed before you start framing the deck, you have to know the exact position of all the main footings. You'll need a more detailed version of the plan that includes a side view, and also shows the size of the footings, the beams, and the joists, if a permit has to be pulled for the job.

# LAYING IT OUT

Once the plan is finished, you generally begin by pounding in the stakes, and then lay out the string lines to find the positions of the footings. The stakes are installed in pairs, with a crossbar between them. Then the strings are attached to the crossbars. You have to do an accurate job when doing the layout, otherwise the posts won't be centered on the footings. I've seen way too many decks, especially those built by contractors, where the posts have sat on the very edge of the footings. This may still work, but it doesn't look very nice.

This photo shows the layout of the stakes and the string lines. The string on the right, that runs perpendicular to the house, is the master line, and it stayed in place until the framing was finished. The other strings are centered over the footings, and were positioned by either measuring off the house or the master line. These will be removed and then put back up, when needed, as the footings are installed.

A mark is made on each crossbar to show the position of the string. These marks should be rechecked every now and then, in case the stakes move. Then once the strings are in place, a magic marker is used to mark the string to show the location of each footing.

As the strings are removed and then put back up, the marks for the footings have to be in the same place, every time. In this case, where the strings are parallel to the house, the position of the footings was measured off the master line, so the strings were tied off on that side. Then every time the strings were retied, the marks had to be rechecked. While doing this, if you stretch the string so the mark that's closest to where it's tied off is positioned correctly, you'll find that the other marks will generally also be in the right place.

The orange spots, beneath the strings, are surveyor tape that's pinned with nails to mark the position of each footing. Make sure the stakes are far enough to the side, so they won't be in the way when digging the holes.

On most decks there will only be a few footings, and only one or two string lines will be needed. This makes the layout much simpler, so a master line, like the one used here, generally isn't necessary.

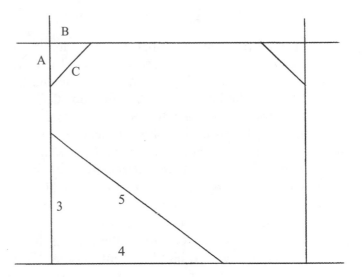

When laying out the string lines, the 3-4-5 method is used to set the strings at a right angle (90 degrees) to the house, or to each other. These measurements only have to be proportionate to 3-4-5. They could also be doubled (6-8-10), or they could be multiplied by 1 1/2 (4 1/2 - 6 - 7 1/2), etc.

To find 45 degrees, measure an equal distance from both sides of a square corner. For instance, if A = B, then C is a 45 degree corner.

On some decks, it's not practical to run string lines. For instance, you might be on a hill where it'd be difficult to lay them out accurately. Here it might be best to install the ledger board and the perimeter of the frame, and then temporarily hold everything up with 2x4s or 2x6s for the posts. After the frame is squared up, drop lines can be used to find the position of the footings.

In this photo, from a different job, the strings were attached to ladders when laying it out.

## FOOTINGS

The size of a footing is determined by the load it supports, and the type of soil at that location. The rules for building a deck in your area should include a table that shows the size of the footings required, and also how deep they have to be in areas where the ground freezes. One of these tables is shown on page 449. It's also used to determine the size of the beam(s).

By studying the table, you can see by using more footings to support the deck, the base of each one can be smaller. This may also reduce the size of the beam required, since the span between the posts will be less. Here you have to consider the cost of the materials, how much time it takes to dig the holes for the footings, and what's going to look better. Then try to come up with the best option while working on your plan.

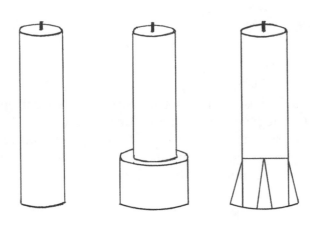

Under the main supports, the footings are generally all the same size at **ground level**. The diameter of the **base** of each footing is what's determined by the table. To make the base larger than the tube that extends above the ground, I cut a 1-foot section from a different form tube, and splice in extra, if needed, to get the diameter I want. Then the other tube lays on top of it.

Years ago, I used to bell out the bottom of the form tubes by splicing in pie-shaped pieces that were cut from the same material. It worked, but it was slow. I prefer the method that I use now. For 6x6 posts, I use 12 inch tubes for the upper part of the footing that extends above the ground. For 4x4 posts, I use 8 inch tubes. Around here, local building centers carry form tubes in sizes up to 16 inches in diameter. When you need a larger size, such as 24 inch, they may have to be ordered, or look on the internet to find a distributor.

Another option is to use Bigfoot footings. These are large plastic bases that attach to the end of the form tubes. Different sizes are available for the different sized tubes. I've only used them on one deck, and my only problem with them, besides the cost, was that larger holes were needed, and also more concrete.

On most of the decks that I've worked on, there were only a few footings, and they were dug by hand with a post hole digger. This deck has 25, so a neighbor came over with his Bobcat and drilled the holes with a bit that we got from a local rental center. Then after the holes were drilled, the string lines were put back into place.

You can see in this photo, that when doing this, the holes don't always end up where you want them to be. All it takes is a rock near the surface to move the drill bit over. Even when the holes are positioned correctly, they still need to be cleaned up. The sides may have to be shaved, and dirt is removed until the hole is the proper depth. When finished, the bottom of the hole should be undisturbed earth, if possible, so the footing won't settle. Any loose dirt should be tamped and compacted.

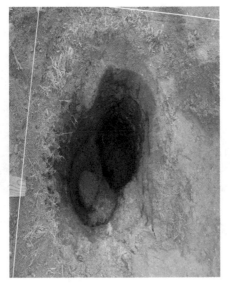

As the holes are dug and/or cleaned up, the depth is measured, and they're checked with a drop line that's tied at the mark to see if there's enough room for the form tube to center on the string. When doing this, I tie an anchor bolt nut to the lower end of the string, and then hold the string at the right height and tie it on with a half-hitch.

Once it's close, the tube is dropped into place and checked with both a measuring tape and 4 foot level. After the hole is finished, I use a post to pound and compact the ground at the bottom of the hole, and try to get the base reasonably level as I do this. Then the tube is held in position by packing dirt around the side of it, before the concrete is mixed.

On this deck, the homeowner bought a used cement mixer for doing the footings. Normally I'd just mix up the bags of concrete in a wheelbarrow, using a hoe. But here we needed a lot of concrete, and it wouldn't have worked out to have it delivered by a cement truck.

When mixing the concrete for the larger holes, I'll fill the lower section, which already has dirt packed around it, and then drop the upper tube into place. A drop line is used to position the tube, and then it's held in place as dirt is also packed around it. It's good to have help when doing this, since it's much easier when one person holds the tube, as someone else shovels the dirt.

The upper tube is filled before the mix starts to set up in the lower section. I also stab the concrete with a stake as I go along, to make sure there aren't any voids in the mix. On footings where the upper tube will be added after the base has already hardened, I'll leave several pieces of rebar hanging out of the lower section to make the connection. Scrape the outside edge of the lower section, so there isn't any concrete hanging out that the frost could grab onto and raise the footing.

Once the form tubes are filled, smooth down the surface of the concrete, and then install the anchor bolts. It may help to let the concrete set up a bit, before putting them in, to keep them from sinking deeper after they're installed. Position the anchor bolts by using drop lines, the same as when positioning the tubes. Then on ones that try to move, hold the bolts in place by pinching them between short pieces of 2x4s.

# LEDGER BOARD

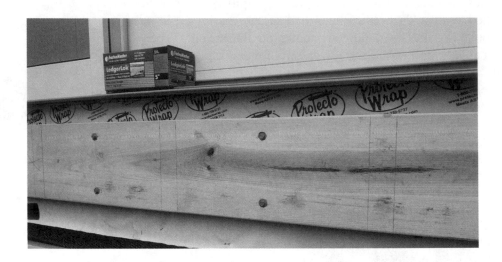

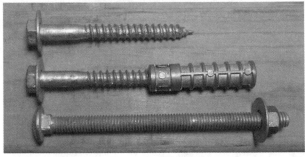

If the deck is getting attached to the house, the joists will be nailed to a ledger board. This board is generally the same width as the joists, and it's attached to the wall with galvanized lag screws or carriage bolts. When using lag screws, they should be long enough to fully penetrate the rim joist, to get a good bite. If the ledger board is attached to concrete, lead anchors are used.

Two 3/8 inch lag screws or bolts every 16 inches was the old rule for attaching the ledger board. In my area, 1/2 inch is now required. There may also be specific spacing requirements that are based on the joist span. Recent products, such as LedgerLok fasteners, are made from a higher quality steel. They're less than 3/8 of an inch in diameter, but are advertised as having more strength than a standard 1/2 inch lag screw. By using them, it also eliminates the need for a separate washer. You don't to have to predrill when using these fasteners, though I still do when I'm at the end of a board, to prevent splitting. All screws, nails, and joist hangers that are used on decks have to be rated for the new types of treated wood, since it can be more corrosive.

In the upper photo, the lag screws are directly above each other. Under the current rules, they have to be staggered with specific requirements for positioning them: * Upper row, 2 inches (center) minimum from the top edge of the board. * Lower row, 3/4 inch minimum from the bottom edge, and a minimum of 5 1/2 inches (2x8), 6 1/2 inches (2x10), and 7 1/2 inches (2x12) from the top. * 2 inches minimum from the ends. * 5 inches maximum between the two rows. * Upper and lower row must be staggered at least 1 5/8 inches.

When the deck is against an inside corner of the house, the joists are generally just attached to a ledger board on one side of the corner. This side carries the load, and is the one that the code requirement concerns. The board on the other wall is only supporting the edge of the deck, so it doesn't have to be as securely attached. Here a double row of nails would probably be sufficient, though I still like to use lag screws, as nails have a tendency to work loose over the years. On this side, I spread them out a little farther, and generally install them around 24 inches on center.

The height of the ledger board is determined by the thickness of the decking, and where you want to end up relative to the interior floor. Here the two surfaces could be around the same height, or you could have one or more steps that go from the deck to inside the house. I generally build a deck so the finished height is about 1 1/2 inches below that of the interior floor. This is low enough to help keep rain and melting snow from coming inside, but not so much that it causes someone to trip.

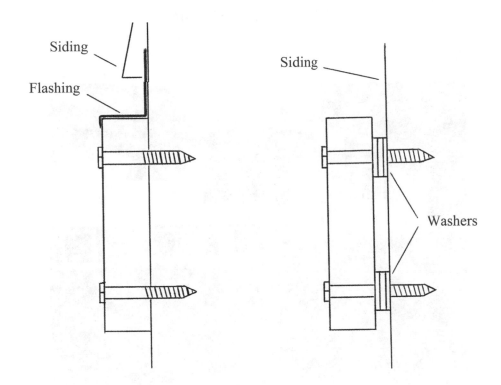

The ledger board is generally installed over the sheathing. Then flashing goes over the top of it to keep rain or snow from getting behind it, which could lead to water damage. Then the siding overlaps the flashing. If the house has already been sided, the rows in the immediate area will have to be removed for the time being. The first row of decking is screwed to the joists, not the ledger board, so there aren't any holes in the flashing. For the same reason, the flashing is attached by just nailing it to the wall. If the flashing sticks out past the ledger board, the upper corner of each joist will have to be notched to clear it.

Another option is to space the ledger board off the finished wall. This is easily done by sliding extra-large galvanized steel washers over the lag screws, between the ledger board and the wall.

Joist hangers are used to attach the joists to the ledger board. When installing them, I use an end that was cut from one of the joists to help set the height. This board should be about the same width as the majority of the other joists. Once I know the correct height, I measure down from the top of the ledger board, and use a pencil to mark the position for the upper edge of each joist hanger. I also use the board to make sure the openings are the right size, so the joists can slip into place.

On most decks, I nail the joist hangers on while I'm waiting for the concrete to cure. I also mark the position of the joists on the ledger board, before it's installed. This keeps me from putting a lag screw in the wrong spot.

## POSTS AND BEAMS

I generally start on the posts and the beams once the footings have had a few days to cure. Where it's allowed, I prefer to rest the posts directly on top of the footings. When doing this, I begin by cutting the lower end on each post. Then I drill a hole in the base, and make the hole a little bigger than the diameter of the anchor bolt. This will allow for any bolts that sit at an angle. For 1/2 inch anchor bolts, I'll use a 5/8 inch drill bit. The hole is centered on the post, unless the anchor bolt is out of position. In that case, the hole would be offset to bring the post back into line.

Once the hole is drilled, the post is set in place on top of the footing, and then checked with a level to see if it's plumb. If it isn't, rotate it to face in different directions to see if that helps. If it's still off, the bottom will have to be planed to remove the wood that's causing the problem. A planer works good for this, but set it for a shallow cut. Once the post sits plumb, it's numbered, and the direction that it should face is marked on it.

Then the end of the post is dipped in wood preservative, such as Cuprinol, to help prevent rot, while I start on the next post. You only have to dip the very bottom of the post, since it will be pulled up into the wood. I generally use an old joint compound bucket or ice cream container for this, and let each post sit in the preservative for about 5 minutes. This particular brand may not be available, as they quit selling it around here a few years ago. I've looked for it on the internet, without success, but found a couple of other brands that may serve the same purpose. It seems that wood preservatives are now water-based, but still have copper in them. I don't know if they work as well.

After all the posts have been plumbed up and dipped, they're cut to length. To do this, I'll start by setting one of the corner posts on its footing. Then I'll slip a joist into the hanger that's the closest to lining up with it, and clamp the other end of the joist to the post with a bar clamp, so it's held level. Then I'll mark the height for cutting the post, take the joist down, and do the same at the other corners.

If the beam is going to rest on top of the posts, measure down the height of the beam from the lower edge of the joist, and then draw a line at that point for cutting the post. If the beam is getting attached to the side of the posts, draw the line right at the lower edge of the joist. Allow for shrinkage when doing this. Even though a doubled-up 2x8 beam might be 7 1/2 inches high when it's first nailed together, it will probably shrink down to around 7 1/4 inches. For the same reason, when I'm attaching the beam to the side of the posts, I'll mount it a little high so the posts don't end up sticking up above it. Sometimes I'll also cut posts that are taller a little long to allow for shrinkage.

Once the corner posts have been marked, draw the lines all the way around the posts. Then cut them off at that point. When cutting with a circular saw, I'll use a speed square as a guide. You'll have to cut from both sides to get through a 4x4. With 6 inch posts, you'll have to cut from every side, and then finish up with a hand saw. It's important that you get a square cut, so the beam won't sit at an angle as it rests across the top of the post. Use a sharp block plane to clean up the cut, if necessary. After the posts are cut, they're positioned on the footings. Then, where needed, they're held in place by attaching diagonal braces, with the lower end of each one screwed to a stake driven into the ground.

Now the height of the other posts can be marked by stretching a string between the corner posts. Then the posts are cut to length, and positioned on the footings so they face in the right direction.

You could also use a laser level for marking the posts. On this deck, I measured down the height of the beams from the lower edge of the ledger board. Then the laser level was adjusted so the beam was at that height, so all I had to do was to pivot it to mark where each post had to be cut.

Years ago, I read that a deck should have a slight slope to it, for the water to run off. So, for a while, that's how I did it. Then I realized it takes a lot of slope for that to happen, -- much more than I'd be willing to give. Now I cut the posts so the deck will be level.

The beams can be installed once the posts have been cut to length. They generally consist of two or three boards that are nailed together, which are matched up along the lower edge, and then nailed with at least two nails every 16 inches. Screws or bolts could also be used. Any joints in the beam should be over a post. After the beam is finished, make sure the lower edge is square wherever it's going to rest on a post. Otherwise, the beam could tip to one side.

361

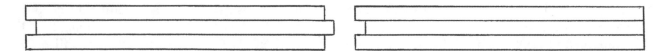

When a beam consists of three boards, and is installed in sections, the center board can be offset to form a tongue and groove to keep everything in line. This also makes it easier to nail the sections together, by going into the tongue from each side. When using this method, use 6 inch posts so there's enough overlap under the joints.

On this deck, we used 16 foot boards for the longer beams. Then, by overlapping the seams and cutting some of the boards in half, we were able to build the beams in one piecc, while still keeping every joint over a post.

I center the beams on the posts, and then attach them by driving screws though the posts at an angle. This way, it's easy to replace a post if it ever becomes necessary. On decks where the beams are getting bolted to both sides of the posts, the boards are clamped into place. Then holes are drilled to install the bolts. When doing this, first I drill a pilot hole by coming from both sides with a smaller bit.

Once the beams are in place, go over the upper surface with a level, and plane off any high spots. As you do this, check the height of each beam, as this may determine the amount of wood that can be removed. For instance, if the center board on one of the beams is wider than the others, but it isn't any taller than the other beams, then the center board would have to stay as it is.

On this deck, two of the beams for the upper level are supported on one end by the lower level. In the photo, you can see how the end of the beam is supported by 2x4 blocks in the short wall. The beam was also notched to clear the upper plate.

A circular saw can help when notching a board. Besides marking the depth, the saw cuts make the job a lot easier, since you only have to slice off the narrow strips between the cuts. This is especially helpful if there's a knot or the wood grain isn't straight.

## JOISTS

After the beams are finished, the joists can be installed. The size of the joists is determined by their length, and how far they're spaced apart. Generally the spacing will be either 16 or 24 inches on center. If you plan on installing the upper surface (decking) diagonally, the joists will have to be spaced within 16 inches, since the screws will be almost 2 feet apart at that measurement. When using 1 1/2 inch thick 2x6s for the decking, that run perpendicular to the joists, it can be increased to 24 inches on center.

Cantilevering the joists, which means the joists overhang the beam, may allow you to use smaller joists for the same size deck. The distance that you can cantilever will vary. Where I live, until recently, only a 2 foot overhang was allowed without special design approval, regardless of the joist size. When doing this, the beams will also overhang the posts, but generally by less than one foot.

From what I've read, there are two rules of thumb to follow when cantilevering the joists. The first is that the length of the joists, between the house and the beam, have to be at least twice as long as the overhang. With 12 foot joists, that would mean a maximum overhang of about 4 feet. The other rule is that the overhang can't be more than 4 times greater than the depth of the joist. So, instead of 4 feet, you can only overhang the beam by 37 inches when using 2x10s, since they're actually only about 9 1/4 inches wide. This rule only works for decks that don't have a heavy load along their outer edge. If you plan on building a porch, an overhang may not be allowed. In my experience, building inspectors tend to be on the conservative side concerning cantilevers, though recent changes to the rule in my area now allow more overhang.

Most of the time, joists are installed with the crown side up. Books will tell you to put the crown side down when cantilevering a joist, but that would depend on the size of the cantilever. Myself, I treat a 2 foot overhang the same as if there wasn't any, but I also won't use boards that are badly crowned, as they cause too many problems.

When installing the joists, the ends are trimmed to remove any splits, and also to make sure the ends are square. Then they're slipped into the joist hangers, and positioned on the marks that were drawn across the beam. On joists that are cantilevered, it's generally best to cut them to length once they're all in place.

Double-shear joist hangers are designed so the nails go into the joists at an angle, which allows you to use longer nails that also toenail the joists to the ledger board. The problem is that the angled holes tend to push the joists away from the ledger board, which leaves a gap. To keep this from happening, you may have to toenail the joists to the ledger board, from the top, before you put the other nails in. When using standard length nails, I generally don't have a problem if I drive the nails as square as I can into the side of each joist.

On most decks, I like to run the end joists tight to the house by attaching them to the end of the ledger board. If they're being doubled up, I'll screw the inside board to the face of the ledger board by going in at an angle. Then I'll overlap the ledger board with the outside board, and drive the screws into the end of it. I generally also install a corner bracket or a cut off joist hanger on the inside corners, whether the boards are doubled up or not.

When using larger sized joists, you'll commonly end up with some that are noticeably wider than the others. Since your goal is to have the upper edge of the joists line up, here you have to decide whether to notch the end of the joist to lower it in the hanger, or to nail it on as is. Let's say the width of most of the joists is a little over 9 1/4 inches, but one of them is 9 1/2 inches wide. When working with treated wood, I base my decision on how much moisture is in the board. If the board felt really wet, and was a lot heavier than the others, I might nail it on as is, figuring that it was going to shrink quite a bit. If it wasn't quite as wet, I'd probably split the difference by shaving a little wood from the lower edge, so it still sat a bit high. Then by only nailing into the joist through the lowest holes in the joist hanger, it will allow the joist to shrink down into the pocket. Later on, the rest of the nails can be put in. You also have to consider the height of the joists where they pass over a beam. Here I'll notch the joist at that point if one is extra wide, but most of the time, I'll just plane down the high spots after the framing is finished.

String lines are commonly needed along the edge when framing a deck. This is especially true when the joists run at an angle to the perimeter. Here it's easy to lose the line, so you end up with a hump or a dip in the edge, and without the string, you won't notice it until it's too late.

Stretch the string a lot tighter than you would think is necessary. Then wrap it around the nail at least a half a dozen times, and tie it off with a half hitch and a loop, like a shoe lace. This way, you can remove the string by just pulling on the end and then unwrapping it. Space the string off the board by slipping a nail under each end. Here the nail was stapled into place because it kept falling out.

To cut the joists to length, mark both ends of the deck, and then snap a chalk line across the joists while holding the string against the marks. After snapping the line, check to make sure that it looks straight. Then use a large speed square to draw the lines, and cut the ends off.

Now the joists can be capped. Cut the board to length, and mark the position of all the joists. Then with someone helping, hold the board in place, and attach it to the joists as you pull them into position.

Once the joists are capped, check to see how square the deck is by measuring diagonally from opposite corners. Hopefully the measurements will be close. But, if the measurements are different, there are a few things that you can do to bring the deck back to square. First, check the posts to see if they're plumb, as they could actually be leaning one way or the other. If they're tipped, you can pull them back to plumb by resetting the diagonal braces. You'll want help when doing this on a large deck, since you'll be dealing with a lot of weight.

You can also slide the deck over on the beam, though I'd still want the end joists to overlap the beam by 1 1/2 inches. This could mean that an end joist might have to be doubled up. Another option is to pull the screws, and slide the beam across the posts. This is easier than it sounds. On a large deck, you don't actually slide the beam over. You move each post by tapping it with a sledge hammer. Then you push on the deck to reset the diagonal braces. Now the posts won't be centered on the beam, but it generally isn't that noticeable if the beam overhangs the posts at each end. On decks that aren't cantilevered, you may also be able to shift the posts over by redrilling the holes in the bottom, if the footings are big enough.

Also consider that on most decks, it doesn't really matter if they're actually square or not. Myself, I always try to build things neat and accurate, but the most important thing here is that the deck is built strong enough. It would be hard to see if it's only a little out of square. The thing that I really notice is when the posts aren't centered on the footings.

After the deck has been squared up, it's locked into position by either attaching diagonal braces across the joists, or with ones that go between the posts and the beam. When that's finished, I toenail the joists to the beam. While doing this, you may find that some of the boards are sitting up a little bit. That's to be expected. The wider the joists, and the more crowns you have, the more this will be a problem. Joists around the right width can be pulled into place with clamps. Shims can fill the gap on boards that are too narrow.

Before you start on the upper surface, go over the framing one more time to see if anything's been missed. Then lay a straightedge across the joists, and check for high spots. The straightedge should be at least 4 feet long. When you come across a joist that sits up above the others, check to see if it's crowned. If it is, try to determine whether or not it will be pulled into place as the decking is screwed on. The board could also be wider because it has a higher moisture content than the others. In that case, it will probably shrink down as it dries. If you think the hump will remain, it should be planed off. This is easy to do with a planer. Adjust it so that it doesn't take off too much with each pass, and keep checking with the straightedge as you go. Other places to check are at the ends of the joists, or any place where the boards come together or overlap each other. Don't expect the joists to line up perfectly. Decks move, and the wood is still drying. Just try to get it close. By just checking, you've already done more than most people.

Once that's finished, everything has to be pulled into place, so the boards are straight and centered properly. Nail 1x2s or 1x3s across the deck, and pull the joists into position as you go. In this photo, the 1x3 sits directly over the beam. Since the joists were already nailed to the beam, by placing the board here, it helped to straighten any joists that were twisted. These joists were extended by butting the ends together, instead of overlapping them, so short boards were attached over the splices.

# THE UPPER SURFACE

When the perimeter of the deck (joists) is getting covered to finish it off, the boards can be screwed on from the back. This will give it a cleaner look, since the only place where the screws will generally show is at the corners. Composite boards, though, have to be screwed through the face.

Before you start on the upper surface, string lines should be run along any edge that runs parallel to the joists. Then edges that aren't straight should be pulled into position and held in place with boards that are either nailed or screwed on. These boards are removed as the surface is installed. Even edges that are already straight should be pinned to keep them from moving. Once that's done, you can start on the decking.

To begin, I always lay out a few of the rows, and gap the boards the same as they'll be when installed. Then I measure the total width that I have to cover, and make sure to include any overhang. Now based on the distance that's covered by the rows that are laid out, I can determine where the last row will end. At that point, if I feel that too much will have to be trimmed from the last row, I'll also cut the first row to split the difference.

If the boards are going to be laid perpendicular to the joists, sometimes I'll start one row out from the house. Then I'll use straight boards for the first couple of rows, and screw them into place with two screws going into each joist. On this deck, the upper surface was nailed on with galvanized ring-shank nails, instead. The boards are cedar 2x4s, and it didn't look right having screws that close together.

Once you have a straight line established, the boards are pulled into place as they get screwed on. Then you measure off one of the other rows to check your work. Small bends can be pulled out by hand, or by using a pry bar. On the bad ones, you might have to use pipe clamps. That's the reason for leaving out the row closest to the house. There are also pry bars made specifically for this, though I've never had the chance to use one.

I generally space the boards by lightly tacking 8D nails against the side of the row that was just done, and then hold the next row tight against them as it's screwed into place. Then the nails are pulled and moved over a row, and the process is repeated.

Deck boards commonly have a lot of moisture in them, so the gaps between the rows will get larger as they dry. If a screen porch is going over the deck, you might be concerned about insects coming up between the boards.

When I helped one of my sisters build a deck, that included a screen porch, there were a couple of options that were considered to keep the bugs out. One was to install screen under the deck boards. I've never liked this idea, since dirt and other crud is always going to be falling between the boards and collecting against it. The method we chose was to dry the wood first, so it would shrink before it was installed. If the boards were just loosely laid out across the deck, there would have been problems with them warping. To prevent this, we laid everything out with the rows tight against each other. Then the last row was screwed down to hold the boards in place. If I remember correctly, we let them sit for around a week. Then we installed the boards with a narrow gap between each row. This deck has held up better than most of the ones I've worked on. The gaps between the rows have stayed about the same size, and the butt joints are still tight after all these years.

When installing the rows, let the boards hang over the edge, and then trim them to length once you're finished. To do this, make a mark for the cut every few feet, while allowing for any overhang. Then use a pencil and a straightedge to draw a line between the marks. If the edge of the deck isn't straight, I'll adjust the marks to straighten up the line. You could also just snap a chalk line, but chalk lines are a little coarse for my taste, and they tend to disappear as you're making the cut.

For the straightest edge, cut it with a circular saw and a cutting jig. On this deck, the upper surface was cut flush to the joists, since a board was going to be installed around the perimeter. Generally, I leave at least an inch for the overhang, and then lightly round off the cuts with a sanding pad.

## STAIRS AND HANDRAILS

Once the upper surface is finished, it's time to build the stairs and install the handrails. For the handrails, see what's available at stores, and then go through books and magazines until you find a style that you like. Another way is to check out other decks in your area.

Shown here are three types of handrails. The upper photos show a style that was more common in the past. On this one, the lower end of the balusters is screwed to the edge of the deck, while the upper end is attached to the handrails. One thing different about this style is that it doesn't need any posts, so the balusters can go around the deck in one continuous run. The photo on the left shows a 2x4 in the corner, but this was done strictly for looks.

The center photos show a deck that belongs to one of my sisters. This type of handrail is a good design. The rails keep the balusters from turning, and the gap beneath it helps for cleaning the deck. The posts are also spaced close enough, at about 5 feet on center, so the handrails feel solid.

In the lower photo, metal handrails were used instead. This gives it a more open look and doesn't obstruct the view as much.

369

For this deck, we ended up going with the second style of handrails. The rules concerning the height of the handrails and the spacing of the balusters are the same, whether you're building a deck or working on stairs indoors. This deck was getting three sets of stairs. The main ones, that go from the deck down to the ground, were already described in the section on building stairs. On this page are the steps that go between the two levels. Here there was plenty of room, so we made the stairs with extra wide treads. This idea turned out a lot better than I expected. With the wide treads, and their sides cut at an angle, it makes the two sections of the deck flow together. Besides being comfortable to walk on, the stairs are also a nice place to sit.

On these stairs, the treads are 19 inches wide, and were framed with 2x8s that had been cut to the correct width on a table saw. After the cedar 2x4s were nailed to the lower step, the upper frame was stacked on top of it. Then it was finished off with the 2x4s running at a right angle to the ones on the step below, the same way it was done on the two levels of the deck.

The third set of stairs are next to the swimming pool. The problem here was building one end at an angle to follow the edge of the pool. To do this, the rest of the stringers were drawn out and cut in the usual manner. Then, once they were in position, I was able to make the last stringer by projecting the lines from the others. There's a little guesswork when doing it this way. You make a cut, and then see how it fits. Then you readjust the angle, and check it again, so you need a board that's extra long to begin with.

Here I started by cutting the upper end of the stringer to fit against the deck, so the lower edge was parallel to the other stringers. This line was drawn at a slightly different angle than that used for the other stringers, since this one would be a little longer because it was coming down at an angle. To make the cut, I also adjusted the blade on the circular saw to match the angle that the board was to the deck, while looking down at it.

Once that was done, I cut the bottom and notched it for the treated 2x6 that the stringer was going to rest on. I did this by holding the board against the deck, as I used a level to draw a horizontal line. Then it was just a matter of cutting off the right amount, parallel to the horizontal line, so the stringer sat at the correct height.

Now with the board in place, I laid the level across the other stringers to project and mark the lines for the tread and the riser cuts. Two marks were needed for every line that had to be drawn. When cutting out the stringer, the blade was set at an angle to make the cuts for the risers. Here the riser cuts had to be made by going backwards. To do this, I clamped a board to the stringer, for the saw to follow, to give me a little more control. Then once the stringer was finished, it was just a matter of cutting the treads and risers to fit.

# POSTS

After the stairs were done, we started on the layout for the posts and the handrails. Some things to consider were the height and the positions of the posts, the spacing between the posts, the spacing between the balusters, the height of the handrails and how much higher we wanted the posts to extend above them, and also, how the handrails should end against the house.

## POSITIONING THE  POSTS ON 45 DEGREE CORNERS

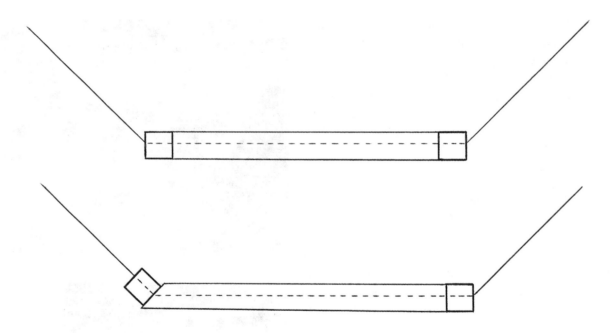

When building a deck that has 45 degree corners, at each corner you'll have to decide where it's best to position the post. Ideally, the posts can be installed so they're either both on the near side or the far side of the corner for each section of handrail, as shown in the upper drawing.

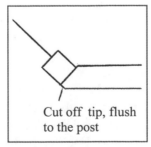

Cut off tip, flush to the post

The other drawing shows what happens when the posts aren't done in the same manner. As you can see, the ends are different. When the rail is cut at an angle, the length of the cut becomes longer, so on rails that lay flat, they'll overhang the post on both sides. One solution is to flush up the inside edge of the rail with the post, and then saw off the corner that overhangs. But now you'll have a different problem because the rail won't be parallel to the edge of the deck. What I generally do is to compromise, and let the rail overhang the post a little bit on the inside edge, so it's not so far out of parallel that it's noticeable. Then I cut the outside edge to match up with the post. By putting some thought into it when doing the layout, you can keep mismatched corners to a minimum.

Once the layout was finished, we started on the posts. The following photos show how it's done.

After cutting the posts to length, the notch was drawn on each post. Then the depth of the cut was adjusted to 1 1/2 inches on the circular saw, and the end of each notch was cut using the speed square.

I generally make the long cuts by just following the line, but here there were going to be 25 posts. To make it easier, I clamped a board to the base of the circular saw to be used as a guide, so every notch would be ripped to the same size. This works well on the first side; but, when the post is turned over, the second cut has to be made by either loosening the depth stop for the blade and then lowering the saw into the cut, or by resetting the board that's used as a guide. Holding the guard out of the way and then cutting backwards can be dangerous, as the blade may try to climb up out of the cut. After using the circular saw, the cut has to be finished with a hand saw.

The notch will generally have to be cleaned up with a chisel and/or a block plane, so it's flat. Sometimes the center will dip in, and that part will have to be left alone. This isn't a problem, as it won't be seen anyhow. Also make sure that the notch is cut to the same depth on both sides, so the post will be square to the deck. As you clean up the edge, check your progress with a straightedge.

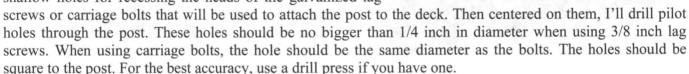

A table saw can also be used for cutting the notch. This should eliminate most of the cleanup. When doing this, set the blade as high up as it will go, so you cut more of the notch.

Once the notch is finished, I use a spade bit to drill shallow holes for recessing the heads of the galvanized lag screws or carriage bolts that will be used to attach the post to the deck. Then centered on them, I'll drill pilot holes through the post. These holes should be no bigger than 1/4 inch in diameter when using 3/8 inch lag screws. When using carriage bolts, the hole should be the same diameter as the bolts. The holes should be square to the post. For the best accuracy, use a drill press if you have one.

On this deck, the cedar 2x4s were cut flush to the outside edge. Normally that isn't the case, and the surface will overhang the framing. Then a jig saw would be used to cut off the overhang wherever a post is going. When the post is going **through** the decking, draw the outline for the post and then cut the hole out, again using the jig saw. If there isn't a place to get the blade started, you'll have to drill a starting hole.

After the holes have been drilled and the upper surface is notched or cut out, if needed, the post is put into position and held with a clamp. Then a level is used to make sure it's plumb, and the same drill bit is used to continue the holes, going all the way through the framing. When using bolts, the post can be attached at this point. When using lag screws, I generally take the post down and drill out the holes in the post to the diameter of the lag screws. Then I put the post back into position and install it. These holes could also be drilled with the post in place, but you have to be careful when doing this, so you don't drill too deep. If you go past the post and into the framing, the lag screw may not have enough holding power and could strip the threads.

Once the bolts or the lag screws have been tightened, check the post for plumb, on the side and also the face of it. If it leans to one side, just hit it so it's straight. Posts that are tipped in or out can be straightened by loosening the lag screws and then inserting felt paper or wood shims behind it. Cut off any shims that show, once the post is in the correct position.

Posts should line up on the edge of 45 degree corners.

This post was notched to center it on a 90 degree corner. When doing this, you'll need a sharp chisel or an oscillating saw to finish up the cuts.

An extra long notch, with a second cut, was needed for this post that goes next to the stairs.

# BALUSTERS AND HANDRAILS

On most decks, it's easier to build whole sections of handrails and balusters, and then install them in one piece. To do this, start by cutting the boards for the top and the bottom rail of each section. Then determine how you want to position the balusters along these boards by laying out the balusters and moving them around until you find the spacing that looks best, while staying within any local rules. Once that's been determined, draw lines across two boards that show the position of the balusters at this spacing. I call these spacer boards.

When using a spacer board, all you have to do is to lay the rail along the side of it and then center it between the marks, so the spacing is equal on both sides. Then the position of each baluster can either be marked on the rail, or the balusters themselves can be laid between the lines.

By using a pair of spacer boards, you can quickly lay out a section and screw it together.

After being assembled, each section was held at the correct height by laying it on blocks, and then it was screwed to the posts. The upper photo shows the sections as they were being installed, while the others show the deck after it was finished. On this deck, solar lights were installed at each corner of the stairs, and also to every other post around the deck.

There are rules concerning the size and shape of handrails over the stairs. According to the building code, you can't use a 2x4 or a 2x6 for a handrail unless the narrow side is up and a groove is cut into the side of it for your fingers to grab. This rule isn't always followed. I've built decks where the inspector followed the letter of the law, and others where I was told that they didn't care. Here the 2x4 handrails were laid flat. To satisfy the building code, an inside handrail would have to be added to the stairs.

In these photos, you can also see the trim boards that cap the outside edge of the deck. The original plan was to use cedar 2x10s, but they were too expensive, so instead, we used standard 5/4 deck boards that were paired up and cut to width on a table saw.

Another view of the finished deck

## OTHER DECKS

This deck is one that I helped build around fifteen years ago, for one of my sisters. Originally, it started with just the upper deck and the screen porch on one end of it.

My sister wanted the porch to blend in with the house, so we matched the siding and also the shingles, soffit, and fascia. As you can see in the upper left photo, the inside of the porch was finished off with tongue and groove cedar, and a fan was installed.

Later on, a pool was added, which was also going to get a deck around part of it. The deck would be framed with treated wood, but instead of cedar, like on the upper deck, we were using plastic boards for the surface. The problem was how to bring it all together. What we ended up doing was to cut off the original stairs at the height of the lower deck, and then switched over to the other surface at the landing.

These photos show a different type of deck, where the beam runs along the outside edge. This deck needed work because it wasn't built strong enough or stiff enough to begin with. It only had one diagonal T-brace going across it, and when you were on the deck, you could feel it sway. There was also too much bounce to it. To stiffen it up, I pulled off the decking and added a second T-brace, coming from the opposite side. Then to strengthen it, I added a 2x12 to the beam. I also replaced the original 4 inch posts with 6x6s. The upper end of the posts were notched to support the beam.

# DECK STABILITY

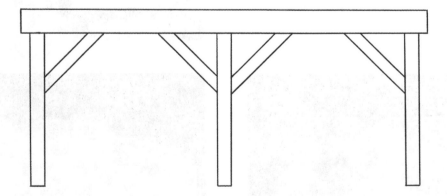

On most decks, the upper surface runs perpendicular to the joists. While the deck feels solid at first, as the wood dries out it may start to move, swaying back and forth. The larger the deck, and the higher it is off the ground, the more you'll feel it. The reason that it's able to move is because it's a parallelogram, which has little structural rigidity. Now if the same deck had the boards put on diagonally, it wouldn't move the slightest bit. That's because it's triangulated, and a triangle is the most rigid shape there is.

Here I'm talking about the rigidity of a deck that's attached to the house. If the platform doesn't move, then the posts won't move either. Now if the same deck was freestanding, this wouldn't necessarily be the case. When a deck isn't connected to anything solid, even if it had a rigid platform, it could still move if it sat on wobbly posts. The way to fix either problem is to brace it using triangulation.

If you're not installing the upper surface diagonally, there are other ways to stabilize the deck. You can either brace the platform, or brace the posts. The least visible way that I know of to stiffen the platform is to run diagonal T-braces under the decking, as shown in the drawing. These work best if they're installed in pairs. Because they're made out of thin metal, they're strong when under tension, but can bend when compressed. When paired up, one of them is always going to be under tension, any time the deck tries to move. To install them, snap chalk lines, and make shallow cuts across the top of the joists. Then slip the T-braces into the cuts, and attach them to every joist.

**WALL**

Wood braces could also be run diagonally across the bottom of the joists. This wouldn't look very nice on a deck that you could walk under, but on a deck that's low to the ground, no one is going to see them. When doing this, I'd use treated 2x4s or 2x6s, and put two screws into every joist.

No matter how the braces are run, the longer they are, the more leverage they'll have to prevent any movement. Both ends of the brace should be attached to the perimeter of the frame. Install the braces so they oppose each other. Ideally, the braces would run to the outer corner, but many decks are too big for that. The drawing shows braces that are set at 45 degrees. Changing the angle would get them closer to the corner, but at some point they'd start to lose there leverage, so you'll have to find the best compromise. In the photo, you can see how T-braces are also used on walls.

To brace the posts, diagonal boards are run from the posts to the beam, as shown in the drawing on the last page. The braces may have to be notched, and on a deck of any size, bolts or lag screws are used to attach them. As with other braces, longer ones have more leverage.

Another thing to consider is the shape of the deck itself. The deck shown on page 386 is rigid without any bracing because the ends are cut off at 45 degrees, so the framing forms a triangle. So is the two-level deck that's shown in most of the photos. To be honest, I never even considered this when they were designed, so I was pleasantly surprised when both decks felt solid, before we even started on the upper surface.

## WORKING ALONE ON A DECK

When building a deck, without help, you have to figure out ways to do certain things by yourself. This deck is only about 8x12 feet; but there were still times when I could have used an extra set of hands. Building it was a lot harder than I expected. I knew it was going to be a problem when I couldn't even pound the stakes into the ground to run the string lines for the footings. As you can see, what I ended up doing was to tie the strings to an old 6x6 that was laying around.

Here I started by attaching the strings to the ledger board, so they were 10 1/2 inches from each end. Then I measured the distance between them and made marks that were the same distance apart on the 6x6, and tied the strings off at those points. To square the strings up, I used the 3-4-5 method. To do this, I marked the strings 3 feet out from the wall. Then I marked the ledger board 4 feet in from the strings, on both sides, and measured between the two points. Now all I had to do was to slide the 6x6 back and forth until both sides measured diagonally at 5 feet. Once that was done, I marked the position of each footing on the strings by measuring out 6 feet from the ledger board.

The 6x6 was the same distance from the wall on both ends, and lined up with the edge of the saw horses. Without this reference point, the mark on each string would have to be remeasured every time the board was moved. If I had help, I probably would have used a 6-8-10 instead, and only measured from one side. But working alone, it was hard enough trying to accurately measure the 5 feet.

When I started this deck, I thought I'd have the holes dug and the footings finished within a day and a half, and that was allowing extra time for doing the digging. I wish that was the case. These were the hardest holes that I've ever had to do, and the photos make the rocks look a lot smaller than they actually are. I couldn't even get the first one out of the hole until I'd dug deep enough to get beneath it. I would guess it weighed around 120 pounds. After that, the rocks got smaller, but continued to the bottom of the hole.

On this deck, which is in northern Minnesota, the footings had to be at least 5 feet deep. With all the rocks, a post hole digger wasn't any good, so I used a shovel for the first couple of feet, and then had to get down into each hole and dig with a little garden shovel. Because of the rocks and the depth, the holes ended up being much larger than what was needed. It took four days before the two holes were finished and filled with concrete.

I would have preferred to let the concrete set up for a few days. However, my time was limited because it took so long to dig the holes. I ended up not touching the footings for two full days, and then I started on the deck, while being careful not to do any pounding on it. This was standard 4000 pound mix. You should really use 5000 pound mix when you don't have much time, as it reaches a higher strength much sooner.

In the meantime, I could nail on the joist hangers and build the beam. The ledger board was installed several years earlier, before we knew the actual size of the deck, so a 2x10 was used.

The beam was made up from three 2x8s that were nailed together. When building it, the boards were clamped together while using a square to line up their lower edges. Then once it was nailed, the beam was turned upright, and any high spots on the upper edge were planed off.

On the third day, I started on the posts. I cut them a little long to begin with, and drilled the holes in the bottom. Then they were placed on the footings and checked for plumb with a level. After planing the bottoms where needed, they were dipped in wood preservative.

Then the posts were cut to length. To do this, I nailed a strip of wood to the ledger board, and marked the height on it that was needed for the two posts. I didn't have a tripod with me, so I put the laser level on a bucket, and then adjusted the height of the bucket so the beam would line up with the mark. Now all I had to do was to pivot the laser level until it was aimed at the posts, and mark each one where it had to be cut off.

Once the posts were in place, the beam was laid on top of them so the overhang was the same on each side, and both ends were the same distance from the ledger board. I also used a level to make sure the beam was sitting straight. Then I installed one of the end joists so it was flush to the end of the beam, and checked it for square, again using the 3-4-5 method. If the string lines were done accurately, it should be close. At most, the beam should only have to be slid over a little bit to square it up. At this time, I also used a level to make sure the beam was at the correct height.

Now the rest of the 2x6 joists could be installed. These were positioned on lines that were drawn across the beam, and then nailed to the joist hangers. Normally I'd also nail the joists to the beam, but here I was trying to go easy on the concrete, so I used screws instead. Since the cantilever on this deck is pretty short, I installed the joists with the crown side up.

This deck didn't have to be a specific size, so before the joists were cut to length, I laid out several of the boards that were being used for the upper surface. After determining how much of a gap I wanted between the rows, I came up with the average distance that each row would cover. Then by using a calculator, I was able to determine

where the joists had to be cut, so I'd end up with a 1 inch overhang on the last row.

To mark the end cuts, I could have either snapped a chalk line or stretched a string across the joists to get a straight line. I ended up using a string, and held a speed square next to it to draw the line across each joist. I also used the speed square to make the cuts.

After cutting the joists to length, a 2x6 was attached to the end of them. To help support it, I clamped a board to the bottom of both end joists. Then each joist was pulled into position against the line as the screws were driven in. Joists that are twisted can be hard to pull into place when you're alone. By attaching a clamp to the board, and then pulling on it, it will give you more leverage.

On this deck, cedar 2x8s were installed around the perimeter to finish it off. The sides were done first. I cut the boards so they overlapped the ledger board, and also stuck out a little bit past the 2x6 that was just installed. This would allow for shrinkage, so the corners wouldn't open up as the wood dried. Then the boards were clamped into place, and screwed on from the back side to hide the screws. When doing this, I used 2 3/4 inch screws, so they wouldn't go all the way through the boards.

The front edge was capped last, and the 2x8 was supported in the same manner by clamping a board to each end joist, as shown in the photo. This was also attached from the back side, except at the corners, where 3 inch screws were driven through the face.

I generally install the upper surface by spacing the rows with small nails, but this deck was different since I'd already determined the distance that each row would cover, and knew exactly where the last row would end. What I did here was to start by installing the row that went against the house, and made sure it was on in a straight line. Then I marked the position of every other row, on every other joist. Starting against the first row, marks were made every 11 5/16 inches.

Now with the marks drawn, I screwed every other row into place, while holding each board against the marks as I went along. Since these boards were long enough to span the deck, butt joints weren't needed. At first, I only put in enough screws to hold each board in position.

Once that was done, I did the other rows by slipping the boards between the ones that were already installed. I used a pry bar to center the boards when necessary, and also used shims to hold them in place until they were screwed down. Then once I'd finished, I went back and put in the remaining screws.

Using this method won't work if the deck boards vary in width or they're badly warped, but here it made everything go much faster. I also used this method on the deck that's shown on the next page.

Once the boards were installed, I marked the ends and cut the edge so there was about a 1 inch overhang. When doing this, I used the cutting jig to get a straight line. Then the deck was ready for the stairs and the handrails to be installed.

Here are some photos from when we built the main deck on the other side of the cabin. On this one, large rocks were in the way, so a backhoe was used to dig the holes for the footings. We also doubled up some of the joists where the span was greater.

# NOT ATTACHING THE DECK TO THE BUILDING

If a deck isn't allowed because of setback requirements for a lake, property line, etc., you may be able to get around the rule by not attaching it to the building. It may take a few extra footings to do it this way, but you won't even notice the difference if the edge of the deck is close to the wall.

This lake cabin belongs to a friend, and the deck isn't attached to it for that reason. In this case, it was actually too close to the wall on part of it, and leaves got stuck between the deck and the siding. To increase the gap, we removed the decking and took off the board that was attached to the end of the joists. Then we cut a little off the joists, reinstalled the board, and cut the edge on the rows that were against the wall when we put the decking back on. In the lower photo, you can see how the joists are cantilevered over a beam.

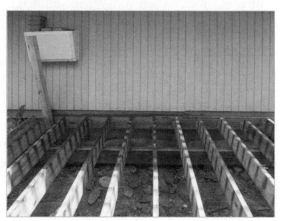

This deck has composite boards for the surface that were installed by using metal fasteners that are attached to the joists between each row. With this system, to replace an interior board, you have to start on one end of the deck, and then remove the other rows until you get to the one that has the bad board. In our case, we had to remove 26 rows, just to trim the edge. Another friend tried a different brand of this type of fastener, but he used treated wood instead for the surface. His deck squeaks every time you take a step, so do your research before using one of these systems.

# REMODELING AND ADDITIONS

Once you know how to frame, and do the wiring, plumbing?, etc., you might consider taking on a major remodeling project, which could involve pretty much anything that's been gone over in this book. If you're thinking about it, first you have to come up with a plan. Then decide if you're capable of doing it and/or who you can get to help. Many times, a job can be pretty intimidating if you look at the whole thing, but it generally isn't as bad when you break it down into parts.

If you've decided to go ahead with the project, where do you start? What I do is to go over each step of it in my head, so I know what has to be done, and in what order. This also helps me come up with a list of what's needed for materials. At this time, I also draw up plans if they're needed or required.

Anytime you're remodeling, you're probably going to have to tear something out before you can get started on the new part. Before you begin, decide what exactly has to be removed, as it's easy to get carried away once you get going. If that happens, you might take something out that ends up having to be replaced. Then while working, use common sense, so you don't cut something off and have it come crashing down on your head. Before you cut or remove any wiring, shut the breaker off, and put a wire nut on the end of each wire before the power is turned back on. Do the same on the plumbing. Shut the water off, and drain the pipes before you cut into the supply lines. Then cap them so you can turn the water back on. When drain lines are cut, they should be plugged to prevent sewer gas from getting into the house.

For most jobs, you'll need a Sawzall and a circular saw, along with a hammer, sledge hammer, pry bar, cats paw, screw drivers, etc. When taking out studs, sometimes the easiest way is to knock out the lower end with a sledge hammer, and then move the stud back and forth a few times to pry it off the nails on the upper end. If you're cutting the studs off, a Sawzall is generally the best thing to use. If you use a circular saw, the blade can get pinched, which could cause the saw to kick back. I learned this the hard way. Years ago, I was cutting through a stud with my new Makita circular saw, when it kicked back and cut through the cord.

# SHORING UP A WALL

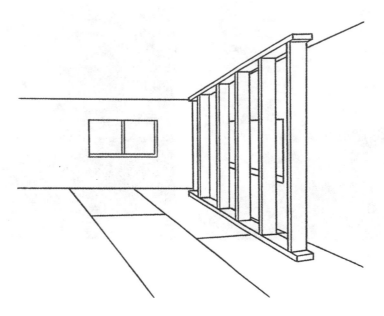

If you're cutting into or removing a load-bearing wall, you may have to shore up the ceiling or the roof to prevent it from sagging down or collapsing. This is shown in the drawing above, where studs are being used to temporarily support the ceiling. In the drawing, there's a plate at each end of the studs, which are used to spread out the load, and also to protect the floor and the ceiling as the studs are tapped into place. Depending on the location, the plates may not be needed on either one or both ends. When the framing is exposed on the ceiling, all you have to do is to put a stud under every joist or rafter, or under every other one if you think that will be strong enough.

This photo shows the front of a garage being supported with 2x4s, so we could replace the header. In this case, the supporting studs had also rotted out on the bottom, so we had to jack the building up to its original height before the studs and the new header could be installed. This was done by moving the jack back and forth as the 2x4s were slipped into position and screwed to the trusses. Then the boards were shimmed up a little bit at a time, until we got to the correct height. Normally I would have put a lower plate across the concrete, but here the height was right at 8 feet, and I didn't want to cut the studs any shorter.

The following pages show some projects where major changes were made to the building. Doing this is generally easier than you'd think, and most of the time, all it takes is some common sense and basic carpentry skills. Then you have to come up with a plan, and be willing to put in some hard work.

## CHANGING THE ROOF

BEFORE                    AFTER

A friend of mine bought this cabin several years ago, and it's been an ongoing project ever since. The next few pages show how we redid part of the roof. As you can see, before we started, the left side of the cabin had a low-pitched roof with very little headroom on the lower end. Our plan was to cut off that part of the roof and then reframe it, so it was a gable roof that matched the other side of the cabin. In the upper left photo, you can see that a beam and new footings have been already installed to support the porch. The old ones had settled, so the cabin had to be jacked up to straighten it out.

To begin, we tore off the shingles, and then cut the rafters so they were flush to the wall. Once that was done, the ridge board was installed. This had to be positioned correctly, since the new roof would flow into the lower-pitched section on each side. To do this, string lines were used as we adjusted the height and moved the ridge board back and forth, until we found the exact spot where both sides lined up. Then the ridge board was squared up to the building using the 3-4-5 rule, and also by taking diagonal measurements from both sides to see if they matched up.

The upper photo gives you a good look at how the roof was framed. You can also see how the new rafters line up with the original roof on the lower end. Here the ridge board was supported in two places to handle the weight until the walls were installed. The rafters are 2x8s that were thinned down on the overhang for installing the soffit and fascia. The height of the front wall was determined by holding a rafter in place, and then measuring what was needed. We also built a couple of headers to support the lower end of the roof. The longer one won't actually span this far once the wall is reframed for a new window.

The original walls on the gable end were in good shape, so we left them in place. Then we ran studs up to the new roof by sistering them to the ones that existed. When the sheathing was installed, it was shimmed out to match the other boards, which were 7/8 inch thick.

In the lower left photo, you can see how part of the original roof was left in place. This gave us something to stand on as we framed up the new one. It was taken out once the rafters were finished. In the other photo, the shingles have been removed on the rest of the cabin, and the new part is sheathed. At this point, the roof was covered with tarps, in case it rained.

This shows how the corners were framed to continue the slope of the original roof.

These photos show the cabin at different stages of the project. In the first one, we're installing the shingles. In the second, the porch has been stripped, and the new windows have been delivered. You can also see that the wall has been built to support the gable end of the new roof. In the next photo, the front wall has been sheathed, a new window is in place, and the porch is being reframed. In the last one, the windows and the siding have been installed on the porch.

On the back side of the cabin, this floor had to be leveled up before the new sheathing could be installed. Originally, it had been an exterior porch, so the floor was sloped. It also sat at three different heights. In order to do this, I found the highest point and used that as the base line. Then I put my laser level on the floor at that spot, and drew lines to mark the position of each floor joist.

Once that was done, I simply pivoted the laser level and measured the height needed at both ends, and also the center, of every joist. I did this by holding the measuring tape against the floor, and then seeing where the laser beam hit. Then I subtracted 3 1/4 inches from that amount, which is the distance that the beam is above the base on my laser level. Let's say, for instance, that I got a measurement of 4 inches. After subtracting 3 1/4 inches from it, that meant the floor was 3/4 of an inch low at that point.

After marking the heights for every joist, I used a circular saw to cut strips of wood that were tapered to those measurements. Then they were laid in place and checked by laying a straightedge across them, and any high spots were planed down. After that, construction adhesive was applied to the strips, and they were nailed to the floor.

## STRENGTHENING A BEAM

When we worked on the interior, we noticed that the beam that holds up the roof on the other end of the building had sagged a little over an inch. To strengthen it, first we installed the largest micro-lam that would fit (18 inches) on one side of the beam. Then on the other side, we sheathed the wall with two layers of 1/2 inch plywood. The first layer was securely nailed to the beam, and to any studs that were above it. Then the second layer was installed with the seams offset by several feet. On this one, we also applied construction adhesive every 8 inches, and then nailed it. The lower edge was kept straight by following a string that was stretched across the 25 foot opening.

393

In the upper photo, a friend wanted to move a post over to open up the basement. After an engineer calculated what was needed, we glued and bolted three micro-lams to the original beam, with a single board on one side of it, and two on the other. An 8 inch post was used, and the footing is 3 feet by 4 feet to handle the estimated 20,000 pound load.

The lower photos show a beam that was installed by the guys who are working on the building where I'm living at this time. Here the joists were cut so the beam could slip between them. Then joist hangers were used to attach them to the beam. On the left, you can see that some of the micro-lams are lower than the others because the framing is at two different heights. On the other side of the beam, some of the joists had to be sistered, as shown on the right.

## SAWING OFF A ROOF

On projects where you're adding another level to the building, you'll have to saw the roof off. This is generally done by using a Sawzall to cut the sheathing between the rafters. Then once you've cut on both sides of a rafter, that section is removed. On a small roof, you might take off the whole section in one piece by sawing through the rafter and the sheathing at both ends, while on a larger roof, it may have to be done in two or three pieces. You'll still be left with the lower end of the rafter that's been nailed to the upper plate, but this can easily be removed with a wonder bar or a crowbar. If you're just removing the rafters, you may be able to pry them off by cutting the upper end, and then raising and lowering them.

When doing this, the shingles are the biggest problem, since they're heavy and can quickly dull the blade. It's nice to have the shingles off, but that's not always an option. Sometimes they can easily be removed by simply pulling them off one at a time. At other times, the best way to take them off is with a bladed pitch fork or a shovel that's specifically made for this purpose.

On a small roof, you can quickly saw it off and then start framing. But that won't be possible on a larger roof, if there's any chance of rain. Here you want to have the roof as ready as it can be for removing it, while still being weathertight. In that case, what I do is to remove the shingles and the sheathing in advance, but leave the rafters in place with tarps stretched across them. Then, when there's a break in the weather, the tarps are removed, and the rafters are quickly sawn off.

The last time I sawed off a roof was a few months ago, when we tore down a garage. What I did there was to rip a slot through the shingles on both sides of a rafter, using the claw on my hammer, and then sawed down the slots. Then I'd cut that section off, and my brother and a nephew would throw it into the dumpster. This went pretty fast. The whole garage was taken down, and the area cleaned up, in about six hours.

This house used to belong to one of my brothers. Originally, it was a one-story house with a 4-12 pitched roof. To increase the living space, we sawed off the roof and reframed it with 2x12s at a 12-12 pitch. There's also a small dormer on the back side.

Since this is a small house that's only about 24 x 32 feet, the upstairs isn't that big. My brother's plan was for it to be a large bedroom, and have another bathroom. The lower photos show how it's mainly one area, with a small room next to the stairs where the dormer is. The width of the main room is about 16 1/2 feet. The bathroom was planned out, but never installed, so this room could also be used as a small office or a walk-in closet.

It was just the two of us doing the work, so everything had to be done according to the weather. If I remember correctly, there were several days with no chance of rain, so that's how long we had to saw off the roof and put up the new 2x12s. Removing the old roof went pretty fast. It was just a matter of taking it off in sections with a Sawzall, and then throwing it into a dumpster. When doing this, use a demolition blade, which is thicker so it won't bend.

After everything was removed down to the top plate, except for the ceiling joists, we put up the ridge board at the correct height to get a 12-12 pitch, and then started on the rafters. To get the right length, we measured from the ridge board to the top plate at all four corners, and split the difference between the measurements. When necessary, the ridge board was shifted over to center it between the walls. Then once the rafters were up and braced, tarps were stretched across the roof until the sheathing was installed.

On this project, my brother and I didn't agree on how the overhang should be done. You can see in the upper photo that there's about a 2 foot overhang at the bottom, with the soffit running parallel to the rafters. Homes in this area generally have a short overhang, with the soffit running horizontally. If it was done that way, the edge of the roof would be higher up. I also felt that the lap siding should continue up to the peak, and the upstairs needed larger windows.

The house in the middle is another one where we sawed off the roof. But here, we left the front of the house as is, and only removed about the last 25 feet. Originally, the roof on the back of the house looked about the same as the one on the last page does now. In this case, we needed more room, so we added walls and built a second floor. At first, I was against the idea of sawing off the roof. I wanted a large dormer instead to fit in better with the neighborhood, but my friend's view was that he wanted all the space he could get. "Besides," he said, "the only place that you can get a good look at the back of the house is from the yard."

On this project, we removed the shingles and the sheathing in advance, so the rafters could be quickly sawed off. Then on a weekend, with about six guys helping, we removed the old rafters, put up the walls, and installed the trusses.

We almost lost the house. On the first morning, the sky was blue and the weather looked perfect. But once the old rafters were removed, we noticed a large cloud to the northwest. We hoped it would stay to the north, but it didn't take long before it was over us, and we were getting pounded by both rain and hail as we held tarps up over our heads, just trying to keep it out. Luckily, the storm only lasted about ten minutes before the sky was blue again, and there wasn't much damage, as we were able to roll the water off wherever it pooled on top of the tarps that we had spread out across the floor. One of my sisters lives about ten miles north. At her house, the storm lasted about an hour.

To have enough headroom, and also match the height of the old roof, we kept the walls short, at about 6 feet 4 inches, and used scissors trusses. The original part of the roof has a 12-12 pitch, while the new section is somewhere between 4 and 6-twelve.

By doing this addition, we added three bedrooms, two bathrooms, and a small room for a second furnace with central air. The footprint of the house is only around 1000 square feet, yet it has a total of four bathrooms, and six rooms that could be used as bedrooms.

One problem that you may run into when adding a second floor is how to attach the exterior walls. If you're just repitching the roof, it's easy. Put a rafter next to each ceiling joist, or every other one, with another rafter between them, if you're on 24 inch centers. When walls are being added, you may find that the ceiling joists have either been cut at an angle, or are too short on each end to set the walls on top of them. Depending on what's easier, you could install boards to support the walls and/or install a rim joist around the house, or just toenail the studs to the top plate. On the house shown here, if I remember correctly, we were able to rest the walls on the ceiling joists as is, which were also long enough to attach the sheathing to them.

This house had an addition added to the back of it, giving it an extra four rooms, not counting the stairs and the basement. In this case, care was taken to maintain the original style. About the only place that you can see where anything was changed is the diagonal seam in the soffit. Here I just worked on the interior, doing plumbing, trim, flooring, finishing the stairs and the basement, etc., and didn't even show up until most of the exterior work was done. Many of the photos in this book are from this house.

 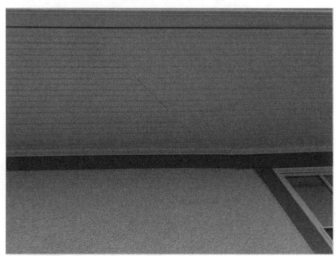

I use this jig for making straight cuts with a circular saw. It can either be clamped to the board that you're cutting, or held in place by just kneeling on it. Some uses include: cutting the edge on a deck, taking a little off a door, and making clean cuts on plywood. I make these jigs by gluing and temporarily nailing a thin strip of wood to a piece of plywood or masonite. The strip must be installed in a straight line, and should be far enough away from one side, so the edge can be trimmed by running the saw down the strip, as shown in the lower left photo. After that's done, the saw will cut along the edge of the jig.

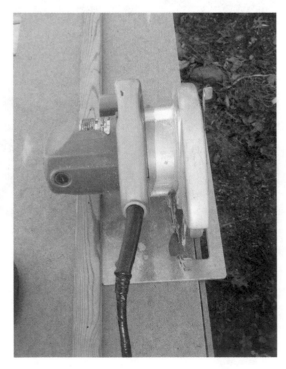

The jig is positioned on the line.      The edge of a deck, after it's been cut.

# JIG FOR SQUARE CUTS

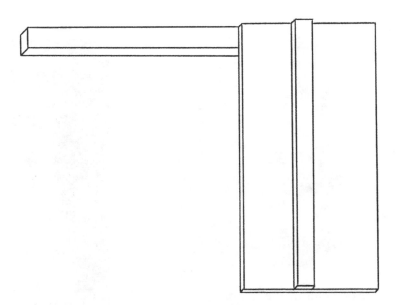

This is just a cutting jig with a board attached to one end.
I use it for cutting aluminum soffit and vinyl siding.

# STAIR JIG

I made this jig for cutting the treads and risers on the stairs in the lower photo. It's simple to use. Just lay it in place, extend the ends so they fit tight against both sides, and tighten the wing nuts to lock it in that position. Then all you have to do is to lay the jig across the board that you're using, and draw the lines for the cuts by running a sharp pencil along both ends of it. This will give you the exact length and the angle of the cuts. This jig cost me about two dollars to make. The version that I've seen in a catalog is around two hundred dollars.

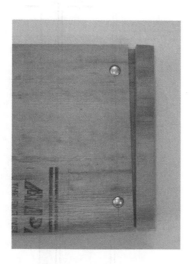

These photos show one end of the jig, on the side that faces down. On the right, it's extended partway out.

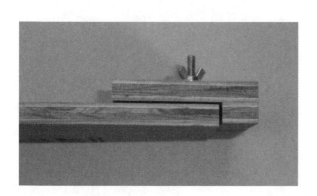

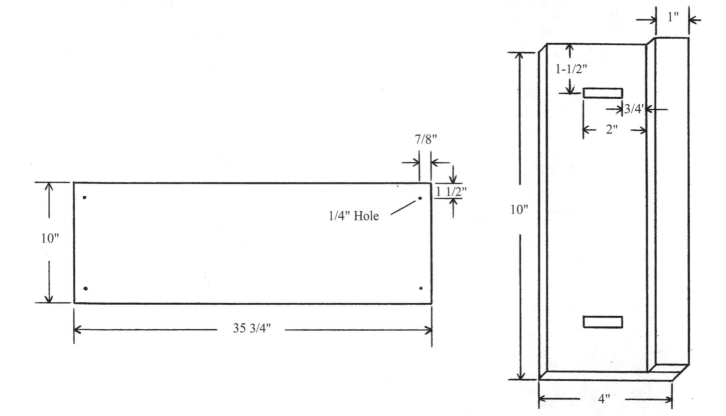

Before the 1/4 inch hole was drilled at each corner on the center board, a 5/8 inch forstner type bit was used to drill a shallow, flat-bottomed hole, so the head of the carriage bolts would be slightly below the surface. To cut the slots in the end boards, I just drilled a series of 1/4 inch holes, and then cleaned up the slots with a chisel and a file.

When making this jig, the length of the center board will mainly determines its size. On the one that's drawn here, the length of the center board is 35 3/4 inches. The jig is 37 3/4 inches long when the ends are pushed in, and 39 3/4 inches when they're fully extended. To give it more adjustment, cut the end boards wider and have longer slots. This is the second center board that's been used on this jig. The first one, which was used to cut the treads and risers for the stairs in the lower photo on the last page, was 3 inches shorter. The current one was used on the stairs in the photo above it.

# SIDING SPACER

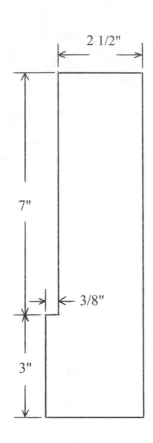

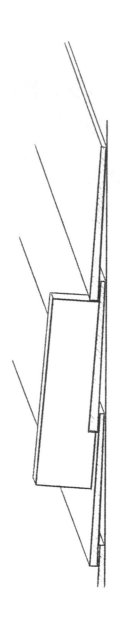

This simple jig is used for spacing the rows when installing lap siding. Have enough so that everyone involved in the project has one in their pouch or their back pocket. When cutting them out, the most important thing is to make sure they're all the same size, otherwise the siding will end up higher on one side than the other. The measurements shown here are for a spacer that will be used to install siding with a 7 inch exposure. Using them will make the job a lot easier, but you should still measure how far you've gone every few rows, as the siding will sometimes move as it's being nailed.

# ROUTER TABLE

While on a job, years ago, I had to round off some boards one day, so I made this simple router table from a couple of scrap boards, and then clamped it to saw horses. When using router bits that have a pilot bearing, the router can be used freehand. But without a bearing, you need a router table to keep from burning the edge.

As you can see, there isn't much to the router table. It's just a piece of 3/4 inch plywood, with a 2 inch hole for the router bit, and a 7/8 x 1 1/2 inch board for the fence. To mount the router, the plastic base was removed, and then used to mark the holes in the plywood. Then flathead screws were used to connect the router to the plywood.

Sheetrock screws were used to attach the fence. Most of the time, it's adjusted so the bearing (if there is one) is barely touching the board. When necessary, the fence is moved over and the screws are reset.

# SCAFFOLDS

For most projects, all you need is a step ladder, or maybe an extension ladder for higher work on the exterior. But once in a while, you'll do a job where a ladder isn't enough, and what you really need is a scaffold. When a scaffold is required, I usually make my own. I like to come up with simple, inexpensive platforms that are made from construction lumber that's been screwed together. These are easily taken apart once the job is finished and they aren't needed anymore.

## ROLLING SCAFFOLD

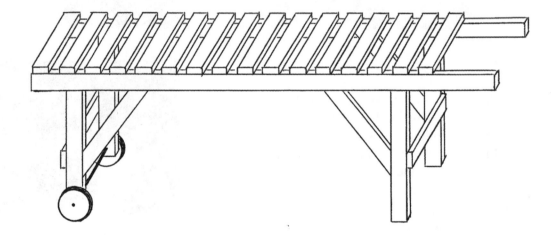

I don't own a pair of stilts, so I use a rolling scaffold on jobs where I'll be doing a lot of work on tall ceilings. The only size requirement is that it's big enough to let me tape a 12 foot sheet of sheetrock before it has to be moved, and that it's at a comfortable working height. I generally make the platform so it's at least 8 feet long and 16 inches to 2 feet wide. On 10 foot ceilings, I like the scaffold to be about 3 feet tall, since 7 feet is a comfortable height for me to do the taping.

On the scaffold that's shown in this drawing, it's mainly constructed out of 2x4s that are attached with deck screws. The wheels only go on one end. These are inexpensive, and can be purchased at a hardware store or local building center. The axel is a piece of 5/8 inch threaded rod. In the drawing, there's only a cross board connecting the legs at each end of the platform. To stiffen it up, a diagonal brace should be added. Plywood could also be used instead.

To move the scaffold, you just lift up on the handles and then roll it around. This makes it a little harder to move, than if it had four wheels that pivot. But this way, you have a solid platform without having to lock the wheels into place. To get on top of it, I generally use an upside-down joint compound bucket for the first step. On taller scaffolds, you'll need a step ladder.

This past winter, I needed a scaffold for insulating and hanging the sheetrock on the second floor of my brother's cabin. It also had to be at a comfortable height for taping the peaks, which, in this case, meant it had to be a little over 8 feet tall. This is what I came up with for doing the job. Here the legs and the upper frame are either 2x4s or 2x6s, and the top is 3/4 inch plywood. At first, I only had pivoting wheels on one end of the scaffold, but it was too hard to move it around. So, instead, I bought an inexpensive dolly, like the one on page 228, and used the wheels from it, The only problem is that there aren't any locks on the wheels. To hold the scaffold in place, I insert a shim between the wheel and the housing on two of the wheels.

# WAR LADDERS

This ladder is the one that's shown on the cover. I call them war ladders because they remind me of something that you'd use to storm a castle in the old days. When they were built, we needed two platforms for installing the ridge boards and the rafters on my brother's cabin. A standard ladder was out of the question, since the peak was 19 feet above the floor, and the rafters were 20 foot long Douglas Fir 2x12s. This simple design gave us a platform that was 14 feet high, and was strong enough for three of us to be up on it at the same time. Once the main rafters were installed, the legs were shortened for working on the lower peaks.

For the main supports, we used 18 foot 2x6s, while 2x4s were used for the other members. In this case, the 2x6s were a little short, so we extended them with 3/4 inch plywood.

When building the ladders, I didn't know how wide the base should be, so I went with a slightly narrower angle than that of the step ladders we were using. On the side that the steps were on, they ended up being around 5 feet wide.

Because of their height, the ladders were tipped up with a bare minimum of braces in place. Then once they were up, the other boards were added, with several screws used to attach each end. At the time, we didn't know what was actually needed, so we just started at the bottom and screwed on boards until the ladders felt safe (solid). Then the platforms were installed, using 3/4 inch plywood, and guardrails were added. These ladders were pretty heavy, but could easily be moved around with two guys.

# LADDERS WITH A PLANK

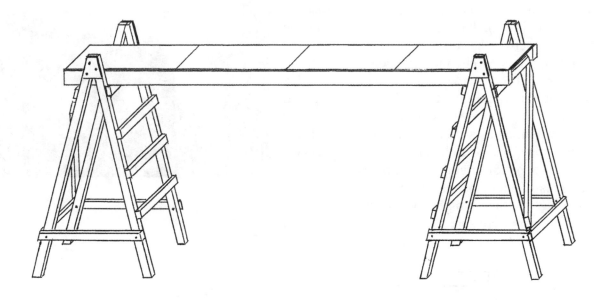

A few years ago, while working on the house that's shown in the photo, we needed scaffolding to install the soffit and fascia on the front porch. Renting it would have cost around 200 dollars for a month. Since the project was being done in stages, that wouldn't be long enough for us to finish the job. The scaffolding would also block the driveway while it was set up, so we decided to build our own, and this is what we came up with.

Here the ladders were made out of 2x4s, and the main supports are 8 foot studs. They're connected at the top with plywood brackets, so the two sections can fold together by disconnecting one end of the lower braces. The horizontal boards are securely attached, and are spaced close enough to allow adjustment for working at different heights. Although they could also be used as steps, their main purpose is to support the plank (platform). The plank is pretty simple. Just a pair of 16 foot 2x8s that are covered with 3/4 inch plywood. I think this one is around 16 inches wide.

This idea ended up working a lot better than if we had rented the scaffolding. It was easy to move everything as we worked our way around the porch, and the driveway could still be used. The total cost for materials was around 50 dollars.

# ROOF CATWALK

On this roof, a catwalk was installed along the peak to work on the chimney. The catwalk consists of three parts: the plywood panels, 2x4 blocks, and the boards that run across the top. To make the panels, the first thing I did was to cut the plywood to match the slope of the roof. Then cuts were made to clear the ridge cap. After that, three short lengths of 2x4s were attached to each panel. The longest one went along the upper edge. This was used to stiffen it up and to provide a place for the upper boards to be attached. The other two were screwed to the lower edge where the panels rest on the roof. This would spread out the load and help prevent damage to the shingles. Then once they were finished, the panels were spread out across the peak, and 2x6s were screwed to the top of them.

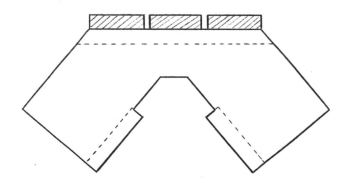

On a steep roof, a roof ladder can be used to safely get on it to make repairs, install a new vent, work on the skylight, etc. This is pretty much the same as a regular ladder, except for the hook on the top that's used to catch on the ridge. To keep the weight down, the ladder is generally made using 2x3s or 2x4s, since it has to be carried up to the peak.

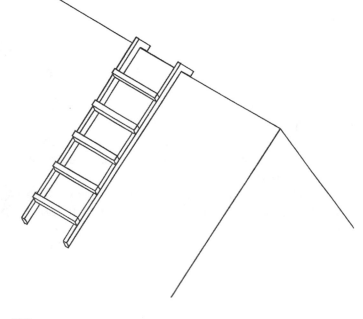

These photos show a platform that was made to go over a stair opening. This allowed me to use a scaffold for working on the vaulted ceiling. It also shut off the second floor, so it didn't have to be heated until the insulation was installed. To go upstairs, you could just use the trap door. Then, when the sheetrock was brought up, the sections were tipped up against the wall, so they were out of the way.

The platform was made in three sections, and it rested on 2x4s that were screwed to the perimeter. A board was also attached to the section that's against the exterior wall to support the one that's hinged for the trap door. To build the platform, I used boards that were just laying around. The main supports are 2x6s, and the upper surface is 3/4 inch plywood. 2x4s and thinner plywood could have been used instead.

# MITER SAW STAND

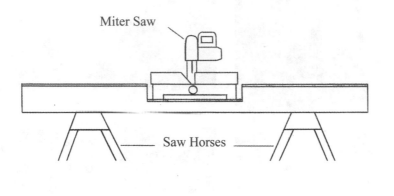

Miter Saw

Saw Horses

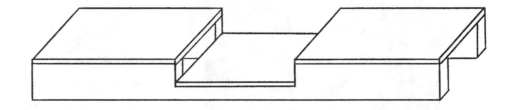

Out of all the different miter saw stands that I've used over the years, this is my favorite. I can't take any credit for the design. I never saw this type until one was quickly assembled by another carpenter who happened to be working on the same house. It's about as simple as you can get, and again, it was constructed out of materials that were just laying around. We're still using it. This stand will handle almost anything. Every manufactured one that I've tried has sagged too much whenever I cut a heavier board.

To build it, the main supports are notched to create a pocket that's the same height as the base of the miter saw. On the first stand, 2x6s were used, and the notches are 3 inches deep. The upper surface consists of thin masonite, though most anything could be used. The stand in this photo is a heavy duty version, and we used 2x8s with 3/4 inch plywood on top. It was used to cut 1 1/2 inch thick siding that was up to 18 feet long.

410

# USING A SPEED SQUARE

I always carry a speed square when I'm framing. I use it for drawing lines, finding angles, and for cutting studs and floor joists to length with a circular saw. While it's easy to get a decent first cut by following a pencil line, using this tool is faster and more accurate. But where it really helps is when the board is little long, and it's necessary to cut off just a bit more.

When cutting a board, hold the square with one hand as you run the saw along the edge of it. In the upper photo, my left hand was busy with the camera, otherwise it would have been holding the square. When using a speed square, it generally isn't necessary to draw a line across the board. Just mark the near edge of the board where you want to make the cut.

In the center photo, the smaller speed square is metal, and the larger one is made out of plastic. I keep the smaller one in my pouch for cutting studs and checking for square, while the larger one is used for cutting floor joists, siding, etc. The reason the larger one is plastic is because, when working outdoors, metal squares can get so hot in the sun that you can't even pick them up.

The lower photo shows a speed square being used to draw a line at a 20 degree angle from the end of the board. To do this, hold the corner of the square against the board, and line up the 20 degree mark with the edge. Then draw the line by following the edge of the square (X). For a 45 degree angle, just hold the square tight against the board, and use the other edge. If you want to find the angle of a cut or a line that's already been drawn, line up the edge (X) with the cut or the line, and then see which number lines up with the edge of the board.

You can also use a speed square to make rafter cuts. That's what the other numbers are for. The numbers on one side of the slot are for making cuts on common rafters, while those on the other side are for hip and valley rafters. On steep roofs, I generally use a framing square instead, because it's more accurate.

# USING A CIRCULAR SAW

Except for finish-work or installing wood siding, on most of my jobs, almost all of the cutting is done with a circular saw. In order to do quality work with this tool, you have to be able to cut in a straight line. This is mainly learned from experience, and means spending enough time actually using your saw to get the feel of it. Most people aren't going to pick one up for the first time and do good work. You also have to know the best way to make the different cuts.

For cutting studs and joists to length, using a speed square is generally the best way, both for speed and accuracy.

When cutting plywood or ripping boards to the correct width, the accuracy of the cut depends on the skill of the person that's making it. This is where it helps to know your saw. On long cuts, once I get started, I seldom look at the saw blade. Instead, I hold the notch on the base of the saw against the line as I make the cut. With my saw, the blade will run down the right side of the line. When doing this, it helps to have the blade extended out as far as possible, so the saw tracks better. Other saws may be different.

For instance, while this method works with my saw, which is a Makita, model number 5007, the less expensive model with the smaller motor has a different base. When using one of those, I always have to watch the saw blade as I cut, since I don't know how to line up the marks. When making short cuts, or cutting on the left side of the line, I still have to look at the blade when using my saw. But whenever I can, I'll hold the notch against the line, since it's faster and more accurate.

When cutting doors, or anything that needs a straight cut, a cutting jig is often the best choice. You could also clamp a straightedge to the surface, and then make the cut by running the saw along it. But the advantage of using the cutting jig is that it's faster and also protects the finish, since the saw is on top of the jig.

The easiest way to make accurate or repetitive ripping cuts is by either using a rip fence or clamping a board to the base of the saw. Then you hold it against the other board as you make the cut. In the lower left photo, I'm cutting long strips to the same thickness. Since I was working alone, I used concrete blocks to hold the boards in place. On page 373, I used this method to notch the posts for a deck.

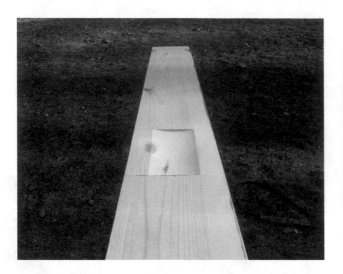 

In these photos, I clamped a board to the base of the saw, perpendicular to the blade, and used the saw to notch a board in order to clear a pipe. While I'm sure that this isn't recommended, it actually worked pretty well. I just held the guard out of the way, and then moved the saw from side to side as I slowly lowered it to the board.

# TOOLS

Years ago, all of my tools, except for the level, hand saw, and the circular saw, would fit into a small box. Actually, when I first started, I didn't even own a circular saw, and used one that belonged to one of my brothers. Now, sometimes I'll spend half an hour loading up the tools to go to a job, and what I have is nothing compared to that of many homeowners.

There are a lot of tools that you might need for a home remodeling project. Some you'll be using everyday, while others are rarely needed. Whenever you're buying a power tool, spend the money to get one that's decent, since you'll have it a long time. At first, ones that are inexpensive may seem to be just as good. But once you use a quality tool, you'll realize that corners were cut to make the cheaper ones cost less. Generally, you get what you pay for. I've had some of my tools for over thirty years.

You don't have to buy every tool that you'll be using. After all this time, there are still many that I don't own, but, if needed, I can borrow from friends or a family member. In return, mine are available to them. Renting is another option. The following is a list of tools that are commonly used for working on a house.

| | |
|---|---|
| Hammer | 16 ounce is a good all-around weight. Heavier is better for framing, but only if you can comfortably handle the extra weight. Milled-face heads are strictly for framing. I've used "Plumb" hammers for around forty years. I think wood handled hammers have better balance and just feel better. |
| Measuring tape | I recommend a standard 25 foot tape. It's more rigid than shorter ones. Fat tapes are a hindrance on most jobs. |
| Pouch | Any sturdy pouch with pockets to hold measuring tape, small tools, pencil, nails, hammer, etc. |

414

| | |
|---|---|
| <u>Pencil</u> | Carpenter pencils are good for framing and sheetrock. For trimming, you'll want a sharp writing pencil. I always carry a separate pink eraser. |
| <u>Utility knife</u> | I prefer one with a retractable blade. |
| <u>Screw driver</u> | The ones with the replaceable bits are tough to beat. |
| <u>Speed square</u> | It's used to check for square or determine angles, and as a guide to cut off studs and joists. When framing walls, I always carry an 8 inch metal square. I use the 12 inch plastic version for working on decks, as it stays cooler in the sun. |
| <u>Chalk line</u> | Either red or blue chalk. Use the color that shows up best. |
| <u>Nail set</u> | 3-pack Stanley nail set. I've never damaged one yet, even though I've abused them many times. I used another brand that was destroyed in one day. |
| <u>Level</u> | Bare minimum for building would be a torpedo level and a 4 foot. A 2 - 3 foot would also be good for checking window sills, while a 6 foot would help when installing doors, tipping up the walls, and straightening walls and ceilings. On some projects, a laser level can be invaluable Get one that shoots both a horizontal and a vertical spot or line. |
| <u>Pull saw</u> | General purpose model. They cut fast and clean, and they're compact. |
| <u>Block plane</u> | Necessary for trimming, scribing, shaving down doors that stick, etc. You'll need a sharpening jig and a stone to keep the blade sharp. Low-angle model is better for planing end grain. |
| <u>Chisels</u> | Set of four, 1/4 - 1 inch. Metal caps on the handles, so you don't need a mallet. If you're only going to buy one, get a 3/4 or a 1 inch. |
| <u>Sheetrock square</u> | I like the heavy duty version that's thicker, so it doesn't bend as easy. |
| <u>Sheetrock saw</u> | Pointed saw for cutting holes, larger blade for straight cuts. I use an old short crosscut saw for this. |
| <u>Rasp</u> | For shaving down sheetrock and cleaning up the edge. |

**TOOLS**

| | |
|---|---|
| Files | 4-in-1 file for all around use. Small files for coping. |
| Framing square | For laying out stair stringers and rafters. |
| Plumbing tools | Pipe wrenches, tubing cutter, push-button torch for either propane or mapp gas, solder, flux, and emery cloth or a wire brush for cleaning copper. |
| Electrical tools | Wire cutter, stripper, needle-nose pliers, voltage tester. |
| Drill | Cordless drill, hammer drill for concrete. Heavy duty slow speed drill is used for mixing buckets of thin set or joint compound. Impact driver is best for driving in Tapcons. |
| Circular saw | 13-15 amp motor for serious use. 10 amp motor weighs less. |
| Jig saw | Make sure it has an orbital action for better cutting. There's a big difference between an inexpensive saw, and a high quality one. |
| Screw gun | For hanging sheetrock or building decks. |
| Reciprocating saw | (Sawzall) For demolition work, sawing off pipes, or anywhere you have to reach in to make a rough cut. |
| Miter saw | A regular 10 inch miter saw or compound miter saw is good for cutting 2x4s or small trim. If you're going to get serious about building, buy a quality sliding miter saw for its greater work potential. |
| Table saw | Used for making accurate rip cuts on boards. Also good for cutting plywood. If you don't plan to have a serious workshop, get a good portable model like a Bosch. I prefer the folding base. |
| Planer | The best tool for planning down high spots on studs and joists. |
| Sander | Orbital finish sander, random orbit sander, belt sander. |
| Oscillating saw | For making stab-cuts on most materials when remodeling or doing repair work. Once you own one, you'll wonder how you got along without it. |

Extension cord — 12-gauge wire for longer cords, or any tool that draws a lot of power.

Air compressor and nail guns — The important number on air compressors is their SCFM @ 90 PSI rating. A framing gun needs at least 2 cubic feet per minute at 90 psi.

Shop vacuum — Quiet models are available. 10 gallon is easier to haul around than a larger one.

Router — For installing hinges, cutting slots, rounding off edges, etc.

Diamond blade — Used for cutting concrete or Durock with a circular saw or a grinder.

Drywall cut-out tool — For cutting around boxes when installing sheetrock.

Coping saw — Used for installing baseboard.

Staple gun — Duo-fast is the only brand that I can recommend. The power is adjustable, and it rarely jambs. It's the best I've seen.

Tile saw — Needed for cutting some types of tile. Buy a good quality saw, or rent one.

Pry bar — Wonder bar, crowbar (wrecking bar) for tough jobs.

Nail puller — (Cats paw) For pulling nails.

Sharpening stone — Diamond, oil, or water stones. A sharpening jig will help to maintain the same angle on planes and chisels.

Clamps — Spring clamps, wood clamps, bar clamps, pipe clamps, C-clamps, etc.

Straightedge — I always have one on hand. The one that I use the most is just a 2 inch wide piece of aluminum that's about 4 1/2 feet long and 1/8 inch thick. I use it for drawing lines, and also clamp it to doors or plywood to make straight cuts with a circular saw. If you're buying one that's also a ruler, get a 5 foot. Many times, 4 feet isn't quite long enough.

Extra long nail set — When framing, I keep an 8 inch piece of 3/8 inch diameter steel rod in my pouch. I use for driving in nails that I can't reach with a standard nail set.

# NAILS AND SCREWS

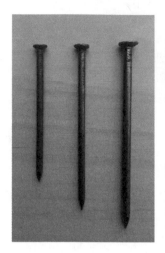 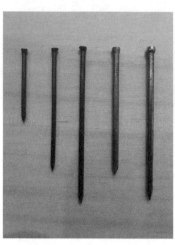 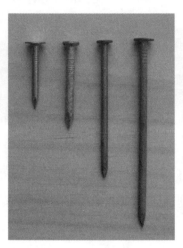 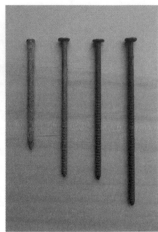

On this page are some of the nails and screws that are available, and what they're used for. On the upper left are an 8D, 10D, and 16D coated sinker, which are used for framing. To the right are trim nails for interior work, starting with a 1 1/4, 2, and a 2 1/2 inch hardened trim nail, followed by a 6D and an 8D standard finish nail. Hardened trim nails are thinner than standard finish nails. The shank on the 1 1/4 and the 2 inch are the same size, which helps when drilling pilot holes. Next are galvanized nails for exterior work. On the left is a 1 inch roofing nail, followed by a 1 1/2 inch joist hanger nail, and then an 8D and a 16D box nail. To the right is a 6D casing, followed by a 2 1/2 inch small diameter galvanized split-less ring shank nail that's used for both siding and trim. Next to it are the painted version in 2 1/2 and 3 inch.

On the lower left are several sheetrock screws is different lengths, followed by a trim screw, which requires a number 1 square bit. Then to the right is a ground screw for metal electrical boxes, followed by an interior zinc-plated construction screw, a couple of deck screws, and an exterior trim screw. The last photo shows some of the different heads that are available for screws. On the left is a Phillips, followed by a number 2 square head and a Torx head. The last two are combo-heads, where you can either use a number 3 Phillips or a number 2 square bit.

 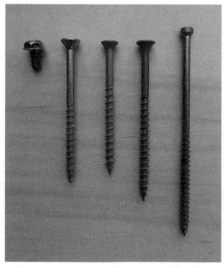 

# REPLACEMENT WINDOWS

While working on the book, I helped a friend install replacement windows on the second floor of his house. The only surprising thing about this is that it was the first time I'd ever done it. In the past, I've always installed complete window units with either brick molding or nailing fins attached. These were Marvin windows. Similar ones are made by other companies, such as Anderson Renewal.

The Original Windows

To take out the old windows, we began by pulling off the window stops inside the house. In this case, the side stops were held on with screws, while the upper ones were nailed on. To remove them, a utility knife was used to cut through the paint. Then the upper stops were pried off by slipping a stiff putty knife beneath them.

Now the only thing that prevented the inner window from coming out were metal slides that were attached to both sides. These were held in place with a single nail at each end. To remove the window, we cut through one of the upper nails by slipping a heavy duty putty knife between the slide and the jamb, and then hit it with a hammer. Once the nail was cut, the inner window was slipped out, and the slides were removed. Other windows may not have this, or they might have a different style.

When I removed the first window, I cut the cord for the balance weight, without hanging on to it. That was a mistake, as the weight fell all the way down to the first floor. Many older homes are balloon-framed, which means long studs were used that extend between two floor levels. Modern houses are built with each floor level having its own wall sections. On the windows that followed, I held on to each cord as it was being cut. Then I tied a knot to keep it from getting past the pulley.

The outer window was held in place by a strip of wood that had been slipped into a groove on each jamb. With the window slid all the way up, a pry bar was pounded into one of the strips, and the lower part of it was pried out and snapped off. Then the window was slid down and removed, and the cords were cut. With the window gone, what remained of the strips was taken out. These windows also had combination windows installed on the exterior, so they were removed at this time.

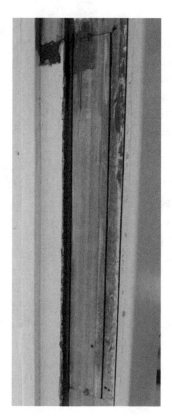

One of the problems with older double-hung windows is the heat loss through the cavities that contain the window weights, which are hidden behind a wood cover. On these windows, the covers were held in place with a screw at each end. The screw heads were filled with paint, so a screw driver blade was pounded in from the side to clean them out. Then the covers were taken off, and the weights were removed. After that was done, we took out the pulleys.

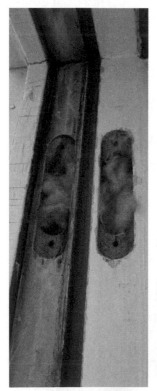

Our original plan was to insulate the cavities by just stuffing fiberglass into each one. That didn't work out, as these cavities went all the way down to the first floor. So, instead, the insulation was cut into pieces. Then each piece was folded over a flexible strip of wood that was about 4 feet long, and slid into place with each piece butted up against the one that went before it. There were two sizes to the cavities, with the larger ones between windows that were mounted together, since they contained four window weights. The insulation was installed full thickness for the larger openings, and was split in half for the smaller ones. Small pieces were used to fill the pulley holes. Once the cavities were insulated, the covers were reinstalled.

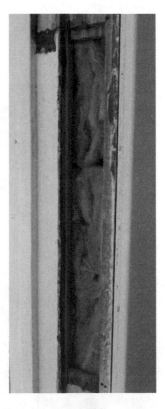

Before we installed the new window, a thick bead of caulk was applied to the inside edge of the exterior stops. Then another bead was laid across the bottom, against the sill, and also on the lower corner of each side, connecting the beads.

After that was done, the window was lifted up and held tight against the sill as it was tipped into place. Then the upper window stop was reinstalled, and shims were put at each corner to hold the window in position, so it was plumb.

The replacement windows weren't quite as deep as the openings they were going into. Because of that, we had to choose whether they'd go against the interior or the exterior stops. We ended up pulling them tight against the sill and the upper interior stop.

In this case, the first three windows sat side by side. After lifting the first one into place, we found that the wall had shifted over time, so each opening was out of plumb, even though the sills were still level. Since none of the openings were square, there wasn't any way to install the windows so that everything lined up with the stops and the sill. Here it was more a matter of what looked the best. We ended up shimming the windows to line up with the sill, so both sides are a little bit off. You can see this in the photo.

At this point, each window was checked for square by measuring from opposite corners to see if the measurements were equal. Then, if the measurements were off, the window was shifted over to square it up by adjusting the shims. At this time, we also opened and closed the window to make sure it worked smoothly, and checked the gap between the window and the jambs when it was closed.

Sometimes you'll end up with a window that wasn't assembled correctly. Though the measurements say it's square, you can clearly see that the window is off, or vice versa. When that happens, you have to go with what looks right.

Once the window was positioned correctly, screws were driven in through predrilled holes at each corner. While doing this, we pulled in on the window to make sure it stayed tight up against the inside stops.

On these windows, the sashes had to be taken out to do the center screws. This was done by releasing each side, which allowed them to be tipped in and then removed.

The center screws were a little different, as they also moved the jamb in or out by turning them. In our case, it didn't always work, so we shimmed the center of the window when needed.

After each window was locked into place, we checked for any light that was coming in around the perimeter, as this would indicate a gap in the caulk. It seemed that no matter how much caulk was used, on almost every window there was light showing on one of the lower corners. We filled these gaps from the exterior side. When the gap was too narrow for the tip of the caulk gun to reach in, a short piece of 5/16 O.D. clear plastic tubing was taped to the end of the caulk tube to extend it.

To finish up the windows on the inside, the shims were cut off flush to the jambs, and the side stops were reinstalled. Then the handles were screwed on. This photo shows one of the windows after it was done.

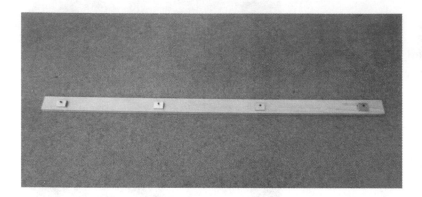

Once we were finished inside, we moved on to the exterior, since metal trim strips still had to be installed around the perimeter of the windows. These would cover the gap between the windows and the original trim on the house. The problem was that the size of the gap varied, so I made a jig that allowed us to cut the strips to whatever size was needed.

As you can see in these photos, the jig consists of short lengths of aluminum channel that are screwed to a straight 1x4. The idea here is pretty simple. Let's say that you've determined a strip should be 3/4 of an inch wide. To cut that size, the strip is marked at 3/4 inch on each end, and positioned on the jig so the marks are sitting right over the edge of the board. Then the strip is locked into place by tightening the screws on the aluminum channel, and it's cut on a table saw that has the fence adjusted so the blade sits just off the edge of the board. This way, anything that hangs over will be cut off. When doing this, a metal-cutting blade is used.

When installing the strips, we found that most of them had to be tapered. Some would need a straight taper from one end to the other, while others would be one width for first half, and then taper the rest of the way. For instance, the first half might be 1 inch, and then taper down to 13/16 at the far end. Because of this, we measured at several points for each strip. On strips that were pretty narrow, the metal would flex enough to allow us to make the cut in one pass. On wider strips that were more rigid, each half was cut separately.

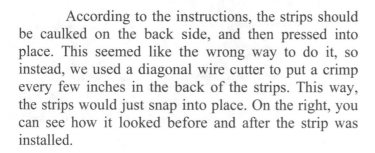

According to the instructions, the strips should be caulked on the back side, and then pressed into place. This seemed like the wrong way to do it, so instead, we used a diagonal wire cutter to put a crimp every few inches in the back of the strips. This way, the strips would just snap into place. On the right, you can see how it looked before and after the strip was installed.

# INSTALLING KITCHEN CABINETS

When installing kitchen cabinets, they should be level and in a straight line, even if the floor and/or the wall is off. Begin by going over the floor and the wall with a level to see what you have to work with. Generally you start on the upper cabinets. These are installed by first drawing a level line across the wall to mark the position of the lower edge of the cabinets. It helps to attach a board to the wall, following this line, so the cabinets will be supported at the correct height by simply resting them on top of it.

Since there could be a lot of weight, two screws are driven into each stud behind the upper cabinets. To avoid unnecessary holes, find the position of every stud before you get started, so you know exactly where to put the screws. This way, the upper cabinets can be lifted up into position and quickly attached to the wall.

As the cabinets go into place, the face frames are lined up and clamped together. Then they're attached to each other with screws. When using flathead screws, you'll need three different drill bits: a pilot bit for drilling the full length of the screw, one that's the outside diameter of the screw for drilling through the first cabinet, and a countersinking bit for recessing the screw head. By going through the first cabinet with a larger bit, after the pilot hole is drilled, the screw will pull the two together. Drill bits are also available that are specifically made for this purpose, so you can do everything in one step. If the screws are hard to drive in, or feel like they're going to break, it helps to lubricate them. I keep a chunk of bees wax or paraffin for this purpose, and rub the threads against it.

When installing the lower cabinets, you begin by putting the first one into place, and shim it so it's level across the top. Then the second cabinet is put into position, and it's shimmed to line up with the first. Then the third one goes in, as do any others that follow. By the second or third cabinet, you'll see how important it is to get the first one right.

On floors that aren't level, it's easier to start on the high side, so the first cabinet will be against the floor, and others that follow will be raised up on shims. One exception to this is when there's a corner cabinet. In that case, the corner cabinet would generally be installed first.

Where the cabinets are against the wall, they're attached with a single screw going into each stud along the upper edge of the cabinets. Then other screws are added, if needed, to pull the end cabinet(s) tight against the wall. The face frames should be attached to each other in the same manner as the upper cabinets.

Besides being level and lining up along the upper edge, the front of the cabinets should also be in a straight line. This is done by inserting shims between the cabinets and the wall at any stud where it's needed.

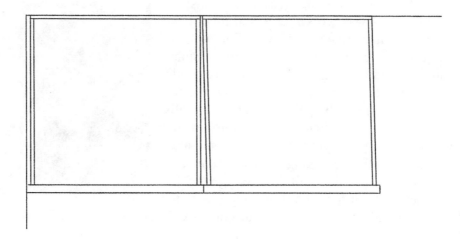

While doing the lower cabinets, you may find that some of them are racked, which means they're out of square. You'll see this by the gap being uneven between the cabinets, as shown in the drawing. A little out of square isn't much of a problem, but at some point the drawers won't track right, and they'll stick out farther on one side than the other. The overhang on the end of the countertop will also be off if the end cabinet is racked.

On cabinets that start at a corner, this is easy to fix, since you can force them into place as you screw each cabinet to the studs. On island cabinets, or ones that are only attached to one wall, you can't always totally straighten them. Putting shims between the cabinets will even up the gap; but, if one of the cabinets is way off, it could pull the others out of position. In this case, the only way that I can think of to square up the cabinet that's racked is to hold it in the correct position with a long clamp, and then attach a wire or a sheet metal strap between the two corners to hold it in place. Since it would be up against the countertop, you'll never notice it.

If the walls aren't plumb, you'll be left with a tapered gap between the end cabinet(s) and the wall. If you know this in advance, you can have the end cabinet(s) made so that the face frame overlaps the side, or the side overlaps the back. This will allow you to plane it to match the wall. This is also done for the upper cabinets.

When the cabinets are installed over a finished floor, shimming them up will leave you with a gap to hide. On the front edge, a kick plate is generally installed that goes tight against floor. This may have to be planed or belt-sanded to get a tight fit. On the side, or the back, you'll have to determine what works best in that location. Base shoe may be all that's needed. Another option is to use a thin board that matches the kick plate.

When installing a vanity in a bathroom, sometimes it better to level it by removing wood from the bottom. A plane or a belt sander can be used for doing this. On tile floors, you might have to scribe the lower edge to match the tile.

# CAULK

Years ago, I thought caulking was easy. I'd just lay a bead around whatever I was working on, and then move on without giving it much thought. Now I find it more difficult, as I've learned to appreciate a professional looking job, and that's harder to achieve. When saying this, I'm not talking about exterior caulk. It's one thing to caulk an exterior joint that's going to be painted over, and totally another to do the seams in a kitchen or a bathroom that you'll be seeing every day for years to come. Sometimes I'll hear someone say that caulking is easy, but I've generally found that those people don't do a very good job.

One summer, back in the 70's, I did some work for the HRA, installing windows at an apartment complex. Then, once the windows were in, two of us caulked around them. We worked as a team, with one guy applying the caulk, while the other followed behind, smoothing it down. At first, we switched off on who did what, but it didn't take long to see that it was much easier for him to smooth the caulk. Those joints were pretty wide, but he had no problem wiping them down in a single pass. When it was my turn, some of the caulk was getting past the side of my finger, making a mess of it. My joints also dipped in too much compared to his. It turned out that his fingers were fatter, which was an advantage in this case. After that, I began to pay more attention any time I caulked a joint, and tried to learn what it takes to do a good job.

I've read instructions where it says to push the caulk gun as you fill the joint. I've always pulled it, and so have most of the people that I've watched. When pulling it, you get a better look at the bead. When pushing the gun, any lumps and unevenness in the caulk will be somewhat smoothed out by the tip, but the caulk tends to get on both sides of the joint, which is what I'm trying to avoid.

When you cut the tip on a new cartridge, consider how wide you want the seam to be. For a narrow bead of caulk, the hole in the tip should be smaller. You're only going to make the job more difficult if the hole is too big, since the bead will be too wide to begin with, and you'll end up removing most of the caulk as you wipe it down. On a wide seam, it's the opposite, where having a small hole is a problem because it takes too long to fill the joint. It's also more difficult to get an even bead.

If there's a trick to getting a good joint, it's to start by laying out a nice even bead, without any gobs or lumps. Then, as you smooth it down, don't let the caulk squeeze out past your finger. On longer joints, excess caulk will build up against your finger as you go along. Before it gets to the point where it starts to squeeze out on the side, stop and wipe it off with a paper towel. Then continue on, smoothing the joint and wiping the excess off your finger as you go. After doing this, you'll be able to see every place that you stopped, so you'll have to make at least one more pass. Try to smooth it down in one continuance sweep. Don't press too hard, or you'll just dig out more caulk.

It helps to lubricate your finger on a long pass. If the caulk is latex or siliconized acrylic, dip your finger in water. When using silicone, wet your finger with mineral spirits (paint thinner). This will dissolve the surface of the caulk, smoothing it down and helping your finger slide easier. Then after you're finished, use a paper towel to clean up any residue on each side. When doing this, I like to dampen the paper towel with whatever I used on my finger. Be sure to stay away from the joint itself, or you'll wreck the edge of it.

In some locations, it's important for a caulked joint to look perfect, with a smooth bead and straight edges. This would include: kitchen counters, vanities, sinks and tub surrounds, etc., especially where the color isn't a match. For joints like this, sometimes I'll tape the outside border where the caulk is being laid. This is the best way that I know of to control the edge. Another place where I'll use tape is when going around a toilet on a rough tile floor. Once caulk gets into tile like that, it's hard to get it out. I know, by mentioning tape, some people are going to be rolling their eyes, thinking that I'm a little crazy, but the results are noticeably better.

When doing this, I either use blue masking tape (painters tape) or Frog tape, since it's less likely to pull the paint off when taping a wall. Make sure there's a seam at each corner, and try to lay the pieces of tape in the same order that they'll be removed. This way, the tape can quickly be pulled, since each piece will lift up the one that was laid after it.

Before taping, first I'll determine the width that I want the seam to be. To my eye, a thin bead of caulk looks better that a wide one, so I won't go any wider than I have to. If there isn't much of a gap, I generally run the tape about an eighth inch off each side of the corner. When caulking around the base of a toilet or a pedestal sink, I think it looks best if the caulk doesn't extend out from the base. A toilet is caulked on the front edge and along both sides, but it's left open in the back.

I generally do one side at a time when caulking a kitchen countertop, vanity, tub, etc. Once I've applied the caulk to the first side, I'll quickly begin to smooth it down. On the first pass, I just want to remove most of the excess. On the next pass, I try to do it in one continuous sweep. I want to get it right in the fewest passes. If the caulk sits too long, it tends to ripple as it's wiped down. It also does this if you make too many passes when smoothing it. Lubricating your finger will buy you extra time, but it won't eliminate the problem. Once it looks right, I'll quickly pull the tape. Then, if it looks good, it's done. But if the edge is too thick on either side, it will need another pass. To do this, I'll lubricate my finger, and gently do it in one continuous sweep to smooth down both edges. Then I'll move on to the next side.

As you smooth down the caulk, your finger should generally be held at an angle, so the caulk ends at the edge of the tape, on both sides. On toilets, come straight from the side, so the caulk doesn't extend out from the base.

Caulk shrinks as it dries, so large gaps may have to be done a second time. If that's the case, there's no sense trying to be too neat on the first coat. I'll also keep the first coat a little narrow, so the second one will overlap it.

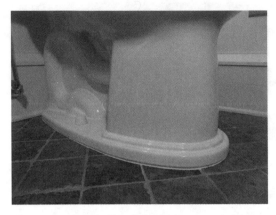

In the kitchen or a bathroom, prepare the surface by wiping it down with rubbing alcohol. Even after I've scraped off the old caulk and washed everything, I'll still give the area a final wipe down with alcohol. This will help to remove any soap scum, mineral spirits, or anything else that could prevent the caulk from getting a good bond. Mineral spirits leaves an oily film that can also keep the tape from sticking to the surface.

Where interior caulk will be left unpainted, such as in kitchens and bathrooms, it's best to use a caulk that has a glossy finish. It will be easier to keep clean, and looks better over time. Kitchen and Bath siliconized acrylic has a glossy finish. So does silicone caulk. One advantage of acrylic caulk is that it can be painted, while silicone can't. I generally use silicone caulk on sinks and faucets, or anyplace where it's always wet. It's also used on drains where plumber's putty can't be used.

Last weekend I helped a friend replace three toilets, because the original ones had plugged way too often. By the time they were installed, it was late in the day, and I still had to caulk around them. Because of that, I had to work fast, so using tape wasn't an option since it would take too long. What I ended up doing was to use Kitchen and Bath siliconized acrylic, and used water for the cleanup. Then I cut the tip so there was only a small hole in the end of the cartridge. One of the problems when caulking around toilets is that sometimes there isn't enough room to hold the caulk gun at the right angle, so on part of it, the caulk was thicker than I would have liked.

After the caulk was applied, I quickly smoothed it down and cleaned my finger when needed. Then I kept dipping my finger in a bowl of water as I quickly made several passes around the toilet, pressing hard enough so the caulk wouldn't extend past the base. Once it looked right, I cleaned any residue off the toilet and wiped down the floor, making sure that I stayed just off the edge of the caulk. When doing this, I used a paper towel that been dipped in the water, with the excess squeezed out. If I found any bad spots or accidentally touched the caulk, I wet my finger and smoothed it down, and then cleaned around it. On tile floors, clean up the edge if the caulk spreads out too far as it passes by a grout line. To prevent this, sometimes I'll put a piece of tape over each grout line where I want the caulk to end.

Every now and then, a new device comes on the market that's advertised to make it easy for anyone to lay a perfect bead of caulk. I've tried some of them, but so far, I've been disappointed with the results. When applying caulk, smoothing the bead is the easy part. Controlling the outside edge is the problem, and that's where every device that I've tried has failed. As the caulk is being smoothed down, the tool has to prevent it from squeezing out on both sides of the joint. To do this, it has to be flexible enough to follow both surfaces when the contours are uneven, such as with tile. The ones that I've used weren't able to do the job. I've also tried other things that were laying around the house, such as spoons, which will work sometimes on larger joints on the exterior, and are good for collecting the excess caulk as it's being smoothed down.

# CONCRETE

This section is different than the others, as there aren't any instructions on how to pour concrete. I'm nowhere near qualified enough to tell anyone how to do this, so instead, I'm going to concentrate on what can go wrong. It's sad to say, but I know more about that side of it.

On most jobs, the only time I work with concrete is to mix up bags of pre-mix for deck footings, or to patch a basement floor that's been cut into for running new drain pipes. When working on slabs, I've generally just been a laborer for friends or family members, where I was called, and then showed up on the day the concrete was coming. Some of those jobs turned out good, while others went bad, and always for the same reasons.

You can generally tell how a job is going to go as soon as you get out of your vehicle. On bad days, you'll find the homeowner all alone, still putting in the forms, as he tells you the concrete should be here any minute. At this point, you already know you're in trouble. The forms should be in ahead of time, and where are the other guys that are supposed to be helping?

When things are going smoothly, pouring concrete isn't bad at all. Myself, I like working with it. But once you get behind, it becomes one of the most unforgiving materials that you'll ever work with. If the concrete is starting to set up, and there aren't enough people to do the different jobs, the finish is going to come out bad, and there isn't anything that you can do about it. To prevent this from happening, don't be stubborn. If you can't get everything prepared in time, or can't get enough help on a certain day, postpone the job. That's what you'd do if there was a heavy rain, so there's no reason that you can't do it because of this.

Although it bothers me when everything isn't ready, the jobs I've been on that went the worst were mainly caused by not having enough help. This was partly from not trying hard enough when calling people, and partly from underestimating the number of people that it takes to do the job. If you're pouring a slab that requires four guys who are professionals, many homeowners assume that with three friends helping, they can do the same thing. Unless you're all experienced at this, how in the world do you think you're going to do the same job with the same number of people. This is one of my pet peeves, and something that I've never understood. A professional does this every day. He knows exactly what to do, and doesn't waste any time. Because of that, he's probably worth more than two guys with less experience.

Let's break a job down to see how many guys are needed. Since I'm just an amateur with limited experience, I might be wrong on this. On this job, we'll be pouring a basement floor where wheelbarrows will be used to haul the concrete for part of it. Chalk lines are snapped on the walls, and pipes have been laid across stakes in the center, so they're at the same height as the lines. To begin, two guys will be needed to man the wheelbarrows. As they're doing this, someone has to form a curb of concrete along the chalk line to be used for screeding the slab. Someone will also have to pull the mesh up off the ground, if it's being used, as the wheelbarrows are being emptied. That person will also have to move the concrete where it's needed. Then, once you've gone a little ways, two of you will have to start screeding. So now, at the same time, you're hauling concrete, lifting the mesh, moving the mix where it's needed, and screeding it. After a section's been done, someone also has to go over it with a bull float.

When the first half is finished, the pipes and the stakes are removed, and the second half is done in the same manner. Then you have to wait until the concrete has set up enough, and then hand trowel the corners and around any drain pipes, and go over the slab with a power trowel.

By my count, at least five guys are needed for this. If there's less than that, you'll have to keep switching jobs, so it would go a lot slower. I've been on similar jobs where we were two guys short. These were some of the most frustrating days that I've ever had. There wasn't anyone to pull the mesh up, so it didn't do any good, and by the time you started to screed and bull float, the mix had sat too long, so it was twice as hard to do the job. After a while, I just hoped that the slab wouldn't look like crap once it was finished.

The following is a list of things to do or to consider.

* Don't call in the order if you're not going to be ready. Have the forms in, and your tools ready to go before the truck gets there. This is not the time to be rushing around, trying to finish up. The concrete can only sit in the truck for so long.

* Order enough, so you're not short. If the floor has dips or humps in it, your calculations on the amount of concrete that's needed may be off. You should also have a plan, in case you have extra. Maybe you could use a stoop, or an apron by the door. If so, have the ground prepared and the wood for the forms ready to go.

* Get plenty of help. This might be the time to call in favors. If you're short even one person, you could have a big problem. Also, consider how dependable your friends are. Will they show up? The concrete may have to be hauled in wheelbarrows, and concrete is heavy. Are the helpers strong enough to handle a loaded wheelbarrow? Everyone should have rubber boots. On jobs that I've been on, where there was plenty of help, there was almost a relaxed atmosphere about it. On others, where there weren't enough people, you had to hurry the entire time, just hoping the job would turn out decent.

* Don't let your ego get in the way of common sense. If you're not experienced at this, get someone to help who is, and put them in charge. The job will go smoother this way, and you'll get better results.

* On larger slabs, you may want to use a power trowel to finish the concrete. Try to find someone who has experience using one, and knows how the blades should be adjusted. If you don't know what you're doing, you could end up spinning in circles and digging up rocks. I'm a little torn when I see this happen. While I know that the slab is taking a beating, it's kind of funny to watch.

* On some jobs, it might be best to pump the concrete.

* Tools that you may need are shovels, rake, wheelbarrows, trowels, floats, edger, bull float, tamper, power trowel, chalk line, string, level, laser level or transit, etc. Also needed are form boards, screed board, stakes, and a large hammer for pounding them in.

* Have a spare wheelbarrow, in case one gets a flat tire. Watch out for the cut ends on reinforcing mesh, as they can go right through a tire. You can make a catwalk for hauling the concrete using wide boards or strips of plywood.

* Ground preparation: Compact and level the sand before the concrete is poured. If there's only a thin layer of sand, or you're patching a floor, just spray it down with water. If it's a thick layer and/or for a larger slab, you should probably use a power tamper. These can be rented at most rental centers. It's surprising how much the sand can settle. Sand is easily leveled by dragging a 2x4 across it.

\*      Footings for houses and garages should be reinforced with rebar. Steel mesh is used for reinforcing concrete slabs. It won't stop cracks from forming, but it will help to keep them from getting larger. Expansion joints are used to prevent cracks from starting, and to contain them. You can also order concrete with polypropylene fibers mixed in, which helps to prevent cracks in slabs.

\*      If the concrete floor is going to be in a heated area, putting insulation under it will make it noticeably warmer and save on the heating bill. Two inches of high density extruded foam is what's commonly used. When in-floor heat is being installed, the insulation is a necessity.

\*      When patios or walkways are next to the house, they should be lower than the inside floor, and also sloped away from the house. This will keep rain and melting snow from coming in. You should consider the slope, anytime you're pouring concrete outdoors.

# ROOFS

It's raining outside as I'm working on the book, which reminds me that I have a couple of things to say about roofs. One of the first things I notice when looking over a roof are the edges. What you want to see are edges that were cleanly cut and are in a straight line. If metal drip edge isn't used, the shingles should hang out past the edge of the wood trim. This keeps the water from coming in along the outside edge as the it runs down the roof. Shingle manufacturers like to recommend a 3/8 inch overhang, though I can't remember ever seeing any that were done that way. Most of the time, I see shingles that overhang the trim by at least an inch, and sometimes as much as two. A potential problem with a longer overhang is that there's more for the wind to catch. The shingles could also curl down and possibly crack. When using wood trim for the edge, I generally set the overhang at 3/4 - 1 inch, which is enough to hide small variations in the trim. On a edge that isn't straight, you may need a little more. Myself, I'd rather have more overhang with a straight edge, than a short overhang that's crooked.

When using metal drip edge, the instructions will tell you to run the shingles flush to the outside edge. This is easier to do, though I still prefer a short overhang. When using it, I generally give the shingles about a 1/2 inch overhang, and go a little bigger if the metal drip edge is crooked.

On many jobs, the shingles are installed so they run long on one end. Then the edge is trimmed after the roof is finished by snapping a chalk line, and then cutting along the line with a utility knife that has a hook blade in it. The temperature of the shingles makes a big difference in how easy they are to cut. In the spring or the fall, it's best to make the cuts before it gets too cold in the evening, otherwise it's much harder to pull the blade through the shingles. There can also be a problem if the shingles are too hot, as the tar tends to gum up the blade.

When cutting the shingles, keep the blade centered on the chalk line, and try to cut square to the shingles. If you were only cutting through one shingle, the angle wouldn't matter, but on a roof you're cutting through two or three layers, one at a time, so the angle that you hold the blade at will make a noticeable difference in how straight the edge looks. When you're cutting the shingles to length, before they're installed, use a framing square and a utility knife with a standard blade in it, and cut from the back. Do the cutting on top of a scrap piece of plywood or OSB.

Sometimes an edge can come out bad. Maybe you weren't careful when following the line, or maybe the cut was made at an awkward angle, or the shingles were cold. If this is an edge that you'll be seeing every day, you may want to clean it up. To do this, I clamp my aluminum straightedge along the edge of the shingles, using spring clamps, and position it where I want the cut to be made. Then I'll slice off the high spots by running a standard utility blade along the straightedge, coming from underneath.

# ROOF VENTS

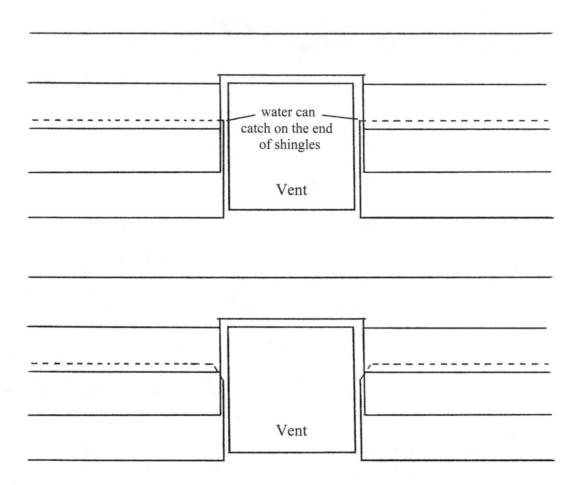

Years ago, right after roofing a friend's cabin, it rained hard all night and water leaked in around a couple of the vents. These vents were on the lower slope of a double-pitched roof, so a lot of water was running past them. To stop the leaks, I put roof cement under the shingles where they went around the vents. Later on, I learned that water going by the vents can catch on the end of the shingles, and then run back along the upper edge. From there, it could either come in under the vents, or run down the roof between the shingles and the felt paper, and then leak in at the first hole that it found.

This is shown in the first drawing. Here you can see how water could catch the edge of a shingle, and then run back along it. The second drawing shows the correct way to install the vent, by trimming the shingles that could cause the problem. By cutting off the upper corners, there's nothing to catch on, so the water will continue to run down the roof.

Another place where you could have the same problem is in the valleys. Cutting the tips off the shingles, on both sides of the valley, will eliminates this potential problem. I do this with a hook blade after I've finished cutting the edge, following a chalk line, and slip my straightedge under the shingles to protect the valley. This probably isn't necessary if ice and water shield has been installed in the valleys, since the water would have to run back a long ways to get past it.

# ALUMINUM FASCIA

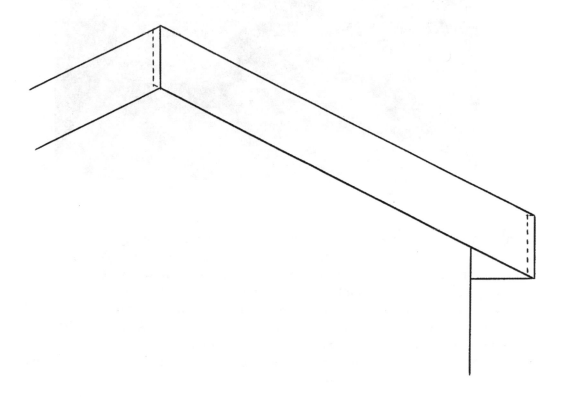

In this drawing, aluminum fascia runs along the lower edge of the roof, and then wraps around the corner, where it gets overlapped by the fascia coming down from the peak. That piece is cut to fit flush on the lower end, and overlaps the peak. Then that piece is overlapped by the one that follows, which is cut so it's centered on the peak. On both pieces, you want a clean cut where it's going to show. Though it can be done with a tin snips, I find that making several passes with a sharp utility knife will give you a better edge. This only works on the main surface of the fascia. The lower edge will still have to be cut with a tin snips. When using this method, the blade doesn't go all the way through the metal, but it cuts deep enough so that you only have to bend it back and forth a few times for it to snap off cleanly. When doing this, use a straightedge, and position it so it rests on the side of the line of what you'll be using. This way, the fascia will be protected if the utility knife happens to slip.

# SHARPENING TOOLS

These days, there are so many different power tools available that using hand tools has almost become a lost art. But even so, there are still times when the best tool for the job is a chisel or a hand plane. Some of the things they're used for include: cutting pockets for hinges and striker plates, planing doors that stick, shaving down high spots on jambs and framing, scribing edges, and notching boards.

Every now and then I'll be at someone's house, going through my tools looking for a block plane or a chisel, and the homeowner will say, "I have one of those, use mine." Almost always, the tool they hand me is dull and/or out of adjustment. In this condition, it's just about worthless.

One thing about cutting-tools is that the sharper they are, the better they work, and the easier they are to use. Sharpening planes and chisels is pretty simple. You just need a sharpening stone, and a jig helps for holding the blade at a fixed angle. There are several types of sharpening stones. There are oil stones, water stones, diamond, and ceramic. You can also use Wet-or-dry sandpaper for sharpening.

A whole chapter could be devoted to sharpening, and books have been written on it, but here I'm going to keep it as short as I can. When sharpening a tool, the idea is to use something abrasive to grind and polish the edge, so it comes to a sharp point. A course abrasive will cut the metal faster, but for an edge to be truly sharp, it has to be smooth and have a polished look to it. That's the reason for having different stones, such as course and fine grit. You start sharpening with a courser stone, to get the edge, and then switch over to one that's smoother to finish it off. Medium grit stones are in between. They don't cut as fast, and the edge will never be as sharp as one that's more polished.

So what's sharp? That depends on the person, and what you're using the tool for. My tools take a beating, and many times they're used for things that they weren't designed for. Because of that, I just need them sharp enough to do the job at hand. If I'm using a block plane to take off high spots on the framing, my main concern is that I'm able to remove wood quickly. This is hard on a blade if you keep hitting knots, so here there's no reason to have the best edge. On window jambs, I'd want a sharper, more polished edge for a smoother finish. When using a chisel to cut hinge pockets on an oak jamb, I want it to be razor sharp, so it's sharp enough to finish off the pockets without having to use a mallet or a hammer.

Sometimes a plane will feel sharp, but it still won't cut right. This is generally caused by the edge being turned on the blade, which means it's curled up slightly, so that it's sliding over the board instead of digging in. This is easily fixed with some light sharpening. You could also roll the edge back by giving it a few strokes with a sharpening steel.

While sharpening, use the same angle that was originally ground on the blade. Then keep it at the same angle on every stroke, so you don't round it off. As the edge is getting close, a burr will start to form on the other side of the blade. At that point, you may want to shift over to a smoother stone.

Once you've got a good edge, the blade could also be raised up slightly, so you're only sharpening the very tip of it. When doing this, use light strokes and a smooth stone. Then anytime the edge is resharpened, go back to the original angle to begin with. If I'm in a hurry, sometimes I also do this to quickly touch up an edge.

The stone can also be used on the back side of the blade. This could be to be flatten out the back if the edge is rounded off, to polish off the grinding marks, or just to remove the burr. When doing this, it's important that the blade is held flat against the stone.

When using a jig for sharpening, the blade is generally moved forward and back, because of the wheel. Otherwise, you can go any direction you want: forward and back, strictly forward, in circles, or by going backwards, as long as you maintain the same angle. I've read that you'll get the sharpest edge by going backwards. When sharpening a knife, I generally push it across the stone in an arc, and switch sides every so many strokes. If I'm trying to concentrate on one part of the blade, I'll go in circles.

In the photo on the last page, a sharpening jig is being used to sharpen a plane blade on a diamond stone. With this jig, the angle is determined by the height of the wheel, and by how far the blade extends out from the sharpener. Other types of jigs are also available. On some, the wheel will roll across the stone itself. When setting the angle, sometimes it's hard to determine where the stone is actually making contact with the blade. Coloring the edge with a Sharpie, and then seeing where it gets rubbed off, will help.

In the photo above, I'm sharpening a chisel freehand, because it won't fit on my jig. This is a little more difficult, since it's hard to maintain the same angle on every stroke. The photo is also misleading, because I actually use both hands. But here, one was needed to hold the camera. What I generally do is to use my other index finger to lightly press the beveled edge against the stone. For me, this helps to keep a consistent angle. When that isn't enough, I still keep a finger on the end of the blade, but I'll change my grip with the other hand, and either have my thumb or a finger hang over the side so that it just barely touches the stone as I'm sharpening.

A grinder would be faster, but using a high speed grinder is a good way to destroy a blade if you don't know what you're doing. One reason is because the edge could lose it's temper if it gets too hot. Another is that the blade may only be properly hardened at the very end. I've owned chisels and planes that held a good edge at first, but after sharpening them many times, they just weren't the same. After that, I couldn't get them as sharp, and the edge would quickly dull.

On the other hand, a slow speed grinder that uses water was designed for sharpening. There should be a guide to keep the blade at the same angle, and you won't lose the temper since the blade doesn't get hot.

# SAWING OPENINGS IN CONCRETE WALLS

When finishing off a basement, you'll commonly have to install an egress window (shown in the upper photo) if you plan on having a bedroom. This generally isn't a problem with wood framing, since all you have to do is to frame the opening and then cut it out, or cut the opening first, and then frame around it.

Sawing through concrete is a little more difficult, but still within reason for the average homeowner. To begin, lines have to be drawn for cutting out the opening. Lines will be needed on both sides of the wall, and they have to match up with each other. To do this, you have to find a spot that every measurement will be based off. This could be the edge of an existing window, the corner on one of the blocks, or anything else that can be seen from both sides of the wall. Then once you've determined a base point, you measure off it, and draw the lines with a magic marker and a level. Sometimes there isn't such a spot. In that case, you'll have to drill a hole through the wall, while making sure that the bit is held square to the wall. Then that hole is used as the base point. When drawing the lines, make sure you allow for any boards that will be attached to the perimeter, and also for the gap around the window,

The best way to cut the hole is with a diamond blade. Abrasive blades are cheaper, but diamond blades cut faster, and the cost is reasonable. On block walls, a circular saw with a 7 inch blade works fine. Cut from both sides, and then knock out the blocks with a sledge hammer. Since you can't cut all the way through, some of the webbing may have to be chiseled off to finish the opening.

The other photos show a poured concrete wall where the opening was enlarged. Originally, the area behind it was just a crawl space, but we dug it out down to the footings so it could be used as a storage area. This was the same as sawing an opening for an egress

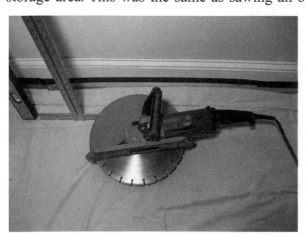

window, though in this case, the wall was thirteen inches thick. To make the cuts, we rented a heavy duty saw with a 14 inch blade. This was the first time that I used a saw this big, and at the start, I wasn't sure who was in control, me or the saw. Even with a 14 inch blade, the saw only cut 4 1/2 inches deep, so we were still left with 4 inches in the middle that wasn't cut. Luckily, the concrete was soft, and it wasn't too hard to break it off.

In this case, the lines matched up, and the cuts came out pretty good. Then, once they were cleaned up, we mixed up bags of concrete and poured a floor in the storage area.

When installing egress windows in block walls or poured concrete, 2x pressure-treated boards are generally installed around the perimeter using Tapcons and/or construction adhesive. This provides a nailing surface for installing the window and attaching the trim. With poured concrete, you'll have a solid edge for attaching the boards, but on block walls, there will be gaps and holes because of the webbing. Depending on their location, they may have to be filled with mortar or concrete, either to fill in spots that are missing, or for attaching the boards along the edge.

Years ago, I'd stuff fiberglass into the open cavities if I thought it would stay dry. I've also used foam that was either injected or cut to fit, trying to cut down on the amount of heat loss around the window. These days, I seldom do it, and insulate the whole wall instead, if it needs it.

On this wall, a door was being installed, so once the opening was cut, we moved the copper pipes so they went above the ceiling, and then installed 2x6s around the opening for attaching the jambs. The lower photo shows how it looked after it was finished.

441

# POOR MAN AIR FILTER

When we cut the opening in the basement wall on the last two pages, we were working in an area that was already finished. Because of that, the furniture was covered, and plastic was hung around the immediate area to enclose it. Then we put a shop vacuum on the outside of the enclosure, and slipped the hose through a small hole in the plastic to suck out the dust. To provide air, we also cut a larger hole in the plastic on the opposite side.

For mixing the concrete, we used a homemade air filter instead, since it would take a while for us to mix up the fifty bags of concrete that were needed for the floor. To build the filter, cardboard was cut and then taped together to make a box that was just slightly larger than the fan. Then one end was folded over, and an opening was cut into it. Over this opening, we attached an inexpensive furnace filter using vapor barrier tape. Then the plastic was cut out for the box to slip through, and the edge of it was taped to the cardboard, so there was a good seal. Once that was finished, the fan was slipped into the box, with it turned so that it would blow out towards the main room. This way, the air would be pulled through the filter, and remove any dust that was in the air.

442

# DRILLING HOLES IN CONCRETE AND TILE

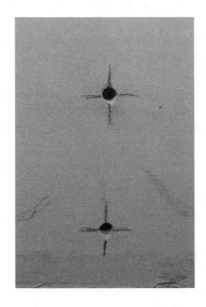

For drilling holes in concrete, you'll need a masonry bit, which is a carbide bit that's specifically designed for this purpose. You'll also need a hammer drill, unless the concrete is really soft. Sometimes it doesn't matter if the hole is off to one side or the other, such as when drilling into a basement floor to attach the walls, while at other times, it's important that the hole is in exactly the right spot. In that case, I've found that it's best to draw intersecting lines (crosshairs) that are centered where you want the hole to be. If you only marked the center of the hole, the mark would disappear as soon you as you started to drill. By having intersecting lines, you can still see where the hole should go, and then shift the drill bit over as needed. Any adjustments have to be made in the very beginning. After that, you just try to keep the bit square to the surface. In the upper left photo, you can see that the holes are pretty well centered on the lines. In the photo on the right, you can see why the holes had to be drilled accurately. Here, new baseboard was being installed by driving trim screws into plastic anchors that werc inserted into the holes. Two holes were drilled every 2 feet, so around a dozen holes had to line up with the ones in the baseboard.

When drilling into tile, you might need a diamond bit if it's a large hole, or you don't want to risk hurting the tile. Some tile, such as porcelain, can be so hard that a masonry bit can barely go into it. One time, before I owned any diamond bits, it took me most of a day trying to drill six holes for installing a shower door. A diamond bit would have gone right through it. Now I have a couple of them. I use a 1/4 inch bit to run screws and Tapcons through tile or for installing plastic anchors, and a 1 inch for going through tile with 1/2 inch and 3/4 inch copper pipe.

The lower photo shows a couple of masonry bits. The carbide tip is what allows them to drill into concrete. On the left is a 1 inch diamond bit. When using this bit, you can't just stab it into what you're drilling, because it won't stay in place. One way to do it is to tip the bit so that it only makes contact on one side. Then, once you've got the hole started, the bit is slowly straightened. Another method is to drill the same size hole through a board, and then position the board where you want the other hole to be to keep the bit from moving. With either method, use water to keep the diamond bit cool.

# BUILDING PEMITS

In many areas, building permits are required to work on your house, though when they're needed will vary, depending on where you live. For large projects, such as when building an addition, it makes sense to have someone go over the plan to make sure it's sound and that everything is sized correctly. On others, to me it seems totally unnecessary, and appears to be just another way for the local government to get more money. For example, where I live, a permit is required to install a water heater. For a gas water heater, it costs around 100 dollars. Sometimes it's also not practical. If you have a family, and your water heater goes out on Friday evening, there's no way that you're going to wait until Monday, just to pull a permit. Most likely, a new water heater will be installed on Saturday, and you're not going to waste your money pulling a permit after the job is already done. Besides, you already spent a lot on the water heater.

Once a permit has been pulled, the job will probably have to be inspected. The number of inspections will also vary, depending on where you live. I've worked on houses where there was an inspection for the footings, the framing, two for the wiring, and another for the plumbing. Added to that were inspections for the heating, the insulation and the vapor barrier, and two for the deck. I've also been on jobs where there weren't any inspections. My brother's cabin is on a popular lake in northern Minnesota, and the only inspection that was required was for the electrical work. While I can't recommend that you skip the permit and quietly do the job, that's how it's done quite a bit of the time, and sometimes it's a lot easier that way.

The good thing about having a permit, provided you have a friendly building inspector, is that now you have someone to answer questions concerning the job, -- whether it's the size that something has to be, or the required way for a job to be done. Just don't ask too many questions. If it appears that you have the general idea on how to do something, you shouldn't have a problem. But on the other hand, if it looks like you're in over your head, and you ask too many stupid questions, the inspector may get sick of answering them and tell you to talk to a professional.

While most building inspectors are decent people who know what they're doing, once in a while you'll find one who's totally unqualified for the job, or in some cases, make up their own rules. I remember one time that I was shingling a roof, and an inspector stopped by and told me that I had to use shorter nails so they wouldn't go through the sheathing, because water could then weep down through the wood. I told him that once the water got under the shingles, you already had a problem, but it didn't make any difference. So while he was there, I had to switch over to 1/2 inch long roofing nails that I happened to find, and then switched back to the original ones as soon as he left. It turned out that what the code actually said was that the nails "had" to be long enough to go through the sheathing on this particular roof. Another time, I was working on a friend's deck when the building inspector stopped by and said there couldn't be any gaps over 3 inches between the balusters. I didn't question it, since this house was used for Daycare, so I assumed it was a special rule because of that. A year later, a different inspector asked why the boards were so close together.

Over time, I've found that it's best to find out what the rules and requirements are before you get started on a project, so mistakes aren't made, causing work to be stopped or from having to be redone. More than once, I've assumed that I knew the rules, and then found out later that the rules had changed.

Originally, the reason for building codes was for safety. These days, unions have used their influence to make it more difficult for homeowners to do their own work. That doesn't sit too well with me, since I don't like being told what to do. Personally, I think you should be able to do whatever you want on your own house, as long as the work meets reasonable safety standards. I've also read that in some states, a homeowner can't make any changes to the original plumbing, in their own home. In Minnesota, homeowners can work on the wiring and plumbing if they sign an affidavit that says they're going to do the work themselves. This rule is broken all the time, and building inspectors generally look the other way. But, in my opinion, it shouldn't matter who does the work, as long as the job is done right. That's enough ranting. Following are some code rules and sizing tables for working on your projects. The residential deck information sheets that are shown have been handed out for years in my area. Recently, some changes have been made concerning: footings, cantilevering, ledger bolt size and placement, joist length, etc. Check the current rules for your area.

# MAXIMUM SIZE OF NOTCHES AND HOLES IN STUDS

Load Bearing    Non-Load Bearing

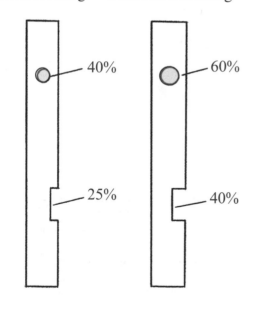

## LOAD BEARING WALLS

|  | 2x4 | 2x6 |
|---|---|---|
| NOTCHES | 7/8" | 1 3/8" |
| HOLES | 1 3/8" | 2 3/16" |
| HOLES IN DOUBLED STUDS | 2" | 3 1/4" |

## NON-LOAD BEARING WALLS

|  | 2x4 | 2x6 |
|---|---|---|
| NOTCHES | 1 3/8" | 2 3/16" |
| HOLES | 2" | 3 1/4" |

Holes no closer than 5/8" to face of stud

Holes not in the same stud section as cuts or notches

60% holes OK in doubled-up studs in load bearing walls, but limited to no more than two successive studs

# MAXIMUM SIZE OF NOTCHES AND HOLES IN JOISTS AND RAFTERS

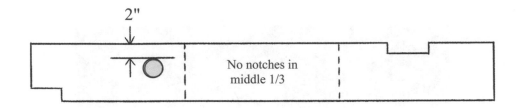

| | NOTCHES | | HOLES |
| --- | --- | --- | --- |
| | END | OUTER 1/3 | 2 INCH TO EDGE MINIMUM |
| 2x6 | 1 3/8" | 7/8" | 1 1/2" |
| 2x8 | 1 7/8" | 1 1/2" | 2 3/8" |
| 2x10 | 2 3/8" | 1 1/2" | 3 1/8" |
| 2x12 | 2 7/8" | 1 7/8" | 3 1/2" |

Holes 2" minimum to top or bottom, or notch

No notches in middle 1/3

Notches are only allowed on the upper edge of a board $\geq 4$", except at ends

Notches in sawn lumber, max 1/3 length and 1/6 depth of member

## I-JOISTS

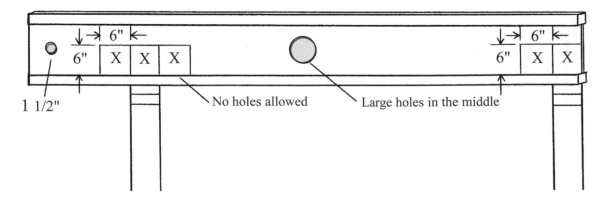

No holes allowed in areas with an X

Check with manufacturer for large holes

Holes up to 1 1/2" allowed anywhere outside of areas with an X

# Residential Decks
# Information Sheet

## Building permits

Required for any deck attached to a structure or any detached deck more than 30 inches above grade.

## Setbacks

*Decks not higher than 5 feet above grade* at any point may encroach 10 feet into the required front setback, 5 feet into the required side setback and 20 feet into the required rear setback, **provided** that a front setback of at least 20 feet, a side setback of at least 5 feet and a rear setback of at least 10 feet is maintained.

*Decks higher than 5 feet above grade* at any point may encroach 5 feet into the required front setback and 10 feet into the required rear setback, **provided** that a front setback of at least 25 feet and a rear setback of at least 20 feet is maintained. Such decks are permitted in the side yard if the setback of at least 10 feet is maintained. Encroachment into public easements of record requires written approval from the Public Works Department.

## Frost footings

Required for any deck attached to a dwelling, porch or garage that has frost footings. The minimum depth to the base of the footing is 42 inches.

## Live load

All decks shall be designed to support a live load of 40 pounds per square foot.

## Guards/guardrails

Required on all decks or stairs more than 30 inches above grade or a lower deck. *See page four for illustration.* *Exception:* On a open stairway, the triangular opening formed by the riser, tread and bottom element of a guardrail must be sized so that a six inch sphere cannot pass through.

## Cantilevers: Overhanging joists and beams

Joists should not overhang beams by more than two feet, nor should beams overhang posts by more than one foot unless a special design is approved.

## Framing details

Header beams and joists that frame into ledgers or beams shall be supported by approved framing anchors such as joist hangers.

## Flashing

All connections between deck and dwelling shall be weatherproof. Cuts in exterior finish shall be flashed.

## Nails and screws

Use only stainless steel, high strength aluminum or hot-dipped galvanized.

## Wood required

All exposed wood is required to be approved wood with natural resistance to decay (redwood, cedar, etc.) or approved treated wood. This includes posts, beams, joists, decking and railings.

Any composite or plastic decking materials must be approved by Building and Inspection prior to installation.

## Stairs

Minimum width is 36 inches. Maximum rise is 7-3/4 inches, minimum rise is 4 inches. Minimum run is 10 inches. Largest tread width or riser height shall not exceed the smallest by more than 3/8 inch. Maximum 4 inch opening at risers greater than 30 inches above grade. See *Single-Family Stairways/Guards.*

## Illumination

All exterior stairways shall be illuminated at the landing to the stairway. Illumination shall be controlled from inside the dwelling **or** automatically activated.

## Handrails

The top shall be placed not less than 34 inches or more than 38 inches above the nosing of the treads. Stairways having four or more risers shall have at least one handrail with handrail ends returned or terminated in posts. Circular hand grips shall be between 1-1/4 inches to 2 inches in cross-sectional dimension or the shape shall provide an equivalent gripping surface. See *Single-Family Stairways/Guards.*

## Special design note

Some designs may not be appropriate if a screen porch or 3-season porch on the deck platform is a future consideration. Porch and deck setbacks are not the same.

**Footings inspection required before pouring concrete.**

**Framing inspection required prior to decking if joists are less than 24 inches off the ground.**

**Final inspection of completed work required.**

## Joist span

Based on No. 2 or better wood grades.
(Design Load = 40#LL + 10#DL, Deflection= L/360)

| | Ponderosa pine | | | Southern pine | | | Western cedar | | |
|---|---|---|---|---|---|---|---|---|---|
| | 12"OC | 16"OC | 24"OC | 12"OC | 16"OC | 24"OC | 12"OC | 16"OC | 24"OC |
| **2x6** | 9-2 | 8-4 | 7-2 | 10-4 | 9-5 | 7-10 | 8-10 | 8-0 | 7-0 |
| **2x8** | 12-1 | 11-0 | 9-0 | 13-8 | 12-5 | 10-2 | 11-8 | 10-7 | 9-2 |
| **2x10** | 15-4 | 13-6 | 11-0 | 17-5 | 15-10 | 13-1 | 14-11 | 13-6 | 11-3 |
| **2x12** | 18-1 | 15-8 | 12-10 | 21-2 | 18-10 | 15-5 | 18-1 | 16-0 | 13-0 |

## Sample calculations for using joist span, beam size and footing size tables

**Case I solution:**

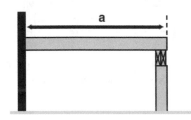

**Case II solution:**

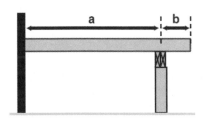

**Case III solution:**

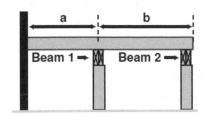

*Refer to tables for joist, beam and footing size requirements.*

Example: a = 12 feet; Post spacing = 8 feet

Use the **joist span** table to find the acceptable joist sizes for a 12 foot span, 2x8s at 12 inches O.C., 2x10s at 16 inches O.C. or 2x12s at 24 inches O.C.

Use the **Beam and footing sizes** table and find the 8 foot post spacing column. With a 12 foot deck span, the beam may be either two 2x8s or two 2x10s, depending on wood used. Depending on the type of soil, the footing diameter at the base must be a minimum of 12 inches, 10 inches or 9 inches for the corner post and 17 inches, 14 inches or 12 inches for all intermediate posts.

*Use "a" to determine joist size and "a" + "2b" to determine beam and footing sizes. The length of "b" is restricted by both the length of "a" and the size of the joists.*

Example: a = 8 feet, b = 2 feet, Post spacing = 10 feet

Refer to the **joist span** table. For an 8 foot joist span, either 2x8s at 24 inches O.C. or 2x6s at 16 inches O.C are acceptable.

For sizing the beam, use a joist length of 12 feet (8 feet + 4 feet) and a post spacing of 10 feet. The **beam and footing sizes** table indicates that the beam may be either two 2x10s or two 2x12s, depending on wood used. Depending on the type of soil, the footing diameter at the base must be a minimum of 15 inches, 12 inches or 11 inches for the corner post and 20 inches, 17 inches or 15 inches for all intermediate posts. Note that because of the 2 foot cantilever all footing sizes were increased by 1 inches as required by footnote 2 at the end of the table.

*Use "a" or "b", whichever is greater, to determine joist size. Use "a" + "b" to determine the size of Beam 1 and the post footing size for the posts supporting Beam 1. Use joist length "b" to determine both the size of Beam 2 and the post footing size for the posts supporting Beam 2.*

Example: a = 6 feet, b = 7 feet, Post spacing = 9 feet

Joist size is determined by using the longest span joist (7 feet). The **joist span** table indicates that 2x6s at 24" O.C. would be adequate for this span.

For Beam 1 and footings, use a joist length of 13 feet (6 feet + 7 feet) and a post spacing of 9 feet. The **beam and footing sizes** table indicates that the beam may be two 2x10s or two 2x12s, depending on the wood used. Depending on the type of soil, the footing diameters for Beam 1 posts shall be 13 inches, 11 inches or 9 inches for the corner (outside) post and 19 inches, 15 inches or 13 inches for all intermediate posts. For Beam 2 and footings use a joist length of 7 feet and post spacing of 9 feet. The beam may be two 2x8s or two 2x10s, depending on wood used. Depending on the type of soil, the footing diameters for Beam 2 shall be 10 inches, 8 inches or 7 inches for the corner posts, and 14 inches, 11 inches or 10 inches for all intermediate posts.

# Beam and footing sizes

Based on No. 2 or better Ponderosa Pine and Southern Pine

| Joist Length | | Post spacing 4' | 5' | 6' | 7' | 8' | 9' | 10' | 11' | 12' | 13' | 14' |
|---|---|---|---|---|---|---|---|---|---|---|---|---|
| **6'** | Southern Pine Beam | 1-2x6 | 1-2x6 | 1-2x6 | 2-2x6 | 2-2x6 | 2-2x6 | 2-2x8 | 2-2x8 | 2-2x10 | 2-2x10 | 2-2x10 |
| | Ponderosa Pine Beam | 1-2x6 | 1-2x6 | 1-2x8 | 2-2x8 | 2-2x8 | 2-2x8 | 2-2x10 | 2-2x10 | 2-2x12 | 2-2x12 | 3-2x10 |
| | Corner Footing | 6 5 4 | 7 6 5 | 7 6 5 | 8 7 6 | 9 7 6 | 9 7 6 | 10 8 7 | 10 8 7 | 10 9 7 | 11 9 8 | 11 9 8 |
| | Intermediate Footing | 9 8 7 | 10 8 7 | 10 9 7 | 11 9 8 | 12 10 9 | 13 10 9 | 14 11 10 | 14 12 10 | 15 12 10 | 15 13 11 | 16 13 11 |
| **7'** | Southern Pine Beam | 1-2x6 | 1-2x6 | 1-2x6 | 2-2x6 | 2-2x6 | 2-2x8 | 2-2x8 | 2-2x10 | 2-2x10 | 2-2x10 | 2-2x12 |
| | Ponderosa Pine Beam | 1-2x6 | 1-2x6 | 1-2x8 | 2-2x8 | 2-2x8 | 2-2x10 | 2-2x10 | 2-2x10 | 2-2x12 | 3-2x10 | 3-2x10 |
| | Corner Footing | 7 5 5 | 7 6 5 | 8 7 6 | 9 7 6 | 9 8 7 | 10 8 7 | 10 8 7 | 11 9 8 | 11 9 8 | 12 10 9 | 12 10 9 |
| | Intermediate Footing | 9 8 7 | 10 8 7 | 11 9 8 | 12 10 9 | 13 11 9 | 14 11 10 | 15 12 10 | 15 13 11 | 16 13 11 | 17 14 12 | 17 14 12 |
| **8'** | Southern Pine Beam | 1-2x6 | 1-2x6 | 2-2x6 | 2-2x6 | 2-2x6 | 2-2x8 | 2-2x8 | 2-2x10 | 2-2x10 | 2-2x10 | 2-2x12 |
| | Ponderosa Pine Beam | 1-2x6 | 2-2x6 | 2-2x8 | 2-2x8 | 2-2x8 | 2-2x8 | 2-2x10 | 2-2x10 | 2-2x10 | 3-2x10 | 3-2x12 |
| | Corner Footing | 7 6 5 | 8 6 6 | 9 7 6 | 9 8 7 | 10 8 7 | 10 8 7 | 11 9 8 | 11 9 8 | 12 10 9 | 13 10 9 | 13 11 9 |
| | Intermediate Footing | 10 8 7 | 11 9 8 | 12 10 9 | 13 11 9 | 14 11 10 | 15 12 10 | 16 13 11 | 16 13 12 | 17 14 12 | 18 15 13 | 18 15 13 |
| **9'** | Southern Pine Beam | 1-2x6 | 1-2x6 | 2-2x6 | 2-2x6 | 2-2x8 | 2-2x8 | 2-2x10 | 2-2x10 | 2-2x12 | 2-2x12 | 3-2x10 |
| | Ponderosa Pine Beam | 1-2x6 | 2-2x6 | 2-2x8 | 2-2x8 | 2-2x10 | 2-2x10 | 2-2x10 | 3-2x10 | 3-2x10 | 3-2x12 | 3-2x12 |
| | Corner Footing | 7 6 5 | 8 7 6 | 9 7 6 | 10 8 7 | 10 9 7 | 11 9 8 | 12 10 8 | 12 10 9 | 13 10 9 | 13 11 9 | 14 11 10 |
| | Intermediate Footing | 10 9 7 | 12 10 8 | 13 10 9 | 14 11 10 | 15 12 10 | 16 13 11 | 17 14 12 | 17 14 12 | 18 15 13 | 19 15 13 | 20 16 14 |
| **10'** | Southern Pine Beam | 1-2x6 | 1-2x6 | 2-2x6 | 2-2x6 | 2-2x8 | 2-2x8 | 2-2x10 | 2-2x12 | 2-2x12 | 3-2x10 | 3-2x10 |
| | Ponderosa Pine Beam | 1-2x6 | 1-2x6 | 2-2x8 | 2-2x8 | 2-2x10 | 2-2x10 | 2-2x12 | 3-2x10 | 3-2x12 | 3-2x12 | Eng Bm |
| | Corner Footing | 8 6 6 | 9 7 6 | 10 8 7 | 10 8 7 | 11 9 8 | 12 10 8 | 12 10 9 | 13 11 9 | 14 11 10 | 14 12 10 | 15 12 10 |
| | Intermediate Footing | 11 9 8 | 12 10 9 | 14 11 10 | 15 12 10 | 16 13 11 | 17 14 12 | 17 14 12 | 18 15 13 | 19 16 14 | 20 16 14 | 21 17 15 |
| **11'** | Southern Pine Beam | 1-2x6 | 2-2x6 | 2-2x6 | 2-2x8 | 2-2x8 | 2-2x10 | 2-2x10 | 2-2x12 | 2-2x12 | 3-2x10 | 3-2x12 |
| | Ponderosa Pine Beam | 2-2x6 | 2-2x6 | 2-2x8 | 2-2x8 | 2-2x10 | 2-2x12 | 2-2x12 | 3-2x10 | 3-2x12 | 3-2x12 | Eng Bm |
| | Corner Footing | 8 7 6 | 9 7 6 | 10 8 7 | 11 9 8 | 12 9 8 | 12 10 9 | 13 11 9 | 14 11 10 | 14 12 10 | 15 12 10 | 15 13 11 |
| | Intermediate Footing | 12 9 8 | 13 11 9 | 14 12 10 | 15 12 10 | 16 13 11 | 17 14 12 | 17 14 12 | 18 15 13 | 19 16 14 | 20 16 14 | 21 17 15 |
| **12'** | Southern Pine Beam | 1-2x6 | 2-2x6 | 2-2x6 | 2-2x8 | 2-2x8 | 2-2x10 | 2-2x10 | 2-2x12 | 3-2x10 | 3-2x10 | 3-2x12 |
| | Ponderosa Pine Beam | 2-2x6 | 2-2x6 | 2-2x8 | 2-2x10 | 2-2x10 | 2-2x12 | 2-2x12 | 3-2x12 | 3-2x12 | Eng Bm | Eng Bm |
| | Corner Footing | 9 7 6 | 10 8 7 | 10 9 7 | 11 9 8 | 12 10 9 | 13 10 9 | 14 11 10 | 14 12 10 | 15 12 10 | 15 13 11 | 16 13 11 |
| | Intermediate Footing | 12 10 9 | 14 11 10 | 15 12 10 | 16 13 11 | 17 14 12 | 18 15 13 | 19 16 14 | 20 16 14 | 21 17 15 | 22 18 15 | 23 18 16 |
| **13'** | Southern Pine Beam | 1-2x6 | 2-2x6 | 2-2x6 | 2-2x8 | 2-2x8 | 2-2x10 | 2-2x10 | 2-2x12 | 3-2x10 | 3-2x12 | 3-2x12 |
| | Ponderosa Pine Beam | 2-2x6 | 2-2x6 | 2-2x8 | 2-2x10 | 2-2x12 | 2-2x12 | 2-2x12 | 3-2x12 | 3-2x12 | Eng Bm | Eng Bm |
| | Corner Footing | 9 7 6 | 10 8 7 | 11 9 8 | 12 10 8 | 13 10 9 | 13 11 9 | 14 12 10 | 15 12 10 | 15 13 11 | 16 13 11 | 17 14 12 |
| | Intermediate Footing | 13 10 9 | 14 12 10 | 15 13 11 | 17 14 12 | 18 15 13 | 19 15 13 | 20 16 14 | 21 17 15 | 22 18 15 | 23 19 16 | 24 19 17 |
| **14'** | Southern Pine Beam | 1-2x6 | 2-2x6 | 2-2x6 | 2-2x8 | 2-2x10 | 2-2x10 | 2-2x12 | 3-2x10 | 3-2x12 | 3-2x12 | 3-2x12 |
| | Ponderosa Pine Beam | 2-2x6 | 2-2x8 | 2-2x8 | 2-2x10 | 2-2x12 | 3-2x10 | 3-2x12 | 3-2x12 | Eng Bm | Eng Bm | Eng Bm |
| | Corner Footing | 9 8 7 | 10 8 7 | 11 9 8 | 12 10 9 | 13 11 9 | 14 11 10 | 15 12 10 | 15 13 11 | 16 13 11 | 17 14 12 | 17 14 12 |
| | Intermediate Footing | 13 11 9 | 15 12 10 | 16 13 11 | 17 14 12 | 18 15 13 | 20 16 14 | 21 17 15 | 22 18 15 | 23 18 16 | 24 19 17 | 24 20 17 |
| **15'** | Southern Pine Beam | 2-2x6 | 2-2x6 | 2-2x8 | 2-2x8 | 2-2x10 | 2-2x12 | 2-2x12 | 3-2x10 | 3-2x12 | 3-2x12 | Eng Bm |
| | Ponderosa Pine Beam | 2-2x6 | 2-2x8 | 2-2x8 | 2-2x10 | 3-2x10 | 3-2x10 | 3-2x12 | 3-2x12 | Eng Bm | Eng Bm | Eng Bm |
| | Corner Footing | 10 8 7 | 11 9 8 | 12 10 8 | 13 10 9 | 14 11 10 | 14 12 10 | 15 12 11 | 16 13 11 | 17 14 12 | 17 14 12 | 18 15 13 |
| | Intermediate Footing | 14 11 10 | 15 12 11 | 17 14 12 | 18 15 13 | 19 16 14 | 20 17 14 | 21 17 15 | 22 18 16 | 23 19 17 | 24 20 17 | 25 21 18 |
| **16'** | Southern Pine Beam | 2-2x6 | 2-2x6 | 2-2x8 | 2-2x8 | 2-2x10 | 2-2x12 | 2-2x12 | 3-2x10 | 3-2x12 | 3-2x12 | Eng Bm |
| | Ponderosa Pine Beam | 2-2x6 | 2-2x8 | 2-2x10 | 2-2x10 | 3-2x10 | 3-2x10 | 3-2x12 | 3-2x12 | Eng Bm | Eng Bm | Eng Bm |
| | Corner Footing | 10 8 7 | 11 9 8 | 12 10 9 | 13 11 9 | 14 11 10 | 15 12 10 | 16 13 11 | 16 13 12 | 17 14 12 | 18 15 13 | 18 15 13 |
| | Intermediate Footing | 14 11 10 | 16 13 11 | 17 14 12 | 18 15 13 | 20 16 14 | 21 17 15 | 22 18 16 | 23 19 16 | 24 20 17 | 25 21 18 | 26 21 18 |

**Notes:**

1. Joist length is total length of joist, *including* any cantilevers.
2. When joist extends (cantilevers) beyond support beam by 18 inches or more, add 1 inches to footing dimensions shown.
3. Requirements for future 3-season porches or screen porches:
   a. Increase corner footing size shown by 90%.
   b. Increase center footing size shown by 55%.
   c. Locate all footings at extremities of deck (no cantilevers).

d. Beam sizes indicated need not be altered.

4. All footing sizes above are base diameters (in inches) and are listed for THREE SOIL TYPES:

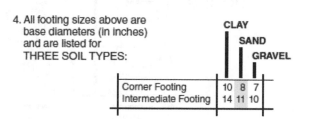

| | CLAY | SAND | GRAVEL |
|---|---|---|---|
| Corner Footing | 10 | 8 | 7 |
| Intermediate Footing | 14 | 11 | 10 |

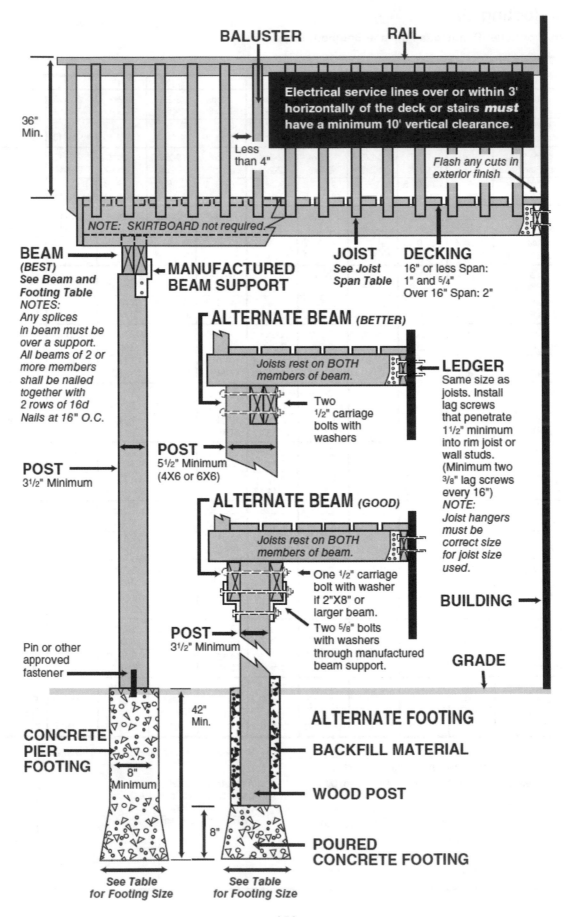

BALUSTER

RAIL

36" Min.

Electrical service lines over or within 3' horizontally of the deck or stairs *must* have a minimum 10' vertical clearance.

Less than 4"

Flash any cuts in exterior finish

NOTE: SKIRTBOARD not required.

**BEAM** (BEST) See Beam and Footing Table NOTES: Any splices in beam must be over a support. All beams of 2 or more members shall be nailed together with 2 rows of 16d Nails at 16" O.C.

← MANUFACTURED BEAM SUPPORT

**JOIST** See Joist Span Table

**DECKING** 16" or less Span: 1" and 5/4" Over 16" Span: 2"

**ALTERNATE BEAM** (BETTER)

Joists rest on BOTH members of beam.

**LEDGER** Same size as joists. Install lag screws that penetrate 1½" minimum into rim joist or wall studs. (Minimum two 3/8" lag screws every 16") NOTE: Joist hangers must be correct size for joist size used.

Two ½" carriage bolts with washers

**POST** 5½" Minimum (4X6 or 6X6)

**POST** 3½" Minimum

**ALTERNATE BEAM** (GOOD)

Joists rest on BOTH members of beam.

One ½" carriage bolt with washer if 2"X8" or larger beam.

Two 5/8" bolts with washers through manufactured beam support.

**BUILDING** →

**POST** → 3½" Minimum

Pin or other approved fastener

**GRADE**

42" Min.

**ALTERNATE FOOTING**

**BACKFILL MATERIAL**

**CONCRETE PIER FOOTING**

8" Minimum

8"

**WOOD POST**

**POURED CONCRETE FOOTING**

*See Table for Footing Size*

*See Table for Footing Size*

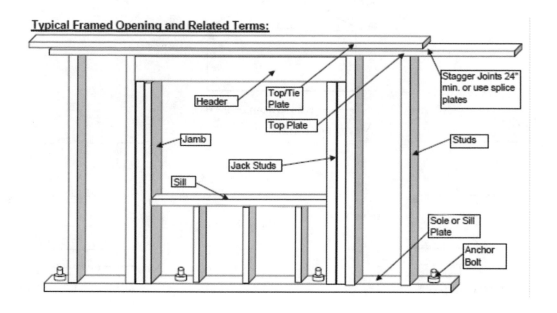

**Typical Framed Opening and Related Terms:**

Header

Top/Tie Plate

Top Plate

Stagger Joints 24" min. or use splice plates

Jamb

Studs

Jack Studs

Sill

Sole or Sill Plate

Anchor Bolt

# IBC HEADER SPANS (INTERNATIONAL BUILDING CODE)

While working on the book, I did a lot of research trying to find specific rules and requirements. One of the things I wanted was a table that showed the required size for headers, since I've always had to guess, or rely on what the building inspector told me to use. When I finally found one, I was surprised at how big some of the headers have to be, and realized that many times I'd installed ones that were too small. As far as I know, none of them have ever sagged, but according to the numbers, they're undersized.

On the next few pages are several tables for sizing headers. Notice that there are three different ones for headers on exterior walls. The reason for this is that it depends on the amount of snowfall in your area. The first table is for 30 pounds per square foot of snow load, the second for 50, and the third is for 70. The last one is the table that's used for Duluth, Minnesota. So if you live in an area that gets a lot of snow, there's a good chance you'll have to use this one.

Besides the length of the opening, another thing that determine the size of the header is the width of the building, perpendicular to the ridge, since a larger building will put a bigger load on the header. In the tables, there are three sizes listed: 20, 28, and 36 feet. When the size of your house is between these numbers, you can average out the maximum span for the header. For instance, let's say the maximum span for a 2x10 header is 10 1/2 feet in a house that's 20 feet wide, just over 9 feet if it's 28 feet wide, and 8 feet if it's 36 feet across. If your house is 24 feet wide, the maximum span would be around 9' - 9".

The number of jack studs that are required to support the header will vary. You would think the reason for this is strictly to hold up the header, but that's not the case. Actually, more jack studs are needed to spread out the load, to keep from crushing the end of the header itself. For the same reason, you shouldn't drill a large hole at the end of a floor joist where it's being compressed between the plate and the wall above it. The numbers shown are for Douglas fir-larch, southern pine, hem-fir, and spruce-pine- fir, #2 or better.

451

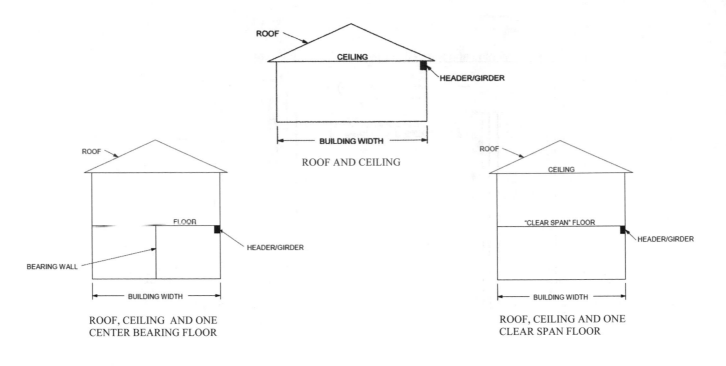

ROOF AND CEILING

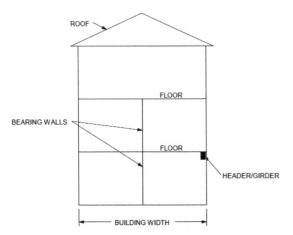

ROOF, CEILING AND ONE
CENTER BEARING FLOOR

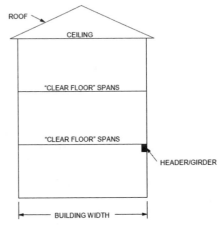

ROOF, CEILING AND ONE
CLEAR SPAN FLOOR

ROOF, CEILING AND TWO
CENTER BEARING FLOORS

ROOF, CEILING AND TWO
CLEAR SPAN FLOORS

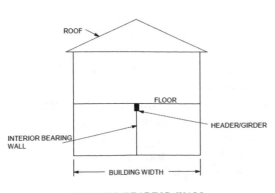

INTERIOR BEARING WALL
ONE FLOOR ONLY

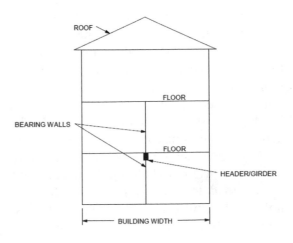

INTERIOR BEARING WALL
TWO FLOORS

| HEADER AND GIRDER SPANS FOR EXTERIOR BEARING WALLS | | | | | | | |
|---|---|---|---|---|---|---|---|
| SNOW LOAD - 30 lbs psf | | BUILDING WIDTH Measured perpendicular to the ridge | | | | | |
| HEADERS AND GIRDERS SUPPORTING | SIZE | 20 | | 28 | | 36 | |
| | | SPAN (feet and inches) | Number of JACK STUDS | SPAN (feet and inches) | Number of JACK STUDS | SPAN (feet and inches) | Number of JACK STUDS |
| Roof and Ceiling | 2 - 2x4 | 3 - 6 | 1 | 3 - 2 | 1 | 2 - 10 | 1 |
| | 2 - 2x6 | 5 - 5 | 1 | 4 - 8 | 1 | 4 - 2 | 1 |
| | 2 - 2x8 | 6 - 10 | 1 | 5 - 11 | 2 | 5 - 4 | 2 |
| | 2 - 2x10 | 8 - 5 | 2 | 7 - 3 | 2 | 6 - 6 | 2 |
| | 2 - 2x12 | 9 - 9 | 2 | 8 - 5 | 2 | 7 - 6 | 2 |
| | 3 - 2x8 | 8 - 4 | 1 | 7 - 5 | 1 | 6 - 8 | 1 |
| | 3 - 2x10 | 10 - 6 | 1 | 9 - 1 | 2 | 8 - 2 | 2 |
| | 3 - 2x12 | 12 - 2 | 2 | 10 - 7 | 2 | 9 - 5 | 2 |
| | 4 - 2x8 | 9 - 2 | 1 | 8 - 4 | 1 | 7 - 8 | 1 |
| | 4 - 2x10 | 11 - 8 | 1 | 10 - 6 | 1 | 9 - 5 | 2 |
| | 4 - 2x12 | 14 - 1 | 1 | 12 - 2 | 2 | 10 - 11 | 2 |
| Roof, Ceiling and 1 Center Bearing Floor | 2 - 2x4 | 3 - 1 | 1 | 2 - 9 | 1 | 2 - 5 | 1 |
| | 2 - 2x6 | 4 - 6 | 1 | 4 - 0 | 1 | 3 - 7 | 2 |
| | 2 - 2x8 | 5 - 9 | 2 | 5 - 0 | 2 | 4 - 6 | 2 |
| | 2 - 2x10 | 7 - 0 | 2 | 6 - 2 | 2 | 5 - 6 | 2 |
| | 2 - 2x12 | 8 - 1 | 2 | 7 - 1 | 2 | 6 - 5 | 2 |
| | 3 - 2x8 | 7 - 2 | 1 | 6 - 3 | 2 | 5 - 8 | 2 |
| | 3 - 2x10 | 8 - 9 | 2 | 7 - 8 | 2 | 6 - 11 | 2 |
| | 3 - 2x12 | 10 - 2 | 2 | 8 - 11 | 2 | 8 - 0 | 2 |
| | 4 - 2x8 | 8 - 1 | 1 | 7 - 3 | 1 | 6 - 7 | 1 |
| | 4 - 2x10 | 10 - 1 | 1 | 8 - 10 | 2 | 8 - 0 | 2 |
| | 4 - 2x12 | 11 - 9 | 2 | 10 - 3 | 2 | 9 - 3 | 2 |
| Roof, Ceiling and 1 Clear Span Floor | 2 - 2x4 | 2 - 8 | 1 | 2 - 4 | 1 | 2 - 1 | 1 |
| | 2 - 2x6 | 3 - 11 | 1 | 3 - 5 | 2 | 3 - 0 | 2 |
| | 2 - 2x8 | 5 - 0 | 2 | 4 - 4 | 2 | 3 - 10 | 2 |
| | 2 - 2x10 | 6 - 1 | 2 | 5 - 3 | 2 | 4 - 8 | 2 |
| | 2 - 2x12 | 7 - 1 | 2 | 6 - 1 | 3 | 5 - 5 | 3 |
| | 3 - 2x8 | 6 - 3 | 2 | 5 - 5 | 2 | 4 - 10 | 2 |
| | 3 - 2x10 | 7 - 7 | 2 | 6 - 7 | 2 | 5 - 11 | 2 |
| | 3 - 2x12 | 8 - 10 | 2 | 7 - 8 | 2 | 6 - 10 | 2 |
| | 4 - 2x8 | 7 - 2 | 1 | 6 - 3 | 2 | 5 - 7 | 2 |
| | 4 - 2x10 | 8 - 9 | 2 | 7 - 7 | 2 | 6 - 10 | 2 |
| | 4 - 2x12 | 10 - 2 | 2 | 8 - 10 | 2 | 7 - 11 | 2 |
| Roof, Ceiling and 2 Center Bearing Floors | 2 - 2x4 | 2 - 7 | 1 | 2 - 3 | 1 | 2 - 0 | 1 |
| | 2 - 2x6 | 3 - 9 | 2 | 3 - 3 | 2 | 2 - 11 | 2 |
| | 2 - 2x8 | 4 - 9 | 2 | 4 - 2 | 2 | 3 - 9 | 2 |
| | 2 - 2x10 | 5 - 9 | 2 | 5 - 1 | 2 | 4 - 7 | 3 |
| | 2 - 2x12 | 6 - 8 | 2 | 5 - 10 | 3 | 5 - 3 | 3 |
| | 3 - 2x8 | 5 - 11 | 2 | 5 - 2 | 2 | 4 - 8 | 2 |
| | 3 - 2x10 | 7 - 3 | 2 | 6 - 4 | 2 | 5 - 8 | 2 |
| | 3 - 2x12 | 8 - 5 | 2 | 7 - 4 | 2 | 6 - 7 | 2 |
| | 4 - 2x8 | 6 - 10 | 1 | 6 - 0 | 2 | 5 - 5 | 2 |
| | 4 - 2x10 | 8 - 4 | 2 | 7 - 4 | 2 | 6 - 7 | 2 |
| | 4 - 2x12 | 9 - 8 | 2 | 8 - 6 | 2 | 7 - 8 | 2 |
| Roof, Ceiling and 2 Clear Span Floors | 2 - 2x4 | 2 - 1 | 1 | 1 - 8 | 1 | 1 - 6 | 2 |
| | 2 - 2x6 | 3 - 1 | 2 | 2 - 8 | 2 | 2 - 4 | 2 |
| | 2 - 2x8 | 3 - 10 | 2 | 3 - 4 | 2 | 3 - 0 | 3 |
| | 2 - 2x10 | 4 - 9 | 2 | 4 - 1 | 3 | 3 - 8 | 3 |
| | 2 - 2x12 | 5 - 6 | 3 | 4 - 9 | 3 | 4 - 3 | 3 |
| | 3 - 2x8 | 4 - 10 | 2 | 4 - 2 | 2 | 3 - 9 | 2 |
| | 3 - 2x10 | 5 - 11 | 2 | 5 - 1 | 2 | 4 - 7 | 3 |
| | 3 - 2x12 | 6 - 10 | 2 | 5 - 11 | 3 | 5 - 4 | 3 |
| | 4 - 2x8 | 5 - 7 | 2 | 4 - 10 | 2 | 4 - 4 | 2 |
| | 4 - 2x10 | 6 - 10 | 2 | 5 - 11 | 2 | 5 - 3 | 2 |
| | 4 - 2x12 | 7 - 11 | 2 | 6 - 10 | 2 | 6 - 2 | 3 |

## HEADER AND GIRDER SPANS FOR EXTERIOR BEARING WALLS

| SNOW LOAD - 50 lbs psf | | BUILDING WIDTH Measured perpendicular to the ridge | | | | | |
|---|---|---|---|---|---|---|---|
| **HEADERS AND GIRDERS SUPPORTING** | | 20 | | 28 | | 36 | |
| | SIZE | SPAN (feet and inches) | Number of JACK STUDS | SPAN (feet and inches) | Number of JACK STUDS | SPAN (feet and inches) | Number of JACK STUDS |
| Roof and Ceiling | 2 - 2x4 | 3 - 2 | 1 | 2 - 9 | 1 | 2 - 6 | 1 |
| | 2 - 2x6 | 4 - 8 | 1 | 4 - 1 | 1 | 3 - 8 | 2 |
| | 2 - 2x8 | 5 - 11 | 2 | 5 - 2 | 2 | 4 - 7 | 2 |
| | 2 - 2x10 | 7 - 3 | 2 | 6 - 3 | 2 | 5 - 7 | 2 |
| | 2 - 2x12 | 8 - 5 | 2 | 7 - 3 | 2 | 6 - 6 | 2 |
| | 3 - 2x8 | 7 - 5 | 1 | 6 - 5 | 2 | 5 - 9 | 2 |
| | 3 - 2x10 | 9 - 1 | 2 | 7 - 10 | 2 | 7 - 0 | 2 |
| | 3 - 2x12 | 10 - 7 | 2 | 9 - 2 | 2 | 8 - 2 | 2 |
| | 4 - 2x8 | 8 - 4 | 1 | 7 - 5 | 1 | 6 - 8 | 1 |
| | 4 - 2x10 | 10 - 6 | 1 | 9 - 1 | 2 | 8 - 2 | 2 |
| | 4 - 2x12 | 12 - 2 | 2 | 10 - 7 | 2 | 9 - 5 | 2 |
| Roof, Ceiling and 1 Center Bearing Floor | 2 - 2x4 | 2 - 9 | 1 | 2 - 5 | 1 | 2 - 2 | 1 |
| | 2 - 2x6 | 4 - 1 | 1 | 3 - 7 | 2 | 3 - 3 | 2 |
| | 2 - 2x8 | 5 - 2 | 2 | 4 - 6 | 2 | 4 - 1 | 2 |
| | 2 - 2x10 | 6 - 4 | 2 | 5 - 6 | 2 | 5 - 0 | 2 |
| | 2 - 2x12 | 7 - 4 | 2 | 6 - 5 | 2 | 5 - 9 | 3 |
| | 3 - 2x8 | 6 - 5 | 2 | 5 - 8 | 2 | 5 - 1 | 2 |
| | 3 - 2x10 | 7 - 11 | 2 | 6 - 11 | 2 | 6 - 3 | 2 |
| | 3 - 2x12 | 9 - 2 | 2 | 8 - 0 | 2 | 7 - 3 | 2 |
| | 4 - 2x8 | 7 - 5 | 1 | 6 - 6 | 1 | 5 - 11 | 2 |
| | 4 - 2x10 | 9 - 1 | 2 | 8 - 0 | 2 | 7 - 2 | 2 |
| | 4 - 2x12 | 10 - 7 | 2 | 9 - 3 | 2 | 8 - 4 | 2 |
| Roof, Ceiling and 1 Clear Span Floor | 2 - 2x4 | 2 7 | 1 | 2 - 3 | 1 | 2 - 0 | 1 |
| | 2 - 2x6 | 3 10 | 2 | 3 - 4 | 2 | 3 - 0 | 2 |
| | 2 - 2x8 | 4 10 | 2 | 4 - 2 | 2 | 3 - 9 | 2 |
| | 2 - 2x10 | 5 11 | 2 | 5 - 1 | 2 | 4 - 7 | 3 |
| | 2 - 2x12 | 6 10 | 2 | 5 - 11 | 3 | 5 - 4 | 3 |
| | 3 - 2x8 | 6 1 | 2 | 5 - 3 | 2 | 4 - 8 | 2 |
| | 3 - 2x10 | 7 5 | 2 | 6 - 5 | 2 | 5 - 9 | 2 |
| | 3 - 2x12 | 8 7 | 2 | 7 - 5 | 2 | 6 - 8 | 2 |
| | 4 - 2x8 | 7 0 | 1 | 6 - 1 | 2 | 5 - 5 | 2 |
| | 4 - 2x10 | 8 7 | 2 | 7 - 5 | 2 | 6 - 7 | 2 |
| | 4 - 2x12 | 9 11 | 2 | 8 - 7 | 2 | 7 - 8 | 2 |
| Roof, Ceiling and 2 Center Bearing Floors | 2 - 2x4 | 2 - 6 | 1 | 2 - 2 | 1 | 1 - 11 | 1 |
| | 2 - 2x6 | 3 - 8 | 2 | 3 - 2 | 2 | 2 - 10 | 2 |
| | 2 - 2x8 | 4 - 7 | 2 | 4 - 0 | 2 | 3 - 8 | 2 |
| | 2 - 2x10 | 5 - 8 | 2 | 4 - 11 | 2 | 4 - 5 | 3 |
| | 2 - 2x12 | 6 - 6 | 2 | 5 - 9 | 3 | 5 - 2 | 3 |
| | 3 - 2x8 | 5 - 9 | 2 | 5 - 1 | 2 | 4 - 7 | 2 |
| | 3 - 2x10 | 7 - 1 | 2 | 6 - 2 | 2 | 5 - 7 | 2 |
| | 3 - 2x12 | 8 - 2 | 2 | 7 - 2 | 2 | 6 - 5 | 3 |
| | 4 - 2x8 | 6 - 8 | 1 | 5 - 10 | 2 | 5 - 3 | 2 |
| | 4 - 2x10 | 8 - 2 | 2 | 7 - 2 | 2 | 6 - 5 | 2 |
| | 4 - 2x12 | 9 -5 | 2 | 8 - 3 | 2 | 7 - 5 | 2 |
| Roof, Ceiling and 2 Clear Span Floors | 2 - 2x4 | 2 - 0 | 1 | 1 - 8 | 1 | 1 - 5 | 2 |
| | 2 - 2x6 | 3 - 0 | 2 | 2 - 7 | 2 | 2 - 3 | 2 |
| | 2 - 2x8 | 3 - 10 | 2 | 3 - 4 | 2 | 2 - 11 | 3 |
| | 2 - 2x10 | 4 - 8 | 2 | 4 - 0 | 3 | 3 - 7 | 3 |
| | 2 - 2x12 | 5 - 5 | 3 | 4 - 8 | 3 | 4 - 2 | 3 |
| | 3 - 2x8 | 4 - 9 | 2 | 4 - 1 | 2 | 3 - 8 | 2 |
| | 3 - 2x10 | 5 -10 | 2 | 5 - 0 | 2 | 4 - 6 | 3 |
| | 3 - 2x12 | 6 - 9 | 2 | 5 - 10 | 3 | 5 - 3 | 3 |
| | 4 - 2x8 | 5 - 6 | 2 | 4 - 9 | 2 | 4 - 3 | 2 |
| | 4 - 2x10 | 6 - 9 | 2 | 5 - 10 | 2 | 5 - 2 | 2 |
| | 4 - 2x12 | 7 - 9 | 2 | 6 - 9 | 2 | 6 - 0 | 3 |

## HEADER AND GIRDER SPANS FOR EXTERIOR BEARING WALLS

| SNOW LOAD - 70 lbs psf | | BUILDING WIDTH Measured perpendicular to the ridge | | | | | |
|---|---|---|---|---|---|---|---|
| HEADERS AND GIRDERS SUPPORTING | SIZE | 20 | | 28 | | 36 | |
| | | SPAN (feet and inches) | Number of JACK STUDS | SPAN (feet and inches) | Number of JACK STUDS | SPAN (feet and inches) | Number of JACK STUDS |
| Roof and Ceiling | 2 - 2x4 | 2 - 10 | 1 | 2 - 6 | 1 | 2 - 3 | 1 |
| | 2 - 2x6 | 4 - 2 | 1 | 3 - 8 | 2 | 3 - 3 | 2 |
| | 2 - 2x8 | 5 - 4 | 2 | 4 - 7 | 2 | 4 - 1 | 2 |
| | 2 - 2x10 | 6 - 6 | 2 | 5 - 7 | 2 | 5 - 0 | 2 |
| | 2 - 2x12 | 7 - 6 | 2 | 6 - 6 | 2 | 5 - 10 | 3 |
| | 3 - 2x8 | 6 - 8 | 1 | 5 - 9 | 2 | 5 - 2 | 2 |
| | 3 - 2x10 | 8 - 2 | 2 | 7 - 0 | 2 | 6 - 4 | 2 |
| | 3 - 2x12 | 9 - 5 | 2 | 8 - 2 | 2 | 7 - 4 | 2 |
| | 4 - 2x8 | 7 - 8 | 1 | 6 - 8 | 1 | 5 - 11 | 2 |
| | 4 - 2x10 | 9 - 5 | 2 | 8 - 2 | 2 | 7 - 3 | 2 |
| | 4 - 2x12 | 10 - 11 | 2 | 9 - 5 | 2 | 8 - 5 | 2 |
| Roof, Ceiling and 1 Center Bearing Floor | 2 - 2x4 | 2 - 7 | 1 | 2 - 3 | 1 | 2 - 0 | 1 |
| | 2 - 2x6 | 3 - 9 | 2 | 3 - 3 | 2 | 2 - 11 | 2 |
| | 2 - 2x8 | 4 - 9 | 2 | 4 - 2 | 2 | 3 - 9 | 2 |
| | 2 - 2x10 | 5 - 9 | 2 | 5 - 1 | 2 | 4 - 7 | 3 |
| | 2 - 2x12 | 6 - 8 | 2 | 5 - 10 | 3 | 5 - 3 | 3 |
| | 3 - 2x8 | 5 - 11 | 2 | 5 - 2 | 2 | 4 - 8 | 2 |
| | 3 - 2x10 | 7 - 3 | 2 | 6 - 4 | 2 | 5 - 8 | 2 |
| | 3 - 2x12 | 8 - 5 | 2 | 7 - 4 | 2 | 6 - 7 | 2 |
| | 4 - 2x8 | 6 - 10 | 1 | 6 - 0 | 2 | 5 - 5 | 2 |
| | 4 - 2x10 | 8 - 4 | 2 | 7 - 4 | 2 | 6 - 7 | 2 |
| | 4 - 2x12 | 9 - 8 | 2 | 8 - 6 | 2 | 7 - 7 | 2 |
| Roof, Ceiling and 1 Clear Span Floor | 2 - 2x4 | 2 - 5 | 1 | 2 - 1 | 1 | 1 - 10 | 1 |
| | 2 - 2x6 | 3 - 6 | 2 | 3 - 1 | 2 | 2 - 9 | 2 |
| | 2 - 2x8 | 4 - 6 | 2 | 3 - 11 | 2 | 3 - 6 | 2 |
| | 2 - 2x10 | 5 - 6 | 2 | 4 - 9 | 2 | 4 - 3 | 3 |
| | 2 - 2x12 | 6 - 4 | 2 | 5 - 6 | 3 | 5 - 0 | 3 |
| | 3 - 2x8 | 5 - 7 | 2 | 4 - 11 | 2 | 4 - 5 | 2 |
| | 3 - 2x10 | 6 - 10 | 2 | 6 - 0 | 2 | 5 - 4 | 2 |
| | 3 - 2x12 | 7 - 11 | 2 | 6 - 11 | 2 | 6 - 3 | 2 |
| | 4 - 2x8 | 6 - 6 | 1 | 5 - 8 | 2 | 5 - 1 | 2 |
| | 4 - 2x10 | 7 - 11 | 2 | 6 - 11 | 2 | 6 - 2 | 2 |
| | 4 - 2x12 | 9 - 2 | 2 | 8 - 0 | 2 | 7 - 2 | 2 |
| Roof, Ceiling and 2 Center Bearing Floors | 2 - 2x4 | 2 - 4 | 1 | 2 - 0 | 1 | 1 - 9 | 1 |
| | 2 - 2x6 | 3 - 5 | 2 | 3 - 0 | 2 | 2 - 8 | 2 |
| | 2 - 2x8 | 4 - 4 | 2 | 3 - 9 | 2 | 3 - 5 | 2 |
| | 2 - 2x10 | 5 - 3 | 2 | 4 - 7 | 3 | 4 - 2 | 3 |
| | 2 - 2x12 | 6 - 1 | 3 | 5 - 4 | 3 | 4 - 10 | 3 |
| | 3 - 2x8 | 5 - 5 | 2 | 4 - 9 | 2 | 4 - 3 | 2 |
| | 3 - 2x10 | 6 - 7 | 2 | 5 - 9 | 2 | 5 - 3 | 2 |
| | 3 - 2x12 | 7 - 8 | 2 | 6 - 9 | 2 | 6 - 1 | 3 |
| | 4 - 2x8 | 6 - 3 | 2 | 5 - 6 | 2 | 4 - 11 | 2 |
| | 4 - 2x10 | 7 - 7 | 2 | 6 - 8 | 2 | 6 - 0 | 2 |
| | 4 - 2x12 | 8 - 10 | 2 | 7 - 9 | 2 | 7 - 0 | 2 |
| Roof, Ceiling and 2 Clear Span Floors | 2 - 2x4 | 2 - 0 | 1 | 1 - 8 | 1 | 1 - 5 | 2 |
| | 2 - 2x6 | 2 - 11 | 2 | 2 - 7 | 2 | 2 - 3 | 2 |
| | 2 - 2x8 | 3 - 9 | 2 | 3 - 3 | 2 | 2 - 11 | 3 |
| | 2 - 2x10 | 4 - 7 | 3 | 4 - 0 | 3 | 3 - 6 | 3 |
| | 2 - 2x12 | 5 - 4 | 3 | 4 - 7 | 3 | 4 - 1 | 4 |
| | 3 - 2x8 | 4 - 8 | 2 | 4 - 1 | 2 | 3 - 8 | 2 |
| | 3 - 2x10 | 5 - 9 | 2 | 4 - 11 | 2 | 4 - 5 | 3 |
| | 3 - 2x12 | 6 - 8 | 2 | 5 - 9 | 3 | 5 - 2 | 3 |
| | 4 - 2x8 | 5 - 5 | 2 | 4 - 8 | 2 | 4 - 2 | 2 |
| | 4 - 2x10 | 6 - 7 | 2 | 5 - 9 | 2 | 5 - 1 | 2 |
| | 4 - 2x12 | 7 - 8 | 2 | 6 - 8 | 2 | 5 - 11 | 3 |

# IBC HEADER SPANS FOR INTERIOR BEARING WALLS

| HEADER AND GIRDER SPANS FOR INTERIOR WALLS | | | | | | | |
|---|---|---|---|---|---|---|---|
| HEADERS AND GIRDERS SUPPORTING | | BUILDING WIDTH Measured perpendicular to the ridge | | | | | |
| | | 20 | | 28 | | 36 | |
| | SIZE | SPAN (feet and inches) | Number of JACK STUDS | SPAN (feet and inches) | Number of JACK STUDS | SPAN (feet and inches) | Number of JACK STUDS |
| One Floor Only | 2 - 2x4 | 3 - 1 | 1 | 2 - 8 | 1 | 2 - 5 | 1 |
| | 2 - 2x6 | 4 - 6 | 1 | 3 - 11 | 1 | 3 - 6 | 1 |
| | 2 - 2x8 | 5 - 9 | 1 | 5 - 0 | 2 | 4 - 5 | 2 |
| | 2 - 2x10 | 7 - 0 | 2 | 6 - 1 | 2 | 5 - 5 | 2 |
| | 2 - 2x12 | 8 - 1 | 2 | 7 - 0 | 2 | 6 - 3 | 2 |
| | 3 - 2x8 | 7 - 2 | 1 | 6 - 3 | 1 | 5 - 7 | 2 |
| | 3 - 2x10 | 8 - 9 | 1 | 7 - 7 | 2 | 6 - 9 | 2 |
| | 3 - 2x12 | 10 - 2 | 2 | 8 - 10 | 2 | 7 - 10 | 2 |
| | 4 - 2x8 | 9 - 0 | 1 | 7 - 8 | 1 | 6 - 9 | 1 |
| | 4 - 2x10 | 10 - 1 | 1 | 8 - 9 | 1 | 7 - 10 | 2 |
| | 4 - 2x12 | 11 - 9 | 1 | 10 - 2 | 2 | 9 - 1 | 2 |
| Two Floors | 2 - 2x4 | 2 - 2 | 1 | 1 - 10 | 1 | 1 - 7 | 1 |
| | 2 - 2x6 | 3 - 2 | 2 | 2 - 9 | 2 | 2 - 5 | 2 |
| | 2 - 2x8 | 4 - 1 | 2 | 3 - 6 | 2 | 3 - 2 | 2 |
| | 2 - 2x10 | 4 - 11 | 2 | 4 - 3 | 2 | 3 - 10 | 3 |
| | 2 - 2x12 | 5 - 9 | 2 | 5 - 0 | 3 | 4 - 5 | 3 |
| | 3 - 2x8 | 5 - 1 | 2 | 4 - 5 | 2 | 3 - 11 | 2 |
| | 3 - 2x10 | 6 - 2 | 2 | 5 - 4 | 2 | 4 - 10 | 2 |
| | 3 - 2x12 | 7 - 2 | 2 | 6 - 3 | 2 | 5 - 7 | 3 |
| | 4 - 2x8 | 6 - 1 | 1 | 5 - 3 | 2 | 4 - 8 | 2 |
| | 4 - 2x10 | 7 - 2 | 2 | 6 - 2 | 2 | 5 - 6 | 2 |
| | 4 - 2x12 | 8 - 4 | 2 | 7 - 2 | 2 | 6 - 5 | 2 |

# HEADERS NOT REQUIRED OVER NON-LOAD BEARING WALLS

According to the IRC (International Residential Code), a single flat 2x4 may be used as a header on exterior or interior non-load bearing walls. The maximum opening may not exceed 8 feet. The vertical distance to the parallel surface above shall not be more than 24 inches. No cripples or blocking are required above the header. On exterior walls, cavities above the headers must be insulated.

In new construction, headers are generally sized the same on the exterior walls, regardless of which side they're on. I've always questioned this, since it doesn't make any sense why headers for a certain size opening have to be the same size on every wall, when there's less load on the non-load bearing side. Even though it seems wrong, I'd still run it by the building inspector before I followed this rule or changed the size on one of the headers. The inspector may not agree with it, and what they say goes.

## Floor joists — 40#LL + 10#DL — L/360

| | 2 x 6 | | | 2 x 8 | | | 2 x 10 | | | 2 x 12 | | |
|---|---|---|---|---|---|---|---|---|---|---|---|---|
| | 12"OC | 16"OC | 24"OC | 12"OC | 16"OC | 24"OC | 12"OC | 16"OC | 24"OC | 12"OC | 16"OC | 24"OC |
| Douglas Fir-Larch | 10-9 | 9-9 | 8-1 | 14-2 | 12-7 | 10-3 | 17-9 | 15-5 | 12-7 | 20-7 | 17-10 | 14-7 |
| Hem-Fir | 10-0 | 9-1 | 7-11 | 13-2 | 12-0 | 10-2 | 16-10 | 15-2 | 12-5 | 20-4 | 17-7 | 14-4 |
| Ponderosa Pine | 9-2 | 8-4 | 7-0 | 12-1 | 10-10 | 8-10 | 15-4 | 13-3 | 10-10 | 17-9 | 15-5 | 12-7 |
| Southern Pine | 10-9 | 9-9 | 8-6 | 14-2 | 12-10 | 11-0 | 18-0 | 16-1 | 13-5 | 21-9 | 19-0 | 15-4 |
| S-P-F | 10-3 | 9-4 | 8-1 | 13-6 | 12-3 | 10-3 | 17-3 | 15-5 | 12-7 | 20-7 | 17-10 | 14-7 |
| S-P-F (South) | 9-6 | 8-7 | 7-6 | 12-6 | 11-4 | 9-6 | 15-11 | 14-3 | 11-8 | 19-1 | 16-6 | 13-6 |
| Western Cedars | 9-2 | 8-4 | 7-3 | 12-1 | 11-0 | 9-2 | 15-5 | 13-9 | 11-3 | 18-5 | 16-0 | 13-0 |
| TJI®/15 | Flange Width = 1 1/2" | | | | | | 18-9 | 17-2 | 15-1 | 22-4 | 20-5 | 15-1 |
| TJI®/25 | Flange Width = 1 3/4" | | | | | | 19-7 | 17-11 | 15-9 | 23-4 | 21-4 | 18-4 |
| LPI™ 32 | Flange Width = 2 1/2" | | | | | | 19-0 | 18-6 | 15-11 | 23-9 | 22-0 | 18-10 |

## Rafters: Flat ceiling rooms; attached garages — 40#LL + 7#DL — L/180

| | 2 x 6 | | | 2 x 8 | | | 2 x 10 | | | 2 x 12 | | |
|---|---|---|---|---|---|---|---|---|---|---|---|---|
| | 12"OC | 16"OC | 24"OC | 12"OC | 16"OC | 24"OC | 12"OC | 16"OC | 24"OC | 12"OC | 16"OC | 24"OC |
| Douglas Fir-Larch | 12-8 | 11-0 | 9-0 | 16-1 | 13-11 | 11-5 | 19-8 | 17-0 | 13-11 | 22-9 | 19-9 | 16-1 |
| Hem-Fir | 12-6 | 10-10 | 8-10 | 15-10 | 13-9 | 11-3 | 19-4 | 16-9 | 13-8 | 22-6 | 19-5 | 15-11 |
| S-P-F | 12-8 | 11-0 | 9-0 | 16-1 | 13-11 | 11-5 | 19-8 | 17-0 | 13-11 | 22-9 | 19-9 | 16-1 |
| S-P-F (South) | 11-9 | 10-2 | 8-4 | 14-11 | 12-11 | 10-6 | 18-2 | 15-9 | 12-10 | 21-1 | 18-3 | 14-11 |

## Rafters: Vaulted ceilings — 40#LL + 15#DL — L/240

| | 2 x 6 | | | 2 x 8 | | | 2 x 10 | | | 2 x 12 | | |
|---|---|---|---|---|---|---|---|---|---|---|---|---|
| | 12"OC | 16"OC | 24"OC | 12"OC | 16"OC | 24"OC | 12"OC | 16"OC | 24"OC | 12"OC | 16"OC | 24"OC |
| Douglas Fir-Larch | 11-9 | 10-2 | 8-4 | 14-10 | 12-11 | 10-6 | 18-2 | 15-9 | 12-10 | 21-1 | 18-3 | 14-11 |
| Hem-Fir | 11-5 | 10-0 | 8-2 | 14-8 | 12-8 | 10-4 | 17-11 | 15-6 | 12-8 | 20-9 | 18-0 | 14-8 |
| S-P-F | 11-9 | 10-2 | 8-4 | 14-10 | 12-11 | 10-6 | 18-2 | 15-9 | 12-10 | 21-1 | 18-3 | 14-11 |
| S-P-F (South) | 10-10 | 9-5 | 7-8 | 13-9 | 11-11 | 9-9 | 16-10 | 14-7 | 11-11 | 19-6 | 16-11 | 13-9 |
| TJI®/15 | Low Slope: Roof Pitch 6:12 or less | | | | | | — | 17-4 | 15-1 | — | 20-11 | 17-1 |
| TJI®/15 | High Slope: Roof Pitch greater than 6:12 | | | | | | — | 15-8 | 13-8 | — | 18-11 | 16-5 |
| LPI™ 32 | Low Slope: Roof Pitch 6:12 or less | | | | | | 22-6 | 20-4 | 16-1 | 26-10 | 23-6 | 19-2 |
| LPI™ 32 | High Slope: Roof Pitch greater than 6:12 | | | | | | 22-0 | 19-7 | 16-0 | 26-1 | 22-8 | 17-7 |

## Rafters: Detached garages — 30#LL + 7#DL — L/180

| | 2 x 6 | | | 2 x 8 | | | 2 x 10 | | | 2 x 12 | | |
|---|---|---|---|---|---|---|---|---|---|---|---|---|
| | 12"OC | 16"OC | 24"OC | 12"OC | 16"OC | 24"OC | 12"OC | 16"OC | 24"OC | 12"OC | 16"OC | 24"OC |
| Douglas Fir-Larch | 14-4 | 12-5 | 10-1 | 18-2 | 15-8 | 12-10 | 22-2 | 19-2 | 15-8 | 25-8 | 22-3 | 18-2 |
| Hem-Fir | 13-10 | 12-3 | 10-0 | 17-10 | 15-6 | 12-8 | 21-10 | 18-11 | 15-5 | 25-4 | 21-11 | 17-11 |
| S-P-F | 14-4 | 12-5 | 10-1 | 18-2 | 15-8 | 12-10 | 22-2 | 19-2 | 15-8 | 25-8 | 22-3 | 18-2 |
| S-P-F (South) | 13-1 | 11-6 | 9-4 | 16-9 | 14-6 | 11-10 | 20-6 | 17-9 | 14-6 | 23-9 | 20-7 | 16-10 |

## Ceiling joists — 20#LL + 10#DL — L/240

| | 2 x 4 | | | 2 x 6 | | | 2 x 8 | | | 2 x 10 | | |
|---|---|---|---|---|---|---|---|---|---|---|---|---|
| | 12"OC | 16"OC | 24"OC | 12"OC | 16"OC | 24"OC | 12"OC | 16"OC | 24"OC | 12"OC | 16"OC | 24"OC |
| Douglas Fir-Larch | 9-10 | 8-9 | 7-2 | 14-10 | 12-10 | 10-6 | 18-9 | 16-3 | 13-3 | 22-11 | 19-10 | 16-3 |
| Hem-Fir | 9-2 | 8-4 | 7-1 | 14-5 | 12-8 | 10-4 | 18-6 | 16-0 | 13-1 | 22-7 | 19-7 | 16-0 |
| S-P-F | 9-5 | 8-7 | 7-2 | 14-9 | 12-10 | 10-6 | 18-9 | 16-3 | 13-3 | 22-11 | 19-10 | 16-3 |
| S-P-F (South) | 8-8 | 7-11 | 6-8 | 13-8 | 11-11 | 9-8 | 17-5 | 15-1 | 12-4 | 21-3 | 18-5 | 15-0 |

The numbers for standard wood are for number 2 grade. The tabulated span for joists is the distance from face to face of supports. On sloped rafters, the span is measured along the horizontal projection, not the length of the rafters. On the next page are the IBC numbers for floor joists of different grades, at two different loads.

# MAXIMUM FLOOR JOIST SPANS   LIVE LOAD 40 psf

| JOIST SPACING (inches) | SPECIES AND GRADE | | DEAD LOAD 10 psf | | | | DEAD LOAD 20 psf | | | |
|---|---|---|---|---|---|---|---|---|---|---|
| | | | 2x6 | 2x8 | 2x10 | 2x12 | 2x6 | 2x8 | 2x10 | 2x12 |
| 12 | Douglas fir - Larch | SS | 11 - 4 | 15 - 0 | 19 - 1 | 23 - 3 | 11 - 4 | 15 - 0 | 19 - 1 | 23 - 3 |
| | Douglas fir - Larch | # 1 | 10 - 11 | 14 - 5 | 18 - 5 | 22 - 0 | 10 - 11 | 14 - 2 | 17 - 4 | 20 - 1 |
| | Douglas Fir - Larch | # 2 | 10 - 9 | 14 - 2 | 17 - 9 | 20 - 7 | 10 - 6 | 13 - 3 | 16 - 3 | 18 - 10 |
| | Douglas Fir - Larch | # 3 | 8 - 8 | 11 - 0 | 13 - 5 | 15 - 7 | 7 - 11 | 10 - 0 | 12 - 3 | 14 - 3 |
| | Hem - Fir | SS | 10 - 9 | 14 - 2 | 18 - 0 | 21 - 11 | 10 - 9 | 14 - 2 | 18 - 10 | 21 - 11 |
| | Hem - Fir | # 1 | 10 - 6 | 13 - 10 | 17 - 8 | 21 - 6 | 10 - 6 | 13 - 10 | 16 - 11 | 19 - 7 |
| | Hem - Fir | # 2 | 10 - 0 | 13 - 2 | 16 - 10 | 20 - 4 | 10 - 0 | 13 - 1 | 16 - 0 | 18 - 6 |
| | Hem - Fir | # 3 | 8 - 8 | 11 - 0 | 13 - 5 | 15 - 7 | 7 - 11 | 10 - 0 | 12 - 3 | 14 - 3 |
| | Southern Pine | SS | 11 - 2 | 14 - 8 | 18 - 9 | 22 - 10 | 11 - 2 | 14 - 8 | 18 - 9 | 22 - 10 |
| | Southern Pine | # 1 | 10 - 11 | 14 - 5 | 18 - 5 | 22 - 5 | 10 - 11 | 14 - 5 | 18 - 5 | 22 - 5 |
| | Southern Pine | # 2 | 10 - 9 | 14 - 2 | 18 - 0 | 21 - 9 | 10 - 9 | 14 - 2 | 16 - 11 | 19 - 10 |
| | Southern Pine | # 3 | 9 - 4 | 11 - 11 | 14 - 0 | 16 - 8 | 8 - 6 | 10 - 10 | 12 - 10 | 15 - 3 |
| | Spruce - Pine - Fir | SS | 10 - 6 | 13 - 10 | 17 - 8 | 21 - 6 | 10 - 6 | 13 - 10 | 17 - 8 | 21 - 6 |
| | Spruce - Pine - Fir | # 1 | 10 - 3 | 13 - 6 | 17 - 3 | 20 - 7 | 10 - 3 | 13 - 3 | 16 - 3 | 18 - 10 |
| | Spruce - Pine - Fir | # 2 | 10 - 3 | 13 - 6 | 17 - 3 | 20 - 7 | 10 - 3 | 13 - 3 | 16 - 3 | 18 - 10 |
| | Spruce - Pine - Fir | # 3 | 8 - 8 | 11 - 0 | 13 - 5 | 15 - 7 | 7 - 11 | 10 - 0 | 12 - 3 | 14 - 3 |
| 16 | Douglas fir - Larch | SS | 10 - 4 | 13 - 7 | 17 - 4 | 21 - 1 | 10 - 4 | 13 - 7 | 17 - 4 | 21 - 0 |
| | Douglas fir - Larch | # 1 | 9 - 11 | 13 - 1 | 16 - 5 | 19 - 1 | 9 - 8 | 12 - 4 | 15 - 0 | 17 - 5 |
| | Douglas Fir - Larch | # 2 | 9 - 9 | 12 - 7 | 15 - 5 | 17 - 10 | 9 - 1 | 11 - 6 | 14 - 1 | 16 - 3 |
| | Douglas Fir - Larch | # 3 | 7 - 6 | 9 - 6 | 11 - 8 | 13 - 6 | 6 - 10 | 8 - 8 | 10 - 7 | 12 - 4 |
| | Hem - Fir | SS | 9 - 9 | 12 - 10 | 16 - 5 | 19 - 11 | 9 - 9 | 12 - 10 | 16 - 5 | 19 - 11 |
| | Hem - Fir | # 1 | 9 - 6 | 12 - 7 | 16 - 0 | 18 - 7 | 9 - 6 | 12 - 0 | 14 - 8 | 17 - 0 |
| | Hem - Fir | # 2 | 9 - 1 | 12 - 0 | 15 - 2 | 17 - 7 | 8 - 11 | 11 - 4 | 13 - 10 | 16 - 1 |
| | Hem - Fir | # 3 | 7 - 6 | 9 - 6 | 11 - 8 | 13 - 6 | 6 - 10 | 8 - 8 | 10 - 7 | 12 - 4 |
| | Southern Pine | SS | 10 - 2 | 13 - 4 | 17 - 0 | 20 - 9 | 10 - 2 | 13 - 4 | 17 - 0 | 20 - 9 |
| | Southern Pine | # 1 | 9 - 11 | 13 - 1 | 16 - 9 | 20 - 4 | 9 - 11 | 13 - 1 | 16 - 4 | 19 - 6 |
| | Southern Pine | # 2 | 9 - 9 | 12 - 10 | 16 - 1 | 18 - 10 | 9 - 6 | 12 - 4 | 14 - 8 | 17 - 2 |
| | Southern Pine | # 3 | 8 - 1 | 10 - 3 | 12 - 2 | 14 - 6 | 7 - 4 | 9 - 5 | 11 - 1 | 13 - 2 |
| | Spruce - Pine - Fir | SS | 9 - 6 | 12 - 7 | 16 - 0 | 19 - 6 | 9 - 6 | 12 - 7 | 16 - 0 | 19 - 6 |
| | Spruce - Pine - Fir | # 1 | 9 - 4 | 12 - 3 | 15 - 5 | 17 - 10 | 9 - 1 | 11 - 6 | 14 - 1 | 16 - 3 |
| | Spruce - Pine - Fir | # 2 | 9 - 4 | 12 - 3 | 15 - 5 | 17 - 10 | 9 - 1 | 11 - 6 | 14 - 1 | 16 - 3 |
| | Spruce - Pine - Fir | # 3 | 7 - 6 | 9 - 6 | 11 - 8 | 13 - 6 | 6 - 10 | 8 - 8 | 10 - 7 | 12 - 4 |
| 19.2 | Douglas fir - Larch | SS | 9 - 8 | 12 - 10 | 16 - 4 | 19 - 10 | 9 - 8 | 12 - 10 | 16 - 4 | 19 - 2 |
| | Douglas fir - Larch | # 1 | 9 - 4 | 12 - 4 | 15 - 0 | 17 - 5 | 8 - 10 | 11 - 3 | 13 - 8 | 15 - 11 |
| | Douglas Fir - Larch | # 2 | 9 - 1 | 11 - 6 | 14 - 1 | 16 - 3 | 8 - 3 | 10 - 6 | 12 - 10 | 14 - 10 |
| | Douglas Fir - Larch | # 3 | 6 - 10 | 8 - 8 | 10 - 7 | 12 - 4 | 6 - 3 | 7 - 11 | 9 - 8 | 11 - 3 |
| | Hem - Fir | SS | 9 - 2 | 12 - 1 | 15 - 5 | 18 - 9 | 9 - 2 | 12 - 1 | 15 - 5 | 18 - 9 |
| | Hem - Fir | # 1 | 9 - 0 | 11 - 10 | 14 - 8 | 17 - 0 | 8 - 8 | 10 - 11 | 13 - 4 | 15 - 6 |
| | Hem - Fir | # 2 | 8 - 7 | 11 - 3 | 13 - 10 | 16 - 1 | 8 - 2 | 10 - 4 | 12 - 8 | 14 - 8 |
| | Hem - Fir | # 3 | 6 - 10 | 8 - 8 | 10 - 7 | 12 - 4 | 6 - 3 | 7 - 11 | 9 - 8 | 11 - 3 |
| | Southern Pine | SS | 9 - 6 | 12 - 7 | 16 - 0 | 19 - 6 | 9 - 6 | 12 - 7 | 16 - 0 | 19 - 6 |
| | Southern Pine | # 1 | 9 - 4 | 12 - 4 | 15 - 9 | 19 - 2 | 9 - 4 | 12 - 4 | 14 - 11 | 17 - 9 |
| | Southern Pine | # 2 | 9 - 2 | 12 - 1 | 14 - 8 | 17 - 2 | 8 - 8 | 11 - 3 | 13 - 5 | 15 - 8 |
| | Southern Pine | # 3 | 7 - 4 | 9 - 5 | 11 - 1 | 13 - 2 | 6 - 9 | 8 - 7 | 10 - 1 | 12 - 1 |
| | Spruce - Pine - Fir | SS | 9 - 0 | 11 - 10 | 15 - 1 | 18 - 4 | 9 - 0 | 11 - 10 | 15 - 1 | 17 - 9 |
| | Spruce - Pine - Fir | # 1 | 8 - 9 | 11 - 6 | 14 - 1 | 16 - 3 | 8 - 3 | 10 - 6 | 12 - 10 | 14 - 10 |
| | Spruce - Pine - Fir | # 2 | 8 - 9 | 11 - 6 | 14 - 1 | 16 - 3 | 8 - 3 | 10 - 6 | 12 - 10 | 14 - 10 |
| | Spruce - Pine - Fir | # 3 | 6 - 10 | 8 - 8 | 10 - 7 | 12 - 4 | 6 - 3 | 7 - 11 | 9 - 8 | 11 - 3 |
| 24 | Douglas fir - Larch | SS | 9 - 0 | 11 - 11 | 15 - 2 | 18 - 5 | 9 - 0 | 11 - 11 | 14 - 9 | 17 - 1 |
| | Douglas fir - Larch | # 1 | 8 - 8 | 11 - 0 | 13 - 5 | 15 - 7 | 7 - 11 | 10 - 0 | 12 - 3 | 14 - 3 |
| | Douglas Fir - Larch | # 2 | 8 - 1 | 10 - 3 | 12 - 7 | 14 - 7 | 7 - 5 | 9 - 5 | 11 - 6 | 13 - 4 |
| | Douglas Fir - Larch | # 3 | 6 - 2 | 7 - 9 | 9 - 6 | 11 - 0 | 5 - 7 | 7 - 1 | 8 - 8 | 10 - 1 |
| | Hem - Fir | SS | 8 - 6 | 11 - 3 | 14 - 4 | 17 - 5 | 8 - 6 | 11 - 3 | 14 - 4 | 16 - 10* |
| | Hem - Fir | # 1 | 8 - 4 | 10 - 9 | 13 - 1 | 15 - 2 | 7 - 9 | 9 - 9 | 11 - 11 | 13 - 10 |
| | Hem - Fir | # 2 | 7 - 11 | 10 - 2 | 12 - 5 | 14 - 4 | 7 - 4 | 9 - 3 | 11 - 4 | 13 - 1 |
| | Hem - Fir | # 3 | 6 - 2 | 7 - 9 | 9 - 6 | 11 - 0 | 5 - 7 | 7 - 1 | 8 - 8 | 10 - 1 |
| | Southern Pine | SS | 8 - 10 | 11 - 8 | 14 - 11 | 18 - 1 | 8 - 10 | 11 - 8 | 14 - 11 | 18 - 1 |
| | Southern Pine | # 1 | 8 - 8 | 11 - 5 | 14 - 7 | 17 - 5 | 8 - 8 | 11 - 3 | 13 - 3 | 15 - 11 |
| | Southern Pine | # 2 | 8 - 6 | 11 - 0 | 13 - 1 | 15 - 5 | 7 - 9 | 10 - 0 | 12 - 0 | 14 - 0 |
| | Southern Pine | # 3 | 6 - 7 | 8 - 5 | 9 - 11 | 11 - 10 | 6 - 0 | 7 - 8 | 9 - 1 | 10 - 9 |
| | Spruce - Pine - Fir | SS | 8 - 4 | 11 - 0 | 14 - 0 | 17 - 0 | 8 - 4 | 11 - 0 | 13 - 8 | 15 - 11 |
| | Spruce - Pine - Fir | # 1 | 8 - 1 | 10 - 3 | 12 - 7 | 14 - 7 | 7 - -5 | 9 - 5 | 11 - 6 | 13 - 4 |
| | Spruce - Pine - Fir | # 2 | 8 - 1 | 10 - 3 | 12 - 7 | 14 - 7 | 7 - 5 | 9 - 5 | 11 - 6 | 13 - 4 |
| | Spruce - Pine - Fir | # 3 | 6 - 2 | 7 - 9 | 9 - 6 | 11 - 0 | 5 - 7 | 7 - 1 | 8 - 8 | 10 - 1 |

* bearing length increased to 2 inches

# HOME DESIGN AND HAVING A PLAN

Over the years, some of the projects that I've worked on have turned out really well, while others, in my opinion, have gone bad. On some of those, it was partly my fault. If I had more experience at the time, I might have known when something wasn't going to work, or wouldn't look right, or been able to come up with a better way to do the job. The problem is that you're never really sure how a project will end up until it's actually finished. One thing I have learned, though, is that having a good design or a good plan can be more important in determining the final result, rather than good workmanship. If the design is bad, even the best work is not going to save it. The projects I've been on that went the smoothest and ended up the best were generally where the homeowner put a lot of thought into it, and had a vision of what the finished result would be. This includes everything, from framing, to trim, to how it will be furnished. The worst results tend to come from making it up as you go. Though this can be fun, many times you'll wish that you had a better plan to begin with, so things could have been done a little different, or to keep from having to redo something when you change your mind.

Sometimes I sit back and try to figure out what I like about certain houses, and dislike about others. What is it that gives one a quality look, and makes another look cheap, and what could have been done differently? Here I'm just going to throw out my thoughts and opinions on different subjects. Let's start with decks. My feeling is, if you're going to build a deck, you should design something nice that you'll be proud of. Don't build a deck, just so you have one. There are way too many like that. Many are also built on the wrong side of the house, and get so hot in the summer that you can't even use them during the daytime. In that case, building a porch would be a better choice. I don't remember even seeing a deck until I was a teenager. Houses in my part of town had porches.

When determining where to put the deck, consider whether you want it to be in the sun, or would you rather stay in the shade. You can have a little of both by building it on the east or the west side of the house. On the east side, you'll get the rising sun, but the deck will become shaded as the sun goes around the corner of the house. Built on the west side, you'll be in the shade until the sun shifts to the south, but the deck could still get too hot if it's against a wall that's in the sun all afternoon. I grew up in a house that had an open porch on the east side of it. The sun could come in earlier in the day, but the porch stayed cool, as it was mainly in the shade when things heated up. Another thing to consider is whether or not you want privacy.

Also, is a there any chance that the deck will be changed in the future? If the deck is ever turned into a porch, you'll need larger footings to handle the extra weight, so this has to be considered before you get started. Porches also tend to be changed. Screen porches become 3-season porches, and 3-season porches get better windows and insulation to become 4-season rooms.

When building a deck, make sure it's large enough. I remember a deck that I once built for a young couple. They wanted it to be 10 x 14 feet, so they could put a pair of chaise lounges on it to lay in the sun. But between the chaise lounges and a small table, there was hardly any room left over. As soon as the deck was finished, the couple already wished that it was a little bigger.

Try to design the deck so you can use the materials efficiently. For instance, on a deck that extends 15 feet out from the house, you'll need 16 foot joists. By using 14 foot joists instead, with a ledger board, a doubled-up end and a 1 inch overhang, you'd finish out at 14 feet 5 1/2 inches, minus the thickness of the siding. The same goes for the length. When decking can cost up to several dollars a linear foot, it doesn't make sense to be cutting it off and throwing it away on purpose. Remember that cantilevering the joists may allow you to build a larger deck without increasing the size of the framing, though this may not be allowed with a porch.

When building a house, people don't consider the climate enough when thinking about windows. I live in Minnesota. In this area, large windows on the north side of the house are a big heat loss in the winter, while those on the south side let heat in from the sun. Large windows on the west side can overheat the house, late on a summer day.

People tend to forget these things as they worry about how everything will look from the street. Since curtains and drapes are being used less these days, the size of the windows and how they're positioned is even more important. Windows are also made for specific purposes. Low-E glass or reflective window film can restrict heat gain where it's needed. Because of this, you may want to sit down with a salesman to go over your options when buying windows for different sides of the house.

I'd swear that some architects are in a contest to see who can put the most complicated roof on a house. This is one of my pet peeves about current home design. I think a house should have a reasonably simple roof, like that on some of the nicer, older homes. It shouldn't be so plain that it looks like the roof on a garage, but it also shouldn't be as complicated as some of the designs that you see today. Maybe you could take the money that you save by having a less complicated roof, and put it somewhere else that will do more good. Also, why have all those angles on the roof, when inside the house you mainly have flat ceilings. Some of the most beautiful ceilings are in older homes that have hand-framed roofs with dormers.

Years ago, more expensive homes tended to have bigger and better windows, but these days, I don't think that's quite as true. Now I see lots of good size windows in homes of all price ranges. One thing in common with the houses I like is that they have more than one story. To me, a house with taller walls just looks better, but then I don't mind walking up stairs, either. Houses are generally larger than they used to be, though some are getting awfully big. Actually, it's getting a little crazy, two people thinking they need 4000 - 6000 square feet to live in. In some places, that would probably be a hotel.

Let's go over materials. I would guess that today, millions of homes have vinyl siding. This stuff is easy to install and maintenance free. But one thing against it is that it doesn't always stay on in a bad storm, and once you get close, it looks a little cheap. No matter what color it is, or what kind of texture it has trying to duplicate wood grain, it's not going to have the quality look of some of the other materials.

When I look around my area, the homes that look the best to me are some of the older ones that were built around a hundred years ago, that have brick, stucco, or lap siding. Brick and stucco are high buck items, very labor intensive, and not something the average homeowner has the skill to do. Years ago, I didn't care for stucco, though I've grown to like it more over time. But I only like houses where the stucco has a smoother texture. Stucco with deep swirls, or a rough pattern that hangs out, doesn't do a thing for me.

I have no idea what it costs to build a brick house, but I'm sure it's a lot. Basically, you're building the walls twice, since there's generally wood framing behind the brick. My oldest brother had a neighbor who built a brick house when he retired. If I remember right, on his, there wasn't any wood framing on the walls, and he insulated it by attaching 2 inches of foam. I remember him saying that he was disappointed with how high his heating bills were. I also see houses where the brick runs to just under the windows. Above that is other siding. Myself, I've never really cared for this look, and would rather see the brick go all the way up.

This leaves lap siding. I really like the look and feel of wood lap siding, but it's expensive, and it's a lot of work to maintain, when you consider that you'll have to scrape and repaint it every so many years. Other choices are fiber cement siding, such as HardiePlank, and LP SmartSiding, which is an engineered wood that looks similar and costs about the same. I've helped install fiber cement siding on a few houses, but still have some reservations about using it because the material is brittle. What if the wall gets whacked by something? SmartSiding can take more abuse, but may not be the best choice in a damp climate. Both materials are commonly installed with hidden nails, so repairing it could be a problem. On the plus side, the price is reasonable, it's easy to install, and looks good when painted. It's also being installed on some of the nicer homes.

For the trim, I generally prefer real wood. Fiber cement board and other composites are cheaper and more stable, but what I dislike about these materials is that they don't hold a nail like wood does. On some of them, the nail heads also stick out. When using wood, it should be good quality. That's the problem these days, trying to find decent wood that's affordable.

Wood soffit and fascia can be a pain, since it will have to be repainted. Here, metal is nice, because it's maintenance free. I've seen expensive homes where it doesn't look very good, though I've also seen others where you hardly even notice that they have metal soffit and fascia. On the ones where it looked bad, I think the main reason was because it was the wrong color, or the color had too much contrast, so it stood out instead of blending in, or vice versa. I haven't tried LP SmartSide soffit panels yet, so I don't have an opinion on it.

Since the 1970s, architectural shingles have gradually taken over the market. I see them going on homes in all price ranges. They're easier to install, since you don't have to worry about lining them up vertically like you have to with 3-tab shingles, but they certainly seem to be getting a lot more expensive.

Now let's move inside the house. Here, most of the materials that are used in a less expensive home are basically the same as those used in one that costs more, though the more expensive one will have better woodwork and/or a lot more tile. This is something to consider if you're trying to increase the value of your home. The nice thing here is that much of the increase will come from the labor that you put into it, provided you have good taste, so the finished project has a quality look that blends in with the rest of the house.

Inside the house, one thing that stands out to me are good-sized rooms with nice trim that's either painted or varnished. I prefer wood floors, but also like carpeting or large rugs in certain areas. To me, red oak has more warmth than maple. I also like ceilings that are finished flat, with a good paint job that isn't hidden by sprayed-on popcorn texture. I tend to like a more open floor plan on the main floor. This includes having a spacious kitchen that's open to the dining area. In the bedroom, I want privacy. I don't want to hear what's going on in the rest of the house. I also want the window sill to be at the right height, so the bed can be pulled up against it to feel the night air during the summer, and to listen to what's going on outside. I also want the bedrooms to be upstairs. Some people don't like stairs, and want everything to be on the first floor. Others want a less open floor plan with more doors.

In most stores, you'll find narrow wood trim, though sometimes there's also a style that's a little wider, sort of a cross between the old and the new. To my eye, this isn't much different, and doesn't look as nice as the two-piece trim that you generally find in an older home. But these days, the price of good trim can be scary, so that also has to be considered. For a time, it was popular to trim houses by using ornamental blocks at the corners of windows and doors. Though this makes the trimming a lot easier, I've always preferred the look of trim, without the blocks.

Tile is one thing that really improves the look of a house, and the most beautiful bathrooms have lots of tile with built-in showers. You don't see many tub surrounds in a high-buck house. About the only place that I see a problem with tile is on kitchen counters, since the grout starts to look grubby after a while. With all the information that's available on this subject, a homeowner should be able to do a nice looking tile job. The price of tile can really vary. It can go from dirt cheap for some of the plain varieties, to ridiculously expensive on others. By looking around and putting some thought into it, you should be able to come up with nice tile that doesn't cost an arm and a leg. Besides going to stores, see what's available on the internet.

Not that long ago, most kitchens had Formica counter tops. Now you have many choices, some natural and some manmade, and all of them have their good points and their bad points. Of these, my favorite is granite. The price has come down quite a bit in the last few years, making it a more affordable option. You don't hear much about Formica these days, but the look has improved quite a bit, with different options available on how the edges are finished.

Always measure to see if something is going to work. Even though I've been doing this a long time, I still have to constantly measure to make sure that things will fit. Some areas appear to be larger than they actually are, and vice versa.

Beware of sales -- and yes, I'm being serious. I've been on some remodeling jobs that didn't turn out as well as they should have. Even though the design itself was good, the overall result turned out bad because the homeowner bought something that was just too good to pass up. It doesn't matter how cheap you can get something. If the style or the color is wrong, it's only going to screw up the project. Commonly, items that are on "Clearance" aren't returnable.

In most homes, there's generally a room or two where people tend to gather. While there may be larger and much nicer rooms, I find it interesting that in some houses, everyone gathers in a small area that has a TV, even though there's also one in another room. This reminds me of how we're linked to our past, with everyone huddled around the fire, except that here, the fire is replaced by the television. Sometimes it seems a shame that the other rooms aren't used as much. If there's a point to this, it's that you never know for sure if something will actually be used as much as you think it will.

Take decks, for instance. Many sit there year after year, with people seldom going on them. The money would have been better spent somewhere else. Another one is Jacuzzi tubs. I don't know of any that I've helped install that are used regularly. They just sit there, taking up space. I've always considered this a waste, and wish that a really nice shower was built instead. Do you ever notice that in some rooms, there's a chair that no one ever sits on. Even though there doesn't appear to be anything wrong with it or how it's positioned, people will go out of their way to sit somewhere else.

Let's move on to heating. In the last few years I've done quite a bit of work on heating systems. I've worked on forced-air systems, ones with radiators, and also in-floor heat. When I first read about in-floor heat, I thought it sounded like the best idea. But after working on these systems, and spending some time in houses that have them, I'm not quite as sure. For one thing, there's a lot of bad information out there. I've read, and heard people say, that with in-floor heat you can set the heat to a lower temperature, so you'll save on the heating bill. I spent most of last winter in a cabin with heated floors. With the heat set at 65 degrees, I always had to wear a warm shirt, so I don't know why people believe this. I could see the thermostat being set a little lower than normal (maybe a couple of degrees) when the pump is running, but even during the winter months, the heat isn't always on. It's turning on and off as needed, and in a well-insulated house, it's off more than it's on. So don't believe any wild claims about miraculous savings because of lower thermostat settings. In-floor heat works great for heating concrete slabs and tile floors, but can take a long time to warm up, and sometimes has a problem putting out enough heat on a cold winter day when installed under carpeting or a hardwood floor. Putting rugs on the floor will only make it worse, because they act as insulation and block the heat.

As I sit here, I'm not sure which type of system I'd choose if I had to pick one, since they all have their advantages and disadvantages. Some people complain about the noise from the fan on a forced air furnace, but this type heats the fastest, filters the air, and let's you install central air conditioning and/or an air infiltration system using the same ducts. In-floor heat isn't always as silent as claimed, either, as PEX tubing can be noisy as it expands when the water is being heated. Old fashioned radiators don't have that problem, and are quiet as long as there isn't any air in the system. But they're very heavy, often weighing several hundred pounds apiece. On the other hand, baseboard radiators are very light, but will hang out wherever they run along the walls. Recently, I learned that the thermostat on a high efficiency forced-air furnace shouldn't be set lower than 60 degrees during the daytime. This might make it a bad choice for a cabin that sits empty part of the year. As you can see, there's a lot to consider when choosing a heating system, and which one is best would depend on the circumstances.

I was at a friend's cabin one day as he talked to a guy about having it insulated with foam insulation, since the walls and ceilings were opened up. There are some advantages to this method. For one, the R-value of foam is much higher than that of fiberglass. Another is that it prevents air from moving through the walls. That's one of the biggest problems with fiberglass. On a house that isn't sealed properly, there's so much air movement on a windy day that the heat is sucked right out. As the guy made his sales pitch, he talked about the benefits of foam, and basically trashed fiberglass. As he rattled off numbers to back it up, he pretty much said that fiberglass had no insulation value once it got down to twenty below zero. Now I know that isn't true, otherwise heating bills would be humongous during the winter months in the northern part of this country, but it shows how numbers can be used to make anything sound better. This is something to keep in mind when you're making a purchase or deciding how something should be done.

So back to my original question. What gives a house that quality look? It turns out that it's not one particular thing, but rather a combination of how everything comes together. Putting all your time and money into the kitchen or a bathroom, new siding, etc., even though it looks great, won't mean much if the rest of the house looks like a dump. Mixing different styles can also be a problem. Some people have a knack for it, and it ends up looking really nice. For others, it just looks wrong and nothing goes together. I feel this is harder to achieve in a small house, since everything is more jammed together. Once the building becomes a little bigger, everything gets spread out. You also have more options on how to lay out the different rooms. Either way, it's all a balancing act, and this requires a lot of thought and planning.

# THE END

These days, technology is rapidly changing the world that we live in, and people in general aren't learning how to do their own work. That's one of the reasons why I got started on this book in the first place. Years ago, it'd be rare to find a guy that couldn't make repairs on his own house. Now many can hardly pound in a nail. It's sad to see this happen, and while I have nothing against some of the new technology, I hate to see it come at the cost of skills and knowledge of other things being forgotten.

I remember when I was little, and my dad and an older brother built the porch on our cabin. This was a different time, when people did pretty much what they wanted, even though they didn't always know how some things should be done. Years later, I realized that there weren't any headers over the windows, which explains why they always stuck, and also that the rafters on the ceiling were a couple of sizes too small. At the time it was built, I was too young to do anything but watch, and just spent my time trying to pound nails into scraps of wood that weren't needed. I don't know if that's when the seed was planted, but I've always been amazed at how you can take a pile of wood and turn it into a building.

Working on this book has been a real learning experience. When I first envisioned it, I was only going to cover a few subjects, and there weren't going to be any photos, just drawings. At the time, I didn't even know if there'd be enough for a book. Well, as they say, times have changed, as this project has taken on a life of its own. When I first started, I told myself that the book would be done within a year, but as I worked on it I kept coming up with more subjects to cover, which meant more drawings that I had to make. Then I bought a camera, and everything kind of took off from there, and one year ended up being over six.

While working on it, I've learned quite a few things from doing research, talking to friends, and asking a lot of questions. I also had help from others, so here I'd like to thank anyone who had a part in it. This was my first serious attempt at writing. Even while in high school, I can't remember doing anything more than maybe a half-page book report that was hand written with the lines spaced way out. You get the picture. This was also the first time that I took any photos since I brought a camera to school when I was in kindergarten. This isn't counting the times that people have shoved a phone or a camera in my hand and had me take their picture. Most of the photos in this book were taken as I worked, with a compact camera, with many of them being shot with one hand as I was either holding a light or a tool in the other. In general, I'm pretty satisfied with them, considering the camera and the conditions that the photos were taken under, although there are some that I wish I could go back and reshoot.

Between the writing, the photos, and the drawings, I hope I've done a good enough job in trying to explain the many things that are covered in this book. Building something, when you know what you're doing, can be very satisfying and also kind of relaxing at times, but when you don't, it can be pretty frustrating. I've always felt that the problem was a lack of information, so hopefully I've helped in this regard.

Neil Tschida